FOR REFERENCE

786.10922

KU-223-134

HARTLEPOOL BOROUGH
WITHDRAWN
LIBRARIES

0012634026   0012634026

RETAIN

A Dictionary of
PIANISTS

Ferruccio Busoni; drawing by Edmond X. Kapp

A Dictionary of
PIANISTS

by
WILSON LYLE

County Libraries
Cleveland

HZ
516

786.
10922

0012634026

K O   709 017 499.

ROBERT HALE : LONDON

© *Wilson Lyle 1985*
First published in Great Britain 1985

Robert Hale Limited
Clerkenwell House
Clerkenwell Green
London EC1R 0HT

British Library Cataloguing in Publication Data

Lyle, Wilson
   A dictionary of pianists.
   1. Pianists—Biography
   I. Title
   786.1′092′2   ML397

ISBN 0–7090–1749–9

All rights reserved. No part of this publication may be reproduced, stored in a retrieval system, or transmitted in any form, or by any means, electronic, mechanical, photocopying, recording or otherwise, without the prior permission of the Copyright holder.

Photoset in Plantin by
Kelly Typesetting Limited
Bradford-on-Avon, Wiltshire
Printed in Great Britain by
St Edmundsbury Press
Bury St Edmunds, Suffolk
Bound by Woolnough Bookbinding Limited

Contents

List of Illustrations

Frontispiece
Ferruccio Busoni (*City Art Gallery, Manchester*)

Between pages 96 and 97
Pedalhammerflügel (*c*. 1795) of a type used by Mozart, by Johann
    Schmidt, Salzburg (*Germanisches National Museum, Nürnberg*)
Piano used by Chopin in London, 1848 (*John Broadwood & Sons Ltd*)
Liszt's piano in the Weimar Museum (*C. Bechstein*)
Beethoven's piano by Konrad Graf (*The Curator, Beethoven-Haus,
    Bonn*)
Claudio Arrau (*Blüthner*)
Vladimir Ashkenazy (*Decca Records*)
Bernard d'Ascoli (*Daily Telegraph*)
Wilhelm Backhaus (*Bösendorfer Klavierfabrik A.G.*)
Frédéric Chopin (*Chopin Society, Warsaw*)
Johannes Brahms (*C. Bechstein*)
Van Cliburn (*John H. Steinway*)
Teresa Carreño (*C. Bechstein*)
Alfred Cortot (*drawing by Myrrha Bantock*)
Jeanne-Marie Darré
Percy Grainger (*Gregor Benko, by permission of John Bird*)
Edvard Grieg (*Eilif Thomassen*)
Josef Hofmann (*drawing by Myrrha Bantock*)
Amparo Iturbi (*Blüthner*)
Vladimir Horowitz (*John H. Steinway*)
Gyula Kiss (*Interkoncert, Budapest*)
Josef Lhevinne (*John H. Steinway*)
Katia and Marielle Labèque (*Cynthia Hampton*)
Franz Liszt (*Bösendorfer Klavierfabrik A.G.*)

Prelude

So far as is known this is the first dictionary devoted to professional pianists and players who composed for the instrument.

It spans Beethoven to Cage, Clementi to Pogorelich, Johann Christian Bach to the Labèque sisters: some four thousand pianists in all, many of them memorable performers in a distinguished profession earning, or having earned, their living by playing classical or romantic or contemporary music. It takes on the aspect of a specialist work since, in the case of all-round musicians, most non-pianistic activities have been deliberately omitted.

The musical scene, like any other, undergoes constant change. Because travel is an important part of the career most musicians are nomadic. To the listener who resides in one place, they tend to go into obscurity as they journey across foreign lands, perhaps settling down there to teach, possibly compose: out of sight and out of mind unless their name appears in the *Radio Times* or on a record sleeve. And with the best will in the world, cultural attachés of embassies and staff of high commissions cannot always provide data although they have given splendid help which I gratefully acknowledge.

A reference work is judged by its capacity to inform instantly. The reader is frustrated when a book says A studied under Z, then draws a blank on looking for Z's name. This book has very few entries which do not contain cross-references as well as essential biographical detail. My purpose has been to collate a web of linked activity over roughly two centuries. I have made this collection of persons a generous one in a conscious endeavour to avoid gaps in the web. To give one instance: the composer Arnold Schoenberg, whose instrument was the cello, has been included because of the significance of his piano works in the new school of composition that emerged in Vienna and equally because, for cross-reference purposes, they became milestones in the careers of pianists like Stadlen and Steuermann.

Had I included everyone who ever gave a piano lesson or who ever wrote a piano concerto or piece, whether sometime published or condemned to remain in manuscript, this work would have become wholly unwieldy, and still inevitably incomplete.

It is a fact of life that most musicians have given birth to a concerto or string of pieces or songs with piano accompaniment. Often gestation has happened during the formative years while budding genius awaits the call of the true vocation and therefore rarely merits detailed listing. The existence of youthful zeal or indiscretion in the form of a piano work does not *ipso facto* entitle the perpetrator to space here even if he/she is worthy of full coverage in some other book for a different reason. It is also a fact of life that most professional pianists have tried a hand at composition. The total must run into hundreds of thousands of pieces, published and unpublished.

Throughout peace, war, pestilence, drought and famine musical man has never run short of music paper, finding the means to buy it in large quantities while going hungry. With this in mind I have endeavoured to balance space in accordance with relative values and main essentials.

So too with the treadmill repertoire of a pianist's public activities. It adds nothing to his cause to emphasize his daily dependence upon Beethoven, Chopin, Liszt and Ravel, any more than it does to relate that he ate, drank and slept. First performances of important works are a different matter, therefore, many are here recorded.

One feature of this book which I believe to be unique and which I hope will prove useful, is the listing under teachers of their better-known pupils: those, that is to say, who themselves went on to achieve distinction as pianists. A note of warning: it will be apparent in the case of, say, Liszt, that many more pupils must have passed through his hands than my list shows. Most teachers have taught other musical subjects beside piano technique and interpretation, and examination of available records does not always clarify what musical aspect X studied under Y: e.g., young Felix Weingartner studied orchestra (and very probably conducting) under Liszt, not piano; and since there appears to be no record he ever played the instrument professionally his name does not figure under W nor under Liszt's pupils.

Again, some pupils, after studying piano under a master, have launched out upon an entirely different vocation even though at a later date they may have applied piano technique to some composition. So should they be included? Other individual factors have been weighed before each decision was taken.

Some recording information is given. By no stretch of imagination can it be claimed complete: and only names of labels are shown.

Makers of 78 rpm discs are given in italics, of long play in Roman type. Because of proliferation in marketing channels only original manufacturers are included. For instance, most of Rachmaninov's discs were marketed in Europe under the HMV label but, as far as is known, he never entered an HMV studio, recording only for Edison and then Victor (as RCA was then known). With early electricals it is often impossible to distinguish between some Pathé and Columbia; Odeon and Parlophone: French and English Columbia; French, English and German HMV. It is a modern custom for artists to appear on various labels and in such cases I have hidden behind that adjective. On aesthetic grounds I have omitted all reference to piano rolls and their transfer to electrical 78s and LP. If the reader is a connoisseur in the matter then he will already know as much as, if not more than, me.

At the end of the book will be found lists of prizewinners and gold medallists of major piano competitions. This supplement is as up-to-date and comprehensive as possible, and the assembly of these data for the first time is, to the best of my knowledge and belief, another unique feature of the work.

Sooner or later a lexicographer is obliged to test the growing accumulation of facts with other sources of reference – just to try to be on the safe side of history. In this context there is no such thing as safety, and sometimes the amount of disparity has alarmed me. Here and there, when wider research has proved abortive, I have accepted a majority opinion without always being confident it was the right decision.

This dictionary is a British creation, and so it is considered right to spell the names of musicians in the style customarily found in English-speaking regions of the world. Where national boundaries have been changed as a result of peace treaties following war (this applying especially to central European countries where someone may have been born in a town which at the time was in, say, Italy, but is now in Yugoslavia, and either spelt differently or bears an entirely different name), I have used the style of the time of occurrence. And where the title of, say, a royal conservatoire was changed because a kingdom went republic, again I have used the original title of the school applicable to the period of the pupil's attendance. This also applies to references to the Royal Manchester College of Music which has lately become known as the Royal Northern College of Music.

In the case of lesser mortals there will, alas, always be gaps in biographical information, and here it is necessary to say that some likely sources treated requests for help with stony silence. And so, at the end, I am left with names and scraps of news which defy resolution for the time being. If any feel they or any others have been served unjustly I offer a contrite apology and ask for assistance in putting matters right at a later date by sending details to me through the publishers.

At one time I had hoped to include biographies of popular professionals – players of jazz, ragtime, blues and pop. This, however, would have stretched the covers to bursting point, and it is by no means clear that such entries mixed in with mainstream would have been appreciated by devotees of jazz and pop, or that the person for whom the dictionary has been primarily prepared would find use for the popular scene. These entries have therefore been excluded but may appear in their own book form at a later date.

It remains for me to express the hope that my dictionary will be found useful and enjoyable. Great care has been taken over its compilation: equal care will continue to be taken in any subsequent edition. The publishers will be as pleased as I shall be to hear from any reader who can assist by putting right any fact or omission that is apparent to him or her, if not to us.

During the prolonged period this book has been under way, information has come from many sources, verbal as well as from books, newspapers, journals and the Press. In the circumstances it is impossible to make a detailed list of obligations. I do, however, gratefully acknowledge help from the following: musicians – too numerous to list; most concert agencies and record companies as well as catalogues and lists; the British Foreign Office and British embassies; British High Commissions; foreign embassies in London; music departments of universities at home and abroad, and of libraries including the British Library and Birmingham Central Library; various who's whos of European and American origin; musical dictionaries and writings on musical subjects, much of the material long out of print; as well as the scores of music publishing houses providing details of dedications and of composers' output, editors and arrangers. In a work of this nature, necessarily dependent upon material derived from numerous sources, it is often difficult to ascertain whether or not particular information is in copyright. If I have unwittingly infringed copyright in any way, I offer my sincere apologies and will be glad of the opportunity, upon being satisfied as to the owner's title, to make appropriate acknowledgement in future editions. As to the illustrations, individual acknowledgements appear in the List of Illustrations. In the preparation of a number of them I must gratefully give recognition to the cheerful and expert assistance received from Carole Mason ARPS, of Harborne, Birmingham.

Wilson Lyle

Acad.	Academy
Coll.	College
Comp.	Competition
Cons.	Conservatoire
Inst.	Institute
Int.	International
ISCM	International Society for Contemporary Music
Nat.	National
Orch.	Orchestra
Pf	Piano
Phil.	Philharmonic
PO	Philharmonic Orchestra
Prof.	Professor
R.	Royal
SO	Symphony Orchestra
Soc.	Society
Univ.	University

ABBADO, Marcello (1926–   )
b. Milan, Italy. Studied at Cons. there under a pupil of Pizzetti for pf. From 1951 taught at Venice Cons. and in 1966 was made Director of Rossini Cons. Pesaro. Composed pf pieces and a double concerto for violin pf and two chamber orchs.

ABRAM, Jacques (1915–   )
b. Lufkin, USA. Pf pupil of D. Saperton at Curtis Inst., then of E. Hutcheson at Juilliard School. Prizewinner 1938 followed by successful concert career. Recorded EMI and *Musicraft*.

ABRÁNYI, Cornelius (1822–1903)
b. Szentgyorgy-Abrányi, Hungary. Left his homeland in 1843 to study music in Europe at large. Met Liszt, then studied for a short time in Paris, one source claims with Chopin and Kalkbrenner (unable to confirm). After returning home in 1846, went to Vienna for further tuition. Thereafter performed in public at home, taught pf and studied composition. Through the founding of a musical journal in 1860 he launched the Hungarian music movement on a nationwide basis. Composed songs and numerous pf pieces and wrote several books including an autobiography.

ACHRON, Isidor (1894–1948)
b. Warsaw, Poland. Studied there and later at St Petersburg Cons., pf teacher A. Essipova. Became pianist, teacher and conductor. Younger brother of the violinist Joseph A, whom he followed to USA in 1922, where he settled. Wrote a pf concerto and pieces; was especially noted as accompanist to celebrities and as such recorded on various labels.

ACHUCARRO, Joaquin (1932–   )
b. Bilbao, Spain. Studied locally and at Madrid Cons. Début Bilbao at the age of 13. Winner of Liverpool (UK) Piano Concerts Comp. 1959. Performed in Europe and USA thereafter. Recorded RCA.

ACKERMANN, Anton Jacob (1836–1914)
b. Rotterdam, Netherlands. Studied at R. School, The Hague. Became concert pianist and was appointed pf teacher there in 1865, later similar at Rotterdam Cons. Composed for solo pf and duets, also songs.

ADAM, Louis (1758–1848)
b. Müttersholz, Germany. Little is known of his student days except that he settled in Paris around 1775. Was pf prof. at Paris Cons. 1797–1842 and wrote a considerable quantity of pf pieces which were popular with his contemporaries; also two textbooks on pf method. Edited the first *Méthode de Pianoforte* published by Paris Cons. in 1804.
Pupils included: Ferdinand Hérold, Friedrich Kalkbrenner, Charles Poisot.

ADDINSELL, Richard (1904–   )
b. Oxford, UK. Pupil of R. Coll. of Music, London. Most famous for *Warsaw Concerto* in the film *Dangerous Moonlight* (pf played by Louis Kentner).

ADLER, Agnes Charlotte (1865–1935)
b. Copenhagen, Denmark. Pupil of E. Neupert, Copenhagen Cons. Début there 1882 under baton of Niels Gade. Taught pf thereafter and confined her concert activities mainly to Scandinavian countries.

ADLER, Clarence (1886–1969)
b. Cincinnati, USA. Studied at Coll. of Music there, then with L. Godowsky, R. Joseffy and R. Gorno. Successfully toured with leading orchs. and as soloist. Played chamber music,

founding New York Trio in 1919. Was pf prof. at Coll. of Music, Cincinnati. Composed pf music and arranged.

Pupils included: Aaron Copland, Jascha Zayde.

ADLER, Vincent (1828–71)
b. Raab. Studied in Vienna and toured Europe many times. Taught at Vienna Cons. from 1865.

ADNI, Daniel (1951–)
b. Haifa, Israel. Pupil of Paris Cons., début 1970 Wigmore Hall, London. Performed with most British orchs. also recitals. Recorded EMI.

AESCHBACHER, Adrian (1912–)
b. Langenthal, Switzerland. Studied pf in Zurich under Emil Frey, then under A. Schnabel in Berlin. Performed in Europe prior to World War II; continued his career in Switzerland. Later pf prof. at Bienne School of Music. Recorded Heliodor.

AGAY, Denes (1911–)
b. Budapest, Hungary. Studied at Acad. there, graduated 1933. Settled USA 1939 as teacher, New York. Additionally edited journal for pf pupils.

AGGHÁZY, Károlyi (1855–1918)
b. Budapest, Hungary. Student of Cons. there; later a pupil of F. Liszt. Début 1878 in Paris followed by recital tours throughout Europe. Pf prof. Budapest Cons., 1881–3, then prof. at Stern's Cons., Berlin, returning to Budapest in 1889 to take over advanced pf class. Composed mostly chamber music, also pf pieces in the idiom of Liszt.

Pupils included: Johannes Doebber.

AGNEW, Roy (1893–1944)
b. Sydney, Australia. Trained in Australia as pianist and composer. Prolific from an early age, many of his pieces being published from around the age of 25. Came to UK in early 1930s and enjoyed a passing vogue, performing in London in concerts of contemporary music. Compositions included a number of pf sonatas, some bearing descriptive prefixes e.g. *Poem*- and *Fantaisie*-, a book of preludes, as well as duets and songs. Later returned to Australia and taught at NSW Cons., Sydney.

AGNILLO, Corradino d' (1868–1948)
b. Agnone, Italy. Student of Naples Cons., before settling in Buenos Aires for a time. Returned to Naples for four years before removing permanently to S. America where he taught at Cattelani Cons. and later became pf prof. at St. Cecilia Inst. A fine pianist who also composed two operas.

AGOSTI, Guido (1901–)
b. Forli, Italy. Studied at Bologna Cons.; teachers included F. Busoni. Made numerous appearances in Europe and the Americas solo and with orch., and in chamber music which he taught. Pf prof. Milan, Venice, then St. Cecilia Cons. Rome, also held master-classes abroad and adjudicated. Wrote technical works on pf playing and made Beethoven and Chopin editions. Transcribed movements of Stravinsky's *Firebird* for pf. Gave a lecture-recital of Beethoven sonatas as recently as 1983 in Rome.

Pupils included: Omar Mejia, Peter Noke, Victor Sangiorgio, Allan Schiller, Charles Timbrell.

AGUILAR, Emanuel Abraham (1824–1904)
b. London, UK, of Spanish descent. Remembered for an album of canons and fugues composed as preliminary study to the keyboard works of J. S. Bach.

AGUILAR-AHUMADA, Miguel (1931–)
b. Huara, Chile. Studied at Santiago Cons., then in Europe at Cologne. Returned home to teaching post at Concepción Cons. Has composed much for pf in avant-garde form.

AGUIRRE, Julián (1869–1924)
b. Buenos Aires, Argentina. Spent early years in Madrid where he studied pf and composition at the Cons. Was a distinguished pianist who became Director of Cons. at Buenos Aires. Studied his national folk-music which he used in pf pieces, chamber music and songs.

Pupils included: Ernesto Drangosch, Roberto Morillo, Celestino Piaggio.

AITKEN, Webster (1908–)
b. Los Angeles, USA. Pupil in Europe of E. von Sauer and of A. Schnabel. Début Vienna, 1929; thereafter performed in Europe. US début New York, 1935; career there since as soloist and as chamber-music player. Intro-

duced Elliott Carter pf sonata 1947. Recorded Lyrichord.

AKIMENKO, Feodor Stevanovich
(1876–1945)
b. Kharkov, Russia. Studied Petrograd Cons. (1896–1901). Became Director of Tiflis Music School, then lived for a time in Paris, before returning to Petrograd Cons. Later settled in France. Wrote many works for pf, chamber music and songs.

ALBANESI, Carlo (1858–1926)
b. Naples, Italy. Pupil of his father, Luigi A. Gave recitals in Italy and in France before settling in London 1882 where he became pf prof. at R. Acad., 1893, as well as a distinguished pf examiner to principal British music schools. Was associated with R. Phil. Soc. for years. Married Maria A, well-known novelist. Wrote mainly pf pieces, songs and chamber music, also six pf sonatas.
    Pupils included: Norman Fraser.

ALBANESI, Luigi (1821–97)
b. Rome, Italy. Pianist and composer.
    Pupils included: Carlo Albanesi.

ALBÉNIZ, Isaac (1860–1909)
b. Camprodon, Andalusia, Spain. Began playing in public from the age of 4. Was said to have been a brilliant prodigy who also composed copious quantities of pieces from instinct rather than formal education. Discerning his talent for music, his parents forced him to practise, and when he was 6 his mother took him to Paris to study privately with A. Marmontel.
    Returning home in 1868, when the family settled in Madrid the boy was made to study at the Cons. there. But he ran away, roaming the countryside and playing the pf to subsist meagrely. When hauled before the authorities in Cadiz and threatened with being sent home, he sought refuge in a ship bound for the Americas, eventually landing in Buenos Aires. Once more he adopted a nomadic existence, relying on his pianistic skill as he made his way northwards in what eventually took shape as a successful concert tour. From Cuba he went to the USA and proceeded to carry out a coast-to-coast tour and back.
    When he returned to Europe, now a teenager, he went to Germany and took lessons with S. Jadassohn and K. Reinecke in Leipzig, later obtaining a grant to study at Brussels R.

Cons. under L. Brassin for pf and F. Arbós for composition. He also received tuition from F. Liszt by accompanying him on his travels.
    His adult début occurred in 1880 and was followed by tours of Europe and the USA. From 1892, however, he turned increasingly to composition, settling, the following year, in Paris to study composition with d'Indy and Dukas. And there he became further acquainted with the French movement through friendships with Chausson, Fauré and others. He taught for a time at the Schola Cantorum.
    Throughout his life he was a prolific composer, mostly for pf, although he did spend time on operas and wrote an orch. suite, *Catalonia*. Spanish rhythms predominate. He composed an enduring masterpiece in *Iberia*, a suite of twelve pieces in four books and inspired by the playing of J. Maláts, whom he greatly admired. This suite and the *Cantos de España* reflect a mature style that benefited from formal tuition in composition in Paris, while giving the instrument a glitter which caused Albéniz to achieve the reputation of being one of the first of the great modern Spanish composers for the pf. *Iberia*, belonging, like *Navarra*, to the end of the composer's life, was first performed in Spain in 1916 by Arthur Rubinstein, whose disinclination to play such nationalistic music in the country of origin was overcome by the composer's widow after hearing him privately. The suite includes *Evocation, El puerto, Fête-Dieu à Séville, Almeria, Triana, Albaicin, El Polo, Malaga* and *Jerez. Cantos de España*, dating from around 1895 or after his return home from Paris, has five pieces: *Prelude, Orientale, Baja la Palmera, Cordoba* and *Seguidillas*. All reflect in musical terms the warmth and colour of life in Spanish regions. They also mirror the glittering dexterity of his technique at the keyboard.
    Around the time he was living in Paris he gave a series of concerts in London. G. B. Shaw described his playing of the Chopin *Berceuse* and an *Impromptu* as 'dainty without triviality' but considered Albéniz 'has not the temperament for Beethoven or Schumann, nor the inhumanity to visit Brahms on us'. A accompanied the violinist (and former teacher) Arbós in the Mendelssohn concerto in E minor which G.B.S. described as 'by no means the least interesting part of the performance'.
    de Falla dedicated his *Four Spanish Pieces* (1908) to A.

ALBÉNIZ, Pedro (1795–1855)
b. Logroño, Spain. Studied pf in Spain, then later in Paris with F. Kalkbrenner and H. Herz. Was one of the original Spanish pianists who became a prof. at Madrid Cons. and wrote a method which was used there for many years. Composed numerous works for pf.

ALBERDI, Juan Bautista (1810–84)
b. Tucuman, Argentina. A reputedly excellent pianist and composer of mostly salon music. Founded the first S. American musical journal, *Boletín Musical*, at the age of 17.

ALBERSHEIM, Gerhard (1902–)
b. Cologne, Germany. Studied at Vienna Cons., settling in USA 1940, working as accompanist to great singers on tour. Taught at California Univ. and California State Coll.

ALBERT, Eugen Francis Charles d' (1864–1932)
b. Glasgow, UK. Pupil of M. Pauer in London where he made successful début 1880. In 1881 premièred his 1st pf concerto at R. Phil. concert under Hans Richter. Spent a year in Europe and received lessons from F. Liszt. After a world tour settled in Germany, later assuming that nationality. Toured extensively as virtuoso and was rated powerful yet poetic, his interpretations conceived on a grand scale. Married several times, including T. Carreño. He died in Riga on tour. Wrote much music including two pf concertos, a sonata, chamber music and pf pieces. Transcribed some Bach organ works. Under the composer's baton played both Brahms pf concertos in Leipzig in 1894 and in Vienna in 1895. Recorded *Odeon*.
    Pupils included: Wilhelm Backhaus, Theodor Bohlmann, Ernst v. Dohnányi, Otto Hegner, Evlyn Howard-Jones, Selma Jansen, Frederick Loewe, Karl Prohaska, Walter Rehberg, Édouard Risler.

ALDEN, John Carver (1852–1935)
b. Boston, USA. Studied there, also in Leipzig with L. Plaidy. Performed and taught at New England Cons. and later in New York. Composed pf concerto and pieces.

ALDERIGHI, Dante (1898–1968)
b. Taranto, Italy. Pf pupil of G. Sgambati, then of T. Teichmüller in Leipzig. Performed, taught and wrote on musical topics. Pf prof. S. Cecilia, Rome, from 1936. Composed several works for pf and orch.

ALEXANDER, Arthur (1891–1969)
b. Dunedin, New Zealand. Studied at R. Acad. with Tobias Matthay, winning the Macfarren Prize and Chappell Gold Medal for his playing. Début 1912, in which year he was appointed pf prof. at Matthay School. Appeared in Europe in recitals. Became prof. at R. Coll. of Music, 1920. His musical tastes were catholic, and he gave a number of first performances including the Bax 2nd sonata. In 1921 married Freda Swain.
    Pupils included: Ruth Gipps, Elizabeth Maconchy, Helen Perkin, Bernard Pinsonneault, Freda Swain.

ALEXANDER, Haim (1915–)
b. Berlin, Germany. Studied there and also at Israeli Cons. After graduation taught pf and composition at the New Jerusalem Cons. and Acad. Became prof. Compositions include six *Israeli Dances* for pf.

ALEXANDER, Marjorie (–)
b. Wellington, New Zealand. Studied there and R. Coll. of Music, London; début 1944 London. Remained in Britain where she performed and taught, her career including a spell at Toynbee Hall.

ALEXANDROV, Anatole Nicolaevich (1888–?)
b. Moscow, Russia. Studied at Moscow Cons. where his pf teacher was C. Igumnov. Graduated 1915. Had a spell as teacher and concert pianist, then, in 1922, was appointed pf prof. at Moscow Cons. Composed much pf music including 12 sonatas, chamber music and songs. Loaded with Soviet honours as artist, worker and composer.

ALEXEEV, Dmitri (1947–)
b. Moscow, USSR. Showed promise from age of 5 and was taught at the Central Music School of Moscow Cons., entering the latter full-time in 1963 and graduating in 1973. Four years earlier he had gained second prize in the Marguerite Long Comp. in Paris and in 1970 the 1st prize in a competition in Bucharest. Four years later he was awarded 5th Prize in the Tchaikovsky Int. Comp. in Moscow, and the following year 1st prize at the 5th Leeds contest. Afterwards played with leading orchs. throughout Europe and the Far East as well as America where his recital début took place in New York in 1978. Recorded Melodiya. In 1981 a London critic described him as: 'an

artist of impressive seriousness and maturity whose playing nevertheless rejoices in an enormous muscular technique and a youthfully reckless keyboard address'.

ALKAN, Charles Henri Valentin (1813–88) (real surname **MORHANGE**)
b. Paris, France. Pupil of P. Zimmerman at Paris Cons. from age of 6, winning 1st Prize four years later. From the age of 18 was mainly composer and teacher, with only occasional appearances as virtuoso in semi-private recitals. Because of that, and the technical difficulties of his complex works which are conceived on a grand scale, his reputation has undoubtedly suffered, although from time to time he has had devoted advocates. Compositions included *études*, preludes, a *Grande Sonate*, duets, chamber music and a number of pieces for the pedal-piano.

Pupils included: Ignacio Cervantes, Élie Delaborde, Franz Stockhausen, Josef Wieniawski.

ALKAN, Napoléon (1826–88)
b. Paris, France. Younger brother of Charles A and a notable pianist in own right although overshadowed by Charles. Also composed for the instrument.

ALLEN, Creighton (1900–)
b. Macon, USA. Pupil of E. Hutcheson, H. Bauer and R. Goldmark. Established successful career as pianist and composer of chamber music, pf pieces and songs.

ALLEN, Gregory (1949–)
b. USA. Studied at Oberlin Coll., then Peabody Inst. under D. Fleisher. In 1973 began teaching at Texas Univ. and performed throughout the USA solo and with major orchs. New York début 1978, in which year he won 2nd Prize in the Concours Musical Int. Reine Elisabeth in Brussels and toured Belgium; in 1980 was awarded 1st Prize and Gold Medal in the Arthur Rubinstein Int. Pf Master Comp. in Tel-Aviv. Recorded DG.

ALLER, Victor (1905–)
b. New York, USA. Student at Juilliard School. Performed and taught.

ALMASY, László (1933–)
b. Budapest, Hungary. Student of F. Liszt Acad. where he won diploma. Début 1959.

Became prof. at Liszt Acad. and performed throughout Europe, Africa and USSR.

ALPAERTS, Jef (1904–)
b. Antwerp, Belgium. Son of composer Flor A (1876–1954). Studied pf in Paris with I. Philipp and A. Cortot. Became prof. at Antwerp, toured widely as concert pianist and founded a pf trio under his name.

ALPENHEIM, Ilse von (1927–)
b. Innsbruck, Austria. Pupil of Salzburg Mozarteum, appearing in public from the age of 9. Performed throughout the world and specialized in the music of Haydn and Mozart. Married the famous conductor Antal Dorati. Recorded the complete keyboard works of Haydn for Vox; also recorded Philips.

ALSLEBEN, Julius (1832–94)
b. Berlin, Germany. Took up oriental languages before turning to music: studied pf with F. Zech in Berlin at Kullak's. Developed career as concert pianist and teacher; also edited music journals.

ALVANIS, Louis (–   )
Request to last-known concert agents for biographical details met with no response.

ALVAREZ, Carmen (1905–)
b. Madrid, Spain. Studied at R. Cons. there under J. Tragó and F. Fuster. Appeared in European capitals, taught and specialized in music of Spanish composers.

ALWIN, Karl (1891–1945)
b. Königsberg, Germany. Pianist and conductor, trained in Berlin. Accompanist, especially of the soprano Elisabeth Schumann who was his wife, 1920–36. Recorded *HMV* as such.

AMADA, Kenneth (1931–)
b. New Jersey, USA. Pupil of M. Rosenthal, H. Kanner-Rosenthal, E. Steuermann and I. Philipp. Début 1951 in New York. Leventritt Comp. winner twice, 1959–60, won 12th place in Concours Reine Elisabeth, 1960, and the Harriet Cohen Music Award, London, 1961. Performed mainly in USA.

AMADÉ, Thaddaus Graf von (1783–1845)
b. Pressburg, Hungary. A Councillor of State who was an excellent pianist and who heard the

young Liszt and provided the means for his protégé to receive training.

AMATI, Orlanda (–)
b. New Jersey, USA. Student of Juilliard School and of K. Friedberg, L. Epstein and D. Saperton. Performed and taught.

am BACH, Rudolf: *see* BACH, Rudolf am

AMES, John Carlowitz (1860–1924)
b. Bristol, UK. Studied pf in Stuttgart and Dresden. London début 1881 featuring a recital of own compositions. Became interested in the Jankó keyboard and introduced it in London in 1888. Besides successful concert career, composed two pf concertos, chamber music, pf pieces and songs.

ANDA, Géza (1921–76)
b. Budapest, Hungary. Pupil of E. von Dohnányi there, winning Liszt Prize. Left Hungary during World War II, went to Switzerland, thereafter touring and recording. US début 1955, taking Swiss nationality same year. Distinguished pianist with catholic tastes. Recorded *Columbia*, Columbia and DG.
 Pupils included: Philibert Mess, Zsuzsanna Sirokay.

ANDERSEN, Diane (1934–)
b. Copenhagen, Denmark. Student of Brussels R. Cons. Début 1941. Has since toured worldwide and is noted exponent of contemporary Hungarian pf music. Married the violinist A. Gertler, lived and taught in Brussels. Recorded Hungaroton and Supraphon.

ANDERSEN, Stell (1897–)
b. Iowa, USA. Initial studies at Chicago musical colleges, then pf pupil of J. Lhevinne in New York, and I. Philipp in Paris. Début New York followed by appearances in USA and Europe and later in Central America. Reputation mainly as teacher.

ANDERSON, Lucy (Mrs) (1790–1878)
b. Bath, UK. Was pf teacher to Queen Victoria and the royal household and was the first woman pianist to appear at a concert of the (R.) Phil. Soc., giving the first performance in Britain of the Hummel pf concerto in B minor. Was highly popular with that audience, appearing nineteen times, her last in 1862 aged 72 in Beethoven's *Choral Fantasia*. Wessel & Co, one-time London publishers of first edition

of Chopin's works, caused the F minor concerto score to be dedicated to her when the composer was totally unaware of her existence. A contemporary report spoke of her 'delicate touch and legitimate style'.
 Pupils included: Kate Loder.

ANDERSON, Ronald Kinlock (1911–84)
b. Edinburgh, UK. Studied at the Univ. there, and later in Germany with C. Hansen and E. Fischer. Début London 1938. Was pianist of the Robert Masters Quartet 1939–71. Served in the RAF in World War II and was prof. Trinity Coll. 1946–63. Became artistic director of EMI in 1971, and was harpsichordist and writer.

ANDERSSON, Richard (1851–1918)
b. Stockholm, Sweden. Pf pupil of J. Boom at Stockholm R. Cons. 1867–74, then in Berlin with K. Schumann and H. Barth. Returned to Stockholm where he taught and performed. Became a member of R. Acad. and was pf prof. at R. Cons. from 1912. Composed pf pieces including a sonata and songs.
 Pupils included: Knut Bäck, Astrid Berwald, Gustav Heintze, Wilhelm Stenhammar, Adolf Wiklund, Victor Wiklund.

ANDREA, Genaro Maria d' (1860–1937)
b. Naples, Italy. Studied at the Cons. there under B. Cesi, making his début in 1875 at the age of 15. Built up successful career as pianist and went on a tour of Argentina in 1898 which met with so much acclaim that he decided to settle there, teaching and performing in between return visits to Europe. In 1905 he co-founded the Cons. Fracassi-d'Andrea in Buenos Aires and used the principles of his old master Cesi.

ANDREOLI, Carlo (1840–1908)
b. Mirandola, Italy. Brother of Guglielmo A and an excellent pianist who studied at Milan Cons. before becoming a pf prof. there. Toured as concert pianist and was in Britain in 1858.

ANDREOLI, Guglielmo (1835–60)
b. Mirandola, Italy. Studied at Milan Cons. and during a short life acquired fame as a pianist because of his poetic style. Visited Britain 1856–9. Brother of Carlo A.

ANDREOLI, Guglielmo (1862–?)
b. Modena, Italy. Of musical family as well as an all-rounder. Concert pianist, composer,

founder of popular concerts in Milan, played viola in quartets and was pf prof. at Milan Cons. from 1891. Wrote manual on harmony.
Pupils included: Edmundo Piazzini.

ANDRIESSEN, Willem (1887–1964)
b. Haarlem, Netherlands. Studied pf at Amsterdam Cons., where he won 1st Prize. Was appointed pf prof. at Hague Cons. 1910–18, then Director at Amsterdam Cons. from 1937. Compositions include a pf concerto in D minor.
Pupils included: Ro Van Hessen.

ANFOSSI, Giovanni (1864–?)
b. Ancona, Italy. Active as concert pianist before founding, in Milan, his own pf school which he named Pasquale Anfossi Cons. after his kinsman of that name (1727–97), once famous as a prolific composer of operas and Masses.

ANGELELLI, Carlo (1872–?)
b. Florence, Italy. Noted concert pianist and teacher of the time, also composer and transcriber.
Pupils included: Edmundo Piazzini.

ANGELET, Charles François (1797–1832)
b. Ghent, Belgium. Studied at Paris Cons. under P. Zimmerman. Took up concert career and studied composition with Fétis after being appointed to Brussels Cons. in pf teaching capacity. Court pianist to Dutch royal family from 1829. Composed mainly pf pieces.

ANIEVAS, Agustin (1934–   )
b. New York, USA, of Spanish-Mexican parentage. Child prodigy. Student of Juilliard School, took prize in Chicago 1958, giving six appearances with orchs. US début 1959; performed thereafter. Recorded EMI.

ANSORGE, Konrad (1862–1930)
b. Buchwald, Silesia. Studied at Leipzig Cons., then with F. Liszt 1885–6, being one of his last pupils. Toured Europe extensively then made US début 1887. Settled in Berlin where he enjoyed a brilliant reputation as an interpreter of Beethoven and Liszt. Taught for a time at the Klindworth-Scharwenka Cons. After World War I had a teaching post in Prague, but ill-health caused him to relinquish it. Composed a pf concerto, a sonata, chamber music and pf pieces. Recorded *Polydor*.
Pupils included: Dorothea Braus, Joseph

Challupper, Ernesto Drangosch, Eduard Erdmann, Sverre Jordan, Selim Palmgren, James Simon.

ANTHEIL, George (1900–59)
b. Trenton, USA. Pf pupil in Philadelphia of C. Sternberg; also of E. Bloch for composition. Early career as concert pianist touring Europe and USA after World War I. In 1920s composed a pf concerto, also for pf *Airplane Sonata* and *Sonate Sauvage*, as well as several chamber works. Later, after working in Europe on a Guggenheim Fellowship, turned to films, being involved in production of musicals in Hollywood. Wrote with insight on contemporary music, achieving at least one epigram: 'Art is not a question of precedence but of excellence.' Wrote *Bad Boy of Music* (1945).

ANTHIÔME, Eugène (1836–1916)
b. Paris, France. Student of Paris Cons., where he later taught during a long and successful career as pianist.
Pupils included: Maurice Ravel.

ANTON, Max (1877–1939)
b. Bornstedt, Germany. Pupil of B. Stavenhagen and J. Kwast. Performed widely and taught at Conss. of Munchen-Gladbach and Detmold. Also conducted. Compositions include pf concertos, pf pieces and songs.

ANTONELLI, Pina (–   )
Request to last-known concert agents for biographical details met with no response.

APPIANI, Vincenzo (1850–1932)
b. Monza, Italy. Pianist and pf prof. Milan Cons. Founder of Milanese Trio. Was highly esteemed as a concert artist.
Pupils included: Edmundo Piazzini.

ARCHER, Violet (1913–   )
b. Montreal, Canada. Studied there and in Europe, afterwards teaching and performing in USA. Was at Alberta Univ. from 1962. Compositions include chamber music and pf pieces.

ARCO, Annie d' (1920–   )
b. Marseilles, France, of Italian father. Pupil of M. Long. Varied career as recitalist and chamber-music player, and with leading orchs. Recorded L'Oiseau Lyre (Grand Prix de Disque), Erato and Calliope.

ARDÉVOL, José (1911–)
b. Barcelona, Spain. Studied pf there and was a prodigy. At age of twenty settled in Cuba where he made career as concert pianist and composer. Founded series of chamber-music concerts. His compositions include a concerto for three pfs and orch.

ARGERICH, Martha (1941–)
b. Buenos Aires, Argentina. Studied there, also with F. Gulda, N. Magaloff and A. B. Michelangeli. Prize-winnings include 1st Prize in the Chopin Comp. in Warsaw in 1965. Toured Europe and Americas extensively. Recorded Muza and DG.

ARIANI, Adriano (1880–?)
b. Macerata, Italy. Studied pf at Pesaro under M. Vitali and composition with Mascagni. Toured Italy as concert pianist and was acclaimed. Settled in USA after World War I for a few years where he had success with the baton.

ARIELI, Celia (1927–71)
b. Istanbul, Turkey. Studied in Jerusalem, at R. Acad., London, and at Juilliard School, New York. Performed widely.

ARMA, Paul (1905–)
b. Budapest, Hungary. Pupil of B. Bartók at R. Cons. there. Recitalist throughout Europe and USA both solo and as pianist in the Budapest Trio. Lecturer and conductor. Worked in Paris from 1935. Composed a pf concerto, chamber music, sonatas and pf pieces.

ARMBRUSTER, Karl (1846–1917)
b. Andernach, Germany. Studied pf at Cologne Cons., début at age of 9, settling in London when 17. Besides career as solo pianist, became increasingly involved as a conductor of Wagner's operas.

ARNAUD, Yvonne (1890–1958)
b. Bordeaux, France. Studied at Paris Cons. from the age of 9, winning 1st Prize for playing three years later. Toured extensively solo and with orch. under celebrated conductors before settling in London, marrying and taking up a successful career on the stage. Made occasional appearances on the concert platform. Probably the only pianist to have a theatre named after her (in Guildford, UK); certainly was the only

actress to play the pf in the famous Hoffnung series of concerts. Recorded *HMV* and EMI.

ARNOLD, Mary (1906–)
b. Newcastle, UK. Student of Newcastle Cons. (pupil of E. Bainton) and of Oxford Univ. Performed widely as soloist and in ensemble, also lecturer.

ARRAU, Claudio (1903–)
b. Chillan, Chile. First recital at 5. At 10 went to study at Stern Cons., Berlin, under M. Krause, winning the Liszt and Ibach Prizes. Came first in Int. Congress of Pianists in Switzerland in 1925, and so the long and world-wide career began. Noted for bold technique and broad, poetic readings, in his repertoire keeping to the mainstream. US début 1923, settling there 1941. *Conversations with Arrau* by Joseph Horowitz (1982) contains full biographical information. Recorded *Odeon, Columbia, Polydor*, Philips and others.
    Pupils included: Cyril Huvé, Philip Lorenz, Jan Odé, Charmion Ross-Oliver, Hilde Somer, Brigitte Wild.

ARTIMIW, Lydia (–)
b. Philadelphia, USA, of Ukrainian origin. Was a pupil of Curtis Inst. and of G. Graffman. Début Philadelphia at the age of 8, European début 1975, Rome, and first appeared in London in 1979. Was third in Leeds Int. Pf Comp. of 1978. Has given concerts solo and with orch. on both sides of the Atlantic. Recorded Chandos.

ASCHER, Joseph (1831–69)
b. London, UK. Studied pf with I. Moscheles in Leipzig, settling in Paris in 1849 where he later became court pianist. Is remembered for his facile salon pieces.

ASCOLI, Bernard d' (1958–)
b. Aubagne, France. Became blind at age of 3. First took to the organ but turned to the pf at the age of 12. Studied assiduously at Marseille Cons. and under P. Barbizet. Performed from the age of 14. Entered pf competitions and gained distinctions including the M. Long-J. Thibaud, Paris, 1979, and Leeds Int. Comp. 1981, where he came third. Performed throughout Europe. Hobbies include skiing. Is committed to playing works of the French School. Recorded EMI.

ASHKENAZY, Vladimir (1936–)
b. Gorki, USSR. Studied Moscow Cons. under
L. Oborin. Won 2nd Prize in Int. Chopin
Comp. Warsaw, 1955, and 1st in the Concours
Reine Elisabeth, Brussels, the following year.
In 1962 joint Gold Medallist (with J. Ogdon) of
the Int. Tchaikovsky Comp. Moscow. Left
Russia the following year, settling first in
London, later Iceland, then Switzerland.
Toured worldwide as renowned all-round
interpreter and later additionally conducted.
Recorded Saga, Everest and Decca.

ASHTON, Algernon (1859–1937)
b. Durham, UK. Studied at Leipzig Cons. and
was a pf pupil of K. Reinecke. Later was a
composition pupil of Raff in Frankfurt. Pf
prof. of R. Coll., London, 1885–1910. A fine
and cultured pianist who for many seasons
successfully toured Europe and UK. Was
prolific composer in many fields including over
200 pf pieces. Had a penchant for writing
letters to the Press on any and every subject,
claiming some 2,000 successes in print which
later he caused to be reprinted in book form.

ASKENASE, Stefan (1896–)
b. Lwow, Poland. Studied privately then with
E. von Sauer in Vienna. Was called up in
Austrian army during World War I, resuming
with von S in 1919. Début Warsaw 1920
followed by extensive tour. Taught Cairo
Cons. 1922–5 when he returned to Europe,
settling in Brussels. Became Belgian citizen
1951. Has toured throughout world. Recorded
DG, Nimbus and others.
  Pupils included: Ilan Rogoff, Joel Shapiro,
Andre Tchaikovsky, Mitsuko Uchida, Ro van
Hessen, Janice Williams.

ASPULL, George (1813–32)
b. Manchester, UK. Prodigy who gave his
début at the age of 9, appearing the following
year in London amid acclaim. Toured British
Isles and gave British première of Weber's
Konzertstück. Received an enthusiastic reception in Paris when he appeared there in 1825.
Composed pf pieces which were posthumously
published by his father.

ATKINSON, Leslie John (1929–)
b. Wellington, New Zealand. Studied there,
also in Rome and at the R. Coll. of Music,
London, where he settled. Toured Europe and
performed in UK and NZ.

AUBERT, Louis (1877–1968)
b. Parame, France. Was pupil of Paris Cons.
from age of 10. Taught pf by L. Diémer, who
tried to persuade him to become a virtuoso. For
a time pursued career of pianist, then turned to
composition, had successes and thereafter
devoted his energies to that field. Wrote *Suite
Brève* for two pfs (1900) and a *Fantaisie* (1901)
for pf and orch., also chamber music all with
pf parts. Is however principally remembered
for the opera *La Forêt Bleue*. Ravel's *Valses
Nobles et Sentimentales* are dedicated to A, who
gave the première in 1911.

AUER, Edward (1941–)
b. New York, USA. Studied at Juilliard School
there. Won 1st Prize in M. Long-J. Thibaud
Int. Comp., Paris, 1967; was fifth in the
Chopin Int. Comp., Warsaw, 1965: joint fifth
in the Tchaikovsky Int. Comp., Moscow,
1966; and seventh in the Concours Reine
Elisabeth, Brussels, 1968. Performed
throughout N. America, Europe and Japan.

AUS DER OHE, Adele: *see* **OHE, Adele aus
der**

AVELING, Valda (1920–)
b. Sydney, Australia. Pupil at New South
Wales State Cons. there. Début 1936, Sydney.
Widely toured concert pianist; also noted
harpsichordist.

AX, Emanuel (1949–)
b. Lwow, Poland. Son of Jewish parents who
survived World War II and who emigrated to
Canada before settling in New York when A
was 10 years old. He studied at the Juilliard
School and was a pupil of M. Münz. He competed in the Maryland Int. Pf Festival of 1971,
winning a Baldwin pf, and the following year
came 7th in the Concours Int. Reine Elisabeth
in Brussels. His real competitive triumph came
in 1974 when, in the inaugural A. Rubinstein
Int. Pf Master Comp. in Tel-Aviv, he came
first. Début in New York in 1975, and thus his
concert career began solo, with orchestra, in
chamber music, and in two-pf recitals with his
wife Yoko. In 1979 he won the Avery Fisher
Prize. That same year he told James Roos in an
interview that there is no simple way to ensure
a successful concert career: it is necessary to
know someone, a conductor or manager, or
win prizes. 'All performing artists are in a real
quandary. When a Rubinstein played what was
new music years ago, he just sat down and

learned it. Today, when we talk about contemporary music, we're talking about spending three or four years learning a whole new system of notation.' Recorded RCA.

AZANCHEVSKY, Mikhail Pavlovich
(1839–81)
b. Moscow, Russia. Studied in Leipzig, then with F. Liszt. Settled in Paris in 1866 where he acquired the d'Anders music collection which he gave to St Petersburg Cons. when appointed there as Director in 1870, a post he held for six years. Composed chamber music and pf works for one and two instruments.

BABADZHANIAN, Arno (1921–)
b. Erevan, USSR. An Armenian who studied at Erevan Cons. until 1947 when he went to Moscow Cons. under C. Igumnov, graduating as pianist the following year. Became pf prof. at Erevan Cons. from 1950. Pf compositions include a concerto, chamber works and pieces.

BABIN, Victor (1908–72)
b. Moscow, Russia. Student of A. Schnabel in Berlin from 1925 at the same time as Vitya Vronsky. Remained there as composer, subsequently marrying V. V. So began a famous duo career. They emigrated to the USA in 1937, where they speedily established a pre-eminent reputation. B composed mainly for pf, making a number of brilliant arrangements for two pfs. Was Director at Cleveland Cons. from 1961. Recorded *HMV*, American Columbia, RCA and Brunswick.

BACH, Carl Philipp Emanuel (1714–88)
b. Weimar, Germany. A brilliant keyboard player who embraced the cause of the early pf and wrote extensively for it in later years, developing the symphonic structure of sonata form as opposed to the then prevailing suite. Has been described as the father of modern pf playing. He wrote in a treatise: 'During the last few years my chief endeavour has been to play the pianoforte in spite of its deficiency in sustaining the sound, so much as possible, in a singing manner, and to compose for it accordingly. This is by no means easy, if we desire not to leave the ear empty or to disturb the noble simplicity of the cantabile by too much noise.'

BACH, Johann Christian (1735–82)
b. Leipzig, Germany. Eighteenth child of J.S.B. Also known as 'the English Bach' because he settled there and made a career as performer, composer, conductor and music master to the royal household. Played keyboard duets with W. A. Mozart who held him in high regard. Originally harpsichordist and in 1768 was the first musician to play a piano forte in public in London. In association with a string player, Karl Abel, organized most successful concerts both indoors and outside in gardens, e.g. Vauxhall. Did much through public performance and by composition to popularize the new keyboard instrument, and from 1775 used Hanover Square Rooms for concerts. His compositions for the pf included sets of concertos.

Pupils included: Wilhelm Bach, Joseph Mazzinghi.

BACH, Johann Christoph Friedrich (1732–95)
b. Leipzig, Germany. J.S.B's ninth son. Composed *c*. 1757 a sonata inscribed on front as for harpsichord or piano forte.

BACH, Johann Sebastian (1685–1750)
b. Eisenach, Germany. Played early hammer instruments on occasion, especially those made by Silbermann at the court of Frederick the Great at Potsdam; but did so without enthusiasm and did not compose for them. His music for keyboard instruments preceding the pf have always been consistently performed on the pf, and other works have been transcribed for the instrument by Liszt, Tausig, Brahms, Rachmaninov, Busoni, M. Hess *et al*.

BACH, Leonhard Emil (1849–1902)
b. Posen, Germany. Studied in Berlin and was pf pupil of T. Kullak, at whose Cons. he taught from 1869 until 1874 when he became court pianist in Prussia. Settled in London in 1882 and taught at Guildhall School. Composed pf pieces.

BACH, Rudolf am (1919–)
b. Trogen, Switzerland. Student of Zurich Cons. and later a pupil of E. Frey and F. Lamond. First male prizewinner in the Geneva Int. Comp. of 1940, and became successful concert pianist.

BACH, Wilhelm Friedrich Ernst (1759–1845)
b. Bückeburg, Germany. Son and pupil of Johann Christoph Friedrich Bach, ninth son of J.S.B.; also pupil of his uncle Johann Christian in London, becoming successful pianist, organist and teacher. Pianist to Queen Louise and teacher to her household. Composed pf works.

BACHAUER, Gina (1913–76)
b. Athens, Greece. Pupil of Athens Cons., then at École Normale, Paris, under A. Cortot. Received some tuition from S. Rachmaninov. Won Int. Comp. Vienna 1933 and thereafter toured as concert pianist. Settled in London and married the conductor Alec Sherman. Recorded EMI, Desmar and Erato.
See also Appendix of winners of piano competitions under UNITED STATES OF AMERICA – Salt Lake City.

BACHE, Constance (1846–1903)
b. Birmingham, UK. Studied pf at Munich Cons. and later with K. Klindworth. An accident in 1883 ended her career as concert pianist, and she became a teacher, writer and translator. Sister of Francis B and Walter B.

BACHE, Francis Edward (1833–58)
b. Birmingham, UK. Eldest of the Bache trio of pianists. Studied in London under Sir W. S. Bennett and abroad. Died at a tragically early age after showing great promise.

BACHE, Walter (1842–88)
b. Birmingham, UK. Most famous member of one-time family of notable musicians. Pupil of F. Liszt and well-known pianist who propagated the music of Liszt, though at his Phil. Soc. début in London in 1880 he played the Mozart pf concerto for two pfs with Anna Mehlig. In April 1886 gave a reception in Liszt's honour when that composer visited Britain for last time. Persisted in advocating Liszt's music despite opposition, and shortly before his death gave an all-Liszt recital, an avant-garde pursuit in those days. Was pf prof. R. Acad., London.
Pupils included: Mary Carmichael.

BACKER-GRÖNDAHL, Agathe Ursula (1847–1907)
b. Holmestrand, Norway. Studied pf initially in Norway; then, from 1866, with T. Kullak in Berlin, with H. von Bülow, then with F. Liszt. Début 1868 in Oslo in the Beethoven *Emperor* under Grieg's baton. Appeared in Leipzig 1871 at start of tour of Europe. Specialized in music of the Romantic period, an approach reflected in her pf works and songs. Was associated with performances of Grieg including the concerto under his baton. Later taught. Deafness ended concert career, and she died in the same year as Grieg. Her only appearance for the R. Phil. Soc. had been in the Grieg concerto in March 1889.
Pupils included: Fridtjof Backer-Gröndahl, Bertha Feiring-Tapper, Judith Heber, Martin Knutsen, Edvard Kreutz, Johan Lunde, Nanne Storm, Dagmar Walle-Hansen.

BACKER-GRÖNDAHL, Fridtjof (1885–1959)
b. Oslo, Norway. Son of Agathe Ursula B-G who taught him pf. Later studied in Berlin under E. Rudorff, K. Barth and E. von Dohnányi. Début Oslo 1903 and subsequently appeared regularly throughout Europe, latterly residing in London. Composed pf pieces. Described by Edvard Grieg as taking 'everyone by storm with his magnificent art, his noble and modest character'.
Pupils included: Odd Grüner-Hegge.

BACKHAUS, Wilhelm (1884–1969)
b. Leipzig, Germany. Studied at the Cons. there. At the age of 10 attended a concert at the Gewandhaus at which E. d'Albert played both Brahms pf concertos with the composer conducting. The event made a deep impression on the boy, who later studied with d'Albert in Frankfurt. His début was in 1900. The Brahms B flat was in his repertoire by 1902, and the following year he played it under the baton of Hans Richter who had often conducted it when the composer was soloist. The performance Backhaus gave of both works during his lifetime as well as three different recordings of each made over three decades may be said to have historical authenticity.
In 1905 he won the Rubinstein Prize in Paris for pf-playing, B. Bártok coming second. The same year he took on teaching work at R. Manchester Coll. He left after a year, the call of his art being too important to stay in provincial Britain (as indeed happened in the case of his

successor, Egon Petri), having already established a reputation as an international artist of immense technical accomplishment as well as being an ardent poet of the instrument.

He became a star of the gramophone in its infancy, wholeheartedly believing in its future as an art form and means of education, and made a number of first-ever recordings including a potted version of the Grieg concerto; the Beethoven *Emperor* as well as both books of Chopin's *Études*. Over a period of forty years he recorded the Beethoven concertos and sonatas twice, the 4th and 5th concertos and several sonatas three times each.

He toured the musical centres of the western world regularly and was much esteemed solo and with orch. He taught little. His repertoire ranged through the German classics to the Romantics but he hardly ventured into the contemporary scene. He was one of the great Beethoven exponents of his generation and was regarded as the darling of Vienna while Schnabel was the darling of Berlin. B was always popular in the UK and after World War II remade his reputation in the USA. He was one among few German pianists possessing the capacity to play Chopin beautifully.

In the '30s he suffered a spell in a concentration camp on Hitler's orders for refusing to accompany the Berlin Phil. with W. Fürtwangler on a prestigious tour through occupied Europe. On release he settled in Switzerland and resumed his concert career. His appearances gradually reduced with the onset of advancing years, but he was working to the end, dying after being suddenly taken ill in the middle of a recital. He had been before the public constantly for just on seventy years.

When he played the *Emperor* in London in 1960 at the age of 76, Donald Mitchell wrote: 'I do not think I have heard an interpretation of this work in which the figuration for piano sounded more beautiful, either rich or slender in tone as the occasion demanded. No less remarkable was the subtle ebb and flow of Backhaus' tempi, a rubato which arose most naturally and happily from the character of the passage or the phrase concerned.'

Z. Kodály attributed to B the ability at any time to play any Bach Prelude and Fugue in any key. He regularly used a dummy keyboard for most of his mechanical practice.

In *Speaking of Pianists* Abram Chasins wrote: 'There was never a time when Backhaus could not toss off any or all of the Chopin etudes or the Brahms-Paganini Variations with an imperturbable calm, an implacable security that left one open-mouthed. Not everyone . . . knew how to measure such achievement.'

Recorded *Polydor, HMV, Decca*, Decca and possibly others; the only known pianist whose recording history spanned from cylinder to stereo disc.

Pupils included: Ellen Ballon, William Busch.

BACON, Denise (–   )
b. Newton, USA. Pupil of M. Horszowski. Début 1942, Boston. Concert pianist, lecturer and writer. Director of Kodály Inst. from 1969.

BACON, Ernst (1898–   )
b. Chicago, USA. Studied there and in California, then later in Vienna. Won Pulitzer Prize 1932 and Guggenheim Memorial Fellowship 1939. Held a number of teaching posts and professorships in USA as well as performing there and in Europe. Composed chamber music, a first symphony for pf and orch., *Riolama* for the same, *Saws* for chorus and pf and two volumes of songs. Solo pf works include duets. Wrote *Words on Music* (1960) and *Notes on the Piano* (1963).

Pupils included: Enrique Solares.

BACON, Katherine (1896–   )
b. Chesterfield, UK. Went to USA, studied at Peabody Cons., Baltimore, and later in New York with Arthur Newstead, whom she married. Début New York, 1921. During Beethoven centenary in 1927 she gave series of historical recitals embracing the 32 sonatas and the following year commemorated Schubert's centenary by playing all the pf works. Taught at Juilliard Summer School.

BADURA-SKODA, Paul (1927–   )
b. Vienna, Austria. Pf pupil of E. Fischer and of Vienna Cons. Début 1948, Vienna, and has toured extensively since, being well known through many gramophone recordings. Specializes in Mozart but has also been identified with modern works, being the dedicatee of Martin's 2nd pf concerto which he premièred. Recorded Nixa, Unicorn, Europa and others. Wrote *Interpreting Mozart on the Keyboard* (1957).

Pupils included: Zsuzsanna Sirokay.

BAGBY, Albert Morris (1859–1941)
b. Rushville, Ill., USA. Studied pf in Europe,

and was a pupil of F. Liszt. Became a performer on returning to USA, additionally taking up concert management, being well-known for the Bagby morning musicales in New York which he ran until his death.

BAGNATI, Cayetano (1840–1904)
b. Tropea, Italy. Student at Naples where he was a prodigy, completing training at the Cons. there. Performed with great success. Visited Argentina and later settled there, founding Almagro Cons. in 1890. Composed chamber music, pf works and songs.

BAILEY-APFELBECK, Marie Louise (1873–1927)
b. Nashville, USA. Studied pf in Leipzig Cons. under K. Reinecke, then in Vienna with T. Leschetizky. Début 1893, Leipzig. Returned to USA, making her New York début, which was followed by coast-to-coast tour and appearances in Canada.

BAINES, William (1899–1922)
b. Horbury, UK. Apart from a few lessons locally, was self-taught and forced by family circumstances to work as cinema pianist from age of 16. Was prolific composer mainly for pf and gave recitals locally. Died prematurely from tuberculosis, leaving a wealth of music, published and in MS that, if rather derivative, nevertheless shows original talent which, had he lived, might well have produced an important British composer.

BAINTON, Edgar Leslie (1880–1956)
b. Coventry, UK. Studied at R. Coll., London. Appointed pf prof. Newcastle-upon-Tyne Cons. 1901 and was Principal 1912–34. Conducted Newcastle PO during that period. An examiner to the Associated Board, R. Schools of Music, London, also adjudicator at major competitions in UK and abroad. His *Concerto-Fantasia* for pf and orch. was premièred at a R. Phil. Soc. concert in 1922 by Winifred Christie, the composer conducting. Became Principal of New South Wales State Cons. of Music, Sydney, 1934–46.
Pupils included: Mary Arnold, Charles Newby.

BAIRD, Martha (1895–1971)
b. Madera, USA. Pupil of N. England Cons. and later of A. Schnabel in Berlin. Performed in Europe and USA. Married John D. Rockefeller Jr in 1937.

BAJARDI, Francesco (1867–1934)
b. Isnello, Palermo, Italy. Student of Cons. there and later of S. Cecilia Cons., Rome, in the pf class of G. Sgambati, winning the Boisselot Prize. Was accounted one of S's best pupils and began a distinguished career as soloist. London début 1894. In addition to concert tours became pf prof. at S. Cecilia Cons. Composed pf pieces of note.
Pupils included: Carlo Zecchi.

BAKST, Rysard (1926–　)
b. Warsaw, Poland. Pupil of Moscow Cons. and gained 6th Prize in the Int. Chopin Comp. Warsaw in 1949. Toured extensively throughout the world and taught in Warsaw and in Manchester, UK. Recorded EMI and Muza.

BALABAN, Emanuel (1895–　)
b. Brooklyn, USA. Pf pupil of S. Stojowski. Accompanied international instrumentalists and taught, especially the art of accompanying.

BALAKIREV, Mily Alexeievich (1837–1910)
b. Nijny-Novgorod, Russia. Apart from a few lessons from his mother and from A. Dubuc, a pupil of J. Field, was self-taught, making his pf début in 1855, the year in which he completed his *Reminiscences of Glinka's 'A Life for the Tsar'*, a brilliant fantasia written in the operatic-transcription-Liszt-Thalberg style. His creative life fell into two sections separated by a period of seclusion. The pianistic triumph of the first part was the Oriental Fantasy *Islamey*, and the achievement of the other period was the long and beautiful pf sonata in B flat minor in the first movement of which he introduces fugal form. There are also two pf concertos, the second of which was completed by S. Liapunov after the composer's death. Amongst late compositions are a *Suite* and a set of arrangements of Russian folk-songs for pf duet. Tchaikovsky regarded B as the most gifted of the 'Big Five' St Petersburg composers who tended to dissipate his talents for music in other directions.

BALDWIN, Dalton (　–　)
b. New Jersey, USA. Student of Juilliard School and of Oberlin Univ. Completed musical training in Europe. Has specialized in accompanying and became one of the world's leading exponents of the art.

BALLON, Ellen (1898–1969)
b. Montreal, Canada, of Russian parentage. A

child prodigy who was a pupil of McGill Cons. from age of 6. From 1906 studied with R. Joseffy in New York, where her début took place 1910 with New York SO and Walter Damrosch. Later a pupil of J. Hofmann, W. Backhaus and A. Jonas. Became notable concert pianist and teacher. Toured Europe 1927–8 and settled in London until World War II, when she returned to Canada, pursuing the dual career until she died in Montreal. Had extensive repertoire and propagated the pf music of Villa-Lobos, commissioning his 1st pf concerto and giving the première 1946 in Rio under the composer's baton. Recorded V-L on *Decca* and Decca.

BALMER, Hans (1903–)
b. Birrwil, Switzerland. Studied at Basle Cons. and, later in Paris, with R. Casadesus for pf and N. Boulanger for composition. From 1932 taught pf at Basle Acad., performed and also played the organ. Composed mainly chamber music and songs; also wrote upon technical aspects of the art.

BALMER, Luc (1898–)
b. Munich, Germany. Pf student of E. Petri at Basle, also of E. Levy 1915–19; later studied composition with Busoni in Berlin. Taught in various Swiss cons.; also conducted. Composed *Concertino* for pf and small orch., pf pieces and songs.

BALOGH, Erno (1897–)
b. Budapest, Hungary. Studied Cons. there under B. Bartók for pf and Z. Kodály for composition. Won Franz Liszt Prize and graduated 1914. Studied further with L. Kreutzer in Berlin; début there 1920. After touring Europe settled in USA as soloist and accompanist. Composed pf pieces and songs.

BALOGHOVA, Dagmar (1929–)
b. Ilava, Switzerland. Studied in Prague; début 1952 there. Has toured Europe, Near East and USA. Recorded various.

BALSAM, Arthur (1906–)
b. Warsaw, Poland. Pupil of Lodz Cons., in which city he made his début in 1918. Toured widely before settling in the USA. Accompanied celebrities in sonata recitals and had a very wide repertoire. Recorded Westminster, Philips, Nixa, Decca and Oiseau-Lyre.

BÁNHALMI, Gyorgy (1926–)
b. Hungary. Studied in Budapest and won 9th Prize in the Reine Elisabeth Comp. Brussels in 1956. Emigrated to USA and settled in Chicago, performing and teaching.

BARBER, Samuel (1910–81)
b. West Chester, Pa, USA. At age of 6 became pf pupil of William Green, a former pupil of T. Leschetizky. Went on to study at Curtis Inst. under I. Vengerova for pf where, in 1928, he won a prize for a violin sonata. The most important works for pf are the sonata Op. 26 in four movements premièred by V. Horowitz in 1950 and the concerto Op. 38 which earned him the Pulitzer Prize and which had its first performance in 1962 with John Browning and the Boston SO. Also wrote *Excursions*, a set of four pieces (1944), and chamber music including an early cello sonata (1932). Was also songwriter.

BARBIZET, Pierre (1922–)
b. Arica, Chile. Studied Paris Cons. and settled in France from where he toured world-wide.
Pupils included: Bernard d'Ascoli, Jacques Gauthier.

BARBOUR, Florence Newell (1867–1946)
b. Providence, USA. Enjoyed long public career as recitalist as well as concerto and chamber-music player. Composed many pf pieces and songs.

BARBOUR, Lyell (1897–1967)
b. UK. Studied in London and was awarded the Tobias Matthay Gold Medal. Toured Europe and USA as concert pianist. A musician of great sensibility and with splendid technique, who excelled in the works of Chopin and Debussy. Was also a teacher, working in California where he died. No further details discovered.

BARENBOIM, Daniel (1942–)
b. Buenos Aires, Argentina. Pupil of father, then of N. Boulanger and E. Fischer. Was child prodigy who went on to become an international artist of the front rank. Took up conducting additionally. Married the cellist Jacqueline du Pré in 1967. Recorded EMI and DG.

BARENTZEN, Aline van (1897–)
b. Somerville, USA. A child prodigy who studied with E. Delaborde at Paris Cons. and

later in Vienna with T. Leschetizky. Toured as concert pianist and was also a teacher. Made first recording of de Falla's *Nights in the Gardens of Spain*, Casella conducting – *Victor*.

BARERE, Simon (1896–1951)
b. Odessa, Russia. Studied from the age of 11, showing phenomenal technical ability. At 15 became a pupil of A. Essipova at St Petersburg Cons., later completing his studies with F. Blumenfeld. Graduated 1919 with the Rubinstein Prize and commenced concert career. In 1929 settled in Berlin, moving to Stockholm during World War II. London début 1934; New York début 1938. Became one of the greatest virtuosi of his generation. In 1951 collapsed and died on Carnegie Hall platform during a concerto. His wife was an excellent pianist and teacher. He recorded *RCA*.
    Pupils included: Eline Nygaard.

BARGIEL, Woldemar (1828–97)
b. Berlin, Germany. Step-brother to Klara Schumann. Pupil of Leipzig Cons. and under I. Moscheles for pf. Taught in Berlin before being appointed prof. Cologne Cons. Taught for a time in Rotterdam before returning to Berlin 1874 as prof. at the Hochschule. Was esteemed in his day as a composer in the Schumann idiom, including chamber music, suites for two and four hands, numerous pf pieces and songs.

BAR-ILLAN, David (1930–   )
b. Haifa, Israel. Studied at Haifa Cons. then in USA at Juilliard and Mannes. Début 1960, New York; thereafter toured widely throughout USA and Europe. Taught, held masterclasses and contributed to musical journals.

BÄRMANN, Karl (1839–1913)
b. Munich, Germany. Studied there, also with F. Liszt in Weimar. After a spell as concert pianist settled in USA. Also taught and composed pf music.
    Pupils included: Mrs H. H. A. Beach, George Copeland, Bruno Klein, Max Schwarz.

BARNARD, Trevor (1938–   )
b. London, UK. Student of R. Acad. of Music, and R. Coll., London. Performed widely with no known speciality or preferences.

BARRATT, Edgar (1877–1928)
b. Lincoln, UK. Studied pf at Leipzig Cons. mainly under R. Teichmüller. Settled in

Glasgow as pianist and accompanist to Scottish Orch. for many years. Was noted as chamber-music player and accompanied Emma Albani on several extended tours. Prolific composer for pf and for voice, mostly in Scottish idiom. Much of it was published and became popular.

BARRATT, Mary Louise (1888–1969)
b. Oslo, Norway. Studied at Lindeman's School, Oslo, then at S. Cecilia under G. Sgambati, and in London with P. Grainger. Début 1908, Oslo. Toured Scandinavia regularly thereafter and in 1916 married the violinist Henrik Due.

BARTH, Hans (1897–1956)
b. Leipzig, Germany. At age of 6 won scholarship at Gewandhaus; studied with K. Reinecke. Went to USA 1907; début same year. Held a number of teaching posts in New York while performing and inventing, developing the first quarter-tone pf which he eventually demonstrated in Carnegie Hall in 1930. Finally lived and worked in Jacksonville, Florida, where he died. His published compositions include sonatas. Recorded *RCA*.
    Pupils included: Richard Andersson, Howard Brockway, Karl Ekman, Wilhelm Kempff, Karl Preyer, Edward Schneider.

BARTH, Karl Heinrich (1847–1922)
b. Pillau, Germany. Pupil of H. von Bülow, H. von Bronsart and K. Tausig. Was fine concert pianist who toured, visiting Britain in 1876 for a number of recitals and concerts including a Henselt pf concerto at a Phil. concert. Founded Barth Piano Trio which gave many successful recitals, and taught in Berlin at Stern's Cons.; then later at the Hochschule, became head of pf dept in 1910. Retired 1921.
    Pupils included: Fridtjof Backer-Gröndahl, Theodor Bohlmann, Dagny Knutsen, Martin Knutsen, Leonard Liebling, Edward Noyes, Bronislaw Pozniak, Rudolph Reuter, Arthur Rubinstein, Ernest Schelling, Wilhelm Stenhammer.

BARTHOLD, Kenneth van (1927–   )
b. Java. Début Bournemouth, UK. Recitalist, teacher and adjudicator but probably best known to British public for television documentaries on ancient pfs into which he has done much research, playing and recording (various). Wrote several works on the history and construction of the pf.

BARTLETT, Ethel (1900–78)
b. London, UK. Pupil of R. Acad. of Music; there under Tobias Matthay, then later with Artur Schnabel. Début London, 1916. Established duo-team with Rae Robertson whom she married, and thereafter toured regularly as duettists in solo recitals and with orch. First performance of Bax two-pf sonata ISCM, London, 1931. Benjamin Britten's early pf works *Scottish Ballad, Introduction and Rondo alla Burlesca*, and *Mazurka elegiac* were all dedicated to the Bartlett-Robertson team. Recorded *HMV, Columbia* and others.

BARTÓK, Béla (1881–1945)
b. Nagyszentmiklos, Hungary (now in Romania), of musical parents. Studied pf from 5, composed from the age of 9, and played in public at 11. Pupil of a teacher called Lázló Erkel in Pressburg, through whom he heard good musical performances and used his own virtuosic gifts to gain access to chamber music, a factor reflected in his output. There he also met E. von Dohnányi. As a teenager he played advanced Liszt in public and in 1899 entered Budapest R. Acad. under S. Thomán for pf and Hans Koessler for composition. Owing to difficulties in outlook and temperament with Koessler he concentrated on developing pf technique and made his Budapest début in 1900. By that time he had acquired a remarkable ability to sight-read complicated scores and memorize at one reading. He graduated in 1903, exempted from final examinations on grounds of proficiency. That same year he appeared in Berlin and Vienna and met influential musicians in both cities. In 1905 he entered the Rubinstein Comp. in Paris, coming second to W. Backhaus, who won 1st Prize for pf playing. He also fulfilled in 1906 a concert tour with the Hungarian violinist Ferenc Vécsey. So far he had chosen a virtuosic path, his creative work having been somewhat derivative. All that changed when he met Z. Kodály.

Together they began collecting genuine folk-music which became an inevitable outlet for B's mental energy and intense patriotism. He listed the music in minute detail, and it became the basis for his monumental pf work *Mikrokosmos*. In 1907 he succeeded Thomán at the Acad., and for a time this additional work reduced his creative output. He was a meticulous and extremely gifted pf teacher but as a composer was meeting with opposition and criticism, even with his revised Op. 1,

Rhapsody for pf and orch., first performed in its new guise in 1909 in Budapest.

The collecting of folk-music material gradually extended into Romania, whence came the *Two Romanian Dances* premièred by the composer in Paris in 1910. He toured Europe as a pianist in between academic duties, becoming recognized as a player of distinction. Kodály said: 'Bartók was a phenomenal pianist but he was not attractive enough to become popular.'

World War I temporarily ended his research in the Balkans. When the old political order collapsed, his patriotism was questioned because his research had taken him outside Hungary. For a time he contemplated leaving his country but resumed extensive tours as pianist, especially in western European countries, and his works came increasingly to be performed at festivals. In 1926 he composed the pf sonata and 1st pf concerto, and the following year made his first tour of the USA. It tired him, as did a tour of USSR in 1929.

The 2nd pf concerto was written in 1930. In 1934 he relinquished teaching at Budapest Acad., devoting time to *Mikrokosmos*, which had been started in 1926 and was destined to be completed just before World War II. The sonata for two pfs and percussion belongs to 1937.

By 1940, when his mother died, there was nothing to detain him in Hungary, so early that year he went to the USA to fulfil an already arranged tour with the violinist Joseph Szigeti, and just stayed on there. The USA was now very ready to accept and fête him, and give him work, research facilities and honorary degrees.

In 1942 leukaemia developed, and his last work for his instrument, the 3rd pf concerto, was completed all but for a few bars of orchestration when he died in New York.

One source claims that in his lifetime B collected folk-melodies to the extent of some 3,000 Hungarian, 3,500 Romanian and 200 Arabic pieces. Besides arrangements in that field and early unpublished pieces, pf solo works include *Rhapsody No. 1* (arranged also for pf and orch. as well as for two pfs, and also for violin and pf), *Four Piano Pieces*, Op. 4, *Bagatelles*, Op. 6, *Allegro barbaro, Sonatina, Suite*, Op. 14, three *Études*, Op. 18, a sonata, *Mikrokosmos* (150 progressive studies), another suite *Out of Doors*, also miscellaneous pieces comprising folk-songs, dances, improvizations and sketches. Bartók composed three pf concertos (Nos. 1 and 2 arranged for two pfs); a *Sonata for two pianos and percussion* which is also available in the form of a concerto for two pfs and orch., a suite No. 2 for two pfs, two sonatas for violin and pf, a second *Rhapsody* for violin and pf, and *Contrasts* for violin, clarinet and pf. His stage work *The Miraculous Mandarin* was arranged for pf duet.

B married twice: his second wife, Ditta (née Pásztory), was a piano pupil of his at the Acad. and later often appeared with him in performances of his works for two pfs, besides propagating his solo works. Recorded *Columbia, Patria, Qualiton, HMV* and Bartók labels.

Pupils included: Paul Arma, Ernö Balogh, Josef Gát, Elisabeth Klein, Lili Kraus, Katalin Nemes, Árpád Sándor, György Sándor, Sándor Veress.

BARTÓK, Ditta (1903–82)
b. Rimaszombat, Hungary. Studied pf at Royal Acad., Budapest under B. Bartók whose second wife she became at the age of eighteen. Appeared with him in many concerts of music for two pfs and accompanied him to USA in 1940, returning to Hungary after his death in 1945. Recorded Vox.

BASLIK, Miroslav (1931–   )
b. Czechoslovakia. Spent a number of years studying music at Bratislava Cons. as well as the Acad., graduating in 1961. Wrote a pf sonata, a set of five *Bagatelles* and other works.

BASSFORD, William (1840–1902)
b. New York, USA. Concert pianist and organist who also composed and is credited with having completed *Estrella*, an opera by William Wallace.

BATALINA, Alexandra Ivanova: *see* **HUBERT, Alexandra Ivanova**

BATE, Stanley (1912–59)
b. Plymouth, UK. Pupil of R. Coll., London, and of A. Benjamin for pf before studying with P. Hindemith in Berlin and N. Boulanger in Paris. Pianist and composer. In 1938 married Peggy Glanville-Hicks, Australian-born composer, critic and writer who had also trained at R. Coll., London. They went to New York in 1942; there was a divorce in 1948 and Mrs Bate became US citizen. Among his compositions are several pf concertos, pieces and music for two pfs for which he had toured Australia with his wife in 1939.

BATH, Hubert (1883–1945)
b. Barnstaple, UK. Student R. Acad., studying pf under O. Beringer. Composed much pf music and film music especially *Cornish Rhapsody* for pf and orch. from *Love Story*.

BAUER, Harold (1873–1951)
b. New Malden, UK, of German father and British mother. Studied violin until 1892 when I. Paderewski advised him to take up pf. Largely self-taught but received some lessons from the Pole in Paris where B lived chiefly until World War I. Piano début 1893 when he achieved rapid fame in Europe. US début 1900 with Boston SO. Besides solo and concerto work B was a good chamber-music player, on occasion forming trio with Thibaud and Casals, also duo recitals with Elman and Kreisler (see also under latter). RPS Gold Medal 1912. Settled in USA during World War I where he began to exercise an immense influence upon its musical life, in 1918 founding the Beethoven Soc. of New York with which he was connected until 1941 and which promoted unfamiliar chamber music. Directed pf section of Manhattan School of Music. His repertory ranged very widely, and his pre-1914 Paris days are reflected in the fact that Ravel's *Ondine* is dedicated to him and he gave first Paris performance of Debussy's *Children's Corner Suite*. Later gave New York première of Ravel's *Concerto in G*. Made arrangements for solo pf including Franck's organ works; also edited Brahms and Schumann for Schirmer. Recorded *RCA, HMV* and *Schirmer*.

Pupils included: Creighton Allen, Winifred Christie, George Copeland, Patrick O'Sullivan, Elizabeth Quaile, Frank Sheridan, Eleanor Spencer.

BAUER, Kurt (1928–   )
b. Kempten, Germany. Pf teachers included W. Gieseking. Début 1952. Prizewinner of international competitions. Performed intensively and was pf prof. at Hanover Musikhochschule.

BAUME, Émile (1903–   )
b. Toulon, France. Pupil of his father, then of Paris Cons., winning Diémer Prize 1927. After studying conducting with F. Weingartner, performed in Europe for some years during 1930s then settled in USA before returning to Europe after World War II.

BAUMFELDER, Friedrich (1836–1916)
b. Dresden, Germany. Pupil of Leipzig Cons. under I. Moscheles and E. Wenzel. Concert pianist and taught in Dresden. Was prolific composer of mainly lightweight pieces.

BAUMGARTNER, Paul (1903–)
b. Altstätten, Switzerland. Pf pupil of E. Erdmann. Was pf prof. at Cologne for eight years, returning to Switzerland 1937 to become head of pf dept at Basle Cons. As concert pianist has a wide repertoire and is a fine technician.
Pupils included: Alfred Brendel, Radoslav Kvapil.

BAX, Sir Arnold (Edward Trevor)
(1883–1953)
b. London, UK. Pupil of R. Acad. there, and of T. Matthay. Was credited with the ability to transcribe complicated orch. scores at the pf keyboard but rarely appeared in public, usually in performances of own works. Compositions include *Symphonic Variations* and *Winter Legends* (both for pf and orch.) four pf sonatas and many pf pieces for solo and two pfs, also chamber music. R. Phil. Soc. Gold Medal 1931; knighted 1937; Master of the King's Musick 1942. Harriet Cohen pioneered his pf works, including a concerto for the left hand which was written for her after she injured her right arm and which she premièred at Cheltenham Festival, 1950. Wrote autobiography, *Farewell my Youth* (1943). Recorded *HMV*.

BAY, Emmanuel (1891–1967)
b. Crimea, Russia. Lived in Lodz, Poland, and was student of St Petersburg Cons. 1908–13 when he graduated with 1st Prize. Toured Europe and took lessons from L. Godowsky in Vienna. His long concert career was mainly that of accompanist to celebrities, especially such great string-players as Heifetz, Elman and Piatigorsky. Died suddenly of heart failure on tour in Israel. Recorded various labels as accompanist.

BEACH, Mrs H. H. A. (née Cheney)
(1867–1944)
b. Henniker, USA. Pf pupil of E. Perabo and K. Bärmann, self-taught in composition. Début 1883, Boston, began successful career which was relaxed somewhat after her marriage in 1885 when she turned increasingly to composition. After becoming a widow in 1910,

returned to concert platform, appearing in Europe a number of times. Composed chamber music, pf pieces and many songs.

BEAN, David (–)
b. Rochester, N.Y., USA, of Russian-USA parentage. Student of Oberlin Cons., and later worked under E. Steuermann at the Juilliard School, New York. Début there in 1957, and as soloist and concerto player appeared in USA, Europe, USSR and S. America. Prof. at Miami Univ., Oxford, Ohio. Recorded RCA and ABC Westminster.

BEATON, Isabella (1870–1929)
b. Iowa, USA. Pupil of M. Moszkowski in Berlin. Taught pf in Iowa, 1892–3, then spent next four years teaching in Berlin. Returned to USA where she taught and performed in Cleveland. Established the Beaton School of Music.

BECKER, Gustav Louis (1861–1959)
b. Richmond, USA. Appeared in public at the age of 11. Studied in New York and then in Berlin under M. Moszkowski and X. Scharwenka. Returning home, he taught at National Cons. On the day after he was ninety-one, he gave a recital in New York commemorating eighty years from his début. Appeared again in public in 1955 – America's Francis Planté! Composed pf works and wrote on technique.

BECKER, Rainer (1955–)
b. Heidelberg, W. Germany. Student of Hanover High School for Music and pupil of H. Leygraf.

BECKMAN-SCHERBINA, Elena
(1881–1951)
b. Russia. Pf pupil of C. Igumnov and adhered mostly to the classical repertoire.

BECKWITH, John (1927–)
b. Victoria, BC, Canada. Studied there and in Paris. Performed; also taught at Univ. of Toronto. Composer of chamber works and pf pieces.

BEECHAM, Lady Betty Humby-: *see*
HUMBY-BEECHAM, Lady Betty

BEETHOVEN, Ludwig van (1770–1827)
b. Bonn, Germany. Received early musical instruction from his father, a singer and

teacher of music. Received help also from others, but as a pf-player was largely self-taught. Composed his first three keyboard sonatas by the age of 12, and his abilities were praised by both W. A. Mozart and F. J. Haydn. Played a number of instruments and on occasion took his place among strings in orchs.

From an early age showed remarkable talent for improvisation in an era when it was a popular pastime, not to add serious sport, for pianists to compete in public in this spontaneous art of which we know nothing today. The young B was always willing to enter into the spirit of a contest and was usually declared the winner. But he was also renowned for his interpretation of the Bach '48'. His lifespan coincided with the early development of the pf, and so the Bonn records are blurred as to the extent to which he played instruments whose strings were plucked and those which were struck with hammers. (First editions of his pf sonatas up to Op. 27 were endorsed 'for harpsichord or piano', for it should be remembered that the change-over in the home from harpsichord to pf did not take place overnight.)

It is known that a number of pfs by Johann Stein (1728–92) of Augsburg were in use in Bonn in 1787 and that B was quite at home on them. Mozart had used Stein's instruments from 1777 when pedal mechanism was operated by the knees. The change-over to foot-operated mechanism occurred around 1789. At that time the instrument's action was 'shallow', giving a delicate sound, and the keyboard compass was only 5 to 5½ octaves. Editors of music of that period broadened the sound effect of the original scores by extending the bass, so using more of the keyboard as we now know it.

B went to Vienna late in 1792 to study with Haydn. In fact he settled there. Haydn claimed him as a pupil but B never acknowledged the fact, although he admitted receiving help. He also studied composition with Albrechtsberger, Salieri and Förster. It seems he was a difficult student and that, while still learning, he began to teach F. Ries. At this time he would have become familiar with the instruments of the Viennese maker Andreas Streicher (1761–1833), for it is on record that he induced the latter to research and improve his action mechanism.

His public début was in Vienna in 1795 in the first performance of his 2nd pf concerto, first of five but subsequently held back for revision so that it was overtaken by the one in C major which has become known as No. 1 in order of publication. Both concertos were played by the composer in the Austrian capital in a concert in 1800. Meantime, in 1796 he had made a concert tour including Nürnberg, Prague and Berlin, returning to Prague two years later when he indulged in a battle of extemporization with a couple of concert pianists.

Around 1800, aged 30 and at the height of his powers, he became aware of a defect in hearing which was to develop into total deafness. A new dimension thus came to be added to this turbulent character. He premièred the C minor pf concerto (No. 3) in 1803, and the G major (No. 4) in 1808, by which time his concert days were numbered on account of deteriorating hearing.

The year 1800 marks the end of what has become known as his first period of composition. In terms of pf music the period embraces the first three concertos as well as pf sonatas up to and including the one in B flat Op. 22. His second period goes to 1809 and enfolds the last two concertos and pf sonatas up to and including the E flat Op. 81a, plus the *Choral Fantasia* and the *Triple* concerto. Works of the third and final period include the last five pf sonatas, the *Archduke Trio* and the G major violin sonata Op. 96.

Musicians of the time judged his pf touch heavy and his style of playing powerful, and a glance at a typical B score will suffice to bear this out. In 1798 Johann Wenzel Tomášchek called him 'a giant among pianoforte players'. Czerny described his powers of improvization as 'brilliant and astonishing in the extreme'; and noted how B could alternate passionate strength with the charm of a smooth *cantabile*. He also commented that, while his great contemporary was not faultless in execution, no one equalled him in the performance of scales, trills and leaps. The powerful fingers were not long (apparently he could span a tenth only with difficulty), and he made more use of the sustaining pedal than his scores would seem to indicate. Ferdinand Ries recorded that B played his music capriciously but that his beat was even. He would 'retard the tempo in a crescendo which produced a very beautiful and striking effect'.

Thus he heralded a new dimension in the art of pf-playing, aided by the efforts of the instrument-makers. Even before deafness had engulfed him, he was always exhorting manufacturers to strengthen the construction of the instrument, to make it sound more powerful and to improve the action in specific respects such as rapid repetition (*vide* the opening page of the *Waldstein* sonata which could not have been at all easy to execute with sharp rapidity on early pfs). Undoubtedly those exhortations influenced the continual efforts at improvement which went on, and thus B unwittingly acted as a precursor of the Romantic Era whose leaders were born around the time his third period of composition was under way and who stood as young men ready to usher in that era as B lay dying.

With increasing deafness he treated instruments unmercifully and, according to contemporary accounts, had grown wildly inaccurate. This was of course a turbulent spirit trying desperately to get sounds through an aural mechanism that had gone silent for ever. The deafness itself caused musicians around, even some of the greatest, to conclude that a deaf composer could not logically compose music, and so they roundly condemned as uncouth and incomprehensible noise those later works of B's which are now held in the greatest veneration.

For some time after he died, his works were rarely played in public simply because they were not understood. They were also far too serious for the popular taste of the day, moulded as it was on the empty if glittering fare served up by keyboard lions bent on using the emerging pf as an instrument for self-glorification. Liszt arranged the B symphonies for pf solo and included a couple of isolated and unrelated sonata movements in recitals when the fancy took him. The symphonies happen to be exceedingly good arrangements, among the best Liszt did with other people's music, but his manner of introducing B to his (Liszt's) public must forever remain deplorable.

Even Chopin was not over-keen on B's sonatas beyond the *Moonlight* and set his pupils to work on early ones; and K. Schumann was accused of unladylike behaviour when she ventured to play the *Hammerklavier* in public. Glinka, incidentally, did not care for the manner in which Liszt played Beethoven sonatas. Hallé and A. Rubinstein were two rare figures who in public played the works complete. It may be added that only in the last fifty years have the '32' come to be regarded by the public as a set; and it was the great and popular examples like Opp. 13, 27/2, 53 and 57 which

secured the happy outcome and final vindication of the '32'.

His compositions include five pf concertos, *Fantasia* for pf, chorus and orch., and concerto for pf, violin, cello and orch. Solo works include 32 pf sonatas (plus movements making up six more which are not published in the set); a score of sets of variations ranging from one written at the age of 12 to the *Diabelli* set of 1823; numerous miscellaneous pieces; sets of *Bagatelles*. Pf duets include a teenage duet sonata. There are five cello and pf sonatas plus three sets of variations; ten for violin and pf plus miscellaneous works; nine pf trios plus separate movements and two sets of variations; four early works for pf quartet and other chamber music with a pf part; numerous songs with pf accompaniment. And B arranged his violin concerto as a pf concerto at the instigation of M. Clementi.

Pupils included: Karl Czerny, Ferdinand Ries.

BEKLEMISCHEV, Grigorii Nikolayevich (1881–1935)
b. Moscow, Russia. Studied at Cons. there under V. Safonov; also spent a year with F. Busoni. Held various teaching posts in Russia in addition to performing at home and abroad.

BELLAMANN, Henry Hauer (1882–1945)
b. Fulton, USA. Studied there, then in Paris with I. Philipp. Taught and performed, with especial interest in French music. Became chairman of examining board at Juilliard and later held similar position at Curtis Inst. Composed pf concerto and a sonata, chamber music and other pieces. Wrote a *Music Teacher's Note Book*.

BELLEVILLE-OURY, Emilie (1808–80)
b. Munich, Germany. Pupil of K. Czerny, becoming highly successful pianist. London début 1831, where she married the violinist Oury and where they settled. Composed pf pieces. One of the first women pianists to tour widely and to enjoy a fine reputation for her technical ability and musicality.

BENBOW, Charles Edwin (1904–)
b. St Leonards, UK. Pupil of R. Coll. of Music, London. Recitalist, teacher, accompanist and adjudicator. Compositions include chamber music, pf pieces and songs.

BENDA, Sebastian (1926–   )
b. Switzerland. Was a prodigy who studied at Geneva Cons., winning 1st Prize. Was also pupil of E. Fischer. Has performed widely. Recorded Candide.

BENDEL, Franz (1833–74)
b. Schönlinde, Czechoslovakia. Studied pf in Prague, then with F. Liszt in Weimar. Taught at Kullak's, Berlin, from 1862 until death. Composed pf pieces and songs.

BENDIX, Otto (1845–1904)
b. Copenhagen, Denmark. Studied locally then with T. Kullak in Berlin and F. Liszt in Weimar. Taught for a time in Copenhagen, then settled in Boston, USA, in 1880, where he taught pf at NE Cons. In 1895 established own pf school.

BENEDICT, Sir Julius (1804–85)
b. Stuttgart, Germany. Son of wealthy banker. Pf pupil of J. Hummel and later studied composition with K. M. von Weber, becoming all-round musician. Settled in London from 1835, establishing a reputation as concert pianist, teacher, conductor and composer. Was an important figure in the musical life of the capital. Knighted 1871. Wrote two pf concertos, one of which received its première in 1850 at a Phil. concert with the composer as soloist. He also wrote a vast quantity of pf music in the style of fantasias and in the idiom of the times. One of them, *Remembrances of Scotland*, received a review in the musical press of 1842: 'This fantasia belongs to the very best school; it is written with the skill and taste of a master, and contains beauties worthy of the name which appears upon its title-page. The commencement is spirited introducing the well-known air "Charlie is my darling", followed by "O Nanny" and "Lewie Gordon". A Scotch reel is then ushered in, simply at first but, as it progresses, more floridly arranged and worked up in a very effective and charming manner. We recommend this fantasia to all with the will and ability to overcome some difficulty, promising them that their efforts will be rewarded by a rich musical treat.'
Pupils included: Sir Henry Cowen.

BEN-HAIM, Paul (1897–1984)
Original surname Frankenburger.
b. Munich, Germany. Attended High School, Acad. and Univ. there, pf teacher being B. Kellermann. Spent some time conducting, settling in Palestine from 1933 as teacher of composition and pf at Tel Aviv Cons. One of Israel's important composers whose works include a pf concerto (1949), chamber music and pf solos including a sonatina (1946).

BENJAMIN, Arthur (1893–1960)
b. Sydney, Australia. Student at R. Coll., London and of Frederick Cliffe for pf. Was pf prof. at State Cons., Sydney, 1920–2. Returned to R. Coll. of Music and settled in London as teacher and composer. Most celebrated pupil was Benjamin Britten. Wrote *Concertino* for pf and orch. (1927) with jazz influences. Went to Canada and for five years was conductor in Vancouver of CBR SO., later becoming resident lecturer at Reed Coll., Oregon. Returned to London after World War II. In 1950 was invited back to Australia to commemorate fiftieth anniversary of his pf début, and took his *Concerto quasi una fantasia* which he performed a number of times under the baton of Sir E. Goossens. Its first British performance was in 1956 with L. Crowson as soloist. Composed pf pieces including the well-known *Jamaican Rumba*, also chamber music. Dedicatee of Britten's *Holiday Diary* suite for pf solo.
Pupils included: Benjamin Britten, Jean Coulthard, Lamar Crowson, Robert Fleming, Irene Kohler, Joan Trimble, Valerie Trimble.

BENNETT, Richard Rodney (1936–   )
b. Broadstairs, UK. Pupil of R. Acad., London, continuing studies in Paris. Has successfully performed his pf concerto many times and amongst a prolific output are pf pieces. CBE 1977.

BENNETT, Sir William Sterndale (1816–75)
b. Sheffield, UK. Studied at R. Acad. of Music, London, from 1826, and in 1833 performed his D minor pf concerto there. The pf firm of Broadwood subsidized two periods of study in Leipzig, where he came to know Schumann and Mendelssohn, both of whom profoundly influenced him musically. On returning to Britain, he performed, taught and composed. He played with great refinement and his compositions had a vogue in Victorian times but are now forgotten. Was Prof. of Music, Cambridge, 1856–75, knighted in 1871 and in the same year received the R. Phil. Soc. Gold Medal.
Pupils included: Francis Bache, Sir William Cusins, Eaton Faning, Tobias Matthay,

Sebastian Mills, Arthur O'Leary, Simon Waley, Thomas Wingham.

BENOIST, André (1881–1953)
b. Paris, France. Studied at Cons. there under C. Saint-Saëns for composition and R. Pugno pf. Toured globally as accompanist to celebrities and finally exclusively with the violinist Albert Spalding.

BENSON, Clifford (1946–)
b. Grays, UK. Student at R. Coll. of Music, London; and with Cyril Smith and L. Crowson. Début 1970, London. Has since performed solo, in chamber music and as accompanist. Recorded CRD and Pearl.

BENTZON, Niels Viggo (1919–)
b. Copenhagen, Denmark. Pianist-composer who has written prolifically for the instrument including a dozen sonatas.

BERENS, Hermann (1826–80)
b. Hamburg, Germany. Studied in Dresden, also with K. Czerny in Vienna. Settled in Sweden as pianist and teacher. Composed a set of pf studies that were once popular in teaching circles.

BERG, Alban (1885–1935)
b. Vienna, Austria. Largely self-taught and protégé of A. Schoenberg. Composed pf sonata Op. 1 and later revised, also small quantity of songs and a chamber-concerto for violin, pf and wind instruments. Chiefly remembered for association with Schoenberg and also the operas *Wozzeck* and *Lulu*.

BERGER, Francesco (1834–1933)
b. London, UK. Studied in Trieste, then in Leipzig with I. Moscheles and with L. Plaidy. Was for years pf prof. at R. Acad., London, and Guildhall. Secretary of R. Phil. Soc. from 1884. Influential musician of his day. Edited Beethoven pf sonatas and composed many pf pieces. Wrote autobiography *Reminiscences, Impressions and Anecdotes* (1913), as well as several pedagogic works.

BERGER, Ludwig (1777–1839)
b. Berlin, Germany. Pf pupil of M. Clementi, then J. B. Cramer in London 1812–15. Returned to Berlin where he settled and became renowned as teacher. Heard J. Field and was profoundly influenced by the experience. One of the original thirty members of the

Phil. Soc. in London and among the first pianists to play at its concerts. Dedicatee of Mendelssohn's *Seven Characteristic Pieces*. Composed a quantity of pf works of technical merit.
Pupils included: Fanny Hensel, Adolf von Henselt, Henriette Kunze, Anna Laidlaw, Albert Loeschhorn, Felix Mendelssohn, Martin Nottebohm, Wilhelm Taubert.

BERGER, Roman (1930–)
b. Cieszyn, Poland. Studied at Bratislava Acad. Début there 1956; performed thereafter and pf prof. at Bratislava till 1965. Has composed chamber music and two pf sonatas.

BERGSON, Michael (1820–98)
b. Warsaw, Poland. Studied with F. Schneider at Dessau and with W. Taubert in Berlin. Toured Europe for a time; then, from 1863, taught pf in Geneva before settling in London where he died. Wrote numerous works for pf, also chamber music.

BERINGER, Oscar (1844–1922)
b. Furtwangen, Germany. Studied pf with I. Moscheles and with K. Tausig. Settled in London 1871 and rapidly achieved a reputation as concert pianist and teacher, directing own school of advanced pf playing. From 1885 taught at R. Coll. of Music, London, in which year he appeared at a Phil. concert in the Schumann pf concerto. Gave first British performance of the Dvořák pf concerto. Was a famous examiner, producing a number of works of educational value and a book, *Fifty years' Experience of Pianoforte Teaching and Playing* (1907).
Pupils included: Hubert Bath, Gordon Bryan, Mary Carmichael, Winifred Christie, Herbert Fryer, Katharine Goodson.

BÉRIOT, Charles Wilfrid de (1833–1914)
b. Paris, France. Son of the famous violinist Charles de Bériot, a Belgian who settled in Paris in 1821. Pf prof. at Paris Cons. and wrote pf concertos and pieces. Ravel dedicated the *Rapsodie Espagnole* to de B.
Pupils included: Justin Elie, Enrique Granados, Joaquin Maláts, Manfred Malkin, Maurice Ravel, J. Roger-Ducasse, Ricardo Viñes.

BERKOWITZ, Paul (1948–)
b. Montreal, Canada. Studied pf from age of 6, including McGill Univ. After graduation there

became scholarship student at the Curtis Inst. under R. Serkin and additionally studied chamber music. Début 1960 with CBC Montreal Orch. after which appeared in Canada and USA. Settled in UK 1972; British début following year. Was pf prof. at Guildhall School from 1975.

BERKOWITZ, Ralph (1910–)
b. New York, USA. Pupil of Curtis Inst. Has instructed at Tanglewood Center where he became Dean. Performed throughout USA and toured Europe. Has edited and arranged for pf.

BERLINSKI, Herman (1910–)
b. Leipzig, Germany. Student of Cons. there, graduating 1932 when he began touring Europe. Settled in Paris for a time for further study and on the fall of France went to New York as concert pianist and composer.

BERMAN, Boris (1948–)
b. Moscow, USSR. Student of Moscow Cons. under L. Oborin, graduating in pf and harpsichord. Emigrated to Israel and began a distinguished career as soloist. Début New York and London 1980, and appeared with leading orchs. On the faculty of Tel-Aviv Univ. and taught in the USA including Boston Univ.

BERMAN, Lazar (1930–)
b. Leningrad, USSR. First appeared in public at the age of 4. Student of A. Goldenweiser and of Moscow Cons., graduating 1953. Toured the West from 1976. Possessed large repertoire and pronounced romantic style of playing. Recorded various.

BERN, Julian (1911–)
b. Skuodas, Lithuania. Studied in Memel then at École Normale, Paris, under A. Cortot for pf. Has toured widely and was prof. Cornell Coll., USA. Composed for the instrument.

BERNARD, Anthony (1891–1963)
b. London, UK. Pf pupil of J. Holbrooke and L. Borwick. For a time accompanied celebrated artists, and became known later as a conductor.

BERNARD, Émile (1843–1902)
b. Marseille, France. Pf pupil of A. Marmontel at Paris Cons. Distinguished composer, organist and pianist who wrote chamber music and pf pieces.

BERNARD, Paul (1827–79)
b. Poitiers, France. Pupil of Paris Cons., then of S. Thalberg. Performed, composed pf works and wrote musical criticisms.

BERNATHOVA, Eva (1932–)
b. Budapest, Hungary. Student at Liszt Acad. there, and has performed worldwide. Recorded Supraphon. Prof. Liszt Acad., Budapest.

BERNSTEIN, Leonard (1918–)
b. Massachusetts, USA. The pf figures quite prominently in the career of this composer-conductor. His first teacher was Helen Coates; then, after Harvard, he studied music at Curtis Inst., New York, under H. Gebhard, then I. Vengerova. Became a brilliant all-round musician: composer-conductor-pianist-lecturer-TV personality. As a pianist specialized in playing concertos which he conducted from the keyboard. Of his compositions the 2nd symphony contains a long and difficult pf solo in the jazz idiom. As chamber-music player premièred the Poulenc clarinet sonata with Benny Goodman in New York in 1963. Recorded RCA and CBS.

BÉROFF, Michel (1950–)
b. Epinal, France. Studied Paris Cons., where he won 1st Prize 1966. Début there same year. Has performed throughout Europe and USA and is identified with French music. Recorded EMI and Erato.

BERTINI, Benoit-Auguste (1780–1843)
b. Lyons, France. Studied pf with M. Clementi in London where he settled to teach pf and write about music.

BERTINI, Henri (1798–1876)
b. London, UK. Pf pupil of his father and of a brother. Début at the age of 12. Toured France and Germany; then, after further studies in Paris, resumed his concert career, and from 1821–59 was successful. An artist of great refinement. Composed much pf and chamber music and is now remembered for books of technical studies. Arranged Bach's '48' for two pfs.

BERTRAM, Georg (1882–1941)
b. Berlin, Germany. Pupil of E. Jedlicka. Thereafter taught in Berlin and performed mainly in Germany, where he had a reputation for excellence. Recorded on Odeon, and joined

forces with K. Szreter in the Saint-Saëns *Variation on a theme of Beethoven for two pianos*.

Pupils included: Astrid Berwald, Natalia Karp, Salvador Ley.

BERWALD, Astrid (1886–)
b. Stockholm, Sweden. Pupil of R. Andersson 1895–1908, also of Stockholm Cons. before studying with E. von Dohnányi and G. Bertram in Berlin. Taught at R. Andersson Music School 1911–65, becoming Principal 1935, in which year she was made a member of Swedish R. Acad. of Music. Well-known soloist and ensemble player, granddaughter of the composer Franz Berwald.

BESSIE, Rosina: *see* **LHEVINNE, Rosina**

BETANCOURT, Carmen (1949–)
b. Mexico. Studied at the Univ. there and later in Paris. Winner of 3rd Prize of Arnold Schoenberg Piano Concours 1981.

BETHUNE, Thomas (*c.* 1850–1908)
b. Georgia, USA. A unique character who was born blind and a black slave in Georgia. Made numerous concert tours, organized by his master, performing the European classical and romantic repertoire. American records of his time testify to his sense of perfect pitch and faultless memory.

BETTINELLI, Bruno (1913–)
b. Milan, Italy. Pupil of Cons. there, where he taught. Noted as concert pianist and composer. Works include two pf concertos and one for two pfs and orch., chamber music, songs and pf pieces.

BEVILACQUA, Francisco Alfredo (1846–1927)
b. Rio de Janeiro, Brazil. Studied in Italy initially, then with T. Leschetizky in Vienna and G. Mathias in Paris. Toured Europe for a time, then returned to Rio, where he was active at the Nat. Inst. reorganizing the pf dept.

BIBALO, Antonio (1922–)
b. Trieste, Italy. Studied there; début 1937. Appeared London 1954. Besides performing, has composed three pf concertos and chamber music.

BIGG, John (1930–)
b. West Wickham, UK. Pupil of M. Long

School, Paris, also of I. Kabos. Performed and taught in USA and in UK.

BIGOT, Marie (1786–1820)
b. Colmar, Germany. Famous pianist of her time who lived and taught pf in Vienna for a number of years where she formed friendships with Haydn and Beethoven. The last twelve years of her life were spent in Paris, where young Mendelssohn received tuition from her during a business trip by his father whom he had accompanied. Wife of secretary to Count Rasoumovsky.

Pupils included: Felix Mendelssohn.

BIMBONI, Alberto (1882–1960)
b. Florence, Italy. Trained there and went to USA before World War I. Besides conducting opera, was well-known accompanist to celebrity recitalists.

BINDER, Fritz (1873–)
b. Baltimore, USA. Was child prodigy who toured Europe till eleven. He then received tuition including T. Leschetizky, finishing at Cologne Cons. Later became a conductor and Director of Danzig Cons.

BINGHAM, John (1942–)
b. Sheffield, UK. A prodigy who gave first recital at 9 and broadcast at the age of 13. Studied at R. Acad., London, and was pupil of H. Craxton and M. Foggin later in Rome and Berlin, and finally spent two years in Moscow with S. Neuhaus. Won distinctions in the Int. Busoni Comp. and the Concours Clara Haskil in Lucerne. Début as adult, London, 1967. Four years later was a prizewinner in BBC Pf Comp. Has since performed widely, solo and with orchs., and taught at Trinity Coll., London. Has very wide concert repertoire. Recorded Meridian.

Pupils included: Ronald Brautigam.

BINNS, Malcolm (1936–)
b. Nottingham, UK. Studied R. Coll., London, winning Chappell Gold Medal 1956. Début London, 1957. Concert pianist, solo and concerto player. Among novelties performed was the Gerhard pf concerto at 1963 London Proms. Has toured Europe and is interested in performing on early instruments. Recorded Saga, EMI, L'Oiseau-Lyre, Pavilion and Decca.

BIRD, Arthur (1856–1923)
b. Cambridge, USA. Studied pf at Kullak's Acad., Berlin, under H. Urban before going to F. Liszt (1885–6), being one of his last pupils. Début 1886, Berlin. Performed in Europe and USA before settling in Berlin. Composed numerous and varied works including pf pieces.

BIRET, Idil (1941–)
b. Ankara, Turkey. Educated in Paris and studied with A. Cortot and W. Kempff. Awarded prizes for pf playing. Début 1952 Paris. Has since appeared worldwide and at leading festivals. Known as an adjudicator. Recorded WEA Finnadar. Dedicatee of Jean Françaix's sonata for pf solo.

BISCHOFF, Hans (1852–89)
b. Berlin. Studied pf with T. Kullak. From 1872 taught at Kullak Acad. in Berlin and later at Stern's Cons. Was fine pianist, teacher and academician.
   Pupils included: Karl Bohm.

BISHOP-KOVACEVICH, Stephen
(1940–)
b. Los Angeles, USA. Studied there and made his début in 1951. Later settled in Britain and was a pupil of M. Hess. Toured Europe, USA and Japan. Recorded Philips.

BISSET, Catherine (1795–1864)
b. London, UK. Student of J. B. Cramer; début 1811, London. Performed there and in Paris, and latterly preferred private engagements.

BIZET, Georges (1838–75)
b. Paris, France. Pupil of Paris Cons. from the age of 9, and under A. Marmontel for pf. Won 1st Prize for playing in 1852 and was a brilliant pianist who wrote dozens of pf works of which the duet suite *Jeux d'Enfants* retains popularity, being forerunner of similar works by Debussy, Fauré and Ravel.

BLACKBURN, Marjorie (1916–)
b. Manchester, UK. Studied at Leipzig Cons. and under R. Teichmüller. Performed solo and with orch. and taught.

BLACKSHAW, Christian (1949–)
b. Cheshire, UK. Student of G. Green at R. Manchester Coll. Later studied at R. Acad., London, and for two years at Leningrad Cons.

Awarded 1st Prize in Alfredo Casella Comp., 1974. British début in 1980 in London followed by tours of Europe and the USA. Also toured USSR several times. Has also played in Israel.

BLAHETKA, Leopoldine (1811–87)
b. Vienna, Austria. Studied in Paris with F. Kalkbrenner and I. Moscheles. Had successful career as brilliant pianist and was prolific composer. Chopin records he met her in Vienna in 1829 and received kindnesses in form of copies of her works and letters of introduction from her father. From 1840 she resided in France. Besides pf concertos and sonatas she wrote numerous works and songs. On a visit to Britain in 1832 she played her *Concertstück* for pf and orch. in London.

BLANCAFORT, Manuel (1897–)
b. La Garriga, Barcelona, Spain. Studied there and was a pupil of J. Maláts. Came under the influence of French Impressionism and of Stravinsky. Won prizes for composition 1927 and 1928, and in 1935 his *Sonatina antigua* was premièred at the ISCM. R. Viñes gave first performance of *El Parque de attracciones*. Composed also two nocturnes (1930), two pf concertos (1943 and 1946), various other pieces and songs.

BLANCARD, Jacqueline (1909–)
b. Paris, France. Pf pupil of A. Cortot. Established career solo and with orch. and toured widely. Recorded *Polydor* and was first artist to record the Debussy *études*.

BLANCARD, Jane (1884–)
b. Paris, France. Student of Paris Cons., where she won 1st Prize for pf in 1899.

BLANCHET, Émile (1877–1943)
b. Lausanne, Switzerland. Pupil first of his father and later of F. Busoni in Weimar. Taught for many years, alternating between Lausanne and Paris, spending the winter in the French capital. Was rated a fine concert pianist and composed prolifically for the instrument: ballads, preludes, studies etc.

BLITZSTEIN, Marc (1905–64)
b. Philadelphia, USA. Student of Univ. of Pennsylvania and of N. Boulanger in Paris, A. Schoenberg in Berlin, and A. Siloti in New York. Taught and composed, being best remembered for his stage works. Compositions

include a pf concerto and a sonata, *Percussion Music* for pf (mostly in experimental vein), and songs. In 1965 friends and colleagues of the deceased formed a trust in his memory with the object of making an annual award to encourage the creation of musicals in the theatre.

BLOCH, Ernest (1880–1959)
b. Geneva, Switzerland. Not strictly a concert pianist but wrote important works for the instrument including *Concerto grosso* for strings and pf, two violin sonatas, a large-scale pf sonata, and other chamber music and a quantity of pf pieces, including *Visions and Prophesies*, 1936.
Pupils included: Roger Sessions.

BLOCK, Michel (1937–)
b. Antwerp, Belgium. Studied with Wilma Erenyi and later B. Webster. Début at age of 9 and completed his training at Juilliard School in 1958. His performance in the Int. Chopin Comp. in Warsaw in 1960 elicited high praise from Arthur Rubinstein. Afterwards established his reputation as a concert pianist. Recorded DG.
Pupils included: Terence Judd.

BLOOM, Tessa (–)
b. New York, USA. Studied pf there, also with T. Matthay in London, where she made her début 1935. Toured Europe and USA (New York début 1937). Settled in UK.

BLOOMFIELD-ZEISLER, Fannie (1863–1927)
b. Bielitz, Austria. The family settled in Chicago when she was 5. By the age of 13 she was already playing in public. Then, in 1878, she went to Vienna to study with T. Leschetizky for five years. From 1883 made regular annual tours of the USA and was hailed as one of the great pianists of her time. A European début in 1893 was equally successful, and thereafter she performed regularly on both continents, with her British début in 1898.
Pupils included: Nina Mesierow-Minchin.

BLUMENFELD, Felix Mikhailovich (1863–1931)
b. Kovalevska, Russia. Pupil of St Petersburg Cons. 1881–5, winning Gold Medal. Taught there until 1918, then at Kiev for four years, and at Moscow Cons. from 1922 until his death. Had reputation of being a distinguished pianist both solo and in ensemble. Wrote 24

Preludes for pf, a symphony and other diverse compositions. Brother of Olga Neuhaus.
Pupils included: Simon Barere, Mme Simon Barere, Iso Elinson, Maria Grinberg, Vladimir Horowitz, Wiktor Labunski, Pierre Luboschutz, Heinrich Neuhaus.

BLUMENFELD, Olga: *see* **NEUHAUS, Olga**

BLUMENTHAL, Felicja (–)
b. Warsaw, Poland. Studied at Cons. there; début 1938. Escaped from Europe in 1942 and made her way to S. America from where she has operated since. Reappeared in Europe in 1955. The next year gave première of Villa-Lobos 5th pf concerto (dedicated to her) with London PO. Has wide repertory and appears to specialize in disinterring forgotten works.

BLUMENTHAL, Jakob (1829–1908)
b. Hamburg, Germany. Studied pf locally then in Vienna, and finally with H. Herz in Paris. Settled in London in 1848 because of the political troubles in France. Became a highly successful pianist and teacher, being employed by Queen Victoria and aristocratic circles. Wrote a great deal of salon music which had a vogue at the time.

BOCCACCINI, Pietro (1843–1919)
b. Comacchio, Italy. Studied first in Rome, then in Naples under Beniamino Cesi. His claim to fame is founded on a vast tome, *The Art of Playing the Pianoforte* (1913).

BOCKLET, Karl Maria von (1801–81)
b. Prague, Czechoslovakia. Studied pf, violin and composition there, beginning career in a theatre orch. in Vienna, where he settled from 1820. Went over to pf and gave concerts and lessons. Friend of Beethoven and Schubert.

BOEHM, Mary Louise (1928–)
b. Sumner, USA. Pupil of mother, later of R. Casadesus in Paris and of W. Gieseking at Saarbrücken Cons. Well-known recitalist and broadcaster who has specialized in pf music of the Moscheles-Hummel era. Recorded Vox. Is also a batik artist whose work has been exhibited.

BOEKELMANN, Bernardus (1838–1930)
b. Utrecht, Netherlands. Studied pf with father before going on to I. Moscheles. In 1862 went to Berlin for two years' study with various

teachers including H. von Bülow. A visit to the USA in 1866 was so successful and promising that he settled in New York as concert pianist and teacher. Wrote much for the instrument and made a curious edition of the Bach '48' in a colour scheme for the purpose of analysis.

BOGIANCKINO, Massimo (1922–)
b. Rome, Italy. Student of S. Cecilia Cons., Rome, and of École Normale, Paris, where his pf teacher was A. Cortot. Established a career as concert pianist with especial interest in contemporary music, and was associated with the ISCM movement. Held teaching posts in Italy and the USA.

BOHLMANN, Theodor (1865–1931)
b. Osterwieck, Germany. Pf pupil in Berlin of K. Barth, K. Klindworth, E. d'Albert and M. Moszkowski. Début 1890 there, followed by tour of Germany. Settled in USA same year where he became pf prof. Cincinnati Cons. and also had successful concert career.

BOHM, Karl (1844–1920)
b. Berlin, Germany. Studied pf with A. Loeschhorn and H. Bischoff. Lived all his life in Berlin as pianist and composer of chamber music, songs and light pf pieces.

BOILDIEU, François Adrien (1775–1834)
b. Rouen, France. Studied pf, organ and composition, achieving a name in the operatic field. Was a pf prof. at Paris Cons. when his most famous opera, *The Caliph of Baghdad*, was produced.

BOLET, Jorge (1914–)
b. Havana, Cuba. Studied from the age of 5, appearing in public when he was 9. Won scholarship to Curtis Inst. and was a pupil of D. Saperton. After his graduation the Cuban Government provided means for study in Europe. Début with the Philadelphia Orch. Served in Cuban army during World War II and afterwards toured worldwide with success. Became naturalized US citizen. Pianist in the film *Song without End*, based on the life of Liszt with whose music he has been much identified. Recorded Genesis, Everest, RCA and Decca.

BOMPTEMPO, João Domingos (1775–1842)
b. Lisbon, Portugal. Studied there before moving to Paris in 1802, where he lived for a time before settling in London as concert pianist and teacher. Prepared a pf method that was published in the British capital. His name is on the list of original 25 Associates of the Phil. Soc. In 1815 he returned to Lisbon and founded an orch. society. Appointed Director of Lisbon Cons. in 1833.

BOND, Margaret (1913–72)
b. Chicago, USA. Graduate of North-western Univ. and pupil of the Juilliard School. Studied with F. Price and was a black artist who toured widely as soloist and accompanist. As a composer ranged from a Mass to a suite for pf, to 'He's Got the Whole World in His Hands'.

BONNEAU, Jacqueline (1917–)
b. St Astier, France. Student of Paris Cons. and pupil of L. Lévy. Was a distinguished soloist, concerto player, accompanist and chamber-music musician. Pianist for RTF Paris. Recorded *Decca* and Decca.

BONYNGE, Richard (1930–)
b. Sydney, Australia. Student of NSW Cons. Became distinguished accompanist as pianist and as conductor for leading operatic stars, including his wife, Joan Sutherland. Recorded Decca. CBE 1977.

BOOM, Jan (1807–72)
b. Utrecht, Netherlands. Studied pf with J. N. Hummel and I. Moscheles. Début 1824. During European tour visited Sweden and settled in Stockholm as concert pianist and teacher. Wrote chamber music, songs and pf works.
Pupils included: Richard Andersson.

BORCHARD, Adolphe (1882–1967)
b. Le Havre, France. Pupil of L. Diémer, Paris Cons. where he won 1st Pf Prize 1903. Début there 1907. Thereafter toured; US début 1910. Became Director of the École Universelle and performed governmental work.

BORDES-PÈNE, Léontine Marie (1858–1924)
b. Lorient, France. Pf pupil of Paris Cons. and married a brother of the composer Charles Bordes (who had studied with A. Marmontel and C. Franck). The latter dedicated his *Prélude, Aria et Finale* to her, and she premièred it in 1898.

BORGE, Victor (1909–)
b. Copenhagen, Denmark. Student of father (Bernard Rosenbaum) then of V. Schioler. In 1940 settled in USA where he developed his performance with humour, tending to obscure the fact that underneath was a serious and very accomplished pianist. Recorded CBS and others.

BOROWSKY, Alexander (1889–1968)
b. Libau, Russia. Taught by his mother, who had been a pupil of V. Safanov; and later with A. Essipova at St Petersburg Cons., winning a Gold Medal and the Rubinstein Prize in 1912. Was pf prof. at Moscow Cons. from 1915, and between the two World Wars toured widely as concert pianist. Settled in USA from 1941. A catholic repertoire with perhaps an emphasis upon the works of Bach and Liszt. Recorded *Polydor*.
Pupils included: Eugen Indjic.

BORTKIEVICZ, Sergei Eduardovich (1877–1952)
b. Kharkov, Russia. Pupil of St Petersburg Cons. 1896–9, then from 1900 of A. Reisenauer in Leipzig. Début 1902, Munich. Thereafter toured Europe, living in Berlin until 1914 and for a time teaching at the Klindworth-Scharwenka Cons. Returned to Russia on outbreak of World War I and after the revolution moved successively to Turkey and Vienna before finally settling once more in Berlin. Composed four pf concertos and pf solos of salon style, a few of which were once performed by his contemporary Russian friends.

BORUNSKI, Leon (1909–42)
b. Poland. Came seventh in the second Chopin Int. Comp. in Warsaw in 1932. No further details uncovered.

BORWICK, Leonard (1868–1925)
b. Walthamstow, UK. Studied first with Henry Bird, then, for six years from 1883, at Frankfurt Cons., allegedly under K. Schumann. Début 1889 in Frankfurt in the Beethoven *Emperor*. London début 1890. Toured Europe regularly thereafter, solo and playing concertos under leading conductors. Appeared with the Joachim Quartet and in 1923 played the entire pf works of Brahms in a series of recitals in London. Arranged for pf works by Bach and Debussy, including *Fêtes* (Nocturnes No. 2) and *L'Après-midi*.
Pupils included: Anthony Bernard.

BOS, Coenrad Valentyn von (1875–1955)
b. Leyden, Netherlands. Pupil of J. Röntgen at Amsterdam Cons., then at Berlin Hochschule. Accompanied Anton Sistermann in première of Brahms' *Four Serious Songs*, realized accompanying was his métier and thereafter specialized in *lieder*, becoming famous in Europe and USA with artists of the calibre of Gerhardt, Culp and Farrer as well as instrumentalists like Casals, Kreisler and Thibaud. Worked on *The Well-Tempered Accompanist*, as told to Ashley Pettis (1949). Recorded various labels.
Pupils included: Ivor Newton.

BOSKOFF, Georges (1882–)
b. Jassy, Romania. Studied first at Bucharest Cons., later at Paris Cons. under L. Diémer where he won 2nd Prize in 1904. Gave a series of historical recitals under the style *From Bach to Debussy* and decided to settle in Paris as pianist-composer. Was first to record Mozart pf concerto No. 19 in F, and composed sonatas, *études*, preludes, *valses* etc and *Variations sur un chant polonais de Chopin*. Recorded *Parlophone*.

BOSKOVICH, Aleksander Urija (1907–64)
b. Cluj, Romania. Studied Vienna and Paris. Performed as pianist and conductor, also taught, settling in Israel in 1939.

BOSMANS, Arturo (1908–)
b. Belgium. Settled in Portugal and then went to Brazil *c.* 1940. Pf works included a *Sonata in Colours* – and a sonatina using Portuguese folktunes.

BOSMANS, Henriette (1895–1952)
b. Amsterdam, Netherlands. Pianist and composer who wrote a pf concerto (1929), chamber music and pieces.

BOSQUET, Émile (1878–1958)
b. Brussels, Belgium. Studied in Brussels, where he won a diploma 1898, then Vienna, where he received the Rubinstein Prize in 1900. Performed throughout Europe, showing great delicacy and skill, specializing in unfamiliar compositions. Taught pf at Antwerp Cons. from 1905 and, later, at Brussels Cons.
Pupils included: Marinus de Jong, Pauline Marcelle.

BOUKOFF, Yuri (1923–)
b. Sofia, Bulgaria. Studied at Sofia Music Cons., winning 1st Prize, then later in Paris (another 1st Prize) and studied with Y. Nat and M. Long. Performed throughout the world with great success. Became naturalized French 1964. Recorded Philips.

BOULANGER, Lili (1893–1918)
b. Paris, France. Of musical family and younger sister of Nadia B. Was dogged by ill-health, in consequence of which her education was fitful. Followed in her sister's footsteps, learning to play several instruments, including pf, and appearing in public as pianist while quite young. Attended Paris Cons. and came under the influence of great names there, also Debussy, Ravel and Pugno. Composed from early age, and the Paris set was greatly impressed with her all-round musicianship which was crowned with success by winning the Grand Prix de Rome at the age of 20, being the first woman to receive the award. Compositions included a few pf pieces, chamber works and songs. It has been said that "her music is remarkable not so much for its novelty as for a certain sensitivity and purity of feeling."

BOULANGER, Nadia Juliette (1887–1979)
b. Paris, France. Graduated from Paris Cons. and won 2nd Prix de Rome, 1908, having studied pf with A. Duvernoy and accompaniment with P. Vidal. Played and taught pf earlier in career. Was on a joint tour of Russia with R. Pugno in 1914 when he died there. Was also organist, and taught harmony, counterpoint and history. A centre of musical attraction for leading musicians throughout the world of her generation and younger, and widely esteemed for erudition and teaching ability. Served on juries of ISCM Festivals and international pf competitions. Lectured and conducted worldwide.

BOURGUIGNON, Francis de (1890–1961)
b. Brussels, Belgium. Pupil of Cons. there and of A. de Greef. Started career as touring virtuoso; also accompanied celebrities. Turned to teaching and composing as well as writing. Wrote a pf concertino, pieces and songs.

BOURNE, Una Mabel (1882–1974)
b. Mudgee, NSW, Australia. Prodigy by the age of 4 when the family moved to Melbourne, and by the age of 10 was playing with orch. Began touring and in 1905 went to study in

Europe, at the end of which she appeared in London. Toured with Dame Nellie Melba performing solo groups in the soprano's recitals. During World War I gave many charity performances in Britain and afterwards confined her activities largely to USA and Australia, in which latter country she gave charity concerts in the cause of World War II. Later founded master-class at Melbourne Cons. Recorded *HMV*, making over forty acousticals of what we would regard as encore pieces, and later violin sonatas with Marjorie Hayward.

BOUTRY, Roger (1932–)
b. Paris, France. Pupil of Paris Cons., graduating 1948 with 1st Prize. Awarded Premier Prix de Rome in 1954, and Grand Prix Musical of Paris in 1963. Toured successfully as pianist and also conductor. Works include a pf concerto and other compositions for the same comb. as well as pieces.

BOVY-LYSBERG, Charles Samuel (1821–73)
b. Geneva, Switzerland. Studied music in Paris where it was claimed his pf teacher was F. Chopin. Taught at Geneva Cons. and composed many pf pieces in the romantic Victorian idiom.

BOWEN, Edwin York (1884–1961)
b. London, UK. Student R. Acad. there 1898–1905 under T. Matthay. Subsequently taught there. Was distinguished pianist; orch. début at a Phil. concert in London in 1907, giving first performance of his pf concerto in one movement. Was also prolific composer including four pf concertos, chamber music and pf pieces. In 1927 played pf part in the *Choral Fantasia* in the London Beethoven Centenary concert. In 1928 gave first performance of Walton's *Sinfonia Concertante* in London under Ansermet. On occasion accompanied his wife Sylvia Y.B, soprano. Wrote *Pedalling the Modern Pianoforte* (1936).

Pupils included: Kathleen Dale, Joan Last, Charles Lynch, Wesley Weyman.

BOYKAN, Martin (1931–)
b. New York, USA. Student of Harvard who was deeply committed to the contemporary scene as interpreter and composer. Own works included chamber music.

BOYLE, George Frederick (1886–1948)
b. Sydney, Australia. Was taught by parents

before being taken to Berlin in 1905 to study with F. Busoni, having already toured Australia in 1902 in company with the Hambourg brothers. Settled in London 1908–10, then in the USA, teaching successively at Peabody, Curtis and Juilliard. A frequent performer who composed a pf concerto and many pieces.

Pupils included: Otto Ortmann.

BRABELY, Seraphine von, *see* **TAUSIG, Seraphine**

BRADSHAW, David (1937–)
b. Washington, DC, USA. Studied pf there and at the Juilliard School of Music (B.S. 1960), also later with L. Kraus. Début Lincoln Centre NYC 1970, having made concerto début with National SO in 1950 in Mozart No. 24 K.491. Gave world première of a concerto by T. Leschetizky in 1977, also same year of *Forward and Fugatto* by O. W. Wargrave which is dedicated to him. Teamed up in 1979 with his pupil Cosmo Buono, début as such 1981 NYC. Since appeared with great success in USA as well as Europe (London début 1983). Gave première of two-pf. version of *Fantasy & Fugue on the Chorale Ad nos, ad salutarem undam* by Liszt, NYC 1983. With C. Buono made transcriptions of *God's Time is Best* (from Cantata No. 106, by Bach), waltzes from '*Der Rosenkavalier*' by R. Strauss. Artist in Residence at Molloy College, New York.

Pupils included: C. Buono.

BRADSHAW, Susan (1931–)
b. Monmouth, UK. Studied at R. Acad., London and in Paris. Performed widely throughout Europe; also accompanied and lectured. Recorded various.

BRAHMS, Johannes (1833–97)
b. Hamburg, Germany. Received first music lessons from his father, a double-bassist and horn-player in orchs. When he was 7 he began learning the pf and became a pupil of E. Marxsen. His début took place in 1847 in Hamburg. The next few years were spent in relative obscurity, giving pf lessons and taking poorly paid engagements. He also began composing some astonishingly mature pf works including the three sonatas written around 1853–4. In 1853 he embarked on an extensive tour with a Hungarian violinist, Eduard Remenyi, which developed into a rather turbulent experience for B because of his com-

panion's temperament and imperfect technique.

He met Joseph Joachim in Hanover, and they became lifelong friends. The violinist was immensely impressed with the younger man's abilities and gave him a letter of introduction to Liszt, who spoke favourably of B's compositions although the meeting did not lead to the formation of a friendship. Remenyi and B parted company.

Joachim, who had given immense help to the young composer in matters of string writing, gave him another letter to Robert Schumann in Düsseldorf, and there he played his works to Robert and Klara Schumann, who expressed amazement and delight with all they heard and pressed him to stay awhile. One of Schumann's critiques extolling B aroused hostility in the Liszt-Wagner circle, but by then Breitkopf & Härtel had begun publishing his music.

After spending Christmas 1853 at home in Hamburg, B went to Hanover, where Joachim was living, and resumed composition. When news came of Schumann's attempted suicide, B rushed to Düsseldorf. So began the lifelong association with Klara. With seven children to support she was obliged to undertake long and tiring concert tours. B's sojourn in Düsseldorf made him short of money, and he also turned to performing, playing mainly Beethoven concertos without, apparently, causing a sensation because what he was offering the public was not popular fare; also his pf style was that of a composer-pianist rather than a virtuoso. He had by this time acquired a substantial repertoire and, besides completing some chamber music and pf pieces, was at work on a symphony parts of which were later incorporated in the D minor pf concerto.

After the death of Schumann B took a post at Detmold as court pianist, conductor and teacher. This post provided ample time for pursuing his other interests, and with Joachim's assistance he went on developing chamber-music composition. At Detmold also he played concertos from his repertoire.

His 1st pf concerto, in D minor, was duly completed and premièred in 1859 at Hanover. He played the solo part and Joachim conducted. Five days later it was repeated in Leipzig. Initially the work was not a conspicuous success because it lacked the showy pf part which audiences of the day had come to expect. In Hamburg, his home ground, however, it was enthusiastically received.

His list of compositions was growing, and he

was being performed. After relinquishing the Detmold post, he spent his time between Hamburg and Hanover. Then in 1862 he visited Vienna and stayed some months, appearing as soloist. His concert repertoire at the time included such works as the Beethoven *Diabelli Variations*, Schumann's *Fantaisie* and 3rd sonata, as well as his own F minor sonata and *Variations on a theme of Handel*, Op. 24. Of B's performance of the *Fantaisie* Eduard Hanslick wrote: 'The forceful and the distorted are simply impossible. I cannot imagine a more profoundly, more genuinely effective performance than that which Brahms gave it. What pleasure it is to hear him play! The instant he touches the keys one experiences the feeling: here is a true, honest artist, a man of intelligence and spirit, of unassuming self-reliance.'

Other eye-witness accounts reflect B's attitude towards the keyboard as that of composer rather than pianist and, further, that he tended to think orchestrally and was concerned more with passion than accuracy. As a player he could very probably have been compared with Beethoven. Others reported that in later years this monumental approach became softened.

In the autumn of 1865 he toured Germany and Switzerland. Then he returned to Vienna, giving sold-out recitals there and in Budapest. About this time also he wrote the *German Requiem* in memory of his mother. The work proved a turning-point in his fortunes because around 1870 he progressed beyond the need to play in public other than for performing his own works although he continued to conduct in Vienna and elsewhere.

At this period he was engaged on large-scale works and no pf pieces were written between the *Paganini Variations*, Op. 35, and the *Klavierstücke*, Op. 76: that is to say, between 1865 and 1875.

The 2nd pf concerto, in B flat, was completed in 1881, receiving its première later that year in Budapest with the composer at the pf. Unlike the D minor it was a success from the start. He continued to perform the pf role in most new works either solo or containing a pf part. His powers as a performer are said to have declined towards the end of his life through lack of practice and the exercise of that last degree of intense concentration. On the other hand Dame Ethel Smyth wrote of his playing in the last years: '. . . to my mind the most wonderful I have ever heard. Overwhelming in power, it was never noisy, and the look on his face when lifting some warm and tender passage out of a tangle of sound is one of the things one can never forget.'

He was awarded the R. Phil. Soc's Gold Medal in 1877 but declined to visit Britain to receive it in person. Similarly he refused to visit Cambridge to receive an honorary degree as well as a tempting fee to conduct a series of concerts in London.

His long friendship with K. Schumann ended with her death in 1896. For all his alleged agnosticism (now largely dispelled), he grieved acutely whenever someone close passed on and was already mortally sick when he hurried to Bonn for her funeral, dying the following year in Vienna. Her death may have hastened his own end for by then he was sorely aware of gaps in his circle of friends through natural causes.

His compositions include the three early pf sonatas, Opp. 1, 2, and 5; a number of sets of variations including those on themes of Handel and Paganini, Opp. 24 and 35; the two massive pf concertos Opp. 15 and 83; two full-bloodied *Rhapsodies*, Op. 79; and late *Klavierstücke*, Opp. 76, 116, 117, 118 and 119. There are sets of lovely waltzes, famous *Hungarian Dances*, solo and arranged for duets, and the *Liebeslieder*, Opp. 52 and 65 for four voices and pf duet. The Viennese ¾-lilt was never very far away from the creative mind of Brahms, embracing every mood from gaiety to nostalgia. His chamber music included three violin and pf sonatas, two cello and pf sonatas, four trios including one for violin, horn and pf; three pf quartets; a pf quintet (not forgetting its version for two pfs); a trio for pf, clarinet (or viola) and cello; two sonatas for pf and clarinet (or viola); and many *lieder* with pf accompaniment. He arranged works by Bach, Weber, Schubert and Chopin for pf. Unlike Busoni's arrangement of the *Chaconne in D minor* which is for two hands, the B version is for left hand. Quite simply he felt that the pianist should be more or less on the same terms as the violinist is in the original version. The Chopin F minor *Étude* of Op. 25 is reworked in sixths and is a companion to the Weber *Rondo*, the well-known *presto* last movement from the 1st sonata in C major. He also arranged the Gavotte from Gluck's *Iphigénie en Aulide*. Early variations and *Ballades* receive indifferent attention from modern pianists. B composed some 50 technical studies for piano as well as cadenzas for Mozart and Beethoven concertos.

Pupils included: Elisabeth von Herzogenberg, Florence May.

BRAILOWSKY, Alexander (1896–1976)
b. Kiev, Russia. Pupil of T. Leschetizky in Vienna from 1911. Début Paris, 1919, and became successful international concert pianist; US début 1924. Specialized in music of Chopin and in playing the complete works in a cycle of recitals, first performed in Paris in 1924 and subsequently repeated there as well as USA, S. America and elsewhere. Was noted for strong virtuosic approach to music. Recorded *Polydor*, *HMV*, and RCA.

BRAINE, Robert (1896–1940)
b. Springfield, Ohio, USA. Pupil of Cincinnati Coll. of Music, graduating in 1915. Accompanist at celebrity recitals, and staff pianist N.B.C. from 1929. Besides orch. and stage works composed chamber music and much pf music including *Barbaric* sonata and numerous songs.

BRANDÃO, José Vieira (1911–)
b. Cambuquira, Brazil. Pianist-composer educated at the Nat. Music School, Rio de Janeiro (1925–9). Song-writer and composer of pf pieces.

BRANDON, Erna (1899–)
b. Bromberg, Germany. Studied there and in Berlin. Performed solo and accompanying; also taught. After World War II settled in Kenya, E. Africa.

BRANSCOMBE, Gena (1881–1977)
b. Ontario, Canada. Studied in Chicago and New York and was pf pupil especially of R. Ganz. Was awarded BA Chicago Musical Coll. After performing, later turned to composition, teaching and conducting. Prolific composer including pf works and songs.

BRANSON, David (1909–)
b. King's Lynn, UK. Student at R. Coll., London, under H. Samuel. Début London, 1920. Performed and composed, including *Pavane and Toccata* for pf and orch., pf pieces and songs.

BRASSIN, Leopold (1843–90)
b. Strasbourg. Studied pf with his brother Louis B with whom he toured; also taught in Switzerland, Russia and Turkey and was for a time court pianist at Coburg. Composed pf pieces.

BRASSIN, Louis (1840–84)
b. Aachen. Germany. Studied piano with I. Moscheles at Leipzig Cons. Made concert tours for a time; then, in 1866, took teaching post at the Stern Cons., Berlin. 1869–79 was prof. at Brussels Cons. and for last five years of life at St Petersburg Cons. Was fine concert pianist and teacher: composed two pf concertos, *études* and other original works, an *École moderne du piano* and a transcription of the Wagner *Magic Fire* music that was in the repertoire of many famous pianists. Recorded *G & T*.

Pupils included: Isaac Albéniz, Leopold Brassin, Paul Ertel, Arthur de Greef, Gennari Korganov, James Kwast, Paul Mickwitz, Franz Rummel, Vassily Safonov, Vassily Sapellnikov, Edgar Tinel.

BRAUNFELS, Walter (1882–1954)
b. Frankfurt, Germany. Studied there, also with T. Leschetizky in Vienna. Was a noted pianist, composed pf music and for a time was Director of Cologne Cons.

BRAUS, Dorothea Marcella (–)
b. Heidelberg, Germany. Pupil of K. Ansorge. Début Berlin and has appeared since solo and with leading orchs. Recorded *Decca*.

BRAUSS, Helmut (1930–)
b. Milan, Italy. Studied at Munich and Heidelberg music schools, then with E. Ney and E. Fischer. Début 1952, Munich. Toured widely, specializing in German Classical and Romantic music.

BRAUTIGAM, Ronald (1954–)
b. Amsterdam, Netherlands. Pf student of Sweelinck Cons. where he obtained a diploma in 1978. Later studied at R. Acad. of Music, London, under G. Green and J. Bingham. Gave recitals throughout Europe; also appeared with Concertgebouw and other orchs. London début 1982, when he was described as 'an exciting and intrepid young pianist, a true virtuoso whose technique enabled him to generate an unusual degree of tension in the three big works.'

BREITHAUPT, Rudolf Maria (1873–1945)
b. Brunswick, Germany. Studied in Leipzig and Berlin under R. Teichmüller and S. Jadassohn. Performed, taught and wrote essays for musical journals. Was pf prof. at Stern's Cons. from 1918. Wrote *Die natürliche*

Klaviertechnik in three parts which was highly successful, being translated into English, French and Russian.

BRENDEL, Alfred (1931–)
b. Weisenberg, Czechoslovakia. Studied at Zagreb and Graz, then received tuition from P. Baumgartner and was in master-classes of E. Fischer and of E. Steuermann. Won 4th Busoni Prize 1949 and is now recognized as one of the great pianists of his generation. Recorded Vox and Philips. Author of *Musical Thoughts and After-Thoughts* (1976).

Pupils included: Imogen Cooper, Zsuzsanna Sirokay.

BRENNAN, John (1911–)
b. Tunstall, UK. Studied at R. Manchester Coll. and Trinity Coll., London. Broadcast from 1932 and made public début 1934 in Birmingham. Wide experience as soloist, chamber-music player and lecturer.

BRESLAUR, Emil (1836–99)
b. Kottbus, Germany. Pupil at Stern's, Berlin. Taught at Kullak's Acad., 1868–79, the year in which he launched a music teachers' society. Besides teaching, wrote a number of books on technique which once had a vogue.

BRIGHT, Dora (1863–1951)
b. Sheffield, UK. Pf pupil of R. Acad., London. Performed in Europe and launched two pf concertos in Germany and Britain. Turned mainly to composition after marriage in 1892. It is claimed she was the first woman pianist to give an 'all-English' pf recital. In later life wrote for musical journals. Of her performance of one of her concertos in London in 1891 Shaw said that she wrote them better than she played them. Performed throughout Europe and composed three works for pf and orch., chamber music, pf solos, songs and a duo for two pfs.

BRISSLER, Friedrich Ferdinand (1818–93)
b. Insterburg, Germany. Pupil of Berlin Acad. and received some musical tuition from R. Schumann. Performed; also taught at Stern's Cons.

BRITTEN, Benjamin (Lord) (1913–76)
b. Lowestoft, UK. Played pf from early age. Won scholarship to R. Coll., London, 1930, where he studied pf under A. Benjamin and H. Samuel. Graduated 1934 and awarded ARCM

for prowess as pianist. Known now as the greatest and most prolific British composer of his time, whose works include an early pf concerto, chamber music and pf pieces, also *Scottish Ballad* for two pfs and orch. In addition to solo work was distinguished accompanist. Gave the première of his pf concerto in London in 1938; it was subsequently revised and reappeared in 1946. CH 1953. R. Phil. Soc. Gold Medal 1964. OM 1965. Life Peer 1976. Recorded *Decca* and Decca.

BROCKWAY, Howard (1870–1951)
b. Brooklyn, USA. Studied initially in New York; then from 1890–95 was in Berlin with Hans Barth for pf and Boise for composition. Returned to New York where he performed and taught. Was a prolific composer, mainly for pf.

BRODSKY, Vera (1909–)
b. Norfolk, Va, USA. Pupil of A. Lambert, then of J. and R. Lhevinne at Juilliard School. Toured Europe and USA thereafter and formed duo-team with H. Triggs. Gave première of Richard Arnell pf concerto 1947 with CBS SO in New York.

BROMAN, Natanael (1887–1966)
b. Kolsva, Sweden. Student of Stockholm Cons. and later studied piano with I. Friedman and W. Kempff. Concert pianist and teacher, mainly in own country. Composed chamber music and a small number of pf pieces.

BROMLEY, Tom (1904–85)
b. Birmingham, UK. Pupil at School of Music there, LRAM and BA (London). Pf prof. Birmingham School from 1926 until retirement. Concert pianist and broadcaster. Gave first British performance of Chavez pf concerto.

BRONARSKI, Ludwig (1890–1975)
b. Poland. Pupil of T. Leschetizky. Pianist, teacher and member of the editorial committee (with I. Paderewski and J. Turczynski) of the Fryderyk Chopin Inst. definitive edition.

BRONFMAN, Yefim (1958–)
b. Tashkent, USSR. Taught at first by his mother. When he was 15, the family emigrated to Israel and he won a scholarship to study at the Acad. of Music, Tel Aviv. Played in the USA from 1976 when he appeared in the Marlboro Music Festival, and continued to

give concerts while studying with R. Serkin. Gave performances throughout the Americas and Europe.

BRONSART, Hans von Schellendorff (1830–1913)
b. Berlin, Germany. Student of Berlin Univ., receiving pf lessons from T. Kullak and later from F. Liszt at Weimar. Made successful tours of Europe but from age of thirty turned increasingly to conducting and, finally, composing. Married Ingeborg Starck, 1862. Composed a pf concerto, chamber music and pf pieces.
Pupils included: Karl Heinrich Barth.

BRONSART, Ingeborg von (née STARCK) (1840–1913)
b. St Petersburg, Russia, of Swedish parentage. Pf pupil of A. Henselt there and later of F. Liszt at Weimar. Toured widely until 1862, in which year she married Hans von Bronsart, and thereafter acquired a second reputation as a composer with pf concertos, chamber music and pf pieces; also had success during her lifetime in the operatic field.

BROSTER, Eileen (1935–)
b. London, UK. Pupil at R. Coll. there and pupil of F. Merrick and C. Smith. Performed widely as soloist and in concertos. Taught at R. Coll.

BROUNOV, Platon (1869–1924)
b. Elizabetburg, Russia. Student of Warsaw Cons., then at St Petersburg Cons. where A. Rubinstein taught pf. Settled in USA as lecturer, concert pianist and teacher. Composed pf pieces and wrote *Ten Commandments of Piano Practice*.

BROWN, Lawrence (Larry) (1893–)
b. Philadelphia, USA. Professionally trained and of Negro origin. In London in 1922, where he was working on Negro folk-music, met Paul Robeson, who was then training for law while touring as an actor in a play, *Voodoo*. Robeson's magnificent voice had a profound effect upon B. In 1925 they met again in the USA, and out of that meeting developed a unique musical association. Besides being Robeson's accompanist, Brown arranged the Negro spirituals which became so much a part of Robeson's life and work. Recorded *HMV, RCA*, Vanguard and CBS.

BROWNING, John (1933–)
b. Denver, USA. A prodigy who played in public at the age of 10. Studied with J. and R. Lhevinne for two summers there, also with L. Pattison in California and with R. Lhevinne at the Juilliard School, New York, where he was the Lhevinne memorial scholar, winning awards in 1954 and 1955. The following year he made his adult début with the New York PO and came 2nd in the Concours Musical International Reine Elisabeth in Brussels. Performed thereafter, and in 1962 premièred the Samuel Barber pf concerto, subsequently playing it many times. Toured internationally, especially in 1965 when he carried out a three-month orchestral tour with George Szell, and sponsored by the US Government, taking in Europe and Communist countries. Has also visited Central America. He revealed in an interview that as a student he was obliged to learn and memorize one work per week so that at the end of each year he had added 50 new works to his repertoire. It meant that by the age of 22 'most of the fundamental concert literature was in my musical storehouse.' Held master-classes at Tanglewood, Ravinia and North-Western Univ. Recorded RCA, Columbia and others.

BRUCHOLLERIE, Monique de la (1915–72)
b. Paris, France. Student of Paris Cons., graduating at 13, pupil of I. Philipp. Became a fine concert pianist with international reputation. In 1960s worked on the idea of a curved pf keyboard to bring bass and treble closer to the player's hands, an idea patented without success by the Austrians Staufer and Haidinger around 1824, and by a German named Clutsam earlier this century. Recorded *HMV* and Nonesuch.

BRUGNOLI, Attilio (1880–1937)
b. Rome, Italy. Student of Naples Cons., graduating 1900; taught at Palma (1907–21) and at Florence (1921–37). Won Rubinstein Prize 1905 and was fine pianist and teacher. Wrote important Italian work, *Dinamica Pianistica*, composed for pf a concerto, a suite and divers pieces. Also arranged editions of Chopin and Liszt for Ricordi.

BRUINS, Theo (1929–)
b. Arnhem, Netherlands. Student of mother, then of Amsterdam Muzieklyceum from 1946, in which year he made his début. The following year gave a concert of three concertos.

Studied with Yves Nat in Paris 1948–50. Has since performed throughout the world, and in 1959 was awarded the Harriet Cohen Beethoven medal. Has wide-ranging repertoire and has composed a pf concerto, *études* etc. Premièred pf concerto of Kees van Baaren which is dedicated to him; first British performance 1970, London Proms.

BRÜLL, Ignaz (1846–1907)
b. Prossnitz, Czechoslovakia. Studied music in Vienna including the pf under J. Epstein. Toured as concert pianist until 1872 when he settled in Vienna as pf prof. In 1878 gave a series of twenty concerts in London. Was a member of the Brahms circle. Composed in the late Romantic style and prepared a large part of Mozart's keyboard works for Universal edition.
Pupils included: Karl Stasny.

BRUMBERG, Leonid (1925–   )
b. Rostov on Don, USSR, of Jewish ancestry. Appeared as a prodigy and studied at Moscow Cons. under H. Neuhaus. After graduation taught at the Gnessin Acad., Moscow as assistant to Neuhaus and later as pf prof. Gave many concerts solo and with orch. Claimed a repertoire sufficient to fill a hundred recitals. Studied orchestration with D. Shostakovich who predicted that the 5-year-old would become a great musician. In 1981 quietly removed to Vienna and settled as pf prof. at the Cons. there. Concert activities then extended into Western Europe. UK début Dover 1983.

BRYAN, Gordon (1895–1957)
b. London, UK. Studied with P. Grainger and O. Beringer. Performed at home and abroad, and broadcast regularly. Lived in Bournemouth, where he often appeared under Sir Dan Godfrey. Gave first performance of Bliss concerto for tenor, pf, strings and percussion in 1923 under composer; first British performance in 1930 of Ernest Schelling's *Fantastic Suite* for pf and orch., and other premières of contemporary music including the Constant Lambert pf sonata in London in 1929. Founded Aeolian Players (flute, violin, viola and pf).

BRZOWSKI, Josef (1805–88)
b. Warsaw, Poland. Student at Warsaw Cons. and brother-in-law of the composer Kurpinski. Beholden to Chopin for more than the titles of his compositions, e.g. *Allegro de*

Concert for two pfs, *Mazurkas* and many others, besides chamber music and songs. His daughter Jadwiga B was a well-known pianist who lived and worked in Brussels after her marriage.

BUCHAN, David (1904–   )
b. London, UK. Studied there; his teachers included H. Fryer. Performed and taught extensively. Composed for the instrument.

BUCHAROV, Simon (1881–1955)
b. Kiev, Russia. Emigrated with parents to USA and studied pf in New York with P. Gallico, later with J. Epstein in Vienna. After returning to USA, performed and held various pf teaching posts, finally settling in California. Compositions included *The Trumpeter's Death* for pf and orch., numerous pf pieces and songs. Wrote *The Modern Pianist's Textbook* (1913).

BUCHBINDER, Rudolf (1946–   )
b. Leimeritz, Austria. Pf pupil of Vienna Acad. from age of 10. Début 1961. Won Harriet Cohen Medal, London, 1966, and Bösendorfer Comp., Vienna, 1967. Has toured Europe, Americas and Far East. Recorded Telefunken.

BUCHMAYER, Richard (1856–1934)
b. Zittau, Germany. Pupil of Dresden Cons., then lived in Russia for a time. Returned to Dresden Cons. to teach until 1890, when he transferred to Dresden Music School. Later gave up teaching to concentrate on researching into older klavier music, making his discoveries known in a series of recitals.
Pupils included: Egon Petri.

BUECHNER, David (1959–   )
b. Baltimore, USA. Student of the Juilliard School, New York and a pupil of R. Firkusny.

BUESST, Victor (1885–   )
b. Melbourne, Australia. Younger brother of Aylmer B, the conductor and teacher. Pf pupil of A. de Greef, Brussels, then of R. Teichmüller, Leipzig. Had advice and lessons from F. Busoni and E. Petri. Performed throughout Europe and gave London première of Ravel's *Tombeau*. Composed chamber music and a concerto for three pfs and orch.

BÜHLIG, Richard (1880–1952)
b. Chicago, USA. Studied there and later with

T. Leschetizky in Vienna. Début 1901, Berlin, followed by European tour. R. Phil. début in London in 1906 in Beethoven's 4th pf concerto. US début 1907, New York. Visited Europe again in 1912. In later years played and taught in California. Rated as an extremely poetic artist. Among his creative works is a transcription for pf of *The Art of Fugue*. Dedicatee of Busoni's third version of *Fantasia Contrappuntistica*.

Pupils included: Theodor Chanler, Henry Cowell, Alton Jones, Leon Kirchner, Earl Wild.

BUJANSKA, Maria (1943–)
b. Warsaw, Poland. Studied at Cracow Coll. and Warsaw Acad. Won prizes in 1963, 1966 and 1969. Toured extensively and has specialized in contemporary Polish music.

BÜLOW, Hans Guido von (1830–94)
b. Dresden, Germany. Pf pupil of F. Wieck from 1839. Despite matriculating as a law student at Leipzig Univ. when 18, he continued to study music. Met Wagner, who taught him conducting, also F. Liszt from whom he took pf lessons. Toured Europe for the first time in 1853 and again two years later, in 1855 succeeding Kullak as Head of Stern's Cons., Berlin. In 1856 married Cosima, Liszt's daughter (they separated in 1869). He continued in the dual role of pianist and conductor, also held various appointments as court pianist as well as teaching pf in German Conss. and in St Petersburg. On his first visit to Britain in 1873 he played at a Phil. Soc. concert (Beethoven's *Emperor* and Bach's *Chromatic Fantasia & Fugue*); and received the Society's Gold Medal. As a recitalist he specialized in gargantuan programmes such as the last five Beethoven sonatas at one sitting, and a recital comprising fifteen works of Liszt. Gave the first performance of Liszt's pf sonata in Berlin in 1857 using the first grand pf made by his friend Karl Bechstein. Was reputedly the first pianist to consign his repertoire to memory and thus dispense with music. Edited extensively for Universal Edition including Beethoven, Chopin and Cramer.

Pupils included: Agathe Backer-Gröndahl, Karl H. Barth, Bernardus Boekelmann, Giuseppe Buonamici, Pietro Florida, Wilhelm Fritze, Karl Fuchs, Hermann Goetz, Otto Goldschmidt, Fritz Hartvigson, Alfred Hollins, Frederick Lamond, Otto Lessmann, Frank Liebich, José V. da Motta, Ethelbert Nevin, Rudolf Niemann, John Pattison, Theodor Pfeiffer, Laura Rappoldi, Cornelius Rybner, Hermann Scholtz, Karl Schulz-Schwerin, Albert Werkenthin, Bernhard Wolff.

BUONAMICI, Giuseppe (1846–1914)
b. Florence, Italy. Studied at Munich Cons. under H. van Bülow and later taught advanced pf class there, returning to Florence in 1873 to become pf prof. at the Cherubini Inst. Was a notable pianist, fine teacher and composer of pf pieces and other works. Prepared a complete edition of Beethoven's sonatas which were judged a model for teaching purposes, also some of Schumann's major pf works. Made an isolated appearance in Britain in 1891 playing Beethoven's *Emperor* at a Phil. concert in London.

Pupils included: Lazzaro Uzielli.

BUONO, Cosmo (1952–)
b. Hakensack, N.J., USA. Studied with D. Bradshaw and R. Casadesus. B.A. Bard Coll. 1974 and M.A. New York Univ. 1976. Début NY 1975. Subsequently appeared solo and in 1979 formed duo with D. Bradshaw (for further details see under that entry). Artist in Residence at Molloy College, New York. Dedicatee of *Lament* by B. Lewis.

BURKHARD, Willy (1900–55)
b. Evilard-sur-Bienne, Switzerland. Studied at Berne, then took a pf course in Leipzig with R. Teichmüller. Was pf prof. at Berne from 1928 for a short time, retiring to Davos as a composer.

Pupils included: Urs Voegelin.

BURMEISTER, Richard (1860–1944)
b. Hamburg, Germany. Pf pupil at F. Liszt (1880–3). Taught at Hamburg Cons., then Peabody Institute, Baltimore, USA, and from 1898 head of Scharwenka Cons. in New York for five years. Returning to Germany, he taught at Dresden Cons. 1903–6 when he went to the Klindworth-Scharwenka Cons., Berlin. Performed widely in Europe and USA. Besides original compositions for pf he rescored Chopin's 2nd concerto, giving it a cadenza, also reworked some of Liszt's pf pieces, giving them orch. accompaniment.

BURROWS, Kathleen (1866–1939)
b. Ontario, Canada. Specialist pf teacher to

children; composed and wrote much on the subject. Ran own school.

BUSCH, Fritz (1890–1951)
b. Siegen, Germany. Of poor family: eight children, one of whom, Adolf B, became famous violinist and chamber-music player. Both possessed absolute pitch. Began learning pf privately, playing in public from early age to earn money. Followed Adolf into Cologne Cons., studying pf and composition; eventually pupil of L. Uzielli. Joined conductor class. Already known as accompanist by 1909 when he made his début in Brahms' D minor concerto. Mainly known as conductor but played pf, often in public usually accompanying or in ensemble. Appeared with Reger in two pf works a month before the composer's death. Wrote *Pages from a Musician's Life* (1949). Assumed Swiss nationality after leaving Nazi Germany.

BUSCH, William (1901–45)
b. London, UK. Trained as concert pianist and composer. Pf teachers included W. Backhaus and E. Petri. Début London, 1927. Wrote a number of works for pf, including a concerto.

BUSH, Alan Dudley (1900–)
b. Dulwich, UK. Pupil of R. Acad., London, also studied pf with B. Moiseiwitsch and A. Schnabel; composition pupil of J. Ireland. Performed widely 1927–33 and was prof. and lecturer at R. Acad. Toured widely as examiner for Association Board. Has written chamber music and pf works, also concerto for pf with baritone solo and male voice chorus in last movement (first performance 1938, BBC, with composer as pianist). Wrote a work on strict counterpoint. Recorded Argo.

BUSONI, Anna (née Weiss) (1833–1909)
b. Trieste, Italy. Mother of Ferruccio B. Showed pianistic ability from early age, and from the age of 14 appeared in public solo and with orch. Married a clarinet-player, Ferdinando B, with whom she toured Europe, being especially well received in Paris. From the age of 12 Ferruccio joined her in public recitals of duets. In later years she confined her musical activities to teaching.
Pupils included: Ferruccio Busoni.

BUSONI, Ferruccio Benvenuto (1866–1924)
b. Empoli, Italy. Taught by his mother who was an excellent pianist, and gave his first concert at the age of 7. He played in Vienna in 1876, where his father had intended him to study at the Cons., but left the capital next year after recovering from diphtheria. He proceeded to give concerts with both parents, his father being a clarinet-player of limited prowess and uncertain temperament. In Graz he studied composition with Wilhelm Mayer, from whom he derived his lifelong love of Bach and Mozart. His first big recital was in 1883 in Vienna and included some of his compositions. He became acquainted with Brahms and A. Rubinstein and was as indifferent to the playing of the former as he was enthusiastic about the latter.

He settled for a time in Leipzig from 1886, and it was there that he made friends with the parents of a 5-year-old child called Egon Petri. His recitals at that time included an improvisatory item on a theme given by a member of the audience, thus continuing to demonstrate the gift of spontaneous composition that had been popular at the start of his century.

In 1888 he taught at Helsinki Cons. and while in that city met Gerda Sjöstrand who became his wife. Two years later he was pf prof. at Moscow Cons., where his *Konzertstück* won the inaugural A. Rubinstein composition prize. He did not settle to the life and conditions of Moscow any more than he had to those of in Helsinki, and in 1891 he took a better-paid post in Boston, USA, which gave him the opportunity to give recitals throughout the States. He held the Boston post for one year only because he was dissatisfied with the grade of pupils. Cured for the time being of seeking financial safety in teaching posts, the Busonis returned to Europe in 1894, where they lived in Berlin until 1914.

During that period B consolidated his reputation as a leading performer, teacher, conductor, composer and revisionist of Bach's music. His concert repertoire was enormous; he was much sought after by aspiring pupils; he conducted a series of concerts in the German capital featuring novel works and some first performances including his own pf concerto in 1903 which he played under the baton of Karl Muck. He toured the USA again in 1904 and in the same year held a master-class in Vienna Cons.

He was invited to direct the Liceo Rossini at Bologna in 1912. When the Great War broke out, he was due to visit the USA once more. During that tour he completed his edition of the *Well-tempered Clavier* and *Goldberg Variations*. When Italy entered the war, he felt obliged to return home. His post at Bologna had meantime been filled, so he settled in Zurich, where his operas *Turandot* and *Arlecchino* were produced.

When peace came, he resumed touring Europe, living once more in Berlin, where his recitals were acclaimed sell-outs. The long programmes, like the man, had become austere, making no concession to any public taste for lighter works. He recorded in London, and letters to his wife tell of the ordeal he suffered in sessions which resulted in a mere four twelve-inch 78 rpm, or some thirty minutes of music all told! In 1928 those discs, the only authentic relics of this virtuoso of colossal intellect, were removed from the English *Columbia* catalogue with the onset of electrical recordings and have not been re-issued.

In 1921, with a rebuilt reputation placing him amongst the foremost musicians of his generation, his health began to fail. The next year his appearance in Britain included a recital in London on two pfs with his favourite pupil and colleague E. Petri. His final concert was in Berlin in May 1922 when he played the *Emperor* concerto. Thereafter his physical condition deteriorated.

Dent said: 'Those who heard Busoni play will remember vividly how under his hands the most complicated passages of Beethoven or Liszt seemed transformed into washes of pure colour, although one could not fail to be aware that every single note was accurately played and nothing smudged or blurred.' The critic and priest Basil Maine wrote: 'I remember some of Busoni's recitals in Wigmore Hall. . . . Perhaps he would be playing the sonata Op. 111, and I would have the experience of suddenly perceiving in a clear light an episode which before had been all but meaningless. It did not seem far-fetched to think of such playing as an act of creation.'

Compositions for pf and orch. include the *Konzertstück*, the pf concerto with male chorus (first performed by the composer and later in the repertoire of such as M. Hambourg, E. Petri, P. Scarpino and J. Ogdon); and an *Indian Fantasy*. Works for pf solo run to some 24 opus numbers and many others without opus numbers, of which the four *Indianisches Tagebuch* are occasionally heard. He wrote a set of 24 preludes and 10 variations on the theme of Chopin's C minor prelude; also a sonata, six

sonatinas, *études* and pieces dedicated to friends, pupils and fellow-pianists. His work in the Bach field was immense, the collection edited by him in association with E. Petri running to 25 volumes. The Bach-Busoni edition comprises seven volumes. He made many arrangements and transcriptions, including works by Brahms, Liszt, Schubert and Mozart (including cadenzas to nine concertos). There are compositions for one pf four hands and for two pfs, among them arrangements of Mozart. Chamber music includes two sonatas and a set of *Bagatelles* for violin and pf; a suite, a *Serenata* and set of variations all for cello and pf. There are also songs with pf accompaniment. Recorded *Columbia*.

Pupils included: Guido Agosti, Grigorii Beklemischev, Émile Blanchet, George Boyle, Victor Buesst, Maria Carreras, Harriet Cohen, Augusta Cottlow, Natalie Curtis, Herbert Fryer, Rudolf Ganz, Percy Grainger, Louis Gruenberg, Clara Haskil, Alexander Kelberine, Leo Kestenberg, Frederick Loewe, Johan B. Lunde, Mana-Zucca, Clara Mannes, Mieczyslav Münz, Karl Nissen, Vincento Pablo, Vladimir Padwa, Selim Palmgren, Egon Petri, Lloyd Powell, Beryl Rubinstein, Sigrid Schneevoigt, Vladimir Shavich, Leo Sirota, Eduard Steuermann, Nanne Storm, Theodor Szántó, Gino Tagliapietra, Francesco Ticciati, Dmitri Tiomkin, Vladimir Vogel, Michael von Zadora, Carlo Zecchi.

OWN RULES FOR PRACTISING THE PIANOFORTE

1 Practise the passage with the most difficult fingering; when you have mastered that, play it with the easiest.

2 If a passage offers some particular technical difficulty, go through all similar passages you can remember in other places; in this way you will bring system into the kind of playing in question.

3 Always join technical practice with the study of the interpretation; the difficulty often does not lie in the notes, but in the dynamic shading prescribed.

4 Never be carried away by temperament, for that dissipates strength, and where it occurs there will always be a blemish, like a dirty spot which can never be washed out of a material.

5 Don't set your mind on overcoming the difficulties in pieces which have been unsuccessful because you have previously practised them badly; it is generally a useless task. But if meanwhile you have quite changed your way of playing, then begin the study of the old piece from the beginning, as if you did not know it.

6 Study everything as if there were nothing more difficult; try to interpret studies for the young from the standpoint of the virtuoso; you will be astonished to find how difficult it is to play a Czerny or Cramer, or even a Clementi.

7 Bach is the foundation of piano playing, Liszt the summit. The two make Beethoven possible.

8 Take it for granted from the beginning that everything is possible on the piano, even when it seems impossible to you, or really is so.

9 Attend to your technical apparatus so that you are prepared and armed for every possible event; then, when you study a new piece, you can turn all your power to the intellectual content; you will not be held up by the technical problems.

10 Never play carelessly, even when there is nobody listening, or the occasion seems unimportant.

11 Never leave a passage which has been unsuccessful without repeating it; if you cannot do it in the presence of others, then do it subsequently.

12 If possible, allow no day to pass without touching your piano.

BUTHS, Julius (1851–1920)
b. Wiesbaden, Germany. Studied at Cologne Cons. under F. Hiller. Performed extensively while still studying, touring activities later being curtailed on account of ill-health. Became a guiding light of the Lower Rhine Festivals.

BYFIELD, Jack (1903–77)
b. Croydon, UK. Pf student R. Coll. of Music, London. Notable pianist especially in light field, playing in ensemble, also accompanist. Recorded various. Composed numerous light pieces.

BYK, Ryzard (1892–)
b. Lwow, Poland. Pf pupil of I. Friedman, then of T. Leschetizky. Performed throughout Europe; also taught.

CAAMAÑO, Roberto (1923–)
b. Buenos Aires, Argentina. Studied pf and composition there. Performed and composed a pf concerto and chamber music.

CABUS, Peter Noel (–)
b. Malines, Belgium. Pupil of Brussels R. Cons., winning 1st Prize. Taught, performed and composed, including concertos, chamber music and pf solos.

CAFFARET, Lucie (1893–)
b. Paris, France. Student of Paris Cons., where she won 1st Prize, afterwards settling to a successful concert career.

CAGE, John (1912–)
b. Los Angeles, USA. Pf pupil of Fanny Dillon there, then of L. Lévy in Paris. Had lessons from Schoenberg and has specialized in composition music for 'prepared pf', an instrument whose familiar characteristics have initially been systematically interfered with so as to render it as much unlike the normal aural image of a pf as possible. Has furthermore tried to rule out all subjectivity. One of his methods is to throw dice which have predetermined directions on their sides. Has 'composed' a pf piece called *4 mins 33 secs* where the performer sits at the instrument for precisely that time doing nothing. His first piece in his style was *Bacchanale* (1938), and the longest *Sonatas and Interludes* (1946) which lasts over an hour. There is also *Concerto for pf and orch.* (1957). Wrote *Silence: Lectures and Writings* (1966) and *A Year from Monday* (1969); also, in association with Kathleen Hoover, *Virgil Thomson: His Life and Music* (1959).

CAHEN, Ernest (1828–93)
b. Paris, France. Pf pupil at Paris Cons. Taught there, performed and composed.

CALAND, Elisabeth (1862–1929)
b. Rotterdam, Netherlands. Was musically educated in Berlin and taught there 1898–1915, where she acquired a good reputation. For a time worked in the Rostock area, returning to Berlin, where she died. Wrote a number of excellent pedagogic works on pf technique.

CALLIGARIS, Sergio (1941–)
b. Tosario, Argentina. First played in public at 13. After studying in Buenos Aires, went to USA and became a pupil of A. Loesser at Cleveland Inst., where he taught 1966–7. Studied further in Rome for three years, afterwards teaching at Los Angeles State Coll. Became naturalized Italian. Recorded Orion.

CALZIN, Alfred Lucien (1885–)
b. Vigny, France. Studied music in Brussels, then, 1904–17, became pf pupil of A. Jonás in Berlin. Début Feb. 1907 with Berlin PO. Toured Europe with success before visiting United States and Canada. Settled to teach in Chicago and later in Minneapolis.

CÁMARA, Júan Antonio (1917–)
b. Havana, Cuba. Student of Cons. there, where he taught after graduating. Neoclassical style as composer, mainly for pf.

CAMPANELLA, Michele (1947–)
b. Naples, Italy. Student of Cons. there. Won a number of pf competitions including 1st Prize of the Casella Int. Pf Comp. of 1966. Thereafter commenced concert career touring Europe. Recorded Philips.

CANINO, Bruno (1936–)
b. Naples, Italy. Student of Milan Cons., obtaining diplomas in pf playing and composition. Toured Europe, USA and Japan; also appeared in major festivals solo and with orch.

Harpsichordist and chamber-music player (pianist of Trio di Milano). Recorded Ricordi.

CARMICHAEL, Mary (1851–1935)
b. Birkenhead, UK. Pupil of O. Beringer, W. Bache and others. Was a celebrated accompanist.

CARPENTIER, Adolphe le: see **LE CARPENTIER, Adolphe.**

CARREÑO, Teresa (1853–1917)
b. Caracas, Venezuela. Was taught by her father who was a fine pianist. Début 1862, New York, where the family had settled. The following year was due to give two recitals in Boston but met with such acclaim she gave twelve. Received lessons from L. Gottschalk, then toured Europe 1865–74, in the course of which she had lessons from G. Mathias and Anton Rubinstein. By then she was among the leading women pianists. There was an interlude in the pf career when she discovered she had a voice, had it trained, then went into opera for some years and even conducted. In 1882 she returned to the concert platform and thereafter pianistic reputation was unrivalled. She married four times: (1) Emil Sauret; (2) Giovanni Tagliapietra; (3) Eugène d'Albert and (4) Arturo Tagliapietra, brother of No. 2. By No. 2 she had two children one of whom, Teresita Tagliapietra, became a concert pianist. In 1890 G. B. Shaw wrote of her: 'She is a second Arabella Goddard: she can play anything for you; but she has nothing of her own to tell you about it. Playing is her superb accomplishment, not her mission.'
Pupils included: George Copeland, Ruth Deyo, Alfred Laliberté, Eino Lindholm, Edward MacDowell, Olallo Morales, Alexander Mottu, Egon Petri, Anders Rachlew, Teresita Tagliapietra.

CARREÑO, Teresita: see
TAGLIAPIETRA, Teresita.

CARRERAS, Maria (c. 1872–1966)
b. Italy. Pf pupil of G. Sgambati and F. Busoni. A prodigy who became a celebrity in eastern Europe, playing at courts. US début 1923 in New York and settled there.

CARROLL, Patricia (–)
b. Beckenham, UK. Pupil of R. Coll. of Music, London, completing studies in Vienna. Début 1952, London. Performed throughout Europe.

CARTIER-BRESSON, Hortense (1958–)
b. Igny, France. Studied at Paris Cons. and Indiana Univ. Teachers included J. Doyen and Y. Loriod. 3rd Prizewinner of Liszt–Bartók Comp., Budapest, 1981.

CARVALHO, Dinora de (1905–)
b. Uberaba, Brazil. Pf pupil at São Paolo Cons. and later with I. Philipp in Paris. Active concert pianist who also composed, including a *Fantasia Brasileira* for pf and orch.

CASADESUS, Gaby (1901–)
b. Marseilles, France. Pupil of Paris Cons. Married Robert C. Her concert career covered solo appearances and duos with her husband. Taught Fontainebleau and Curtis Institutes. Recorded CBS and others.

CASADESUS, Jean (1927–72)
b. Paris, France. Son of Robert and Gaby C. Student of Paris Cons. and of parents. Was in USA in 1939 and continued studies. Début 1946, Philadelphia, in Ravel G major. Performed thereafter and in 1954 joined American Cons. at Fontainebleau. Killed in road accident in Canada. Recorded various.

CASADESUS, Robert Marcel (1899–1972)
b. Paris, France. Pupil of Cons. there under L. Diémer. Won Prix Diémer 1913. Began touring 1922, covering most continents in the years before 1939. Settled in USA 1941. Special affinity with music of Mozart, Chopin and the French school. Celebrated his golden jubilee as concert pianist the year he died. Composed pf concertos and sonatas as well as works for one and two pfs. His 24 preludes are dedicated to Ravel. In Paris in 1924 gave the first all-Ravel recital. Recorded *Columbia* and CBS.
Pupils included: Hans Balmer, Mary Boehm, Cosmo Buono, Claude Helffer, Andrew Imbrie, Grant Johannesen, John Simons, Mario Varro, George Walker.

CASALS, Pau (1876–1973)
b. Vendrell, Spain. The pf was one of seven instruments which C mastered, and thus he may be likened to F. Kreisler. Often accompanied his second wife, Susan Metcalfe, the soprano, in recitals.

CASELLA, Alfredo (1883–1947)
b. Turin, Italy. Played pf from age of 4 when his mother gave him lessons. At age of 13 went to Paris Cons. under L. Diémer, where in 1899

he gained 1st Prize. Thereafter made successful tours of Europe playing and conducting. From 1912–15 was prof. of advanced pupils at Paris Cons.; then in 1915 took over pf prof. at S. Cecilia, Rome, on death of G. Sgambati. Gave first performance in 1913 of Ravel's *A la manière de . . .* and *Prélude* and in 1915 took the pf part in the première of Ravel's *Trio*. Was a leading international musical figure of his time and was regarded as the most accomplished Italian composer. A prolific composer in most branches he wrote *Partita* for pf and small orch., also *Scarlattiana* for pf and 32 instruments. His *Sinfonia, Arioso e Toccata* (1936) for solo pf was featured by W. Gieseking. Wrote two sets of pf duets. Made an edition of Beethoven pf sonatas for Ricordi. Recorded pre-war with Pro Arte Quartet (label unknown). Dedicatee of Busoni's *Romanza e Scherzoso* for pf and orch.

Pupils included: Enriques Solares, Lydia Tartaglia.

CASSEL, Sir Francis Edward (1912–69)
b. London, UK. Pf student with T. Matthay. Concert pianist and barrister. Also Chairman of Management Committee, Cassel Hospital for Functional Nervous Disorders. Second Bart. For years announced annual pf recital every autumn in Royal Albert Hall, apparently not appearing in public in between. Never seemingly obtained a write-up from critics, and upon his death left £750,000.

CASTAGNETTA, Grace (1912–)
b. New York, USA. Pupil of Curtis Inst., Philadelphia, also of Berlin Hochschule. Performed, lectured, also composed pf pieces and songs and made arrangements for pf including Gershwin.

CASTELNUOVO-TEDESCO, Mario (1895–1968)
b. Florence, Italy. Studied at Cherubini Musical Inst. there under Edgardo Del Valle de Paz. Toured as concert pianist and conductor, and in 1939 settled in USA. Wrote in most genres, including two pf concertos, chamber music and numerous pf pieces mostly with individual descriptive titles and of considerable difficulty. His 2nd concerto had its première in 1939 in New York with the composer at the pf and New York PO under Barbirolli.

CASTIGLIONI, Niccolò (1932–)
b. Milan, Italy. Student of Cons. there. Successful concert pianist and composer in avant-garde style.

CASTRO, Ricardo (1864–1907)
b. Mexico City, Mexico. Studied pf there and later in Europe, where he performed solo and with orchestra with conspicuous success. Achieved praise for a pf concerto and pieces. A career which had been auspiciously launched was sadly ended when he died shortly after returning home.

CATOIRE, George Lvovich (1861–1926)
b. Moscow, Russia. Studied pf with K. Klindworth in Berlin, and composition with Liadov. His style was influenced by P. Tchaikovsky, who took an interest in his work. A finished craftsman who wrote mainly for pf, chamber music and a pf concerto which had a vogue at the time including a London performance in 1920; also pf pieces. Earned a living teaching composition at Moscow Cons. and at the Scriabin Inst.

CAZDEN, Norman (1914–)
b. New York, USA, Prodigy who appeared in public recital at 12. Pupil of E. Hutcheson and others at Juilliard School, and later at Harvard. Recitalist, teacher, broadcaster, accompanist. Essayist and editor of folk-songs.

CECCATO, Aldo (1934–)
b. Milan, Italy. Pupil of Verdi Cons. there. Int. Comp. prizewinner 1949. Gave recitals while additionally studying conducting, to which he turned in 1964 after winning 1st Prize in an Italian competition on radio. From 1969 worked mainly in N. America.

CELLI, Edoardo (1888–1925)
b. Rome, Italy. Pupil of G. Sgambati, winning pf diploma R. Liceo di S. Cecilia 1904, then studied with E. von Sauer and T. Leschetizky in Vienna. Performed throughout Europe and USA.

CERNIKOV, Vladimir (1882–1940)
b. Paris, France. Studied in Switzerland, then in Berlin. Début 1905, Mülhausen; first London recital 1908. Toured widely and wrote an autobiography, *Humour and Harmony* (1936). Recorded *Columbia and other labels*.

CERVANTES, Ignacio (1847–1905)
b. Havana, Cuba. Pupil of L. Gottschalk, then, at Paris Cons., of A. Marmontel and C. Alkan. Returned home to live as concert pianist and teacher. Composed light music for pf, originating use of Cuban rhythms in his work. Especially noteworthy are 21 *Danzas Cubanas*.

CESI, Beniamino (1845–1907)
b. Naples, Italy. Pupil of Naples Cons., also of S. Thalberg. Took lessons from K. Tausig also. Thereafter made many successful concert tours of Europe. Taught at R. Coll. Naples, 1866–85, in which year he accepted an invitation from Anton Rubinstein to teach at St Petersburg Cons., resigning six years later on health grounds. After a short spell in Palermo he returned to Naples, where he taught until his death. Compiled a pf method and wrote pf works; also edited some of the educational pf scores for the Ricordi edition.
    Pupils included: Cav Andrea, Pietro Boccaccini, Napoleone Cesi, Sigismondo Cesi, Francesco Cilea, Michele Esposito, Pietro Floridia, Alessandro Longo, Giuseppe Martucci, Samuel Maykapar, Luigi Romaniello, Florestano Rossomandi.

CESI, Napoleone (1867–1940)
b. Naples, Italy. Son of Beniamino C, who taught him. Later studied with P. Martucci. Came second in the Rubinstein Comp. of 1890 which was won by F. Busoni. Composed works for pf and orch. and pieces.

CESI, Sigismondo (1869–1936)
b. Naples, Italy. Son of Beniamino C, who taught him, also pupil of A. Longo. Founded Liceo Musicale in Naples 1898. Performed; arranged editions, especially Schumann's pf works, and wrote pedagogic works.

CHABRIER, Emmanuel (1841–94)
b. Ambert, Puy de Dôme, France. Pf pupil of É. Wolff. Composer mainly of opera, ballet music and orch. works. His own pf playing was regarded by contemporaries as of an explosive nature, leading, as in the case of Beethoven, to damage to the instrument. Pf works include *Pièces Pittoresques* and the *Bourrée fantasque*; for two pfs *Trois valses romantiques*; and for duet *Cortège burlesque*, *Souvenirs de Munich* and an arrangement of *España*.

CHAI, Nakyong (1933–)
b. Seoul, S. Korea. Studied in Germany and USA. Performed widely through those countries.

CHAJES, Julius (1910–)
b. Lwow, Poland. Pf pupil of R. Robert and H. Kanner-Rosenthal in Vienna, winning Int. Contest there in 1933. Performed, then taught for two years in Tel-Aviv before settling in USA in 1937, where he became Director of the Jewish Centre, Detroit. Composed *Fantaisie* for pf and orch., first performed by him in 1928, a pf concerto (1952) premièred on Vienna Radio in 1957, as well as chamber music and pf works including a sonata.

CHALLIS, Phillip (1925–)
b. Huddersfield, UK. Pupil of R. Manchester Coll. and of H. Fryer and I. Kabos. Has performed throughout UK and Europe, composed pf pieces, songs and chamber music.

CHALLUPPER, Joseph (1911–)
b. Horowive, Czechoslovakia. Student Paris and Vienna and of pf in particular under K. Ansorge. Début Prague, 1929. Concert pianist, teacher and composer.

CHALOFF, Julius (1892–)
b. Boston, USA. Pupil of I. Friedman, Berlin. Début there 1913. Returned home and became pf prof. at New England Cons.

CHAMINADE, Cécile (1857–1944)
b. Paris, France. Studied pf with F. Le Couppey, who ran a master-class for talented young ladies. Début 1875 and toured as a virtuoso for a quarter of a century. Studied composition under B. Godard and proceeded to compose over 200 pf pieces of light and romantic appeal, many of which enjoyed great popularity during her lifetime. Visited London in 1895 and played her *Concertstück* for pf and orch. at a R. Phil. Soc. concert. Recorded *G & T*.

CHANLER, Theodore Ward (1902–61)
b. Newport, RI, USA. Pf pupil of H. Ebell and R. Bühlig, then had a spell at Oxford Univ., UK, before studying with N. Boulanger in Paris. Among his works are a violin sonata, *Five Short Colloquies* for pf solo, a fugue for two pfs and songs which reflect the style of Fauré.

CHAPPLE, Stanley (1900–)
b. London, UK. Studied there. Held several teaching appointments, especially at Guildhall School. Performed and conducted. Settled in USA and from 1948 was head of music at Washington Univ. Wrote works on technique, harmony etc. Recorded *Vocalion Broadcast* as young man.

CHASINS, Abram (1903–)
b. New York, USA. Student of Juilliard School and of Curtis Inst., teachers being E. Hutcheson, R. Goldmark and J. Hofmann. Début 1929, Philadelphia, playing première of own 1st pf concerto. Gave first performance same city 1932 of 2nd pf concerto, in between the events touring both continents with success (London début 1931). Also taught at Curtis, composed and wrote essays. Author of *Speaking of Pianists* (1957). Solo pf compositions include 24 *Preludes*, *Narrative*, a set of Chinese pieces which enjoyed a passing vogue; also for four hands concert paraphrases on themes from *Carmen* and *Die Fledermaus* respectively. Recorded *RCA*.

CHATTENDEN, Kate (1856–1949)
b. Hamilton, Canada. Noted teacher of pf at Vassar Coll. Composed pedagogic works.

CHAVCHAVADZE, George (Prince) (1905–62)
b. St Petersburg, Russia, second son of Prince and Princess Troubetzkoy. Musically educated from age of 5 in Russia and later in Austria, 'to the Leschetizky method'. During the revolution he was brought to Britain by British officials, and the rest of the family arrived by various routes and settled. London début 1927 and appeared several times in ensuing seasons both solo and with orch. Toured Canada a number of times and also visited Scandinavia. Arranged *El Amor Brujo* (de Falla) for pf solo. Of a three-concerto concert in May 1931 a London critic wrote: 'In the Mozart (K.488) one was free to enjoy a performance of rare delicacy and much tonal beauty.'
Pupils included: Pyta Shrager.

CHEMPIN, Beryl Margaret (–)
b. Birmingham, UK. Pupil of Birmingham School of Music and later of H. Craxton in London. Gave first performance in Birmingham of 2nd pf concerto of Shostakovich.

Soloist, accompanist and became well-known teacher.

CHERKASSKY, Shura (1911–)
b. Odessa, Russia. Studied with his mother then with J. Hofmann. Toured USA as a prodigy of 12, appearing before President Hoover. Became an international artist, though his style belonged more to that of pupils of Leschetizky, being regarded in some critical quarters as idiosyncratic. A fabulous technique, however, as befitting a pupil of the legendary Hofmann. Recorded various.

CHERNIAVSKY, Jan (1892–19)
b. Odessa, Russia. Pupil of father and was prodigy. Studied with A. Essipova, then with T. Leschetizky. With brothers Leo (violin) and Mikhail (cello) formed trio in 1900 and toured globally as highly successful ensemble. Recorded *Columbia* and *Pathé*.

CHEVILLARD, Camille (1859–1923)
b. Paris, France. Studied at Cons. there under G. Mathias, taking 2nd Prize 1880. Took to conducting and taught himself composition; works for pf being mostly chamber music. From 1907 taught chamber music at Cons.

CHIAPUSSO, Jan (1890–1969)
b. Kendal, Java. Musically educated in Netherlands and in Germany, graduating from Cologne Univ. Also received tuition from F. Lamond. Studied later then taught at Chicago Univ., later becoming prof. musical history and pf at Kansas Univ. until 1960. Author of *Bach's World*.
Pupils included: Rosalyn Tureck.

CHING, James (1900–62)
b. Thornton Heath, UK. Studied in Oxford, London and Berlin. Was a fine teacher and founded own school. Composed pf music and wrote a number of textbooks on technique. Married Betty Reeves.

CHISHOLM, Erik (1904–65)
b. Glasgow, UK. Studied there, in Edinburgh and in London – composition under Tovey, pf under L. Pouishnov. Held various teaching posts at home and abroad and was always keenly connected with local contemporary movements. Worked in S. Africa after Second World War, mainly Cape Town. Composed in a variety of genres including pf concertos.

CHLIONSKY, Verdina: *see*
SHOLONSKY, Verdina.

CHODOS, Gabriel (1939–)
b. New York, USA. Studied there and in
Vienna. Début 1970, Carnegie Hall, followed
by appearances in USA, Europe and elsewhere. Recorded RCA and Orion.

CHOPIN, Frédéric (Fryderyk Franciszek)
(1810–49)
b. Zelazowa Wola, Poland, of a French father
and a Polish mother. This great composer for
the pf arrived on the musical scene virtually
fully equipped for his mission at a time when
the instrument had just been evolved sufficiently to cope with the Romantic movement
which proceeded to stream through numerous
pens, and which in turn inspired manufacturers rapidly to develop the mechanism,
power and soul of the pf.

The boy received tuition from an obscure
provincial pf teacher named Adalbert Zywny,
in no discernible manner important in the
history of music other than having been C's
teacher for a short time. He introduced his
charge to keyboard works of Bach, and when it
is considered that this could happen in countryside outside Warsaw, itself scarcely on the
musical map of Europe at the time, and when
elsewhere in more important centres Bach's
works lay hidden under dust, there is something predestined in Zywny's influence on C,
for the music of Bach and Mozart had a profound and lifelong effect on the famous son of
Poland who always remembered his teacher
with respect and affection.

On entering Warsaw Cons. he came under
the guidance of its Principal, Josef Elsner, a
pedagogue whose creative talents lay more with
opera but who, recognizing genius, wisely left
the youth to blossom in his own unerring way.
C left the Cons. in 1829 with only twenty short
years of life ahead in which to accomplish his
immortal task. That same year he wrote a pf
concerto (published as No. 2 in F minor), playing it at his début the following year in
Warsaw, later repeating it at another event
before, in a third concert, giving the première
of his second concerto (No. 1 in E minor).

At the end of 1830 he left Warsaw, never to
return. He journeyed to Vienna, meeting influential musicians and performing his works,
notably the Mozart *Variations* for pf and orch.,
Op. 2, which were well received and which
drew enthusiastic praise from R. Schumann.

By then, except for the *Andante spianato et
Grande Polonaise*, Op. 22, he had composed all
the works for pf and orch., plus the early
sonata in C minor, Op. 4, as well as a number of
pieces in the Polish idiom; and the great sets of
Études, Opp. 10 and 25, were well under way,
probably inspired by impressions from hearing
Paganini play in Warsaw the previous year, an
experience that opened up a whole new world
to the young man whose genius was so far
ahead of pedagogic minds of the day.

His sojourn in Vienna became profitless and
empty, judging by entries in his diary at the
time which have been interpreted as signifying
temporary madness, whereas more probably
they reflect the symptoms of passing through a
'Dark Night of the Soul' when his artistic sensi-
bilities were brought rapidly to maturity
because of pressure of time. At the end of a
barren period of inward searching, he left
Vienna for Paris via Munich and Stuttgart, and
never again in his life do we find stagnation or
uncertainty.

The journey to Paris was an instinctive gravi-
tation towards his father's native land, for he
settled in the French capital, maintaining
himself by teaching wealthy members of
society supplemented by earnings from composition. There he was to remain for the rest of
his life, a Pole in exile, watching from afar the
Russian oppression of his country.

After the French Revolution Paris had
become the artistic centre of Western Europe,
and on his arrival there C moved effortlessly
into the mainstream of music, rapidly becoming a celebrity as an inevitable consequence of a
successful début at the beginning of 1832. His
playing was highly appreciated by leading
musicians of the day, and his pre-eminent position was achieved without entering the arena
occupied by Liszt and Thalberg.

When C played in the Salle Pleyel that same
year, the Belgian musical historian Fétis, then
prof. of composition at Paris Cons., wrote in
Revue Musicale, making a comparison between
what Beethoven had written 'for the piano' and
what C was writing 'for pianists', adding 'it will
without doubt exercise a profound influence on
all future work written for the instrument'.
Fétis found C's style of playing 'elegant,
precise, and full of charm and grace'.

Again at the end of that year, 1832, C played
a movement of his 2nd concerto at a Berlioz
concert at the Cons., but his reception was
cool, and he must thereafter have realized that
his style was suited better to the salon than to

big halls. From then onwards he played rarely other than in conditions with an intimate atmosphere.

Between 1834 and 1839 C made trips abroad, visiting the Lower Rhineland Music Festival at Aachen during which he met Mendelssohn. He met his parents at Carlsbad in 1835, and later that year went to Dresden, and then to Leipzig where he saw the Schumanns whom he met again the following year. He visited London in the summer of 1837. The winter of 1838 was spent in Majorca in company with Mme Dudevant, and the spring of 1839 was spent in Marseilles with a visit to Genoa.

The liaison with the cigar-smoking Mme Dudevant, better known as a writer under the pen-name of George Sand, has been made much of in biographies and romantic novellas. Some of his best work was composed during the Sand episode, which lasted from 1838 until 1846. Early in 1848, and after an interval of six years from his previous concert, he gave his last recital in Paris, assisted by the violinist Delphin Alard and the cellist Auguste Franchomme. Some movements from C's new cello sonata were played in public for the first time. The young Charles Hallé attended and recorded in his autobiography that at the start C was able to move only with difficulty, being bent like a half-opened penknife and in pain. Then, as he began playing, his body relaxed, 'the spirit having mastered the flesh. In spite of his declining strength, the charm of his playing remained as great as ever'.

When revolution broke out in Europe later that year, he joined the stream of migrants to Britain. He played in London, Edinburgh and Manchester under uncongenial conditions and with indifferent success and little self-satisfaction, returning to Paris a broken man. In less than a year he was dead, leaving a rich seam of peerless pf music that ever since has been a source of never-ending interest, fascination and enrichment to pianists and public alike. The style is unique because he was a trailblazer. Those who tried to follow merely flattered him in the dubious art of imitation. It has been pointed out that he used Field, Hummel and Weber as models; yet what evolutionist of whatever branch of art has not taken and used that which is already in existence as a stepping-off point to some better result?

Many pianists and pf composers of his day have left impressions of his playing. On some aspects they conflict, confusing the reader. All are unanimous on one point: that his style was unique, quite unlike anyone else's and, being unique, went with his passing. Charles Hallé, who heard C play many times, said he himself lost all power of analysis and did not for a moment think how perfectly he dealt with particular difficulties but listened, as it were, to the improvisation of a poem, and was under its charm as long as it lasted.

The critic Henry Chorley was present at a private recital given by C on 23 June 1848. It lasted 90 minutes, no less than the average recital does today. Chorley wrote: 'Whereas other pianists have proceeded on the intention of equalising the power of the fingers, M. Chopin's plans are arranged so as to utilise their natural inequality of power, and, if carried out, provide varieties of expression not to be attained by those with whom evenness is the first excellence. Allied with this fancy are his peculiar mode of treating the scale and the shake, and his manner of sliding with one and the same finger from note to note, by way of producing a peculiar *legato*, and of passing the third over the fourth finger. All these innovations are art and part of his music as properly rendered, and as enacted by himself they charm by an ease and grace which, though superfine, are totally distinct from affectation. The delicacy of Chopin's tone, and the elasticity of his passages are delicious to the ear. He makes a free use of *tempo rubato*; leaning about within his bars more than any player we recollect, but still subject to a presiding sentiment of measure, such as presently habituates the ear to the liberties taken. In music not his own we happen to know he can be as strict as a metronome.'

Moscheles said of his playing: 'His *piano* is so softly breathed forth that he does not require any strong forte to produce the wished for contrast.' And Stephen Heller remarked, 'It is a wonderful sight to see Chopin's small hands expand and cover a third of the keyboard. It was like the opening of the mouth of a serpent about to swallow a rabbit whole.'

In his time the solid style of the German school of pianism was at its height, and some of its forthright approach and squareness could be attributed to the example set by Beethoven, especially with the onset of deafness. C's style was the antithesis. Hating violence and mere noise, his hands caressed the keyboard and he applied individual fingering to achieve technical perfection. He was probably the first to enunciate the theory that the scale of B major lies far more naturally under the beginner's hand than does that of C major. He saw nothing wrong in using the thumb to strike black notes, a view which theorists of his day received with horror. Unlike Beethoven he never urged pf-makers to build more powerful instruments. On the contrary he preferred the lightweight actions of Pleyel pfs because they produced congenial and expressive responses. Because of a slight physique and a high degree of sensitivity, he scaled down his performances in perfect proportion, and his large-scaled works like the *Ballades*, the *Scherzi* and the *Barcarolle* are in no way inferior in boldness of thought and power of construction to Beethoven's. To remember that his *Études* Op. 10 were completed within four years of the death of Beethoven is to realize that the old order was closed and that a whole new dimension had opened up in the world of pf music.

His compositions include two youthful pf concertos and the following other works for pf and orch.: *Variations on 'Là ci darem'*, *Fantasia on Polish Airs*, *Krakowiak Rondo* and *Andante spianato et Grande Polonaise*; four sonatas including two big, mature four-movement works for pf, and the late one for cello and pf; two books of highly important and superb *Études*; four *Ballades* and four *Scherzi* – all tone poems of extraordinary power and brilliance; books of polonaises and mazurkas (both dance forms lying at the heart of the composer's work): 14 waltzes, 20 nocturnes, 24 preludes, four impromptus; important pieces like the *Barcarolle*, the *Berceuse*, the *Fantaisie* and the *Polonaise-Fantaisie*; four *Rondos*, including one for two pfs, and several sets of early variations. He composed an early pf trio, a handful of chamber works and 17 *Polish Songs*; and he contributed to the Lisztian *Hexameron*. Other works came to light after his death and were published despite his dying wish that all such should be destroyed.

Pupils included: Charles Bovy-Lysberg, Karl Filtsch, Adolph Gutmann, Wilhelm de Lenz, Ignace Leybach, Georges Mathias, Antoinette Mauté de Fleurville, Karl Mikuli, Thomas Tellefsen, Casimir Wernick.

CHORZEMPA, Daniel (1944–)
b. Minneapolis, USA. Began playing from age of 4 and taught at Minnesota Univ. from age of 17, later becoming PhD of Music there. Is also noted organist and violinist. Is credited with

having memorized a vast repertoire. Recorded Phonogram and Classics for Pleasure.

CHOTZINOV, Samuel (1889–1964)
b. Vitebsk, Russia. Was taken to USA as a boy, where he received his musical training, ending at Columbia Univ. Principal concert work was as accompanist to celebrities with whom he toured. Latterly turned to musical criticism, teaching and lecture tours. Was also with Curtis Inst. and NBC, New York. Husband of Pauline, sister of the famous violinist Jascha Heifetz.

CHOU, Chia (–)
b. Canada. Won 1st Prize, Sydney (Australia) Int. Pf Comp 1981. Enquiries failed to reveal any other details.

CHRAPOWICKI, Victor (1893–1931)
b. Warsaw, Poland. Pupil of Cons. there and of A. Michałowski. A pianist highly regarded in Poland who suffered from ill-health and died of tuberculosis at a comparatively early age.

CHRISTIE, Winifred (1882–1965)
b. Stirling, UK. Pf student at R. Acad., London, on a Liszt Scholarship and under O. Beringer. After graduation she studied abroad, especially with H. Bauer, and began touring in Europe. Resided in USA 1915–19. In 1923 married the pianist-inventor Emanuel Moór, inventor of the Moór-Duplex keyboard of two manuals, an octave apart, with a device for coupling them in order to overcome 'spread' chords and facilitate octave playing. From her marriage until 1939 she toured ceaselessly, demonstrating the invention. After the war she founded the Central Music Library as well as a scholarship at the R. Acad. (of which she was a Fellow) especially to revive interest in the Moór-Duplex keyboard. In an obituary notice Max Pirani, another enthusiast of the principle, described her as: 'a pianist of striking and individual qualities'. Composed concertos, chamber music and pf pieces. Gave première of *Concerto-Fantasia* for pf and orch. by E. Bainton at a R. Phil. Soc., London, concert in 1922, the composer conducting. Wrote technical exercises for the double-keyboard pf. Recorded *Vocalion* and possibly *HMV*.

CHUNG, Myung-Whun (1953–)
b. Seoul, S. Korea. Musically educated in USA at Mannes and Juilliard schools. Début 1960 in Seoul. In 1974 was awarded joint 2nd Prize

(silver medal) at Tchaikovsky Comp., Moscow. Additionally took up conducting. Brother of Kyung Wha Chung, violin, and of Myung Wha Chung, cello, with whom he gave chamber-music concerts. Recorded EMI and Decca.

CIAMPI, Marcel Paul Maximin (1891–1980)
b. Paris, France. Pupil at Paris Cons. under L. Diémer for pf. Won 1st Prize pf 1909. Toured solo, with orch. and as duo with artists of calibre of Casals and Thibaud. Latterly concentrated on teaching only and established own school. Hon. prof. of Paris Cons. Married Yvonne Astruc, distinguished violinist, in 1920. Recorded *Columbia*.

Pupils included: Stanislav Knor, Rosamund Leonard, Hepzibah Menuhin, Jeremy Menuhin, Yaltah Menuhin, Cécile Ousset.

CIANCHETTINI, Pio (1799–1851)
b. London, UK. His mother was pf teacher and member of Dussek family. Was phenomenal prodigy from age of 5 and composed prolifically for the instrument, performing a concerto of own composition in London in 1809 when he was 10. Edited Beethoven's works for British publishers.

CIANI, Dino (1941–)
b. Fiume, Italy. Studied in Italy and with A. Cortot, winning 2nd Prize Liszt–Bartók Comp., Budapest, 1961. Since performed throughout Europe.

CICCOLINI, Aldo (1925–)
b. Naples, Italy. Began learning pf when young and at 9 entered Naples Cons., winning 1st Prize for playing 1940. Début following year in Naples in Chopin F minor concerto. Became pf prof. at his Cons. in 1947. Paris début 1949 and visited USA following year. Subsequently toured Europe, Americas and Far East and became prof. at Paris Cons. Wide repertoire from Bach to modern French. Recorded EMI.

Pupils included: Olivier Leger.

CILÈA, Francesco (1866–1950)
b. Palmi, Italy. Student of B. Cesi at Naples Cons. where he taught 1890–2 before moving to the Cherubini Istituto, Florence, and then, in succession to Palermo and Naples Cons. of S. Pietro a Maiella of which he became Director. Composed refined chamber music,

pf pieces and songs but is best remembered for his opera *Adriana Lecouvreur*.

CLAUSS-SZARVADY, Wilhelmine (1834–1907)
b. Prague, Czechoslovakia. Studied pf there, where she made début 1849. Lived in Paris from 1852 from where she toured regularly, making an isolated appearance that year in London in the Beethoven *Emperor* while not yet 18. Noted for her musicianship and respect for composers' intentions.

CLEMENTI, Marjorie (1927–)
b. Manchester, UK. Pupil of R. Manchester Coll. and of E. Isaacs, also in London with M. Cole. Prof. Manchester Coll. from 1965 and as a pianist has specialized in works of her namesake M. Clementi. Pupils included: Peter Noke, Martin Roscoe.

CLEMENTI, Muzio (1752–1832)
b. Rome, Italy. Showed interest in music from early age and was encouraged by his father, an amateur musician, who provided suitable teachers. At the age of 9 C was appointed a church organist, his other instrument being the harpsichord. When he was 15, an acquaintance of the family, a wealthy Englishman by the name of Beckford, prevailed upon the father to let him take the boy to England where, on an estate in Devonshire, he pursued an intensive education, especially in music. By this time he had turned his attention to the pf, and in 1770, at the age of 18, he arrived in London, where he created a furore with his unrivalled command of the instrument. Socially and musically his acclaim far exceeded anything Handel had enjoyed. His pf sonata Op. 2 took the public by storm, one musician of the day declaring that only the devil and C could have played it.

He enjoyed the adulation of London's musical circle for seven years before making a brilliant tour of Europe, meeting leading musicians as well as crowned heads. In Vienna he met Mozart, and they became acquainted with each other's playing. Mozart regarded C as 'a mere mechanician without a penn'orth of feeling and taste'. C on the other hand was much impressed by Mozart's 'singing touch and exquisite taste', and the experience is said to have led him greatly to reconstruct his own style of playing.

He returned to London, playing and teaching, as well as resting on his laurels, for by now his fame was such that pupils poured from all over Europe to study with him. One of these was an Irish boy, John Field, and in 1802 C took this pupil on a tour through Europe, ending in St Petersburg where Field was lionized so much that he decided to make that city his home, marrying into wealthy aristocracy and rapidly acquiring affluence.

Back in London C bought an interest in a music business, but it failed, saddling him with crippling debts. However, he set up his own firm manufacturing instruments and publishing music, and this flourished until 1807 when it was destroyed by fire entailing a loss of some £40,000. He set about restoring his fortunes but from 1810 gave up the career of concert pianist, turning to composition. He continued to teach as well as supervise the business which was later to be carried on under the house name of Collard. He is credited with doing the most effective research into the construction of the upright pf between 1810 and 1818.

He was probably the most important pedagogue of the time, much admired by Beethoven, and the first teacher to lay down a proper system of keyboard fingering. A prolific composer whose works included over 100 pf sonatas, some of great difficulty. Most famous work was, however, *Gradus ad Parnassum*, a set of studies which undoubtedly influenced pf technique and which for a long time was held to be an important collection of exercises for manual dexterity. The writer has seen records of household accounts of a country seat in Norfolk where, in the early years of the 19th century, C regularly called to give harp lessons to young ladies of the house.

Pupils included: Ludwig Berger, Benoit Bertini, Johann B. Cramer, Karl Czerny, John Field, August Klengel, Charles Meyer, Giacomo Meyerbeer, Karl Zeuner.

CLEVE, Halfdan (1879–1952)
b. Kongsberg, Norway. Studied pf and composition there and later worked in Berlin under X. Scharwenka. Début 1902, Berlin, playing two of his own pf concertos. Toured as concert pianist specializing in Norwegian works and often played the Grieg pf concerto under the composer's baton. Composed five pf concertos and a sonata, chamber music and songs.

CLIBURN, Van (1934–)
b. Shreveport, USA. Pupil first of his mother then later of R. Lhevinne at the Juilliard School, New York, graduating 1954, the year

in which he appeared with the New York PO. This was not, however, his first orch. appearance, for his début had been in 1947 with the Houston Orch.

Won 1st Prize in the Tchaikovsky Pf Comp. in Moscow in 1958 where he was much appreciated by the Russian audience. Because he was the first American to win this prestigious event, he received a tickertape welcome on his return home, and his concert career proper was launched upon a tour of the US and recordings. Toured Europe and became identified with the music of Russian composers, especially Tchaikovsky and Rachmaninov. For a time was regarded among the most celebrated young pianists of his time but was later held in some quarters as having failed to maintain the initial high promise, a colleague once summing up the dilemma by commenting that he was the victim of fame and never got a chance to develop naturally.

C turned, as did many of his contemporaries, to conducting, making his début in 1964. The Van Cliburn Quadrennial Pf Comp. in Texas was instituted in 1962 to commemorate his achievement in Moscow. Recorded RCA.

CLIFFE, Frederick (1857–1931)
b. Lowmoor, UK. A natural pianist and organist, receiving first instruction from his father. In 1876 won scholarship to study under F. Taylor. In 1883 became pf prof. at R. Coll. of Music, London. From 1901 was prof. at R. Acad. as well as a member of the examining boards of both schools.

Pupils included: Arthur Benjamin, John Ireland.

CLOAD, Julia (1946–)
b. London, UK. Studied at R. Coll. of Music, London, and was a pupil of C. Smith, and later at the Liszt Acad. in Budapest under L. Hernadi. Winner of Hopkinson Gold Medal 1966 and other awards. Performed extensively and appeared with leading orchs.

CLOEREC, René Albert (1911–)
b. Paris, France. Studied there, winning 1st Prize for pf playing. Became pf prof. at École Supérieure de Musique and was notable pianist. Has written numerous successful film scores.

CLUTSAM, George (1866–1951)
b. Sydney, Australia. Teachers unknown but was a touring prodigy in Australasia and at age

of 22 toured Far East. Went to London 1889 where he made a reputation as accompanist to celebrities before turning music critic on *The Observer*, 1908–18. Wrote pf pieces and operas but is now remembered for *Lilac Time* (1922) and *Blossom Time* (1942), for both of which shows he arranged Schubert's music.

COCHRANE, Peggy (190?–   )
b. London, UK. Trained in the violin at R. Acad. there (ARAM) alongside studying the pf, and for a time careers in both instruments were continued. Had long and extensive vocation in concerts, theatres and night-clubs as well as radio. Married Jack Payne, band leader and agent. Recorded *Vocalion* and *HMV*. Wrote an autobiography, *We Said it with Music*.

COCKS, Rena (–   )
b. Norwich, UK. Studied at Trinity Coll. and R. Acad., London. Gold medallist. Début London. Performed solo and with orch., also broadcaster.

COELHO, Rui (1891–   )
b. Alcacer do Sal, Portugal. Studied in Lisbon and Germany. Début 1900, Lisbon. Composed chamber music and pf pieces.

COENEN, Willem (1837–1918)
b. Rotterdam, Netherlands. Member of a musical family. After training he performed throughout Europe and the Americas. Lived in London 1862–1909, performing and teaching. Settled in Lugano in retirement. Composed pf works and songs.

COHEN, Arnaldo (1948–   )
b. Rio de Janeiro, Brazil. While learning violin and pf, he studied engineering at Rio Univ., and not until he was 19 did he decide to play the pf professionally. Pupil of J. Klein and winner of a number of local competitions, finishing in Vienna. Début 1972, in which year he toured Europe and also won 1st Prize in the Busoni Comp. Came sixth in the inaugural Arthur Rubinstein Int. Comp. in Israel in 1974. Appeared in most European countries including USSR, also the Americas. In 1982 a London critic said: 'His colossal reserves of power were all the more remarkable because they were used with such total avoidance of outward show and were held in check for those moments that really matter.' Recorded Dischi Ricordi.

COHEN, Harriet (1895–1967)
b. London, UK. Pupil of R. Acad., London, under T. Matthay; also received lessons from F. Busoni. Début 1920, Wigmore Hall, appearing same year in first performance of *Symphonic Variations* by A. Bax. Subsequently toured widely solo and with orch., and was distinguished chamber-music player with Casals, Sammons, Tertis etc, playing in premières of contemporary British chamber works. Besides being a famed exponent of Bach, was also identified with first performances of contemporary British works for pf and orch., e.g. Bax's *Winter Legends* in 1932, Vaughan Williams's pf concerto in 1933, J. Ireland's *Legend* in 1934 and the Bax *Concertante* for orch. with pf solo (left hand) in 1950 when she returned to the platform after some years of inactivity because of an accident to the right arm which left it incapacitated. Dedicatee of the Milhaud *Sonatine* and of Bax's 3rd pf sonata. From 1952 organized the Harriet Cohen Int. Music Awards for talented young musicians. CBE 1938. Wrote *Music's Handmaid* (1936) and *A Bundle of Time* (1967). Recorded *Columbia* and *HMV*.

The Harriet Cohen Memorial Music Awards Trust offers biennial awards to professional musicians up to 30 years old who have shown outstanding promise and are in need of further assistance. By nomination only from various institutions by rota throughout the country. No individual applications considered. The address of the Trust is c/o Rubinstein, Callingham, 6 Raymond Buildings, Gray's Inn, London WC1.

COLE, Maurice (1902–   )
b. London, UK. Student of Guildhall School under C. Sobrino; later pupil of A. de Greef. Début 1922, Wigmore Hall, London, in series of recitals followed by provincial appearances, also in Europe. Prom début 1927, thereafter making regular appearances. Broadcast from its early days in Europe and UK, in 1972 making TV appearance to celebrate his and the BBC's 50th anniversary of broadcasting. Taught at Guildhall School. Recorded *Vocalion*, *Broadcast* and Saga.

Pupils included: Marjorie Clementi.

COLE, Ulric (1905–   )
b. New York, USA, Pf pupil of J. Lhevinne. Performed and composed two pf concertos, chamber music and pf works.

COLLARD, Jean-Philippe (1948–)
b. Mareuil-sur-Aÿ, France. Began winning competitions from the age of 12, and in 1964 achieved 1st Prize at Paris Cons. Appeared throughout Europe, USA, USSR and the Far East. London début 1980. In 1982 a London critic wrote: 'Common to all his playing was an impeccable musical and pianistic clarity, a refinement of sound and texture which even at its most powerful retained an immaculately groomed, typically Gallic finesse.' Recorded EMI.

COLLET, Robert (1905–)
b. London, UK. Studied at R. Coll. there. Début Wigmore Hall, 1930. Performed and taught. Pf prof. at Guildhall School and has written on various aspects of music.

COLLINS, Peter (1961–)
b. New Orleans, USA. Studied at Peabody Cons., Baltimore.

CONCI, Noretta (1931–)
b. Rome, Italy. Studied at S. Cecilia Cons. there and was pupil of A. B. Michelangeli, winning a diploma 1948 and the Harriet Cohen Int. Music Medal 1957. Was joint winner of BBC Comp. 1969. Has performed and taught extensively in Europe and USA.

CONINCK, Jacques Félix de (1791–1866)
b. Antwerp, Belgium. Early Belgian pianist who was pupil of Paris Cons. Performed and also accompanied, notably for Maria Malibran in her US tour 1825–7. Founded Antwerp music society and composed pf concertos, sonatas and pieces.

CONSOLO, Ernesto (1864–1931)
b. London, UK. Pf pupil of G. Sgambati at S. Cecilia, Rome, and later of K. Reinecke in Leipzig. British début 1904 at Phil. concert, giving first performance of *Concertstück* in A flat by Franco da Venezia. Rapidly became esteemed as a leading Italian pianist. Toured Europe, then USA, where he taught at Chicago Coll., 1906–9, before resuming career in Europe, teaching additionally at Florence Cons., where he became pf prof. Was noted chamber-music player especially in a trio with Serato (violin) and Mainardi (cello).
    Pupils included: Luigi Dallapiccola, Rio Nardi.

CONSTANTINIDIS, Nicolas (–)
b. Egypt of Greek parentage. Blind from 6. Début in Cairo when 17 followed by recital tours, raising funds to get to USA on scholarship in 1957.

CONTESTABILE, Emma (1928–)
b. Bologna, Italy. Studied S. Cecilia Cons., Rome, also in Salzburg. Performed widely throughout the world and held a number of teaching posts in Italy.

CONTIGUGLIA, John Joseph (1927–)
b. New York, USA. Student of Yale School of Music, teachers included M. Hess. Performed widely in USA and appeared in Europe from 1962. Elder brother of Richard C (b. 1937, New York), who also studied at Yale School and with M. Hess. They premièred the T. Serly concerto for two pfs in 1965 in Syracuse.

CONUS, Lev (1871–1944)
b. Moscow, Russia. Concert pianist and pf prof. at Moscow Cons., where he had been trained. Fellow-pupil in Arensky's composition class with S. Rachmaninov; became lifelong friends, his nephew Boris marrying Rachmaninov's younger daughter, Tanya. Arranged Tchaikovsky's *Pathétique* Symphony for four hands which he played with Taneyev before the composer in 1893, the year of the latter's death. Emigrated to USA in 1936, where he died. Youngest of three brothers, all musical, who were taught at Moscow Cons. and in turn became profs. there.
    Pupils included: K. Evers, Sergei Conus.

CONUS, Sergius (1902–)
b. Moscow, Russia. Pupil of his father Lev C., before studying at Paris Cons. under A. Cortot and I. Philipp. Lived successively in Bulgaria and Poland, then in France throughout World War II, after which he settled for ten years in Moscow before moving in 1959 to USA where he was pf prof. at Boston Cons. Compositions include a pf concerto and 24 preludes in a style said to reflect the influence of Rachmaninov.

COOKE, William Waddington (1868–1940)
b. West Keel, UK. Studied first at R. Coll., London, then with T. Leschetizky in Vienna. Début London, 1900, then taught at Guildhall School of Music up to his death.

COONS, Minnie (1882–)
b. New York, USA. Studied pf in Berlin and

was a pupil of X. Scharwenka (1900–4). Début 1904 with Leipzig Gewandhaus Orch. and toured Europe successfully before returning to USA. Début with NYSO 1905 and thereafter settled there as concert pianist and teacher.

COOPER, Gaze (Walter Thomas Gaze)
(1895–1981)
b. Long Eaton, UK. Studied in Nottingham and at R. Acad., London, pf teacher F. Dawson. Had splendid technique; also taught and conducted, becoming leading musical figure in Nottingham through founding in 1933 what grew to become Nottingham SO. Taught Midland Cons. from 1925. Was prolific composer including a pf concerto that was premièred 1923 by Bournemouth Orch., and a set of *Nocturnes* first performed by Liza Fuchsova in 1950. He also wrote pf sonatas, songs and pf pieces.

COOPER, Imogen (1949–)
b. London, UK. Student of K. Long, then at Paris Cons. with J. Février and Y. Lefébure, winning 1st Prize there in 1967. Afterwards studied with A. Brendel. Since then has performed solo and with orch., with increasing success. Has also appeared in Germany and Austria. Recorded Erato and Philips.

COOPER, Joseph (1913–)
b. London, UK. Studied pf and organ, received lessons from E. Petri. London début postponed from 1939 to 1947 on account of war service. Performed but achieved fame on British TV in series *Face the Music* where as question-master he rattled out pf music on dummy keyboard for panel to try to guess its identity. OBE 1982. Recorded Decca.
   Pupils included: Charmion Ross-Oliver.

COOPER, Peter (1918–)
b. Christchurch, New Zealand. Studied at R. Acad., London, then with I. Friedman and E. Fischer. Début 1939, Christchurch. Toured as virtuoso. Recorded Pye and EMI. Wrote *Style in Piano Playing* (1975).

COPELAND, George (1882–1971)
b. Boston, USA. Pf pupil of K. Bärmann, T. Carreño and H. Bauer. Début Boston, 1905, and thereafter toured USA and Europe. Introduced Debussy's pf music in Boston and other US cities. During a European tour in 1911 met Debussy and as a result spent some months

studying music with the composer. C published his account of the episode in *Atlantic Monthly* for Jan. 1955. Propagated the works of Debussy and Ravel in recitals and arranged *L'Après Midi* for pf. Gave Golden Jubilee recital in New York, 1957.

COPLAND, Aaron (1900–)
b. Brooklyn, USA. Pf pupil of C. Adler. Pianist, composer, teacher and lecturer. Principal works for pf include a concerto (1926), piano variations (1930), piano sonata (1941) and fantasy (1957). All were premièred by the composer. Of the first performance of the concerto in 1927 the *Boston Post* wrote: 'Since there must be a bit of jazz in all American music nowadays, Mr Copland has his measures in that view, but as one young man in the audience remarked: "No dance-hall would tolerate jazz of such utter badness." ' There is also a violin sonata, *Vitebsk* for pf trio, four *Piano Blues* (written over two decades and each dedicated to a different pianist) and *Danzon Cubano* for two pfs, written in 1942 and first performed that year by the composer and L. Bernstein in New York. Wrote *Our New Music* (1941). Recorded various.

COREA, Chick (1941–)
b. Massachusetts, USA. Studied pf from age of 4, working at Columbia Univ. and Juilliard School. Turned to jazz as his principal career but as a composer has used jazz in serious works.

CORNIL, Dominique (1953–)
b. Mons, Belgium. Studied at R. Cons. there, also Paris Cons., and was a prizewinner in the 1975 Concours Musical Int. Reine Elisabeth, Brussels. Toured throughout Europe solo and with orch. Recorded DG.

CORTOT, Alfred (1877–1962)
b. Nyon, Switzerland, of French father and Swiss mother. They had four children and removed to Paris when the younger son was 9 years old so he could study at the Cons. with E. Decombes and, later, with L. Diémer. In 1896 he won 1st Prize for pf playing, in works by Beethoven and Liszt – composers who virtually disappeared from his later repertoire.
   After graduation he immersed himself for some years in the cause of Wagner, working as *répétiteur* in Bayreuth, and later conducting some of the operas in Paris, much to the disdain of Debussy. In 1905 he returned to pf

playing: as soloist, accompanist and in two pf recitals with other pianists like Diémer, Planté, Risler and Saint-Säens. That same year the Cortot–Thibaud–Casals Trio was formed and became the most illustrious and famous ensemble of its kind ever. In 1907 he was appointed head of the pf dept at the Cons., a post he held for a decade.

Over the years he occupied a unique position in the art and in the hearts and minds of musicians and public. He accomplished an incredible amount of work: annual tours of Europe, the USA and the USSR; recording sessions, teaching, lecture-recitals, accompanying; writing erudite yet lively books and articles that are a delight to read; even occasionally taking up the baton. Always, throughout his long career, he laboured to propagate French pf music. Then, in maturity, his repertoire came to rest within the Romantic output plus the then modern French School. Because of such a workload the technical finish of his playing often left much to be desired. The interpretation always had tensile strength characterized by a refined, even fragile beauty, although in the writer's experience the gossamer poetry of his most inspired moments was not always reliably captured on gramophone records, of which he left us a comprehensive legacy.

The gramophone recording machine of the 1930s, which, in retrospect, seems to reflect vividly and sympathetically the art of persons like Rachmaninov, Backhaus, Petri and Lhevinne, distorted the impulsive side of C's nature without catching that delicacy which in concert halls freely took flight. It exposed with permanent cruel emphasis his essentially evanescent use of *rubato* which in public came over as a sigh, a momentary catch of breath. Wrong notes are, of course, bearable in a live recital where they soar into the rafters and are lost forever, whereas as permanent features on wax they become obtrusive and eventually abhorrent. The writer heard C in person on many occasions and several times in concertos, including the Chopin No. 2, and cannot really believe now that he customarily took such hair-raising liberties with *rubato* as appear on the *HMV* recording of 1935. On the other hand, the recording of Chopin's two *études* in G flat, made before the First World War, are glorious examples of the gossamer web he *could* weave so breathtakingly.

During World War II he involved himself in politics by holding a post in the Vichy Government; and an isolated concert tour of Germany did not further endear him to the French resistance movement. When peace returned, he was called to account but forgiven by his countrymen before returning to the concert platform in long tours despite the affliction of glaucoma, visiting countries as far afield as S. America and Japan. It has been estimated that in the period between the end of the war and 1958, when he finally retired, C gave almost 1,000 recitals.

In the Edinburgh Festival of 1948 he presented a Chopin recital corresponding as near as research could reveal to the programme assembled by the composer for his sole public appearance in the Scottish capital exactly 100 years before. And his wartime quarrel with his other colleagues of the celebrated Trio was partly reconciled when, in July 1958, he appeared with the cellist at the Prades Festival, Thibaud having perished in an airplane crash five years previously. Prades marked C's final appearance. He had received the RPS Gold Medal in 1923 and became Commandeur de la Légion d'Honneur in 1934. In 1919, two years after he had vacated the Cons. post, he founded the École Normale de Musique in Paris where he held master-classes during summer months. He produced fresh editions of the pf works of Chopin and Schumann for the Paris publishing firm of Salabert, some of them being published in Boston, USA. He collected original Chopin MSS and wrote a book, *In Search of Chopin* (1951). His most notable and abiding achievement in this field, however, must remain *French Piano Music* (1932). Recorded *HMV*, Japanese *Victor*, and EMI.

Pupils included; Jef Alpaerts, Gina Bachauer, Julian Bern, Idil Biret, Jacqueline Blancard, Massimo Bogianckino, Halina Czerny-Stefanska, Dino Ciani, Sergei Conus, Jean-Michel Damase, Leopold Damrosch, Evelyne Dubourg, Alfred Ehrismann, Samson François, Gunnar de Frumerie, Eric Gaudibert, Henri Gil-Marchex, Clara Haskil, Eric Heidsieck, Franz Hirt, Leonard Isaacs, Václav Kaprál, Julian von Károly, Dagny Knutsen, Jean Laforge, Yvonne Lefébure, Jean Leleu, Rosamund Leonard, Dinu Lipatti, Peter Maag, Thomas Manshardt, Marcelle Meyer, Vlado Perlemuter, Elaine Richepin, Jesus Sanroma, Ruth Slenczynska, Solomon, Kyril Szalkiewicz, John Vallier, Marie Varro, Janine Weill.

CORY, Patrick (1910–)
b. Berkhamsted, UK. Pf pupil of R. Acad. of Music, London, becoming pf prof. there from 1948. Performed and adjudicated throughout the countries of the old British Empire, lectured and gave recitals on radio. Composed pf pieces.

COSTA, Sequeira (1929–)
b. Africa, of Portuguese parentage. Studied Lisbon Acad. and with J. V. da Motta and E. Fischer, and then in Paris with M. Long. Début 1937, Lisbon, and has since performed extensively. Recorded Supraphon.

COTTLOW, Augusta (1878–1954)
b. Shelbyville, USA. Was a prodigy who studied in Chicago, appearing with orch. at the tender age of 10. Performed for six years, then went to Berlin and studied with F. Busoni, afterwards touring Europe with great success. Made a return home at the beginning of the century where her reputation preceded her then returned to Berlin until 1917, going home when the US entered World War I.

COUPPEY, Félix LE: *see* **LE COUPPEY, Félix.**

COVERDALE, Miles (1914–)
b. Hull, UK. Studied pf in London and was pupil of H. Craxton and T. Matthay. Won Matthay Memorial Prize 1937. Performed, accompanied and taught in Glasgow from 1958.

COWDEROY, Peter (1918–)
b. London, UK. Studied R. Acad. of Music there, and pf with M. Pirani, F. Reizenstein and others. Won numerous prizes for pf playing and other musical subjects. Developed successful career as pianist, accompanist and teacher at various schools before working privately. Compositions include choral music, pf pieces and songs.

COWELL, Henry Dixon (1897–1965)
b. Menlo Park, California, USA. Received some pf lessons from R. Bühlig. Regularly toured Europe and America 1923–33 and held teaching posts. His concert appearances aroused controversy because he was one of the innovators of the use of tone-clusters or, as he called it, secundal harmonies. A prolific composer in modern idioms using the tone-cluster idea of striking the keyboard with elbow, hand

or forearm as well as fingers. Wrote books and contributed frequently to musical journals on varied topics. Involved himself in polyrhythms and with associates worked upon the Rhythmicon, a machine to work out all manner of intricate rhythms and patterns. Made a lifelong study of folk-music and gave lecture tours on the subject using many of the tunes which took his fancy in own compositions. Output included numerous pf pieces; also wrote a number of works including *Charles Ives and his Music* (1954) and *New Musical Resources* (1969).

COWEN, Sir Frederick Hymen (1852–1935)
b. Jamaica, West Indies. When he was 4, his parents moved to London. Pupil of J. Benedict, then of Leipzig Cons. and of I. Moscheles for pf, finishing his musical education in Berlin. A fine pianist who turned to conducting, holding principal posts at home and abroad. Conducted the first concert in the new Queen's Hall in 1893. Composed in all genres from opera to songs, including a *Concertstück* for pf and orch., solos and chamber music, all in a refined but light-hearted style. His overture, *The Butterfly's Ball*, survived for a time but it too is now forgotten. Knighted 1911. Toured widely at one time with celebrated singers.

COWLES, Cecil Marion (1898–1968)
b. San Francisco, USA. Worked on her career in New York and in California, private pf pupil of S. Stojowski and C. Deis. Turned composer, mainly pf works and songs.

COXE, Nigel (1932–)
b. Jamaica, West Indies. Pf pupil at R. Acad., London. Début 1956, London. Performed, broadcast, taught. US début 1971, New York. Now resident there.

CRAMER, Johann Baptist (1771–1858)
b. Mannheim, Germany. Had several pf teachers of whom the most illustrious was M. Clementi. Commenced touring as pianist 1788, working from his home in London. Beethoven held him in the highest regard as a performer. In 1824 he established a publishing house in London in association with Addison and Beale. From 1832 C spent a good deal of his time in Paris. After his death, the London firm went into the field of pf manufacture, and thus his name was continued on instruments. Was a founder member of (R.) Phil. Soc., London.

Was steeped in the keyboard works of J. S. Bach and played them in public at a time when there was little interest in them.

Pupils included: Ludwig Berger, Catherine Bisset, George Onslow, Rudolf Schachner.

CRANE, Meade (1955–)
b. San Antonio, USA. Studied at Peabody Cons., Baltimore, also at Interlochen Arts Acad. Teachers included L. Fleischer.

CRANMER, Philip (1918–)
b. Birmingham, UK. Son of the distinguished singer Arthur Cranmer and, at the age of 13, accompanied his father in German *lieder* and English songs at a London recital in 1932. Student at Oxford and of R. Coll. of Music, London. Held successive teaching posts in Birmingham, Belfast and London. Prof. as well as extremely fine accompanist. Compositions included sonatina for pf duet first performed by the composer and Priscilla Naish at Wigmore Hall, London, in 1982.

CRAWFORD, Ruth Porter (1901–53)
b. East Liverpool, Ohio, USA. Studied in Jacksonville and at the American Cons., Chicago, among her teachers being H. Levy. Won a Guggenheim Fellowship and spent it in Europe 1930. Settled in Washington DC. Performed, taught and composed. Works included a set of preludes for pf, chamber music and songs.

CRAXTON, Harold (1885–1971)
b. Devizes, UK. Pupil of T. Matthay and became pf prof. at the T.M. School from 1914, then of R. Acad., 1919–60. Was for many years a distinguished accompanist to artists like Clara Butt, Melba, Gerhardt, Thibaud etc. Gave recitals of early British pf music, also prepared editions for Associated Board of R. Schools of Music, and taught in USA. OBE 1960. As accompanist recorded various labels. Father of the well-known oboe-player Janet C (Mrs Alan Richardson, 1929–81).

Pupils included: John Bingham, Beryl Chempin, Miles Coverdale, Christian Darnton, Iain Hamilton, Robin Harrison, John Jenkins, Denis Matthews, Nina Milkina, Alan Richardson, John Simons, Sergio Varella-Cid, Nancy Weir, Janice Williams, Arnold van Wyk.

CRESTON, Paul (1906–)
b. New York, USA. Pf pupil of G. Randegger

and organ pupil of G.-M. Déthier. Composer, teacher, pf accompanist and organist. Compositions include two pf concertos and two two-pf concertos, chamber music, pf pieces and songs. Wrote *Principles of Rhythm* and *Creative Harmony*.

CROCHET, Evelyn (1934–)
b. Paris, France. Studied at Paris Cons., winning 1st Prize in 1954, where she was a pupil of Y. Lefébure. Later received tuition from E. Fischer and R. Serkin. Settled in USA. Recorded Turnabout.

CROSSLEY, Paul (1944–)
b. Leeds, UK. Studied pf locally then in Paris with Y. Loriod. Performed from 1968, when he won the Concours Olivier Messiaen. Wide-ranging repertoire, especially identified with Tippett's sonatas. Taught Trinity Coll., London. Recorded RCA, Decca Gp, EMI and others.

CROWSON, Lamar (–)
Pupil of R. Coll. of Music, London, and of A. Benjamin, whose *Concerto quasi una fantasia* he premièred in 1956. Dedicatee of Racine Fricker's 12 pf studies of which he gave first performance in Cheltenham in 1961. Record labels included Argo, Lyrita and L'Oiseau Lyre. Request to artist for biographical details met with no response.

Pupils included: Clifford Benson, Howard Shelley.

CSALOG, Gabor (1960–)
b. Budapest, Hungary. Studied at the Liszt Acad. there and was pupil of P. Kadosa, D. Ranki and Z. Kocsis.

CUBILES, José (1894–1970)
b. Cadiz, Spain. Studied pf at Madrid Cons. where he won 1st Prize before becoming a pupil of L. Diémer at Paris Cons. Début Paris, 1914. Became concert pianist and a noted advocate of Spanish and French contemporary music, giving première of de Falla's *Nights in the Gardens of Spain* in Madrid 1916. Toured widely and broadcast.

Pupils included: Rafael Orozco.

CURTIS, Natalie (1875–1921)
b. New York, USA. Studied with A. Friedheim at the National Cons., New York; also with F. Busoni in Berlin. Became interested in

the culture of N. American Indians, lectured and wrote extensively on her research.

CURZON, Sir Clifford (1907–82)
b. London, UK. Studied at R. Acad., London, then with A. Schnabel, K. Goodson and W. Landowska. Appeared at Queen's Hall under Sir H. Wood at the age of 16 and founded a secure and successful career internationally. Toured Europe 1936 and made US début 1939, appearing with leading orchestras. Repertoire became tilted in favour of Beethoven, Mozart and Schubert, but he did play works by Britten and gave the première of Alan Rawsthorne's 2nd pf concerto in 1951. Other first performances included Lennox Berkeley's *Sonata in A* which is dedicated to C. A notable chamber-music player. Married the American harpsichordist Lucille Wallace. Was soloist at the centenary concert of the Hallé Soc. in 1958, in which year he was made CBE. Knighted 1977 and received RPS Gold Medal 1980. His will revealed gross assets of £1.6m. Recorded *Decca* and Decca.

CUSINS, Sir William George (1833–93)
b. London, UK. Studied at Brussels Cons. and R. Acad., London, under Sir W. S. Bennett and C. Potter, where he later became pf prof. Made Phil. Soc. début in 1858 playing Bennett's 4th pf concerto; many subsequent appearances as pianist and also as conductor. His own pf concerto in A minor was played by Arabella Goddard under his baton in 1872. Taught at Guildhall School. Knighted 1892. Composed chamber music, pf pieces and songs. Master of the Queen's Music from 1870 until his death.

CUSTER, Laurenz (1930–)
b. Frauenfeld, Switzerland. Studied pf with M. Long. Performed widely solo and in ensemble.

CZAJKOWKA, Teresa (1920–)
b. Radom, Poland. Student of state music schools at Cracow and Wroclaw. Début 1959 Radom. Toured thereafter as soloist and accompanist, also taught.

CZAPIEWSKI, Bogden (1949–)
b. Gdynia, Poland. Studied there and at Warsaw Cons. Successful competitor at several European piano competitions. Well-known recitalist in Poland.

CZERNY, Karl (1791–1857)
b. Vienna, Austria. After initial tuition from father had lessons from L. Beethoven with whom he was on intimate terms, also Clementi and Hummel. In early years was a famous concert pianist but gave up touring, confining himself thereafter assiduously to teaching and composing. His pf studies will presumably always interest aspiring students, but larger works have fallen by the wayside.
   Pupils included: Emilie Belleville-Oury, Hermann Berens, J. Dachs, Theodor Döhler, Anton Door, Jules Egghard, Karl Haslinger, Theodor Kullak, Louis Lacombe, Theodor Leschetizky, Franz Liszt, Leopold v. Meyer, Albert Seyfried, Adalbert Sowinski.

CZERNY-STEFANSKA, Halina (1922–)
b. Cracow, Poland. Pupil of S. Czerny, a descendant of Karl C. In 1932 won a prize for a limited amount of tuition in Cortot's masterclass at the École Normale, Paris, then resumed studies with J. Turczynski until 1939. When the Int. Chopin Pf Comp. in Warsaw was resumed in 1949, she won 1st Prize jointly with Bella Davidovich, making her London début the same year. Performed and taught. Recorded Supraphon, Erato and Muza.

CZIFFRA, György (1921–)
b. Budapest, Hungary. Was something of a prodigy, whose father was his first teacher. In 1930 entered Franz Liszt Acad. under E. von Dohnányi. Studies interrupted by army service in World War II. Thereafter appears to have pursued a popular musical career for a time before recommencing classical calling in 1953, winning the Franz Liszt Prize in 1955. After Hungarian uprising in 1956, went to France via Vienna where he settled, initiating, in 1969, the Cziffra Comp. at Versailles. Recorded EMI.
   Pupils included: Cyril Huvé.

DACHS, Joseph (1825–96)
b. Regensburg, Austria. Pupil of K. Czerny. Pf prof. Vienna Cons.

Pupils included: Jan Drozdowski, Vladimir de Pachmann, Laura Rappoldi, Josef Rubinstein, Theodor Szantó, Isabella Vengerova, Julius Zarembski.

D'AGNILLO, Corradino: *see* **AGNILLO, Corradino d'.**

DAHL, Ingolf (1912–70)
b. Hamburg, Germany, of Swedish parentage. A composer and teacher who played pf. Composed a *Sonata Seria* and chamber music, also *Sonata Pastorale*. Arranged for two pfs Stravinsky's *Danses concertantes*.

DAHL, Viking (1895–1945)
b. Osby, Sweden. Studied at Stockholm Cons., then at Paris Cons., where his pf teacher was R. Viñes. Is supposed – uniquely – to have had dancing lessons from Isadora Duncan. Wrote chamber music.

D'ALBERT, Eugène Francis Charles: *see* **ALBERT, Eugène Francis Charles d'.**

DALBERTO, Michel (1955–   )
b. Paris, France. Student of Paris Cons. under V. Perlemuter, winning 1st Prize in 1972. Won Clara Haskil Prize at Vevey in 1975 and in 1978 was first in Leeds Comp. Has since successfully toured throughout Europe. Recorded RCA, Erato.

DALE, Benjamin James (1885–1943)
b. London, UK. Studied at R. Acad., London, and was under E. Howard-Jones for pf. Later became prof. of composition at R. Acad. Wrote fine pf sonata in D minor (1905) which

had a one-time vogue, being propagated by Myra Hess; also chamber music and pf solos.

Pupils included: Florence Spencer-Palmer.

DALE, Kathleen (1895–1984)
b. London, UK. Private pupil of York Bowen and Fanny Davies. Was noted accompanist and taught at Tobias Matthay School. Later connected with Workers' Educational Assn. and with Soc. of Women Musicians. Composed chamber music, pf works and songs published under maiden name of Kathleen Richards. Also wrote extensively on musical subjects especially pf., including *19th-Century Piano Music* (1954).

DALLAPICCOLA, Luigi (1904–75)
b. Pisino, Istria, Italy (now Yugoslavia). Learned pf from age of 6, studying in Trieste before entering Cherubini Cons., Florence, in 1922, studying pf with E. Consolo, graduating with honours 1924. Worked on composition there until 1931 when he became involved in contemporary movements and was Italian representative as ISCM. Continued from 1934 as pf prof. at Florence Cons. His major pf composition is *Piccola Concerto* with which he made his US début in 1952 on NBC network. Also wrote a work for three pfs, a sonata based on Paganini *Caprices*, and songs. Dedicatee of L. Berio's revised *Cinque Vars* (1966).

DAMASE, Jean-Michel (1928–   )
b. Bordeaux, France. Student of pf and composition at Paris Cons., winning the Prix de Rome in 1947, in which year he made his pf début. US début 1954. Noted as a composer whose works include two pf concertos and a sonata, chamber music, pf pieces and songs. Recorded French Decca.

DA MOTTA, José Vianna: *see* **MOTTA, José Vianna da.**

DAMROSCH, Clara: *see* **MANNES, Clara Damrosch.**

DAMROSCH, Leopold: *see* **MANNES, Leopold Damrosch.**

D'ANDREA, Genaro Maria: *see* **ANDREA, Genaro Maria d'.**

DANIEL, Erno (1918–)
b. Budapest, Hungary. Pf pupil at Franz Liszt Acad. there, also of E. von Dohnányi. Début Budapest, 1940. Taught at Liszt Acad. until 1948 and toured Europe solo and with leading orchs. After 1948 settled in USA as pf prof., successively at Midwestern and California Univs. Specialized in Hungarian pf music.

DANNREUTHER, Edward (1844–1905)
b. Strasbourg. At the age of 5 was taken by his parents to Cincinnati, USA. Studied at Leipzig Cons. 1859–63 under H. Richter, I. Moscheles and Hauptmann. A visit to London in 1863, during which he gave first British performance of Chopin's F minor pf concerto, was such a success that he decided to settle there. Gave other first British performances including Liszt A major concerto. Championed Wagner's cause and founded the London Wagner Soc. 1872, conducting its first concerts. Toured USA several times. Became pf prof. at R. Coll., London, 1895. Frequently wrote essays for musical Press, lectured and composed for the pf. Wrote a once esteemed work on *Musical Ornamentation* (two volumes).
Pupils included: James Friskin, William Y. Hurlstone, Sir Walter Parratt, Harold Samuel.

d'ARCO, Annie: *see* **ARCO, Annie d'.**

DARNTON, Christian (1905–81)
b. Leeds, UK. Studied pf with H. Craxton at Tobias Matthay School, and composition with Benjamin Dale and Gordon Jacobs. Début 1927 in London in recital of own compositions. Chiefly known as composer-pianist and teacher, especially at Stowe School. Works include a pf concerto and a *Concertino* for pf and strings, film music and a suite for violin and pf, later using twelve-tone system.

DARRÉ, Jeanne-Marie (1905–)
b. Givet, France. Studied in Paris where she was pupil of M. Long and I. Philipp. Enjoyed long and successful career as concert pianist with wide range of repertoire, remarkable pianism as well as impeccable taste and poetry. Pf prof. at Paris Cons. from 1958. US début 1962, New York, which she took by storm. Recorded *Vocalion* as early as 1923, then *HMV* and *Polydor*, EMI, RCA and Saga.
Pupils included: Maria de la Pau, Jacques Gauthier, Charles Timbrell, Ilana Vered.

d'ASCOLI, Bernard: *see* **ASCOLI, Bernard d'.**

DAVEY, Winifred (1900–)
b. Bristol, UK. Studied pf in Bristol, then in London with V. Langrish. Well-known recitalist and accompanist especially for BBC.

DAVID, Annie Louise (1891–1960)
b. Boston, USA. Pf pupil of A. Foote, E. MacDowell and H. Gebhard. Début Boston, 1900 followed by tour of USA and Europe. Additionally played and taught harp.

DAVID, Luise: *see* **DULCKEN, Luise.**

DAVIDOVICH, Bella (1928–)
b. Baku, USSR. Pupil of C. Igumnov and Y. Flier. Joint 1st Prizewinner Chopin Comp., Warsaw, 1949. Had distinguished career in USSR, specializing in Chopin, before appearing in the West in 1966 with the Leningrad PO. Settled in USA in 1978. When she reappeared in London in 1982, one critic wrote: 'Her playing was of a flawless accomplishment, strong, decisive and rigorously unsentimental.' Recorded various.

DAVIES, Fanny (1861–1934)
b. Guernsey, Channel Islands, UK. Pf pupil of Leipzig Cons. under K. Reinecke and O. Paul, and at Frankfurt under Klara Schumann, 1883–5. London début 1885, thereafter toured Europe regularly, becoming especially noted for her playing of Schumann (she was rated Klara's most distinguished pupil), though her concert repertory was much wider, embracing Beethoven, Chopin, Brahms (then new music) and British works. Gave first performance of Ethel Smyth's violin sonata with Adolf Brodsky in Leipzig in 1887. Had the honour of playing to Queen Victoria at Balmoral, and the rare distinction for a British musician of being awarded a civil list pension of no less than £90 p.a. in 1932. At her request Elgar composed a

Concert Allegro around 1901 that became 'lost' after several performances and was rediscovered about 1970 and recorded by John Ogdon. Recorded *Columbia*, all-Schumann and included the concerto. In obituary notices Tovey spoke of her high spirits and brilliant powers of mimicry, while Wood called her 'a most admirable musician and a delightful woman' who never received quite her full due.

Pupils included: Kathleen Dale.

DAVIES, Ffrangcon (1925–)
b. Cardiff, UK. Studied there and at R. Acad. of Music, London. Performed and taught. Compositions included a pf sonata and a set of variations.

DAVIES, Lyndon (1944–)
b. Cardiff, UK. Studied pf in Bournemouth and at R. Acad., London, pupil of F. Reizenstein. Début 1957, Bournemouth. Concert pianist, teacher and broadcaster.

DAVIES, Sir Walford (1869–1941)
b. Oswestry, UK. Organist, lecturer and composer, a musician of many parts; became famous to the public in a pianistic capacity through his work for BBC in early days, first in *Music for Schools* programmes and later in *Foundations of Music* series which he organized and in which he often played. Knighted 1922; KCVO 1937. Wrote two works for pf and orch., chamber music and songs. Recorded *HMV*. Master of the King's Musick 1934–41.

DAVIS, Ivan (1932–)
b. Texas, USA. Studied music at N. Texas State Univ., then in Rome under C. Zecchi, and later with V. Horowitz. Prize winnings include the Busoni, Bolzano 1957, and the Liszt, New York 1960. New York début 1959, London première 1968. Has appeared regularly with leading orchs. in USA and Europe as well as solo recitals. Professor of Music at Miami Univ. 1974–. Recorded Columbia, Decca and others.

DAVIS, John David (1870–1942)
b. Birmingham, UK. Studied pf and composition at Raff Cons., Frankfurt, then at Brussels, where his pf teacher was A. de Greef. Thereafter was prof. successively at Guildhall School, London, Birmingham School of Music and Int. Cons., London. Composed in various genres including chamber music and pf pieces.

DAWSON, Frederick (1868–1940)
b. Leeds, UK. Pf pupil of C. Hallé; also received tuition from A. Rubinstein. Was one of the original pf teachers at Manchester Coll. when established by Hallé and returned later in 1930s. Had fine technique, big repertoire and an excellent concert reputation throughout European capitals. Second half of his life was increasingly dogged by ill-health. Should also be remembered for having in his repertory back in the 1890s the Tchaikovsky No. 1 pf concerto when it was relatively obscure.

Pupils included: Gaze Cooper, Thomas Johnson, Dorothy Wilson.

DAWSON-LYELL, Julian (1947–)
b. UK. Studied pf from early age and was a pupil of L. Crowson and A. Benjamin of the R. Coll. of Music, London, and privately with L. Kentner. Performed throughout Europe, and in London in 1982 gave première of sonata (1981) by the American composer Corey Field, which is dedicated to him. Requests to London agents for further biographical information met with no response.

DE BOURGUIGNON, Francis: *see* **BOURGUIGNON, Francis de.**

DEBUSSY, Claude Achille (1862–1918)
b. St Germain-en-Laye, France. Taught by F. A. Mauté de Fleurville, who saw talent in the boy of 8 and continued to teach freely when family funds dried up. The father had visions of his son becoming a concert pianist so he entered Paris Cons. at 10, studying pf with A. Marmontel and composition with Ernest Guiraud. His academic career was undistinguished as he was altogether highly idiosyncratic, but he did win the Prix de Rome. There he met F. Liszt who, with G. Sgambati, played the Saint-Saëns *Variations on a theme of Beethoven*, and D performed for the aged Hungarian. He cut short the three-year period returning to Paris at the end of two years. The works of that period ought to have been performed in the Cons. under the terms of the Prix, but the academics were so outraged and D was so unpenitent that he went his way. His output during the next 25 years is one of the glories of music, let alone French music, and he revolutionized the pf idiom. Many writers, especially French ones, have sought to do justice in words to the precision of his technique by which new and beautiful effects were achieved, although he became a some-

what limited executant, preferring those in the top flight of the playing profession to demonstrate his marvellous work. As a student he was a somewhat rumbustious player; as a mature musician he played softly and produced charming effects. The sets of pf music were spaced throughout his career and thus show continual development. During World War I the French publishers Durand et Cie asked him to prepare a new edition of Chopin. Having always admired the Pole's music, he undertook the task. It led to his own set of *Études*, dedicated to the memory of Chopin, and a happy outcome Durand's could not have foreseen when commissioning the work. Alfredo Casella called D 'a most admirable pianist' without 'the virtuosity of the specialist, but his touch was extremely sensitive'. Works for pf include *Children's Corner Suite, Deux Arabesques, Estampes, Suite bergamasque, Images, Pour le piano, 24 préludes, L'Isle joyeuse, Masques* and 12 *études*. There is an early *Fantaisie* for pf and orch., and chamber works, the most important of which were written during World War I. The splendid pf writing accompanying the songs should also not be forgotten. Recorded *G & T* as accompanist to Mary Garden.

DE CARVALHO, Dinora: *see* **CARVALHO, Dinora de.**

DECKER, Konstantin (1810–78)
b. Fürstenau, Germany. Studied pf in Berlin, performed and composed, including pf sonatas and songs.

DECOMBES, Émile (*c*.1830–1912)
b. Paris, France. A somewhat shadowy pianist-teacher whose name was linked with the Chopin circle as a listener and who taught a junior class at Paris Cons., some of whom later became famous.
Pupils included: Alfred Cortot.

DECREUS, Camille (1876–1939)
b. Paris, France. Student at Paris Cons. under R. Pugno, winning 1st Pf Prize in 1895. Was accompanist to the opera class of the Cons. for two years before becoming *répétiteur* at the Opéra 1898–1900. Début as concert pianist in Paris in 1906 and then commenced touring Europe and the USA as soloist and accompanist to artists like Renée Chemet whom he married in 1909. They lived in the USA during World War I, later returning to France.

Became pf prof. at the American Cons. at Fontainebleau. Composed pf works and songs.
Pupils included: Ulvi Erkin.

DEERING, Henri (1894–19)
b. St Louis, USA. Pf pupil of A. Schnabel and I. Philipp. Début 1925, New York. Toured USA and Europe both as soloist and in chamber music and concertos.

DEERING, Richard (1947–)
b. London, UK. Studied there, where he made his début 1973. Toured solo and widely known as adjudicator, lecturer and accompanist. Recorded Saga.

DE FRANCMESNIL, Roger: *see* **FRANCMESNIL, Roger de.**

DE FRUMERIE, Gunnar: *see* **FRUMERIE, Gunnar de.**

DE FUSCO, Laura: *see* **FUSCO, Laura de**

DE GRAY, Julian: *see* **GRAY, Julian de.**

DE GREEF, Arthur: *see* **GREEF, Arthur de.**

DE GROOT, Cor: *see* **GROOT, Cor de.**

DE GROOTE, André: *see* **GROOTE, André de.**

DE GROOTE, Steven: *see* **GROOTE, Steven de.**

DE HARTMANN, Thomas: *see* **HARTMANN, Thomas de.**

DEIS, Carl (1883–1960)
b. New York, USA. Began pf at 4 and from age of 8 spent a year at Nat. Cons. and a year at New York Coll., otherwise self-taught. Recitalist – solo and chamber, as well as accompanist. From 1917 was editor-in-chief for the publishers G. Shirmer, editing many of their pf scores, especially Brahms.
Pupils included: Cecil Cowles.

De KONTSKI, Antoine: *see* **KONTSKI, Antoine de.**

DELABORDE, Élie Miriam (1839–1913)
b. Paris, France. Pf pupil of C. Alkan and I. Moscheles. Toured Europe as concert pianist and during Franco-Prussian War settled in

London. Returned to Paris and became pf prof. at Paris Cons. Wrote pf pieces and songs. Dedicatee of Saint-Saëns 3rd pf concerto. During his sojourn in London, gave public demonstration of the Pedalier-Pianoforte, 'a pedal keyboard attached to the piano', an invention developed for a time by the house of Broadwood. Son of C. Alkan.
  Pupils included: Amina Goodwin.

DE LARA, Adelina: *see* **LARA, Adelina de.**

DELACROIX, Léon Charles (1880–1938)
b. Brussels, Belgium. Pf pupil of J. Wieniawski, studied composition with Théo Ysaÿe and V. d'Indy. Turned theatre conductor until 1927 when he concentrated on composition. Wrote an award-winning pf quartet, a *Fantasia on a Breton theme* for pf and orch., much chamber music and pf solos. Wrote a biography of Josef Wieniawski.

DELIOUX DE SAVIGNAC, Charles (1830–80)
b. Lorient, France. Pupil of Paris Cons. Prolific composer of pf pieces. Performed and taught; wrote a pf method.

DELIUS, Frederick (1862–1934)
b. Bradford, UK. Composed a pf concerto which was first performed in 1904. It underwent revision and became a one-movement work, receiving its première at the London Proms of 1907 with the pianist T. Szántó, to whom the concerto is dedicated and who assisted the composer in the revision work. Also composed chamber music with a pf part, and two groups of pf pieces. Learned violin and pf but was not an able pianist.

dello JOIO, Norman: *see* **JOIO, Norman dello.**

DEL VALLE DE PAZ, Edgardo (1861–1920)
b. Alexandria, Egypt. Studied at Naples Cons. with B. Cesi, thereafter touring Italy and Egypt as concert pianist before settling in Florence. Was pf prof. at the Cons. there from 1890. Founded and edited the journal *La Nuova Musica*, and composed a pf sonata as well as technical exercises. Also prepared an edition of Handel's keyboard works.
  Pupils included: Mario Castelnuovo-Tedesco.

DEMUS, Joerg (1928–   )
b. St Poelten, Austria. Studied at Vienna Acad. and with A. B. Michelangeli, W. Gieseking, E. Fischer and Y. Nat. Début 1943, Vienna. After World War II, began touring widely. Preferred using instruments of the original period (e.g. for Mozart) and was also known as an accompanist. Recorded various.
  Pupils included: Zsuzsanna Sirokay.

DENÉE, Charles (1863–1946)
b. New York, USA. Pupil of New England Cons., Boston, where he taught after graduating. Also a highly successful concert artist until 1897 when damage sustained to right arm caused him to retire from the platform and concentrate on pedagogic career.

DENTON, Oliver (1886–1928)
b. Hempstead, USA. Undertook pf studies in Europe. Début 1913, Berlin. Toured thereafter and taught.

DE PACHMANN, Adrian: *see* **PACHMANN, Adrian de.**

DE PACHMANN, Vladimir: *see* **PACHMANN, Vladimir de.**

DE PACHMANN-LABORI, Marguerite: *see* **PACHMANN-LABORI, Marguerite de.**

DEPPE, Ludwig (1828–90)
b. Alverdissen, Germany. Pupil of E. Marxsen in Hamburg and later studied in Leipzig. Took up career of pf teacher and conductor in Hamburg from 1857. Wrote works on pf technique and had strong views on correct playing, posture, muscle control etc. Evolved a method on which Sir Donald Tovey, in one of his analytical essays, says he was trained.

DE ROSA, Dario: *see* **ROSA, Dario de.**

DESCAVES, Lucette Hélène (1906–   )
b. Paris, France. Student at the Cons. there, winning 1st Prize for pf playing 1923. Became established concert pianist, teacher and adjudicator. Prof. at the Cons. 1941–76. Gave première of Jolivet pf concerto in Strasbourg in 1951 and first New York performance in 1953. Recorded *French HMV*.
  Pupils included: Pascal Rogé.

DE SÉVÉRAC, Déodat: *see* **SÉVÉRAC, Déodat de.**

DESSOFF, Felix Otto (1835–92)
b. Frankfurt, Germany. Pupil of Leipzig Cons. and of I. Moscheles for pf. Taught at Vienna Cons. and conducted the Phil. In later years was mainly a conductor. His compositions included chamber music, each of which had a pf part, also pieces for solo pf.
Pupils included: Heinrich Herzogenberg.

DE VALMALÉTE, Madeleine: see **VALMALÉTE, Madeleine de.**

DEVOYON, Pascal (1953–   )
b. France. Entered Paris Cons. at the age of 16, was a pupil of L. Gousseau and graduated in 1971 with 1st Prize. Entered a number of European pf competitions, gaining joint 3rd at Leeds in 1975, and joint 2nd at the Tchaikovsky Comp., Moscow in 1978. Toured Europe and the USSR subsequently, and made his US début in 1980 in Carnegie Hall. Recorded Erato.

DE VRIES, Alexander: see **VRIES, Alexander de.**

DEYANOVA, Marta (19 –   )
b. Bulgaria. A prodigy who won 1st Prize at a Sofia competition for young performers in 1964. Distinguished winner in other adult competitions, e.g. the Busoni, Italy, and 1970 'Alessandro Casagrande'. Appeared solo and with leading orchs. throughout the world. Recorded Harmonia Mundi and Nimbus.

DEYO, Felix (1888–1959)
b. New York, USA. Studied pf with mother, then at Brooklyn Cons., where he taught after graduation. Became Director of the Baldwin Cons. Composed pf sonatas and pieces. Related to Ruth D.

DEYO, Ruth Lynda (1884–1960)
b. New York, USA. Studied pf with W. Mason and T. Carreño. Was composition pupil of E. MacDowell. Début 1893, Chicago, after which had successful career as concert pianist solo and in celebrity duo-recitals. From 1925 lived in Cairo. Related to Felix D.

DIABELLI, Anton (1781–1858)
b. Salzburg, Austria. Originally destined for priesthood but his musical abilities received encouragement from Michael Haydn, and he settled in Vienna as pf teacher and composer. Later went into the music-publishing business

for 30 years. A composer of small merit, his sonatinas were once used for elementary teaching purposes, and Beethoven used one of his waltzes for the *33 Variations* Op. 120.

DIBDIN, Charles (1745–1814)
b. Southampton, UK. Largely self-taught as singer, instrumentalist and composer. Was working at Covent Garden when, in 1787, according to an announcement of the time, he accompanied a singer on 'a new instrument called a piano-forte'. It is also claimed that J. C. Bach in 1768 played a pf in public for the first time in Britain.

DICHTER, Mischa (1945–   )
b. Shanghai, China, of Russian parents whose initial wish was that he should become a doctor. The family settled in the USA in 1947, and he became naturalized in 1953. Educated in Los Angeles, studying pf with a Schnabel pupil, then, from 1963, with R. Lhevinne at the Juilliard School in New York. Won 2nd Prize in the Tchaikovsky Int. Pf Comp., Moscow, in 1966 which laid the foundation of a successful career. Toured widely in subsequent years (British début 1971) but later confined appearances mainly to the USA, Europe, Israel and the Far East. In addition to recitals and orch. appearances he has appeared in two-pf recitals with his wife Cipa, as well as chamber concerts. Taught master-classes at Aspen and Ravinia. Composed cadenzas for Mozart concertos.
Because of the background of his teachers, D was described by one writer as a legatee of both German and Russian traditions of pf-playing since his style reflected the German respect for structure and clarity and at the same time the Russian search for heroic proportion. Recorded RCA and Philips.
Pupils included: Vanessa Latarche.

DIÉMER, Louis (1843–1919)
b. Paris, France. Studied at Cons. there under A. Marmontel, winning 1st Pf Prize at 13. Took prizes in other branches. Had very successful career as concert pianist and in 1887 succeeded Marmontel as pf prof. at the Cons. A series of historical recitals led him to form the *Société des anciens instruments*; was highly successful teacher, composed a pf concerto and chamber music. Dedicatee of Saint-Saëns 5th pf concerto and gave première of Franck's *Les Djinns* in Paris in 1885 under Colonne and of the *Variations symphoniques* in 1886.

Pupils included: Louis Aubert, Adolphe Borchard, Georges Boskoff, Robert Casadesus, Alfredo Casella, Alfred Cortot, Felix Dyck, Armand Ferté, Roger de Francmesnil, Emil Frey, Marius Gaillard, Henri Gil-Marchex, Gabriel Grovlez, Vincent d'Indy, Léon Kartun, Lazare Lévy, Robert Lortat, Yves Nat, Édouard Risler, Elie Schmitz, Sigismund Stojowski, Joseph Thibaud.

DILLER, Angela (1877–1968)
b. New York, USA, Pupil of E. MacDowell, then spent largely pedagogic life of teaching, editing and writing on musical theory. After working in David Mannes School, 1916–21, became co-founder of Diller–Quaile School, New York. Wrote numerous educational textbooks.

DILLON, Fannie Charles (1881–1947)
b. Denver, USA. Studied in California, then with L. Godowsky in Berlin and with R. Goldmark in New York, where he made his début 1908. Became mainly teacher and composed pf pieces with pretty titles.
Pupils included: John Cage.

D'INDY, Vincent: *see* **INDY, Vincent d'**.

DIXON, Cecil Edith (1891–1979)
b. New Zealand, where she was educated. Student of R. Coll., London, and of T. Matthay. Won Challen Gold Medal 1915, Hopkinson Silver 1917 and Hopkinson Gold Medal 1918. Pf prof. at R. Coll.; also on staff of BBC (being the original 'Aunt Sophie' for *Children's Hour* up to 1939) until 1943. MBE 1939. Soloist and accompanist. Recorded *Columbia*.

DOBROWEN, Issay (1894–1953)
b. Nizhny-Novgorod, Russia. Studied Moscow Cons. under C. Igumnov for pf, later finishing with L. Godowsky in Vienna. Was prof. at Moscow 1917–21, thereafter becoming known as conductor and composer. Wrote reputedly fine music including a pf concerto, chamber works and pf pieces including two sonatas and *études*.

DOBRZYNSKI, Ignacy Felicks (1807–67)
b. Romanov, Poland. Pupil at Warsaw Cons. under J. Elsner and was fellow-pupil of F. Chopin. Toured as concert pianist before returning to Warsaw as pianist-composer-

conductor. Wrote chamber music, pf works and songs.

DOEBBER, Johannes (1866–1921)
b. Berlin, Germany. Pupil of Stern's Cons. there under K. Aggházy. Taught at Kullak's Acad., then for a while took up opera conducting. Returned to Berlin 1908 as teacher, pianist and music critic. Wrote chamber music, pf pieces and songs.

DOENHOFF, Albert von (1880–1940)
b. Louisville, USA. Studied pf with A. Lambert, also X. Scharwenka and R. Joseffy. Début New York, 1905. Became successful concert pianist and composed for the instrument.

DÖHLER, Theodor (1814–56)
b. Naples, Italy. Studied pf and composition there, then became a pf pupil of K. Czerny in Vienna. Was appointed pianist to the Duke of Lucca in 1831, and for the next fifteen years made highly successful concert tours of Europe. In 1846 was ennobled by the Duke, married a Russian countess and, in 1848, settled in Florence. Wrote a collection of pf works with titles in keeping with Romantic times. Heine wrote of his playing as 'neat, cute and pretty; graceful weakness, elegant impotence, interesting pallor'. Was seemingly not a concerto player since he appeared twice in London (1838 and 1840) at Phil. Soc. orch. concerts, playing both times his *Fantasia* for solo pf on themes from *William Tell*.

DOHNÁNYI, Ernst von (1877–1960)
b. Bratislava, Slovakia (Poszony, Hungary). Student of R. Hungarian Acad., Pest, from 1893 and under S. Thomán for pf. Graduated 1897 and spent that summer receiving further tuition from E. d'Albert. As a student he had already begun to compose and a pf quartet of his was performed at the Acad. in the presence of Brahms, who was impressed and took a lively interest in the promising student.

His pf début in Berlin in 1897 was so successful that he began a tour of Europe that was to extend over the next five years. At his British début in 1898 he played Beethoven's G major pf concerto. He went to the USA for the first time the following year. In 1900 in Britain, within the space of two months, he gave no less than 32 concerts.

He was appointed pf prof. of Berlin Hochschule 1908–15, at the same time continuing his career as virtuoso and composer. Then he returned to Budapest in a similar capacity at the School of Music, later being appointed Director. By now he had built up an extensive repertoire including the entire Beethoven sonatas. He was the first concert pianist to have all the Mozart pf concertos in his repertoire, and he usually played them conducting the orch. from the keyboard, a practice that in his day was frowned upon by critics. He became an influence on the Hungarian music scene along with B. Bartók and Z. Kodály, although his compositional style leaned towards Brahms, and his musical outlook was conditioned by his career as virtuoso and teacher. He was therefore in no sense a national musician like the other two.

He was conductor of Budapest PO for many years, and Director of Hungarian Radio for a time from 1931. After World War II, and because of past German connections, as well as having held important posts under the Horthy Government, D fell into disgrace with the new Communist régime. He left his native land for good in 1948 and was in Britain for a short time, premièring his 2nd pf concerto under Sir T. Beecham in a number of places, before settling in the USA, where he taught at Florida State Univ. His last appearances in UK were in 1956 at Edinburgh Int. Festival, solo and in a joint recital with the violinist Alfredo Campoli.

His playing, if not highly disciplined, was nevertheless imbued with romantic warmth and great humanity. He composed in most *genres* including chamber music which is occasionally heard, as are a handful of brilliant pf pieces and paraphrases of Strauss waltzes, some of which once found favour with leading pianists.

He died in New York in the middle of a recording session of his own works. Recorded *Columbia*, *HMV*, EMI, Varèse and Everest.

Pupils included: Géza Anda, Fridtjof Backer-Gröndahl, Astrid Berwald, György Cziffra, Erno Daniel, Annie Fischer, Andor Foldes, Boris Goldowsky, Lajos Hernadi, Lydia Hoffmann-Behrendt, Julian von Karólyi, Edward Kilenyi, György Kosa, Mischa Levitzki, Ervin Nyiregyhazi, Miklos Schwalb, Sir Georg Solti, Helen Stanley, Max Trapp, Imre Ungar, Tamas Vásáry, Balint Vazsonyi, Josef Weingarten.

DOMANIEWSKI, Boleslaw (1857–1925)
b. Gronowek, Poland. Student of Warsaw Cons. with J. Wieniawski for pf. Toured as concert pianist for a while, then resumed studies at St Petersburg Cons. Became prof. of pf at Cracow 1890, staying there until 1900 and thereafter at Warsaw. Was fine virtuoso and composed a number of pf solos.

DONOHOE, Peter (1953–)
b. Manchester, UK. Studied pf from age of 4. Début 1965, Manchester, in a Beethoven concerto. Student of R. Coll. of Music, Manchester, and later studied with Y. Loriod. Soloist, accompanist and ensemble player. Came 6th in Leeds Int. Pf Comp. in 1981, and joint 1st (Silver Medal) in Tchaikovsky Pf Comp. in Moscow in 1982. Recorded EMI.

DONSKA, Maria (1912–)
b. Lodz, Poland. Studied there, and with A. Schnabel in Berlin; then later at R. Coll. of Music, London, where she became pf prof. Performed widely and specialized in Polish music. Recorded Saga.

DOOR, Anton (1833–1919)
b. Vienna, Austria. Pf pupil of K. Czerny. A successful début there in 1850 ensured a touring vocation for some years. During a visit to Scandinavia (1856–7) he was appointed court pianist in Stockholm. Two years later he succeeded N. Rubinstein, becoming pf prof. at Moscow Cons. in 1864. From 1869 to 1901 taught master-classes at Vienna Cons. In a successful concert career gave first performances of pf music by Brahms and Raff, and in 1877 made highly acclaimed European tour with Pablo Sarasate. Dedicatee of Saint-Saëns 4th pf concerto in C minor.

Pupils included: August Främcke, Rubin Goldmark, Adele Margulies, Felix Mottl, Benno Schönberger, Fritz Steinbach, August Stradal, Marguerite Volavy, Erich Wolff.

DOPPLER, Arpad (1857–1927)
b. Budapest, Hungary. Studied in Stuttgart, spent some years in New York, then returned to Stuttgart Cons. as teacher. Composed pf pieces.

DORATI, Ilse: *see* **ALPENHEIM, Ilse von.**

DORFMANN, Ania (1899–)
b. Odessa, Russia. Studied locally then with I. Philipp in Paris. Toured extensively from 1920. British début 1933; US début 1936,

settling there same year. Has appeared with leading orchs. Recorded *Columbia* and *RCA*. Pupils included: Marian Migdal.

DÖRING, Heinrich (1834–1916)
b. Dresden, Germany. Studied at Leipzig Cons., his pf teacher being L. Plaidy; subsequently taught there before moving to Dresden Cons. in 1858 where he remained the rest of his working life. Composed much music of educational value and wrote pedagogic works.

DORRELL, William (1810–96)
b. London, UK, son of a watercolour painter. Student of R. Acad. and of C. Potter, then in Paris of F. Kalkbrenner. Was pf prof. at R. Acad. of Music for over forty years, a concert pianist and conductor. Founder member of Bach Soc. and member of Phil. Soc., London. His sister Jane D (1813–83) was a pupil of Mrs L. Anderson and of C. Potter and was a noted pianist also.

DOSSOR, Lance (1916–)
b. Weston-super-Mare, UK. Pupil at R. Coll., London, under H. Fryer. Won Liszt Prize, Vienna, 1937, also 4th Prize in Warsaw same year. London début 1937 and performed thereafter. Resided in Australia from 1953, principal of pf at Univ. of Adelaide.

DOUCET, Clement: *see* **WEINER, Jean.**

DOUGHERTY, Celius (1902–)
b. Minnesota, USA. Student of Univ. there and later at Juilliard School under J. Lhevinne. Concert pianist and accompanist. Played one pf part in the première of P. Hindemith's Sonata for two pfs.

DOUGLAS, Barry (1960–)
b. Belfast, UK. First appearance in public at age of 10. Studied at R. Coll. of Music, London, on scholarship and was successful in a number of competitions including R. Over-Seas League (1979) and Paloma O'Shea (1980). London début Wigmore Hall 1981, when he gave first British performance of Bernstein's *Touches*.

DOYEN, Ginette (1921–)
b. Paris, France. Studied at Nat. Supérieur Cons., winning 1st Prize for pf playing and other prizes. Performed extensively throughout the world. Recorded Westminster and other labels. Married to the violinist Jean Fournier.

DOYEN, Jean (1907–)
b. Paris, France. Student at Paris Cons. and with Marguerite Long for pf. 1st Pf Prize 1922. Début Paris 1924. Began touring. London début 1931. Performed and taught. Awarded Grand Prix du Disque 1938. Recorded *HMV* and Erato.
Pupils included: Hortense Cartier-Bresson, Marie-Thérèse Fourneau, Jean Laforge, Arthur Lima.

DRAESEKE, Felix August (1835–1913)
b. Coburg, Germany. Pupil of Leipzig Cons. and later of F. Liszt. Taught for ten years at Lausanne Cons. and lived for many years in Dresden, teaching, composing and performing. Was prolific composer in most fields including pf. There is a *Sonata quasi fantasia* in C sharp minor, and *Fata Morgana*, a set of pieces in the style of *ghasel*, a Persian type of poetry in which every alternate line ends with the same word: D attempted the equivalent with music.
Pupils included: Karl Ehrenberg, Egon Petri, Percy Sherwood.

DRANGOSCH, Ernesto (1882–1925)
b. Buenos Aires, Argentina. Studied first with J. Aguirre at the Cons. there, and later in Berlin with K. Ansorge. Appeared several times solo and with the Berlin PO, toured Europe and the Americas for some years until 1905 when he settled in Buenos Aires and became pf prof. Compositions include a pf concerto, several sonatas, studies and many other pieces.

DRESEL, Otto (1826–90)
b. Andernach, Germany. Studied pf with F. Hiller and composition with Mendelssohn. Went to USA in 1848, settling in New York as teacher and concert pianist. Became a leading artist in that country, where he introduced some of the best German composers.

DRESEL, Otto (–)
b. Germany. Pupil of father Richard D, later of A. Friedheim. Appointed to Guildhall School, London, in 1905 as teacher of pf in succession to father. Had successful concert career. Guildhall records show he taught there up to 1926.

DRESSEL, Richard (–)
b. Germany. Taught pf at Guildhall School, London, until 1905 when his son Otto D succeeded him.

DREWETT, Nora: *see* **KRESZ, Nora Drewett de.**

DREYSCHOCK, Alexander (1818–69)
b. Zack, Czechoslovakia. A legendary virtuoso of early 19th century. Pupil of J. Tomáschek in Prague, having performed in public from age of 8. Toured Germany 1838 and Russia 1840–2 followed by extensive performing in W. Europe. Prof. at the new Moscow Cons. 1862–8 and pianist to the Tsar. Ill-health caused his resignation, and he went to Italy, where he died. His digital dexterity was legendary, and he is reputedly the first pianist to use the left hand for solos. Wrote numerous pf pieces now of small value. Hanslick said D 'completed the succession of those virtuosi whose bravura was capable of attracting and fascinating a numerous public which admired technical magic and was happiest in – astonishment!' Berlioz wrote of him as 'astounding', and as one whose 'talent is fresh, brilliant and energetic, with immense technical skill and musical feeling of the highest order'. Composed *Fantasy on God Save the King for the left hand alone* which was enormously popular in his lifetime.
   Pupils included: Felix Dreyschock, Sarah Heinze, Julius Melgounov, Albert Payne, Seraphine Tausig, Martin Wallenstein, August Winding.

DREYSCHOCK, Felix (1860–1906)
b. Leipzig, Germany. Nephew of Alexander D, with whom he studied pf initially, later in Berlin with H. Ehrlich, K. Taubert and F. Kiel. Performed and taught in Berlin for many years. Composed pf pieces and songs.
   Pupils included: Bruno Walter.

DROUCKER, Sandra (1876–)
b. St Petersburg, Russia. Studied with Anton Rubinstein and subsequently taught in Berlin following début 1894. Toured Europe and established reputation as virtuoso. Married Gottfried Galston 1910 and was divorced eight years later. Re-settled in Berlin. Wrote memoirs on Rubinstein which were published in 1904.

DROZDOWSKI, Jan (1857–1918)
b. Cracow, Poland. Studied there, then later in Vienna under J. Dachs. Returned to Cracow and was appointed pf prof. at Cons., where he spent the rest of his life. Wrote works on pf technique.

DRZEWIECKI, Zbigniew (1890–1971)
b. Warsaw, Poland. Studied pf there, then later in Vienna. Taught at Warsaw Cons.; also worked hard propagating contemporary music especially by Polish composers. Recorded Muza.
   Pupils included: Jan Ekier, Ken Sasaki, Regina Smendzianka, Roger Woodward.

DUBLANC, Emilio (1911–)
b. La Plata, Argentina. Student at Buenos Aires Nat. Cons. Performed and taught in Mendoza. Composed chamber music and pf pieces.

DUBOURG, Evelyne (1929–)
b. Paris, France. Studied at Geneva Cons. with D. Lipatti, also worked on interpretation with A. Cortot and N. Magaloff. Performed and taught thereafter.

DUBUC, Alexander Vassilievich (1812–98)
b. Moscow, Russia. Pf pupil of J. Field and taught at Cons. there 1865–72. Performed and composed pf pieces and songs. Wrote an autobiography, also treatise on pf technique.
   Pupils included: Mily Balakirev, Alexander Villoing, Nikolai Zverev.

DUCASSE, Jean Jules ROGER-: *see* **ROGER-DUCASSE, Jean Jules.**

DUCHARME, Dominique (1840–99)
b. Montreal, Canada. Pupil of P. Letondal and later in Paris of A. Marmontel. On return home became notable teacher and organist, neglecting his undoubted talents as a pianist. Taught in the Leschetizky method.

DUE, Mary Louise: *see* **BARRATT, Mary Louise.**

DUFFEY, Beula: *see* **HARRIS, Johana.**

DUKAS, Paul (1865–1935)
b. Paris, France. Pupil of Paris Cons., 1882–8, studying pf under G. Mathias. Compositions include the E flat minor pf sonata which received advocacy at one time by É. Risler and

B. Selva, and *Variations, interlude et finale* on a theme of Rameau which are still occasionally performed.

DUKE, John (1899–)
b. Cumberland, USA. Studied at Peabody Cons., also New York; then with A. Schnabel in Europe. Became pf prof. and composer, including a concerto for pf and strings, chamber music and songs.

DUKE, Vernon (1903–69)
b. Pskov, Russia. Originally Vladimir Dukelsky. Student of his mother, then of Kiev Cons., where he neglected pf studies for composing. After the Russian Revolution the family reached the USA via Turkey. In the USA he earned a living playing and writing light music. Met G. Gershwin and achieved success on Broadway and in London under the assumed name Vernon Duke which he acquired for good when he became an American citizen in 1939. His serious works include a pf concerto, a *Ballade* for pf and orch., *Dedicaces* for soprano, pf and orch., chamber music and pf pieces including a sonata. Under the other name of John Duke, he is best remembered for *April in Paris* and *This is Romance*. Wrote entertaining autobiography, *Passport to Paris* (1955) under Vernon Duke name.

DUKELSKY, Vladimir: *see* **DUKE, Vernon.**

DULCKEN, Ferdinand Quentin (1837–1901)
b. London, UK. Pf pupil of I. Moscheles, Leipzig, and of F. Hiller, Cologne. Taught at Warsaw Cons. and subsequently in Russia until 1876 when he settled in the USA as pianist, teacher and composer of mostly salon pieces. Son of Luise D and nephew of F. Hiller.
Pupils included: Michael Hertz.

DULCKEN, Luise (*née* **David**) (1811–50)
b. Hamburg, Germany. Sister of Ferdinand David. Pupil of Friedrich Grund, whose pf *études* were esteemed by Schumann. Début as a prodigy at age 11. Went to London on her marriage in 1828 where she attained the reputation of a brilliant pianist. Gave lessons to Queen Victoria and in 1843 gave what has been claimed as the first British performance of Chopin F minor concerto at Phil. Soc. concert.

DULEBA, Josef (1842–69)
b. Nowy Sacz, Poland. Studied pf in Warsaw, went to Paris at 16 under A. Marmontel. Début Prague, 1863, followed by European tour. A promising career was ended when he died of wounds following a duel.

DUMESNIL, Maurice (1886–1974)
b. Angoulême, France. Student of Paris Cons. and of I. Philipp. Performed in Europe and USA and in 1930 toured Spain demonstrating the Moór Duplex keyboard. Also taught. Settled in the USA where he died. Knew Debussy, was an exponent of his music and wrote a book on how to play and teach D, and later a biography.

DUMONT, Jeanne Louise: *see* **FARRENC, Jeanne Louise.**

DUNHILL, Thomas Frederick (1877–1946)
b. London, UK. Studied at R. Coll., London, from 1893 and was pf pupil of F. Taylor. Subsequently became prof. of composition there. Ran series of Thomas Dunhill Concerts of chamber music in London 1907–19 at which important contemporary works were performed. Wrote much chamber music, also a student's manual on the subject.

DUNN, John Petrie (1878–1931)
b. Edinburgh, UK. Pf pupil of T. Matthay, London; studied theory with Niecks at Edinburgh Univ. Awarded scholarship 1899 and studied at Stuttgart Cons. with M. Pauer for pf. Taught there for a time, and in 1904 toured Europe with Jan Kubelik. Taught at Kiel Cons. 1909–14, then returned to Britain. From 1920 was prof. at Edinburgh Univ. until his death. Wrote a book on Chopin's ornamentations, and another on the secret of the pianist's hand.

DUPARC, Henri (1848–1933)
b. Paris, France. Pf pupil of C. Franck. Pf works destroyed save the accompaniments to his *Mélodies* which are exquisite models of the genre. His orch. nocturne *Aux Étoiles* was arranged for two pfs by Saint-Saëns and for four hands on one pf by C. Franck.

DUPONT, Auguste (1827–90)
b. Ensival, Belgium. Pupil of his father, then of Liège Cons., and thereafter toured as concert pianist until 1852 when he was lured into teaching by being asked to become pf prof.

at Brussels Cons. Was said to have become so devoted to his task that he had a profound influence on Belgian pianism. Composed four pf concertos, a *Polonaise* for pf and orch., studies, duets and pieces, some of which earned popularity at the time because they were well written. Was an editor for the publishers Gevaert & Sandré.

Pupils included: Camille Gurickx, Émile Mathieu.

DUSEK, Milan (1931–)
b. Ustinad Orlici, Czechoslovakia. Pupil Prague Cons. Début 1943. Now pf prof., Prague State Cons., in addition to performing.

DUSSEK, Johann Ladislaus (1760–1812)
b. Czaslau, Czechoslovakia. Reached his early twenties before, having studied with C. P. E. Bach, he decided to make the pf his career. Was renowned throughout court circles in Europe, even, it is said, playing before Marie Antoinette. Fled to London from the French Revolution, where he married a singer and took on his father-in-law's music business. When it failed, he evaded creditors by escaping back to France and resumed his playing career. Composed a prolific amount of music especially pf sonatas which once had a vogue for teaching purposes. According to Johann Tomáscek, D was the first pianist to place the instrument on the platform so that he showed the audience his right profile. In 1794 Broadwoods produced the first six-octave grand, and he was the first concert pianist to use that size instrument in public.

Pupils included: Vincenz Masek, George Onslow, Camille Pleyel.

DUTILLEUX, Henri: *see* **JOY, Geneviève.**

DUVERNOY, Victor Alphonse (1842–1907)
b. Paris, France. Studied at Paris Cons., including pf under A. Marmontel, taking 1st Prize in 1855. Became pf prof. there. Played often in chamber-music concerts, wrote criticisms and composed pf music.

Pupils included: Nadia Boulanger, Nora Drewett de Kresz, Alexander Winkler.

DVOŘÁK, Antonin (1841–1904)
b. Mühlhausen. National composer of Bohemia who was no concert pianist so far as can be traced but who composed a pf concerto, chamber music with piano parts, and numerous pf works mostly in dance form for solo and duet.

DVORSKY, Michel: *see* **HOFMANN, Josef.**

DYCK, Felix (1893–)
b. Bremen, Germany. Studied in Berlin under M. Mayer-Mahr, winning the Blüthner Prize 1909; and later with L. Diémer at Paris Cons., where he won 1st Prize in 1912. Settled in Berlin as pianist-composer. Recorded *Odeon*.

DYGAT, Zygmunt (1894–)
b. Cracow, Poland. Studied there at first then with J. Lalewicz at Vienna Cons., followed by a spell with I. Paderewski in Switzerland. Toured as concert pianist from 1919, especially France and Poland, where he was popular. Appeared also in USA.

DYMMEK, Zbigniew (1896–1948)
b. Warsaw, Poland. Pupil of A. Michałowski, pf at Warsaw Cons., then of St Petersburg Cons. Studied theory in Leipzig. Entered the Paderewski Comp. at Lublin in 1919 and won 1st Prize. Described as having a splendid technique.

EAMES, Henry Permort (1872–1950)
b. Chicago, USA. After study in the USA he
went to Europe for further instruction from K.
Schumann and I. Paderewski. Toured both
sides of the Atlantic for some years as concert
pianist before settling at home to a pedagogic
career.

EBELL, Hans (1888–1934)
b. St Petersburg, Russia. Student of the Cons.
there, continuing privately with S. Rachmaninov, J. Hofmann and L. Godowsky. Début
Vienna, 1912. Toured Europe until World
War I, when he settled in the USA, becoming
pf prof. at the Mary Wheeler School.
Pupils included: Theodore Chanler.

EBERL, Anton Franz Josef (1766–1807)
b. Vienna, Austria. An early pf composer
whose operas attracted the attention and
friendship of Mozart. Somehow some of E's pf
works, including a pf sonata, were published
under Mozart's name. In 1795 he commenced
touring and reached St Petersburg 1796, where
he took post of *Kapellmeister* for five years.
Composed many pf works.

ECHANIZ, José (1905–69)
b. Havana, Cuba. Studied there, and early in
his career performed throughout Americas and
Europe. For a while taught at Eastman School
of Music. Was Artistic Director of Lake Placid
Music Festival from inception in 1963 until his
death, as well as being solo performer and
member of trio around which the festival was
organized. Recorded *Columbia*.

ECKARDT, Johann Gottfried (1736–1809)
b. Augsburg, Germany. Early German pianist
who settled in Paris from age of 22 and wrote pf
works including sonatas.

ECKERBERG, Sixten (1909–)
b. Hjaltevad, Sweden. Pupil of Stockholm
Cons.; later studied with E. von Sauer in
Vienna and I. Philipp in Paris. Later added
composing and conducting to pf career. Compositions included pf concertos and pieces, also
songs.

ECONOMOU, Nicolas (1953–)
b. Cyprus. Studied in Moscow for 8 years, and
now living in Munich as pianist, composer and
conductor. Compositions include an arrangement of Tchaikovsky's *Nutcracker Suite* for two
pfs. Recorded DG.

EDELMANN, Johann Friedrich (1749–94)
b.   Strasbourg.   Pianist-composer-teacher
whose works were widely published in his lifetime and included pf concertos and sonatas.
Was denounced by a pupil during the upheaval
in France and went to the guillotine – the only
pianist known to suffer that fate.

EDEN, Bracha (1928–)
b. Israel. Student of Jerusalem Cons., with A.
Schroeder, a pupil of A. Schnabel. Formed
duo partnership with A. Tamir, making their
US début in 1955 which developed into an
international career with tours throughout the
world. Recorded Decca.

EGGE, Klaus (1906–)
b. Granskerad, Norway. Pupil of Oslo Cons.,
where his pf teacher was N. Larsen. Known
mainly as a composer of strongly national style.
Principal works for pf: 1st concerto (1937),
Trio (1941), 2nd concerto (1944) and a *Sonata
Patetica* (1934). President of Norwegian Composers' Soc.

EGGELING, Eduard (1813–85)
b. Brunswick, Germany. Studied pf, taught it

and lived there. Wrote studies and pedagogic works which were much esteemed in his day. Composed other pf pieces.

EGGHARD, Jules (1834–67)
b. Vienna, Austria. Pf pupil of K. Czerny. Concert pianist and composer of light pieces.

EGNER, Richard (1924–   )
b. St Louis, USA. Studied at Inst. of Music there and later at Chicago Coll. Début 1949, New York. Has appeared solo and with leading orchs. Paderewski Gold Medal 1951. Compositions include pf sonatas.

EGOROV, Youri (1954–   )
b. Kanzan, USSR. Pf pupil of J. Zak. Performed in Europe and USA. Now resident in Netherlands. Recorded Melodiya. British début 1980, London.

EHLERS, Alice (1887–   )
b. Vienna, Austria. Studied pf there with T. Leschetizky, and later harpsichord with W. Landowska in Berlin. Toured Europe frequently; then, in 1936, US début. Settled in California in 1939.

EHLERT, Louis (or Ludwig) (1825–84)
b. Königsberg (now Kaliningrad, USSR). Studied with R. Schumann and F. Mendelssohn and, later, in Berlin and Vienna. Resided Berlin 1850–63 as pf teacher and critic. Taught in the Tausig School 1869–71, finally settling in Wiesbaden. Compositions included pf pieces and songs.
Pupils included: Edward MacDowell.

EHRENBERG, Karl (1878–1962)
b. Dresden, Germany. Pf student of A. Wieck then at the Cons. there under F. Draeseke. Later took up conducting. Composed pf pieces, chamber music and songs.

EHRISMANN, Alfred (1926–   )
b. Winterthur, Switzerland. Pupil of L. Lévy, E. Fischer and A. Cortot. Début Winterthur. Distinguished recitalist and ensemble player.

EHRLICH, Alfred Heinrich (1822–99)
b. Vienna, Austria. Studied under A. Henselt and S. Thalberg there. Taught pf at Stern's Cons., Berlin, after holding appointments as court pianist and various teaching posts in Germany and UK. Composed technical works and was a prolific writer on technique and

reminiscences, as well as several novels.
Pupils included: Felix Dreyschock, Severin Eisenberger, Paul Jankó, Bruno Walter.

EHRLICH, Friedrich Christian (1807–87)
b. Magdeburg, Germany. Pf pupil of J. Hummel. Performed and taught. Composed pf pieces and songs.

EHRLING, Sixten (1918–   )
b. Malmo, Sweden. Studied pf and composition at Stockholm Cons., then conducting in Dresden and Paris. For a decade toured widely as concert pianist and conductor, gradually relinquishing keyboard work.

EIBENSCHÜTZ, Albert (1857–1930)
b. Berlin, Germany. Student of Leipzig Cons., where he later taught for a time before becoming pf prof. at Cologne Cons. Was at Stern's Cons., Berlin, from 1896. Composer of pf sonatas, pieces and songs.

EIBENSCHÜTZ, Ilona (1872–1967)
b. Budapest, Hungary. Was a prodigy, and it is said F. Liszt played a duet with her when she was 6. Studied at Vienna Cons. and graduated at the age of 12. Then spent four years with K. Schumann, where she met Brahms and subsequently much assisted his cause by playing his works. Toured Europe. London début 1891, of which G. B. Shaw wrote: 'She is too young to have yet acquired the *sang-froid* necessary for the complete management of her great musical energy.' Proceeded to have a brilliant concert career for another ten years until her marriage, when she retired from the platform, living quietly in London. Recorded *G & T*, never issued in her lifetime. Some Brahms pieces are to be found on an historical IPA LP.

EISENBERGER, Severin (1879–1945)
b. Cracow, Poland. Pupil of H. Ehrlich and T. Leschetizky. Pf prof. at Cracow Cons., 1914–21, then at Vienna Cons. until 1933 when he settled in the USA, performing solo and with orch., as well as teaching. Held to be a fine artist of his day, especially renowned for his Schumann.

EISLER, Paul (1875–1951)
b. Vienna, Austria. Pupil of Vienna Cons., début 1893. Toured mainly as accompanist to celebrity artists. Studied conducting with A. Bruckner and later took up baton as well.

EISNER, Bruno (1884–1947)
b. Vienna, Austria. Pupil of Cons. there. Career mainly as pf prof. at Stern's Cons., Berlin, then later at Hamburg until 1933 when he emigrated to USA. Reputedly a fine concert pianist.
Pupils included: Konrad Wolff.

EKIER, Jan (1913–   )
b. Cracow, Poland. Pf pupil of Z. Drzewiecki. Performed and taught at State Coll., Warsaw. Recorded Muza.

EKMAN, Karl (1869–1947)
b. Kaarina, Finland. Studied in Helsinki at first; then 1892–5 with H. Barth in Berlin and A. Grünfeld in Vienna. Returned to Helsinki where he taught pf at the Cons., becoming Director there. Was also conductor and organized chamber-music concerts in capital. Wrote a textbook on pf technique.

ELGAR, Sir Edward (1857–1934)
b. Worcester, UK. Not perhaps a professional pianist but the instrument figured in his early musical studies and he did play in public as a boy. That he used the instrument consistently in the course of composing can be adduced from photographic records, and the pf pieces, chamber music and accompaniment to his many songs testify to his skill in that direction. Knighted 1904. Baronet 1931. OM 1911. R. Phil. Soc. Gold Medal 1925. Made arrangements of his own orch. works including *Enigma Variations* Op. 36.

ELIE, Justin (1883–1931)
b. Cap Haitien, Haiti. Student Paris Cons. under A. Marmontel and C. de Bériot. Appeared in Europe and toured N. and S. America before returning to Haiti where he taught and composed, including a pf concerto.

ELINSON, Hedwig (*née* STEIN) (1907–83)
b. Jena, Germany. Pf pupil at Stern's Cons., Berlin. Performed and taught. Married Iso E. Taught at R. Manchester Coll. from 1947.

ELINSON, Iso (1907–64)
b. Moghilev, Russia. Pupil first of his mother, who had been taught by A. Rubinstein, then of F. Blumenfeld in Leningrad. Became teacher and concert pianist at the outset of career, addicted to series like the Beethoven '32' and Bach '48'. London début 1936, becoming British citizen, and from 1944 taught pf at R. Manchester Coll. of Music. Recorded Pye.
Pupils included: David Wilde.

ELIZALDE, Frederico ('Fred') (1907–79)
b. Manila, Philippines. Had classical training at Madrid R. Cons., winning 1st Prize for pf at age 14. In 1927 he suddenly launched into musical life of rhythm pianist and hot jazzband leader, working in Savoy Hotel, London, for two years. Composed ballet music for Diaghilev during same period and in 1930 reverted to serious career. Wrote songs, a pf concerto which he performed and one for violin which Campoli took up. Recorded as soloist and with band, *Brunswick* and *Decca*.

ELLEGAARD, France Marguerite (1912–   )
b. Paris, France, of Danish parentage. Pupil of Paris Cons. 1922–33. Thereafter performed in Europe and taught. Recorded *Polydor* and *Decca*. Taught at Sibelius Acad., Finland.

ELLIS, Vivian (1904–   )
b. London, UK. Student at R. Acad., London, and pf pupil of Myra Hess. Commenced career as concert pianist, had a song published at 18, turned to composition and became one of Britain's great composers for musical theatre. Wrote music for some of the most resoundingly successful West End shows. CBE 1984 Recorded *Columbia* and HMV.

ELSNER, Josef Xaver (1769–1854)
b. Grottkau, Silesia. A contemporary of Beethoven and one of the fathers of Polish music. Teacher of F. Chopin and other pianists, yet himself had no traceable tuition on that instrument. Was in fact a composer of opera and cantatas whose instrument was the violin and who founded a school in Warsaw which grew into the Cons. Composed chamber music, a sonata for pf for four hands, many pf pieces and songs. Dedicatee of Chopin's unsuccessful first sonata in C minor, Op. 4.
Pupils included: Frédéric Chopin, Ignacy Dobrzynski, Julian Fontana, Josef Nowakowski, Édouard Wolff.

ENCKHAUSEN, Heinrich (1799–1885)
b. Celle, Germany. Pupil of A. Schmitt. Excellent executant and one-time court pianist at Hanover. Composed music with emphasis on technique.

ENESCO, Georges (1881–1955)
b. Liveni, Romania. A many-sided musician now principally known as composer-violinist-teacher. Received training in pf at Paris Cons. along with organ and cello, and performed often in that capital on violin and pf, giving master-classes in the former at École Normale. On violin he gave the première of his 1st violin sonata with A. Cortot in 1898, and two years later was pianist to Jacques Thibaud's violin in the first performance of his 2nd sonata. After World War II he taught in New York, giving, in 1950, a farewell concert in which he appeared in the four roles of composer, conductor, pianist and violinist. Compositions include three pf sonatas, three violin sonatas, two cello sonatas, a pf quintet, a pf quartet and other miscellaneous chamber works; also two pf suites, and a set of *Variations on an Original Theme* for two pfs. There is also an early *Fantaisie* for pf and orch. Recorded Hungaroton (with D. Lipatti).

ENGEL, Karl (1818–82)
b. Hanover, Germany. Was pf pupil of J. Hummel. Taught successively in Hamburg, Warsaw and Berlin, then settled for a time in Britain, first in Manchester then in London. Became interested in the history of instruments and published many books and essays. Committed suicide, leaving behind a vast manuscript in the form of a history of musical instruments the world over.

ENGEL, Karl Rudolf (1923–)
b. Basle, Switzerland. Student of Cons. there, winning diploma. Has toured Europe and taught in Paris. In recitals has featured entire cycles of sonatas by Mozart and by Beethoven.

ENGLAND, Leslie (1902–71)
b. Barrow-in-Furness, UK. Went to London at age of 8 to study with private teachers and won open scholarship at the R. Acad. there, whose staff he joined on graduation. Appeared regularly before the public and toured overseas. A heart condition curtailed his activities from 1950. Recorded *Columbia*.
    Pupils included: Dennis Murdoch, Charmion Ross-Oliver.

ENTREMONT, Philippe (1934–)
b. Rheims, France. Studied with M. Long and at Paris Cons., where he graduated with highest honours. Entered the Concours M. Long-J. Thibaud in 1951 and 1953, coming 5th and joint 2nd respectively. Was 10th in the Concours Reine Elisabeth, Brussels, of 1952. Toured all over the world exhibiting his poetry and fine technique. Later turned additionally to conducting Vienna Chamber Orch. and New Orleans SO. Also became Director of the Ravel Acad. at St Jean de Luz. Recorded *RCA* and CBS.

EPSTEIN, Julius (1832–1926)
b. Agram, Austria. Pupil of A. Halm in Vienna. Was pf prof. at the Cons. there 1867–1901 and was esteemed as teacher and concert pianist. Assisted in the Breitkopf & Härtel edition of Schubert works. At once discerned Brahms' stature when the latter arrived in Vienna, and took active steps to assist the cause.
    Pupils included: Ignaz Brüll, Simon Bucharov, Richard Epstein, Wesley Forsyth, Paolo Gallico, Sigmund Herzog, Alexander Lambert, Eduard Poldini, Hugo Reinhold, Josef Schalk, Gino Tagliapietra.

EPSTEIN, Lonny (1885–)
b. Frankfurt, Germany. Student of Cons. there and later of J. Kwast and K. Friedberg at Cologne Cons. Début 1903, Stuttgart. Toured for some years, then taught at Cologne 1912–25. Settled in USA from 1926 where she lived in New York, teaching and performing.
    Pupils included: Orlanda Amati.

EPSTEIN, Richard (1869–1919)
b. Vienna, Austria. Son of Julius E, who taught him pf at Vienna Cons. Spent two years in Berlin in further study before returning to teach at the Cons. Lived in London 1904–14, teaching and performing, then went to USA and settled in New York. Excelled in ensemble work and accompanied some of the greatest singers and instrumentalists, as well as playing in chamber-music recitals.

ERDMANN, Eduard (1896–1958)
b. Wenden, Latvia. Studied initially in Riga; then, in 1914, went to Berlin under K. Ansorge. Had fine bold technique and played the classics as well as contemporary works. Gave première of Schnabel's pf sonata at ISCM; 1925. That year became head of master-class of Cologne Cons. until 1950 when he went in same capacity to Hamburg Cons. Toured extensively and composed in variety of genres. Recorded Brahms for *Parlophone* and French works for *Polydor*.

Pupils included: Paul Baumgartner, Alfons Kontarsky, Aloys Kontarsky, Lottie Krebs.

ERKEL, Ferenc (1810–93)
b. Gyula, Hungary. An important 19th-century figure in Hungarian music who founded the national opera in Pest in 1837 and was its first conductor. Composed a number of operas and also founded the Budapest Phil. Soc, of which he was first conductor. He was also Director and pf prof. of the Music Acad. from its inception in 1875 until 1889 (it later became the R. High School). Composed the Hungarian national anthem in 1845.
Pupils included: Ladislaw Erkel.

ERKEL, Ladislaw (1844–96)
b. Budapest, Hungary. Son of Ferenc E, who taught him. Performed as pianist and conductor.

ERKIN, Ulvi Camel (1906–   )
b. Istanbul, Turkey. Studied there before winning scholarship to Paris Cons. and later École Normale; teachers included I. Philipp and C. Decreus. Returned to Turkey in 1930, teaching and performing. Wrote a pf concertino (1932) and a concerto (1942), chamber music and pf works including a sonata, also songs.

ERLEBACH, Rupert (1894–   )
b. London, UK. Pf pupil of R. Coll. of Music and especially of F. Taylor and E. Howard-Jones. Performed and composed pf music, songs etc.

ERSKINE, John (1879–1951)
b. New York, USA. After studying pf and composition initially went off on literary career. Took up pf again comparatively late, becoming pupil of E. Hutcheson in 1923. Besides a concert career and private teaching, he held high offices in Juilliard School up to his death.

ERTEL, Paul (1865–1933)
b. Posen, Germany. Pf pupil of L. Brassin and later of F. Liszt. Interrupted his career as pianist to take a course of law in Berlin where he had settled. Subsequently became pf teacher and music critic. Composed chamber music and pf works.

ERTMANN, Dorothea (1781–1849)
b. Offenbach, Germany. An early pianist who

features in Beethoven's life as an accomplished player who propagated his pf works once he was beset by deafness. Dedicatee of his pf sonata Op. 101.

ESCHENBACH, Christoph (1940–   )
b. Breslau, Germany. Initially taught by step-mother, herself a pianist. Subsequently trained in Cologne and at Hamburg Music Univ. Having launched successful career as pianist, especially noteworthy in Mozart, embarked additionally on conducting. In 1983, in a London recital with J. J. Frantz, gave a world première of some of Brahms' *Hungarian Dances* in the composer's version for two pfs, the MS of which had recently been discovered. Recorded DG, Europe and EMI.

ESCHMANN, Johann Karl (1826–82)
b. Winterthur, Switzerland. Pf pupil of I. Moscheles and F. Mendelssohn. Taught subsequently at Cassel, then Zurich. Performed and composed chamber music, songs and pf pieces. Wrote pedagogic works that were popular in their day.

ESPOSITO, Michele (1855–1929)
b. Castellamare, Naples, Italy. Pupil of the Cons. S. Pietro a Maiella, Naples, studying pf with B. Cesi. Subsequently gave recitals and taught the instrument. Lived in Paris 1878–82, in which year he moved to Dublin as pf prof. at the R. Irish Acad. Composed in most genres including chamber works and many pf pieces.
Pupils included: Sir Hamilton Harty.

ESSIPOVA, Annette Nicolaievna
(1850–1914)
b. St Petersburg, Russia. Pupil of T. Leschetizky, whom she married 1880. Gold Medal winner 1870. Début 1874, St Petersburg. Then began long concert tours, visiting London 1874, Paris 1875, USA, 1876. Was appointed pf prof. at St Petersburg Cons. 1893, where she remained until her death. In the words of one critic: 'Passion and poetry are the chief characteristics of her playing.' The style of her more renowned pupils could well reflect her own distinctive qualities of technical facility and interpretative power. Arranged Tchaikovsky's *1812 Overture* for pf and his *Nutcracker Suite* for pf duet.
Pupils included: Isidor Achron, Simon Barere, Alexander Borowsky, Jan Cherniavsky, Thomas de Hartmann, Ignace Hilsberg, Jerzy Lalewicz, Alfred Mirowitsch, Edward

Noyes, Marie Paur, Lev Pouishnov, Serge Prokofiev, David Rabinovich, Max Rabinovich, Artur Schnabel, Sergei Tarnowsky.

ESTEBAN, Julio (1906–)
b. Shanghai, China, of Spanish parentage. Studied in Barcelona where he graduated at 18. Performed there until 1925 when he taught at Philippines Univ.; also pursued concert career in the East. Joined Peabody Cons. in 1955.

Pupils included: Jonathan Plowright, Teresa Walters.

ESTRELLA, Arnaldo (1908–1980)
b. Rio de Janeiro, Brazil. Pupil of National Music School there. After graduating commenced touring. Won Columbia Prize, New York, 1942. European début 1948. Became pf prof. at Nat. School, Rio.

EVANS, Bradley (1958–)
b. New South Wales, Australia. Studied at State Cons. there (Mus.Bac. 1981). Won a number of prizes in competitions including joint Australian Musical Overseas Scholarship for an Australian pianist at The Royal Overseas League Music Festival, London, 1984. Also studied with B. Kaplan in London.

EVANS, Lindley (1895–1982)
b. Cape Town, S. Africa. Concert pianist; also accompanist to leading soloists. Pf prof. at New South Wales State Cons., Sydney, 1928–66. Composed works for pf and orch., chamber-music, pf pieces and songs.

EVERS, Karl (1819–75)
b. Hamburg, Germany. Studied pf there and later with F. Mendelssohn in Leipzig. Was rated fine pianist and carried out numerous and extensive tours. Lived successively in Paris, Graz and Vienna, where he died. Composed elegant music (sonatas, songs without words etc) all somewhat beholden to Mendelssohn.

EVSEIEV, Sergei Vassilievich (1894–1956)
b. Moscow, Russia. Pupil of Moscow Cons.; studied pf with L. Conus and A. Goldenweiser. From 1922 taught pf at Moscow Cons. and composed small amount of pf music and songs.

FAELTON, Karl (1846–1925)
b. Ilmenau, Germany. Received tuition from a teacher who had been a pupil of J. Hummel but was in the main self-taught. Worked at Frankfurt Cons. until emigrating to USA, where he worked successively at Peabody Inst., Baltimore, and New England Cons., Boston, in which city he founded his own pf school in 1897. Composed and published studies, technical treatises and transcriptions.

Pupils included: Cedric Lemont.

FAELTON, Reinhold (1856–1949)
b. Ilmenau, Germany. Younger brother of Karl F. Studied in Weimar and joined Karl in Frankfurt, emigrated to USA, where he taught at Peabody Inst., Baltimore, and New England Cons., Boston; also co-founder of the school in Boston with the brother in 1897. Wrote technical works on pf playing.

FALCKE, Henri (1866–1901)
b. Paris, France. Pf pupil at Paris Cons., where he later taught. Wrote several works on technique.

FALLA, Manuel de (1876–1946)
b. Cadiz, Spain. Began to learn the pf from an early age, with opportunities to play chamber music privately. Studied with J. Tragó and soon commenced composition, some of it being performed in a music showroom in Cadiz. The family removed to Madrid in 1896. He entered Madrid Cons. and precociously accomplished the seven-year course in two, graduating with honours and being tipped for a virtuoso's career. Around this time he was studying composition with Felips Pedrell, a composer who was at the time busily establishing a new school of Spanish composition. F always acknowledged a deep spiritual debt to his mentor. In 1905 he won a pf competition in Madrid,

beating other contestants by sheer musicianship. The performance was repeated at a public concert. Around then he was also playing concertos and chamber music.

The Four Spanish Pieces (*Aragonesa, Cubana, Montañesa* and *Andaluza*), were in hand when he went to Paris for further study and to expand his musical horizon. There he supported himself by taking on work in an obscure theatre, conducting a small band from the pf. He met Turina as well as Debussy, Fauré and Dukas, who introduced him to Albéniz. This was a rich period of his formative years following on the groundwork of Pedrell. He was also befriended by R. Viñes through whom he met Ravel. Durand et Cie published the four pieces which are dedicated to Albéniz and which received their première in Paris by Viñes. F was composing other music including songs and opera, besides teaching and playing. *La Vida Breve* was staged in Nice and Paris.

He visited London in 1911 to participate in a concert of Spanish music and had already begun work on *Nocturnes* for pf, later expanded on the suggestion of Viñes into *Nights in the Gardens of Spain* for pf and orch., to whom this important work is dedicated.

On the outbreak of war in 1914 he returned to Spain, where he continued to develop his style, which is noted for great precision of craftsmanship as well as Spanish flavour. He toured the regions of the country, imbibing local culture and especially colour in music. Performances of his works followed in Madrid, including the successful *La Vida Breve*. Work on *El Amor Brujo* began, and a pf version was published in 1921 including the famous *Ritual Fire Dance*. Cubiles premièred *Nights* in Madrid, and Viñes played it in San Sebastian. The composer also played it, notably in London in 1921. He also wrote *Fantasia Baetica*, dedicated to Arthur Rubinstein.

The other major work, *Concerto for harpsi-chord (or pf) and five instruments* (flute, oboe, clarinet, violin and cello) belongs to 1926, premièred the same year at a concert of F's works given in Barcelona by the Casals Orch. He played *Nights* before conducting W. Landowska at the harpsichord, with soloists from the orch. F performed the concerto in Paris and London and later recorded it. In 1935 he composed the short *Hommage à Paul Dukas*, the year in which his old friend died.

When the political scene in Spain flared in the 1930s, F toured in search of peace, spend-ing time in Mallorca in between spells in Granada and Barcelona. His health was deter-iorating and he was ill in Granada throughout the Civil War. In 1939 he accepted an invita-tion to conduct in Buenos Aires because it meant reunion with his sister. He stayed on there in straitened circumstances and poor health until his death. Recorded for *Columbia* (only traceable works being the concerto and some songs sung by Maria Barrientos with the composer's accompaniment).

FALVAI, Sandor (1949–   )
b. Budapest, Hungary. Student of Liszt Ferenc Acad. there; graduated 1972 before continuing studies at Moscow Cons. Came 4th in the Liszt–Bartók Int. Pf Comp. in Budapest in 1971. Has since performed throughout Europe. Recorded Hungaroton.

FANING, Eaton (1850–1927)
b. Helston, UK. Studied at R. Acad., London, under Sir W. S. Bennett and others, winning Mendelssohn Prize 1876. Taught at R. Acad., becoming pf prof., also at Cambridge, Guild-hall School, R. Coll., Harrow School and else-where. Composed in many fields including chamber music and pf pieces.

FARJEON, Harry (1878–1948)
b. New Jersey, USA of British parents. Studied with L. Ronald then attended R. Acad., London, 1895–1901. Earned his living mostly as prof. of composition but is remem-bered for pf works of which he composed many, ranging from a concerto in D which had its première at London Proms in 1903, to suites, sonatas, variations and smaller pieces all characterized by good workmanship and perfect taste. Wrote *The Art of Piano Pedalling* (1923).

FARNADI, Edith (1921–73)
b. Budapest, Hungary. Pupil of Franz Liszt Acad. there. Début 1933 in Budapest at age of 12, playing Beethoven's C major concerto which she conducted from the keyboard. Graduated at 16 and taught at the Acad. in addition to extensive concert tours. Was a chamber-music player of note. Recorded Westminster and EMI.

FARRELL, Richard (1927–58)
b. Auckland, New Zealand. Educated in Wellington and spent five years at New South Wales Cons., Sydney, before going to Juilliard School, New York, for three years under O. Samaroff. Début New York, 1948; also appeared in own country same year. Per-formed in English-speaking countries from 1951 and established secure reputation for musicianship both solo and with orch. Died tragically in road accident in UK.

FARRENC, Jeanne Louise (*née* **Dumont**) (1804–75)
b. Paris, France. Pupil of A. Reicha. Developed a reputation as concert pianist and married Jacques F, who was a music publisher and who began compiling *Trésor des Pianistes*, a vast collection of pf music with biographical details of the composers. The undertaking was continued by Jeanne after her husband's death in 1865. Additionally she was pf prof. at Paris Cons. and composed numerous pf works.

FAURÉ, Gabriel Urbain (1845–1924)
b. Pamiers, France. In 1854 entered École de Niedermeyer whose curriculum was geared to produce organists and pf teachers. Saint-Saëns taught pf there and was probably the pianistic influence in F's young life. He graduated in 1865, spent four years in Rennes, then returned to Paris in 1872 to teach at Nieder-meyer's. In 1896 became prof. of composition at Paris Cons. and its Principal 1905–20. His principal pf compositions are five *Impromptus*, thirteen *Nocturnes*, thirteen *Barcarolles*, and *Thème et Variations*. Besides the *Ballade* and the *Fantaisie* both for pf and orch. there are a number of chamber works with pf part and many songs. The style is beautiful, rich, highly individual but perhaps introspective. A public concert of his works was organized by friends and given in the Sorbonne in Paris in June 1922. The programme included *Shylock*, *Caligula*, and *Pelléas*, and *Cantique de Racine*. A. Cortot was soloist in the *Ballade*, and Pablo

Casals in the *Élégie*, *chansons* were sung by Claire Croiza accompanied by A. Cortot, Jeanne Raunay accompanied by Robert Lortat; Charles Panzera gave the première of *L'Horizon chimerique* accompanied by his wife. Lortat also played the 6th *Nocturne*, 5th *Barcarolle* and 2nd *Impromptu* as well as the pf part of the 2nd *pf quintet*. The orch. was the Société des Concerts du Conservatoire under various conductors. Half a century after his death his work stands alone and quietly secure in terms of recognition and esteem. He wrote for pf duet the well-known *Dolly Suite* and collaborated with A. Messager in *Souvenirs de Bayreuth*, a skit on Wagnerian influences of the time.

FAVARGER, René (1815–68)
b. Dun-sur-Auron, France. Pf pupil at Paris Cons. Toured Europe, eventually settling in London as pianist, teacher and composer of pf pieces under typical titles.

FAY, Amy (1844–1928)
b. Bayou Goula, USA. Studied pf in Berlin with K. Tausig and T. Kullak; thence to Weimar with F. Liszt. When she returned home, she resided in New York, lecturing on music and teaching pf. Her claim to immortality, however, lies in a volume of reminiscences, *Music-study in Germany*, which was first published in 1881 and throws interesting light on some great European musical figures when she was a student.

FAZER, Edvard (1861–1943)
b. Helsinki, Finland. Studied there and later in Germany under B. Stavenhagen. Toured Europe as virtuoso. Later founded Finnish opera in the capital and established own concert agency. Managed first European tour of Anna Pavlova with Imperial R. Ballet.

FEINBERG, Samuel Eugenievich
(1890–1962)
b. Odessa, Russia. Student of Moscow Cons. under A. Goldenweiser, where he graduated 1911 and thereafter quickly established a reputation as concert virtuoso. His compositions include a dozen sonatas, the 6th being performed at ISCM, Venice, 1925; also chamber music and pf pieces. Recorded *Polydor*.

FEIRING-TAPPER, Bertha: *see* **TAPPER, Bertha.**

FERBER, Albert (1911–)
b. Lucerne, Switzerland. Studied pf there, and later with W. Gieseking and M. Long. Performed and taught, settling in UK 1939. Recorded *Decca*, Saga, Rosicrucian and Meridian labels.

FERGUSON, Howard (1908–)
b. Belfast, UK. Pf pupil of H. Samuel. His early F minor pf sonata (first performed by Myra Hess in 1940) was dedicated to the memory of his teacher. Other compositions include chamber music, a *Partita* for orch. and *Concerto in D* for pf and strings. Edited Schubert pf sonatas and wrote *Keyboard Interpretation*.
Pupils included: Keith Humble.

FERGUSON, Robert Stanley (1948–)
b. London, UK. Student at R. Coll. there and of C. Smith. Prizewinner. Début London, 1973. Performed solo and duo including demonstrations on early instruments.

FERRARI, Gustav (1872–1948)
b. Geneva, Switzerland. Pianist, accompanist and composer. Settled in London 1900; also wrote for musical Press.

FERRATA, Giuseppe (1865–1928)
b. Gradoli, Italy. Studied pf from early age, entering Rome R. Acad. at 14. Graduated 1885 with Gold Medal, having made his début two years earlier. Pupil of G. Sgambati and F. Liszt, becoming travelling companion to the latter as well as often playing second pf for the aged composer. Had successful concert career with a wide repertoire including own compositions. Prolific composer in most genres and especially for own instrument including arrangements.

FERROUD, Pierre (1900–35)
b. Lyons, France. Studied pf from early age and was a pupil of F. Schmitt. Played in public but was better known as music critic. Was killed in road accident in Hungary when on holiday. Compositions include pf and chamber music.

FERTÉ, Armand (1881–)
b. Paris, France. Pupil of L. Diémer, winning 1st Prize at 16. Début at Concerts Colonne in 1900. Toured as soloist and with orch., and taught, deputizing for his old master. Founded

a concert society in Grenoble which he conducted.

FESCA, Alexander Ernst (1820–49)
b. Karlsruhe, Germany. Pf pupil of W. Taubert. Successful concert pianist whose compositions included chamber music and songs. A Victorian biographer said he 'succumbed to the effects of a disorderly life' and that his compositions showed talent but were lacking in substance.

FÉTIS, Adolphe Louis (1820–73)
b. Paris, France. Younger son of François Joseph F, the great 19th-century musicologist. Studied with H. Herz. Performed and taught, living successively in Brussels, Antwerp and Paris. Composed much pf music that is forgotten.

FÉVRIER, Jacques (1900–79)
b. St Germain-en-Laye, France. Studied with M. Long and É. Risler. A fine pianist and interpreter, especially of modern French music. Identified with Ravel who later chose him in preference to Wittgenstein in the LH pf concerto. With composer premièred the Poulenc Concerto for two pfs at Venice Int. Festival 1932 and was staunch propagator of the works of that composer. Prof. at Paris Cons. In his autobiography Arthur Rubinstein regarded him as an excellent musician and the best sight-reader he ever met. Recorded *French Col*, EMI, Nonesuch, Everest.

Pupils included: Imogen Cooper, Norma Fisher, John Jenkins, Robert Johnson, Bernard Ringeissen, Valerie Tryon.

FEW, Margerie (1914–   )
b. Jamaica, West Indies. Studied R. Coll. of Music, London, and in Vienna. Settled in London, performed widely and broadcast.

FIALKOWSKA, Janina (1951–   )
b. Montreal, Canada. Studied pf from age of 5, passing her music degrees at the Univ. there in 1968. Subsequently studied with Y. Lefébure in Paris, then at the Juilliard School of Music, New York, with S. Gorodnitzki. Came 6th in the 1971 Montreal Int. Pf Comp. and joint 3rd in the Arthur Rubinstein Comp. in 1974. Afterwards toured widely throughout the western world with a catholic repertoire. In 1982 a London critic wrote of 'the exhilarating verve' of her Chopin: 'Her heroic vigour and colossal technical resource in the First Ballade

and fifth Polonaise were brilliantly successful.' Recorded RCA.

FIBISCH, Zdenko (1850–1900)
b. Seborsitz, Czechoslovakia. Pupil of Leipzig Cons. with S. Jadassohn for pf. Received lessons from I. Moscheles. Was both precocious and possessed enormous creative energy. Wrote many pieces for pf as well as some chamber music which now are never played. Also wrote a pf method.

FICKENSCHER, Arthur (1871–1954)
b. Aurora, USA. Studied at Munich Cons. and graduated 1895. Début Munich same year. In addition to performing solo and with orch., he became accompanist to celebrated vocalists and instrumentalists and did a great deal of teaching in Europe and USA. Inventor of the 'Polytone', an instrument in which each octave is subdivided into sixty tones.

FIEDLER, Max (1859–1939)
b. Zittau, Germany. Studied pf with father, then at Leipzig Cons. Began auspicious career as concert pianist before gradually turning to conducting at which he excelled, occasionally appearing as pianist thereafter only in chamber concerts and as accompanist. Composed pf pieces and songs.

FIELD, Henry Ibbot (1797–1848)
b. Bath, UK. West-Country trained, where he played and taught. Appeared at Phil. concerts, London, in Hummel's concertos where he gave the first British performance of the A minor in 1822. Was evidently addicted to that composer's music, playing other Hummel works at his two subsequent appearances with the Soc.

FIELD, John (1782–1837)
b. Dublin, Eire, of a musical family, his grandfather being his first pf teacher. Appeared there as prodigy. His father was a theatre violinist who moved to London when the lad was 11, and so it came about that he was apprenticed to M. Clementi as a pf pupil and demonstrator of instruments in Clementi's showrooms. It has been said that the master was hard on his pupil, but it should be remembered that in those days children were not exactly cossetted. According to testimonies of a number of persons, Clementi was certainly parsimonious, but at the same time he did give the young F a solid technical foundation for a successful career. F's London début was in

1794, and by the time he premièred his first pf concerto in 1799, the Press was hailing him as one of the finest exponents of the day.

In 1802 master and pupil took the long trip through Europe to St Petersburg. All the way F gave concerts, establishing a reputation as a foremost pianist-composer. When Clementi decided to return to Britain, F stayed on, becoming the darling of society as well as establishing a fashionable teaching practice.

He married in 1810. There was a son but the couple separated after ten years, and in 1822 he settled in Moscow, where he made much money from concerts and teaching as well as from a number of tours of Europe. He had a feckless streak and was not businesslike. To fecklessness can be added intemperance and unwise affaires. His most concentrated period for touring was 1832–4, and it was while he was in Italy in the latter year that he was taken ill in Naples. After a slow recovery F returned to Russia via Austria, where he was fêted. He died early in 1837 in Moscow of bronchitis.

His pf playing was much admired for delicacy and fluency of technique. When Glinka said that 'his fingers, like great drops of rain, poured over the keys as pearls on velvet', he was not only mixing similes; he was indicating that technical fluency but also in effect reminding the reader that piano actions in F's day were 'shallow', taking less than half the weight to depress keys than it does to depress the keys of a modern instrument.

F composed fantaisies, rondos, seven pf concertos, four pf sonatas of which three are student works, a quintet for pf and strings, and around twenty *Nocturnes*, being the accredited originator of the genre. From time to time the music has had its champions, notably Frank Merrick in recent times.

Pupils included: Alexander Dubuc, Antoine de Knotski, Charles Mayer, Charles Neate, Edvard Passy, Maria Szymanowska.

FIELDS, James (1948–)
b. Los Angeles, USA. Pf pupil of E. Leginska and others. Child prodigy; mature début in 1964 at 16.

FILTSCH, Karl (1830–45)
b. Hermannstadt, Hungary. Remarkable prodigy who studied with F. Chopin 1841–3 and who was rated the most talented and promising of all the master's pupils. Had some of Chopin's most important works in his repertoire and performed them before distinguished

audiences, appearing in public in London and Paris in 1843. Died in Venice from tuberculosis at tragically early age.

FINE, Vivian (1913–)
b. Chicago, USA. Teachers included R. Sessions. Performed and taught at Bennington Coll. Compositions include a pf concerto, chamber music and pf pieces.

FIORENTINO, Sergio (1928–)
b. Naples, Italy. Pf student of Cons. there. Prizewinner at Naples and Genoa; 2nd at Geneva Int. Comp. 1947. Toured Europe and established reputation for interpretation of romantic composers. Recorded Saga, Dover.

FIQUÉ, Karl (1867–1930)
b. Bremen, Germany. Student of Leipzig Cons. and of K. Reinecke for pf. Emigrated to USA 1887 as concert pianist; also gave lecture-recitals. Composed pf pieces.

FIRKUSNY, Rudolf (1912–)
b. Napajedla, Czechoslovakia. Family moved to Brno, where he studied before moving to Prague Cons. Pupil of V. Kurz and of A. Schnabel. In early days greatly influenced by L. Janáček. Début in Prague in 1920 in Mozart's *Coronation Concerto* and thereafter toured Europe. US début 1938, where he settled after the fall of France in 1940. First introduced the Menotti pf concerto in 1945 with Boston SO; gave first performance of sonata by C. Floyd in 1957, and première of Yardumian pf concerto in Philadelphia the following year under Ormandy. Also propagated Martinu's works; giving many first performances, including the 2nd pf concerto, *Les Ritournelles: Fantaisie and Rondo* which is dedicated to him. Taught at Juilliard School. Composed a pf concerto and pieces. Recorded various.

Pupils included: David Buechner, Carlisle Floyd.

FISCHER, Annie (1914–)
b. Budapest, Hungary. Pupil of F. Liszt Cons. there, and of E. von Dohnányi. Début 1922, Budapest, at age of 8. Adult début 1926, Zurich. Began performing. In 1933 won the Liszt Prize in Budapest and has continued successful concert career since. Recorded EMI.

Pupils included: Tamas Vásáry.

FISCHER, Edwin (1886–1960)
b. Basle, Switzerland. Pupil of H. Huber there, then of M. Krause in Berlin. Taught at Stern's Cons., 1905–14. Besides being one of the great pf teachers of his day, he regularly toured in programmes largely confined to German masters and was a celebrated interpreter of Bach and Beethoven. Obtained a remarkable wealth of sonority from the instrument. Had his own chamber orch. for some years and played concertos conducting from the keyboard. Was pf prof. at Berlin Cons. for many years and played chamber music with artists of the calibre of G. Kulenkampff. With E. Mainardi there was a fine trio. Despite a reputation based on German classics, he pioneered first performances of the Hans Pfitzner pf concerto in E flat, giving the London première in 1937. Made editions of Bach and Beethoven and wrote *Reflections on Music*. Recorded *HMV*, EMI and Cetra.

Pupils included: Ronald Anderson, Paul Badura-Skoda, Daniel Barenboim, Sebastian Benda, Helmet Brauss, Alfred Brendel, Peter Cooper, Sequeira Costa, Evelyn Crochet, Joerg Demus, Alfred Ehrismann, Konrad Hansen, Egil Harder, Gunnar Johansen, Lionel Nowak, Dario Raucea, Robert Riefling, John Vallier, Rosemary Wright, Yentsislav Yankov.

FISCHHOF, Josef (1804–57)
b. Butschowitz, Czechoslovakia. Studied in Vienna and taught pf to supplement concert work. Succeeded so well as a teacher that he was appointed pf prof. at Vienna Cons. in 1833. Acquired papers and records from the Beethoven family with the intention of using them for an official biography of the composer. He set about adding to them before passing them to the safe custody of the State Library in Berlin. These papers became the basis of A. Thayer's great work on Beethoven. F prepared Mendelssohn's pf works for Universal edition.

Pupils included: Leopold von Meyer.

FISHER, Esther (–)
b. Christchurch, New Zealand. Studied there and at Paris Cons. Début 1923, London. Performed and taught. Prof. at R. Coll., London, and elsewhere.

FISHER, Norma (1940–)
b. London, UK. Pupil of Guildhall there, of S. Harrison, I. Kabos and J. Février, winning a Busoni Prize, Bolzano, 1961, and Harriet

Cohen Memorial Prize. Début 1956, London. Performed extensively, touring Europe and USA solo and with orch.

FISSOT, Alexis Henri (1843–96)
b. Airaines, France. Pupil of Paris Cons., studying with A. Marmontel, winning 1st Prize. From 1887 pf prof. there. Also composed much pf music.

Pupils included: Johanne Stockmarr.

FLAGELLO, Nicolas (1928–)
b. New York, USA. Studied in New York; also in Italy with I. Pizzetti. Has taught at Manhattan School and Curtis Inst.

FLAVELL, Charles Edwin (1817–79)
b. Birmingham, UK. Studied there and later in Frankfurt with A. Schmitt. Returned home and began successful career as concert pianist and teacher, settling in London in 1873, where additionally he sold instruments.

FLEISCHER, Leon (1928–)
b. San Francisco, USA. Was prodigy. Studied locally, then with A. Schnabel in Berlin before World War II. Début 1944, New York, under Monteux, subsequently touring with success. Gave first performance of Leon Kirchner 2nd pf concerto in Seattle in 1963. The following year he turned to conducting because of a physical handicap which developed in the right hand. Recorded Columbia Odyssey.

Pupils included: Gregory Allen, Meade Crane, Max Lyall, Alan Marks, Liliane Questel, Piet Veenstra, André Watts.

FLEMING, Robert (1921–)
b. Prince Albert, Canada. Musical education at R. Coll., London, under A. Benjamin for pf. After World War II completed studies at Toronto Cons. Notable as composer for film music. Wrote pf concerto and songs.

FLEURVILLE, Mauté de: *see* **MAUTÉ DE FLEURVILLE, Antoinette Flore.**

FLIER, Yakov Vladimirovich (1912–78)
b. USSR. Student of Moscow Cons., where on graduation he instructed, 1937–47. Won 1st Prize Vienna 1936 and many other prizes and medals. Toured extensively as solo and with orchs.

Pupils included: Bella Davidovich, Mark Zelter.

FLORES, Noel (1935–   )
b. Goa, India. Student of the Cons. of Madrid and of Vienna. Pupil of H. Graf. Performed throughout Europe and the Iberian peninsula, S. America and India. Taught at Vienna Cons. from 1974. Appeared on juries of international pf competitions.
Pupils included: Avedis Kouyoumdjian.

FLORIDIA, Pietro (1860–1932)
(Hereditary style Barone Napolino di San Silvestro.) b. Modica, Sicily. Studied at Liceo, Naples, 1873–9, under B. Cesi. While a student he wrote an opera and also had some pf pieces published which sold well. After the opera was produced, he toured as concert pianist 1885–90 and was pf prof. at Palermo Cons. 1888–92. Toured, taught and composed in Italy until 1904 when he settled in the USA, performing, teaching and conducting.

FLOYD, Carlisle (1926–   )
b. S. Carolina, USA. Pf pupil of R. Firkusny among others, to whom he dedicated his pf sonata written in 1957 and first performed by Firkusny. Taught pf at Florida State Univ. from 1947.

FOGEL, Helen: *see* **SCHNABEL, Helen.**

FOGGIN, Myers (1908–   )
b. Newcastle-on-Tyne, UK. Student of R. Acad., London, where he was prof. from 1936. Concert appearances in Europe and broadcast numerous times on BBC. Principal of Trinity Coll. from 1965. Has also conducted widely. Recorded *Decca*.
Pupils included: John Bingham.

FOLDES, Andor (1913–   )
b. Budapest, Hungary. Pupil of E. von Dohnányi at Cons. there, winning Liszt Prize 1933. Performed in Europe until 1939, when he settled in USA, being naturalized 1948. Wrote *Keys to the Keyboard* (1948). Recorded *Continental* and DG.

FOLVILLE, Eugénie Émilie (1870–1946)
b. Liège, Belgium. Famous pianist and violinist in France and Low Countries whose career extended over many years. Conducted and additionally composed including a pf concerto, sonatas and pieces.

FONTAINE, Henri Mortier de: *see* **MORTIER de FONTAINE, Henri Louis Stanislav.**

FONTANA, Julian (1810–69)
b. Warsaw, Poland. Student of J. Elsner at Warsaw Cons., where he was friend and fellow-pupil of Chopin. Like Chopin, settled in Paris 1830, teaching pf there and in London. Toured USA with Sivori. Dedicatee of the Chopin polonaises Op. 40. Looked after Chopin's affairs when the latter was away from Paris, and after the composer's death sorted out certain MSS which, with family's permission, were published as posthumous works in 1865. F composed pf pieces and songs in Chopin idiom. Committed suicide.

FONTOVA, Conrado (1865–1922)
b. Barcelona, Spain. Studied there and at Brussels Cons. under A. de Greef. Toured mainly as accompanist to his brother Leon F, a renowned violinist, until 1905 when they founded the Fontova Inst. in Buenos Aires. Composed songs and pf pieces.

FOOTE, Arthur William (1853–1937)
b. Salem, USA. Pf pupil of B. J. Lang. For many years was well-known in area as recitalist and chamber-music player. Prolific composer in divers fields and wrote several textbooks on pf-playing and harmony.
Pupils included: Annie Louise David.

FORBES, George (1813–83)
b. London, UK. Pupil of brother Henry F and of others including Sir G. Smart. Performed for many years in London, organizing his own events. Composed a pf sonata and other works.

FORBES, Henry (1804–59)
b. London, UK. Elder brother of George F. Studied with Sir G. Smart before going to Europe to work under J. Hummel, I. Moscheles and H. Herz. Pianist, conductor and organist, giving concerts with his brother. Composed pf pieces.
Pupils included: George Forbes.

FORBES, Robert Jaffrey (1878–1975)
b. Stalybridge, UK. Student of R. Manchester Coll., became accompanist to international celebrities and was successful concerto player. Joined his old college in 1909 as pf prof., becoming Principal in 1929. Also lecturer.

Historic instruments: (*above left*) Pedalhammerflügel (*c.*1795) by Johann Schmidt, Salzburg, of a type used by W. A. Mozart in concert; (*above right*) piano used by Chopin in London in 1848; (*left*) Liszt's piano in the Weimar Museum; (*right*) Beethoven's piano by Konrad Graf

Claudio
Arrau

Vladimir
Ashkenazy

Bernard
d'Ascoli

Wilhelm
Backhaus

Frédéric Chopin; drawing by Eliza Radzewill

Johannes Brahms

Van Cliburn

Teresa Carreño

Alfred Cortot; drawing by Myrrha Bantock

Jeanne-Marie Darré

Percy
Grainger

Edv. Grieg.

Edvard
Grieg

Josef Hofmann; drawing by Myrrha Bantock

Amparo Iturbi

Vladimir Horowitz

Gyula Kiss

Josef Lhevinne

Katia and Marielle Labèque

Franz Liszt performing at the Royal Court, Vienna, c.1872

Served on important music committees. CBE 1948.

FORD, Michael (1953–)
b. Philadelphia, USA. Student of the Musical Acad. and Coll. of Performing Arts there. Teachers included Suzan Starr.

FORGE, Frank La: see **LA FORGE, Frank.**

FORINO, Hector (1875–1933)
b. Rome, Italy. Pupil of G. Sgambati. Settled in Buenos Aires 1899, assisting his brother Luigi, the cellist, who had started the S. Cecilia Cons. Was successful concert artist and teacher.

FÖRSTER, Anton (1867–1915)
b. Zengg, Croatia. Pupil Leipzig Cons. Performed and taught successively at Stern's Berlin, and the Scharwenka Cons., before settling in Chicago, USA.

FORSYTH, Wesley Octavius (1863–1937)
b. Toronto, Canada. Trained there and then in Leipzig under M. Krause and S. Jadassohn, and in Vienna with J. Epstein. Returned home and developed career as concert pianist and teacher. Became Director of Metropolitan School of Music. Contributed to musical Press and composed for pf. Is regarded as one who did much to assist the cause of the pf in Canada.

FORTESCUE, Virginia (1922–)
b. UK. Pupil of R. Acad. of Music, London. Besides a concert career was also a lecturer, working in Cape Town, S. Africa, from 1955.

FOSS, Lukas (1922–)
b. Berlin, Germany. Studied in Paris 1932–7, in latter year settling in USA and taking US citizenship 1942. Graduate of Curtis Inst., where his pf teacher had been I. Vengerova. From 1944 was Boston SO pianist for six years, a post offering scope for composing. Was prof. at Univ. of California, and from 1963 conductor of Buffalo PO. Compositions include two pf concertos, pf solos and chamber music. *Echoi* (1961) for pf, clarinet, cello and percussion is in four movements, goes beyond notation and permits players to 'do their own thing' in what are described as beatless and barless periods. Recorded Brunswick.

FOSTER, Sydney (1917–77)
b. Florence, USA. Pf pupil of I. Vengerova and D. Saperton, winning Leventritt Award 1941. Début same year, New York. Has toured extensively, introducing new works especially sonatas by N. dello Joio. Became pf prof. at Indiana Univ. 1952.

FOURNEAU, Marie-Thérèse (1924–)
b. St Mandé, France. Studied with M. Long and J. Doyen. Gained 2nd Prize in the Concours M. Long–J. Thibaud 1943, and Grand Prix de Disque 1947.

FOURNIER, Suzanne (1953–)
b. Quebec, Canada. Student of Montreal Cons. and pupil of Y. Lefébure, C. Helffer and Aloys Kontarsky. Won 2nd Prize of Arnold Schoenberg Pf Comp. 1981.

FOU TS'ONG (1934–)
b. Shanghai, China. Studied pf with Mario Paci and Ada Bronstein. Won prizes in international pf competitions including 3rd in the Chopin, Warsaw, in 1955. A pianist of exquisite sensitivity who became domiciled in UK. Recorded EMI, CBS and other labels.

FOWKE, Philip Francis (1950–)
b. Gerrards Cross, UK. Studied at R. Acad. of Music, London, and with G. Green. Début London, 1974. Two years later was awarded a Fellowship to study with R. Tureck. Came 5th in Sydney Int. Pf Comp. 1977. Appeared with British orchs. and at festivals. Recorded EMI and Unicorn.

FOX, Felix (1876–1947)
b. Breslau, Germany. Pupil at Leipzig Cons. with K. Reinecke, then with I. Philipp in Paris. Went to USA 1897, settling in Boston and establishing a pf school with others. Wrote pf pieces and songs, edited works and was an early propagator of music of MacDowell.
Pupils included: Miriam Gideon.

FRAGER, Malcolm (1935–)
b. St Louis, USA. Was prodigy, making his début there with the St Louis SO at the age of 10. Later studied with K. Friedberg at Juilliard School. Awarded joint 2nd Prize at Geneva Comp. 1955; won a Leventritt Prize in 1959, and was 1st in the Concours Reine Elisabeth, Brussels, in 1960. Studied languages at Columbia Univ. and spoke seven fluently. Became established concert pianist in

USA and Europe, claiming in 1978 to be the most-travelled pianist of his generation. Recorded RCA, EMI, Vox and others, including a two-pf recital with V. Ashkenazy on Decca.

FRÄMCKE, August (1870–1933)
b. Hamburg, Germany. Studied at Hamburg Cons., then at Vienna Cons. under A. Door. Won prizes in competitions. Début Hamburg, 1886 and performed throughout Europe. Settled in USA, where for many years was a Director of New York Coll. of Music.

FRANÇAIS, Jean (1912–)
b. Le Mans, France. Showed ability from early age, his first pf works being published when he was 10. Studied pf at Paris Cons. with I. Philipp, where he won 1st Prize. His *Eight Bagatelles for string-quartet and pf* received first performance at ISCM 1932, the *Concertino for pf and orch.* in Paris in 1934, and the *Concerto in D* for same combination in Berlin in 1936, all with composer as soloist. The concerto proved so popular in Europe and USA that F retained sole rights of performance for two years. His work has been described as witty, graceful and suave if somewhat brittle. Recorded *HMV* and Decca.

FRANCESCHI, Vera (1928–66)
b. San Francisco, USA. Studied in USA and Europe. Début 1939, Paris; New York début 1948.

FRANCK, César (César Auguste Jean Guillaume Hubert) (1822–90)
b. Liège, Belgium of Flemish–German parentage. Pupil of Liège R. Cons. from 1830, winning prizes, including a 1st for pf in 1834, and began short concert career. Also continued pf studies with P. Zimmerman at Paris Cons., where he won another 1st Prize for a brilliant performance. From 1844 settled in Paris as teacher and organist, becoming prof. at the Cons. in 1872. Performed regularly as pianist for some years. His pf compositions fall into two phases, an early group which were never published in his lifetime and which are not in pianists' repertory, and great works of maturity upon which his reputation stands: *Prélude, Chorale et Fugue*, *Prélude, Aria et Finale*, Sonata for violin and pf (also transcribed for cello and pf), the Pf Quintet; *Les Djinns* and *Variations symphoniques* both for pf and orch. Assumed French nationality 1873.

Pupils included: Henri Duparc, Alberto Williams.

FRANCK, Eduard (1817–93)
b. Breslau, Germany. Pupil of F. Mendelssohn and friend of R. Schumann. Composed chamber music and pf works, including sonatas, in style much influenced by his early associations. Was distinguished teacher, holding professorships of pf at Cologne Cons., Berne and Stern's in Berlin. Not related to César Franck.

FRANCK, Richard (1858–1938)
b. Cologne, Germany. Musically educated by his father and also at Leipzig Cons. Spent some time in Switzerland performing and teaching before returning to Germany to continue the joint career first in Kassel and later Heidelberg. A notable performer of Beethoven. (His father, Eduard F (1817–93) had been a pupil of F. Mendelssohn and was a friend of R. Schumann.) Besides performing and teaching, he composed much music in the idiom of that setting.

FRANCMESNIL, Roger de (1884–1921)
b. Paris, France. Pupil of Paris Cons., studied pf with L. Diémer and won 1st Pf Prize 1905. Gave concerts and composed.

FRANÇOIS, Samson (1924–70)
b. Frankfurt, Germany. Frenchman whose father was a diplomat, hence his studying in Italy (playing a Mozart concerto under Pietro Mascagni at the age of 5), Yugoslavia and then Nice where he won 1st Prize at the Cons. Later studied in Paris under A. Cortot at the École Normale, and with M. Long at the Cons., where he took another 1st Prize in 1941, the year of his début. Had an international career, visiting China in 1964. Recorded *Decca* and EMI.

FRANK, Claude (1925–)
b. Nuremberg, Germany. Studied at Columbia Univ., USA, and later with A. Schnabel. Début 1950 New York, and has since established himself as successful concert pianist. Taught at Yale, made regular appearances at US festivals and gave duo recitals with his wife Lilian Kallir. Recorded RCA.

Pupils included: Ian Hobson, Randall Hodgkinson, Vanessa Latarche.

FRANKEL, Benjamin (1906–73)
b. London, UK. Learned pf from Victor Benham; after World War I studied in Germany. In 1923 returned to London as teacher and pianist, and gradually attained notice as a composer including pf pieces, chamber music and *Passacaglia* for two pfs.

FRANKL, Peter (1935–   )
b. Budapest, Hungary. Began early, and his pf teachers included Ilona Kabos, and Marguerite Long in Paris. Won a number of international prizes for pf playing including the Liszt Prize in Budapest in 1958. Toured Europe, appearing in London in 1962, where he settled, taking British nationality in 1967. Recorded *Vox*.

FRANKLIN, Norman (1905–   )
b. Hereford, UK. Student of R. Acad., London, and of T. Matthay, at whose school he became pf prof. Was primarily accompanist to leading British singers and also taught pf and singing.

FRASER, Norman (1904–   )
b. Valparaiso, Chile. Studied there and at R. Coll., London, under C. Albanesi, also in Paris with I. Philipp. Début 1928 followed by European tour. Settled in London, then taught in Chile before returning to UK in 1936 to work for BBC. Later worked abroad for British Council and for Int. Folk Music Council. Composed chamber music, pf pieces and songs.

FREED, Isadore (1900–   )
b. Brest Litovsk, Russia. Parents settled in USA when he was young. Studied pf at Univ. of Penn., graduating MB. Also studied with J. Hofmann and later in Paris with E. Bloch and V. d'Indy. Returned to USA 1934 and taught at Curtis Inst. before being head of music dept. at Temple Univ. Fine Arts School. Also interested in organizing and conducting local concerts. Various compositions, include pf pieces, a sonata and chamber music.

FREEDMAN, Jack (1930–   )
b. Birmingham, UK. Studied there, playing in public from an early age. London début 1957. Performed extensively in Europe and USA solo and with orch. Later became pre-eminent as soloist on luxury liners cruising worldwide. Composed pf pieces and songs and for the theatre, and in his repertoire specialized in

Chopin, Debussy, Ravel and Rachmaninov. Recorded various labels.

FREIRE, Nelson (1944–   )
b. Brazil. A prodigy, playing from age of 3 with début at 5. In 1957 won a pf competition in Rio and scholarship to study in Vienna. Concert career began two years later. In 1964 won Lipatti Medal and the da Motta Comp. in Lisbon. Has appeared with leading orchs. of Europe, USA and Israel. Recorded Telefunken, CBS, Pye.

FREUDENTHAL, Otto (1934–   )
b. Gothenberg, Sweden. Studied pf at Trinity Coll., London, also with I. Kabos; won a Harriet Cohen Memorial Medal for interpretation. Début Wigmore Hall. Thereafter performed throughout Europe and taught at Manchester R. Coll.

FREY, Adolf (1865–1938)
b. Landau, Germany. Pf pupil of K. Schumann; was pianist to court of Hesse 1887–93. Later went to USA and from 1893 was pf prof. at Syracuse Univ. and was connected with teaching there for 40 years in between concert tours and appearances. In 1935 established own pf school in New York.

FREY, Emil (1889–1946)
b. Baden, Switzerland. Studied there and later at Paris Cons. under L. Diémer, winning 1st Prize in 1904. Lived in Berlin and toured Europe as concert pianist. In 1910 won the Rubinstein Prize in St Petersburg, plus honorary degree for a pf trio. Was pf prof. at Moscow Cons. 1912–17 before returning to Zurich. Continued to tour Europe and made several trips to USA. His compositions include pf works. Brother of Walter F.
Pupils included: Adrian Aeschbacher, Rudolf am Bach.

FREY, Walter (1898–1938)
b. Basle, Switzerland. Pupil at Zurich Cons., where he taught after graduating. Also received lessons from W. Rehberg. Toured extensively as concert pianist, specializing in contemporary music. Brother of Emil F. Was on *Decca* label.
Pupils included: Walter Lang.

FRICKENHAUS, Fanny (1849–1913)
b. Cheltenham, UK. Studied pf in London and Brussels. Début London 1879, becoming

notable and successful pianist there, where she played much chamber music and was a leading British pianist of her day.

FRID, Géza (1904–)
b. Marmarossziget, Hungary. Pf pupil of mother, then at Budapest High School with T. Szántó, graduating 1924. Toured extensively. After World War II settled in Amsterdam as teacher and concert pianist. Composed concerto for pf, chorus and orch., chamber music and pf works include a sonata and studies; also songs.

FRIEDBERG, Karl (1872–1955)
b. Bingen-am-Rhine, Germany. Pf pupil at Frankfurt Cons. under J. Kwast, J. Knorr and K. Schumann. Début 1892 Vienna, thereafter integrating a successful concert career with teaching, in which capacity he was at Frankfurt 1893–1904 and at Cologne 1904–14 when he went to USA, staying for the duration of World War I. He duly returned to Munich but by 1940 was teaching at Juilliard School, having been a member of its original Faculty when it was formed in 1923.
  Pupils included: Orlanda Amati, Lonny Epstein, Malcolm Frager, Percy Grainger, Gerard Hengeveld, Bruce Hungerford, Ethel Leginska, Ernest Lush, William Masselos, Yaltah Menuhin, Franz Mittler, Elly Ney, Erwin Schulhoff, Jascha Zaydc.

FRIEDBERG, Manna (1901–)
b. Byalistock, Russia. Pupil of S. Stojowski and of Juilliard School, New York. Début 1927, New York. Concert pianist and teacher.

FRIEDENTHAL, Albert (1862–1921)
b. Bromberg, Germany. Pf pupil of T. Kullak, Berlin. Thereafter toured globally, even Far East, finally settling in Berlin as teacher and composer.

FRIEDHEIM, Artur (1859–1932)
b. St Petersburg, Russia. A prodigy who first played in public at the age of 9. Studied with Anton Rubinstein and then with F. Liszt, of whose music he later became a famed interpreter. Performed and taught in N. America for several years before settling in London in 1889. Was pf prof. at R. Coll., Manchester, in addition to performing. Moved in 1921 to Canada, where he taught at the Canadian Acad., Toronto. (Played at inaugural concert of Massey Hall, Toronto, 1894.) Finally settled

in New York. Recorded *Columbia* and *Emerson*.
  Pupils included: Natalie Curtis, Colin McPhee, Julius Prüwer.

FRIEDMAN, Ignace (1882–1948)
b. Podgorze, Poland. After initial tuition in Cracow became a pupil of T. Leschetizky in Vienna. Début 1904, rapidly becoming famous throughout Europe and America for his brilliant technique. In the years between the two World Wars lived successively in Germany and USA, dying in Australia. Composed numerous works for pf and made a number of transcriptions. Edited the complete Chopin for Breitkopf & Härtel (1912), and works of Schumann and Liszt for Universal. Performed chamber music with Huberman and Casals including the Beethoven trios, and is credited with having given over 3,000 concerts. Recorded *Columbia*.
  Pupils included: Natanael Broman, Ryzard Byk, Julius Chaloff, Peter Cooper, Algot Haquinius, Bruce Hungerford, Karl Maria Savery, Victor Schiøler.

FRIEDMAN, Victor (1938–)
b. Moscow, USSR. Pupil of Cons. there, graduating with Gold Medal 1962. Thereafter performed widely, solo and with orch. Settled in the West.

FRIEMANN, Witold (1889–)
b. Kalisz, Poland. Student of Warsaw Cons., then studied later with J. Pembauer in Berlin. Became head of pf dept at Lwow Cons. until 1932 when he went to Katowice Music School as Director. Composed mainly for pf, including a concerto.

FRIML, Rudolf (1884–1972)
b. Prague, Czechoslovakia. Pupil of Cons. there under J. Jiránek for pf and A. Dvořák for composition. Undertook world tours as accompanist to J. Kubelik (violinist). In 1904 in USA decided to settle and toured solo as well as pianist-composer, featuring his pf concerto. Turned to light composition in 1912 at the invitation of A. Hammerstein and became highly successful in popular field of musical comedy and operetta. Settled in Hollywood. Composed much serious music as well. Recorded *Columbia*.

FRISARDI, Nicola (1957–)
b. Andria, Italy. Studied at Bari Cons. and at

Mozarteum, Salzburg. Teachers included H. Leygraf.

FRISKIN, James (1886–1967)
b. Glasgow, UK. Studied at R. Coll., London from 1900 under E. Dannreuther and F. Hartvigson. Taught at R. Coll. for the Blind 1909–14 when he went to USA, settling in New York as a concert pianist and teacher at Inst. of Musical Art. Was member of the original Faculty of Juilliard School of Music when founded in 1923. Composed chamber music and pf works and wrote *The Principles of Pianoforte Practice*.
Pupils included: Fernando Laires.

FRITZE, Wilhelm (1842–81)
b. Bremen, Germany. Studied there and later at Leipzig Cons. with H. von Bülow. Began touring, living successively in Berlin and Stuttgart. Composed a pf concerto, sonatas, and works for two and four hands, also songs.

FRUGATTA, Giuseppe (1860–1933)
b. Bergamo, Italy. Concert pianist, prof. at Milan Cons. and composer of chamber music and pf pieces.

FRUGONI, Orazio (1921–)
b. Davos, Switzerland. Pupil of Verdi Cons., Milan, also of Geneva Cons. and of S. Cecilia, Rome. Début 1947, New York. Recitalist and lecturer. Pf prof. of Cherubini Cons., Florence. Recorded Vox.

FRÜH, Huldreich Georg (1903–45)
b. Zurich, Switzerland. Pupil of Cons. there, later teaching, performing and playing in night club. Compositions include chamber music, a pf sonatina and other pieces.

FRÜHLING, Karl (1868–1937)
b. Lemberg. Pupil at Vienna Cons. Noted chamber-music player and accompanist to celebrities. Lived and taught in Vienna. Compositions include a pf concerto, chamber music, pf pieces and songs.

FRUMERIE, Gunnar de (1908–)
b. Nacka, Sweden. Studied at Stockholm Cons., then with E. von Sauer in Vienna and with A. Cortot in Paris. Taught at Stockholm Cons. from 1945; also concert pianist and composer, works including pf concertos, a set of variations and fugue, and other pieces.

FRUSCIANTE, John Augustus (1945–)
b. New York, USA. Pupil of Juilliard School there, teachers including J. Lateiner. Graduated and made début 1971, Vienna. Toured thereafter, taught and was adjudicator.

FRYER, Herbert (1877–1957)
b. London, UK. Pf pupil of O. Beringer at R. Acad. there 1893–5, when he won scholarship to R. Coll., studying with F. Taylor until 1898. Spent that summer in Weimar with F. Busoni. Début November 1898, London, and thereafter toured Europe with success. Was pf prof. at R. Acad. 1905–14, in the latter year touring Canada and USA. Pf prof. New York 1915–19, when he returned to London to teach at the R. Coll. and continue his concert career in Europe. Also toured extensively in Australia, Canada, Ceylon, India and S. Africa, adjudicating as well as giving concerts. Recorded *Vocalion*. Composed pf pieces including *Suite* Op. 11, also songs. Transcribed works of Bach and old English ballads.
Pupils included: David Buchan, Phillip Challis, Lance Dossor, Leonard Isaacs, Constant Lambert, George Malcolm, Leo Quayle, Cyril Smith, Kendall Taylor.

FUCHS, Karl Dorius Johann (1838–1922)
b. Potsdam, Germany. Studied in Berlin, pf teacher H. von Bülow. Taught thereafter in Berlin and from 1897 in Danzig. Was fine concert pianist, sound teacher and writer of a number of books on musical subjects.

FUCHSOVA, Liza (1913–77)
b. Brno, Czechoslovakia. Studied at Prague Cons. and taught there after graduation. Performed throughout Europe. Settled in UK 1939.

FUGA, Sandro (1906–)
b. Mogliano Veneto, Italy. Pf pupil at Verdi Cons., Turin; pf prof. there from 1932. Composed *Divertimento* for pf and orch.

FULEIHAN, Anis (1900–70)
b. Kyrenia, Cyprus. Went to USA in 1915 to continue musical studies, becoming a pupil of A. Jonás in New York. Début there 1919; toured that continent for next five years. Visited Europe and Near East in 1925, and for next three years lived in Cairo. Wrote two pf concertos, 14 sonatas and many pf pieces of technical difficulty.

FUMAGALLI, Adolfo (1828–56)
b. Milan, Italy. One of four musical brothers.
Studied pf at Milan Cons. Became brilliant
artist and undertook highly successful tours.
Was known as 'the Paganini of the piano' and
composed light but intelligent pf works that
enjoyed a vogue at the time. A short but very
concentrated career.

FUMAGALLI, Luca (1837–1908)
b. Milan, Italy. Younger brother of Adolfo F.
Also pupil of Milan Cons. and a brilliant
concert pianist as well as a composer of lightweight pf works.

FUSCO, Laura de (1946–)
b. Castellammare di Stabia, Italy. Student of
Cons. San Pietro a Maiella, Naples. Came 4th
in the Ettore Pozzoli Int. Pf Comp. 1960.
Toured Europe, USA and S. America.
Recorded Dischi Riscordi.

FUSTER, Francisco Virto (1887–)
b. Valencia, Spain. Studied music at Cons.
there, then at R. Cons., Madrid (pf under José
Tragó), where he won 1st Prizes for pf-playing
and composition. Taught there for a time, later
becoming prof. at Bilbao Cons.
 Pupils included: Carmen Alvarez.

GABRILOWITSCH, Ossip (1878–1936)
b. St Petersburg, Russia. Studied at the Cons.
there 1888–94 and was taught by Anton
Rubinstein, graduating with the Rubinstein
Prize. He then spent two years with T.
Leschetizky in Vienna. Début Berlin in 1896
and proceeded to build a reputation in Europe
before making his US début in 1900. Featured
a series of six concerts showing the development of the pf concerto from Bach onwards
which proved popular in Europe and USA.
Added conducting to his US activities before
World War I, where he settled as pianist-
conductor. Was esteemed as a chamber-music
player, making a now legendary recording of
the Schumann pf quintet with the Flonzaley
String Quartet in 1927. Married Mark Twain's
daughter, Clara Clemens, a soprano whom he
frequently accompanied in recitals and who
wrote *My Husband Gabrilowitsch*. Recorded
Victor.

GAETANO, Robert de (1946–)
b. New York, USA. Pupil of A. Weissenberg.
Début 1971 followed by tour of N. America.
No further details ascertainable.

GAGNEBIN, Ruth (1921–)
b. Neuchâtel, Switzerland. Student of Geneva
Cons., winning diploma. Performed throughout Europe.

GAILLARD, Marius-François (1900–73)
b. Paris, France. Pupil of Paris Cons. and of L.
Diémer, winning 1st Prize for pf at age of 16. In
1917 in the Salle Gaveau performed Granados'
Goyescas which he had studied with the com-
poser. As young pianist specialized in music of
Debussy (some of which was recorded on
HMV and *Odeon*) and Ravel. His programmes
had wide range, but abroad he propagated
French music. Later took up conducting addi-

tionally, in 1928 founding a series devoted
entirely to contemporary music. Composed
Images d'Épinal for pf and orch., several
chamber works with pf part, and pf pieces.

GAITO, Constantino (1878–1945)
b. Buenos Aires, Argentina. Student there and
later at Naples Cons. Toured Europe before
returning home, taking up mainly chamber-
music career. Was also prof. of Cons. in
Buenos Aires.

GALAJIKIAN, Florence (1900–)
b. Maywood, USA. Studied at North-Western
Univ. School of Music and Chicago Coll. Performed widely and taught at Chicago Cons.

GALLET, Luciano (1893–1931)
b. Rio de Janeiro, Brazil. Student of Nat. Inst.
of Music there; gold medallist 1916. Became
interested in Negro influence on Brazilian
music.

GALLICO, Paolo (1868–1955)
b. Trieste, Italy. Gave his first recital when he
was 15. Studied in Vienna under J. Epstein,
winning the Gold and the Gesellschafts Medals
at 18. Toured Europe for a number of years
with success then, in 1892, settled in USA,
where he toured as soloist and with leading
orchs., and taught in New York.
　Pupils included: Simon Bucharov, Augusta
Schnabel-Tollefsen, Elinor Warren.

GALLON, Noël (1891–1966)
b. Paris, France. Pf pupil of Paris Cons. and of
É. Risler and I. Philipp. Won 1st Prize 1909
and in 1910 Prix de Rome. Taught at Paris
Cons. and wrote a number of works including a
Sonata breve and a sonatina.
　Pupils included: Sergei Lancen.

GALSTON, Gottfried (1879–1950)
b. Vienna, Austria. Pf student of T. Leschet-izky 1895–9 before spending a year at Leipzig Cons. under S. Jadassohn and K. Reinecke. Taught in Berlin for four years before working at St Petersburg Cons. and in Munich. Performed extensively throughout Europe and made his US début in 1912. After World War I he made Berlin his home until 1927 when he settled in the USA. Featured a series of historical recitals and was renowned for his intellectual breadth and fine technique. Married Sandra Droucker 1910, divorce 1918.
    Pupils included: Charles Griffes.

GALYNINI, German (1922–   )
b. Tula, USSR. Taught himself to play several instruments including pf. Went to Moscow Cons. in 1938 and during a first spell there developed Scriabin tendencies in composition. Served in Soviet Army 1941–3, then returned to the Cons. to continue under Shostakovich. Composed pf works including *Variations* (1943), *Suite* (1944), a sonata (1945) and a concerto (1945–6). A controversial figure, he was included in the famous purge of artists of 1948, and his subsequent works remained un-published. No pianist in the West has seem-ingly studied the collection of works written when G was studying with Shostakovich.

GAMMON, Philip (1940–   )
b. Chippenham, UK. Student of R. Acad. of Music; winner of MacFarren Gold Medal. Performed solo and as accompanist, also worked extensively in ballet. Also lecturer.

GANCHE, Edouard (1880–1945)
b. Baulon, France. French musicologist who spent much time and effort as a Chopin expert. Wrote a number of works on the composer including *La Vie de Chopin dans son Oeuvre*; was also editor of the Oxford edition of Chopin's works (1932).

GANDINI, Gerardo (1936–   )
b. Buenos Aires, Argentina. Teachers in-cluded A. Ginastera. Concert pianist, teacher and composer who has worked in New York. Compositions include pf pieces, works for pf and orch. and chamber music.

GANZ, Eduard (1827–69)
b. Mainz, Germany. Taken to London 1840 where father (Adolf G) conducted. Pupil of I. Moscheles and S. Thalberg. Later settled in Berlin as concert pianist and teacher. Founded pf school there 1862.

GANZ, Rudolf (1877–1972)
b. Zurich, Switzerland. Studied music in Switzerland and later pf with F. Busoni in Berlin, where he made his début with the Berlin PO in 1899. Rapidly became successful soloist in tours throughout Europe and USA. Was head of pf dept of Chicago Music Coll. for a time, returning there in 1940 as Director. Became naturalized American citizen. Eagerly propagated contemporary pf music and is dedicatee of Ravel's *Scarbo*. Recorded Veritas.
    Pupils included: Gena Branscomb, Charles Haubiel, Guy Johnson, Nils Larsen, Jeffrey Seigel, Harold Zabrack.

GANZ, Wilhelm (1833–1914)
b. Mainz, Germany. Studied there but made London his home from 1850. Was soon in demand as a pianist with fine technique, and Jenny Lind used his services as accompanist on her later tours. Organized a series of orch. concerts in London in which works by Liszt and Berlioz were featured; also introduced for first time soloists who were to become inter-nationally famous. Taught at Guildhall School for years and wrote an autobiography: *Memories of a Musician*.

GARDINER, Balfour (1877–1950)
b. London, UK. Took to the pf early and studied it before starting to compose. Continued with both disciplines in Frankfurt, with L. Uzielli for pf. Compositions included pf works and songs.

GARGUREVICH, Louise (–   )
b. Australia of Yugoslavian–French parentage. Début Melbourne at age of 14. London début 1932. Toured British Empire with success.

GARRATT, Percival (1877–1953)
b. Oxfordshire, UK. Studied in Vienna and Berlin and was pf pupil of K. Klindworth. Toured Europe and S. Africa many times, solo and as accompanist to celebrated singers and instrumentalists. Composed much pf music of a popular style that was played during his life-time. Dedicatee of *Variations on a Theme of Schumann* (1930) by Maurice Jacobson.
    Pupils included: Charmion Ross-Oliver.

GÁT, Josef (1913–67)
b. Hungary. Pupil of B. Bartók at R. Acad.,

Budapest, where he subsequently taught. Mainly known as a pedagogue who wrote *The Technique of Piano Playing* (1965) and who researched the gymnastical aspects of practising.

GAUDIBERT, Eric (1936–)
b. Vevey, Switzerland. Student of Lausanne Cons. and of École Normale, Paris, being a pf pupil of A. Cortot. From 1975 pf prof. at Geneva Cons., also composition.

GAUTHIER, Jacques (1953–)
b. Martinique. Was brought up in France and studied at Marseille Cons., and as pupil of P. Barbizet. Later went to Paris Cons., where he was a pupil of J.-M. Darré, winning 1st Prize in 1974. Performed throughout Europe and as far afield as Japan. Recorded Erato.

GAVEAU, Colette: *see* **MALCUZYNSKI, Witold.**

GAVRILOV, Andrei (1956–)
b. Moscow, USSR. Studied at Cons. there, winning Tchaikovsky Prize and Gold Medal 1974. Has toured Europe and possesses extensive repertoire. Recorded Melodiya.

GAWRONSKI, Wojciech (1868–1910)
b. Sejmony, Poland. Pf pupil Warsaw Cons. and later in Berlin and Vienna where he also studied composition. Toured as concert pianist and founded a school in Russia which he ran for some years before returning home. Composed chamber music, pf pieces and songs.

GAZELLE, Marcel (1907–69)
b. Ghent, Belgium. Pf student at École Normale, Paris, also at Ghent Cons. Prof. there from 1938. A noted soloist, chamber-music player and accompanist. Recorded numerous labels mostly as accompanist to celebrities.
Pupils included: Jeremy Menuhin.

GEBHARD, Heinrich (1878–1963)
b. Sobernheim, Germany. Emigrated to USA with parents when 10. Studied pf in Boston, then with T. Leschetizky in Vienna for four years. Début Boston 1900. Thereafter performed and taught. Composed works for pf and orch., chamber music and pf pieces. Wrote *The Art of Pedalling*.
Pupils included: Leonard Bernstein, Annie Louise David, Alan Hovhaness, Henry Levine.

GEEHL, Henry (1881–1961)
b. London, UK. Pf pupil of father, then of B. Schönberger. Performed for a time but turned his attention to conducting, composing, lecturing and editing. Composed pf works and songs including the famous 'For you Alone', in the repertoire of most tenors of the time from Caruso downwards. In later life experimented with twelve-tone system. Recorded *Parlophone*.

GEIGER, Ruth (1923–)
b. Vienna, Austria. Pf pupil there of J. Isserlis, later of J. Lhevinne at Juilliard School of Music, USA, where she was made an honorary graduate. Début 1944 New York and has since performed extensively in USA and Europe.

GELINEK, Josef (1758–1825)
b. Selé, Bohemia. An early pianist whose pf playing is said to have been admired by Mozart. Performed before, and taught, the nobility. It is said of him that he fell foul of Beethoven for purloining phrases and style of the Master of Bonn. His *fantaisies* and variations have been described as 'fabricated by him in large numbers', and publishers were alleged to have ordered many similar to be written by others but published under his name. Noted for ability to extemporize.

GENSS, Hermann (1856–1940)
b. Tilsit, Lithuania. Pf pupil of L. Köhler, also of K. Taubert at Berlin Hochschule. Performed and taught successively in Lübeck and Hamburg, later Director of Mainz Cons. and from 1893 of Scharwenka–Klindworth Cons. in Berlin. Settled in USA in 1899 as pf prof. at Irving Inst., San Francisco.

GENTY, Jacques (1921–)
b. Paris, France. Studied there, teachers including L. Lévy. Début 1941 Paris. Has had distinguished career as soloist, ensemble player, teacher and conductor. Recorded important works of the pf repertoire.

GEORGIADIS, Georges (1912–)
b. Salonika, Greece. Student of Athens Cons., where he became pf prof. in 1943. Made successful appearances as soloist, and his compositions include a *Concertino* for pf and orch., chamber music, pf solos and songs.

GEORGII, Walter (1887–1967)
b. Stuttgart, Germany. Studied at the Cons.

there under M. Pauer. Performed, then taught Imperial Russian School of Music, Voronesh, before moving to Halle. In addition to concert career, taught successively at Leipzig and Cologne. Made a special study of Weber's pf works, propagating them in public as well as editing some; also obtained a PhD for a paper on *Weber as a Piano Composer* (1914). Wrote essays on other musical subjects.

GERDINE, Leigh (1917–)
b. N. Dakota, USA. Studied at university there and in Oxford. Pf pupil of L. Kentner. Mainly academic career.

GERHARD, Roberto (1896–1970)
b. Valls, Spain. Pf pupil of E. Granados, then, after 1916, with Pedrell for five years. In 1923 he went to Schoenberg and stayed five years. For next ten years, until 1938, he taught in Barcelona, becoming supervisor of the music section of the Catalan Library. At the end of the Spanish Civil War he left Spain in 1938, went to UK and settled in Cambridge on a research scholarship at King's Coll. Wrote variety of music including a Piano Trio (1918), pf solos and songs.

GERMER, Heinrich (1837–1913)
b. Sommersdorf, Germany. Student of Berlin Acad. Concert pianist who lived in Dresden and wrote technical works that were highly esteemed; edited and arranged for publishers; also selected works for teaching purposes.

GERNSCHEIM, Friedrich (1839–1916)
b. Worms, Germany. Student of Leipzig Cons. and of I. Moscheles for pf. Became pf prof. at European music colleges. Compositions include pf concertos, chamber music and songs.

GERSHWIN, George (1898–1937)
b. Brooklyn, NY, USA. Pupil of E. Hutcheson, turning to popular music in 1917 while working as pianist for Victor Herbert and Jerome Kern. Produced *Rhapsody in Blue* (1924) which proved so popular that Walter Damrosch commissioned him to write a pf concerto which was premièred in 1925. A *Second Rhapsody* was premièred under Serge Koussevitzky in 1932. Besides composing songs and musical comedies, he made regular appearances playing his works in USA and Europe. His last work for pf and orch., *Variations on 'I Got Rhythm'*, was written in 1934. Recorded

Columbia and *RCA*. The *3 Preludes* are occasionally performed by concert pianists. His *Songbook* (1932), published in two editions, contains eighteen of his songs, each followed by short improvisations for pf solo and demonstrates his accomplishment in this field.

GERSTMAN, Blanche (1910–)
b. Cape Town, S. Africa. Pupil of SA Coll. of Music. Played a number of instruments and taught. Composed chamber music, pf pieces and songs.

GHYS, Henri (1839–1908)
b. Toulon, France. Pupil of Paris Cons. under A. Marmontel, gaining 1st Prize in 1854. Soon became celebrated pf teacher in society circles as well as a prolific composer of largely salon pieces.
    Pupils included: Maurice Ravel.

GIBB, James (–)
b. Monkseaton, UK. Studied in Edinburgh and London. Début 1949 London and has since performed and taught, playing solo, with orch. and in ensemble.

GIBSONE, Guillaume Ignace (1826–97)
b. London, UK, of Scottish parentage. Studied with I. Moscheles and from 1845 performed from Brussels for a time. Returned to London in 1850 where he worked as concert pianist, teacher and composer of chamber music, pf pieces and songs.

GIDEON, Miriam (1906–)
b. Colorado, USA. Pf pupil of F. Fox. Her musical life was spent mainly teaching and composing, including suites for pf, a sonatina for two pfs and a number of chamber works.

GIESEKING, Walter Wilhelm (1895–1956)
b. Lyons, France, of German parentage. Played pf from early age but did not receive any real formal training until he became a pupil of Hanover Cons., 1911–16. Début 1915, then was on war service 1916–18. Resumed career touring Europe. London début 1923; New York début 1926. Became established as a foremost interpreter of German classics and of French impressionism especially Debussy, which was still novel to the musical public and for which his remarkable command of nuances and general refinement was ideal. Gave many first performances, and it was claimed he had the ability to memorize a new score merely by

reading it through with concentration. Composed chamber music and pf pieces; also transcribed Richard Strauss songs and wrote articles on pf subjects. Recorded on *Odeon, Parlophone, Columbia*, EMI, Saga and IPA., including works of Ravel and Debussy.

Pupils included, Kurt Bauer, Mary Boehm, Joerg Demus, Albert Ferber, Stewart Gordon, Werner Haas, Antonio Tauriello, Herbert Ruff, Malcolm Troup.

GILELS, Emil Gregorevich (1916–)
b. Odessa, Russia. Pf pupil of Cons. there, then of Moscow Cons. and of H. Neuhaus. First recital outside USSR 1933 in Vienna where he later won 2nd Prize in Pf Comp., 1936. Winner 1st Prize Ysaÿe Comp., Brussels, 1938. Pf prof. at Moscow Cons. from 1951. UK début 1953; US début 1955. Gave première of Prokofiev 8th pf sonata 1944 which is dedicated to him. Recorded various labels. A daughter, Elena G, is also a pianist who appeared solo and in duos with her father.
Pupils included: Milena Mollova.

GILLESPIE, Rhondda (1941–)
b. Sydney, Australia. Studied at Sydney Cons., then in London with L. Kentner and D. Matthews, winning H. Cohen Medal 1966. Recorded Vista and Argo.

GIL-MARCHEX, Henri (1894–1970)
b. St Georges d'Esperanche, France. Pupil of Paris Cons. and of L. Diémer and A. Cortot. Toured and became well known especially in French music, sponsoring it at the Int. Festival of Chamber Music, Salzburg, 1923. Played in an all-Ravel concert in Aeolian Hall, London, 1924; made pf transcriptions of contemporary French orch. works and composed songs etc. Recorded *Columbia*.

GIMPEL, Jakob (1906–)
b. Lwow, Poland. Studied there and with E. Steuermann. Settled in USA, performed and held professional teaching appointments. Was one of three brothers who formed a pf trio. Recorded *EMI* and various.

GINASTERA, Alberto (1916–83)
b. Buenos Aires, Argentina. Studied privately and at the Cons. Williams, becoming an excellent pianist. Visited USA 1945 where he spent a year absorbing the musical scene, meeting influential people and composing. On his return home founded a Cons. for music and dance; also created local branch of ISCM. His compositions, which reflect North as well as South American styles, include two pf concertos, 3 sonatas and pieces like the early *Argentine Dances* (1937). Settled in Switzerland from 1971.
Pupils included: Gerardo Gandini.

GINZBURG, Dov (1906–)
b. Warsaw, Poland. Student of Warsaw Cons. Début there 1925. Performed successfully and later settled in Israel. Additionally percussionist and composer.

GIORNI, Aurelio (1895–1938)
b. Perugia, Italy. Pf pupil of G. Sgambati at Rome Cons. Début there 1912; thereafter toured Europe. Emigrated to USA 1915, where he performed solo and as member of Elshuco Trio. Held a number of teaching posts, wrote chamber music, pf *études* and songs.

GIPPS, Ruth (1921–)
b. Bexhill, UK. Student of R. Coll. of Music, London; pf pupil of A. Alexander and of T. Matthay. 'Adult' début at 10 in Haydn pf concerto. Has written pf pieces and chamber music, also pf concerto. Contributed to musical Press.

GIUSTINI, Luigi (–)
Composed a volume of sonatas published in 1732 under the title *12 Sonate da cembalo di piano e forte detto volgaramente dei martellati*, believed the first pf music to be written, republished in London in 1933 by R. Harding.

GLAZER, Frank (–)
Request to last-known concert agents for biographical details met with no response.

GLAZOUNOV, Alexander (1865–1936)
b. St Petersburg, Russia. Principal teachers N. Yelenkovsky for pf and Rimsky-Korsakov for composition. Appeared little in public as soloist but composed an appreciable amount including two pf concertos and two pf sonatas, variations and chamber works, plus a cantata for women's chorus, solo and two pianos (eight hands). The main pf works came later in life, Op. 72 and upwards.

GLINKA, Mikhail Ivanovich (1804–57)
b. nr Smolensk, Russia. Pf training from C. Mayer, apart from one or two lessons from J.

Field. Wrote chamber music, pf pieces and songs. Pianists now remember him only as the composer of *The Lark*, a song which Balakirev transcribed for pf with great effect. Wrote *Memoirs* (1855).

GLOCK, Sir William (1908–)
b. London, UK. Student at Cambridge Univ. and later pf pupil of A. Schnabel. Developed reputation as critic, lecturer and administrator in BBC music, but was also solo pianist, concerto and chamber-music player. Knighted 1970.

GLORIEUX, François (1932–)
b. Courtrai, Belgium. Studied there and at Ghent Cons., graduating at the age of 21. Subsequently toured the Americas, Europe, Africa and the Middle East. Composed a pf sonata as well as pieces, also *Mouvements* for pf, brass and percussion which received its première in Brussels in 1964.

GLOVER, Sarah Ann (1785–1867)
b. Norwich, UK. Pf teacher who invented tonic sol-fa notation through a wallchart known as 'the Norwich sol-fa ladder'. The chart was later taken up and developed by John Curwen, founder of the firm of London music publishers.

GNATTALI, Radames (1906–)
b. Porto Alegre, Brazil. Studied in Rio de Janeiro; pf gold medallist 1924. Pianist and viola-player. Composed a concerto and a concertino for pf and orch., chamber music, pf pieces and songs.

GOBBAERTS, Jean Louis (1835–86)
b. Antwerp, Belgium. Pupil of Brussels Cons. and reputed to be splendid concert pianist. Prolific composer in light field, publishing under several pen-names.

GOCKEL, August (1831–61)
b. Westphalia, Germany. Studied at Leipzig Cons. under F. Mendelssohn and L. Plaidy. Toured from 1848, making an extensive visit to USA.

GODDARD, Arabella (1836–1922)
b. St Servan, France. Began lessons with F. Kalkbrenner at age of 6; later studied with S. Thalberg; finally with J. W. Davidson whom she married in 1859. Played to Queen Victoria when she was 8 and made her début in 1850 in London, soon becoming equally famous on the Continent as one of the foremost women pianists; also amongst the first artists to play from memory and dispense with the music sheets in public. Was great favourite with audiences of the Phil. Soc., London, appearing no less than seventeen times between 1856 and 1878 during which she was addicted to playing Sterndale Bennett concertos, and twice played a Bach *Prelude and Fugue* under the extraordinary programme title 'à la Tarantella'. Was awarded the Society's Gold Medal in 1871.

GODOWSKY, Leopold (1870–1938)
b. Vilna, Lithuania. At the age of 3 he passed into the care of an uncle who had studied violin with Henryk Wieniawski. By his own efforts this small boy found his way around his uncle's pf, acquiring mastery of the keyboard to such effect that he made his début at the age of 9. Years later he recalled that in some way, in a manner seemingly as perfectly natural as learning to eat, he gained masterly control of the instrument. He denied ever being a pupil of Ernst Rudorff in Berlin or of Saint-Saëns in Paris, although he acknowledged indebtedness to both for befriending him.

As a teenager he gave recitals in western Europe without creating overmuch stir in musical circles and in 1884 sailed for the USA, making his début there in Boston. He was more successful, the critics were kindly, and he stayed in America for two years. The period 1886–90 was spent in London and Paris, and it was at this time that his friendship with Saint-Saëns developed. Then he returned to New York, married and became a US citizen. In 1900 he made his Berlin début and achieved a sensational success which made him internationally famous. He remained in Berlin for some time, teaching and using the city as a base from which to tour. He was Director of the Master School of the Imperial R. Acad., Vienna, from 1909 to 1912, then went back to New York which thereafter became his home. In 1910 he had been engaged by the R. Phil. Soc. in London for their Chopin Centenary concert to play the E minor concerto, also the *Barcarolle* and 3rd scherzo.

He was numbered amongst the very greatest musicians of his generation, and his company was sought by fellow-pianists of the calibre of Hofmann and Rachmaninov. His studio in New York became a sort of musical Mecca wherein the finest playing and most stimulating conversation were to be heard by those lucky enough to gain entrance. Contemporaries said that he came to prefer performing before a private gathering to playing in large halls and that under salon conditions fantastic feats were performed (ref. *Speaking of Pianists* by Abram Chasins). He continued to teach.

Godowsky once said: 'Technique properly concerns itself with the discriminating use of the tools, the employment of the tones in making a masterly musical picture, whether that picture be a composition or an interpretation. What if painters spent all of their time contemplating or discussing their brushes? There would be very little art in the world. The main thing is creation. The preservation of personality is the all-important thing in the interpretative artist. The best teachers are those who give most thought to this.'

In 1930 he suffered a stroke in London during a session of extensive gramophone recordings and never played again. Recorded *Brunswick* and *Columbia* (American and British).

His compositions are fantastically complex, especially the 53 studies based on Chopin's own sets, and transcriptions of Strauss waltzes. He arranged pieces by Bach, Brahms and Weber, and *lieder* by Schubert. Also wrote a long and difficult sonata and the *Java Suite*, as well as instructional works.

Pupils included: Clarence Adler, Fannie Dillon, Issay Dobrowen, Hans Ebell, David Guion, Harold Henry, Leonard Liebling, Clarence Loomis, Mana-Zucca, Nina Mesierow-Minchin, John Mokreis, Heinrich Neuhaus, Felix Petyrek, Walter M. Rummel, Augusta Schnabel-Tollefsen, Vladimir Shavich, Zadel Skolovsky, Jan Smeterlin, Noel Straus, Paul Wells, Wesley Weyman.

GODZINSKY, George (1914–)
b. St Petersburg, Russia. Student at Helsinki Cons. and of S. Palmgren. Toured as accompanist and composed.

GOEDICKE, Alexander Fedorivich (1877–1957)
b. Moscow, Russia. Pupil of Cons. there whose pf teacher was V. Safonov. Won the Gold Medal 1898. His *Concertstück* for pf and orch. won the Rubinstein Prize in Vienna in 1900. Later became pf prof. at Moscow Cons.

GOEPFART, Karl Eduard (1859–1942)
b. Weimar, Germany. Pupil of father and later

of F. Liszt. Composed chamber music and songs.

GOETZ, Hermann (1840–76)
b. Könisberg (now Kaliningrad, USSR). Pf pupil of L. Köhler there, later studying in Berlin 1860–63, where his pf teacher was H. von Bülow. Worked thereafter from Switzerland, performing and composing. Also conducted and played the organ. Composed a pf concerto, chamber music, pf pieces and songs.

GOLDBECK, Robert (1839–1908)
b. Potsdam, Germany. Studied with L. Köhler and with H. Litolff. Resided successively in London, New York and other American cities. Returned to Europe 1899–1903 but finally settled in St Louis. Concert pianist and teacher who founded a number of schools. Wrote a book on harmony, also an *Encyclopaedia of Music* in two volumes.

GOLDE, Walter (1887–1963)
b. New York, USA. Studied pf there and later in Vienna; then went on to study voice, 1922–31. Formed excellent career teaching and conducting, also accompanying many celebrated singers and instrumentalists. Wrote pf pieces and songs.

GOLDENBERG, Franciszek (1896–1960)
b. Sumatra of Polish parentage. Studied pf in Hamburg, then later with A. Schnabel in Berlin. Début 1915 under Mengelberg followed by European tour away from war zones. Settled in USA after World War I.

GOLDENWEISER, Alexander Borissovich (1875–1961)
b. Moscow, Russia. Pupil of Cons. there and of L. Pabst and A. Siloti, graduating with Gold Medal 1897. Commenced career as touring pianist then was prof. at the music school of the Moscow Phil. Soc. 1904–6, in the latter year joining Moscow Cons. as pf prof., and Director from 1922. Was a lifelong advocate of Scriabin's cause, and dedicatee of Rachmaninov's 2nd *Suite* for two pfs Op. 17.

Pupils included: Lazar Berman, Sergei Evseiev, Samuel Feinberg, Dmitri Kabalevsky, Tatiana Nikolayeva, Nikolai Petrov, Isabella Vengerova, Oxana Yablonskaya.

GOLDMARK, Karl (1830–1915)
b. Keszthely, Austria. Largely a self-taught pianist. Début 1858 Vienna, playing own pf

concerto. Subsequently wrote much chamber music and pf works for two and four hands. Uncle of Rubin G.

GOLDMARK, Rubin (1872–1936)
b. New York, USA. Nephew of Karl G. Studied pf in New York, then in Vienna under A. Door. On returning to USA he continued studies with R. Joseffy. Later taught at the Nat. Cons. and was for a time Director of the Cons. of Colorado. There followed a spell of lecturing throughout N. America. Taught at Juilliard School from 1924. Composed pf works, chamber music (of which a pf quartet won the Paderewski Prize 1910) and songs.
Pupils included: Creighton Allen, Abram Chasins, Fannie Dillon, Solomon Pimsleur, Frank Sheridan, Jascha Zayde.

GOLDOWSKY, Boris (1908–)
b. Moscow, Russia. Pf pupil of P. Luboschutz, then of A. Schnabel in Berlin and of E. von Dohnányi in Budapest. Début 1921 with Berlin PO. US début 1930, where he settled.

GOLDSAND, Robert (1911–)
b. Vienna, Austria. Pupil of H. Kanner-Rosenthal. Début Vienna 1921. New York début 1927. Also appeared in UK. Resided in USA, teaching at Cincinnati Cons. and Manhattan School. Specialized in music of Chopin to which he brought a refined style and great musicality. Recorded *Decca*, Nixa and Desto.

GOLDSCHMIDT, Otto (1829–1907)
b. Hamburg, Germany. Studied there and later at Leipzig Cons. under H. von Bülow for pf and F. Mendelssohn for composition, afterwards residing for some time in Paris. London début 1849 in a concert with Jenny Lind for whom he acted as accompanist during her US tour of 1851, marrying her in Boston the following year. Later settled in London where he busied himself with the affairs of the Phil. Soc., took a post at the R. Acad. in 1863 and founded the Bach Choir in 1875. As conductor is credited with having given the first British performance of the Bach *Mass in B minor*. Composed a pf concerto, a pf trio, studies etc.

GOLDSCHMIDT, Sigmund (1815–77)
b. Prague, Czechoslovakia. Pf pupil of J. Tomásek. Toured Europe and made an especially favourable impression on Paris. At height of career turned amateur in order to take over management of father's mercantile affairs.

GOLDSTONE, Anthony (1944–)
b. Liverpool, UK. Pupil at R. Manchester Coll. of Music. Début 1968 London. Performed in Europe and Americas. Recorded Oryx.

GOLINELLI, Stefano (1818–91)
b. Bologna, Italy. Studied there, becoming pf prof. at the Liceo. Toured Europe many times and was prolific composer including 5 sonatas and 48 preludes.

GOOD, Margaret (–)
b. London, UK. Student of R. Acad.; also received lessons from T. Matthay. Won MacFarren Gold Medal and became ARAM. Début 1930 Rudolf Steiner Hall, London. Thereafter performed throughout Europe. Specialized in ensemble work, playing especially with her husband, cellist William Pleeth. Together they have given numerous premières of works by British composers, especially G. Jacob, Seiber, Rubbra and Wordsworth. Recorded *Decca* and Jupiter.

GOODMAN, Isador (1909–82)
b. Cape Town, S. Africa. Appeared in public from the age of 6 and played a Mozart concerto with the SO there the following year. Studied at R. Coll. of Music, London, from 1919, being appointed a pf prof. in 1927. The following year won the Chappell and Challen Gold Medals. In 1930 joined Sydney Cons., Australia, which country became his home although he toured worldwide solo and with orch. with a repertoire containing little music of this century. A notable teacher who, in one obituary notice, was called 'that grand old man of Australian music'. Recorded *Decca* and other labels.

GOODSON, Katharine (1872–1958)
b. Watford, UK. Student at R. Acad., London, under O. Beringer, later spending four years in Vienna with T. Leschetizky. Début 1897 London and quickly established a reputation as one of the finest British women pianists. Toured Europe and USA and had secure technique and a repertoire solidly based for the most part on the classics, though she did sponsor modern works, e.g. the Delius pf concerto. Married the composer-conductor Arthur Hinton (1869–1941) whose pf concerto she performed at her first appearance for the R. Phil. Soc., London, in 1911.

Pupils included: Sir Clifford Curzon, Michal Hambourg, Frank Laffitte.

GOODWIN, Amina Beatrice (1867–1942)
b. Manchester, UK. Student of K. Reinecke and of S. Jadassohn at Leipzig Cons.; later of E. Delaborde in Paris where she won a scholarship to the Cons. Had already appeared in public in UK when she received lessons from F. Liszt, finally studying with K. Schumann. Reappeared 1892 in London and rapidly became a celebrity as soloist and chamber-music player. Founded Pianoforte Coll. for Ladies in London 1895. Wrote a book on pf technique. Became equally well known in Europe but retired from the platform early.

GOOSSENS, Sir Eugene (1893–1962)
b. London, UK. Student of R. Coll. of Music, London, including pf. Wrote works for the instrument, including the suite *Kaleidoscope* and *Hurdy-Gurdy Man*, chamber music and *Fantasy Concerto* for two pfs and orch., which had its première at London Proms 1944. Knighted 1955. Wrote *Overture and Beginners* (1951).

GORDON, Stewart Lynell (1930–)
b. Olathe, USA. Student of Univs. of Kansas and Rochester, also of W. Gieseking. Toured USA and Europe and taught in N. America. Founder and Director of Maryland Int. Pf Festival and Comp. in 1971.

GORIA, Alexandre Édouard (1823–60)
b. Paris, France. Pupil of Paris Cons., studying pf with P. Zimmerman. Won 1st Prize 1835. Taught mainly thereafter besides composing light salon pf pieces.

GORINI, Gino (1914–)
b. Venice, Italy. Studied pf there, graduating with honours in 1931. Became pf prof. there from 1940 as well as having an international career as pianist. Composed extensively in chamber music genre.

GORNO, Albino (1859–1945)
b. Casalmorano, Italy. Pupil of Milan Cons., winning three Gold Medals. Début there followed by a concert career which included acting as accompanist to Adelina Patti on her US tour of 1881–2. Settled in Cincinnati where he became pf prof. at the Coll. of Music. His pf compositions show a marked interest for two instruments.

GORNO, Romeo (1870–1931)
b. Cremona, Italy. Pupil of Milan Cons. On graduation visited USA and liked it so much that he settled in Cincinnati from which he performed as soloist and member of a trio. Also gave lecture-recitals. Pf prof. at Cincinnati Coll.
Pupils included: Clarence Adler.

GORODNITZKI, Sascha (1905–)
b. Kiev, Russia. His parents emigrated to the USA when he was very young. Studied at the Juilliard School with J. and R. Lhevinne, graduating with honours. Début 1930 with New York PO. Successful concert career followed and in 1932 he joined Juilliard School as pf prof.
Pupils included: Janina Fialkowska, Raymond Jackson, Diana Kacso, Andres Liigand, Garrick Ohlsson.

GOTTSCHALK, Louis Moreau (1829–69)
b. New Orleans, USA. His father was a settler from Europe, his mother of French-Creole origin. Louis Moreau, eldest of five children, showed musical ability from the age of 3 and made rapid progress at the pf as well as studying the violin. Went to Paris in 1842, studying under C. Hallé and later C.-M. Stamaty. There he made his début in 1845 and, with the aid of aunts on his mother's side, rapidly became a favourite entertainer in Parisian salons, being especially noted for his improvisations. Following a bout of typhoid entailing enforced rest, he studied composition with Hector Berlioz, who promoted a series of highly successful concerts for his pupil, and later toured France before spending two years in Spain, a country he found much to his liking. Back in Paris in 1852 he gave farewell concerts before returning to the USA, where his first tour coincided with the US début of S. Thalberg.

As one of the first American-born virtuosos he played many of his own compositions in his recitals. One New York critic even preferred them to the works of Beethoven! At that time his output was indebted to Spanish influences derived through his sojourn in Madrid; later, in the course of touring Central America, he was to use Creole melodies (perhaps learned when a child from his mother). It is possible they were in due course taken up by Negro pianists in New Orleans–St Louis area, becoming a formative influence for ragtime and blues. Peter Gammond, in his book on Scott Joplin and the Ragtime Era says: 'Ragtime is nearer to

West Indian than African origins, where we can find its links with the Creole type of melody exploited by that unusual American composer Louis Moreau Gottschalk.'

In Havana in 1860, in the course of touring the W. Indies, he met up with A. Napoleon, and they proceeded to form a successful duo team. The tour became a nomadic wander throughout the Antilles, and history does not record how G managed to transport instruments let alone tune and maintain them. It is known he enjoyed spells of idleness midst idyllic landscapes, demands on his purse alone causing him to play. During this period records of his repertoire are meagre, but it would seem he performed his own music whether composed or improvised.

In 1862 he returned to the USA and to more formal concert work. Critics began to cavil over the emptiness of his own works as well as his pyrotechnical virtuosity, but the public seemed to love both. A contemporary wrote of him at this time: 'He passed through life as would a splendid wild singing bird, making music because it was the law of his being, but never directing that talent with conscious energy to some purpose beyond itself.'

In 1865 he went south once more, spending four years being fêted in S. America and giving many concerts without apparently sating the appetite of his audiences. The period may have vividly reminded him of the happy days he had spent in Spain almost twenty years before. In the spring of 1869 he suffered an attack of yellow fever in Rio from which he never fully recovered, dying at the end of that year.

George Ferris, one-time music critic, took the view that G's gifts were never more than half-developed: that before his death he showed signs of 'having ripened into more earnest views and purposes'. A contemporary in New York described his playing as 'sparkling, dashing, showy, but, in the judgment of the most judicious, he did not appear to good advantage in comparison with Thalberg, in whom a perfect technique was dominated by a conscious intellectualism, and a high ideal, passionless but severely beautiful'.

In 1969, to commemorate the centenary of his death, the US Louis Moreau Gottschalk Comp. was founded there, sponsored by the Organization of American States. An annual competition was to be held in Puerto Rico, open to pianists and composers of any nationality. Using normal channels of communication, the writer has been unable to trace the whereabouts of the headquarters of this competition.

G's compositions have been catalogued in chronological order by the musicologist Robert Offergold, the numbers appearing in brackets preceded by 'RO'. A diary of G's activities which he kept between 1857 and 1868 was published posthumously in 1881.

Pupils included: Teresa Carreño, Ignacio Cervantes.

GOULD, Glenn (1932–82)
b. Toronto, Canada. Was taught pf by his mother from the age of 3. When he was 10 he entered the R. Cons. there, remaining under A. Guerrero for nine years, in later years describing his lessons as exercises in arguments. Début with Toronto SO in 1946 when he began performing. US début 1955 was followed in 1957 by a European tour, and he claimed he was the first N. American pianist to tour the USSR. He also appeared in a series of concerts with the Israel PO in 1958.

He acquired an enviable reputation upon a mere forty-odd public appearances before falling under the spell of the microphone for broadcasting and recording. Becoming averse to the life of a concert pianist, he retired from the concert platform in 1964 at the age of 32. He in fact predicted the eventual closure of concert halls, insisting that the musical public would come more and more to prefer hearing music electronically.

His radio broadcasts were hugely popular, and he made documentary programmes as well as giving pf recitals. His repertoire ranged from Byrd to Schoenberg, and his reputation came to rest in the main on studio recordings for CBS.

GOULD, Morton (1913–)
b. New York, USA. Student of Juilliard School and of NY Univ., where, at the age of 15, he took a short course of composition while playing the pf anywhere he was asked. In 1931 became pianist in the music hall of Radio City and in 1934 began working in radio as a conductor. Two years later his *Chorale and Fugue in Jazz* for two pfs and orch. was premièred under L. Stokowski with the composer as one of the pianists. Wrote serious and light works for concert hall, films, TV, radio and ballet; and his music attracted the attention of musicians as diverse as Toscanini and Benny Goodman. There are also a pf concerto and three sonatas. He wrote to order *Inventions* for

four pfs and orch. especially for Steinway's centenary concert in Carnegie Hall 1953. Recorded RCA, Columbia, Everest and others.

GOUSSEAU, Lélia (1909–)
b. Paris, France. Student of Paris Cons. and prizewinner. Performed widely throughout the world solo and with orch., also taught. Propagated the Dukas pf sonata among French contemporary music. Prof. at Paris Cons. from 1961.
 Pupils included: Pascal Devoyon, Maria de la Pau, Anne Queffélec.

GRABOWSKA, Clementina (1771–1831)
b. Poznan, Poland. Studied in Poland but was resident in Paris from 1813 as a leading woman concert pianist. Composed pf works. Was a countess. Arthur Hedley mentions in his biography of Chopin that she gave a soirée in 1817 in Warsaw at which the young Chopin played.

GRAÇA, Fernando Lopes (1906–)
b. Tomar, Portugal. Pupil of Lisbon Cons. and completed studies in Paris. Taught in Lisbon, performed and composed, including two pf concertos, chamber music, pf works and songs. Has written extensively.

GRADOVA, Gitta (1905–)
b. Chicago, USA, of Russian descent. A somewhat legendary figure of the pf world who made a distinguished Paris début. Her performance of the Rachmaninov *Rhapsody* under Sir John Barbirolli in New York around 1936 aroused the composer's admiration. Her fashionable home in Chicago became a noted salon for the cream of the musical world, especially of Russian ancestry.

GRAF, Hans (1928–)
b. Vienna, Austria. Student of Vienna Acad. Performed throughout Europe and the Americas and from 1958 conducted own master-class in Vienna Academy. Was on teaching staff of Indiana Univ.
 Pupils included: Noel Flores.

GRAFFMAN, Gary (1928–)
b. New York, USA. Pupil of I. Vengerova at Curtis Inst., also of V. Horowitz and R. Serkin. Début 1936 Philadelphia. European début 1950. Established international reputation. Gave première of pf works of Benjamin

Lees: the 4th sonata of 1963, and the 2nd concerto in 1968. Recorded CBS.
 Pupils included: Lydia Artimiw.

GRAHAM, Alasdair (1934–)
b. Glasgow, UK. Studied in Edinburgh and Vienna, also with P. Katin. Has performed extensively including a world tour 1966.

GRAINGER, Percy Aldridge (1882–1961)
b. Brighton, Australia. Taught by his mother until the age of 10, then was under L. Pabst for two years before his mother took him to Germany to study with J. Kwast in Frankfurt. Toured Germany 1900 and UK 1901. Met Grieg in 1906 in London and played his pf concerto in Leeds and several other cities. US début New York, 1915, where he settled and joined armed forces in World War I. On release resumed concert work and taught pf in various schools. His friendship with Grieg had aroused his interest in folk-music, especially British, which he began researching and arranging. Is now remembered for this work rather than his pianism. Wrote much for pf, including a brilliant transcription of Tchaikovsky's *Valse des Fleurs* which is in no way inferior to any of the 19th-century concert waltz paraphrases. Also made arrangement for pf of themes from R. Strauss's *Rosenkavalier*. Recorded *Columbia* including 1st electrical recording of an instrumental sonata in 1925.
 Pupils included: Mary Louise Barratt, Gordon Bryan, Leo Sowerby.

GRANADOS, Eduardo (1894–1928)
b. Barcelona, Spain. Son of Enrique G. Studied pf and composition at the Granados Acad., taught there 1910–16, then became its Director on the tragic death of his father. Also conducted concerts of their music.

GRANADOS, Enrique (1867–1916)
b. Lerida, Spain. Studied pf at Barcelona Cons., then in Paris with C. de Bériot. Settled in Barcelona in 1899, teaching, composing and establishing a reputation as a brilliant virtuoso. Was for a time pianist in a quartet comprising J. Thibaud (violin), Manén (viola) and Casals (cello). Established a concert society in 1900 and the following year his own pf school, Academia Granados. His most famous work is *Goyescas*, a set of pf pieces inspired by Goya paintings. Later Fernando Periquet provided a libretto and the composer turned the original score into an opera which had its première in

New York in Jan. 1916 attended by G. Returned to Europe in HMS *Sussex* which was torpedoed in English Channel. G was drowned trying to save his wife. Wrote much pf music besides *Goyescas* including four volumes of *Spanish Dances*. Ernest Newman wrote: 'The texture of Granados' music, like that of Chopin's, is of the kind that makes you want to run your fingers over it, as over some exquisite velvet; the flavour of it is something for the tongue almost, as well as the ear. An exceedingly adventurous harmonist, he never writes a chord or a sequence that does not sound well and talk continuous sense; to play through some of his pages is like a joyous wading knee-deep through beds of gorgeous flowers – always with a sure way through, and the clearest of light and air around us.' Recorded *Odeon*.

Pupils included: Roberto Gerhard, Frank Marshall, Baltasar Samper.

GRAY, Edith (1890–1935)
b. Boston, USA. Studied there and later with E. Hutcheson. Toured USA extensively solo and with orch.

GRAY, Isabel (1898–)
b. Dundee, UK. Pupil at R. Acad., London. Début 1918 London. Pf prof. at R. Acad.; also concert recitalist. Gave first performance in London 1921 of *Concertino* for pf and orch. by the American composer John Alden Carpenter.

GRAY, Julian de (1905–)
b. Harrisburg, USA. Pupil of L. Lévy and T. Matthay. Début London 1929. Chappell Gold Medallist. Toured Europe and USA (New York début 1930). Pf prof. in various US appointments, including Bennington Coll. 1932–71.

GREATOREX, Richard (1919–)
b. Calcutta, India. Studied there. Pf prof. at R. Manchester School from 1949. Also performed.

GREEF, Arthur de (1862–1940)
b. Louvain, Belgium. Studied at Brussels Cons. with L. Brassin and later with F. Liszt at Weimar. Was pf prof. at Brussels Cons. from 1885 and toured regularly as renowned performer in Beethoven, Chopin and Liszt. Was a friend of E. Grieg and of C. Saint-Saëns and was noted for playing their concertos in A minor and G minor respectively. From 1916

played in London Proms, often on the opening night. His pf concerto was given by him at the Proms of 1921. Composed also a fantaisie for pf and orch., pf pieces and studies, and songs. Recorded *HMV*.

Pupils included: Francis de Bourguignon, Victor Buesst, Maurice Cole, John D. Davis, C. Fontova, Richard Hageman, William James, Alberto Jonás, Herbert Menges, Raymond Moulart, Edmundo Pallemaerts, Marcel Poot, Lewis Richards.

GREEN, Gordon (1905–81)
b. Barnsley, UK. Pupil of F. Merrick at R. Manchester Coll. and later of E. Petri. Taught at that college from 1945 until becoming pf prof. at London R. Acad. in 1962. Came to be rated as a foremost teacher.

Pupils included: Christian Blackshaw, Ronald Brautigem, Stephen Hough, John McCabe, John Ogdon, Martin Roscoe, David Silkoff, Heather Slade, Martino Tirimo.

GREENBAUM, Kyla (1922–)
b. Brighton, UK. Pupil of R. Acad., London, later studying in Budapest. Toured extensively thereafter, specializing in contemporary music. Gave first British performance of Schoenberg pf concerto in 1945, and the same of Prokofiev 2nd pf concerto in 1955; also had Lambert's *Rio Grande* in her repertoire. Sister of the conductor Hyam Greenbaum. Recorded *Columbia*.

GREENFIELD, Bruce (1948–)
b. Wellington, New Zealand. Studied at Victoria Univ. there. Mus B. Concert pianist, accompanist and teacher.

GREENSLADE, Hubert (1909–)
b. Cape Town, S. Africa. Studied in London, especially at Trinity Coll. Became celebrated accompanist to some of the world's leading artists. Adjudicated and lectured. Recorded various (as accompanist).

GREGOIR, Josef Jacques (1817–76)
b. Antwerp, Belgium. Studied there and in Paris under H. Herz; later pupil of C. Rummel. A successful concert pianist who toured mid-Europe where he also taught. Wrote pf pieces and works on pf technique; also, in association with Vieuxtemps, duets for violin and pf.

GRETCHANINOV, Alexander Tikhonovich (1864–1956)

b. Moscow, Russia. Pf pupil of V. Safonov at Moscow Cons. Was composition prof. there until 1922, when he lived in Paris, later settling in USA. Wrote a large quantity of chamber music, pf works including a sonata, and a vast number of songs. Recorded *HMV* in accompanying role.

GRIEG, Edvard Hagerup (1843–1907)

b. Bergen, Norway, of Scottish ancestry, his birth coinciding with a revival in the nation's art. As a small child he showed interest in the pf and harmony, and his first teacher was his mother, who played the instrument in public. His first compositions date from the time he was 14 and when he first met Olaus (known as Ole) Bull, Norwegian violinist and visionary in the renascent movement. At 15 G went to Leipzig to study at the Cons., but he always maintained he learned little there and that the teachers and curriculum were alike dull and uninspired. His pf tutors were L. Plaidy, E. F. Wenzel and I. Moscheles, and he used to refer to difficulties he had with harmony lessons. However, records in Bergen Library show he worked hard and obediently and obtained a good graduation. In 1862, when his training ended, he appeared at a students' concert at the Gewandhaus, playing his own pf pieces. By then he had begun to write songs. That same year he made his Norwegian début in Bergen.

Dissatisfied with the German influence which Leipzig Cons. had implanted in him, he decided to work with Niels Gade, the Danish composer. In the three years 1863–6 spent in Copenhagen, probably the two most important events affecting his life were his meeting with his cousin Nina Hagerup, whom he married in 1867, and contact with Rikaard Nordraak, who in his short life greatly influenced Norwegian art and artists not least G, who, through him, discovered his national aspirations. In Copenhagen he wrote the pf sonata, the 1st violin sonata and some of the characteristic and beautiful songs that were to come from his pen.

After touring Germany and Italy he settled in Oslo 1866–74 and in the autumn of 1866 made his début there in a highly successful concert devoted to Norwegian composers. He was appointed conductor of the Phil. and established himself as a pf teacher. The following summer, during his honeymoon, he wrote the 2nd violin sonata.

During the Oslo period he relied on teaching as a living; as with Chopin, the best hours of his day were taken up with trying to teach young ladies to play the pf. He also conducted and gave concerts of his works. However, in the summer of 1868 he did compose the A minor pf concerto, which was premièred by Edmund Neupert in Copenhagen in April 1869 and thereafter achieved immediate and enduring success the world over. In the meantime the Griegs had toured Italy on a governmental grant, where G met F. Liszt from whom he received great encouragement; also notables like G. Sgambati.

Gradually he became accepted widely as a composer-pianist whose works had a characteristic harmonic flavour. Because his output has a preponderance of sets of pf pieces and songs, he has been labelled a miniaturist. Simplicity of construction as well as a great charm and freshness made them accessible to the amateur musician; while at the same time neither genre seems to have fitted well into recital programmes, and so they have been largely ignored by professional musicians.

The cello sonata was composed in 1883, and the perhaps best of his chamber works, the third violin sonata, followed in 1887. Thus Grieg provided himself with material for the type of 'mixed' recital once the vogue and where he could appear as solo pianist, as collaborator in ensemble and as accompanist to his wife Nina who, as a concert soprano, did much to popularize his unique songs in the early days.

His last concerts were given in Germany, sold out in advance, to much acclaim. He died in the summer of 1907, and his home at Troldhaugen, near Bergen, has become a shrine. E. von Dohnányi described him as 'very different from Brahms. He was good-natured, rather jovial, and full of feeling and sentiment'. And G. B. Shaw said of him as a concert artist: 'Grieg is a small, swift busy earnest man, with the eyes of a rhapsode, and in his hair and complexion the indescribably ashen tint that marks a certain type of modern Norseman.'

Compositions include the pf concerto in A minor Op. 16; pf sonata in E minor Op. 7; three violin sonatas, one cello sonata and a string quartet in G minor; *Ballade* Op. 24 (a set of variations) for pf solo together with ten books of *Lyrische Stücke*, the *Holberg Suite* Op. 40 and numerous separate pieces for solo, four hands, and two pfs, including arrangements for most of his orch. works; also groups of songs amounting in all to over 140, many with beautifully integrated pf accompaniment. Recorded *G & T*, *HMV*.

GRIFFES, Charles Tomlinson (1884–1920)
b. New York, USA. Musical education began at Elmira Acad. and ended in Berlin under G. Galston for pf, and Humperdinck for composition. Lived there as pf teacher and soloist until 1907 when he returned to the USA. Wrote works for orch., but most of his output was for pf, of which the most important is a large-scale sonata written a few years before his early death. His worth as a composer was recognized posthumously.

GRIFFIN, George Eugene (1781–1863)
b. London, UK. Concert pianist, teacher and composer. Early member of Phil. Soc. Composed two pf concertos, four sonatas, numerous pieces and songs.

GRIFFIS, Elliot (1893–1967)
b. Boston, USA. Pf pupil of Yale School of Music and later New England Cons. Taught and performed thereafter, settling in California. A composer of light pf works.

GRIMAUD, Yvette (1922–)
b. Algiers, Algeria. Was child prodigy and pupil of Paris Cons., where she graduated with 1st Prize 1941. In her compositions has utilized 'Les Ondes Martenot' invented by Maurice Martenot.

GRIMSON, Annie (–)
b. London, UK. Studied at R. Coll. and graduated with Gold Medal. Was also pupil of T. Matthay. Début 1899 London. Pianist and composer. Member of a family which produced six concert artists of whom Jessie G (sister of Annie) was the first woman violinist to play in a Queen's Hall orch.

GRINBERG, Maria (1908–79)
b. Russia. Studied in Moscow and was pupil of C. Igumnov and F. Blumenfeld. Had distinguished concert career and taught. Recorded MK.

GRITTON, Eric William (1890–1981)
b. Reigate, UK. Studied at Cambridge and R. Coll. of Music, London (Mendelssohn Scholar). Pf prof. there, and was well-known accompanist. Compositions include songs. Recorded *Decca*.

GROBE, Charles (*c*.1817–*c*.1868)
b. Weimar, Germany. Origins obscure prior to settling in USA around 1839 when he proceeded to turn out non-stop every conceivable type of pf solo and duet from fantasies to operatic arrangements and from waltzes to variations. Is believed to hold the world record with opus numbers approaching 2,000. Understandably he was an indifferent pianist, lacking the time to apply himself to that side of his career.

GRONINGEN, Stefan van (1851–1926)
b. Deventer, Netherlands. Pupil of Berlin Hochschule. Worked successively in Zwolle and The Hague as touring pianist and teacher. Composed chamber music, pf pieces and works for two pfs.

GROOT, Cor de (1914–)
b. Amsterdam, Netherlands. Student of Cons. there, graduating with honours 1932. Toured extensively before and after World War II, until nerve complaint in arm caused him to confine activities to teaching. Pf prof. at The Hague Cons. from 1938. US début 1956. Recorded *Odeon* and RCA. Compositions include a sonatina and several works for pf and orch.
Pupils included: Peter Hansen.

GROOTE, André de (1940–)
b. Brussels, Belgium. Studied at Brussels Cons. Début Johannesburg, 1955. Came 7th in Int. Tchaikovsky Comp., Moscow, 1966, and 5th in Concours Reine Elisabeth, Brussels, 1968. Appeared widely in Europe including countries behind the Iron Curtain. Pf prof., Brussels Cons. Brother of Steven de G.

GROOTE, Steven de (1953–)
b. S. Africa. Appeared in public as a prodigy, solo and in chamber music with members of his family. Student of Brussels Cons. and of E. del Pueyo, graduating with 1st Prize for pf in 1971; was then at Curtis Inst. 1972–5 under R. Serkin, M. Horszowski and S. Lipkin. New York début 1977, in which year he was a finalist in the Levintritt Comp. and came 1st in the Van Cliburn Pf Comp. In the ensuing years toured worldwide and received highly laudatory criticism. Recorded Finlandia and DG.

GROVLEZ, Gabriel (1879–1944)
b. Lille, France. Pupil of Paris Cons. under L. Diémer, gaining 1st Prize for pf playing. Toured Europe solo and in chamber recitals.

Pf prof. 1900–6. Thereafter turned conductor. Gave Paris première of Ravel's *Sonatine* in 1906. Wrote a sonata for violin and pf, also pf pieces.

GRUENBERG, Louis (1884–1964)
b. Brest-Litovsk, Russia. Went to USA in 1886. Took pf lessons from A. Margulies, then in 1903 went to Berlin to study with F. Busoni. Début Berlin 1912. Was appointed to teach at Vienna Cons. and returned to USA in 1919, where he turned to composition with a jazz flavour. Edited Negro spirituals and composed in most genres including two pf concertos and pf works in jazz style. Although influential artists like Heifetz took up his output, he suffered neglect towards the end of his life.

GRUMMITT, Margaret (1905–)
b. London, UK. Pupil of I. Philipp, Paris. Début London 1936. Performed in London area thereafter, solo and as accompanist.
Pupils included: Homer Simmons.

GRÜNBERGER, Ludwig (1839–96)
b. Prague, Czechoslovakia. Studied in Prague and Dresden. Was well-known pianist, teacher and composer of works for two and four hands.

GRÜNER-HEGGE, Odd (1899–1973)
b. Oslo, Norway. Studied with Nils Larsen and F. Backer-Gröndahl. Pf début 1918. Later added conducting and succeeded Kirsten Flagstad as Director of Norwegian Opera, Oslo, in 1960. Wrote chamber music and a pf suite. His work was popular in Norway on account of its distinctive national qualities.

GRÜNFELD, Alfred (1852–1924)
b. Prague, Czechoslovakia. Studied there at first before becoming pupil of T. Kullak in Berlin. Settled in Vienna in 1873 and speedily became famous as a virtuoso, making extended tours throughout Europe and also USA. His touch was delicate and he was regarded as especially fine in Schubert and Schumann. Wrote a number of pf works in style of the period but is remembered for his Strauss transcriptions and Wagner arrangements which used to be in the repertoire of most virtuosos.
Pupils included: Karl Ekman.

GRUNN, John Homer (1880–1944)
b. West Salem, USA. Pupil of E. Liebling; later in Berlin at Stern's Conservatoire. Returned to USA and took up mainly teaching

career in various centres, finally settling in Los Angeles in 1910.
Pupils included: Homer Simmons.

GUARNIERI, Camargo Mozart (1907–)
b. São Paulo, Brazil. Distant descendant of the Cremona violin makers of that name. Student of pf at the São Paulo Cons. where he taught the instrument from 1927. Also began composing and the 1st pf concerto was performed in São Paulo in 1936. Won a scholarship to study in Paris where he remained until the outbreak of World War II. His USA début was in 1942 when several of his works were played. On a second visit in 1946 his 2nd pf concerto had its world première. Returned in 1960 to Brazil to teach, becoming Director of the Cons. in 1961. Compositions include a pf sonatina (1928), and much music for pf including *Choro Torturado* and dances, five concertos for pf and orch. (some in the style of *choros* of Villa-Lobos), chamber music and songs.

GUERRERO, Alberto Garcia (1886–1959)
b. Serena, Chile. Self-taught pianist whose early enthusiasm set alive Chilean musical circles. Moved for a time to New York but finally settled in Toronto around 1919 as a concert pianist who became celebrated for his wide-ranging programmes. Introduced the work of 'moderns' like Milhaud, Stravinsky and Schoenberg as well as the classics. Became loved as a fine teacher who was working hard up to his death.
Pupils included: Glenn Gould.

GUERVÓS, José Maria (1870–1944)
b. Granada, Spain. Brother of Manuel G. Pupil of his father and later of R. Cons., Madrid, winning 1st Prize for pf playing 1899. Had distinguished career as soloist, accompanist and chamber-music player. Became pf prof. at Madrid Cons. Worked out a new system of notation whereby the two staves were unified by one C clef on the sixth line. Composed pf pieces and songs in the Albéniz idiom.

GUERVÓS, Manuel (1863–1902)
b. Granada, Spain. Pupil first of father then of Madrid R. Cons. winning 1st Prize for pf playing. Début 1875 Madrid and commenced career as concert pianist. In addition to solo work was Sarasate's accompanist. Composed pf pieces which were popular.

GUION, David Wendell (1895–)
b. Texas, USA. Studied at Jacksonville and Fort Worth, then in Vienna with L. Godowsky. Taught pf in Texas for many years, settling in New York as a composer of avowedly popular music and songs.

GULDA, Friedrich (1930–)
b. Vienna, Austria. Studied there and won 1st Prize in Geneva Comp. 1946. Thereafter toured Europe and USA. Researched into period music performed on authentic original instruments; also liked playing jazz. Recorded *Decca*, Decca and DG.
Pupils included: Martha Argerich, Marc Raubenheimer, Bernard Wambach.

GÜLLER, Youra (1895–)
b. Paris, France, of Russian–Romanian parentage. Was a child prodigy at 5 and toured in recitals until 9 when she entered Paris Cons. Studied under I. Philipp and gained a 1st Prize at age of 12. Thereafter performed solo and with leading instrumentalists until World War II, when she suffered ill-health which persisted until 1959. New York début 1971 by which time she had become a legendary figure. Recorded Nimbus.

GUNEYMAN, Meral (–)
b. Turkey. Won 2nd Prize in 1980 Univ. of Maryland Int. Pf Comp. Enquiries addressed to sources in Turkey met with no response.

GUNN, Glenn Dillard (1874–1963)
b. Kansas, USA. Studied initially there, then worked in Leipzig Cons. 1893–1900, pf teachers K. Reinecke and R. Teichmüller. Toured Germany then returned home, teaching at Chicago Music Coll. until 1905 when he founded his own pf school. Made successful concert appearances and in addition lectured and wrote musical criticisms, being music editor of Chicago *Herald Examiner*.

GURICKX, Camille (1848–1937)
b. Brussels, Belgium. Pf pupil of A. Dupont at Brussels Cons. Was granted government funds to visit Germany, where he met Liszt who befriended him. His Paris début in 1874 led to other concerts and a tour of Russia where he came under the beneficial influence of Anton Rubinstein. After working on composition with C. Saint-Saëns in Paris was appointed pf prof. at Mons Cons. On the death of Auguste Dupont in 1890 became head of the pf dept at Brussels.

GURLITT, Cornelius (1820–1901)
b. Altona, Germany. Studied music under the father of K. Reinecke and was an organist and pedagogue who wrote a large quantity of pf works which were once used extensively for teaching purposes.

GURT, Michael (1959–)
b. Ypsilanti, USA. Studied first with his father before obtaining a scholarship at Michigan Univ. where he graduated with highest honours. Later entered the Juilliard School of Music where he won the concerto award and appeared on TV and in recitals in New York, 1982. That same year won 1st Prize in the Gina Bachauer Pf Comp. at Utah. Toured USA and Japan.

GUSTIN, Lyell (1895–)
b. Quebec, Canada. Studied there and in New York. Held important pf teaching posts in Canada and was examiner at Toronto R. Cons.

GUTIERREZ, Horacio (1948–)
b. Havana, Cuba. Studied there, making his début at the age of 11. Family moved to Los Angeles in 1962. Student of Juilliard School where he graduated. Became US citizen 1967. Came 2nd in 1970 Tchaikovsky Comp., Moscow. New York début 1972 and London 1974. Toured successfully thereafter. Recorded EMI.

GUTMANN, Adolph (1819–82)
b. Heidelberg, Germany. Pupil of F. Chopin but accomplished little on own account either as pianist or composer. Stayed close at hand to help during Chopin's dying days. Composed a group of studies for pf. Dedicatee of the *Scherzo in C sharp minor* Op. 39.

GUZMAN, Enrique de Perez: *see* **PEREZ de GUZMAN, Enrique**

GYROWETZ, Adalbert (1763–1850)
b. Budweis, Bohemia. Son of a choirmaster and composition pupil of Nicola Sala in Naples. Precocious composer from an early age credited with 60 symphonies, over 40 ballets, many operas, three dozen pf sonatas, around 100 chamber works and an unspecified number of pf concertos, one of which F. Chopin played at his début in 1818. Said to be in the style of Haydn, all this music has long since been forgotten.

HAAS, Monique (1909–)
b. Paris, France. Pupil of Paris Cons. and of Lazare Lévy for pf. Won 1st Prize 1927. Performed extensively in Europe. Recorded *Decca*, Decca and DG. Married to the composer Marcel Mihalovici.
Pupils included: Charles Timbrell.

HAAS, Werner (1931–)
b. Stuttgart, Germany. Studied pf from an early age and eventually joined the master-class of W. Gieseking. Début in 1955 in Stuttgart. Toured Europe in possession of a wide repertoire. Recorded Philips.

HÁBA, Alois (1893–1972)
b. Visovici, Czechoslovakia. Student of Prague Cons. under V. Novák and later of Vienna Cons. Lived in Berlin where he wrote a string quartet in quarter tones, first of its kind. Taught at Prague Cons. from 1923 and researched into quarter- and sixth-tone techniques, experimenting with a number of works for pf and inventing a quarter-tone instrument. Composed *Symphonic Fantasy* for pf and orch., chamber music and quantity of pf works including two sonatas.

HABERBIER, Ernst (1813–69)
b. Königsberg (now Kaliningrad, USSR). Pupil of his father. Went to St Petersburg in 1832, quickly establishing a reputation as virtuoso and teacher. Appointed pianist to Tsar 1847. London début 1850. Settled in Oslo, from where he made concert tours of Europe. Worked on a system of splitting difficult pf passages between the hands, of great interest to musicians and apparent delight of audiences. Lived in Bergen from 1866 where he died suddenly on the concert platform. Composed much pf music of considerable difficulty.

HACKH, Otto (1852–1917)
b. Stuttgart, Germany. Studied at the Cons. there, then later with A. de Kontski in New York. Extensive concert tours followed until 1880 when he turned to teaching, mainly in USA. Wrote many pf works and songs which had a vogue.

HAEBLER, Ingrid (1926–)
b. Vienna, Austria. Studied at Salzburg and Vienna Academies, also at the Conss. of Geneva and Paris. Performed from 1954 with a wide repertoire. Acquired specialization in Mozart's works. Recorded Philips and Saga. Grand Prix du Disque 1958.

HAGEMAN, Richard (1882–1966)
b. Leeuwarden, Netherlands. Child prodigy. Studied at Brussels Cons., pf pupil of A. de Greef. After working in opera in Amsterdam, toured as accompanist to various celebrities in Europe and USA. In 1907 received offer to work as assistant conductor Metropolitan Opera and turned mainly to the baton. Wrote songs and pf pieces.

HAHN, Reynaldo (1875–1947)
b. Caracas, Venezuela. Was taken to Paris at age of 3 which remained his home. Pupil of Paris Cons. A brilliant and civilized musician who played the pf well both as soloist and as accompanist. Wrote a witty pf concerto, the equal of any similar French work of the 1930s but which is neglected, as well as many pieces and songs. Recorded some of his own songs and those of Fauré to own accompaniment on *Columbia* and accompanied Ninon Vallin in his songs on *Odeon*. Stravinsky once described him as 'a thin, elegant man with motherly manners'.

HAIG, Allan (1925–)
b. Newark, USA. Pupil at Oberlin Coll. and Juilliard School. US and European appearances. Composer in modern idiom; also arranger. Recorded various labels.

HAIGH, Thomas (1769–1808)
b. London, UK. Pupil of J. Haydn there 1791–2. Was early concert pianist who composed violin and pf, and pf sonatas and songs; also arranged some Haydn symphonies for pf.

HAJN, Bronislaw (1934–)
b. Lodz, Poland. Studied Vienna Acad. Début 1956 Kelce. Mainly accompanist.

HÁLA, Josef (1928–)
b. Czechoslovakia. Student of Prague Acad. Toured extensively as concert pianist and in ensemble work. Was pianist of Suk Trio.

HALACZ, Bogna (1934–)
b. Mikolov, Poland. Musically educated in Cracow, Belgium and Italy. Début 1959 Cracow. Known as concert pianist mainly in E. Europe, and specialized in Chopin.

HALFFTER, Cristobal (1930–)
b. Madrid, Spain. Nephew of Rodolfo H. Pupil of Madrid Cons. Composer, conductor and pianist. Has written a pf sonata and a concerto as well as songs.

HALFFTER, Rodolfo (1900–)
b. Madrid, Spain. Self-taught apart from assistance from Falla. Wrote an *Overture Concertante* for pf and orch., two sonatas and other works for pf, all in an advanced style rather than following Spanish tradition. Emigrated to Mexico after Civil War. In later years branched out into twelve-tone system.

HALL, Elsie (1879–1976)
b. Toowoomba, Australia. Was prodigy and won scholarship to R. Acad., London which was not taken up. Did perform there in early teens and earned several notices from G. B. Shaw, the last of which said it was time she went to Leschetizky to put her technique under control. Did study in Berlin, however, with E. Rudorff, winning Mendelssohn prize. Her pf playing was praised by Brahms, and she toured Europe and USA extensively, as well as teaching, including members British royal

family especially Princess Mary. Finally settled in S. Africa. Recorded *Decca*.
Pupils included: Constant Lambert.

HALLÉ, Sir Charles (1819–95)
b. Hagen, Germany. A prodigy who went to Paris in 1836 where he settled into the musical scene, making a reputation as pianist and teacher. Received lessons from F. Kalkbrenner and learned much from friendship with Chopin and Liszt. The 1848 revolution caused him to flee to London. He settled in Britain, finally in Manchester where the concerts and orch. were named after him. He remained very much a pianist as well as conductor and teacher, being among the first pianists to play all Beethoven sonatas in a cycle; also propagated the music of Chopin and Liszt. Wrote an interesting autobiography, and was knighted in 1888.
Pupils included: Frederick Dawson, Louis Gottschalk.

HALLER, Hermann (1914–)
b. Burgdorf, Switzerland. Pupil of Zurich Cons. where he won diploma for pf and composition. Completed studies with N. Boulanger and C. Marek. Pf prof. at Zurich Cons. and composer of two pf concertos and a sonata, chamber music and pf pieces.

HALLIDAY, Anthony (–)
b. Australia. Student of Melbourne Univ. and later, through scholarships, of R. Coll. of Music, London, especially with A. Morrison and C. Horsley. Broadcast on Australian radio and television, winning an ABC competition for his performance of the Bartók 2nd concerto. London début 1980, giving first London performance of Margaret Sutherland's *Chiaroscuro One and Two* in 1982. Has a wide repertoire which includes the works of Malcolm Williamson.

HALLIS, Adolph (1896–)
b. Port Elizabeth, S. Africa. Pf student at R. Acad., London, and performed in Europe before World War I, with special interest in the contemporary scene. Returned to S. Africa 1939. Dedicatee of 2nd pf concerto by E. Chisholm. Recorded *Decca*.

HALSTEAD, Philip (1866–1940)
b. Blackburn, UK. Studied at Leipzig Cons. 1885–8 under K. Reinecke and won the Mozart Prize. Played at the inaugural concert

of the new Leipzig Cons. Studies continued with B. Stavenhagen at Weimar in Liszt tradition. Resided thereafter in Glasgow area where he was a popular concert pianist, solo and with orch. Founded chamber-music concert series and taught.

Pupils included: Rae Robertson.

HAMBOURG, Mark (1879–1960)
b. Bogutchar, Russia. Son of Mikhail H, who was his first teacher. In 1889 family moved to London. Début 1890 Prince's Hall. Studied with T. Leschetizky 1891–5. Won Liszt Scholarship 1894 and played with Vienna PO 1895 at short notice. New York début 1898. Became famous on account of powerful technique and ebullient personality. Prolific recording artist but refused to broadcast until 1935. Gave première of Busoni pf concerto in London in 1910. Composed works for pf, including a set of variations on the A minor *Caprice* of Paganini, and wrote books on the art of pf playing and autobiography. The one-time Hambourg Trio consisted of Mark and his younger brothers Boris, a cellist, and Jan, violinist. G. B. Shaw wrote of his Steinway Hall London recital of 1891 (before Hambourg went to Leschetizky) that: 'He played Bach better than any other composer on his programme.' Recorded *HMV*.

Pupils included: Michal Hambourg, Poldowski, Reginald Stewart.

HAMBOURG, Michal (1919–   )
b. London, UK. Daughter of Mark H. Pupil of K. Goodson and R. Coll., London (and doubtless of father). Début London 1936 and toured UK, initially with Mark H. Recorded *HMV* with father.

HAMBOURG, Mikhail (1856–1916)
b. Yaroslav, Russia. Father of Mark H. and of Boris and Jan. Pupil of St Petersburg and Moscow Conss. Pf prof. Moscow from 1880. Performed and taught in London 1891–1911 when he settled in Canada, founding, with Boris and Jan, the Hambourg Cons. in Toronto.

Pupils included: Mark Hambourg.

HAMBRO, Leonid (–   )
b. New York, USA. Well-known pianist in serious and popular fields. Was pianist of the New York PO, being especially noted for his performances of contemporary music. Also performed on radio and television, solo and in duo appearances with his equally gifted partner Jascha Zayde. Recorded Command.

HAMBURGER, Paul (1920–   )
b. Vienna, Austria. Studied at State Acad. there, also with F. Merrick at R. Coll., London. Career mainly as accompanist; also taught, wrote and translated. Wrote *Frederick Chopin* (1966).

HAMILTON, Iain (1922–   )
b. Glasgow, UK. Student of R. Acad. of Music, London, pf teacher H. Craxton. Won various prizes and awards. Took up composition and was prof. at North Carolina Univ., USA, 1962–71, thereafter at City Univ., New York. Has written a pf concerto, chamber music and solos.

HAMPEL, Hans (1822–84)
b. Prague, Czechoslovakia. Pf pupil of J. Tomásek. Pianist, composer and organist. Numerous pf compositions include a set of variations for left hand only, Op. 26.

HAN, Tong (1941–   )
b. Korea. Showed early promise and studied at Juilliard School of Music, New York, winning the Leventritt Comp. in 1965. Performed and taught at Illinois State Univ.

HANNIKAINEN, Ilmari (1893–1955)
b. Jyväskylä, Finland. Son of Pekka Juhani H and brother of Arvo (violinist) and Tauno (cellist and conductor). Studied in Helsinki, then in Vienna, and finally under A. Siloti in Petrograd, 1915–17. Was appointed principal pf teacher at Helsinki Music Inst. Toured Europe and composed pf works including a concerto and a quartet, also songs. The three brothers gave trio recitals.

HANON, Charles Louis (1820–1900)
b. Rem, France. Pianist, teacher and composer of fine sets of studies as well as other technical works and a Method which achieved worldwide recognition.

HANS, Pierre: see **SMULDERS, Carl**

HANSEN, Konrad (1906–   )
b. Lippstadt, Germany. Pupil and protégé of Edwin Fischer, with whose Chamber Orch. he made his début in 1930. Thereafter toured and worked as teacher with Fischer until 1938 when he went to Stern's Cons. in Berlin; he was

there throughout World War II. Later a co-founder of Detmold Acad.; then in 1960 went to Hamburg to succeed Eduard Erdmann at the Hochschule. Noted chamber-music player. Edited the Beethoven pf sonatas. Recorded *Polydor*.

Pupils included: Ronald Anderson.

HANSEN, Peter (1917–   )
b. The Hague, Netherlands. Pupil of R. Cons. there and of C. de Groot. Performed and taught. Also accompanied leading instrumentalists. Organized school concerts.

HANSLICK, Eduard (1825–1904)
b. Prague, Czechoslovakia. Received first lessons from his father before spending four years with J. Tomáschek, most famous teacher in Prague of the time. Although he took up musicology and became one of the first informed and reliable critics, he was an accomplished pianist by talent and formal training. His write-ups on important pianists of his time are still well worth reading.

HAQUINIUS, Algot (1886–1966)
b. Sveg, Sweden. Pupil of Stockholm Cons., then of M. Moszkowski in Paris and of I. Friedman in Berlin. Toured as concert pianist, taught and composed.

HARASIEWICZ, Adam (1932–   )
b. Chodziez, Poland. Student at Cracow School of Music. Won 1st Prize in Chopin Comp., 1955, Warsaw. Recorded Philips.

HARDER, Egil (1917–   )
b. Norway. Student of R. Cons., Copenhagen 1934–8 and later attended master-classes of E. Fischer. Concert pianist, teacher and adjudicator.

HARGREAVES, Francisco (1848–1900)
b. Buenos Aires, Argentina. Studied locally and in Europe. Performed and composed many pf pieces incorporating Argentinian folk-music and dance rhythms.

HARRIS, Clement (1871–97)
b. London, UK. Student of Frankfurt Cons. and later pupil of K. Schumann. Concert pianist and composer of a number of pf pieces including studies. Joined the Greek forces in Greco-Turkish War and was killed in battle.

HARRIS, Johana (*née* **Beula DUFFEY**) (1913–   )
b. Ottawa, Canada. Studied pf there and at Juilliard School of Music, New York, from where she performed and taught. Married the American composer Roy Harris (1898–1979) in 1936 and helped propagate his pf compositions in the course of her career. Joint dedicatee, with Roy H, of the 1952 Ginastera pf sonata which she premièred in 1952 in Pittsburgh, Pa.

HARRISON, Anita (1902–68)
b. Stockton-on-Tees, UK. Pf pupil of R. Acad., London, then of E. von Sauer. Performed throughout Europe. Resided in Stockholm for many years.

HARRISON, Eric (1918–70)
b. Halifax, UK. Pf pupil of R. Coll., London, and under C. Smith. Had his chance when the Fokine ballet based on Rachmaninov's *Rhapsody on a theme of Paganini* was staged Covent Garden, London, in summer of 1939 when he played the pf part with great success. Performed at home and abroad solo, with orch and in ensemble, teaching in Australia 1960–3. Was successful teacher as well as church organist. Recorded Pye.

Pupils included: Kay Lam.

HARRISON, Margaret (189?–   )
b. London, UK. One of four sisters, all musicians, of whom the eldest, Beatrice, was the famous cellist who propagated the Elgar concerto for that instrument. Trained in violin and pf and became better known as accompanist to her sisters. The later works of Delius for strings were written with the Harrisons in mind, and Margaret took the pf part in the sonatas. Recorded *HMV*.

HARRISON, Robin (1932–   )
b. London, UK. Studied in London with H. Craxton and in Rome with C. Zecchi; also with I. Kabos. Début 1949 London. Afterwards performed and taught.

HARRISON, Sidney (1903–   )
b. London, UK. Studied at Guildhall School, London. Concert pianist, teacher, examiner and adjudicator at home and abroad. Became a T.V. and radio personality. Wrote *Music for the Multitude*, *Musical Box*, *Beginning to Play the Piano* and *You Shall have Music*. Claims to

have made television history by giving first pf lesson in the world on the small screen in 1950.
Pupils included: Norma Fisher.

HARSÁNYI, Tibor (1898–1954)
b. Magyarkaniza, Hungary. Pupil of Budapest Acad. under S. Kovács. Début Vienna 1921, then commenced touring as concert pianist. Composed *Concertstück* for pf and orch., chamber music and much pf music and songs, all of French rather than Hungarian style. Recorded *Columbia*.

HARTE, Ruth (–   )
b. Bristol, UK. Student of R. Acad. of Music, London. Début 1950 London. Has since appeared as soloist, chamber-music player and with orch. Teacher. Married V. Langrish.

HARTLEY, Fred (1905–80)
b. Dundee, UK. Began his professional career as an accompanist at R. Acad. of Music, London, then worked with the BBC from 1927, being in charge of the Light Music Dept during World War II. Besides solo and accompanying work, also ran a quintet and a band bearing his name. Recorded *Decca*.

HARTMANN, Ludwig (1836–1910)
b. Neuss, Germany. Pupil of Leipzig Cons. and later studied with F. Liszt. Became established as concert pianist and later music critic.

HARTMANN, Thomas de (1886–1956)
b. Khoruzhevka, Russia. Pupil of Moscow Cons. and studied pf with A. Essipova. A fine pianist. Taught at Tiflis for a while from 1919 then settled in France. In 1951 went to USA, where he died. Composed a pf concerto and two sonatas, besides pf pieces, chamber music and songs.

HARTVIGSON, Anton (1845–1911)
b. Aarhus, Denmark. Pf pupil of K. Tausig and E. Neupert. Début Copenhagen. Moved to London in 1882 as teacher, concert pianist and lecturer, returning to Copenhagen ten years later.

HARTVIGSON, Fritz (1841–1919)
b. Jutland, Denmark. Elder brother of Anton H. Pf pupil of H. von Bülow, Berlin. Début Leipzig 1861. Worked in UK for a time; later became famous pianist in Russia and Finland.
Pupils included: James Friskin.

HARTY, Sir Hamilton (1879–1941)
b. Hillsborough (N. Ireland), UK. Largely self-taught as pianist and composer though came under the influence of M. Esposito in Dublin who was both friend and adviser whom H deeply respected. Moved to London 1900 and rapidly established a reputation as accompanist and composer. Met the singer Agnes Nicholls in this capacity and they were married in 1904. Became pianist in chamber-music performances before branching out as a conductor which became his principal métier. Gave première of his own pf concerto in Leeds in 1922 with Beecham conducting, also first public performance of *Rio Grande* at a Hallé concert conducted by Constant Lambert in Queen's Hall, 1929. Besides the concerto wrote an amount of chamber music and songs. Knighted 1925. RPS Gold Medal 1934. Recorded *Columbia* in ensemble, in *Rio Grande* and as accompanist.

HASKIL, Clara (1895–1960)
b. Bucharest, Romania. Début Vienna 1902 as child prodigy. Went to Paris as pupil of A. Cortot, and later of F. Busoni in Berlin. Achieved international status as recitalist and concerto-player and in chamber concerts with celebrities like Casals and Ysaÿe. Marcel Dupré dedicated his four pf pieces of Op. 19 to her. Recorded *Decca*, Philips and Nixa.
Pupils included: Tamas Vásáry.

HASLINGER, Karl (1816–68)
b. Vienna, Austria. Son of Tobias H, founder of the publishing firm of that name. Pf student of K. Czerny. An accomplished pianist and composer who took over the family business in 1842 on death of father and published works of Beethoven, Liszt and Strauss.

HÄSSLER, Johann Wilhelm (1747–1822)
b. Erfurt, Germany. Teacher was an uncle who had been a pupil of J.S.B. Was one of the early concert pianists, touring from 1790. Visited London where he performed a Mozart concerto. Settled in Russia from 1792. Prolific composer for pf especially sonatas, which he grouped as big and small, a set of *Études en quatre-vingt valses*, characteristic pieces and a *Grande Gigue* which once had vogue. Also songs.

HAUBIEL, Charles (1892–   )
b. Delta, USA. Pf pupil of R. Ganz, then of J. and R. Lhevinne. Won the US Schubert Cen-

tenary Contest of 1928 with *Karma* symphonic variations. Toured as soloist and as accompanist. Composed extensively, chamber and pf works, also songs.

HAWKINS, Margarete (1906–　)
b. Stuttgart, Germany. Studied music there, was pupil of M. Pauer, also of W. Kempff. Performed, taught and later settled in Nairobi, Kenya.

HAWLEY, Stanley (1867–1916)
b. Ilkeston, UK. Student of R. Acad. of Music, London, 1884–92. London début 1887 in Grieg concerto. Became concert pianist and accompanist and was hon. sec. of R. Phil. Soc. for years up to his death. Wrote a quantity of pf music but specialized in recitations to pf accompaniment.

HAYDN, Franz Josef (1732–1809)
b. Rohrau, Austria. Was taught on keyboard instruments earlier than pf, and of the 51 keyboard sonatas it is not certain for which instruments they were written since he, like W. A. Mozart, lived through the transitional period and before the pf came into its own. These sonatas, as well as the concertos and miscellaneous solos, are usually played on the pf.
　　Pupils included: Thomas Haigh, Franz Lessel, Sigismund Neukomm.

HEAD, Michael Dewar (1900–76)
b. Eastbourne, UK. Student of R. Acad. of Music, London, where in due course he became pf prof. Also singer and composer and gave vocal recitals accompanying himself. Toured USA and most countries of the old British Empire.

HEAP, Charles Swinnerton (1847–1900)
b. Birmingham, UK. Studied music there and in 1865 won Mendelssohn Scholarship to study in Leipzig. From 1868 established himself in Midlands as pianist and conductor, becoming a local celebrity. Composed chamber music, pf pieces and songs.

HEBER, Judith (1880–1919)
b. Gol, Norway. Pupil of Agathe Backer-Gröndahl and of X. Scharwenka, Berlin. Début 1907 Oslo.

HEGDAL, Magne (1944–　)
b. Gerdrum, Norway. Student of Oslo Cons. Concert career as soloist and with orch., and as chamber-music player. Compositions include works for one and two pfs.

HEGEDÜS, Endre (1954–　)
b. Hodmezovasarhely, Hungary. Student of the Liszt Acad., Budapest, and was a pupil of Z. Kocsis. Joint 5th Prizewinner of Liszt-Bartók Comp. 1981.

HEGNER, Otto (1876–1907)
b. Basle, Switzerland. Studied pf there and with E. d'Albert in Berlin, where he appeared as a prodigy. Made a sensation in London in 1888; later toured USA with phenomenal success. Last visit to London was in 1893 when he played 2nd pf concerto by Hans Huber.

HEIBERG, Harold (1922–　)
b. Twin Valley, USA. Studied at Columbia Teachers' Coll. and with K. Schnabel and L. Shure; also took voice training. Début 1971 New York, touring thereafter in variety of roles.

HEIDSIECK, Eric (1936–　)
b. Reims, France. Studied in Paris with A. Cortot; also with W. Kempff. Won 1st Prize, Paris Cons., 1954, and other awards. Performed extensively thereafter. Made own cadenzas for classical concertos. Recorded Decca.

HEININEN, Johannes (1938–　)
b. Helsinki, Finland. Student of Univ. there and of Sibelius Acad. and later of Cologne Hochschule, then Juilliard School, New York. A fine concert pianist whose compositional output contains much music for the instrument including two pf concertos and other works in sonata form.

HEINONEN, Eero (1950–　)
b. Turku, Finland. Studied at the Music Institute there, winning a pf competition in 1966. Afterwards continued for three years in Moscow on a grant provided by the Soviet Govt. Appeared throughout Europe and USA as soloist, with orch., and in chamber music. Taught at the Sibelius Academy in Helsinki. Recorded EMI and BIS.

HEINTZE, Gustav (1879–1946)
b. Jönköping, Sweden. Pupil of Stockholm Cons. and under R. Andersson for pf, at whose pf school he subsequently taught. Composed

two pf concertos and a *Concertstück* for same combination, also concerto for two pfs, chamber music and pf solos.

HEINZE, Sarah (*née* **Magnus**) (1839–1903)
b. Stockholm, Sweden. Pf pupil there, then later under T. Kullak, A. Dreyschock and F. Liszt. Successful concert pianist who lived and worked most of her life in Germany.

HELFFER, Claude (1922–   )
b. Paris, France. Pupil of R. Casadesus. Début 1948. Performed since in Europe and USA. Recorded various labels.
    Pupils included: Suzanne Fournier, Louis Pelletier.

HELLER, Stephen (1813–88)
b. Budapest, Hungary. Studied pf from an early age, and his début at 9 was so successful that he was sent to study in Vienna, playing in public there at the age of 14. Two years later toured Hungary, Poland and Germany. Began composing, and in 1838 went to Paris, becoming a well-known pianist and teacher who moved in the Chopin-Liszt circle. His compositions which had been published in Germany attracted favourable attention from Schumann, with whom he also became friendly. Visited London in 1849 and built on his reputation further. The remainder of his life was spent in Paris. His numerous pf works are skilfully written but too often reflect the influences of Mendelssohn and Schumann.

HELLIWELL, Clifton (1907–   )
b. Farnworth, UK. Pupil at R. Manchester Coll. On BBC staff many years until 1961; afterwards on staff of R. Manchester Coll. and R. Northern Coll. Pianist, accompanist and teacher.
    Pupils included: Heather Slade.

HELLWIG, Klaus
Request to last-known concert agents for biographical details met with no response.

HELPS, Robert (1928–   )
b. New Jersey, USA. Pupil of Juilliard School of Music and has occupied various teaching posts since graduation. Composer of works mainly for pf, including two concertos, chamber music and pieces.

HELY-HUTCHINSON, Victor (1901–47)
b. Cape Town, S. Africa. Won Nettleship Scholarship in music at Balliol College, Oxford, and studied at R. Coll., London. Taught on staff of Cape Town Univ. 1922–5. Joined BBC 1926–34. His *Young Idea* for pf and orch. was first performed at London Proms with composer as soloist 1928. Taught at Birmingham Univ. (UK), 1934–44. Thereafter returned to BBC as Director of Music.

HENDRICKSON, John (1957–   )
b. Montreal, Canada. Studied there and at the Juilliard School, New York. Entered the 1975 Int. Chopin Comp., Warsaw, and his omission from the list of finalists caused great commotion amongst audience. Prizewinner in 1976 Montreal Int. Comp. Has toured Canada and USA and in 1980 performed in European capitals. Recorded Muza.

HENGEVELD, Gerard (1910–   )
b. Kampen, Netherlands. Pupil at Amsterdam Cons, winning prize 1930. Went on to study with K. Friedberg in Zurich. Performed thereafter as soloist, accompanist and chamber-music player. A noted Bach interpreter. Has taught at the R. Cons. at The Hague. Compositions include a concerto, concertino, violin sonata and songs.

HENKEL, Heinrich (1822–98)
b. Fulda, Germany. Pupil first of his father, Michael H, a composer of sacred music, then later of A. Schmitt. Settled in Frankfurt as pianist and teacher. Composed pf pieces and songs and wrote works on technique.

HENKEMANS, Hans (1913–   )
b. The Hague, Netherlands. A doctor of medicine. Studied pf at The Hague; composition under W. Pijper; pf pupil of G. van Renesse. Concert pianist in own works and in duo appearances; also accomplished interpreter of Mozart and Debussy. Composed pf concerto, a *Passacaglia and Gigue* for pf and orch., and chamber-music.

HENNEBERG, Richard (1853–1925)
b. Berlin, Germany. Studied pf there and later with F. Liszt at Weimar. Toured as accompanist to celebrated soloists; also conducted.

HENNES, Aloys (1827–89)
b. Aachen, Germany. Pupil of F. Hiller and K. Reinecke. Had successful career as pf teacher in Germany. Also published *Klavierunterrichtsbriefe*.

HENRIOT, Nicole (1925–)
b. Paris, France. Student of Paris Cons. and pupil of M. Long, graduating with 1st Prize at 14. Began touring Europe after World War II and made US début 1948. Recorded EMI, RCA, Decca.

HENRY, Harold (1884–1956)
b. Kansas, USA. Studied there before taking tuition from L. Godowsky in Berlin and M. Moszkowski in Paris. Début Chicago 1906. Was well-known teacher in New York and composed light pieces and songs.

HENSCHEL, Sir George (1850–1934)
b. Breslau, of Polish stock. Studied at the Music Inst. there, and as a teenager took part with three fellow-pupils in a public performance of Weber's *Concertstück* for four pfs. Also took singing lessons and in 1867 went to Leipzig Cons., studying pf successively under E. Wenzel and I. Moscheles. In 1868 he met F. Liszt and sang *Wotan's Farewell*, accompanied by the Hungarian. In 1870 he joined the Hochschule in Berlin as singing teacher but also gave pf lessons and gradually gathered together a substantial career as baritone, pianist, accompanist, conductor and composer. Was conductor of Boston SO 1881–4, when he returned to London as 1st conductor of London SO, becoming a British subject in 1890. Throughout his subsequent career in Europe and USA he usually accompanied himself in *lieder* recitals, making his last public appearance in London in 1914 at 64. He was well over 75 when he made recordings of German *lieder*. Knighted 1914. Wrote *Musings and Memories of a Musician* (1918). His daughter Helen H also made a career as vocalist, accompanying herself, and as teacher. Mathilde Verne said of him: 'All his long life Sir George carried aloft the torch of complete devotion to the highest ideals, both as a musician and as a man; he was incapable of the smallest dishonesty of those ideals, and he was withal, to the very end, sweet and simple as a child, an inspiration to all with whom he came in contact.'

HENSEL, Fanny (*née* **Mendelssohn-Bartholdy**) (1805–47)
b. Hamburg, Germany. Elder sister of Felix M. Musically educated as pianist and composer under L. Berger. Brilliant pianist who married Wilhelm H, a painter attached to the Prussian court. Her death at an early age was said to have hastened the end of her brother F.

She composed pf music much in the idiom of 'songs without words', as well as songs. Felix rated her a better pianist than himself.

HENSELT, Adolf von (1814–89)
b. Schwabach, Germany. Studied first in Munich then, with help from King of Bavaria, with J. N. Hummel in Weimar. Made successful tour of Germany in 1837. Went to St Petersburg in 1838, settling as virtuoso, teacher and court pianist. Wrote prolifically and brilliantly, his F minor pf concerto being in the repertoire of pianists like von Sauer and Sapellnikov. Only the piece *Si oiseau j'étais* survived. Dedicatee of Schumann's *Noveletten*, Op. 21.

Pupils included: Ingeborg von Bronsart, Heinrich Ehrlich, Karl Lütschg, John Pattison, Robert Pflughaupt, Sophie Pflughaupt, Laura Rappoldi, Johann Zschocher, Nikolai Zverev.

HERMAN, Jan (1885–1946)
b. Neveklov, Czechoslovakia. Studied pf in Prague. Appointed pf prof. at Orel Cons., Russia, for a time before returning to Prague as prof. at Cons. Was fine technician with good temperament and wide repertory, especially of Czech composers. Experimented with quartertone music. Gave première of Martinu's pf concerto No. 1 in 1926 in Prague with Czech PO under V. Talich.

HERNADI, Lajos (1906–)
b. Budapest, Hungary. Student at Liszt Acad. there, winning diploma 1927. Pupil of E. von Dohnányi and in Berlin of A. Schnabel. Début Budapest 1929. Concert pianist and pf prof. at Liszt Acad. Has composed cadenzas to Mozart pf concertos.

Pupils included: Julia Cload.

HÉROLD, Ferdinand (1791–1833)
b. Paris, France. His father, who taught pf and had been a pupil of Karl P. E. Bach, was against his son taking up music but died when the boy was eleven. It was Fétis who discovered a musical aptitude in H, who, in 1806, went to Paris Cons. to study. His pf teacher was L. Adam, and he won 1st Prize. Spent three years in Rome before going on to Naples as court pianist to the Queen. Began composing opera, and thereafter his concertwork as pianist declined, especially after the success of *Zampa*, by which alone he is remembered. Wrote much pf music which is totally neglected.

HERTZ, Michael (1844–1918)
b. Warsaw, Poland. Pf pupil of F. Dulcken, then of T. Kullak. Taught for a time at Stern's Cons., returning to Warsaw in 1869. Composed pf music and songs.

HERZ, Henri (1803–88)
b. Vienna, Austria. Pupil of L. Pradère at Paris Cons., also of A. Reicha. Won 1st Prize for pf playing. Heard I. Moscheles and was so impressed that he tried to model his playing on the pedagogue. Achieved an enormous reputation as composer and teacher, and also as a virtuoso when he proceeded to tour Europe. Went into pf manufacture but lost money which he recouped by an extended tour of the USA, Mexico and W. Indies (1845–51). On returning to exercise his talents in Paris, he made so much money making and selling instruments that he resigned as pf prof. at Paris Cons., a post held since 1842. Moved in the Liszt circle and was one of the virtuosi who contributed to the famous *Hexameron* variations. Wrote much pf music which was popular at the time but which, because of its shallowness, has become forgotten. As an executant he was seemingly likewise fluent but shallow.
Pupils included: Pedro Albéniz, Jakob Blumenthal, Adolphe Fétis, Henry Forbes, Jacques Gregoir, Anna Laidlaw, Marie Pleyel, Henri Rosellen, Charles Salaman, Marie Trautmann.

HERZ, Jacques Simon (1794–1880)
b. Frankfurt, Germany. Elder brother of Henri H. Studied at Paris Cons. under L. Pradère, winning 1st Prize 1812. Taught pf in Paris and London before being appointed to teach at Paris Cons. in 1857.

HERZOG, Sigmund (1868–1932)
b. Budapest, Hungary. Pf pupil of J. Epstein at Vienna Cons., graduating 1885. Studied with R. Joseffy in New York. Performed and taught at Inst. of Musical Art. Composed for pf and prepared a textbook on *The Art of Octave-playing*.

HERZOGENBERG, Elisabeth von (*née* **Stockhausen**) (1847–92)
b. Paris, France. An accomplished pianist who studied with J. Epstein, then, on his advice, with J. Brahms. Married Heinrich von H in 1868. They settled in Leipzig in 1872. She retained deep affection for Brahms and his

work and gave advice in correspondence which continued up to her death.

HERZOGENBERG, Heinrich von (1843–1900)
b. Graz, Austria. Studied pf at Vienna Cons. under F. Dessoff. Performed and taught, living at Graz until 1872 when he settled in Leipzig and became co-founder of the Bach-Verein two years later. Later taught composition at Berlin Hochschule. Prolific composer in most fields apart from opera, many works for two and four hands as well as chamber music with pf parts. Married Elisabeth von Stockhausen (1847–92) who also was professional pianist.

HESS, Dame Myra (1890–1965)
b. London, UK. Pupil of R. Acad. there under T. Matthay. Début 1907 London and slowly consolidated her career. US début 1922, thereafter touring Europe and USA annually apart from World War II, and was popular in the Netherlands. Especial sympathy with German composers. Evoked great warmth of tone from her instrument in interpretations marked by sobriety rather than sheer virtuosity. In World War II organized lunchtime concerts at the National Gallery, London, for which work received DBE 1941. R. Phil. Soc. Gold Medal same year. During first part of her career her repertoire was wider-ranging, and in 1921 she gave first performance in London of the Bliss concerto for pf, tenor, strings and percussion. Also gave première of F. Bridge pf sonata in 1925, and of the Howard Ferguson pf sonata in 1940. Was unaccountably the dedicatee of a pf piece by A. Bax, *In a Vodka Shop*, one of a group of three pieces apparently inspired by a visit to Russia. The violinist Joseph Szigeti gave his first performances in public of Beethoven sonatas with H at the pf and wrote in *Strings Attached*: 'Eloquence born of understatement, a rare gift indeed and, I suspect, a particularly British one – was hers even in that youthful time.' Recorded *Columbia, HMV, EMI* and Philips.
Pupils included: Stephen Bishop-Kovacevich, John Contiguglia, Richard Contiguglia, Vivian Ellis, Howard Ferguson, Joel Ryce, Yonty Solomon, Desmond Wright.
The Dame Myra Hess Trust, administered by the Musicians' Benevolent Fund, makes awards to outstanding instrumentalists aged 18–30 years, preference being given to those wishing to make a professional career. Assist-

ance can be in the form of help towards the purchase of an instrument; assistance with tuition costs and maintenance during study; or by help with the cost of a first recital. Application to the Secretary, Myra Hess Trust, 16 Ogle Street, London W1P 7LG.

HESSE, Marjorie (1911–)
b. Brisbane, Australia. Musically educated at Sydney Cons. Début Sydney 1932. Toured extensively, taught in Sydney and adjudicated. Composed pf pieces.

HESSE-BUKOWSKA, Barbara (1930–)
b. Lodz, Poland. Pf pupil at Warsaw Cons., winning 2nd Prize, Warsaw Chopin Comp., 1949, and later many other prizes. Worldwide tours followed. Besides performing was also teacher. Recorded Muza and Westminster.

HESSELBERG, Eduard Gregory (1870–1935)
b. Riga, Russia. Student of Moscow Cons. and pf pupil of Anton Rubinstein. Settled in USA in 1892 and had a succession of teaching posts. Moved to Toronto for a time where he had a master-class. Composed pf pieces and songs, also made transcriptions of repertoire pf solos for four hands.

HEYMAN, Katherine Ruth Willoughby (1879–1944)
b. Sacramento, USA. Début 1899 Boston. Toured USA and Europe as soloist and as support pianist in celebrity recitals. Was in London 1910 and played the d'Indy *Symphonie*. Among first pianists to play Scriabin's works in USA. Took American pf works to Europe and founded group to further the cause of contemporary music. Besides accompanying, wrote on musical topics and composed pf pieces and songs. Recorded *Friends of Recorded Music* label.

HILDRETH, Dorothy: *see* **POUISHNOV, Lev**

HILL, Granville (1878–1953)
b. Manchester, UK. Studied from early age and at first won distinction on organ. Gave it up in preference for pf and became successful accompanist in Manchester area. Was appointed pf prof. at Leeds Coll. of Music 1936. Worked as music critic.

HILL, Wilhelm (1838–1902)
b. Fulda, Germany. Studied in Frankfurt, where he lived as concert pianist, teacher and composer. Wrote chamber music, pf pieces and songs.

HILLER, Ferdinand (1811–85)
b. Frankfurt, Germany. A prodigy who made his début at 10 in a Mozart concerto. Studied pf with J. Hummel. It is said he was taken to see the dying Beethoven. Settled in Paris 1828–35 as teacher, pianist and composer. Reputedly gave first performance of the *Emperor* in Paris and acquired a reputation as an interpreter of Beethoven. Wrote much music, of which his pf concerto in F sharp minor enjoyed a vogue, and was much esteemed by famous contemporaries. Chopin dedicated the *Nocturnes* Op. 15 to him. A curiosity of his creative output is *Operette ohne Text* for pf duet and following the lines of an operetta with overture, arias etc but of course without words.
Pupils included: Julius Buths, Otto Dresel, Ferdinand Dulcken, Aloys Hennes, Carl Lachmund, Frank Liebich.

HILSBERG, Ignace (1894–1973)
b. Warsaw, Poland. Studied pf at St Petersburg under A. Essipova, then I. Vengerova, graduating 1917. Had lessons from E. von Sauer in Vienna, then taught in Silesia and Greece until 1923 when he settled in USA, holding various teaching posts as well as performing, finally moving to Hollywood where he did work in film industry.

HIMMEL, Friedrich Heinrich (1765–1814)
b. Treuenbrietzen, Germany. An early pianist, contemporary of Beethoven who became locked in the battle of improvisation in Vienna in 1796. He had studied in Dresden on a grant provided by Friedrich II and was highly rated as a pianist. Became *Kapellmeister* in Berlin. Wrote operas and songs, as well as church and chamber music.

HINDEMITH, Paul (1895–1963)
b. Hanau, Frankfurt, Germany. Student of Hoch Cons., Frankfurt. Pf was only one of a number of instruments he learned as a boy, although the mature artist was best known as violinist and violist. As a young man he experienced most types of music including jazz and military band, interests reflected in his piano *Suite 1922*, its five movements entitled 'March', 'Nocturne', 'Shimmy', 'Boston' and

'Ragtime'. Taught at Berlin Hochschule from 1927 until the Nazis tried to purge him in 1934. Was allowed to teach and to tour abroad but eventually left home for the USA, via Switzerland. There he taught and composed, taking American nationality after World War II. In 1951 took an additional teaching post at Zurich Univ. which lasted some six years. In the meantime he had settled in Switzerland. In a large and varied output by this one-time leading figure on the German musical scene pf works include: 2 concertos (1924 and 1945), *Konzertmusik* for pf, brass and 2 harps; 3 pf sonatas (all 1936), as well as numerous chamber-music works and sonatas with pf parts, the already-mentioned *Suite 1922* and the important *Ludus Tonalis* (1943) which was propagated by F. Reizenstein and which consists of a set of twelve 3-part fugues with prelude and postlude, the fugues connected by interludes and following a key-change pattern. H also arranged his symphony *Mathis der Maler* for pf duet, and there is vocal music with pf. Wrote an important modern work on composition in three volumes (the third published after his death), also *A Composer's World*, based on lectures. Recorded RCA (his duet sonata with J. M. Sanroma).

HIOKI, Sumiko (1955–)
b. Tokyo, Japan. Pupil of Toho Gakuen School of Music, Tokyo, and of Indiana Univ. Teachers included G. Sebok.

HIPKINS, Alfred James (1826–1903)
b. London, UK. A technician with the firm of John Broadwood who learned the harpsichord and pf and gave pf recitals. Tuned the famous Broadwood grand No. 17,047 which Chopin used in 1848 on his last visit to Britain and wrote a book on how Chopin played, as well as other works on keyboard instruments. Became an authority on the subject of keyboard instruments, giving lecture recitals in London which became renowned. At one of them in 1886 Anton Rubinstein was present and assisted by turning over the pages.

HIRT, Franz Josef (1899–)
b. Lucerne, Switzerland. Studied with E. Levy in Basle, also with E. Petri and A. Cortot. Returned to Berne as prof. and was also successful concert pianist, solo and in chamber music. Recorded *Electrola*, *HMV* and *Polydor*.

HLAWICZKA, Karol (1894–)
b. Cieszyn, Poland. Student of Warsaw Cons. Début 1912 Cieszyn. Performed and taught. Composed a pf concerto and pieces; also wrote a history of the polonaise.

HOBDAY, Ethel (1872–1947)
b. Dublin, Eire. Studied at R. Irish Acad. there before going to R. Coll., London with F. Taylor. Début London 1891. Subsequently performed in Europe and turned to accompanying in which field she collaborated with most leading British instrumentalists in chamber-music recitals. As such recorded on most 78 rpm labels prior to World War II.

HOBSON, Ian (1952–)
b. Wolverhampton, UK. Studied pf, violin and organ from early age and in 1968 won an open scholarship to Cambridge, completing BA in two years. Studied pf at R. Acad., London, receiving diploma at age of 17, youngest student ever to do so. In 1972 was enrolled at Yale Univ., his principal pf teacher being Claude Frank. Later studied with M. Pressler and became assistant pf prof. at Illinois Univ. Performed in Europe, USA and Israel. Came 5th in Van Cliburn Comp., 1977; 2nd in Arthur Rubinstein Int. Comp., 1980; 4th in Leeds Comp., 1978, and 1st in same comp. of 1981. In June of same year was 2nd in the Int. Beethoven Pf Comp. in Vienna. Recorded EMI.

HODAPP, Frieda: *see* **KWAST, Frieda Hodapp**

HODGKINSON, Randall (1955–)
b. Ohio, USA. Student first of Cleveland Music School Settlement, then of C. Frank. Won scholarship to New England Cons., Boston, where his teachers included L. Shure. Taught at Belmont Music School and won a number of prizes including 1st in the 1971 Int. Music Comp., New York.

HOEHN, Alfred (1887–1945)
b. Eisenach, Germany. Studied with L. Uzielli at Hoch's Cons., Frankfurt. Won Rubinstein Prize of 1910 with his performance of the 'Hammerklavier' against competitors of the calibre of Borowsky, Pouishnov and Arthur Rubinstein. Possessed a fine technique and was accounted more successful in the Classical repertoire than in Romantic music. Recorded Chopin on *Parlophone*.

HOFFMAN, Jan (1906–)
b. Cracow, Poland. Studied at Cons. there, then with E. Petri. Taught at Cracow Cons. and High School of Music there. Was an adjudicator.

HOFFMANN, Joachim (1788–1856)
b. Austria. Was known as a pianist and teacher in Vienna from around 1815. Composed for pf; also wrote a work on harmony which was at one time a standard work of reference in Austria. Provided one of the pf variations for the Diabelli waltz publication.

HOFFMAN, Ludwig (1925–)
b. Berlin, Germany. Studied organ at first, then turned to pf. Pupil of Hinze-Reinhold and Schmidt-Neuhaus; also of M. Long and A. B. Michelangeli. Won pf prizes in Weimar, Cologne and Munich. Established in Germany as a concert pianist whose sympathies lay in the main stream of pf repertoire. Recorded Hallmark, Europa and others.
    Pupils included: Kyoko Koyama, Daniel Rivero.

HOFFMAN, Richard (1831–1909)
b. Manchester, UK. A pupil of his father, then of I. Moscheles, I. Pleyel and Anton Rubinstein. Went to the USA in 1847 where he was so successful that he settled. Made numerous tours solo, and with violinists like Wm. Wallace, composer of the opera *Maritana*. Was a close friend of L. M. Gottschalk, making frequent duo-appearances, and is dedicatee of the latter's *The Banjo*, a once-popular solo with pianists. Also toured USA with the singer Jenny Lind. Composed mainly salon pf pieces, and wrote *Some Musical Recollections of Fifty Years* (1910).

HOFFMANN-BEHRENDT, Lydia (1890–1971)
b. Tiflis, Russia. Went to Berlin as a young girl to study with E. von Dohnányi, then to Vienna. Début Berlin 1911. Thereafter toured Europe. Specialized in contemporary music. Was pf prof. 1923–34 at Stern's Cons., Berlin. In 1934 settled in USA as teacher of pf at New York Coll. of Music.

HOFFMEISTER, Karel (1869–1952)
b. Halůboka, Czechoslovakia. Student of Prague Univ., later taught at Ljubljana, 1891–8, when he returned to teach at Prague Cons. Fine pianist, especially chamber music.

Composed pf works and wrote various books on technical matters, notably *The Piano – its Methods and Masters* (1923).

HOFMANN, Casimir (1842–1911)
b. Cracow, Poland. Pf pupil at Vienna Cons. Taught pf and conducted in Warsaw from 1878. Settled in Berlin 1886. Father of Josef H.

HOFMANN, Heinrich (1842–1902)
b. Berlin, Germany. Pupil of T. Kullak. Did not compose even one pf concerto so far as can be traced.

HOFMANN, Josef Casimir (1876–1957)
b. Podgorze, Poland. Pf pupil of father Casimir, and at the age of 6 made a prodigy appearance at a charity concert which caused a sensation. When he was 9 he undertook a highly successful tour of Europe, repeating the success in 1887 in the USA, beginning in New York. The tour which should have followed was cut short through action by the SPCC, but a wealthy patron offered Casimir financial support for the boy provided he studied intensively until the age of 18 and in the meantime made no public appearances.
    In Berlin he studied with M. Moszkowski, then, 1892–4, with A. Rubinstein. H's biographers imply that he was Rubinstein's only pupil but, since the latter founded St Petersburg Cons. and taught there, the reference may mean that H was the only *private* pupil, a claim not entirely proven. What cannot be gainsaid, however, is that the Russian made a profound impression upon the young Pole, who, in the spring of 1894, made his adult début in Hamburg playing the Rubinstein D minor pf concerto with the composer conducting. That autumn he toured throughout Europe and the USA, and by the end of the season he had become established as one of the world's leading pianists.
    He made his home in the USA from 1898, becoming naturalized in 1926. At the turn of the century he was asked to write a series of articles on pf technique in *Ladies' Home Journal* in New York. The essays went on for a long time and were a popular feature of the journal, later forming the basis of his book *Piano Playing*, which has been republished a number of times and is a mine of information. The philanthropic head of Curtis Publishing who owned the journal, Cyrus Curtis, was musical and in 1924 founded the Curtis Inst. of Music, appointing H as its first Director. The

post curtailed his concert activities, and by the time he revisited Europe in 1933, there had been a gap of twenty-five years. The public had seemingly forgotten the name. His London concerts produced disastrously small audiences. In one of them he played the *Emperor* Concerto, at another the Chopin in E minor, while the third was a recital.

Of his *Emperor* Richard Capell recorded: 'In some respects his playing was unsurpassable in the evenness of his scales and of his trills. Nothing could have been more polished.' Ernest Newman wrote of his: 'smooth perfection of style'. Arthur Loesser heard Hofmann play many times and thought a more flawless pianist had never lived. And in *Speaking of Pianists* . . . his own pupil Abram Chasins devoted a whole chapter to the master.

In the USA his career continued undimmed, and in 1937 he celebrated a half-century on the American musical scene with a grand tour of which his appearance in the New York Metropolitan Opera House was recorded and is an everlasting testimonial to the deeply emotional enthusiasm shown that November day by a capacity audience. That recital which featured one concerto with orch., the Rubinstein D minor, involved him giving fifteen encores. Thus the wheel of his music-making in that country had turned full circle, for it was in that same opera house that he had made his US début back in 1887. His last appearance was in Carnegie Hall early in 1946. When he finally retired to California, he devoted his inventive faculties to the pf and the automobile.

His temperament was mercurial: seemingly he never twice played a work in exactly the same manner. His description of the way he was taught by Rubinstein makes it possible to conclude that the master affected the pupil. According to Hofmann the Russian never demonstrated a point on the keyboard, and the pupil was never allowed to bring a piece more than once because Rubinstein: 'might forget in the next lesson what he told me in the previous one, and by drawing an entirely new picture only confuse my mind.' For the Hamburg début the teacher refused to rehearse the concerto, even run through it with the pupil, on the grounds that 'We understand each other.' Is it surprising H was never wholly satisfied with his gramophone recordings for the simple reason that he had changed his mind about the interpretation of a work between recording it and listening to the playback? It would be wrong to assume that he was capricious in the vein of, say, Pachmann. His playing seems always to have been a miracle of refinement and sudden illumination, in passing wholly convincing because it was founded upon fabulous technique.

He is the dedicatee of Rachmaninov's 3rd pf concerto although so far as is known he never performed the work in public. Under the pseudonym of Michel Dvorsky he composed much music for pf, including five concertos and *Chromaticon*, described as a dialogue for pf and orch.

Pupils included: Ellen Ballon, Abram Chasins, Shura Cherkassky, Hans Ebell, Isadore Freed, Harry Kaufmann, Ruth Slenczynka, Walter Süsskind, Teresita Tagliapietra.

HOLBROOKE, Joseph (1878–1958)
b. Croydon, UK. Student of R. Acad., London, and of F. Westlake. Won the Lucas Prize and Sterndale Scholarship. For many years performed regularly as pianist and conductor. Was among the first British pianists to play the Rachmaninov concerto in C minor, and in 1903 gave first British performance of the Tchaikovsky concerto No. 3 at Bournemouth with Sir D. Godfrey conducting. His 1st pf concerto had its première in London in 1909 with Harold Bauer and the London SO conducted by the composer. His compositions failed to attract public attention, despite his constant pressure on British conductors and the efforts of the Holbrooke Soc. of long standing. Wrote much chamber music with pf part, as well as pf solos. Recorded *Piccadilly*.

Pupils included: Anthony Bernard.

HOLLAENDER, Alexis (1840–1924)
b. Ratibor, Germany. Studied in Breslau and Berlin. Taught pf at Kullak's and was also a teacher of voice. Lecturer at Humboldt Academy from 1903. Composed chamber-music, pf pieces and songs. Edited Schumann's pf works for the Schlesinger edition.

HOLLANDER, Lorin (1944–)
b. New York, USA. Pupil of Juilliard School. Début 1956 New York. Performed thereafter. Toured Europe. Recorded RCA.

HOLLINS, Alfred (1865–1942)
b. Hull, UK. Blind pianist who was a pupil of H. von Bülow. Despite handicap toured most countries throughout the world in the course of

a long career including the USA in 1888 where he played concertos with major orchs. Was also organist and composer and published his memoirs in 1936. Records show he played the Beethoven *Emperor* concerto in London in 1888 at the age of 22.

HOLMES, William Henry (1812–85)
b. Sunbury, UK. Studied at R. Acad., London, winning two medals. Taught there from 1826 becoming principal pf prof. Played at R. Phil. Soc. concerts from 1851. Compositions include a pf concerto (*The Jubilee*), chamber music, pf pieces and songs.

HOLTEN, Karl von (1836–1912)
b. Hamburg, Germany. Pupil of Leipzig Cons. and of I. Moscheles and L. Plaidy. Taught at Hamburg Cons. and was a much sought-after teacher. Composed pf concerto, chamber music, pf pieces and songs.

HOLZKNECHT, Vaclav (1904–)
b. Prague, Czechoslovakia. Student of Prague Cons. 1924–8, taught there becoming prof. 1942 and Director 1948. As a pianist devoted much attention to contemporary works, especially of Czech origin. Wrote extensively on the art in books and periodicals.

HONEGGER, Andrée: *see*
VAURABOURG, Andrée

HOPE, Eric (1920–)
b. Warwickshire, UK. Studied in Vienna, and in London with Solomon and F. Reizenstein. Début there at R. Albert Hall Prom. concert. Toured UK and Europe solo, with orchs. and ensemble with leading instrumentalists. Gave British première of the Respighi *Toccata* for pf and orch. in Birmingham, also first performance of pf concerto by Sergei Lancen in London. Dedicatee of Philip Cannon's *Sonata Champêtre*, Op. 7, and of *Partita* by Peter Wishart. Pf Prof. at R. Acad., London. Wrote *A Handbook of Piano-Playing*. Recorded Decca, Delyse.

HOPEKIRK, Helen (1856–1945)
b. Edinburgh, UK. Studied there to begin with, then went on to Leipzig; also had lessons from T. Leschetizky in Vienna. Début Leipzig 1878. Returned to UK and toured with success. Married a merchant, William Wilson, in 1882 and emigrated to USA the following year where she achieved great success as

pianist. Resided in Vienna 1887–9, performing throughout Europe. She toured Europe and USA until 1897 when she settled in Boston. In USA she propagated the music of MacDowell and also of the French School. Compositions include a concerto and a *Concertstück* for pf and orch., chamber music, pf pieces and songs.

HOPKINS, Antony (1921–)
b. London, UK. Student of R. Coll. of Music, London, and of C. Smith. Was on staff of Morley Coll. and over many years broadcast a weekly talk on music on BBC, thus continuing the educational work on the air begun by Sir Walford Davies and Sir Donald Tovey. Author of a number of textbooks.
Pupils included: Douglas Young.

HORÁK, Adolf (1850–1921)
b. Jankovic, Czechoslovakia. Co-founded with his brother Eduard H the Horák Pf School of Vienna which was remarkably successful for a time.

HORAN, Catherine Anne (1948–)
b. Chicago, USA. Studied there and at N. Western Univ., later in Austria. Recitalist and accompanist.

HOROWITZ, Norman (1932–)
b. New York, USA. Pf teachers included I. Vengerova. Linked up with M. Stecher to form Stecher and Horowitz duo; also co-founder of pf school of same name from 1960. Composed, taught, lectured and wrote, especially for the young. Recorded Everest.

HOROWITZ*, Vladimir (1904*–)
b. Kiev,* Russia. Originally wanted to be a composer. Pf teachers included his mother, S. Tarnowsky and F. Blumenfeld. Pupil at Kiev Cons. 1912–20, his graduation performances including Rachmaninov's 3rd concerto and 2nd sonata, works which remained in his repertoire. Also in 1920 gave two public recitals in Kiev although his début is reckoned to have taken place in Kharkov the following year. During the next four years, and in post-revolution conditions of great difficulty, his concert career in Russia developed unspectacularly, and he left the country on a limited-period visa in 1925, making his Berlin début the following year.

* Date and place of birth are in dispute, the alternatives being 1903 and in Berdichev. The family name was Gorowitz.

In a Germany still trying to recover from a disastrous war he was just one of many pianists until Fate took a hand when he happened to be giving a recital in Hamburg. Asked at short notice to deputize for a pianist who had fallen ill he performed the Tchaikovsky 1st concerto without rehearsal, and caused a sensation which led to appearances in Paris, Rome, London and other European capitals. For a time Paris became his home. In 1928 his US début occurred in New York with the Tchaikovsky concerto on two consecutive evenings, and the highly successful tour of that country which followed on finally established him among the first flight of the profession with a truly formidable technique.

He accompanied Gregor Piatigorsky when the Russian cellist made his Paris début in 1930; and gave duo-recitals with his lifelong friend Nathan Milstein, the Russian violinist. The three joined forces in a trio recital in Carnegie Hall early in 1932. Later that year he made an extensive tour of Great Britain.

In the years before World War II he divided his time between the USA and Europe, and in 1933 married Wanda, daughter of Arturo Toscanini, with whom he performed and recorded. He became especially identified with Tchaikovsky No. 1 and Rachmaninov No. 3, and had a filial relationship with the pianist-composer until the latter's death in 1943. A series of illnesses led to his absence from the concert platform between 1935 and 1938 in which year he resumed his career beginning with a recital in Zurich. On the outbreak of World War II he returned to the USA and as a stateless person assumed US citizenship in 1942.

Further illnesses, said to connect with personal problems, caused further withdrawals from concert activities and later in life his public appearances became rare. In 1951 he returned to Europe, being acclaimed wherever he appeared. Two years later he celebrated the 25th anniversary of his US début by playing the Tchaikovsky then, for his Golden Jubilee in 1978, played the Rachmaninov No. 3 in Carnegie Hall, a performance that was simul-taneously broadcast worldwide, televised and recorded. In May 1982, at the age of 77, he made two sensational appearances before capacity audiences in the Royal Festival Hall, London, the first one being televised in its entirety. Peter Stadlen wrote that in Rach-maninov's 2nd sonata H 'unleashed to the full his stupendous power and virtuosity – age

cannot wither him nor custom stale his infinite variety.'

Many critics have sought to capture on paper the musical character of an unique artist who became a legend in his own lifetime yet whose reputation derived little from a classical reper-toire. They have commented at length upon a prodigious technique and mercurial tempera-ment, both of which were combined to perfec-tion in Scarlatti sonatas of which he was recognized as the supreme exponent on the concert grand. Critics also took him to task for hard hitting and exaggerations of interpret-ation, especially in the Romantics, yet he con-fessed never to play a work twice in the same way, and his gramophone records corroborate this to some extent. But recordings are a poor substitute for personal communion with the living presence of such a practitioner of the art of musical prestidigitation. Similar elements were discernible in Josef Hofmann and if the results were sometimes equally unpredictable they were never dull or unsatisfying.

Two factors contributed to the legendary reputation enjoyed by Horowitz throughout the second half of his career. The first was the rarity of his public appearances; the second was a close affinity with fellow-countryman Rachmaninov, himself a legendary pianist from the old Russia in whose footsteps H in-stinctively trod, if to different effect and result. 'He gave this concerto to me,' H said of the D minor years after the death of the composer. No one alive during the lifetime of the two musicians would dispute the claim. Like all great artists he overwhelmed the listener at the moment of performance by the complete authenticity of his interpretation; and no one should expect more of a virtuoso than that. Throughout a long career he also strove, surely like no one else, to collaborate closely with his favourite piano-makers to produce an instru-ment for concerts and recordings that always sounded dreadful to an ear attuned to the noblest sounds great manufacturers can aspire to.

Although his reputation rests largely upon Romantic pf music he did give a number of first performances in the USA including Proko-fiev's 6th sonata in 1942, the 7th in 1944 and the 8th in 1945; Kabalevsky's 2nd in 1947 and 3rd in 1948; also Samuel Barber's *Excursions* in 1945 and the sonata in 1950.

The biography *Horowitz* by Glenn Plaskin was published in 1983. Compositions include a *Danse excentrique*; arrs of *The Stars and Stripes*

Forever, and Saint-Saëns' *Danse Macabre*; also *Variations on a theme from Carmen*. Recorded *HMV*, *RCA*, RCA and CBS.

Pupils included: Ivan Davis, Gary Graffman, Byron Janis, Ronald Turini.

HORSLEY, Charles Edward (1822–76)
b. London, UK. Son of Sir William H, one-time organist of renown and a founder of the (R.) Phil. Soc. in 1813. Studied pf with I. Moscheles and composition with F. Mendelssohn. Performed in UK 1845–62, when he settled in Australia for a while, moving finally to the USA. Composed pf pieces and wrote *Textbook of Harmony* (1876).

HORSLEY, Colin (1920–)
b. Wanganui, New Zealand. Student of R. Coll. of Music, London. Début London Proms 1942. Worldwide tours followed. Joined R. Manchester Coll. teaching staff 1964. OBE 1963. Recorded *HMV*, *Decca*, EMI and Meridian.

HORSZOWSKI, Mieczyslaw (1892–)
b. Lwow, Poland. Pupil of M. Soltys and of H. Melcer at Lwow Cons., later of T. Leschetizky in Vienna. Child prodigy who toured Europe before resuming study. Adult début 1913. Became internationally known as soloist and ensemble player of front rank. Taught at Curtis Inst. after settling in USA in 1940 and has appeared at most music festivals. Came out of retirement at the age of 91 to give recitals at the Aldeburgh Festival, 1983–4. Recorded RCA and other labels.

Pupils included: Denise Bacon, Steven de Groote, Cecile Licad, Seymour Lipkin.

HORZALKA, Johann (1798–1860)
b. Triesch, Czechoslovakia. Of musical family. Studied pf with I. Moscheles and lived in Vienna from which centre he toured as pianist. Was also theatre accompanist there.

HOUGH, Stephen (1961–)
b. Heswall, UK. Student of Chetham's School, R. Manchester Coll. and G. Green. In 1980 was awarded the Julius Isserlis Scholarship with which he studied at the Juilliard School, New York. Performed with orch. in UK and Germany. Winner of the 1st Terence Judd Award, 1982, and as such gave his Wigmore Hall début same year.

HOVHANESS, Alan (1911–)
b. Somerville, USA. Pf pupil of H. Gebhard. A prolific composer who made study of oriental music and incorporated its basic features in numerous works with pf parts. Recorded Poseidon.

HOWARD, Leslie (1948–)
b. Melbourne, Australia. Studied locally, and although he had pf teachers, his musical education was scholastic and through university gaining BA and MA. Became lecturer at Monash Univ. and won a pf prize in Naples in 1976. Appeared in Europe as well as Australasia, broadcast, appeared on television and recorded various.

HOWARD, William (1953–)
b. London, UK. Studied pf in London and Oxford, and later in Paris. London début 1981. Performed solo and in chamber concerts; played on radio; also taught.

HOWARD-JONES, Evlyn (1882–1964)
b. London, UK. Pupil of R. Coll. of Music, London, and later of E. d'Albert and E. Jedliczka in Berlin. Toured regularly as concert pianist and was noted for his interpretations of Bach, Beethoven and Brahms. Taught at R. Coll. and was pf prof. there. Début 1908 at R. Phil. Soc. concert, London, in the Brahms B flat concerto. Took a leading role in the 1929 Delius Festival in Queen's Hall, playing pf in the chamber works and the pf concerto, and in accompanying the singers. In 1933 devoted four Wigmore Hall recitals to the entire pf works of Brahms on the occasion of the centenary of the composer's birth. Recorded *Columbia*.

Pupils included: Benjamin Dale, Rupert Erlebach, Thelma Robinson.

HOWE, Mary (1882–1964)
b. Richmond, Va, USA. Studied in Boston and Paris (including N. Boulanger for composition). Performed and composed chamber music, pf pieces and songs.

HOWELL, Dorothy (1898–1982)
b. Birmingham, UK. Studied at R. Acad., London, and was pf pupil of T. Matthay. Taught pf and gave recitals. Prof. at R. Acad. from 1924 and also taught at Malvern High School for Girls. Composed a pf concerto in D minor which was premièred in London in 1923, also pf pieces and songs.

HSIEN-MING, Lee (1918–)
b. Shanghai, China. Studied pf in Paris and performed in Europe, settling in USA after World War II. Wife of Alexander Tcherepnin.

HUBEAU, Jean (1917–)
b. Paris, France. Pupil of Paris Cons. from 1926, winning 1st Prize for pf in 1930 at the age of 13. Toured Europe as virtuoso. Director of Versailles Cons. from 1942. Composed pf concerto, chamber music, pf pieces and songs.

HUBER, Hans (1852–1921)
b. Schönenwerd, Switzerland. A prodigy. Studied at Leipzig Cons. with K. Reinecke and E. Wenzel. Was excellent pianist, teacher and composer who influenced the Swiss musical scene of his day. Extensive list of works include pf concertos, chamber music, pf pieces and songs. Most noteworthy opus is a *Well-Tempered Clavier*, comprising another set of 48 preludes and fugues.
  Pupils included: Edwin Fischer.

HUBERT, Alexandra Ivanova (*née* **Batalina**) (1850–1937)
b. Russia. Pf prof. at Moscow Cons., where her husband, Nicolai H, was a theory prof., and became Director there on death of N. Rubinstein. She arranged some of Tchaikovsky's orch. works for pf.

HUGHES, Edwin (1884–1965)
b. Washington, USA. Pf pupil of R. Joseffy and of T. Leschetizky. Taught at Detroit School of Music but settled in Munich, performing and teaching until USA entered World War I, when he returned home to teach, give concerts, edit pf music and write musical essays. Composed songs and works for pf including a paraphrase of the Strauss waltz *Vienna Blood*. Gave two-pf recitals with his wife Jewel Bethany H.

HUGH-JONES, Elaine (1925–)
b. London, UK. Studied at R. Acad., London, and with J. Isserlis. Accompanist and teacher and worked on BBC. Composed songs etc.

HUGLMANN, Josef (1768–1839)
b. Vienna, Austria. Taught and played pf, composed pieces and was associated in music publishing.

HUMBLE, Keith (1927–)
b. Geelong, Australia. Studied at Melbourne

Cons., graduating 1949. Went on to R. Coll., London, under H. Ferguson, later becoming a pf student at École Normale, Paris. Performed solo and as accompanist. Works include a pf sonata (1959), chamber music, pf pieces and songs.

HUMBY-BEECHAM, Lady Betty (1908–58)
b. London, UK. Early beginner who won a scholarship to R. Acad., London, 1918 and was teaching pupils three years later. Received lessons from A. Schnabel and L. Kraus. Continued teaching during early concert career when she made a name as an exponent of Mozart. In this way met Sir T. Beecham. They married (both for second time) in USA during World War II. Besides Mozart she played the Delius pf concerto under his baton many times, and they recorded it for EMI. Her concert career after the war became somewhat intermittent, and announced appearances were frequently cancelled. After much illness she died in Buenos Aires, where Sir Thomas was fulfilling engagements.

HUMMEL, Ferdinand (1855–1928)
b. Berlin, Germany. From early age had equal facility with pf and harp. Studied both at Kullak's Acad., and the Hochschule, Berlin, 1868–75. Appointed director of R. Acad. there 1897. Wrote much pf music.

HUMMEL, Johann Nepomuk (1778–1837)
b. Pozsony, Hungary. A pupil of his father. When W. A. Mozart heard him, he was so impressed that he took the boy into his care for two years, feeding, clothing, sheltering and teaching him. At the end the student appeared in a Mozart concert with such success that H's father took him on an extended tour of Europe including Britain. Returning to Vienna, the lad continued to study, with Albrechtsberger, Haydn and Salieri.
  In 1804 he succeeded Haydn as *Kapellmeister* to the Esterházy household. A recital in Vienna created a sensation, and he was held to be a celebrity inferior to none, not even Beethoven. As such he had a beneficial influence on the musical scene and toured widely with great success as pianist and as composer. He was especially brilliant at extemporization, Spohr holding that 'no other piano virtuoso ever approached him in improvisation'. The young Chopin was tremendously impressed when H played in Warsaw in 1828.
  His own pianistic ability lent lustre to his

creative work, which is elegant and soundly constructed. After his death in Weimar, his esteem as a composer rapidly slumped in comparison with his contemporaries, yet he was a definite stepping-stone between the 'Classical' and 'Romantic' movements.

Since World War II musicians have taken fresh interest in the music; in consequence his reputation has undergone some resurgence, and it has been extensively recorded. His works include seven pf concertos, five sonatas, chamber music and studies. He wrote a textbook, *Anweisung zum Pianofortespiel* (1828), with an important section on fingering.

Pupils included: Julius Benedict, Jan Boom, Karl Czerny, Friedrich Ehrlich, Karl Engel, Louise Farrenc, Henry Forbes, Adolf Henselt, Ferdinand Hiller, Wolfgang Mozart Jnr, Edouard Roeckel, Wilhelm Scharfenberg, Franz Schoberlechner, Sigismund Thalberg, Giuseppe Unia, Heinrich Willmers.

HUNEKER, James (Gibbons) (1860–1921)
b. Philadelphia, USA. Studied locally before going to Paris as a pf pupil of T. Ritter, and then New York for lessons from R. Joseffy. Settled in that city and taught pf at National Cons. before turning to musical criticism. Assisted in the Joseffy edition of Chopin for the publishers G. Shirmer, and wrote a number of books including his autobiography and one of the first intelligent works on F. Chopin.

HUNGERFORD, Bruce (1922–77)
b. Korumburra, Australia. Pf pupil of I. Friedman, then went to New York to study with E. Hutcheson and later K. Friedberg. Début New York 1951. Took master-classes and toured extensively, notably in Beethoven. Recorded RCA and Eterna.

HUNT, John (1905–78)
b. Eltham, UK. Pupil of R. Acad., London, then of A. Schnabel in Berlin. Début 1930 London. Concert pianist and broadcaster. Also pf prof. at R. Acad. of Music, London, Cornell Univ., USA and Tokyo Univ., Japan. Gave first performance of W. Wordsworth pf concerto with London SO, London, 1947. In early 1930s demonstrated the Neo-Bechstein pf incorporating an electrophonic device where sound was amplified into electrical waves from valves. Latterly resided in Rome and was additionally organist. Recorded *HMV* (Neo-Bechstein).

HÜNTEN, Franz (1793–1878)
b. Coblenz, Germany. Pupil of A. Reicha at Paris Cons., where he remained, playing, teaching and composing, including arrangements for pf that were popular for a time. Wrote a *Méthode* for pf.

HURÉ, Jean (1877–1930)
b. Gien, France. Musical education details obscure because when he arrived in Paris in 1898 he was a fully equipped pianist and composer. Gave frequent concerts there and toured Europe with success. In 1912 he founded the famous École Normale for teaching pf, organ and composition. Wrote a quantity of pedagogic works and besides opera composed pf and chamber-music.

HURLSTONE, William Yeates (1876–1906)
b. London, UK. With no formal musical education a set of five waltzes of his were published when he was 9. Went to R. Coll., London at 18 and received pf lessons from E. Dannreuther. Delicate health prevented a concert career, and in the short span left he composed much, mainly chamber music and pf pieces. He gave first performance of his pf concerto in 1896 in London. As a composer of chamber music was regarded as slightly ahead of the British school of Bridge, Ireland etc. Transcribed a suite for harpsichord by Purcell into pf duet.

HURNICK, Ilja (1922–)
b. Ostrava, Czechoslovakia. Prodigy in pf playing and at composition. Début Prague 1942. Performed in Europe generally after World War II and was prof. at Prague Cons. Has composed for pf, including a concerto.

HURUM, Alf (1882–1972)
b. Oslo, Norway. Studied there; also spent four years at Berlin Hochschule, his pf teacher being V. da Motta. Went to Paris where he was influenced compositionally by the Impressionist movement, then to St Petersburg, before beginning to tour as concert pianist. Returned later to Oslo, mainly as composer, and in 1924 settled in Hawaii and took up painting.

HUSS, Henry Holden (1862–1953)
b. Newark, USA. Pupil of father then of Munich Cons. Returned to USA on completion of training and combined concert work with teaching in New York. Composed a *Rhapsody* and a concerto for pf and orch., chamber music, pf pieces and songs.

HUTCHENS, Frank (1892–1965)
b. Christchurch, New Zealand. Studied in London at R. Acad. under T. Matthay for pf, afterwards staying on in a teaching capacity until 1914 when he was appointed prof. at Sydney Cons. Returned to UK in 1922 and gave series of successful recitals. Composed a concerto for pf, *Fantasy Concerto* for two pfs and orch., chamber music and pf pieces.

HUTCHESON, Ernest (1871–1951)
b. Melbourne, Australia. Toured that country as a prodigy before studying in Leipzig under K. Reinecke till 1890 when he received lessons from B. Stavenhagen in Weimar. Pursued practice and study until 1900 when he made a tour of Europe. Dissatisfied with the results, he went into seclusion again until 1912 when a second tour was an unqualified success, as was his New York début in 1915. Thereafter in between concert tours he undertook teaching in various American schools. Composed a concerto for two pfs and sets of pieces, and made transcriptions. Was an original member of Faculty of Juilliard. Wrote *The Literature of the Piano* (1950), revised by Rudolf Ganz (1969).

Pupils included: Jacques Abram, Creighton Allen, Norman Cazden, Abram Chasins, John Erskine, George Gershwin, Edith Gray, Bruce Hungerford, Paul Jacobs, Fernando Laires, Otto Ortmann, Olga Samaroff, Ernest Seitz, Oscar Wagner, Paul Wells.

HUVÉ, Cyril (1954–   )
b. Paris, France. Student of Paris Cons. and pupil of C. Arrau and G. Cziffra.

HYAM, Lottie (1864–?)
b. Sydney, Australia. Studied there and came into prominence through demonstrating Steinway's instruments at Sydney Int. Exhibition 1879. A distinguished early Australian concert artist.

HYDE, Miriam (1913–   )
b. Adelaide, Australia. Studied at Univ. there and then R. Coll., London. Composed two pf concertos which she premièred in London, later performing them in Australia. Composed chamber music and numerous pf works.

HYLLESTED, August (1856–1946)
b. Stockholm, Sweden, of Danish stock. Toured as prodigy at 11, then studied with T. Kullak in Berlin before spending three years with F. Liszt. British début 1883. US début 1885 in course of touring Europe and America. Settled in USA 1886, holding various teaching posts as well as performing. Went to Glasgow, UK, 1903–14, but was in USA during World War I. Retired to Blairmore, Argyll, Scotland, in 1923. Composed in Romantic idiom.

Pupils included: Arne Oldberg.

IBBOTT, Daphne (1918–)
b. London, UK. Pupil at R. Acad. there. Accompanist and teacher; also chamber-music player. Recorded various labels.

IGUMNOV, Constantine Nikolaievich (1873–1948)
b. Liebedian, Russia. Pupil of N. Zverev, then at Moscow Cons. of A. Siloti and P. Pabst. Taught at Tiflis for a time; thereafter pf prof. at Moscow Cons. from 1899.

Pupils included: Anatole Alexandrov, Arno Babadzhanian, Elena Beckman-Scherbina, Bella Davidovich, Issay Dobrowen, Maria Grinberg, Pierre Luboschutz, Lev Oborin, Nicolas Orlov, David Rabinovich, Naum Shtarkman, Jakob Weinberg.

ILES, Edna (–)
b. Birmingham, UK. Studied privately and appeared with leading European orchestras, including British provincial tour of Philharmonia O. in 1949; also recitalist. Was a leading exponent of Medtner's music.

IMBRIE, Andrew (1921–)
b. New York, USA. Pupil of L. Ornstein and R. Casadesus. Compositions included chamber music and a pf sonata.

IMMELMAN, Niel (1944–)
b. Bloemfontein, S. Africa. Student of pf in London of C. Smith and I. Kabos. Chappell Gold Medallist, 1969, at R. Coll. Début with London PO followed by appearances in Europe and N. America.

INDJIC, Eugen (1947–)
b. Belgrade, Yugoslavia, of Russian and Serbian parentage. Studied pf there before family emigrated to the USA where the 9-year-old boy became a pupil of A. Borowsky. Appeared on television aged 10 and made his orch. début in Washington in 1960. Graduated Harvard 1969 and commenced pianistic career. 4th Prizewinner of Int. Chopin Comp., 1970, and came 3rd in the Leeds Int. Comp., 1972. Also won Rubinstein Prize 1974. London début 1980. Appeared in Europe and Far East. Recorded CBS.

INDY, Vincent d' (1851–1931)
b. Paris, France. Pf pupil of L. Diémer 1862–5. Knew most of the great musicians of his time and played a full part in the musical life of France as teacher and composer, influencing younger composers through founding the Schola Cantorum in Paris. Works for pf include *Symphonie sur un chant montagnard français* for pf and orch. (1886), a pf sonata, a *Thème varié, fugue et chanson* and several collections. The *Fantaisie sur un Vieil Air de Ronde français* was completed in the year of his death. British première of *Symphonie montagnard* was during 1907 Proms in London. There is also a *concerto for pf, flute, cello and string orch.*, dating from 1927.

INFANTE, Manuel (1883–1958)
b. Seville, Spain. Studied with E. Morera. Worked mainly as conductor and composer and lived in Paris from 1909. Apart from one opera, his compositions are for pf, mainly dances reflecting the Andalusian idiom. His works were actively propagated by J. Iturbi from 1921.

INNIS, Josephine Console (–)
b. Chicago, USA. Pupil at Cons. there and later with M. Rosenthal. Début 1927. Performed and broadcast solo and as accompanist. Recorded RCA.

INTEN, Ferdinand von (1848–1918)
b. Leipzig, Germany. Pupil of Cons. there, studying pf with I. Moscheles. Toured Europe as concert pianist, then in 1868 settled in USA. Had brilliant début in New York but soon after turned to chamber music which at that time was little performed and understood in America. Went back to Germany 1876 and gave first performance of Liszt's sonata in Leipzig.

IRELAND, John (1879–1962)
b. Bowden, Cheshire, UK. Pupil at R. Coll., London, 1893–1901, studying pf under F. Cliffe. A self-critical composer who destroyed much of his early work. Output includes a pf concerto (1930), an early *Fantasy Trio* in A minor, three violin sonatas, the second of which established the composer's reputation when in 1917 it received a first performance by Albert Sammons and William Murdoch. According to Edwin Evans, the first edition of the score was sold out before publication. There is an important pf sonata in E (1920) and a quantity of pf pieces including *Sarnia* (1941). Recorded *Columbia* and *Decca*.

ISAACS, Edward (1881–1953)
b. Manchester, UK. Studied at R. Manchester Coll., 1894–1903, continuing in Germany and Vienna. Début 1905 in Manchester under Richter and settled there in 1907, performing, teaching, lecturing, broadcasting and composing. Founded and directed chamber concerts as well as a series of Tuesday midday concerts. In 1924 as a result of an accident I became completely blind but did not allow it to curtail his activities, and his public concerts and recitals continued. Wrote a book, *The Blind Piano Teacher*. Premièred his pf concerto in C sharp minor at 1907 Proms. Recorded *Regal-Zono*.
    Pupils included: Marjorie Clementi.

ISAACS, Harry (1902–72)
b. London, UK. Student of R. Acad. there and later appointed to staff. Teacher, concert pianist and broadcaster. Formed a Pf Trio which took his name.

ISAACS, Leonard (1909–)
b. Manchester, UK. Son of Edward I. Pf pupil of R. Coll., London, under H. Fryer; later with A. Cortot in Paris and with E. Petri in Berlin. Was on the staff of the BBC for many years in a variety of capacities. Adjudicated at

home and abroad. Settled in Canada in 1963 as prof. at Manitoba Univ.

ISADOR, Michael (1939–)
b. Philadelphia, USA. Studied at Paris Cons. and Juilliard School, pupil of I. Kabos. Début Philadelphia 1951. Performed in Europe and USA as soloist, also accompanying famous instrumentalists. Taught in USA and S. Africa. Recorded EMI.

ISAKOVICH, Vera Ivanovna: *see* **SCRIABIN, Vera Ivanovna**

ISEPP, Martin (1930–)
b. Vienna, Austria. Studied Oxford, UK. Teacher and noted accompanist; also harpsichordist. Was on Juilliard School Faculty 1973–6. Recorded various labels.

ISHERWOOD, Cherry (–)
b. Preston, UK. Student at R. Acad. of Music, London. Accompanist and harpist. Married the violinist Henry Datyner.

ISSERLIS, Julius (1888–1968)
b. Kishinev, Romanian borders with Russia. Studied at Kiev Cons. under V. Puchalski, then at Moscow Cons. under V. Safonov, winning the Gold Medal 1906. Toured Europe and USA 1907–9. Appointed pf prof. at Moscow Cons. 1913. After the revolution he moved to Vienna, establishing his reputation as virtuoso, teacher and composer. Settled in London prior to World War II. In later life activities curtailed by failing eyesight. Specialized in Chopin and Russian composers, especially Scriabin. Composed pf works including two *Poems* for pf and orch. Recorded Delta.
    The Julius Isserlis Scholarship was established for musical students of either sex and any nationality (but normally living in the UK), aged 15–20, to study abroad for two years. Enquiries to the Administrative Secretary, c/o The R. Phil. Soc.
    Pupils included: Ruth Geiger, Elaine Hugh-Jones, Bernard Pinsonneault.

ISTOMIN, Eugene (1925–)
b. New York, USA, of Russian parentage. Student of Mannes School and later of E. Petri at Curtis Inst. Début 1943 New York in Brahms 2nd concerto. Performed thereafter as soloist. Was member of Istomin-Stern-Rose Trio.

ITURBI, Amparo (1899–1969)
b. Valencia, Spain. Sister of José I. Fine concert pianist who had distinguished career, if somewhat overshadowed by her brother, as he admitted. Recorded RCA.

Pupils included: Bruce Sutherland.

ITURBI, José (1895–1980)
b. Valencia, Spain. Played pf from age of 3, was prodigy by 7. Student of Valencia Cons., winning 1st Prize 1908, and of J. Maláts, then at Paris Cons., where he graduated in 1912 with Grand Prix. Further study in Barcelona. Head of pf dept. Geneva Cons. 1919–23. British début 1923 with great success, followed by tour of Europe and S. America. US début 1928, adding conducting to his activities there in 1933. Broke into the world of Hollywood films. At peak of career averaged 200 concerts a year. A fine artist and humble man who brought great pleasure to many people by his warmth and the dexterity of a superb pianism.

Composed *Fantasia* for pf and orch. as well as pf pieces. Recorded *HMV*, *RCA* and Columbia and Angel.

Pupils included: Richard Yardumian.

IVALDI, Filippo (1874–1939)
b. Alexandria, Egypt, of Italian family. Studied at Bologna Cons. under G. Martucci, where he later became pf prof.

IVES, Charles Edward (1874–1954)
b. Danbury, USA. Learned several instruments, including pf, from his father who was a military band conductor. A Yale graduate, his life was spent mainly in insurance, music being a spare time occupation until 1930. His compositions were published much later, many of them since his death. There are two pf sonatas, the second entitled *Concord* and first performed by J. Kirkpatrick, chamber music, pf solos and more than 100 songs.

JABLONSKA, Oksana: *see*
YABLONSKAYA, Oxana

JACKSON, Frederic Marsh (1905–)
b. Lincoln, UK. Pf pupil of R. Acad. of Music, London. Taught and gave lecture-recitals. Principal work as pf prof. at R. Normal Coll. for the Blind.

JACKSON, Raymond (1933–)
b. Providence, USA. Studied at New England Cons., Boston, and Juilliard School. Pupil of S. Gorodnitzki and B. Webster. Début New York in 1959. Won 4th Prize in M. Long–J. Thibaud Concours, Paris 1965. Toured the Americas and Europe; also taught at Howard Univ.

JACOBS, Paul (1930–83)
b. New York, USA. Pupil of E. Hutcheson and Juilliard School, graduating 1951, and having already made début. Was in Europe 1951–60, performing, lecturing and gaining first-hand experience in contemporary scene in which he has taken lively and active interest. Was appointed to New York Phil. 1961 and has fulfilled teaching posts at Tanglewood and NY Brooklyn Coll. Recorded various, including important sets of Debussy's *préludes* and *études* for Nonesuch.

JACOBSON, Maurice (1896–1976)
b. London, UK. Studied at Modern School of Music, London, resuming training after World War I. Performed, taught and composed, including chamber music, pf solos, duets and duos, also songs. OBE 1971.

JACOMET, Johann Georg (1946–)
b. Graubünden, Switzerland. Blind pianist who studied for a short time under W.

Rehberg. Also organist. Noted for wide repertoire.

JACZYNOWSKA, Katarzyna (1875–1920)
b. Stawle, Poland. Studied pf with Anton Rubinstein 1883–94, and then with T. Leschetizky in Vienna for two years. Toured central Europe as virtuoso and from 1912 taught master-class of Warsaw Cons.
    Pupils included: Isaac Albéniz, Rudolf Breithaupt, Wesley Forsyth, Zdenko Fibich, Gottfried Galston, Amina Goodwin, Jean Kürsteiner, Adele Lewing, Stanislas Niewiadomski, Willy Rehberg, Frank Shepard, Roman Vesely.

JADASSOHN, Salomon (1831–1902)
b. Breslau, Germany. Student of Leipzig Cons. Pupil of F. Liszt 1849–51. Taught in Leipzig thereafter. Composed much including a pf concerto, chamber music, pf pieces and songs. Wrote educational works on aspects of composition.

JADIN, Hyacinthe (1769–1802)
b. Versailles, France. Younger brother of Louis Emmanuel J. Pf prof. at Paris Cons. and composer.

JADIN, Louis Emmanuel (1768–1853)
b. Versailles, France. Was born and reared in household of Louis XVI. Became accompanist and eventually conductor. Survived the Revolution to become pf prof. at Paris Cons. and is said to have performed before Napoleon. Composed assiduously for one and two pfs in the salon vein of the times.

JAËLL, Alfred (1832–82)
b. Trieste, Italy. Pf pupil of I. Moscheles. Début 1843 Venice. Became well-known pianist and composer of pf music. Playing des-

cribed as 'smooth and brilliant and insinuating'. Emigrated to USA 1848 during European revolution of that year, returning 1854. In 1866 married Marie Trautmann, later divorced. J visited Britain regularly 1866–77. Marie Jaëll's name is now principally remembered as dedicatee of Saint-Saëns' *Étude en forme de Valse*, Op. 52/6.

Pupils included: Benjamin Lang.

JAMES, William Garnet (1892–   )
b. Ballarat, Australia. Studied at Melbourne Cons., then in Brussels under A. de Greef. Début London 1915. Became Controller of Australian Broadcasting Commission. Toured Australia, composed pf works and songs. OBE 1960.

JANDÓ, Jenö (1952–   )
b. Hungary. Student at the Liszt Acad. in Budapest where his teachers included P. Kadosa. Graduated 1974 with distinction, and a year later became assistant to Kadosa. That same year was placed 2nd in the Dino Ciani Comp. in Milan. Came 11th in the Sydney (Australia) Int. Pf Comp. of 1977. Toured Hungary and later Europe, as well as Canada and Japan. UK début Wigmore Hall, London, 1984. Ensemble player in addition to recitals and concerts, and has been described as combining 'astonishing technical assurance with a rich expressive palette'. Recorded Hungaroton.

JANIS, Byron (1928–   )
b. Pittsburgh, USA. His mother was Russian, emigrating to the USA when she was quite young. He began studying the pf at the age of 5 and by the time he was 7 was living in New York with his mother and working under the Lhevinnes; he was also tutored by other teachers in addition to studying composition under the American composer Roger Sessions. His début was in Pittsburgh in 1944, performing the Rachmaninov C minor concerto. V. Horowitz happened to be present, and as a result of a conversation Janis became his pupil in New York, accompanying the great Russian pianist on concert tours in order not to interrupt tuition. He remained with Horowitz until 1948, when he was 20. That year his Carnegie Hall début launched his adult concert career. In 1952 he made his European début with the Concertgebouw Orch. before touring the Continent. He visited the USSR in 1960, repeating that visit two years later.

J has always had a strong affinity with Chopin, to the extent of visiting Nohant and meeting George Sand's granddaughter. He appeared in the TV film *A Portrait of Frédéric Chopin* (1975) and has been the recipient of numerous awards, including the Grand Prix du Disque 1962.

His repertoire is catholic, spanning Mozart to Rachmaninov, his special interest in the latter composer doubtless stemming from his association with V. Horowitz. His second wife is the daughter of the film star Gary Cooper (1901–61). Recorded RCA, Philips, Everest, Mercury etc.

Pupils included: Thomas Zaiko.

JANKÓ, Paul (1856–1919)
b. Tata, Hungary. Received comprehensive musical education in Berlin and Vienna, principal pf teacher being H. Ehrlich. From 1892 he resided in Istanbul. The inventor of the Jankó Keyboard, consisting of six rows of keys in rising terraces, the main purpose being to enable a hand to cover a stretch of two or three more keys than on a normal pf keyboard. Around 1886 it was widely publicized and demonstrated by J and other pianists. It failed because the touch was not even and by the nature of the invention could not be made so. Wrote about the ideas in *Eine neue Klaviatur* (1886).

JANOTHA (Marie Cecilia) Natalia (1856–1932)
b. Warsaw, Poland. Studied pf in Berlin, then with K. Schumann. Début Leipzig 1874. Became brilliant concert pianist. Wrote several books on Chopin as well as translating into English the Tarnowski biography. Is supposed to have always laid a prayer-book on the instrument before playing, even at public concerts. Shaw said in 1891 that 'When her playing lost its freshness it did not gain the warmth and sympathy of the mature artist.' He also recorded how beautifully she played the Beethoven 4th when she first toured in 1879.

Pupils included: I. J. Paderewski.

JANSEN, Rudolf (1940–   )
b. Arnheim, Netherlands. Pupil of Amsterdam Cons. and of N. Wagenaar, winning a diploma. Toured as soloist and accompanist.

JAPHA, Louise (1826–89)
b. Hamburg, Germany. Studied there and later, in 1853, had lessons from K. Schumann.

Toured Europe, being especially appreciated in Paris for her playing of Schumann. Married the German violinist Friedrich Langhans 1858. After divorce in 1874 she lived in Wiesbaden, mainly teaching. Lifelong friend of Brahms and played the pf part in the 1st public performance in 1868 of the Brahms F minor pf quintet, Op. 34, in Paris.

JAWUREK, Josef (1756–1840)
b. Benesov, Czechoslovakia. Nothing known prior to début Warsaw 1792, after which toured Poland. Settled in Warsaw as concert pianist. Taught at Cons. there.

JEDLICZKA, Ernst (1855–1904)
b. Poltava, Russia. Student of Moscow Cons. and of N. Rubinstein for pf. Taught pf at Moscow Cons. 1881–8, then went to Berlin, first at Klindworth, later at Stern's.
    Pupils included: Georg Bertram, E. Howard-Jones, Stanislas Lipski.

JEMELIK, Antonin (1930–62)
b. Prague, Czechoslovakia. Student of Prague Cons. and of Prague Acad. of Music. Début in 1947 there and toured Eastern Europe. A pianist of great fire yet sensibility whose early death must be regarded as untimely and tragic. Recorded Supraphon.

JENKINS, John Philip (1940–)
b. Newcastle-under-Lyme, UK. Student of R. Acad., London, and of H. Craxton and J. Février, winning Harriet Cohen Comp. Performed especially chamber music. Pf prof.

JENNER, Alexander (1929–)
b. Vienna, Austria. Student of the Acad. there, and amongst his awards was the Bösendorfer Prize in 1949. Performed internationally, taught in Vienna, adjudicated and broadcast on radio and television.

JENSEN, Adolf (1837–79)
b. Königsberg (now Kaliningrad, USSR). Mainly self-taught though some references suggest he received lessons from F. Liszt. Spent time with Gade, presumably studying comp. Returned to Königsberg in 1860, teaching and composing. Was head of the pf masterclass at the Tausig School in Berlin 1866–8. The rest of his life was spent in Baden. His compositions include many songs at which he was more successful than in the pf music which is formal and colourless.

JENTSCH, Max (1855–1918)
b. Magdeburg, Germany. Student of Stern's Cons., Berlin. Début 1880 there. Toured widely thereafter, living for a time in Istanbul, returning to Germany in 1892. Pf prof. of Vienna Cons. from 1899. Composed a pf concerto, chamber music and pf pieces.

JEZEWSKI, Zbigniew (1921–)
b. Cracow, Poland. Student of Cons. there, graduating with diploma 1946. Concert pianist solo and with orch., also chamber-music player. Pf prof. at Cracow Cons.

JIRÁNEK, Josef (1855–1940)
b. Ledce, Czechoslovakia. Foster-son of B. Smetana, who was his teacher. Besides pf he studied violin, harp and organ. Taught pf at Kharkov 1877–91, becoming pf prof. at Prague Cons. 1891–1923. Enthusiastically propagated Czech pf music, especially the works of Smetana. Composed chamber music and songs.
    Pupils included: Rudolf Friml, Vitezslav Novák.

JOHANNESEN, Grant (1921–)
b. Salt Lake City, USA. Pupil of R. Casadesus, then of E. Petri. Début 1944 New York and first toured Europe 1947. Married the cellist Zara Nelsova. Recorded Golden Crest, Vox, CRI.

JOHANSEN, David Monrad (1888–1974)
b. Vefsen, Norway. Pf pupil of K. Nissen. Studied composition in Oslo and Berlin. Début as pianist 1910. Performed and composed, and in 1915 gave concert in Oslo of own compositions. Was also music critic. As a composer he used national folk-tunes, adapting them to contemporary techniques. Wrote a book on Edvard Grieg which was translated into English (1938). Wrote musical criticism.

JOHANSEN, Gunnar (1906–)
b. Copenhagen, Denmark. Pupil of V. Schiøler, then in Berlin with F. Lamond, E. Fischer and E. Petri. Début 1924. Toured Europe for some years, then settled in USA as touring virtuoso and teacher. Admired Busoni and propagated his music. Recorded Artist Direct.

JOHNS, Clayton (1857–1932)
b. New Castle, USA. Studied in Boston, then in Berlin with F. Rummel. Returned to Boston

where he performed, taught and composed. Wrote memoirs and works on pf technique.

JOHNSON, Guy (1933–)
b. Marinette, USA. Teachers included R. Ganz and G. Sandor. Début Milwaukee 1955. Concert pianist and teacher.

JOHNSON, Robert Sherlaw (1932–)
b. Sunderland, UK. Musically educated at Durham Univ. and R. Acad., London. Also studied pf with J. Février. Performed specializing in contemporary music; also taught at Leeds Univ. and Oxford. Published compositions include two sonatas and pf pieces. Wrote on contemporary composers.

JOHNSON, Thomas A. (1908–)
b. Neston, UK. Pupil of F. Dawson and F. Merrick in Manchester. Performed extensively, often featuring works of neglected composers. Composed pf works including a sonata, studies and a *Theme and Variations*, as well as works for the left hand.

JOHNSTONE, Arthur Edward (1860–1944)
b. London, UK. Educated in New York, studying pf with W. Mason. Led mainly pedagogic career as lecturer and editor. Wrote pf pieces.

JOHNSTONE, John Alfred (1861–1941)
b. Cork, Ireland. Graduated in Dublin, emigrating to Australia 1882 where he directed music and taught pf at the Atheneum, Melbourne, ending his days in Devonshire, UK. Wrote a number of books on aspects of pf technique.

JOIO, Norman dello (1913–)
b. New York, USA. Studied pf with father and was natural sight-reader. Went on to Juilliard School and began playing pf in jazz bands. First major work was pf sonata (1943). Gave première of *Ricercari* for pf and orch. 1945 with New York PO. Wrote a *Concertino* and a set of variations for pf and orch., sonatas and pieces. Used jazz rhythms and has been said to reflect harmonies of Hindemith. Also composed two sets of children's pieces for pf duet.

JOLIVET, André (1905–74)
b. Paris, France. Pupil of Paul le Flem and of Edgar Varèse and a founder-member of 'Jeune France'. Composed a set of six pieces for pf, *Mana*, a concerto with pf part, several pf

sonatas (one dedicated to the memory of B. Bartók) and works for pf and the Theremin, and for Ondes Martenot, as well as chamber music and works for two pfs.

JONÁS, Alberto (1868–1943)
b. Madrid, Spain. Student of Madrid Cons. and from 1886 of Brussels Cons. under A. de Greef, winning 1st Prize for pf-playing in 1888. In 1890 received tuition from Anton Rubinstein in St Petersburg. Début 1891 Berlin. Thereafter toured Europe and USA, holding various teaching posts in the latter country 1894–1904. Taught in Berlin 1904–14 and returned to USA on the outbreak of war. Composed pf pieces and wrote several works on technique.
Pupils included: Ellen Ballon, Alfred Calzin, Anis Fuleihan, Louis Loth, Vincent Persichetti.

JONAS, Maryla (1911–59)
b. Warsaw, Poland. Prodigy at age of 8. Studied with I. Paderewski, E. von Sauer and J. Turczynski. Adult début 1926, in which year she commenced the career of a touring virtuoso. Also taught. After Poland was occupied in 1939, she went to S. America, quickly establishing a fine reputation. US début 1946 in New York and settled there.

JONES, Alton (1899–1971)
b. Fairfield, USA. Studied in New York under R. Bühlig. Début New York 1925. In addition to performing held various teaching posts.

JONES, Martin (1940–)
b. Witney, UK. Pupil of R. Acad. of Music, London, and Chigiana Acad., Siena. Début London 1969. Toured Europe and visited USA. Pianist-in-residence Cardiff Univ. Identified with the music of Szymanowski and of A. Hoddinot whose seventh sonata received its première by M. J. in London in 1984. Recorded Argo and EMI.

JONG, Marinus de (1891–)
b. Osterhout, Netherlands, of Belgian parentage. Student of Antwerp Cons. and of E. Bosquet for pf. Toured widely in the 1920s before settling in Belgium where he was appointed head of pf at Antwerp Cons. Composed several pf concertos and pf sonatas, much chamber music and pieces for pf.

JORDAN, Sverre (1889–1972)
b. Bergen, Norway. Trained in Berlin 1907–14, pf teachers being J. da Motta and C. Ansorge. Début Bergen 1911 where he settled as pianist, teacher, composer and conductor. Became important figure in musical life there and wrote much music including pf pieces which reflect some influence of Grieg. Best known for his songs.

JOSEFFY, Rafael (1852–1915)
b. Hunfalu, Hungary. Studied in Budapest, then spent two years at Leipzig Cons. under E. Wenzel and I. Moscheles. Two more years were spent with K. Tausig, and the summers with F. Liszt at Weimar. Début 1870 in Berlin was immediate success, and so were subsequent tours. US début 1879 was so successful that he decided to settle there. Will always be associated with the work of familiarizing the public with Chopin and with preparing the complete edition for G. Schirmer. He also did much to propagate the works of Brahms. Was pf prof. at the National Cons., New York, 1888–1906. Composed pf music and arranged work of other composers. Of a recital in Vienna in 1874 E. Hanslick wrote: 'The Tausig school is unmistakable in his well-rounded and consummate technique, in the sharply chiselled phrasing, and in the rich nuances of touch.'
   Pupils included: Clarence Adler, Ellen Ballon, Albert von Doenhoff, Rubin Goldmark, Sigmund Herzog, Edwin Hughes, James Huneker, Moritz Rosenthal.

JOSELSON, Tedd (1954–)
b. Belgium. American pianist who studied from age of 5 and who made exciting concerts with major orchs. in his teens. Has appeared widely in USA. Recorded RCA.

JOUKOV, Igor: *see* **ZHUKOV, Igor**

JOURAVLEFF, George: *see* **ZURAWLEW, Georg**

JOY, Geneviève (1919–)
b. Bernaville, France. Pf pupil of Y. Nat and of Paris Cons., where she won 1st Prize 1941. Was especially interested in contemporary French music. Married the composer Henri Dutilleux (1916–), who was also a student at Paris Cons., winning the Prix de Rome 1938. Had distinctive career as composer whose output was not large, and has been described as 'embracing conservative and *avant garde* extremes'. J gave the première of his pf sonata in Paris in 1948 and later performed *Figures de resonances* for two pfs (1970).

JOYCE, Eileen (1912–)
b. Zeehan, Tasmania. Was brought to the notice of P. Grainger at an early age and became a pupil of R. Teichmüller at Leipzig Cons., of T. Matthay in London, then of A. Schnabel in Berlin. Début London Proms. Thereafter performed, broadcast and recorded, giving many concerts for troops in World War II, after which she toured extensively throughout the world. Gave first British performance of Shostakovich's 1st pf concerto in 1936, and of his 2nd in 1958. Also played the Rachmaninov 2nd in the film *Brief Encounter*. Created an innovation of changing gowns during recitals and between concertos, giving added glamour to her stage presence. Was enormously popular and latterly added the harpsichord to her accomplishments. Companion to Order of St Michael and St George 1981. Recorded *Parlophone, Columbia, Decca* and Saga.

JUDD, Terence (1957–79)
b. London, UK. Was prodigy, winning the Nat. Junior Pf Comp. at age of 10. Amongst his teachers was Michel Block, and he played with the Nat. Youth Orch. and other London bands. Won a prize in Tchaikovsky Comp. in Moscow in 1978 and subsequently toured USSR. Died tragically. BBC recitals issued as recordings on Chandos label.
   The Terence Judd Award was established in 1982 and is given biennially to an artist 'of considerable professional experience of any nationality who is clearly on the threshold of an international career.' The winner is offered a recital in both London and Manchester, engagements with the Hallé Orch. and a cash award. Address: Administrator, Terence Judd Trust, Hallé Concerts Society, 30 Cross Street, Manchester M2 7BA.

KAAN-ALBESTU, Heinrich (1852–1926)
b. Tarnopol, Poland. Studied in Prague.
Became pf prof. at Cons. there in 1889 and
later Director. Composed and arranged pf
pieces.

KABALEVSKY, Dmitri Borisovich
(1904–   )
b. St Petersburg, Russia. Learned pf from an
early age and gave lessons while still a boy.
Pupil of Scriabin Inst. until 1925 when he
entered Moscow Cons., studying pf with A.
Goldenweiser. Graduated in 1930, and was a
very fine pianist who toured widely, especially
propagating own works. Composed three pf
concertos (the first gained a Cons. diploma and
was premièred in Moscow in 1931 with the
composer as soloist), three pf sonatas, 24
Preludes and variations etc.

KABOS, Ilona (1892–1973)
b. Budapest, Hungary. Pupil of Budapest R.
Acad., winning Diploma for pf-playing.
Taught there 1930–6 and toured Europe exten-
sively. Married L. Kentner 1931 (divorce
1945), and settled in UK before World War II,
performing and teaching. Played two pfs with
Kentner and later with N. Mewton-Wood.
With Kentner gave première of revised Bartók
sonata for two pfs and percussion in London in
1942. In 1965 settled in USA as pf prof. at
Juilliard School, New York.
   Pupils included: John Biggs, Phillip Challis,
Norma Fisher, Peter Frankl, Otto Freuden-
thal, Robin Harrison, Niel Immelman,
Michael Isador, Finn Nielsen, Marios
Papadopoulos, Howard Shelley, Jeffrey Siegel,
Janos Solyom, Sergio Varella-Cid, Inger
Wilkström.

KACSO, Diana (1953–   )
b. Rio de Janeiro, Brazil. Student of the Cons.

there and later of the Juilliard School and S.
Gorodnitzki; prizewinner of numerous pf
compositions including 6th in the Chopin Int.
Pf Comp., Warsaw, 1975, 2nd Gold in the
Arthur Rubinstein Comp., Tel-Aviv, 1977,
and 2nd in the Leeds Int. Pf Comp., 1978.
Toured Europe and the Americas solo and with
orch. Recorded DG.

KADOSA, Pál (1903–83)
b. Leva, Czechoslovakia. Pupil of Budapest
Acad. and on teaching staff of Fodor School
1927–43, then of Budapest Acad. from 1945.
By platform work consistently promoted the
cause of contemporary music and wrote extensively for the instrument, giving first performance of his pf concerto in 1933 in Amsterdam.
Also wrote a pf concertino, several sonatas and
suites as well as groups of solos.
   Pupils included: Gabor Csalog, Jenö Jandó,
Gyula Kiss, Zoltan Kocsis, Chiseko Minami,
Dezso Ranki, András Schiff, Istvan Székely.

KAGEN, Sergei (1909–64)
b. St Petersburg, Russia. Emigrated to USA
when young and studied at the Juilliard School
1925–30. Joined the Faculty, composed and
edited.

KAHN, Erich Itor (1905–56)
b. Rimbach, Germany. Student of Hochschule, Frankfurt, developing a predominant
interest in ensemble work and accompanying.
Settled in USA during World War II and
founded the Albeneri Pf Trio. Awarded
Coolidge Medal in 1948. Composed chamber-
music and pf works using twelve-tone system.
As accompanist recorded on *Columbia*.

KAHN, Percy (1880–1968)
b. London, UK. Pf pupil of R. Coll. there and
enjoyed worldwide career touring as accom-

panist to celebrities like Richard Tauber and Oda Slobodskaya. Recorded various labels as accompanist.

KAHN, Robert (1865–1951)
b. Mannheim, Germany. Studied there and in Berlin and Munich. Pf pupil of F. Kiel. Taught pf at Berlin Hochschule from 1893 until his retirement in 1931. Composed a considerable amount of chamber music, a *Konzertstück* for pf and orch., pf pieces and songs.

KAHRER, Laura: *see* **RAPPOLDI, Laura**

KALICHSTEIN, Joseph (1946–)
b. Tel Aviv, Israel. Pupil of Juilliard School, New York. Début 1867 there. Won 1st Prize Leventritt Comp. 1968 and successful career as concert pianist followed through USA and Europe. Recorded RCA and Erato.

KALKBRENNER, Friedrich (1785–1849)
b. in a carriage between Cassel and Berlin, Germany. Was taught by his father before entering Paris Cons. in 1799 under L. Adam. Début 1805 in Berlin was followed by a tour of German cities before returning to Paris in triumph. Spent ten years in London, then, after visiting Germany in 1823, settled in Paris as virtuoso and teacher of great renown with a technique well developed in all respects. His compositions are technically well wrought but no longer hold public interest. Dedicatee of the E minor pf concerto by F. Chopin who admired K, for a time considered becoming his pupil and wrote to a friend in 1831: 'If Paganini is perfection Kalkbrenner is his equal, but in quite another style. It is hard to describe to you his calm, his enchanting touch, his incomparable evenness, and the mastery that is displayed in every note. He is a giant walking over Herz and Czerny and all, and over me.'
Pupils included: Pedro Albéniz, Leopoldine Blahetka, William Dorrell, Arabella Goddard, Sir Charles Hallé, Paul Letondal, Ignace Leybach, George Mathias, George Osborne, Marie Pleyel, Ludwig Schunke, Édouard Silas, Camille Stamaty, Sigismund Thalberg, Ambroise Thomas.

KALLIR, Lilian (1931–)
b. Prague, Czechoslovakia, of Austrian parents. As refugees from the Nazi invasion, the family emigrated to USA via Portugal (where as a young girl she first met her future

husband). Studied at the Mannes School and later with I. Vengerova. Won several awards. Début 1949 New York and has since toured Europe regularly in addition to USA, both solo and with orch. Married to Claud Frank and gives duo recitals frequently. Recorded various.

KAMENIKOVA, Valentina (1930–)
b. Odessa, USSR. Lived in Czechoslovakia and became one of the nation's leading pianists. Recorded Supraphon. No further details ascertainable.

KAMENSKY, Aleksander (1900–52)
b. Geneva, Switzerland, of Russian parents. Studied at St Petersburg Cons., graduating in 1924. Spent lifetime performing; also taught at Leningrad Cons. from 1934. Especially famous for the number of recitals given there under dangerous conditions when the city was besieged by the Germans. Composed pf works and transcribed Russian opera for pf solo.

KANN, Hans (1927–)
b. Vienna, Austria. Studied there and was a pupil of F. Wührer. Won a number of prizes for pf playing and performed throughout Europe from 1945. Taught at Vienna Acad. for a time before becoming pf prof. at Tokyo Univ. in succession to L. Kreutzer. Composed pf pieces for one and two pfs, also chamber music and songs.

KANNER-ROSENTHAL, Hedwig (1882–1959)
b. Budapest, Hungary. Studied with T. Leschetizky and M. Rosenthal, whom she married. Début Vienna where she taught for five years. Had her own successful career as concert artist, solo, accompanying, ensemble and in duet recitals with her husband. From 1939 assisted in the pf school he founded in New York.
Pupils included: Kenneth Amanda, Julius Chajes, Robert Goldsand, Charles Rosen.

KAPELL, William (1922–53)
b. New York, USA. Of Russian-Polish parentage. Pupil of Olga Samaroff. New York début 1941. Toured USA thereafter as well as Europe after war ended. Killed in air crash. Recorded *RCA*.
Pupils included: Jaques Klein, Joel Ryce.

KAPLAN, Benjamin (1929–)
b. London, UK. Student of Guildhall School, London, and was a pf pupil of F. Reizenstein and L. Kentner. Won 3rd Prize in the Liszt Soc. Comp. in London, 1961.
Pupils included: Bradley Evans.

KAPRÁL, Václav (1889–1947)
b. Urcitz, Czechoslovakia. Pf pupil of V. Novák in Brünn and later of A. Cortot in Paris. Settled in Brünn as pianist, teacher and composer including four pf sonatas and a *Ballade* for cello and pf.

KARASOWSKI, Moriz (1823–92)
b. Warsaw, Poland. Studied cello and pf there but earned his living playing the former, residing in Germany from 1864. Was friend of the Chopin family and wrote the first definitive biography of Chopin (1877).

KARG-ELERT, Siegfried (1877–1933)
b. Oberndorff, Germany. Pupil of Leipzig Cons., pf teacher being K. Reinecke. Taught for a time at Magdeburg Cons., then returned to Leipzig where he took pf and composition. Besides playing pf and teaching, he studied organ and especially *Kunstharmonium*, for which he composed extensively.

KARÓLYI, Julian von (1914–)
b. Budapest, Hungary. Pupil of E. Von Dohnányi, J. Pembauer and A. Cortot. Performed and taught, specializing in Chopin. Recorded DG.
Pupils included: Lennart Rabes.

KARP, Howard (1929–)
b. Illinois, USA. Studied at Juilliard School there, then Acad. of Music, Vienna. Winner of Fulbright Award. Concert pianist and teacher.

KARP, Natalia (1914–)
b. Cracow, Poland. Pupil of W. Labunski at Cracow Cons., and later in Berlin with G. Bertram and A. Schnabel. Début there 1930 with Berlin PO. Performed successfully until World War II when she spent some years in a German concentration camp, on release returning to Cracow in 1945 and resumed her career. Settled in UK from 1947. Recorded Saga.

KARTUN, Léon (1895–)
b. France. Pupil of Paris Cons. and of L. Diémer. Recorded *Pathé* and *Parlophone*.

KATCHEN, Julius (1926–69)
b. Long Branch, USA. Was pf pupil of D. Saperton. Début Philadelphia 1937. Gave up career to study philosophy, re-emerging 1945 to make successful career as concert pianist on both sides of Atlantic. Settled in Paris and formed a trio with Josef Suk and Janos Starker. Very wide range of repertoire. Recorded *Decca* and Decca.
Pupils included: Pascal Rogé.

KATIN, Peter (1930–)
b. London, UK. Student of R. Coll. there. Début Wigmore Hall 1948 with immediate acclaim from critics. Toured extensively thereafter and had wide repertoire. Gave London première of G. Finzi's *Grand Fantasia & Toccata* for pf and orch., Op. 38, in 1954. Recorded Decca, EMI, Unicorn, Lyrita and others.
Pupils included: Alasdair Graham.

KATWIJK, Paul van (1885–1974)
b. Rotterdam, Netherlands. Studied at Hague Cons. and later in Vienna with L. Godowsky. Went to USA in 1912 and for a time concentrated on teaching and conducting around Dallas, finally taking pf pupils privately 1949–55.

KATZ, Mindru (1925–78)
b. Bucharest, Romania. Student at R. Acad. there and prizewinner in Berlin and Bucharest. Performed throughout the world. Recorded Pye.

KAUFMAN, Harry (1894–1961)
b. New York, USA. Pupil of S. Stojowski, then of J. Hofmann. From 1924 taught at Curtis Inst., specializing in work as accompanist at which he was renowned in addition to recitals, concerts and chamber music.

KEDRA, Wladyslaw (1918–68)
b. Lodz, Poland. Studied pf at Lodz Cons. with A. Dobkiewicz, then at Paris Cons. with M. Tagliaferra. 5th Prizewinner of the 1949 Chopin Int. Comp., Warsaw. Specialized in the music of Chopin. Recorded Muza and Westminster.

KELBERINE, Alexander (1903–40)
b. Kiev, Russia. Studied at Cons. there and later in Vienna; also taught by F. Busoni in Berlin. Went to USA and studied with A. Siloti at Juilliard School. Taught in USA and per-

formed extensively. Prolific composer. Committed suicide.

KELLERMANN, Berthold (1853–?)
b. Nuremberg, Germany. Studied pf privately, then in summertime 1873–8 with Liszt at Weimar. Taught successively at Kullak's and Stern's, Berlin. Went to Bayreuth in 1878 and among other activities was music teacher to Wagner's children. Did some conducting.

Pupils included: Paul Ben-Haim.

KELLEY, Edgar Stillman (1857–1944)
b. Sparta, USA. Studied in Chicago and later at Stuttgart Cons. under W. Krüger for pf. Was teacher, lecturer, music critic and organist, and taught pf in Berlin as well as New York. Composed symphonies and other works for orch., chamber music, pf pieces and songs. Wrote *Chopin the Composer* (1913) which was highly regarded in its day.

KELLEY, Jessie Stillman (Mrs Edgar Stillman Kelley) (1866–1949)
b. Chippewa Falls, USA. Studied pf with X. Scharwenka, theory with Edgar Kelley whom she married. Played pf and taught in USA and Germany 1910–34.

KELLY, Alexander (1929–)
b. Edinburgh, UK. Studied pf there and at R. Acad., London, where he later taught. Soloist, accompanist and chamber-music player.

Pupils included: Vanessa Latarche, J. Plowright.

KELLY, Dorothy (1918–)
b. Tobermore, (N. Ireland), UK. Studied there and at Guildhall School, London. Performed widely, especially in N. Ireland where she was accompanist for Belfast Phil. Soc. and for the BBC.

KELLY, Frederick Septimus (1881–1916)
b. Sydney, Australia. Remarkably gifted from early age and was awarded the Nettleship Scholarship at Balliol, Oxford, in succession to Sir D. F. Tovey, with whom he studied composition. Later continued pf studies at Hoch's Cons., Frankfurt. British début in three recitals at Aeolian Hall, London, 1912. Was killed in action, France, 1916. Composed a violin sonata premièred by d'Aranyi and L. Borwick, London, 1919, and pf works including *Theme, Variations and Fugue*.

KEMPFF, Wilhelm (1895–)
b. Juterborg, Germany. Studied in Potsdam under H. Barth and later at Berlin High School, winning two Mendelssohn prizes. Held teaching posts in Stuttgart and Potsdam but was known internationally as an illustrious concert pianist especially in works of Beethoven and Schumann. A poet with great warmth of tone at his command. Pf compositions include a sonata in four movements. Recorded *Polydor* and DG.

Pupils included: Idil Biret, Natanael Broman, Margarete Hawkins, Eric Heidsieck, Detlef Krause, John O'Conor, Gitti Pirner, Daniel Pollack, Robert Riefling, Mitsuko Uchida, Solveig Wikman, Rosemary Wright, Ventsislav Yankov.

KENDALL, Iain (1931–)
b. London, UK. Studied at R. Acad. of Music there, and won Harriet Cohen Medal in 1958. Performed with special interest in Debussy. Compositions include chamber music, pf pieces and songs. Published educational material for children.

KENNEDY, Spruhan Keith (1901–)
b. Adelaide, Australia. Studied there but has performed and taught mostly in Cape Town, S. Africa; also lecturer. Composer of songs.

KENTNER, Louis (1905–)
b. Silesia. Student of Budapest R. Acad. from 1911. Won 5th Prize in Int. Chopin Comp., Warsaw, in 1932 and came 3rd in the Liszt Comp. in Budapest the following year. Rapidly established a name throughout Europe as one of the leading Hungarian pianists. First appeared in UK in 1935 where he settled, becoming naturalized in 1946. Was married to Ilona Kabos 1931–45, and with her gave première of revised Bartók sonata for two pfs and percussion in London in 1942. Other premières included Bartók's 2nd concerto (1933) in Budapest, Rawsthorne's 1st concerto (1942), Bartók's 3rd concerto (1946 – European); with Y. Menuhin Walton's violin sonata (1950); and Tippett concerto (1956) in Birmingham. Dedicatee of Bliss's pf suite *Triptych* which he first performed in London in 1971. US début 1956. Compositions include three pf sonatinas. Wrote *Piano* in the Yehudi Menuhin Master Music Guide series. Recorded *Columbia, HMV* (as accompanist), EMI and Turnabout.

Pupils included: Leigh Gerdine, Rhondda

Gillespie, Benjamin Kaplan, Iris Loveridge, Omar Mejia, Bernard Pinsonneault, Lennart Rabes, Peter Simon, Marguerite Wolff, Mary Wu.

KERN, Jerome (1885–1945)
b. New York, USA. Studied at New York Coll. of Music and was taught pf by A. Lambert, completing musical studies in Germany 1904–5. Became famous through musical comedies and film scores and developed the musical idiom of these forms through a classical background.

KERR, Muriel (1911–63)
b. Regina, Canada. A prodigy who made her début at the age of 7 and began performing from the age of 9. US début Carnegie Hall 1928. Taught at Juilliard School 1942–9, toured Europe 1948 and was on the staff of S. California Univ. 1955–63. Recorded RCA.

KERR, Thomas (1915–)
b. Baltimore, USA. Student of Eastman School. Became head of the pf department at Howard Univ. School of Music, Washington. Concert career included solo tours and appearances with leading orchs. Compositions include seven *Dancetudes* for pf.

KERSENBAUM, Sylvia Haydée (1944–)
b. Buenos Aires, Argentina. Studied pf at Nat. Cons. there, winning Diploma. Début 1953 Buenos Aires. Toured extensively throughout musical world solo and with orch. Settled in UK. Recorded EMI.

KESSLER, Joseph Christoph (1800–72)
b. Augsburg. Self-taught pianist who became an excellent pedagogue and executant. Lived and taught in Poland a number of years, especially Warsaw 1829–30 where he became friendly with F. Chopin who took part in concerts at K's house. Settled finally in Vienna. Produced sets of pf *études* which were highly rated and used by Moscheles and Liszt. Chopin dedicated the German edition of his Op. 28 preludes to K.

KESTENBERG, Leo (1882–1962)
b. Rosemberk, Hungary. Pf pupil of F. Kullak and of F. Busoni in Berlin. Became teacher at Klindworth-Scharwenka Cons. there. As concert pianist was notable exponent of Liszt's music. Had distinguished academic career in

Germany until 1933 when he took up post with Ministry of Interior, Prague.

KETTEN, Henri (1848–83)
b. Baja, Hungary. Received musical training at Paris Cons. with pf under A. Marmontel. During a short life performed and composed pf pieces that are well turned but of salon style.

KETTERER, Eugene (1831–70)
b. Rouen, France. Pupil at Paris Cons. A one-time famous and prolific writer of salon pf pieces; also teacher.

KHRENNIKOV, Tikhon (1913–)
b. Glet, Russia. Pupil first of Gnessin Music School then of Moscow Cons. A fine pianist; also a composer who conformed to the Russian requirements in composition, having been a leading light of the USSR's Union of Composers from its inception in 1948. Composed a number of concertos, two of them for pf, the first dating from student days and, like Rachmaninov, his Op. 1. The second belongs to 1974, for which he was awarded the Lenin Prize.

KIDDLE, Frederick B. (–)
b. Frome, UK. Pf pupil of R. Coll., London. Was well-known accompanist who toured with celebrities including Gervase Elwes; was also official accompanist at Queen's Hall 1902–27 and was a soloist in the first British performance there of the Mozart concerto for three pfs and orch. (K.242). Recorded with Elwes on *Columbia*.

KIEL, Friedrich (1821–85)
b. Puderbach, Germany. Self-taught pianist who resided in Berlin from 1842 and became extremely reputable teacher. Wrote pf works including four sonatas.
Pupils included: Felix Dreyschock, Robert Kahn, Rikard Nordraak, Max Puchat, Otto Sinder, jnr.

KIHL, Viggo (1882–)
b. Copenhagen, Denmark. Pf student at Leipzig Cons. under R. Teichmüller. Début Copenhagen 1901. Lived in London 1903–13, appearing frequently there and throughout the UK. Thereafter resided in Canada as concert pianist and pf prof. at Toronto Cons.

KILENYI, Edward, jnr (1911–)
b. Philadelphia, USA. Son of Edward K,

Hungarian-born composer. Studied with E. von Dohnányi in Budapest from 1927, and toured with his master in the Schubert Centenary concert celebrations of 1928, graduating in 1930. Début outside Hungary 1929, Amsterdam. Toured Europe (UK 1935 under aegis of Sir T. Beecham) before returning to USA. Served in forces during World War II, then resumed career mainly in Americas. Taught at Florida State Univ. Recorded *Columbia*.

KILPINEN, Margarate (1896–)
b. Helsinki, Finland. Student at Cons. there. Accompanist and principally known as a propagator of works of her husband Yrjö K. Recorded *HMV* as accompanist in Kilpinen Song Soc. edition.

KILPINEN, Yrjö (1892–1959)
b. Helsinki, Finland. Largely self-taught composer who wrote many songs to Finnish and German settings, also pf works including six sonatas, several suites and chamber music.

KING, Oliver (1855–1923)
b. London, UK. Student in London, then later under K. Reinecke in Leipzig. Spent some time in Canada and USA. Returned to UK and in 1893 became pf prof. at R. Acad., London. Wrote pf concerto and pieces.

KING, Reginald (1904–)
b. London, UK. Received formal training as pianist, playing in London Prom concerts and elsewhere. Turned to light field and had own orch. Compositions covered a wide range. Recorded *HMV*.

KINGSLEY, Colin (1925–)
b. London, UK. Studied at R. Coll. of Music there. Performed solo and in ensemble and accompaniment. Lecturer.

KIRCHNER, Fritz (1840–1907)
b. Potsdam, Germany. Pf pupil of T. Kullak where he taught for 25 years before moving on to Berlin. Composed pf works and songs.

KIRCHNER, Leon (1919–)
b. New York, USA. Studied with R. Bühlig in Los Angeles. Later worked at the Univ. of California and on composition with E. Bloch and N. Boulanger. Adopted a largely pedagogic career and composed including two pf concertos, the first of which he premièred in

New York in 1956 under D. Mitropoulos, a pf sonata, chamber music and songs.

KIRCHNER, Theodor (1823–1903)
b. Chemnitz, Germany. Studied with Julius Knorr in Leipzig 1838–42; worked at Winterthur 1843–62, Zurich 1862–72; director of Würzburg Cons. 1873–5, then taught successively in Leipzig, Dresden and Hamburg. Was friend of Schumann and Mendelssohn. Wrote numerous works for pf, also chamber music and songs.

KIRKPATRICK, John (1905–)
b. New York, USA. Studied at Princeton Univ., graduating 1926. Went to Paris and became a pupil of I. Philipp and N. Boulanger. Taught and gave recitals and lecture-recitals. Devoted special study to the interpretation of 17th- and 18th-century chamber music. Made an edition of Bach's *Goldberg Variations* in 1938, and the following year gave the première of Charles Ives' 2nd pf sonata, sub-titled *Concord Mass.*, *1840–60*, a work in four movements each based on famous writers who had lived in Concord: Emerson, Hawthorne, Thoreau and the Alcotts. Arranged for pf Carl Ruggles' *Organum* for orch.

KIRKPATRICK, Ralph (1911–84)
b. Leominster, USA. Noted harpsichordist who, following research in Spain, became foremost authority of his day on Domenico Scarlatti; prepared own edition of sonatas and wrote a book on the composer combining biography and musical analysis. His numbered list of Scarlatti's works has become standard reference superseding Longo's. (This entry has been made because pianists are increasingly using K's numbering.)

KISS, Gyula (1944–)
b. Budapest, Hungary. Studied there at Liszt Acad. under P. Kadosa, graduating in 1967. Following year appeared with great success in Lisbon. Has toured extensively throughout Europe. US début 1973 and the following year toured the Far East. Recorded Hungaroton.

KISS, Krisztina (1958–)
b. Budapest, Hungary. Student of the Liszt Acad. there, and came joint 5th in the Liszt-Bartók Comp. 1981.

KITCHIN, Alfred (–   )
b. London, UK. Studied there and later at

Leipzig and Zurich. Performed and taught at Trinity Coll., London.

KITCHIN, Margaret (1914–)
b. Montreux, Switzerland. Studied at Lausanne Cons., winning prize 1946. Performed thereafter. Dedicatee of Tippett's 2nd pf sonata first performed by her in 1962 in Edinburgh.

KLEE, Ludwig (1846–1920)
b. Schwerin, Germany. Studied pf with T. Kullak, then taught at Kullak's Acad. until 1875 when he worked privately. Wrote several pedagogic works.

KLEEBERG, Clotilde (1866–1909)
b. Paris, France. Student of Paris Cons., winning 1st Prize in 1878 at the age of 12. Paris début 1881; London 1883. Thereafter performed until 1894 when she married Charles Samuel, the sculptor. Played Beethoven's 4th pf concerto in London in 1892 when she was described by Shaw as 'running her hands daintily up and down the keyboard without once awakening the work'.

KLEIN, Bruno Oscar (1858–1911)
b. Osnabruck, Germany. Father was first teacher. Then studied at Munich Cons. under K. Bärmann for pf. Went to USA 1878, touring as concert pianist, settled New York 1883 and was head of pf department at the Convent of the Sacred Heart until his death, interrupted by only one concert tour of Germany 1895. Took up organ in later life and composed much music for pf and organ.

KLEIN, Elisabeth (1911–)
b. Hungary. Pupil of Liszt Acad. of Budapest and of B. Bartók. Début 1946 in Copenhagen. Gave recitals widely and lectured, as well as holding teaching posts in Scandinavia. Exponent of Bartók's pf works.

KLEIN, Jacques (1930–82)
b. Ceara, Brazil. Studied at Rio Cons. and with W. Kapell in New York. Won 1st Prize in International Comp., Geneva, 1953. Toured worldwide solo and with orchs. Held teaching posts in Brazil and was connected with Brazilian SO.
Pupils included: Arnaldo Cohen.

KLENGEL, August Alexander (1783–1852)
b. Dresden, Germany. A pupil of M. Clementi who accompanied his master across Europe in 1805 and reaching St Petersburg where he lived until 1811, playing in public and teaching. After staying in Paris, London and Rome, he returned to Dresden, settling as pianist, organist, teacher and composer, becoming known as 'Kanon-Klengel' because of an addiction for canon writing. Wrote 48 canons and fugues after J. S. Bach (also pf concertos and numerous pieces). When the young Chopin passed through Dresden, he called on K, who regaled his visitor with these works for two hours, an entertainment Chopin received with mixed feelings. Sir D. Tovey described the fugue subjects as 'always good and often charming'. The Phil. Soc. of London records show K played the pf part in a quintet of his in MS at a London concert in 1816.

KLIEN, Walter (1928–)
b. Graz, Austria. Studied pf at Vienna Acad., then with A. B. Michelangeli. Won a Busoni Prize in the Bolzano Comp. and in 1953 came 7th in the M. Long-J. Thibaud Concours in Paris as well as gaining the Bösendorfer Prize in Vienna. Toured worldwide and possessed an extensive repertoire. Recorded Vox.

KLIMOV, Dmitri (1850–)
b. Kazan, Russia. Pupil of T. Leschetizky. Was appointed pf teacher St Petersburg Cons. 1880 and seven years later became Director of Odessa Music School.

KLINDWORTH, Karl (1830–1916)
b. Hanover, Germany. Self-taught, self-willed and precocious young musician who in course of touring met F. Liszt and became his pupil 1852–3. Tried his luck as virtuoso and teacher in London and stayed 1854–68, though the going was slow until in latter year Anton Rubinstein appointed him pf prof. at Moscow Cons. In 1881 settled in Berlin, playing, conducting and establishing the school which bore his name. When he retired in 1893 the school was merged with Scharwenka's. Was a formidable technician who wrote difficult works. In addition transcribed Wagner's *Ring*, the Schubert C major symphony, and Tchaikovsky's *Francesca da Rimini*, as well as an edition of Beethoven pf sonatas and a complete Chopin edition, including revision of the orchestra in the F minor concerto.
Pupils included: Constance Bache, Theodor Bohlmann, George Catoire, Percival Garrett,

Sergei Liapunov, Arthur Nevin, Ethelbert Nevin, Édouard Risler, Otto Urbach.

KNARDAHL, Eva (1927–)
b. Norway. Studied in Oslo and made her début there at the age of 11 with the Phil. Orch., playing three pf concertos. Visited the USA in 1947 and was resident there for some time, performing solo and in chamber-music recitals. Returned to Norway in 1967 where she continued her career. Toured UK in 1982 with Oslo Phil. Orch.

KNOR, Stanislav (1929–)
b. Prague, Czechoslovakia. Studied at the Acad. there and later in Paris with M. Ciampi at the Cons. Début Prague 1944 and has since toured widely throughout Europe including Scandinavia and behind the Iron Curtain. Adopted Swedish nationality in 1966 and since then has held professorships in Oslo and Copenhagen. Composed pf music.

KNORR, Julius (1807–61)
b. Leipzig, Germany. Début there 1831. Friend of R. Schumann, and distinguished concert pianist and teacher whose technical exercises were highly esteemed.
Pupils included: Karl Friedberg, Theodor Kirchner, Hermann Wollenhaupt.

KNUTSEN, Dagny (1890–)
b. Oslo, Norway. Studied locally, at Berlin High School with H. Barth; then in Paris with A. Cortot and R. Lortat. Début Oslo 1914. Through regular tours became well known in Scandinavia. Featured the contemporary French School in her repertoire.

KNUTZEN, Martin (1863–1909)
b. Drammen, Norway. Studied in Oslo with A. Backer-Gröndahl, then in Berlin with K. Barth, and finally with T. Leschetizky in Vienna. Début 1887 Oslo. Performed in Scandinavia and Germany and was renowned as one of the finest Norwegian pianists of his time.
Pupils included: Nils Larsen.

KOCSIS, Zoltan (1952–)
b. Budapest, Hungary. Student of B. Bartók Cons. 1963–8 when he joined Liszt Acad. under P. Kadosa. Two years later won 1st Prize in Hungarian Radio Comp. and his début followed. London début 1973; Japan 1975; USA 1977. Has since toured widely, has fine

technique and is noted exponent of Liszt and Bartók. Recorded Hungaroton and Philips.
Pupils included: Gabor Csalog, Endre Hegedus, Istvan Szekely.

KOCZALSKI, Raoul von (1884–1948)
b. Warsaw, Poland. A remarkable prodigy who toured European capitals giving recitals before he was 10, and was exploited. A court pianist to several German states. Was a noted Chopin exponent, and after World War II returned to Warsaw. Wrote: *Frédéric Chopin* (1936). Recorded *Polydor*.
Pupils included: Detlef Kraus.

KODÁLY, Zoltan (1882–1967)
b. Kecskemet, Hungary. Studied at Budapest High School and Univ. Made a speciality of collecting Hungarian folk-music with B. Bartók and was prof. of theory at Liszt School for many years. One of the major figures of the modern Hungarian musical scene. Wrote pf works and chamber music. R. Phil. Soc. Gold Medal 1967.

KÖHLER, Irene (1912–)
b. London, UK. Pupil of Trinity Coll., then of R. Coll. 1928–32; pf pupil of A. Benjamin. Challen Gold Medal 1932. Obtained scholarship to train one year with E. Steuermann in Vienna. London début 1934 at Proms. Performed widely, broadcast and taught.

KÖHLER, Louis (1820–86)
b. Brunswick, Germany. Studied in Brunswick and Vienna; settled in Königsberg in 1847 and started a highly successful pf school, receiving the honorary title of R. Prof. in 1880. He was an extremely conscientious teacher and was called Czerny's heir on account of his educational writings and compositions which were at one time of great use to pf teachers. Also made editions of other composers' scores.
Pupils included: Hermann Genss, Hermann Goetz, Robert Goldbeck, Alfred Reisenauer.

KOLAŘ, Katharina: *see* **SMETANA, Bedřich**

KOLESSA, Lubka (1904–)
b. Lvov, Poland. Pupil of E. von Sauer in Vienna. Début 1920 at age of 16. Thereafter performed throughout Europe. US début 1938. Settled in Canada and taught at Toronto Cons. Recorded *HMV* and Nixa.
Pupils included: Louis Pelletier.

KOMIAZYK, Magdalena (1945–)
b. Gdansk, Poland. Studied Warsaw Cons. where she made her début 1973. Toured widely.

KÖNEMANN, Feodor (1873–1937)
b. Moscow, Russia. Student of Cons. there, winning Gold Medal 1897. Toured world regularly, principally as Chaliapine's accompanist. Wrote pf pieces and songs.

KONING, David (1820–76)
b. Rotterdam, Netherlands. Pupil of A. Schmitt in Frankfurt, became successful teacher; composer of pf pieces and songs.

KONTARSKY, Alfons and Aloys
(1932/1931–)
b. Iserlohn, Westphalia (both). Studied at Cologne High School for Music and in 1955 won 1st Prize for duo-playing on German radio in Munich. Later both studied with E. Erdmann. Thereafter established a worldwide reputation in duo-playing, regularly touring Europe and America. Also appeared in Asia and Africa. Recorded DG.
Pupils included (Aloys): Suzanne Fournier.

KONTSKI, Antoine de (1817–99)
b. Cracow, Poland. Second of four brothers, all musicians, and the most famous. After studying with J. Field, his perfect technique made his concert tours triumphant. Taught successively in Paris, St Petersburg, then London where an opera of his was produced in 1872. Later toured USA with great success and lived there awhile. At age of 80 he made a worldwide tour stretching over two years. Composed two pf concertos and solos, of which *The Awakening of the Lion* was popular in Victorian drawing-rooms.
Pupils included: Otto Hackh.

KONTSKI, Charles (1815–67)
b. Cracow, Poland. Elder brother of Antoine K. Child prodigy who was exploited in between studies, eventually moving to Paris where he acquired a secure reputation as a teacher.

KONUS, Lev: *see* **CONUS, Lev**

KOPPEL, Hermann (1908–)
b. Copenhagen, Denmark. Student of R. Acad. there where he later became prof. Concert pianist and composer whose output included four pf concertos, chamber music, pf works and songs.

KORBAY, Francis Alexander (1846–1913)
b. Budapest, Hungary. A strange case of an artist pursuing two careers simultaneously: tenor and pianist. Was a pf pupil of F. Liszt. Principal tenor of Pest Opera 1865–70 while also touring Europe as pianist. Visited the USA in 1871 and taught in both capacities, finally settling in London where he taught at the R. Acad. until at the age of 57 he began to work privately. Composed pf pieces and songs, one of which, *Le Matin*, was arranged for orch. by Liszt, who was his godfather.

KORECKA-SOSZKOWSKA, Maria
(1943–)
b. Lwow, Poland. Pupil at State High School, Cracow, winning 1st Prize 1967. Won diploma Vienna 1976. Performed regularly both solo and with orch., mainly in Communist countries.

KORESCHENKO, Arseni (1870–1921)
b. Moscow, Russia. Student of Moscow Cons. under N. Zverev and S. Taneiev for pf and Arensky for composition. Gold Medal 1891 and became prof. there. Wrote chamber music and pf pieces.

KORGANOV, Gennadi Ossipovich
(1858–90)
b. Caucasus, Russia. Pupil of K. Reinecke and L. Brassin. Concert pianist who died at an early age in a railway train while on tour. Compositions included a pf fantasia *Bajati*, based on Caucasian folk-tunes.

KORNGOLD, Erich Wolfgang (1897–1957)
b. Brünn, Austria. Son of a distinguished music critic who was his first teacher. Studied composition and pf and in 1910 had an overture performed by Nikisch. Appeared in Berlin as pianist in a concert of own works in the same year, having at the age of 11 written his first pf sonata. Wrote three all told, as well as a pf concerto, chamber music and a left-hand concerto for P. Wittgenstein. Rewrote a number of Strauss operettas and worked in Hollywood on film music from 1935. Became US citizen 1943.

KÓSA, György (1897–)
b. Budapest, Hungary. Studied composition with B. Bartók and pf with E. von Dohnányi.

Performed mainly as celebrity accompanist. Taught at Budapest Acad. from 1927. Was ill-treated by the Germans during World War II but resumed his career from 1945. Composed chamber works and pf pieces.

KOSAKOV, Reuben (1898–)
b. New Haven, USA. Studied at Juilliard School of Music then with A. Schnabel in Berlin. Compositions include a pf concerto, pf solos including a *Rhapsody*, and songs.

KOSCHAK, Maria Leopoldine (1792–1855)
b. Graz, Austria. Well-known pianist and friend of Schubert and Beethoven, being especially esteemed by the latter on account of the way in which she interpreted his music.

KOSHETZ, Nina Pavlovna (1894–1965)
b. Moscow, Russia. Pf student of Moscow Cons. from 1905 where she graduated 1911, playing Rachmaninov's C minor concerto. Immediately went to Paris and studied singing under Litvinne and so began a fabulous career in opera and the concert hall. Had songs etc written for her by leading composers, especially Russian, and they accompanied her, e.g. Gretchaninov, Rachmaninov, Prokofiev and Tcherepnin. In 1949, ten years after her retirement, she made another appearance as pianist, accompanying at her daughter Marina's New York début. Recorded *Schirmer*, accompanying herself in several songs.

KOUGUELL, Arkadie (1900–)
b. Crimea, Russia. Student at Cons. at St Petersburg and Vienna. Performed and taught thereafter, working in New York from 1951 as well as in Europe. Composed chamber music and works for pf.

KOUYOUMDJIAN, Avedis (Avo) (1960–)
b. Beirut, Lebanon. First appeared in public at the age of 9. Student of Vienna Cons. and N. Flores, winning a diploma in 1979. Attended master-classes of S. Neuhaus and won a prize in the 1979 Vianna da Motta Pf Comp. in Lisbon. Came 1st in the Int. Beethoven Pf Comp. in Vienna 1981. Performed throughout Europe and Asia.

KOVÁCS, Sándor (1886–1917)
b. Budapest, Hungary. Concert pianist who

also taught at Acad. there. Wrote several treatises on technique.
Pupils included: Tibor Harsanyi.

KOVALEV, Paul Ivanovich (1890–1951)
b. Nikolaiev, Russia. Studied at Odessa, Cracow then Leipzig under R. Teichmüller. Performed for a time. Became pf prof. at Odessa Cons. 1919–22 before settling in Moscow. Wrote pf works.

KOWALSKI, Henri (1841–1916)
b. Paris, France. Studied there and was a pupil of A. Marmontel. Toured widely, including N. America a number of times. Wrote an autobiography and composed pf pieces of salon variety.

KOYAMA, Kyoko (1959–)
b. Tokyo, Japan. Studied at National Univ. of Fine Arts and Music there, and Acads. of Warsaw and Munich, teachers including R. Smendzianka and L. Hoffmann.

KOŽELUH, Leopold Anton (1752–1818)
b. Welvarn, Bohemia. A law student who turned to music, studying with his cousin Johann Anton K (1738–1814). Became a renowned pianist and composer, teaching at the Vienna court where he became court composer on the death of W. A. Mozart. Was given to making disparaging remarks in public about his contemporaries, including Beethoven, Haydn and Mozart. Composed a vast quantity of music of all sorts including pf concertos and pieces and chamber music, all of which are now in obscurity. One of the early talented school of Bohemian composers. Year of birth varies according to source of reference.

KRAJNÝ, Boris (1945–)
b. Moravia, Czechoslovakia, where he studied at Kromeriz Cons. and later at Prague Acad. Toured most countries of the western world as recitalist and soloist with major orchs. US début 1972. London début 1978. Wide catholic taste. Recorded Supraphon.

KRANTZE, Eugen (1844–98)
b. Dresden, Germany. Studied at Cons. there, then taught privately until joining the Cons. staff in 1877. Additionally taught singing, later including choral. Bought the Cons. in 1890. Was distinguished concert pianist especially as accompanist.

KRAUS, Detlef (1919–)
b. Hamburg, Germany. Pupil of W. Kempff
and R. von Koczalski. Début Hamburg 1936.
Toured internationally solo and with orch., as
well as radio and television appearances.
Recorded various labels.
Pupils included: Maria de la Pau.

KRAUS, Lili (1908–)
b. Budapest, Hungary. Studied at the Cons.
there 1915–22 (her teachers included Z.
Kodály and B. Bartók) and later was a pupil of
E. Steuermann in Vienna 1925–7, then of A.
Schnabel in Berlin 1930–4. Meantime she
made her début in 1926 and began appearing as
soloist, in concertos, and in chamber-music
recitals with artists of the calibre of the violinist
Szymon Goldberg with whom, before World
War II, she recorded Mozart and Beethoven
sonatas, also an album of Haydn pf trios joined
by the cellist Antony Pini. In 1928 she accepted
pf prof. at Vienna Cons., and became internationally known as she toured worldwide
from 1935.

She and her Austrian husband were abroad
at the time of the *Anschluss*, and it became
impossible for them to return home when they
refused to accept German passport identity. In
1941, in company with her husband, she was
carrying out a tour of the Far East when they
were caught in Djakarta as the Japanese over-
ran the Pacific area. Thus Mme K became a
victim of the Axis powers, just as W. Backhaus
had been, although her period of tribulation
was to be longer and she was forced to do hard
manual work which could have ruined her
hands. She was of course without a pf during
her four years' imprisonment.

After her release, and a period of recuperation and preparation, she toured Australia,
then worked her way westwards to resume her
career. She was head of the pf department of
Cape Town Univ. 1949–50 and held other
teaching posts.

In the 1966–7 season she performed the
complete cycle of Mozart concertos in New
York, the first time such a feat had been done
there. Later recorded them together with the
complete sonatas. Published a complete set of
her own cadenzas for the concertos where none
exist by the composer.

She was especially attuned to the works of
Mozart and Schubert, once remarking to an
interviewer that 'an inspired musician will wed
his life to the essence of the piece, demonstrating the glow, the swiftly-changing visions

through the symbols that were Mozart's
language.'
Recorded *Parlophone*, Vanguard, CBS-Epic
and others.
Pupils included: Betty Humby-Beecham
and D. Bradshaw.

KRAUSE, Anton (1834–1907)
b. Geitain, Germany. Pupil of Leipzig Cons.
and of I. Moscheles. Performed and taught at
the Cons. 1860–97, taking over from K.
Reinecke. Composed pf pieces and songs, and
published 18 volumes of works for two pfs.

KRAUSE, Emil (1840–1916)
b. Hamburg, Germany. Studied at Leipzig
Cons. and was pf pupil of L. Plaidy and I.
Moscheles. From 1860 lived in Hamburg,
teaching pf and theory at the Cons., from 1885
as prof. Wrote musical criticism as well as a
quantity of textbooks.

KRAUSE, Martin (1853–1918)
b. Lobstadt, Germany. Pupil of his father and
later of K. Reinecke and E. Wenzel at Leipzig
Cons. Was launched on a successful career as
concert pianist and teacher when he met F.
Liszt in 1882 and spent some years studying
further in Weimar. Taught successively in
Dresden, Leipzig and Berlin, building an
eminent reputation.
Pupils included: Claudio Arrau, Edwin
Fischer, Wesley Forsyth, Manuel Ponce,
Henry Puddicombe, Rosita Renard.

KRAUSE, Zygmunt (1938–)
b. Warsaw, Poland. Studied at Cons. there,
graduating 1962. Went to Paris for further
studies with N. Boulanger. Taught in USA at
Cleveland State Univ. Pianist with fine technique. Propagated contemporary music. Own
works include a pf *Triptych*, five *Piano Pieces*
and chamber music.

KREBS, Lotte (–)
b. Cologne, Germany. Pf pupil of E. Erdmann
and of W. Rehberg in Cologne. Soloist,
ensemble player and teacher.

KREBS, Marie (1857–1900)
b. Dresden, Germany. Daughter of the philosopher and music critic Karl K. Toured Europe
with success from an early age and was an
especial favourite in London. Toured USA in
1870 as accompanist to Henri Vieuxtemps.

Had Beethoven works in her repertoire, including the *Emperor*.

KREISLER, Fritz (1875–1962)
b. Vienna, Austria. Somewhere through violin training K learned to play the pf and was a very competent performer, keeping technique in order through the years. Frequently played pf versions of his Viennese violin pieces. A story runs that in USA K gave a sonata recital with H. Bauer including the Kreutzer Sonata. Afterwards they attended a reception where they were asked to play. After whispers Bauer took up Kreisler's violin, Kreisler sat down at the pf – and they repeated the Kreutzer, reversing roles. M. Pincherle, in his *Monde des Virtuosos*, said of K. at the pf: 'His tone was exquisite. His bouncing rhythm – a rhythm to raise the dead – soon had all the musicians in the orchestra gathered around him.'

KRENEK, Ernst (1900–)
b. Vienna, Austria. Prolific composer in most genres, member of the second Viennese school. Atonal in style and experimenting with jazz idiom. Toured as concert pianist and accompanist in own works. Composed large-scale concertos, sonatas, sonatinas, suites and sets of variations and of pieces.

KRENTZLIN, Richard (1864–1956)
b. Magdeburg, Germany. Student of Kullak Acad. Taught and composed.

KRESZ, Nora Drewett de (1882–1960)
b. Sutton, UK. Pupil of V. Duvernoy at Paris Cons., also of B. Stavenhagen in Berlin. Toured Europe as concert pianist until her marriage in 1918 when she settled in Canada as soloist, chamber-music player and teacher at Toronto R. Cons. Died in Budapest.

KREUTZ, Edvard (1881–)
b. Oslo, Norway. Studied locally and with Agathe Backer-Gröndahl, later in Berlin and Vienna. Début Oslo 1910. Performed and taught thereafter.

KREUTZER, Leonid (1884–1953)
b. St Petersburg, Russia. Studied at the Cons. there with A. Glazounov for composition and A. Essipova for pf. Lived in Berlin from 1908 as concert pianist and teacher with a master-class at the Hochschule 1921–33. Went to Japan as prof. of master-class at Tokyo Imperial Acad. Wrote textbooks on technique

and made an edition of Chopin. Recorded *Polydor*.
Pupils included: Erno Balogh, Franz Osborn, Georg van Renesse, Karl U. Schnabel, Peter Stadlen, Alexander Zakin.

KRIGAR, Hermann (1819–80)
b. Berlin, Germany. Studied with R. Schumann and F. Mendelssohn in Leipzig. Returned home to teach. Composed pf pieces and songs.

KROLL, Franz (1820–77)
b. Bromberg, Germany. Studied in Berlin, then later had lessons from F. Liszt. Taught in the German capital and assisted in the Bach Gesellschaft edition.

KRONKE, Emil (1865–1938)
b. Danzig, Poland. Studied in Leipzig with K. Reinecke, then with T. Kirchner at Dresden Cons. 1886–7, winning prizes for pf-playing. In Dresden he settled as concert pianist and teacher. One of the first to spread knowledge of Liszt's better works. Composed chamber music and pf pieces; also made an edition of Chopin.

KROSS, Gustav (1831–85)
b. Moscow, Russia. Studied pf there, becoming prof. at St Petersburg Cons. Gave Russian première of Tchaikovsky's 1st pf concerto.

KROUCHEVSKY, Eugueni (1955–)
b. USSR. Of musical family. Began studying the pf from the age of 6. Was student at Moscow Cons. and 1st Prizewinner of Int. Comp., Geneva, 1982.

KRÜGER, Wilhelm (1820–83)
b. Stuttgart, Germany. Studied there. Lived in Paris from 1845 as successful concert pianist and teacher. Franco-Prussian war forced him to return to Stuttgart. Wrote numerous pf works in salon style; also made transcriptions.
Pupils included: Edgar Kelley, Karl Stasny.

KUHE, Wilhelm (1823–1912)
b. Prague, Czechoslovakia. Pf pupil of J. Tomáschek and of S. Thalberg. Visited London as an accompanist in 1847 and decided to settle there. Pf prof. at R. Acad. 1886–1904, and prolific composer of light pf music.
Pupils included: Wilhelm Speidel.

KUHLAU, Friedrich (1786–1832)
b. Ülzen, Germany. Apart from some harmony lessons, largely self-taught. Settled in Denmark in 1810 to escape conscription and made a living by teaching pf. Found a post in court circles, wrote operas which were produced and so acquired title of prof. in 1828. Now remembered for his sonatinas, which have been much used for teaching purposes.

KÜHNER, Konrad (1851–1909)
b. Meiningen, Germany. Pupil of Stuttgart Cons. Taught pf in Dresden and later Brunswick. Wrote pedagogic works and technical exercises. Edited the Schumann pf works for Litolff publishing.

KULLAK, Adolf (1823–62)
b. Meseritz, Germany. Brother of Theodor K. Taught at the Kullak Acad., composed pf pieces and songs, and wrote books on music which ran to several editions.

KULLAK, Franz (1844–1913)
b. Berlin, Germany. Son of Theodor K. Pf pupil of his father's Acad., which he took over in 1882. Had lessons from F. Liszt. When the school closed in 1890, he continued to teach privately.
Pupils included: Leo Kestenberg, Adele aus der Ohe.

KULLAK, Theodor (1818–82)
b. Krotoschin, Germany. His musical gifts as a boy were brought to the notice of Prince Radziwill who arranged lessons under Agthe. Became court pianist in 1829 at age of 11. Later studied in Vienna under C. Czerny. Toured Austria before settling in Berlin as court pianist and teacher. With Stern and Marx formed Berlin Cons. in 1850, leaving it five years later to found the Acad. under his own name. Wrote many pieces of educational difficulty.
Pupils included: Leonhard Bach, Agathe Backer-Gröndahl, Otto Bendix, Hans Bischoff, Amy Fay, Albert Friedenthal, Alfred Grünfeld, Sarah Heinze, Michael Hertz, Heinrich Hofmann, August Hyllested, Fritz Kirchner, Ludwig Klee, Franz Kullak, James Kwast, Emil Liebling, Georg Liebling, Leonard Liebling, Moritz Moszkowski, Edmund Neupert, Rikard Nordraak, Albert Parsons, Edward Perry, Silas Pratt, Julius Reubke, Adolf Ries, Nikolai Rubinstein, Xavier Scharwenka, Peter Shostakovski, Ingeborg Starck, Constantin Sternberg, Karl Wehle, Wilhelm Wolf, Théophile Ysaÿe, Frederick Zech, Johann Zschocher.

KUN WOO PAIK: *see* **PAIK, Kun Woo**

KUNZE, Henriette (1808–39)
b. Leipzig, Germany. Pupil of L. Berger. Became well-known pianist and is dedicatee of Schumann's sonata Op. 22.

KUOSMA, Kauto Einari (1926–)
b. Viipuri, Finland. Pupil at Sibelius Acad. and later Paris Cons. Début Helsinki 1949. Since performed. Taught at Sibelius Acad. Composed chamber music and pf pieces.

KÜRSTEINER, Jean Paul (1864–1943)
b. New York, USA, of French-Swiss parentage. Pupil of S. Jadassohn and of R. Teichmüller in Leipzig. On return to USA in 1893 taught pf in Philadelphia. Composed pf music and wrote a textbook on pf playing.

KURT, Melanie (1880–1941)
b. Vienna, Austria. Pf student of Vienna Cons. 1887–94; won a gold medal and the Liszt Prize. Private pupil of T. Leschetizky 1894–6. Début 1897 Vienna. Performed until 1900 when she decided to go in for operatic career, becoming a famous Wagnerian soprano.

KURYOKHIN, Sergei (1954–)
b. Leningrad, USSR. Studied at Cons. there but left because he did not toe the official line. An accomplished pianist, also *avant-garde* composer, using current techniques including jazz. Pf works include *The Ways of Freedom* in seven parts. Recorded Leo.

KURZ, Vilém (1872–1945)
b. Nemecky Brod, Czechoslovakia. Studied in Prague. Début 1890 and performed until the end of the decade when he took up teaching. Prof. at Lwow Cons. until 1918 when he joined Brno Cons. Retired and settled in Prague in 1928. Was a foremost pedagogue and wrote several works on technique.
Pupils included: Rudolf Firkusny, Ilonka Kursova.

KURZOVA, Ilonka (1899–)
b. Lwow, Poland. Daughter of Vilém Kurz and Rozena Kurzova. Pupil of parents. Début 1907 and was well-known recitalist and teacher, being prof. at Prague Acad. from 1946. Married Vaclav Stepan 1928.

KURZOVA, Rozena (1880–1938)
b. Prague, Czechoslovakia. Wife of Vilém K
and pf teacher of note at Prague Cons.
Pupils included: Ilonka Kurzova.

KVAPIL, Jaroslav (1892–1958)
b. Frystak, Czechoslovakia. Studied at Leipzig
Cons. and was a pupil of R. Teichmüller. Performed widely before World War I, later
becoming pf prof. at Brno Cons.

KVAPIL, Radoslav (1934–)
b. Brno, Czechoslovakia. Pf pupil at Brno
Acad. Début 1954 and graduated 1957. Later
received lessons from H. Neuhaus and P.
Baumgartner. Toured widely and specialized
in Czech pf music. Taught at Prague Cons.
Recorded Supraphon and Genesis.

KWAST, Frieda Hodapp (1880–1949)
b. Bargen, Netherlands. Second wife of James
K. Distinguished Dutch concert pianist. Gave
first performance of the Reger pf concerto in F
minor in Leipzig in 1910 under A. Nikisch.

KWAST, James (1852–1927)
b. Nijkerk, Netherlands. Studied with K.
Reinecke in Leipzig, then with T. Kullak in
Berlin and L. Brassin in Brussels. Taught suc-
cessively at Frankfurt Hoch Cons., Klind-
worth-Scharwenka Cons. and Stern's Cons.
His first wife was Antonia, daughter of F.
Hiller, his second Frieda Hodapp.
Pupils included: Max Anton, Lonny
Epstein, Karl Friedberg, Percy Grainger,
Hans Pfitzner, Adolf Wiklund, Hermann
Zilcher.

LABÈQUE, Katia and Marielle
(1953/1956–   )
b. Bayonne, S. France. Both studied with their mother who had been a pupil of M. Long, and later with J.-B. Pommier at Paris Cons. where they graduated the same year, each receiving a 1st Prize. Début Bayonne in 1961 and early on decided upon a duo career and with a diverse repertoire including jazz. Katia L has also interested herself in synthesizer performances.

LABOR, Josef (1842–1924)
b. Horowitz, Czechoslovakia. Pupil of Vienna Cons., in which city he made his début, thereafter touring Europe extensively, residing in capitals. Returned to Vienna 1868 where he became established as virtuoso teacher. Blind from birth. Wrote chamber music and solos for the instrument.
Pupils included: Frank La Forge, Francis Richter, Arnold Schoenberg, Paul Wittgenstein.

LABUNSKI, Wiktor (1895–1966)
b. St Petersburg, Russia, of Polish parentage. Pupil of the Cons. there and later of F. Blumenfeld and V. Safonov, making his début in 1916. Began performing regularly throughout Europe and was head of the pf department at Cracow Cons. 1920–8. In the latter year made his US début at Carnegie Hall and settled there to a concert career. Head of pf department at Nashville Cons. and later at Memphis Coll. Compositions include a concerto and a concertino, *Variations*, and a concerto for two pfs. Brother-in-law of Arthur Rubinstein.
Pupils included: Natalia Karp.

LACHMUND, Carl Valentine (1857–1928)
b. Booneville, USA. Pupil of Cologne Cons., studying with I. Seiss and F. Hiller. Was pupil of M. Moszkowski in Berlin and, finally, of F.

Liszt. Performed and taught at Scharwenka Cons., Berlin. Toured the USA several times and in 1891 decided to settle in New York.

LACK, Théodore (1846–1921)
b. Quimper, France. Was a prodigy, studying at Paris Cons. under A. Marmontel for pf, graduating 1864 as prizewinner. Taught at Cons. thereafter until his death and held high offices as pedagogue. Wrote much superficial music.

LACOMBE, Louis Trouillon (1818–84)
b. Bourges, France. Studied Paris Cons. and was under P. Zimmerman for pf, winning 1st Prize for playing 1831. A concert tour of Europe followed before he settled in Vienna for a year to study with K. Czerny among others. Toured with the violinist Henri Vieuxtemps in 1834, and in Leipzig Schumann called him 'a small but fiery pianist, full of talent and courage'. Finally settled in Paris as touring pianist, teacher and composer. Works included chamber music and pf pieces.
Pupils included: Édouard Silas.

LACOMBE, Paul (1837–1927)
b. Carcassonne, France. Received some music lessons but was largely self-taught. Appeared in public mainly as composer-pianist. Besides orch. and religious works he composed several for pf and orch., pf solos including *études*, also chamber works, where he was most successful. A friend of Bizet who took no part in the Parisian musical scene.

LADA, Janina (1876–1947)
b. Warsaw, Poland. Pupil of Cracow Cons., then of T. Leschetizky in Vienna. Toured Europe as virtuoso and taught at Cracow Cons.

LAFFITTE, Frank (1901–82)
b. Bromley, UK. Studied Guildhall School, London, also with K. Goodson. Début Queen's Hall, London, 1920 in two pf concertos under Ronald. Taught at Trinity Coll. and Guildhall and had successful concert career, being noted for his Debussy interpretations. Gave first performance of Albert Coates' pf concerto. Fellow Emeritus of Guildhall School, London.

LA FORGE, Frank (1879–1953)
b. Rockford, USA. Student in Vienna of J. Labor and T. Leschetizky. Performed extensively in Europe as both soloist and accompanist to celebrities. Was probably unique accompanist in that he always memorized his part. When he returned to USA, he opened his own studio and taught voice, numbering famous American singers among his pupils. Composed pf pieces and songs.
Pupils included: Elinor Warren.

LAFORGE, Jean (–)
(Details of birth cannot be traced). Studied pf with M. Tagliaferro, A. Cortot and J. Doyen. Won 1st Prize at Paris Cons. and subsequently toured widely with success. Is also known as a conductor and has worked in opera.

LAIDLAW, Anna Robena (1819–1901)
b. Bretton, UK. Studied pf with H. Herz and L. Berger. Lived and performed in Europe and knew R. Schumann who dedicated his *Fantaisiestücke* Op. 12 to her.

LAIRES, Fernando (1925–)
b. Lisbon, Portugal. Studied pf there, also with I. Philipp in Paris, and J Friskin and E. Hutcheson in New York. Harriet Cohen Award, London, 1956. Concertised widely and performed the Beethoven cycle of sonatas. Held teaching posts in USA and Europe.

LAKE, Ian Thomson (1935–)
b. Quorn, UK. Studied at R. Coll., London, winning Chappell Gold Medal 1957. Début London 1961. Prof. at R. Coll. 1967 onwards. Visited most countries as soloist.

LALEWICZ, Jerzy (1877–1951)
b. Suvalki, Poland. Pupil of A. Essipova at St Petersburg Cons., where he graduated in 1901 with a Gold Medal. Won Rubinstein Prize in Vienna in 1900, and was pf prof. at Odessa Cons. until 1905 when he went to Cracow

Cons. In 1912 was appointed to Vienna Acad. where he remained until 1918 when he returned to Poland. Later paid an extended visit to Paris before settling in Buenos Aires where, besides performing, he taught at the Cons. Composed for pf.
Pupils included: Zygmunt Dygat, Mieczyslaw Münz, Josef Rosenstock, Friedrich Wilckens.

LALIBERTE, Alfred (1882–1952)
b. Quebec, Canada. Studied in Montreal and later in Berlin where he won a scholarship and played before the Kaiser. In 1906 in the USA he met A. Scriabin who was on a concert tour, and the composer persuaded L to continue studies in Europe. He spent a year with T. Carreño in Berlin, then went on to Brussels where Scriabin was living, and became enthusiastic over the Russian's music so that on returning to Canada he actively propagated it in his concert work. Composed mainly for pf.

LAM, Kay (–)
b. India. Studied in Bombay, then later in UK with C. Smith; at the R. Coll., London, with E. Harrison and at the Guildhall School. Studied composition with E. Rubbra. London début 1981. Concert tours included the Far East. Possessed perfect pitch and claimed the ability to play his repertoire in any key.

LAMBERT, Alexander (1862–1929)
b. Warsaw, Poland. Was auditioned at 12 by Anton Rubinstein who advised that he should study at Vienna Cons. Later became a pupil of J. Epstein. Début 1881 New York. He returned to Europe and toured Germany and Russia before spending a period with Liszt at Weimar. In 1884 he went back to USA and resumed performing. Became Director of New York Coll. of Music in 1888 and held it until he retired in 1906, having given up concert work in 1892. Composed small-scale works and wrote pf methods.
Pupils included: Vera Brodsky, Albert von Doenhoff, Jerome Kern, Mana-Zucca, Nadia Reisenberg, Beryl Rubinstein.

LAMBERT, Constant (1905–51)
b. London, UK. Studied pf with E. Hall before winning scholarship to R. Coll., working under H. Fryer (pf) and R. Vaughan Williams (composition). Won early recognition in performances of W. Walton's *Façade*; met Diaghilev, from which connection blos-

somed his devotion to ballet, becoming principal conductor Vic-Wells Ballet during World War II, on tour often playing pf when no orch. was available. Wrote and arranged a number of scores for ballet including version of Liszt's *Dante Sonata* for pf and orch. Composed *Elegiac Blues* (1927), a pf sonata (1928) and a pf concerto (1931), also for pf duet *Trois Pièces Nègre*. Most famous, however, is *Rio Grande* (1928), first public performance 1929 by Sir H. Harty at the pf and with the composer conducting.

LAMBERT, Lucien (1858–1945)
b. Paris, France. Concert pianist in his youth, when he toured Europe and USA as virtuoso. Returned to Paris and took up composition, eventually settling in Oporto, where he died. Compositions mainly operas and works for orch., but did write some pf pieces and songs.

LAMM, Pavel Alexandrovich (1882–1951)
b. Moscow, Russia. Student of the Cons. there. Was an accompanist for some years, later becoming preoccupied with publishing. Besides editing the entire output of Mussorgsky, he made two-pf arrangements for eight hands of orch. works by Russian composers from Borodin to Scriabin.

LAMOND, Frederic (1868–1948)
b. Glasgow, UK. Pupil of Raff Cons. from 1882, later spending a year with H. von Bülow and a year with F. Liszt. Début Berlin 1885; London 1886. Taught for many years in Berlin from which he toured, especially noted for his Beethoven and Liszt. During long career had a spell of teaching in Netherlands and in USA, finally in 1940 returning to Scotland. Recorded *HMV* and *Decca*. Wrote *Memoirs* (1949).
Pupils included: Rudolf am Bach, Jan Chiapusso, Gunnar Johansen, Ervin Nyiregyhazi.

LAMPE, Walter (1872–1964)
b. Leipzig, Germany. Pupil of K. Schumann. Was pf prof. at Munich 1919–37. Composed pf pieces and songs; also made fresh edition of Mozart sonatas from original MSS.

LANCEN, Sergei (1922–)
b. Paris, France. Pupil of Paris Cons. under N. Gallon for pf. Lived in Switzerland during World War II, continuing his studies in Paris when peace returned. Prix de Rome 1949. Wrote a pf concerto while a student.

LANDAUER, Walter (1909–83)
b. Vienna, Austria. His teachers included P. Weingarten and E. von Sauer. Performed solo until 1933 when he teamed up with M. Rawicz and toured Europe. British début 1935 was so successful that they settled in UK, becoming naturalized after World War II. The duo toured Europe, the USA, Australia, S. Africa etc, and their repertoire ranged from Mozart to Saint-Saëns; they also made many arrangements. Recorded *Columbia* and EMI.

LANDOWSKA, Wanda (1877–1959)
b. Warsaw, Poland. Pf pupil of Warsaw Cons. with A. Michałowski, later in Berlin with M. Rosenthal. She then taught pf at Schola Cantorum, Paris, until 1913, and toured Europe as pianist. Becoming more interested in the harpsichord, she joined Berlin Hochschule in 1913 as prof. of that instrument. After World War I she returned to Paris and taught privately and at Fontainebleau Cons. Became celebrated as a Bach interpreter but occasionally played Mozart and Beethoven on the pf. She settled in the USA before World War II, where she remained active up to her death. Composers wrote harpsichord concertos for her, notably de Falla, whose example was first performed by her in Barcelona, and F. Poulenc, whose *Concert Champêtre* was premièred by her in Paris in 1929 under Monteux's baton. Recorded pf on *HMV*.
Pupils included: Sir Clifford Curzon, John Simons.

LANE, Piers (1958–)
b. Brisbane, Australia. Studied there and made broadcasts and public appearances from the age of 12. Played in Europe and USA. A pupil of N. Weir and of Y. Solomon in London, winning 1st Prize in the 1982 pf section of the R. Overseas League Musical Festival. Performed Europe, USA and Australia since.

LANG, Benjamin Johnson (1837–1909)
b. Salem, USA. Studied locally, especially with A. Jaëll during the latter's sojourn in the USA on account of the 1948 revolutions in Europe. Studied composition in Berlin and received pf lessons from F. Liszt. Début Boston 1858 where he lived, performing, teaching and conducting. Also an organist. Took great interest in contemporary music, of which he gave many first performances in the USA.

Pupils included: Arthur Foote, Ethelbert Nevin.

LANG, Henry (1854–1930)
b. New Orleans, USA. Studied there, then at Stuttgart under S. Lebert and D. Pruckner. Toured Germany with the violinist E. Remenyi before taking up teaching post at Karlsruhe Cons. where he had studied composition with V. Lachner. Continued career as concert pianist solo, with orch. and in chamber music, returning to USA in 1890, where he lived in Philadelphia teaching and performing. Composed chamber music, pf pieces and songs.

LANG, Walter (1896–1966)
b. Basle, Switzerland. Studied in Geneva, Munich and Zurich, his most famous teacher being W. Frey. Subsequently taught at Basle and Zurich Conss., performed solo and also formed a pf trio which took his name. Composed a pf concerto, chamber music, pf sonatas and other pieces, also songs.

LANGE, Gustav (1830–89)
b. Schwerstedt, Germany. Student of A. Loeschhorn. Lived in Berlin thereafter where he taught and composed many hundreds of pf pieces that enjoyed a one-time fashion on account of tunefulness and salon-like quality.

LANGER, Edouard (1835–1905)
b. Moscow, Russia. Studied at Leipzig Cons. under I. Moscheles for pf. Returned home to teach at Moscow Cons. Composed chamber music and pf pieces, and specialized in arrangements for two pfs.

LANGRISH, Vivian (1894–1980)
b. Bristol, UK. Studied at R. Acad., London, with T. Matthay, winning scholarships which he was unable to take up owing to service during World War I. When peace returned, he resumed a career in solo recitals and with orch. Toured with Dame Clara Butt. In 1924 was elected Fellow of the R. Acad. of Music, where he taught for many years. CBE. See also Ruth Hart.
Pupils included: Winifred Davey, Florence Spencer-Palmer.

LANGSTROTH, Ivan Shed (1887–1971)
b. Alameda, USA. Studied in San Francisco, and in Berlin with J. Lhevinne where he lived for a time. Toured Scandinavia towards the end of World War I. Taught in Vienna until 1928 when he returned to the USA as concert pianist, teacher and lecturer. Composed pf works, chamber music and songs.

LARA, Adelina de (1872–1961)
b. Carlisle, UK. Studied with F. Davies and was one of K. Schumann's last pupils 1886–91. Début London 1891. She played mainly Schumann's works, taught and was Vice-President of the Soc. of Women Musicians. Gave farewell London recital in 1951, the year in which she was awarded OBE. Composed two pf concertos, pf pieces and songs. Wrote autobiography, *Finale* (1955). Recorded A de L Soc.

LARROCHA, Alicia de (1923–   )
b. Barcelona, Spain. Pupil of F. Marshall. First public appearance at age of 5, followed at 11 by her first orch. date in Madrid with F. Arbos in a Mozart concerto. Adult début came in 1940 after the Spanish Civil War, and from 1947 she made European appearances outside Spain. Visited USA 1954 and again in 1965, when she appeared with New York SO, the foundation of her international career. Became a foremost Spanish pianist, and taught at the Academia Marshall, Barcelona. Recorded Decca.

LARSEN, Nils (1888–1937)
b. Oslo, Norway. Pupil of M. Knutzen there. Later studied in Berlin with R. Ganz and J. V. da Motta. Returning to Oslo, he founded his own school. Toured Scandinavia regularly, acquiring a reputation for poetical interpretation. Composed pf works and songs.
Pupils included: Klaus Egge, Odd Grüner-Hegge, Robert Levin, Eline Nygaard.

LASSIMONE, Denise (1904–   )
b. Camberley, UK, of French parentage. Pupil of R. Acad., London, and of T. Matthay. Member of that 'school' who became a well-known recitalist and teacher. Sponsored *Myra Hess by her friends*, a book of affectionate memorial tributes on the death of the subject in 1965. Recorded *Decca*.

LAST, Joan (1908–   )
b. Littlehampton, UK. Pf pupil of M. Verne and Y. Bowen. Début 1926 London. Concert pianist, teacher and adjudicator. Pf prof. at R. Acad., London. Widely travelled in the course of her vocation.

LÁSZLÓ, Alexander (1895–)
b. Budapest, Hungary. Pupil of Acad. and of
A. Szendy. Went to Germany, performed in
Berlin and taught in Munich. Began working
on a Colour Piano which throws colour onto a
screen, first shown at Kiel Festival in 1925
when he performed his own works using a
special colour notation of his own invention.
Published a work on the subject, *Colour Light
Music*. Settled in USA 1938 and worked in
Hollywood from 1945. Wrote many works for
the invention (called sonchromatoscope), including *Hollywood Concerto, Fantasy of Colours*
and *The Ghost Train*.

LATARCHE, Vanessa (1959–)
b. Isleworth, UK. Student at R. Coll. of
Music, London, and of K. Taylor. Other
teachers included C. Frank, M. Dichter, V.
Perlemuter and A. Kelly. Accompanist and
chamber-music player as well as teacher.

LATEINER, Jacob (1928–)
b. Havana, Cuba, of Austrian-Polish parentage. A prodigy who appeared in public at 10;
studied at Curtis Inst., USA, from 1940.
Début 1947 in *Emperor* under Koussevitzky
with immediate success followed by extensive
concert tour. Gave first performance of Elliott
Carter's pf concerto 1967. Recorded RCA.
Pupils included: John Frusciante.

LAUDER, William Waugh (1860–)
b. Toronto, Canada. After studying pf locally,
went to Leipzig. Claimed to be the only
Canadian who was a pupil of F. Liszt, with
whom he studied around 1880. When he
returned home, he developed the lecture
recital, giving several hundreds all told. Also
taught, later settling in Boston where his career
seems to have faded without trace.

LAUKO, Dezider (1872–1942)
b. Bekes, Hungary. Educated locally, then
attended Budapest Acad. under A. Szendy.
Concert pianist and composer of pf pieces in
Slovak dance idiom.

LAUSKA, Franz (1764–1825)
b. Brno, Czechoslovakia. An early virtuoso
pianist, teacher and composer who studied
under Albrechtsberger in Vienna and after
court appointments in Italy and Germany
settled in Berlin to a successful career from
1798. Was held in high esteem for technical
brilliance and fine musicianship. Composed pf

sonatas plus one for four hands, also tuneful
chamber music and songs said to be in the
idiom of Clementi and which had a vogue for a
time.

LAVAGNE, André (1913–)
b. Paris, France. Pupil of Cons. there, winning
1st Prize for pf-playing in 1933 and 2nd Prix de
Rome in 1938.

LAVALLÉE, Calixa (1842–91)
b. Quebec, Canada. Pf pupil of father, then of
P. Letondal. Début in Montreal in 1855 at the
age of 13. Toured Canada and the USA and
after taking part in the American Civil War
returned to Montreal as pianist and teacher,
later settling in New Orleans and touring
widely. In 1873 went to Paris to study with A.
Marmontel. After returning home he became
one of Canada's early leading musicians. Wrote
O Canada, now the only piece for which he is
remembered. Settled in Boston finally where
he died.
Pupils included: Roy Philéas.

LAVER, William Adolphus (1866–1940)
b. Castlemaine, Australia. Took up violin first;
later went to Frankfurt where he learned pf
and conducting. Back home in 1889 began
giving pf recitals and teaching, becoming first
Australian to hold Chair of Music at
Melbourne Univ., where he became prof. and
principal pf teacher. Travelled widely as conductor, concert pianist and examiner. Hon.
member R. Coll., London.

LAVIGNAC, Albert (1846–1916)
b. Paris, France. Pupil of Paris Cons. and
studied pf with A. Marmontel. Taught theory
at the Cons., wrote copiously on musical
subjects and was the first editor-in-chief of the
Encyclopédie de la Musique begun in 1912 at the
instigation of the French Government. A very
minor composer who published his own
arrangements for two pfs of Beethoven's
symphonies Nos. 1 and 2.

LAVROV, Nikolai (1861–1928)
b. Pskov, Russia. Pupil of St Petersburg Cons.,
graduating 1879 and becoming pf teacher
there. Gave première of Rimsky-Korsakov pf
concerto 1884 St Petersburg, also played
Anton Rubinstein's 4th concerto at the
memorial concert to the composer following
latter's death in St Petersburg in 1894.

LAZARE, Martin (1829–97)
b. Brussels, Belgium. Studied there, then at The Hague, and finally at Paris Cons. under P. Zimmerman. Successfully toured Europe and America as concert pianist and composed chamber music and pieces for his instrument.

LAZARUS, Gustav (1861–1920)
b. Cologne, Germany. Student of Cons. there under I. Seiss for pf. Taught at Scharwenka Cons., Berlin, from 1887 to the turn of the century when he took over the Breslau Cons. A successful pianist for many years and a prolific composer for the instrument, solo and for two pfs.

LEBERT, Siegmund (1822–84)
b. Stuttgart, Germany. Studied in Prague under J. Tomásek. Performed and established a teaching reputation in Munich. Was a co-founder of Stuttgart Cons. in 1856 and became highly regarded as a pianist and pedagogue. His teaching works, once popular, are now forgotten. Edited numerous works including Clementi's Gradus.
Pupils included: Henry Lang.

LE CARPENTIER, Adolphe (1809–69)
b. Paris, France. Pupil of Cons. there and prizewinner before graduating and taking up teaching career in that city. Composed studies and other pf pieces as well as a method.

LE COUPPEY, Félix (1811–87)
b. Paris, France. Student of Paris Cons. In 1848 took over the pf class of H. Herz when latter went to USA on tour. Later instructed own class, performed and wrote much music of a pedagogic nature as well as treatises on technique.
Pupils included: Cécile Chaminade, Fanny Montigny-Rémaury.

LECUONA, Ernesto (1896–1963)
b. Guanabacoa, Cuba. Was prodigy at age of 5. Studied at Havana Cons. under J. Nin, graduating 1911. Thereafter turned to light music in which he led orchs. in dance halls and theatres. His compositions spanned both serious and light fields, and all are imbued with Cuban rhythms and colour.

LEDENT, Félix (1816–86)
b. Liège, Belgium. Pupil of Cons. there and later of Paris Cons., where he won 2nd Prix de

Rome. Pf prof. at Liège Cons. and composer of works for pf as well as songs.

LEDGER, Philip (1937–)
b. Bexhill, UK. Student of King's Coll., Cambridge, followed by academic and administrative career. As pianist mainly accompanist. Also harpsichordist. Recorded EMI, and Argo with R. Tear.

LEE, Dennis (1946–)
b. Penang, Malaysia. Educated at London Univ. and R. Coll. of Music. Won 1st Prize in R. Over-Seas League Comp. 1968. Début London 1969, where he settled. Toured Europe and Far East. Recorded CBS.

LEE, Maurice (1821–95)
b. Hamburg, Germany. Studied there, settled in London, taught and composed pf pieces. Youngest of three brothers, the other two being cellists.

LEE, Noël (1924–)
b. Nanking, China, of American parentage. Student of Harvard Univ. and of New England Cons., winning a diploma there 1948. Later studied in Paris. Won prizes for his compositions, performed solo and in duo-recitals with the violinist Paul Makanowizky. Settled in Paris. Compositions included chamber music, pf pieces and songs. Recorded Philips.

LEFÉBURE, Yvonne (1904–)
b. Ermont, France. Studied in Paris, and with A. Cortot. Performed throughout Europe and America. Teacher, lecturer and essayist. Was associated with the École Normale. Recorded Unicorn.
Pupils included: Imogen Cooper, Evelyn Crochet, Janina Fialkowska, Suzanne Fournier, Antony Peebles.

LEGER, Olivier (1957–)
b. Bayonne, France. Student of Paris Cons. under A. Ciccolini.

LEGINSKA, Ethel (1886–1970)
b. Hull, UK. A prodigy with a gift for readily improvising on themes given to her. Was a pupil of J. Kwast at Frankfurt Cons. before spending three years with T. Leschetizky. Début 1907, with a European concert tour followed by appearances in USA. Studied composition in New York and in 1922 gave a recital in London of her works. Additionally took up

conducting. Settled in USA, where she died. Recorded *Columbia*.

Pupils included: James Fields, Daniel Pollack, Bruce Sutherland.

LEIDESDORF, Maximilian Josef (1787–1840)
b. Vienna, Austria. Co-founder of music publishing business there in 1822 which after some 13 years merged with the Diabelli firm. Studied pf and became pianist and teacher, also accompanist. Was for a time court pianist to the Duke of Tuscany, and later pf prof. at Florence Cons., which had been founded around 1815.

LEIMER, Kurt (1920–74)
b. Wiesbaden, Germany. Pupil of Karl Leimer (1858–1944). Successful concert career and composed much including four pf concertos, sonatas etc.

LEITERT, Johann Georg (1852–1901)
b. Dresden, Germany. Studied there and was a pupil of F. Liszt at Weimar. Toured solo and in chamber-music concerts; also taught in Vienna for a time.

LELEU, Jeanne (1898–)
b. Saint-Mihiel, France. Pf pupil at Paris Cons. and of M. Long and A. Cortot. Graduated 1913 with 1st Prize. Wrote a pf concerto, chamber music and songs. Was one of the pianists in the première of the Ravel *Ma Mère l'Oye* in Paris, 1910.

LEMBA, Arthur (1885–)
b. Revel, Estonia. Pupil at St Petersburg Cons., winning the Rubinstein Prize 1908. Taught there from 1910, becoming prof. 1915. Settled in Revel from 1922. Composed a pf concerto and pieces.

LEMOINE, Henri (1786–1854)
b. Paris, France. Early French pianist and pupil of Paris Cons. Performed, taught, also ran family music publishing business. Wrote pedagogic works on technique.

LEMONT, Cedric Wilmot (1879–1954)
b. New Brunswick, Canada. Studied with C. Faelton in Boston. Settled in Chicago, where he played the organ and taught pf. Later taught in New York. Rated as the most prolific Canadian composer, with over 600 works.

LEMOYNE, Gabriel (1772–1815)
b. Berlin, Germany. Spent most of his life in Paris. Early concert pianist who also taught and composed concertos, sonatas and chamber music.

LENORMAND, René (1846–1932)
b. Elbeuf, France. Interesting musical character and a fine pianist wholly taught by his mother, who had been a pupil of P. Zimmerman. Also studied composition. Was a friend of H. Berlioz. Directed a society for developing interest in the song, especially the *chanson* in other countries. Composed some 150 songs reputedly of splendid quality; also numerous pf works for two and four hands, and a pf concerto which received its first British performance at the London Proms in 1903.

LENZ, Wilhelm de (or von) (1809–83)
b. Riga. Went to Paris 1828 to study music, first with F. Liszt, later with F. Chopin. Wrote important works on Beethoven, also an interesting volume of personal reminiscences of great pianists he met during the Paris years.

LÉON, Hélène (1890–)
b. Paris, France. Student of Paris Cons. for five years up to 1906 when she won 1st Prize for pf. Was active concert pianist, teacher and adjudicator. One of the original four pianists in first performance of Stravinsky's *Les Noces* in Paris in 1923.

LEONSKAJA, Elisabeth (1945–)
b. Tbilisi, Georgia, USSR. Began playing pf at the age of 7, her mother being a pf teacher. Attended a music school and played the Beethoven pf concerto in C when she was 11. Her first solo recital followed two years later. Progressed to Moscow Cons. during which time she won a prize in Bucharest, came joint 3rd in the M. Long–J. Thibaud Comp. in Paris in 1965, and 9th in the Concours Musical Int. Reine Elisabeth in Brussels in 1968. Thereafter toured Europe, USA and Far East. Settled in Vienna in 1978.

LEPIANKIEWICZ, Julius (1910–)
b. Lvov, Poland. Student of Cons. there and of E. Steuermann in Vienna. Performed and taught Trinity Coll., London.

LERNER, Tina (1890–)
b. Odessa, Russia. Studied there before

becoming pupil at Moscow Cons. (1899–1904) under L. Pabst. Début 1904 in Moscow was followed by extended tours of Europe. US début 1908 in New York. Settled in America from 1912, performing and teaching. Her name came to life again recently on account of the unearthing of the piano roll of a Chopin study. Married Vladimir Shavich.

LESCHETIZKY, Theodore (1830–1915)
b. Lancut, Poland. Taught first by his father then by K. Czerny in Vienna. Went to St Petersburg in 1852 and helped to found the Imperial Russian Music Soc. Also performed, composed and taught at the Cons., deputizing in Anton Rubinstein's absences on tour. Left Russia in 1878 and went on tour. Two years later married his second wife, A. Essipova, who had been a pupil. They were divorced 1892, and he was to marry twice more. Meantime the desire to teach took fresh hold, so he settled in Vienna and made his final concert appearance in 1886 in Frankfurt. His reputation as a teacher came to rival that of F. Liszt, and the fantastic initial successes of I. Paderewski could not but add lustre to the teacher.

Pupils included: Marie Bailey-Apfelbeck, Aline van Barentzen, Dominirsha Benislavska, Francisco Bevilacqua, Fannie Bloomfield-Zeisler, Alexander Brailowsky, Walter Braunfels, Ludwig Bronarski, Richard Bühlig, Ryzard Byk, Edoardo Celli, Jan Cherniavsky, William W. Cooke, Alice Ehlers, Annette Essipova, Severin Eisenberger, Bertha Feiring-Tapper, Ignace Friedman, Ossip Gabrilowitsch, Gottfried Galston, Heinrich Gebhard, Katharine Goodson, William H. Green, Mark Hambourg, Helen Hopekirk, Mieczyslaw Horszowski, Edwin Hughes, Katarzyna Jaczynowska, Hedwig Kanner-Rosenthal, Dmitri Klimov, Martin Knutzen, Melanie Kurt, Janina Lada, Frank la Forge, Adele Lewing, Stanislas Lipski, Czeslaw Marek, Samuel Maykapar, Henrik Melcer, Paul Mickwitz, Benno Moiseiwitsch, Ethel Newcomb, Elly Ney, Marie Novello, Arne Oldberg, Eugene Pankiewicz, Marie Paur, John Powell, Vladimir Puchalski, Louis Rée, Francis Richter, Marie Rozborska, Vassily Safonov, Jadwiga Sarnecka, Ernest Schelling, Franz Schmidt, Artur Schnabel, Eduard Schütt, Arthur Shattock, Josef Slivinski, Heinrich Spanenberg, Eleanor Spencer, Walter Spry, Evelyn Suart, William Upton, Isabella Vengerova, Adolphe Veuve, Marguerite Volavy, Dagmar Walle-Hansen, Jakob Weinberg, Emerson Whithorne, Alexander Winkler, Paul Wittgenstein, Julius Wolfsohn, George Woodhouse, Dalhousie Young, Michael Zadora, Paul Zynovyev.

LESSEL, Franz (1783–1838)
b. Pulawe, Poland. Went to Vienna in 1800 to study medicine but became involved in the musical scene. Met Haydn, from whom he received lessons including pf, remaining friends up to the composer's death. On returning home, Lessel became one of the first Polish pianists and a composer of sonatas, chamber-music, songs and a pf concerto. Only the songs have survived in the Polish repertoire.

LESSMANN, Otto (1844–1918)
b. Berlin, Germany. Pupil of H. von Bülow and taught for many years at Stern's Cons. One-time proprietor of *Allgemeine Musik-Zeitung*.

LETONDAL, Paul (1831–94)
b. Paris, France. Pupil of F. Kalkbrenner. Emigrated to Canada 1850. Performed a little and taught. His son Arthur L taught pf at Montreal Cons. from its inauguration in 1876.

Pupils included: Dominique Ducharme, Calixa Lavallée.

LEV, Ray (1912–68)
b. Rostov, Russia. Family emigrated to USA 1913, living in New York where in due course she studied pf, in 1930 winning scholarship to study in London with T. Matthay for three years. British début 1932 in London; New York début 1933. Recorded Nixa.

LEVANT, Oscar (1906–72)
b. Pittsburgh, USA. Pf pupil of S. Stojowski. Appeared in serious and popular roles, principally remembered as an interpreter of G. Gershwin; also played jazz for a time. Soloist in the film *Rhapsody in Blue*, a biography of Gershwin. Composed a pf concerto and pieces and wrote *A Smattering of Ignorance*. Made pf arrangement of Khatchaturian's *Sabre Dance* which proved popular in USA. Recorded CBS.

LEVIN, Robert (1912–)
b. Oslo, Norway. Pupil of N. Larsen and others. Début Oslo 1932. Noted soloist in Scandinavia as well as accompanist. Pf prof. at Norwegian Acad.

LEVINE, Henry (1892–1951)
b. Boston, USA. Pupil of H. Gebhard. Performed and taught thereafter. Also worked as editor in music publishing, especially with Boston Music Co.

LEVITZKI, Mischa (1898–1941)
b. Krementshug, Russia. Was sent to Warsaw at the age of 7 to study with the legendary A. Michałowski. In 1908 the family emigrated to USA and he studied with S. Stojowski at the Juilliard School. In 1911 he went to Berlin to have lessons from E. von Dohnányi and won the Mendelssohn Prize. Toured Germany 1914–15, most of Europe the following year, and made his US début in 1916 in New York. Became one of the world's leading virtuosi and composed pf pieces of salon quality, a pf concerto and a cadenza for Beethoven's 3rd concerto. Recorded *Columbia* and *HMV*.

LÉVY, Alexandre (1864–94)
b. São Paulo, Brazil. Studied in Paris and on his return home adopted the life of concert pianist and pedagogue. As a composer he tried to develop the Brazilian idiom, but there is a distinctly underlying European romanticism in his work.

LEVY, Ernst (1895–   )
b. Basle, Switzerland. Studied with E. Petri in Basle, then with R. Pugno in Paris. Taught at Basle Cons. 1916–20, then moved to Paris, finally settling in the USA. Composed chamber music and sets of pf pieces.
Pupils included: Luc Balmer, Lukas Foss, Franz Hirt.

LÉVY, Heniot (1879–1946)
b. Warsaw, Poland. Student of Hochschule, Berlin, where he made his début 1899. Toured for a year before settling in USA. Taught in Chicago and performed. Composed pf concerto and one for two pfs and string orch., chamber music and pf pieces.
Pupils included: John Cage, Ruth Crawford, Clarence Loomis.

LÉVY, Lazare (1882–1964)
b. Brussels, Belgium, of French parentage. Showed great promise at early age so at 12 went to Paris where he attended the Cons. under L. Diémer, winning 1st Prize for pf-playing in 1898. Performed in Europe and taught at the Cons. As young pianist L was regarded as a very finished virtuoso. Composed chamber music and pf pieces.
Pupils included: Jacqueline Bonneau, Alfred Ehrismann, Jacques Gentry, Julian de Gray, Monique Haas, Juliette Poumay, Ruth Slenczynska, Kyril Szalkiewicz, Andre Tchaikovsky.

LEWENTHAL, Raymond (1926–   )
b. Texas, USA. Studied pf with O. Samaroff at Juilliard School, and later with A. Cortot in Paris. Début 1948 Philadelphia. Began touring, establishing a fine reputation. But his career has been periodically affected through ill-health. Specialized in the music of C. Alkan which he broadcast and recorded. Made an Alkan edition for G. Schirmer. Recorded RCA and CBS.

LEWING, Adele (1866–1943)
b. Hanover, Germany. Pupil of Leipzig Cons. under K. Reinecke and S. Jadassohn, graduating 1885. Took lessons from T. Leschetizky in Vienna and toured Europe thereafter, then USA, where she finally settled in New York, performing widely, also teaching, and where she died after a versatile and successful career.

LEY, Salvador (1907–   )
b. Guatemala City. Studied pf in Berlin with G. Bertram 1922–7. Début 1927 in Berlin and performed in Europe, returning home 1934. US début four years later. Taught pf at Guatemala School of Music, becoming Director. Composed pf works and chamber music.

LEYBACH, Ignace (1817–91)
b. Gambsheim, France. Studied pf in Paris under J. Pixis, F. Kalkbrenner and F. Chopin. Settled in Toulouse as pianist, cathedral organist and teacher. Wrote prolifically for both instruments and was a distinguished musician in his day.

LEYGRAF, Hans (1920–   )
b. Stockholm, Sweden. Début as prodigy at the age of 10, before entering Stockholm Cons. Went on to study in Munich and Vienna. Performed widely in Europe and composed pf concerto, chamber music and pf pieces. Married the Austrian pianist Margarete Stehle (1921–   ), born Vienna, Austria.
Pupils included: Rainer Becker, Nicola Frisardi, Marian Migdal.

LHEVINNE, Josef (1874–1944)
b. Orel, Russia. Student of Moscow Cons.
under V. Safonov and fellow-pupil of S.
Rachmaninov and A. Scriabin. In teens came
under musical influence of A. Rubinstein, who
conducted at his début in the *Emperor* concerto
in Moscow in 1899. Won Gold Medal, also
Rubinstein Prize 1895. Performed and taught
in Europe and America before World War I.
US début 1906 under V. Safonov. Played
Tchaikovsky No. 1 under same conductor at
R. Phil. Soc. concert, London, 1913. Resided
in Germany 1907–19 and was interned during
World War I. In 1919 he and his wife Rosina L
emigrated to USA, where they taught at
Juilliard School and toured solo and together.
Was one of the greatest pianists of the golden
age of virtuosi. Wrote *Basic Principles of
Pianoforte Playing* and recorded American
Pathé, RCA Victor and others. Last UK
appearance Wigmore Hall, April 1937, playing
Schumann's *Toccata*, Beethoven's *Waldstein*,
Paganini-Brahms *Variations Op. 35*, Chopin
4th Ballade, Scriabin *Nocturne for left hand*,
Liszt's *Feux Follets* and Balakirev's *Islamey*.
    Pupils included: Stell Andersen, Vera
Brodsky, Ulric Cole, Celius Dougherty, Ruth
Geiger, Sascha Gorodnitzki, Charles Haubiel,
Ivan Langstroth, Nina Mesierow-Minchin,
Ernest Seitz, Harold Triggs, William Upton,
Royal Welch, Paul Wells.

LHEVINNE, Rosina (1880–1976)
b. Kiev, Russia. Student of Cons. there, win-
ning Gold Medal. Début 1895 Moscow and
toured European capitals. Taught pf. Married
Josef L, settling in New York after World War
I. US début 1923. Taught at Juilliard School
and performed solo and in two pf works with
husband. Recorded *RCA* (with J.L.), also solo
on Hallmark, and CBS.
    Pupils included: Vera Brodsky, Van
Cliburn, Mischa Dichter, Sascha Gorodnitzki,
Charles Haubiel, Leonidas Lipovetzky, Edwin
McArthur, Garrick Ohlsson, Ursula Oppens,
Daniel Pollack, Marc Raubenheimer, Roman
Rudnytsky, Jeffrey Siegel, Harold Triggs,
Ilana Vered.

LIAPUNOV, Sergei Mikhailovich
(1859–1924)
b. Yaroslav, Russia. Studied at Moscow Cons.
under K. Klindworth and L. Pabst. Settled in
St Petersburg where in 1910 he became prof. at
the Cons., in the meantime having joined
Balakirev's group of composers. After the

Revolution he settled in Paris. Composed two pf
concertos and a *Rhapsody on Ukrainian Themes*
for pf and orch., as well as chamber music and
songs. His most important work for solo pf is a
set of 12 *Études d'éxecution transcendantes*, dedicated to the memory of F. Liszt. Among orch.
works is a symphonic poem *Zelazowa Wola*,
the name of Chopin's birthplace, and a tribute
to the Pole.

LIBERACE, Walter (1919–)
b. West Allis, USA, of Italian-Polish descent
(and an assumed name). Picked up pf technique and is said to have performed for I.
Paderewski, who encouraged him to continue.
Played in night clubs and gradually developed
the style of light classics in popular arrangements and presented with candelabra and
sequins. Recorded CBS and others.

LIBERT, Henri (1869–1937)
b. Paris, France. Studied pf with A.
Marmontel and L. Diémer; also took organ
with César Franck and C. Widor. Became
mainly organist and composed pf pieces and
songs.

LICAD, Cecile (1961–)
b. Manila, Philippines. Studied pf from age of
4, début three years later. Her subsequent
tuition was in the USA, including eight years at
the Curtis Inst. Her teachers included S.
Lipkin, M. Horszowski and R. Serkin. Won
the Leventritt Foundation prize in 1981, the
year in which she made her New York début.
London début 1982. Recorded CBS.

LIEBICH, Frank (1860–1922)
b. London, UK. Pupil at Cologne Cons. of F.
Hiller and I. Seiss. Later worked with H. von
Bülow. Début 1867 in Brighton. Became
established in Britain as solo pianist and
chamber-music player, devoting much attention to contemporary music. Then, with his
wife's collaboration, he developed a lecture-
recital on Chopin in which she delivered the
lecture and he delivered the illustrations at the
keyboard: an act that was not well received by
G. B. Shaw in 1893.

LIEBLING, Emil (1851–1914)
b. Pless, Silesia, Germany. Studied with T.
Kullak in Berlin and with F. Liszt in Weimar.
Emigrated to the USA 1867 and settled in
Chicago from 1872 until his death. Was suc-
cessful pianist and teacher, and edited *The*

American History and Encyclopaedia of Music. Composed pf pieces and songs. Brother of Georg L.
Pupils included: John Grunn.

LIEBLING, Georg Lothar (1865–1946)
b. Berlin, Germany. Studied with T. Kullak in Berlin, then with F. Liszt in Weimar. Toured from 1881. Berlin début 1884. Set up own school there. Taught at Guildhall School, London 1898–1908 and lived in Munich before emigrating to the USA, eventually settling in Hollywood. Composed a pf concerto, much pf music and chamber works. Brother of Emil L.

LIEBLING, Leonard (1874–1945)
b. New York, USA. Studied at New York City College, then privately with L. Godowsky. Won scholarship to Berlin Hochschule and received further tuition from T. Kullak and K. Barth. Returned home and commenced a successful career as concert pianist. Became interested in musical criticism.

LIE-NISSEN, Erika: *see* **NISSEN, Erika** (*née* **Lie**)

LIIGAND, Andres (1952–)
b. New York, USA. Student of the Juilliard School and pupil of S. Gorodnitzki.

LILL, John Richard (1944–)
b. London, UK. Student at R. Coll. of Music, London. Début 1963 London. Joint winner of 1st Prize Tchaikovsky Pf Comp., Moscow, 1970. Has performed since, also taught, taking master-classes at Trinity Coll., London. He was billed to begin 1984 by giving in California, within the space of 28 days, the Beethoven 32 sonatas, 5 concertos and the Choral Fantasia (with the San Diego SO). His agent claimed no professional pianist 'anywhere in the world has ever attempted this remarkable feat in such a short space of time'. Recorded various. OBE 1978.

LIMA, Arthur Moreira (1940–)
b. Rio de Janeiro, Brazil. Studied pf privately at first, then in Paris with M. Long and J. Doyen. Spent six years at Tchaikovsky Cons., Moscow, during which won 2nd Prize in Int. Chopin Pf Comp., Warsaw, 1965. Subsequently toured Europe and Americas. Recorded Muza, Melodiya and others.

LIMA, João de Souza (1898–)
b. São Paolo, Brazil. Studied there, then at Paris Cons. with I. Philipp and M. Long, where he won 1st Prize 1922. Toured Europe before returning home. Taught at Cons. Carlos Gomes, performed and founded the Trio São Paolo.

LIN, Gillian (1954–)
b. Singapore. Educated in UK, where she was a pupil of C. Smith at R. Coll. of Music, winning prizes and high marks. Début 1968 there and subsequently appeared widely in the Far East and in S.E. Asia. Married a diplomat and settled in the USA. Recorded ABC and Chandos.

LINDEMANN, Fritz (1876–)
b. Wehlau, Germany. Pupil of X. Scharwenka in Berlin, where he stayed, becoming pianist at the Opera, recitalist and chamber music player.

LINDHOLM, Eino (1890–)
b. Finland. Pupil of Helsinki Musikförening, then in Berlin with T. Carreño. Became popular recitalist especially in Scandinavia and taught at the Musikförening.

LINDSAY, Anthony (1934–)
b. London, UK. Studied at Birmingham School of Music and Trinity Coll., London. Pf pupil of A. B. Michelangeli at Rome Acad., Turin, winning prizes. Performed and taught at Trinity Coll.

LIPATTI, Dinu (1917–50)
b. Bucharest, Romania. Studied pf at Cons. there, winning 2nd Prize in pf competition in Vienna in 1933. As a result went to Paris and studied with A. Cortot until 1939 when he returned home, performed solo, with orch. and also with the violinist Enesco. Left Romania in 1943 and after concerts in Scandinavia and Switzerland settled in latter where he had a master-class at Geneva Cons. until 1949. His last public appearance was in Geneva in early 1950 in the Schumann concerto under the baton of Ansermet who years previously had conducted the recording of the same work for F. Davies. Early death cut short the career of a leading artist of the day. Composed a concertino for pf and orch., *Symphonie Concertante* for two pfs and strings; also works for left hand and for two pfs. His wife, Madeleine L. was a

pianist and teacher. Recorded *Columbia*, Decca, and EMI.

Pupils included: Evelyne Dubourg, Andrei Volkonsky.

LIPKIN, Seymour (1927–)
b. Detroit, USA. Studied pf at Curtis Inst. and with R. Serkin and M. Horszowski; 1st Prize Rachmaninov Pf Comp. 1948. Performed and taught at Curtis Inst., additionally conducting.

Pupils included: Steven de Groote, Cecile Licad.

LIPOVETZKY, Leonidas (1944–)
b. Uruguay. Student of Juilliard School and of R. Lhevinne. Début 1965 Washington. Has since performed throughout Americas and Europe.

LIPSKI, Stanislas (1880–1937)
b. Warsaw, Poland. Pupil of Cracow Cons. and of L. Zelenski, later of E. Jedliczka in Berlin and of T. Leschetizky in Vienna. From 1910 taught at Cracow Cons. Performed and composed mainly pf pieces and songs of great beauty and refinement.

LIST, Eugene (1918–85)
b. Philadelphia, USA. Studied there and appeared with Los Angeles SO in 1930, aged 12. Subsequently pf pupil of O. Samaroff, then of Juilliard School. Adult début in 1934 at Philadelphia in Shostakovich's 1st pf concerto, repeated in New York following year. Thereafter toured worldwide as soloist and with orch. Gave first performance of the Carlos Chávez pf concerto 1942 with New York PO under Mitropoulos. In 1979, on the occasion of the 150th anniversary of the birth of L. M. Gottschalk, he organized a 'monster concert' of the composer's works in Carnegie Hall, supported by 19 other pianists and using 10 concert instruments. Recorded Westminster and Vox.

LISZT, Franz (1811–86)
b. Raiding, Hungary. One of the greatest pianists of all time and a leading figure of the Romantic movement whose father was a steward on an Eszterhazy estate as well as an accomplished amateur pianist who became his son's first teacher. Début 1820 in Odenburg playing a Ries pf concerto. The Eszterhazy circle were so impressed that they gave the boy the means to study in Vienna where he was a pupil of K. Czerny and was soon in much demand in the salons of the Austrian capital. He studied composition with Antonio Salieri, whose pupils had included Beethoven and Schubert.

After eighteen months he and his father went to Paris. When Cherubini refused him entry into the Cons. because he was not of French nationality, he took lessons from A. Reicha, and soon Parisian salons were as captivated by the talents of the youngster as the Viennese had been. The adulation worried the father, who in 1825 took his son away on a concert tour of Britain. At that time the young virtuoso was described as a 'pale, fragile, slender boy with deep melancholy stamped on the noble outline of his face, and an appearance of maturity that belied his years'. His return to France was marked by a period of melancholy and immersion in religiosity.

The sudden death of his father in 1827 was a cruel blow to the 16-year-old youth, who had to support his mother by resuming a concert career based on Paris. Early compositions of this period are in a religious vein.

He quickly established a leading reputation through a floridly brilliant technique he brought quite naturally to the keyboard. His only rivals in reputation were Chopin and Thalberg. Any lingering grief over his father's death was put aside to savour a series of passionate love affairs which, with concert successes, seemed to stimulate more extrovert composition. His liaison with the Countess d'Agoult led to their retirement to Geneva, and his withdrawal from the Parisian pf scene created a gap which Thalberg proceeded to fill with such success that L was obliged to hurry back into the gladiatorial arena to display the fruits of his latest compositional efforts at Geneva, taking the form of arrangements of Schubert *lieder* and Beethoven symphonies – amongst the best exercises in musical cosmetics he ever achieved. Three children were born of the liaison with d'Agoult, one of whom, Cosima, was to become the wife firstly of H. von Bülow and later of Richard Wagner. In Geneva also he had given spare-time tuition to selected young lady students at the Cons., reporting on one of them: 'vicious method (if it can be called a method), great zeal, mediocre temperament, grimaces and contortions. Glory to God in the highest and peace to men of good will'.

Once lured back to Paris, he pursued the active life of a touring virtuoso from 1837 until 1849, reigning virtually unchallenged throughout the capitals of Europe. At this period Schumann wrote of him: 'I never found any artist except Paganini to possess in so high a degree this power of subjecting, elevating and leading the public. It is an instantaneous variety of wildness, tenderness, boldness, and airy grace; the instrument glows under the hands of its master.' Yet for the most part his programme material consisted of what in all kindness would be regarded today as deplorably third-rate, even rubbish: frothy *fantaisies* and gushing arrangements designed primarily to demonstrate a glittering technique and titillate the low level of audience appreciation. It can be debated that he was conforming to the conventions of the day. It can also be argued that he did not use his powerful influence to raise the standard of public appreciation while admitting, as Schumann said, his *power* to elevate and lead the public. Of course L was not the only pianist of the time to adore the sensation of dazzling avid listeners with virtually no experience of serious musical fare, and who probably stared agape at feats of keyboard prestidigitation which properly belonged more to the circus. In fairness it must be added that the virtuosi of his time played no mean part in the evolution of the pf as a noble, powerful and sensitive instrument, features that modern writers for the instrument seem to have forgotten.

Marc Pincherle, in his *Le Monde des Virtuoses* (1963), has described how L would put a Beethoven sonata into his programme only if it was surrounded by *fantaisies*, *potpourris* and *souvenirs*; and how, on one occasion when Berlioz was to conduct his *Symphonie fantastique* and L was invited to appear at the concert, he judged the event of no more importance than to present his effervescent version of variations on Moscheles' *Alexander's March*. Usually he broke a Beethoven sonata into fragments by inserting other keyboard material between the movements, presumably not to overtax the mental concentration of the audience.

As an arranger he took liberties with the original text, and since we know that Chopin was later offended at the cavalier manner in which L tampered with his music, it should not be forgotten also that in a letter to Hiller dated 1833 Chopin wrote: 'At this moment Liszt is playing my studies and putting honest thoughts out of my head: I should like to rob him of the way to play my studies.' It is also fair to repeat that L's arrangements of the Beethoven symphonies for pf solo are models of their kind.

After roaming far and wide as the darling of the piano recital, suddenly, in 1849, at the height of his career and in the year of Chopin's death, he retired to Weimar to conduct its orchestra and take an interest in Wagner's works in the original in what might be perceived as a belated act of musical penance. He became a celebrated teacher in the sense that he became the focal point for starry-eyed young virtuosi, of prime quality anyway, all eager to pick up crumbs of wisdom that fell from the table of the master: such as one saying, cited by Lamond, in connection with the left-hand octave passages in the Chopin Polonaise in A flat: 'I vant to hearr ze 'orses' hooves' (BBC talk *c.* 1945).

Liszt made an emphatic impact upon musical style in the last century, on both writing and playing, while remaining an inveterate adaptor of other people's work, re-working for pf solo the polonaise from Tchaikovsky's *Eugene Onegin* as late as the 1880s.

A book on the life of Chopin, purporting to be by L because it bears his name as author, is an extraordinarily poor study, revealing little real knowledge of one who had been an intimate friend. Critical opinion has tended to regard the two composers as equals in the Romantic movement. Chopin did not regard the relationship in that manner since the best and most original of L's compositions saw the light of day only after Chopin's death.

In an interview with Moritz Rosenthal, published in the American *Hifi/Stereo Review* of Feb. 1965, Louis Biancolli quoted that pianist, one of L's last pupils, as saying: 'There is a secret history of Liszt which only I know. It has partly to do with Chopin. You see, there were two Liszts, the Liszt who as a young man had conquered the whole world and was at the height of his fame, and the other Liszt, the one fighting desperately for his existence. Liszt had heard Chopin play. The effect was almost tragic. He was crushed by the overwhelming grandeur of the man. What do you think he did? He retired to study six hours a day for four years. . . . He was trying to develop his individuality so that he could reach Chopin. . . . Before he knew Chopin, Liszt was far from great. Chopin himself spoke of both Liszt and Thalberg as "zeros" compared with Kalkbrenner. After those years of study [coinciding with his sojourn in Geneva: W.L.] even Chopin recognised Liszt as a genius.'

L, like Thalberg, Alkan and others of the time, had little or no regard for the amateur pianist, composing virtually nothing for that once proud section of the musical population. In the case of Liszt, apart from the *Consolations* and some late pieces which as sheet music always tended to remain obscure and not readily available, everything he wrote was far too difficult for the amateur. He composed primarily for himself, unlike Beethoven, Chopin, Schubert, Schumann, Brahms and many other composers. Professional pianists have therefore maintained a virtual monopoly over the performance of his works.

Compositions include two pf concertos and other works for pf and orch., the great and innovatory one-movement sonata in B minor, several sets of *études*, 19 published *Hungarian Rhapsodies*; transcriptions include the Beethoven symphonies, Berlioz's *Symphonie fantastique* and 50 Schubert songs. There are also 12 books of *Technische Studien* for the aspiring student, and 3 sets *Années de Pèlerinage*.

Pupils included: Karolyi Agghàzy, Isaac Albéniz, Eugen d'Albert, Konrad Ansorge, Mikhail Azanchevsky, Walter Bache, Agathe Backer-Gröndahl, Albert Bagby, Karl Bärmann, Franz Bendel, Otto Bendix, Arthur Bird, Hans v. Bronsart, Richard Burmeister, Felix Draeseke, Paul Ertel, Johann Eschmann, Amy Fay, Giuseppe Ferrata, Artur Friedheim, Karl Goepfart, Amina Goodwin, Arthur de Greef, Ludwig Hartmann, Sarah Heinze, Richard Henneberg, Richard Hoffmann, August Hyllested, Salomon Jadassohn, Rafael Joseffy, Barthold Kellermann, Karl Klindworth, Francis Korbay, Martin Krause, Franz Kroll, Franz Kullak, Carl Lachmund, Frederic Lamond, William Lauder, Johann Leitert, Wilhelm de Lenz, Emil Liebling, Georg Liebling, Louis Maas, William Mason, Anna Mehlig, Johannes Merkel, Max Meyer, Sebastian Mills, José V. da Motta, Adele aus der Ohe, Paul Pabst, John Pattison, Edward Perry, Carlyle Petersilea, Robert Pflughaupt, Sophie Pflughaupt, Karl Pohlig, Dionys Pruckner, Laura Rappoldi, Alfred Reisenauer, Julius Reubke, Eduard Reuss, Theodore Ritter, Julie Rivé-King, Moritz Rosenthal, Bertrand Roth, Josef Rubinstein, Emil von Sauer, Ludwig Schytte, Giovanni Sgambati, William Sherwood, Peter Shostakovski, Alexander Siloti, Otto Singer Sr, Alfred Sormann, Ingeborg Starck, Karl Stasny, Bernard Stavenhagen, Constantin Sternberg, August Stradal, Árpád Szendy, Karl Tausig, Stefan Thóman,

Vera Timanova, Anton Urspruch, Rudolf Viole, Josef Wieniawski, Alexander Winterberger, Julius Zarembski, Geza Zichy, Johann Zschocher.

LITOLFF, Henry Charles (1818–91)
b. London, UK. Studied pf with I. Moscheles. Début 1830 at the age of 12. He visited Paris but met with failure, and it was not until he was 22 that a successful concert there established his reputation. He toured Europe for eight years, settling in Brunswick where he married the widow of a music publisher called Meyer. He changed the firm's name to his own, and it became one of the most successful publishing houses. In the last years he devoted his time to composition of which only the *scherzo* from one of his pf concertos remains in the repertoire.

Pupils included: Robert Goldbeck.

LODER, Kate (1825–1904)
b. Bath, UK. Student of R. Acad., London, and of Lucy Anderson. Début 1844 in London, performing works of Mendelssohn in the composer's presence. Subsequently taught at the R. Acad. With C. Potter she gave, in London in 1871, a première of Brahms' *Requiem* in a version for two pfs which she had arranged.

LOESCHHORN, Albert (1819–1905)
b. Berlin, Germany. Student of L. Berger and taught at the R. Inst. for Church Music in Berlin from 1851, becoming prof. in 1858. Performed and wrote much pf music, but is remembered for his one-time indispensable studies for developing technique.

Pupils included: Karl Bohn, Gustav Lange.

LOESSER, Arthur (1894–1969)
b. New York, USA. Pf pupil of S. Stojowski, winning a prize in 1911. Début 1913 in Berlin was followed by a formal appearance in New York in 1916. A world tour followed and from 1921 he performed regularly throughout the USA. Taught at Cleveland Inst. from 1926. Was described as having 'a sparkling technique of uncommon delicacy'. Wrote an autobiography, *Men, Women and Pianos*, and founded IPA (Int. Pf Archives), an organization devoted to the preservation of historical recordings of the art of pf-playing. Part of his 1967 Town Hall, New York, recital is recorded on that label.

Pupils included: Sergio Calligaris.

LOEWE, Frederick (1904–)
b. Vienna, Austria. Studied with E. d'Albert and F. Busoni. Settled in USA in 1924 as concert pianist. Later teamed up with the librettist Alan Lerner to produce highly successful musicals: *Brigadoon*, *Paint Your Wagon*, *My Fair Lady* etc.

LOEWE, Karl Gottfried (1796–1869)
b. near Halle, Germany. Had a remarkable voice from an early age as well as instinct and feeling for composition, especially vocal. Studied theology and music side by side and is remembered as the German composer who first produced the finished song of ballad type to integrated accompaniment, giving public performances at the pf. His setting of *Erlkönig* and others are still performed. Composed in other genres including pf sonatas and chamber music. Was pupil of Daniel Türk.

LOGIER, Johann Bernhard (1777–1846)
b. Cassel, Germany. Pf training obscure and ran away from home at 10 to escape drudgery of practice. Was adopted by an Englishman and taken to UK, where he enlisted as a flautist. Invented the *Chiroplast*, a device for regulating the hands in pf practice which was patented in 1814 and proved highly popular and lucrative when promoted in UK and Germany for private use as well as in music schools, for it enabled a number of pupils to work on the same piece of music, each at own instrument. Settled in Dublin. Later his method came under attack. Published textbooks on the invention and also composed a pf concerto, chamber music, sonatas etc.

LONG, Kathleen (1896–1968)
b. Bury St Edmunds, UK. Student of R. Coll. of Music, London, winning Hopkinson Gold Medal 1915. On graduation was appointed to the teaching staff. Achieved international status both solo and in chamber music and was notably sympathetic to the music of Mozart and of the French School typified by G. Fauré at a time when it was relatively uncommon in British musical circles. In 1957 gave première of G. Finzi's *Eclogue* for pf and string orch., Op. 10, in London. Awarded CBE same year. Recorded *Decca*.
Pupils included: Imogen Cooper, Arthur Oldham, Gerard Schurmann.

LONG, Marguerite (1874–1966)
b. Nimes, France. Pupil of Paris Cons. and of A. Marmontel for pf. Taught there herself from 1906, becoming prof. in succession to Diémer in 1920. Was identified with French pf music, especially Fauré and Ravel. The latter dedicated his G major concerto to her, which she premièred under his baton throughout Europe; also recorded it for *Columbia*. Other 'first' recordings she made of French pf music were the Fauré *Ballade* and the Milhaud pf concerto. Wrote reminiscences and notes on the music of Fauré and Ravel in separate volumes which are historically highly interesting.
Pupils included: Annie d'Arco, Yuri Boukoff, Sequeira Costa, Laurenz Custer, Jeanne-Marie Darré, Jean Doyen, Philippe Entremont, Albert Ferber, Jacques Février, Marie-Thérèse Fourneau, Peter Frankl, Nicole Henriot, Ludwig Hoffman, Jeanne Leleu, Arthur Lima, João de Souza Lima, Bruno Mezzena, Enrique Perez de Guzman, Elaine Richepin, Bernard Ringeissen, Ruth Slenczynska, Daniel Wayenberg, Peter Wallfisch, Janine Weill, Ventsislav Yankov.

LONGAS, Federico (1895–1968)
b. Barcelona, Spain. Studied with E. Granados and J. Maláts. Toured Europe and Americas as solo pianist and accompanist for celebrities. Founded own school in Barcelona. Moved to Paris, later settling in the USA.

LONGO, Alessandro (1864–1945)
b. Amante, Italy. Pf pupil of B. Cesi at Naples Cons., where in due course he became pf prof. Achieved a high reputation as concert pianist both solo and ensemble. Composed chamber works and pieces for his instrument. Founded a journal, *L'Arte Pianistica*, but is now remembered for his edition of the complete keyboard works of D. Scarlatti which bear his numbered sequence. Also edited other music of ancient origin.
Pupils included: Sigismondo Cesi.

LOOMIS, Clarence (1889–1965)
b. Sioux Falls, USA. Pupil at Dakota Univ., then of H. Lévy at Chicago Cons., where he won a gold medal. Went on to study with L. Godowsky in Vienna before returning to Chicago to teach. Held other teaching appointments in USA settling in California in 1960 in private capacity. Composed a *Fantasy* for pf and orch. and pf works.

LOPATNIKOV, Nikolai Lvovich (1903–76)
b. Estland, Russia. Pupil of St Petersburg Cons. 1914–17. Escaped to Finland during the Russian Revolution, settling in Berlin in 1930 to study pf with W. Rehberg and composition with E. Toch. Visited Finland 1933, London 1934, and finally settled in the USA in 1939. Taught at Carnegie-Mellon Univ., Pittsburgh. Wrote a wide variety of music (in neo-classical style) including two pf concertos and one for two pfs and orch., *Variations and Epilogue* for cello and pf, as well as other chamber works and a quantity of pf pieces.

LOPES-GRAÇA, Fernando (1906–)
b. Tamar, Portugal. Studied at Lisbon Cons. Début 1932 Lisbon. In the same year he began teaching at Coimbra Music Inst. Was in Paris 1937–40, when he returned to Lisbon. Became known for his concerts in S. America and also toured Africa and the USSR.

LORENZ, Philip (1935–)
b. Bremerhaven, Germany. Lived in USA from the age of 15 and studied with C. Arrau until 1969, when he joined the faculty of California State Univ.; prof. there from 1974. Gave recitals solo and with Ena Bronstein; held master-classes. Joint editor with C. Arrau of Peter's latest edition of the Beethoven pf sonatas.

LORIOD, Yvonne (1924–)
b. Houilles, France. Student of Paris Cons. under Messiaen, whom she married. As a result of concert tours became internationally famous. Repertoire includes many contemporary works, and she has given first performances of Bartók, Messiaen and others. The solo pf part of her husband's *Turangalila* symphony was written with her in mind, and she premièred the work. Recorded Supraphon, Erato and EMI.
Pupils included: Hortense Cartier-Bresson, Paul Crossley, Peter Donohoe, Bruno Peltre.

LORTAT, Robert (1885–1938)
b. Paris, France. Studied at Paris Cons. under L. Diémer, winning 1st Prize in 1901 and Prix Diémer in 1905. Début 1910 in Paris and later toured Germany. In 1913 played the cycle of Chopin works in Paris and London; the following year gave London the entire pf works of G. Fauré in a series of four recitals. Was wounded in World War I and invalided out. US début 1916. Besides solo tours he gave chamber-music recitals with leading instrumentalists like Jacques Thibaud. Recorded *French Columbia*: Chopin *études*, preludes and sonata Op. 35.
Pupils included: Dagny Knutsen.

LOTH, Louis (1888–)
b. Richmond, USA. Studied pf in New York, then with A. Jonás in Berlin. Performed in Europe before returning to USA. Taught, composed pf works and two pf concertos.

LOUSSIER, Jacques (1934–)
b. Angers, France. Studied pf and in 1947 went to Paris Cons. under Yves Nat leaving at the age of 17. Worked in the Caribbean area until 1959 where he was exposed to other influences besides the classical tradition. After his return to Paris he began to experiment with Bach, whose music he proceeded to treat in the idiom of the day, for the purpose forming a trio which achieved an unique fame and following. Derek Jewell said of the Trio: 'Few artists have done so much to show the common ground which exists between the music of different centuries and different cultures.' Recorded various.

LOVERIDGE, Iris (1917–)
b. London, UK. Pupil of R. Acad. there; also received tuition from C. Smith and L. Kentner. Made many concert appearances and broadcasts. Recorded *Columbia* and others.

LÖW, Josef (1834–86)
b. Prague, Czechoslovakia. Studied there and began touring from the age of 20. Besides performing he composed some 500 salon pieces which once had a vogue.

LOWE, Claude Egerton (1860–1947)
b. London, UK. Student of Leipzig Cons. Became teacher and examiner at Trinity Coll., London.

LOWENTHAL, Jerome
Request to last-known concert agents for biographical details met with no response.

LOYONNET, Paul (1889–)
b. Paris, France. Pupil Cons. there. Début Paris 1906. Leading pianist, solo, with orch. and in chamber music. Toured Europe. Author of critical works on Beethoven. Was member of the Trio Capet.

LÜBBECKE-JOB, Emma (1888–)
b. Germany. Pianist friend of Paul Hindemith who gave première of a number of his works for pf, including the first pf concerto in 1924 in Frankfurt, and the *Konzertmusick* in 1930 in Chicago. Performed Hindemith's 1st pf concerto at a London Prom in 1931.

LUBECK, Ernst (1829–76)
b. The Hague, Netherlands. A natural prodigy who commenced his pianistic career in 1841 and who later toured the Americas in the manner of L. Gottschalk. In 1854 returned to The Hague to teach, settling the following year in Paris, where he established himself as a fine concert artist. Visited London 1860 and 1868.
Pupils included: John Shedlock.

LUBOSCHUTZ, Pierre (1891–1971)
b. Odessa, Russia. Studied at Moscow Cons. under C. Igumnov, graduating 1912, then, later, with F. Blumenfeld in Paris. Début Moscow 1912. Thereafter toured as soloist before settling in USA. Married Genia Nemenoff in 1931. They gave première of Martinu's concerto for 2 pfs in 1943 with Philadelphia under E. Ormandy. Recorded Everest.
Pupils included: Boris Goldowsky.

LUCAS, Brenda: *see* **OGDON, John**

LUCKSTONE, Isidore (1861–1941)
b. Baltimore, USA. Studied pf in Berlin under X. Scharwenka; also took lessons in singing before becoming celebrated accompanist, touring the world several times before settling as teacher and accompanist in New York, where he appeared regularly with artists of calibre of Kreisler.

LUMSDEN, Ronald (1938–)
b. Dundee, UK. Studied there and at R. Coll., London. Mainly academic career and broadcaster. Recorded Vista.

LUNDBERG, Lennart Arvid (1863–1931)
b. Norrköping, Sweden. Student of Stockholm Cons. and later in Berlin, then in Paris where he received lessons from I. Paderewski. His first European tour in 1893 took in London where he was described as showing neatness as well as brilliance. Taught at Stockholm Cons. from 1903 in addition to pursuing a concert career. Composed pf works.

Pupils included: Henning Mankell, Olof Wibergh.

LUNDE, Johan Backer (1874–)
b. Le Havre, France. Studied pf with Agathe Backer-Gröndahl in Oslo, then with F. Busoni in Berlin. Made successful concert tours of Scandinavia, Germany and UK before settling in Oslo as soloist, accompanist and teacher. Wrote pf and orch. music.

LUPU, Radu (1945–)
b. Romania. Début at the age of 12 in a recital of own works before winning scholarship to study at Moscow Cons., where he was a pupil of H. Neuhaus and S. Neuhaus. Won 1st Prize in the Van Cliburn Int. Comp. 1966; and 1st Prize in the Leeds Int. Pf Comp. 1969. Appeared thereafter in leading musical centres, solo and with orch. Dedicatee of a pf concerto by Andre Tchaikovsky which he premièred in London in 1975. Recorded Decca.

LUSH, Ernest (1908–)
b. Bournemouth, UK. Pupil of T. Matthay, also K. Friedberg. Début Bournemouth 1927, in which year joined BBC as principal accompanist and chamber-music player; therefore made few outside concert appearances. As accompanist appeared on various record labels.

LUTOSLAWSKI, Witold (1913–)
b. Warsaw, Poland. Began studying at the age of 11, then attended Warsaw Cons. under J. Lefeld, graduating in 1937 with a diploma for composition, having already a number of works to his credit including a pf sonata. During Nazi occupation he earned a living playing music for two pfs with Andrej Panufnik, making their own arrangements, only one of his appearing to remain: *Variations on a theme of Paganini* (based on the 24th Caprice), which has proved popular with duettists.

LÜTSCHG, Karl (1839–99)
b. St Petersburg, Russia. Studied pf with A. Henselt in St Petersburg, then with I. Moscheles in Leipzig. In addition to a concert career was pf prof. at St Petersburg Cons. Composed works of educational nature.
Pupils included: Waldemar Lütschg, Aleksander Tansman.

LÜTSCHG, Waldemar (1877–1948)
b. St Petersburg, Russia. Son of Karl L and studied pf at Cons. under father. Successful concert pianist and teacher, working in Berlin (1899–1905) after which he taught in USA for two years before returning to St Petersburg.

LYALL, Max Dail (1939–　)
b. Oklahoma, USA. Studied there and was later a pupil of L. Fleischer. After graduation became active in the Nashville area as soloist and composer.

LYAPUNOV, Sergei Mikhailovich: *see* **LIAPUNOV, Sergei Mikhailovich**

LYMPANY, Moura (Mary Johnstone) (1916–　)
b. Saltash, Cornwall, UK. Studied at Liège then at R. Acad., London, under T. Matthay, winning a prize. Spent some time in Vienna before returning to London as a pupil of Mathilde Verne. Début Harrogate 1928 in Mendelssohn G minor; London Prom début 1938, same year as she came 2nd in Ysaÿe Int. Pf Comp., Brussels. Gave 1st British performance of Khatchaturian pf concerto 1940. CBE 1979. Has performed regularly and toured throughout the world. Recorded *Decca*, Decca and EMI. Gold medallist Paris as wine-grower.

LYNCH, Charles (1906–1984)
b. Co. Cork, Eire. Entered Cork School of Music at age of 8. In 1921 won scholarship to R. Acad., London, becoming a pupil of Y. Bowen. Later studied with E. Petri. Début 1932 London. Performed solo and in ensemble. Taught. Was reported having performed in a series all Beethoven symphonies arranged by F. Liszt. Dedicatee of Bax's 4th pf sonata.

LYSBERG, Charles Samuel Bovy-: *see* **BOVY-LYSBERG, Charles Samuel**

MAAG, Peter (1919–)
b. St Gallen, Switzerland. Studied in Zurich and Geneva, later becoming a pupil of A. Cortot. Mainly known as a conductor.

MAAS, Louis Philipp Otto (1852–89)
b. Wiesbaden, Germany. Pupil of Leipzig Cons. under K. Reinecke, followed by three years with F. Liszt. Taught at Leipzig 1875–80, then emigrated to Boston, USA, where he performed and taught. Composed a pf concerto, sonatas, pf pieces and chamber music.

MAAZEL, Israela: *see* **MARGALIT, Israela**

MacDERMID, James (1875–1960)
b. Ontario, Canada. Studied there and in USA, where he settled, becoming naturalized in 1906. Married the soprano Sibyl M and accompanied her recitals.

MacDOWELL, Edward Alexander
(1861–1908)
b. New York, USA. Studied there with T. Carreño; was at Paris Cons. 1876–8 with A. Marmontel, then worked with L. Ehlert in Wiesbaden. Became friendly with J. Raff, through whom he secured an introduction to F. Liszt who liked M's compositions. Taught pf at Darmstadt 1881–2. Lived, played, taught and composed in Germany until late 1888, then returning to USA to settle in Boston, and already known as a composer through performances by Carreño and others. US début Nov. 1888, and the following year was soloist in the première of his 2nd pf concerto in New York. In 1896 became first head of music department of Columbia Univ., performing less but composing more. It was perhaps his best creative period for, from 1902, his health declined and he resigned the teaching post in 1904. Visited the UK once, in 1903. Was the first serious

American composer though his romantic style was deeply imbued with European musical culture, and even in the virtuosic studies for pf he evinced little that was new. His workmanship is always technically competent, and American pianists have included both pf concertos in their repertoire.

Pupils included: Annie David, Angela Diller, Marion Nevins.

MACDOWELL, Marion (*née* **Nevins**)
(1857–1956)
b. New York, USA. Pf pupil of E. Macdowell, whom she married in 1884. She worked tirelessly in his cause after his death, founding the Peterborough Festival and giving her husband's home there to the MacDowell Memorial Association for use by young composers for work during the summer.

MACFARREN, Walter Cecil (1826–1905)
b. London, UK. Brother of Sir G. A. M. Was an early pupil of R. Acad. under C. Potter. Became pf prof. there from 1846 until his death. Was a popular concert pianist; also lectured and conducted. Composed a pf concerto, sonatas and much pf music. Edited a wide range of classical pf music and wrote an autobiography *Musical Memories*.

Pupils included: Dora Bright, Stewart Macpherson, Frederick Westlake.

MACKIE, Jean (1920–)
b. London, UK. Pf. pupil of R. Acad. of Music, London, where she made her début. Performed and taught R. Acad. of Music.

MACNAMARA,   Hilary: *see   under*
SHELLEY, Howard

MACONCHY, Elizabeth (1907–)
b. Broxbourne, UK. Pupil of R. Coll., London

on Blumenthal Scholarship, studying composition with R. Vaughan Williams and pf with A. Alexander. Won Octavia Scholarship in 1929 leading to study in Prague where some of her works, including the pf concerto, were first performed by her. The concerto had its British première in 1936 in London, and *Dialogue* for same genre in 1942. Also wrote chamber music, pf pieces and songs.

MACPHERSON, (Charles) Stewart (1865–1941)
b. Liverpool, UK. Pupil of R. Acad., London, studying pf with W. Macfarren. Became distinguished scholar and toured the world as an examiner to the Association Board. Wrote a number of books on technical aspects and produced complete editions of the Beethoven sonatas, Mozart sonatas and other classics for the publishers Joseph Williams Ltd of London.

MADEIRA, Joaquin d'Azevedo (1851–91)
b. Lisbon, Portugal. Studied there and taught pf as well as performing.
Pupils included: José Vianna da Motta.

MADRIGUERA, Paquita (1900–   )
b. Igualada, Spain. Studied with E. Granados for composition and Frank Marshall for pf. Thereafter concert pianist in Europe and USA and composed pf works.

MAGALOFF, Nikita (1912–   )
b. St Petersburg, Russia, of Russian-Swiss stock. Family moved to France before Russian Revolution. Became pupil of I. Philipp at Paris Cons., graduating with 1st Prize in 1929. Performed thereafter, settling in Switzerland on outbreak of World War II. On staff of Geneva Cons. from 1949. Son-in-law of the famous violinist Joseph Szigeti whom he accompanied in recitals. Composed pf and chamber works, also Mozart cadenzas. A *Toccata Op. 6* is dedicated to V. Horowitz. Dedicatee of Igor Markovich's *Variations and Fugue* on a theme of Handel ('*The Harmonious Blacksmith*'), 1941. Recorded *Radiola*, Decca and Phonogram.
Pupils included: Martha Argerich, Evelyne Dubourg, John O'Conor, Janis Vakarelis.

MAIER, Guy (1892–1956)
b. Buffalo, USA. Studied at New England Cons., then later in Berlin with A. Schnabel. Début 1914 Boston and began performing solo

and also in team with Lee Pattison. Also taught at Juilliard School. Went to Los Angeles in 1946 to teach at Univ. of California.
Pupils included: Leonard Pennario.

MALÁTS, Joaquin (1872–1912)
b. Barcelona, Spain. Pf pupil of F. Pujol in Barcelona, then studied at Paris Cons. under C. de Bériot, winning 1st Prize 1903 and later the Prix Diémer. Performed thereafter mainly in Iberia, where he made a fine reputation as an interpreter of I. Albéniz. Composed pf pieces.
Pupils included: Manuel Blancafort, José Iturbi.

MALCOLM, George (1917–   )
b. London, UK. Studied at R. Coll. there from the age of 7 and was a pupil of H. Fryer. Studied at Balliol Coll., Oxford, 1934–7, returning to R. Coll. in 1938. Wartime service in RAF. Turned to harpsichord, becoming a foremost exponent in UK and abroad. Appearances as pianist became confined largely to chamber-music concerts. CBE 1965.
Pupils included: Andras Schiff.

MALCUZYNSKI, Witold (1914–77)
b. Warsaw, Poland. Pf pupil of J. Turczynski at Warsaw Cons., graduating 1936. Won 3rd Prize in the Int. Chopin Comp., Warsaw the following year. Studied with I. Paderewski in Switzerland. Married the pianist Colette Gaveau and went to Paris in 1939. Was in the Americas during World War II. US début 1942. After the war toured worldwide, returning to Warsaw from 1958. A Chopin exponent. Recorded *Columbia*, EMI and Muza.

MALININ, Eugeny (1930–   )
b. Moscow, USSR. Student of Moscow Cons., also of S. Neuhaus. Came 7th in Chopin Pf Comp., Warsaw, in 1949, and joint 2nd in M. Long-J. Thibaud Concours Int. in 1953. Performed from 1949, touring most countries. From 1957 taught at Moscow Cons. and became a well-known adjudicator at international competitions. Recordings included Columbia.

MALIPIERO, Gian Francesco (1882–1973)
b. Venice, Italy. Studied in Italy and had scholastic career apart from composing. Works include six pf concertos and *Variazioni sensa Tema*, *Dialogo* (two pfs and orch.), besides a triple concerto, chamber music and many works for one and two pfs, also songs.

MALKIN, Manfred (1884–1966)
b. Odessa, Russia. Studied at Paris Cons. and
was pupil of C. de Bériot. Début there 1904
and other European musical centres. Began to
tour the USA in successive seasons; became
established and eventually settled in New
York, performing and teaching. Formed a trio
with his brothers Jacques (violin) and Josef
(cello).

MALOZYOMOVA, Sofia Alexandrovna
(1845–1908)
b. St Petersburg, Russia. Pupil of Cons. there
and of T. Leschetizky and Anton Rubinstein.
Graduated at the Cons. 1866, where she taught
all her life, being especially associated with
Rubinstein's classes.

MANA-ZUCCA (**Augusta Zuckermann**)
(*c.*1887–)
b. New York, USA. Appeared there as a
prodigy and was taught successively by A.
Lambert, L. Godowsky and F. Busoni. Discovered a voice and studied singing before
touring Europe in dual role. Commenced composing and gave première of her pf concerto in
New York in 1919. Became a prolific composer
and, besides chamber works, wrote an
immense volume of 366 pf works called *My
Musical Calendar,* one for each day of the year
incl. leapyear. Discarded the surname Zuckermann around 1916. Exact date of birth
uncertain: sources vary between 1887 and
1894.

MANDEL, Alan Roger (1935–)
b. New York, USA. Studied at Juilliard
School. Début 1948 New York. Won prizes at
Salzburg 1962, Bolzano 1963. Has performed
throughout USA and Europe etc. Recorded
complete pf works of C. Ives for CBS label.

MANES, Stephen (1940–)
b. Vermont, USA. Studied at Juilliard School
New York, and Vienna Acad. Pf prof. and
concert pianist, winner of Leventritt Comp.
Teaching posts include Oberlin and State
Univ., New York.

MANKELL, Henning (1868–1930)
b. Härnösand, Sweden. Student of R. Cons.,
Stockholm 1889–95. Pf pupil of L. Lundberg
for next four years. Afterwards taught, being a
member of Stockholm R. Acad. teaching staff.
Was also music critic and composer, having
studied composition with Hilda Thegerström,

a pupil of F. Liszt. As a composer absorbed
French and Russian influences of the time.
Works for pf include a concerto, chamber
music, and solos, including 4 *Ballads,* most of
which is unpublished.

MANNES, Clara Damrosch (1869–1948)
b. Breslau, Germany. Studied successively in
New York and Dresden before, in 1897,
becoming pupil of F. Busoni. Thereafter performed and taught, marrying David Mannes
the violinist, with whom she additionally
toured as a duo-team. Was popular in Europe
as well as in the USA. From 1940 established
with her husband the Mannes School in New
York. Was daughter of Leopold Damrosch
(1832–85).

MANNES, Leopold Damrosch (1899–1964)
b. New York, United States. Son of Clara
Damrosch Mannes and David Mannes.
Studied in New York, also in Paris with A.
Cortot. Was Pulitzer prizewinner 1925.
Taught in the Mannes School. Later left for a
time as, being a physicist and BA, he did
research at the Eastman Kodak works in
association with Leopold Godowsky Jr., as a
result of which they invented the Kodachrome
colour photography method. Wrote a suite for
two pfs and other works.

MANNHEIMER, Frank (1896–)
b. Ohio, USA. Pf training privately in USA
and Europe. Settled in London 1926; taught at
Tobias Matthay School, became well known
on the concert platform solo and with orch.
Broadcast numerous recitals of an educational
nature and including one given on the 'Chopin'
Broadwood grand. Returned to USA on outbreak of World War II.

MANNINO, Franco (1924–)
b. Palermo, Italy. Student of R. Silvestri at St
Cecilia Cons., Rome. After touring widely,
turned to opera, composing and conducting in
that medium. Prolific composer including pf.

MANSHARDT, Thomas (1927–)
b. Wai, India. Studied in Lausanne, also at
École Normale, Paris, pf lessons from A.
Cortot. Début 1954 Vienna. US début 1964.
Appeared in Europe, India and USA. Taught
in Canada from 1966.

MANTIA, Aldo (1903–)
b. Rome, Italy. Student of S. Cecilia Acad.

there and of Naples Cons. Taught in Rome and Parma and performed. Numerous compositions include pf works, and has written on musical topics.

MANZ, Wolfgang (1960–)
b. Düsseldorf, Germany. Studied in Prague and later Hanover. Won a number of pf prizes in European competitions including Milan in 1979 and Berlin in 1981. Came second in Leeds Int. Pf Comp. in 1981. Gave recitals in countries in which he competed. London début 1981, when one critic said of his Liszt *Mephisto Waltz*: 'Possessed by a gripping demonic fervour, his searching musicianship was as imaginative as his scintillating pianism.'

MAPP, Richard (–   )
Request for biographical details met with no response from NZ Cultural Attaché, London.

MARCELLE, Pauline (1911–)
b. Ixelles, Belgium. Student of Brussels Cons. and of E. Bosquet. Début 1932 there. Has performed solo and with orch. throughout Europe and USA. Distinguished teacher. Order of Leopold 1960. Recorded various labels.

MARCHWINSKI, Jerzy (1935–)
b. Truskolasi, Poland. Pupil of Warsaw Acad. and of C. Zecchi. Soloist, accompanist and lecturer.

MAREK, Czeslaw Josef (1891–)
b. Przemysl, Poland. Student of Lwow Cons., then of Vienna Acad., and pf. pupil of T. Leschetizky. Studied composition with Pfitzner in Strasbourg. Début Lwow 1909, where he taught until 1915, thereafter in Zurich. Toured Europe regularly as Chopin exponent. Has composed and written works on technique and musicianship.
Pupils included: H. Haller.

MARGALIT, Israela (1944–)
b. Haifa, Israel. Student of Israeli Acad., then in Salzburg. Prizes include jt. 4th in Busoni, Italy, 1965. Has toured widely solo and with orch. in Europe and USA and married the conductor Lorin Maazel.

MARGARITIS, Loris (1895–1953)
b. Aigion, Greece. Remarkable prodigy who later studied in Berlin with B. Stavenhagen.

Was pf prof. in Salonika thereafter. Compositions include pf pieces and songs.

MARGULIES, Adele (1863–1949)
b. Vienna, Austria. Pf pupil of A. Door at Vienna Cons., winning 1st Prize three years running. Toured Europe and made US début in 1881 in New York. Returned there two years later and appeared with orchs. Settled in USA and in 1890 founded the Margulies Pf Trio which gave many chamber-music recitals over a long period featuring new compositions. Also taught successively at the National Cons. and in Houston, where she retired in 1936.
Pupils included: Louis Gruenberg.

MARIGO, Francisco (1916–)
b. Padua, Italy. Student at Acad. Chigiana., also of A. B. Michelangeli. Début Padua. Has performed throughout Europe and Latin America. Prolific composer in various genres.

MARKHAM, Richard (1952–)
b. Grimsby, UK. Pupil of M. Pirani. Début 1974 London, followed by appearances solo and with orchs., at home and abroad and including festivals like Aldeburgh.

MARKS, Alan (1949–)
b. Chicago, USA. Studied in St Louis, where he made his début in 1966 before studying further at the Juilliard School of Music (B Mus.). Later was pupil of L. Fleisher and became successful concert pianist. New York début 1971 at Carnegie Hall. Won 2nd Prize in the Univ. of Maryland Int. Pf Festival 1973. Appeared solo and with orchestras in the USA, Europe and Far East. Gave première of *Caprichos* by C. Chavez in 1976.

MARMONTEL, Antoine-François
(1816–98)
b. Clermont-Ferrand, France. Student of Paris Cons. under P. Zimmerman for pf. Won 1st pf prize 1832, and in 1848 succeeded his old master as head of pf class. Many of his pupils were to become famous during his long spell of almost forty years as pedagogue. Was prolific composer, mostly of the study type, and wrote several books on the instrument and its executants, notably one called *Pianistes Célèbres*.
Pupils included: Isaac Albéniz, Émile Bernard, Georges Bizet, Ignacio Cervantes, Louis Diémer, Theodore Dubois, Dominique Ducharme, Josef Duleba, Victor Duvernoy, Justin Elie, Alexis Fissot, Henri Ghis, Henri

Ketten, Henri Kowalski, Théodore Lack, Calixa Lavallée, Albert Lavignac, Rudolf Niemann, Gabriel Pierné, Francis Planté, Alfonso Thibaud, François Thomé, Carlos Vidiella, Emil Waldteufel, Josef Wieniawski, André Wormser.

MARMONTEL, Antonin Émile Louis (1850–1907)
b. Paris, France. Son of A-F M. Teacher of female class at Paris Cons. Pupils believed to include M. Long and O. Samaroff. Mme Long, in her book on Fauré, records her indebtedness for the guidance she received over a long period, not only with her repertory but with aspects of teaching as well.

MARSHALL, Elizabeth (1937–)
b. Philadelphia, USA. Studied at Manhattan, also Vienna Acad. Début 1963, New York. Afterwards became successful concert pianist.

MARSHALL, Frank (1883–1959)
b. Mataro, Spain. Student of Barcelona Cons. under E. Granados for pf, becoming prof. there on completion of training at the age of 17. Toured Europe widely, also the Americas. Gave series of recitals at the Milan Exhibition 1906. Later returned to Barcelona to assist Granados, taking over direction of the Acad. on Granados's death in 1916. Later involved in propagating de Falla's music and was one of the most celebrated teachers of his time. Composed various works for pf, also songs. Recorded *Odeon*.
Pupils included: Alicia de Larrocha, Paquita Madriguera.

MARTENOT, Ginette-Geneviève (1902–)
b. Paris, France. Daughter of Maurice M. Pf pupil of Paris Cons. and travelled widely as pianist in Europe and USA. Lectured and also demonstrated the 'Ondes Martenot' (see M. Marthenot). Composed songs and for stage.

MARTENOT, Maurice (1898–1980)
b. Paris, France. Pf pupil at Paris Cons. and later prof. at École Normale. Invented Ondes Musicales, now called Ondes Martenot, a radio-electronic instrument regarded as in advance of the Theremin and which was patented and demonstrated for the first time in 1928. Composers of the calibre of Florent Schmitt and Arthur Honegger wrote works using it, and at the Paris Exposition of 1937 it was demonstrated by means of the perform-

ance of no less than twenty works. The inventor published a textbook on the instrument with preface by A. Cortot. Has been called 'the father of the present music synthesiser'. The Ondes Martenot has been used by succeeding composers, e.g. Messiaen.

MARTINU, Bohuslav (1890–1959)
b. Policka, Czechoslovakia. Violinist-trained composer whose works include five pf concertos and a triple concertino as well as chamber music and many pf solos.

MARTUCCI, Giuseppe (1856–1909)
b. Capua, Italy. Played in public in Naples at the early age of 11, and studied at the Cons. there until 1872, pupil of B. Cesi. Was appointed pf prof. on graduation, and successfully toured Europe as a concert pianist. Directed Bologna Cons. 1886–1902, and Naples Cons. from 1902 until his death. Became well-known as a conductor and composed in most genres.
Pupils included: Filippo Ivaldi, Paolo Martucci.

MARTUCCI, Paolo (1883–)
b. Naples, Italy. Son of Giuseppe M; his pupil at Bologna Cons. Début 1902. Settled in London 1904–11 when he emigrated to USA. Début New York 1915, and lived there as pianist and teacher.
Pupils included: Napoleone Cesi.

MARVIN, Frederick (1923–)
b. Los Angeles, USA. Studied there and made his début 1939. Received lessons from R. Serkin. Career interrupted by World War II. European début 1954. An authority on Antonio Soler (1729–83) whose harpsichord sonatas (amounting to some 75) are featured in his pf recitals.

MARXSEN, Eduard (1806–87)
b. Nienstädten, Altona, Germany. Pupil of I. Seyfried who had studied with Haydn and Mozart. Played pf and taught in Hamburg. His principal claim to fame now is as a teacher of J. Brahms, whose B flat pf concerto Op. 83 is dedicated to M.
Pupils included: Johannes Brahms, Ludwig Deppe.

MARZO, Eduardo (1852–1929)
b. Naples, Italy. Lived most of his life in New

York. Accompanied celebrity recitalists; also well-known organist of his time.

MASEK, Vincenz (1755–1831)
b. Zwikovecz, Czechoslovakia. Pf pupil of J. Dussek and performed as a very early pianist, certainly one of the earliest of the Bohemians. A younger brother, Paul M, had similar successful career in Vienna. Vincenz additionally opened a music shop in Vienna.

MASON, William (1829–1908)
b. Boston, USA. Studied there and made his début in 1846. From 1849 was a pupil of I. Moscheles and later studied with F. Liszt in Weimar. Toured Germany and appeared in London on his way home, where, in 1855, he settled in New York. Helped form a chamber-music society which flourished for over a decade. Was one of the first purely American concert pianists and teachers and was brother of Henry M, co-founder of the American pf firm of Mason & Hamlin. Published textbooks on pf technique as well as the autobiography *Memories of a Musical Life* (1902).
Pupils included: Ruth Deyo, Arthur Johnstone, Samuel Sanford, Eleanor Spencer, Wesley Weyman.

MASSELOS, William (1920–   )
b. Niagara, USA, of Dutch and Greek parentage. Student of Juilliard School and later of K. Friedberg. Graduated 1943. Début New York same year, then commenced touring as soloist. Has identified himself very much with the contemporary scene. Gave first public performance of Ives' 1st pf sonata, arranged its publication and recorded it. Recorded RCA.

MASSENET, Jules (1842–1912)
b. Montaud, France. Pupil of Paris Cons. where he studied pf with Laurent. Won 1st Prize for pf-playing and was always good pianist though he taught composition at the Cons. and composed numerous operas by which he is chiefly remembered now. Also composed a pf concerto, many songs and pf pieces for two and four hands.
Pupils included: Reynaldo Hahn.

MASZYNSKI, Piotr (1855–1934)
b. Warsaw, Poland. Was a student of the Cons. there and of A. Michałowski. Taught at the Cons. over 40 years, performed, also conducted, being interested in choral music.

MATHIAS, Georges (1826–1910)
b. Paris, France. Student of Paris Cons. and a pupil of F. Chopin; may therefore be presumed to have passed on to his pupils some of the technique acquired from the Pole. Took lessons also from F. Kalkbrenner. Pf prof. at Paris Cons. 1862–93, composed two pf concertos, studies and pieces, as well as chamber music and songs.
Pupils included: Francisco Bevilacqua, Teresa Carreño, Camille Chevillard, Paul Dukas, Isidor Philipp, Raoul Pugno, Erik Satie, Ernest Schelling, Alberto Williams.

MATHIEU, Émile (1844–1932)
b. Lille, France, of Belgian parentage. Pupil of Louvain School then of Brussels Cons. under A. Dupont. Taught at Louvain 1867–96, becoming Director. Took charge of Ghent Cons. 1896–1924. Compositions include *Paysages d'automne* for pf and orch., songs and pieces.

MATHIS, James
Request to last-known concert agents for biographical details met with no response.

MATTEI, Tito (1841–1914)
b. Campobasso, Italy. Studied in Rome, then with S. Thalberg. Became prof. at Academia di S. Cecilia, Rome, and pianist to the Italian court. From 1865 settled in London, where he added composing opera and conducting to his activities. Wrote pf music.

MATTHAY, Tobias (1858–1945)
b. London, UK. Pupil of R. Coll., London, under Sterndale Bennett, Sullivan, Prout and Macfarren. Became pf prof. at R. Acad. from 1880 and founded own school in 1900. Claimed to have developed a new method and was one of the most prestigious teachers of his time. Wrote a number of books on how to play the pf and composed much pf music that seems never to have been in any pianist's repertoire. He was known affectionately by his many pupils as 'Uncle Tobs'. Recorded several of his pieces on *Columbia*.
Pupils included: Arthur Alexander, Ethel Bartlett, Sir Arnold Bax, Tessa Bloom, York Bowen, Martin Burke, Harriet Cohen, Miles Coverdale, Harold Craxton, Cecil Dixon, John Dunn, Norman Franklin, Norman Fraser, Ruth Gipps, Margaret Good, Julian de Gray, Annie Grimson, Dame Myra Hess, Dorothy Howell, Frank Hutchens, Eileen Joyce, Vivian

Langrish, Denise Lassimone, Ray Lev, Ernest Lush, Moura Lympany, Nina Milkina, Eunice Norton, Gertrude Peppercorn, Rene Pougnet, Rae Robertson, Irene Scharrer, Millicent Silver, John Simons, Felix Swinstead, Wesley Weyman, Percy Whitehead, Dorothy Wilson.

MATTHEWS, Denis (1919–)
b. Coventry, UK. Pf pupil of H. Craxton at R. Acad., London. Début 1939 and established himself at Dame Myra Hess' Nat. Gallery lunchtime concerts during World War II, in which he served in RAF. Thereafter resumed career solo and with orch. In 1971 appointed pf prof. at Newcastle Univ. CBE 1975. Wrote *Keyboard Music* and *In Pursuit of Music*. Recorded *Columbia* and EMI.
Pupils included: Rhondda Gillespie, John Ogdon, Allan Schiller.

MAUTÉ DE FLEURVILLE, Antoinette Flore (*née* **Chariat**) (–1884)
b. France. According to biographers of C. Debussy, was a pupil of F. Chopin and was Debussy's first pf teacher. It is said that from her he derived much of his admiration for, and ex-textbook knowledge of, Chopin in the form of handed-down legend. She was mother-in-law of the poet Verlaine and may well have instilled a love of French poetry in Debussy that later bore fruit in his *chansons*.

MAY, Florence (1845–1923)
b. London, UK. A pupil of her father; also received tuition from J. Brahms around 1871, apparently on the recommendation of K. Schumann. Became steeped in the Brahms cult and actively propagated his music in her concert work. Wrote a two-volume work on him which was translated into German, also *The Girlhood of Klara Schumann*.

MAYER, Charles (1799–1862)
b. Königsberg (now Kaliningrad, USSR). Studied pf with J. Field in St Petersburg; toured Europe before returning to settle there until 1850, when he went to Dresden. Toured periodically and was prolific composer whose work is worth an occasional glance.
Pupils included: Mikhail Glinka.

MAYER, Max (1859–1931)
b. Vechta, Germany. Studied in Stuttgart then with F. Liszt in Weimar. Lived in Manchester from 1883 and became naturalized in 1900. Specialized in chamber-music concerts and in

1908 was appointed prof. at the R. Manchester Coll. Compositions included pf music and songs.

MAYERL, Billy (1902–55)
b. London, UK. Came of poor family and played in a cinema while still at school in order to provide private pf studies. Won scholarship to Trinity Coll., London, graduating 1918. Worked in hotel bands. Broadcasting and recordings, especially of his own popular compositions, rapidly established his reputation as one of the world's leading light pianists and composers. Started the Billy Mayerl School of Music which had branches all over the globe. Recorded *HMV, Columbia*.

MAYER-MAHR, Moritz (1869–1947)
b. Mannheim, Germany. Studied music in Mannheim and Berlin. In 1892 was appointed pf prof. at Klindworth-Scharwenka Cons., Berlin. Composed pf pieces and songs; wrote works on pf technique, edited Czerny studies and produced the Simrock edition of Brahms pf works. Recorded *Polydor*.
Pupils included: Felix Dyck, Ernst Roters.

MAYKAPAR, Samuel (1867–1938)
b. Kerson, Russia. Pupil of St Petersburg Cons. and of B. Cesi and T. Leschetizky. Performed and was pf prof. at St Petersburg Cons. Composed small-scale works for pf, much of which had a teaching purpose.

MAYLATH, Heinrich (1827–83)
b. Vienna, Austria. A highly successful pianist who toured widely until around the age of 40 when he settled in New York. Additionally composed, transcribed and taught.

MAZURETTE, Salomon (1848–1910)
b. Montreal, Canada. Studied there and at Paris Cons. Became successful pianist and teacher on return to Canada; additionally organist. Settled in Detroit in 1873. Was also chamber-music player.

MAZZINGHI, Joseph (1765–1844)
b. London, UK. Early pianist, pupil in London of J. C. Bach. Became a successful teacher and is credited in the composition field with half a gross of pf sonatas as well as much else in operatic and vocal works.

McARTHUR, Edwin (1907–)
b. Denver, USA. Studied pf there and later in

New York with R. Lhevinne. Became celebrated accompanist to leading vocalists and instrumentalists. As such recorded various labels.

McCABE, John (1939–)
b. Liverpool, UK. Precocious musician as a child. Studied at R. Manchester Coll. under G. Green. Held pf post in Cardiff 1965–8, then settled in London as composer-pianist. Pf compositions include three *Impromptus*, a set of *Variations*, five *Bagatelles*, *Fantasy on a theme of Liszt*, a pf concerto and four *Studies*. Recorded Saga, Decca, Oryx, Prelude, RCA and others.

McDONALD, Harl (1899–1955)
b. Colorado, USA. Taught initially by mother, then studies continued in Europe. Performed for a time solo and as accompanist, then was on the staff of Pennsylvania Univ. Later became manager of Philadelphia Orch. Composed widely, including a concerto for two pfs and orch., and chamber music.

McGURK, Molly (1929–)
b. Armadale, Australia. From début 1948 became successful pianist, solo and with leading Australian orchs. Later added singing and teaching to her accomplishments.

McINTYRE, John (1938–)
b. Samia, Canada. Pf pupil of Toronto Cons. and Univ. Toured N. America and Europe solo, in ensemble and with orch. besides having a pedagogic career.

McKINNEY, Mathilde (1904–)
b. Indiana, USA Pupil of Juilliard School, New York. Performed and taught at Westminster State Coll., New Jersey. Compositions include pf pieces.

McPHEE, Colin (1901–64)
b. Montreal, Canada. Pf pupil of A. Friedheim and I. Philipp. Made a study of Balinese music and dancing, results of which came out in compositions, e.g. *Balinese Ceremonial Music* for two pfs. Wrote three books as a result of his sojourn on Bali: *A House in Bali* (1946); *A Club of Small Men* (1947), and *Music in Bali* (1966).

MEDTNER, Nicolas (1880–1951)
b. Moscow, Russia, of German parentage. Went to Moscow Cons. where V. Safonov taught him pf and S. Taneyev counterpoint. Followed a mainstream of students destined to

achieve world fame – among them Lhevinne, Rachmaninov and Scriabin – albeit some seven years their junior. Like them was made into a magnificent pianist and like them won the coveted Gold Medal. Also received the Rubinstein Prize in Vienna in 1900, the year of his début.

Safonov saw M as a concert pianist and lined up a European tour. Having visited most capitals and made a favourable impression by demonstrating his prowess in a concerto he disliked, he came to the irrevocable decision that he wanted to be a composer, not a touring virtuoso, this resolution being reached after he had returned to Moscow and taught as a pf prof. at the Cons. As a composer his German blood showed through the Russian background and musical training, and his work has been assessed as showing the influence of Brahms. From 1918 until 1921 he returned to teach at the Cons., assisting through the difficult period of the Russian Revolution. Then he left Russia for good, settling successively in Berlin and Paris; in 1940 he moved to London as France was overrun.

He toured the USA as well as Europe, taught, occasionally played and all the time continued to compose. Because he wrote no popular work to take the musical world by storm and thus attract its attention to him, he lacked box-office appeal despite the fact that he was a magnificent pianist committed to the work of propagating himself as a composer. Famous players whom he reckoned among his friends helped with only a little support now and again, and he was 'a musician's composer' whose writing is undeniably intricate at times, and with subtle and frequent changes of rhythm which would go unheeded by the man-in-the-street. Historically it belongs to the tradition of Tchaikovsky and Rachmaninov rather than to Rimsky-Korsakov, Stravinsky and Prokofiev. By a coincidence, both Rachmaninov and M wrote their 2nd pf concertos in C minor, but whereas the former may have retained Tchaikovsky's mantle around his shoulders while writing music that the public at large could enjoy because of sweeping tunes and dazzling virtuosity, M's C minor is highly intellectual, has fewer luscious moments and does not readily yield up its virtues, requiring some effort on the part of the listener.

M gave the first British performance of the 2nd concerto at a R. Phil. Soc. concert in London in 1928, and a first performance of his 3rd concerto in 1944.

At the time he succumbed to an ailing heart in 1951 it could have been argued he was just about on the musical map – at least more than Scriabin was at the time. This is no longer the case, despite advocacy of his cause by a handful of pianists, in the van of whom must be mentioned Edna Iles. In a tribute on the centenary of his birth, Wilson Lyle wrote: 'He was self-effacing and unassuming, by all accounts a religious man who believed music was a sacred art capable of bringing spiritual refreshment to men's hearts and minds.'

Through the good offices of the Maharajah of Mysore, who underwrote the venture, M made a series of record albums of his works, solo and in concertos, as well as accompanying leading singers of the day in his songs. The pf quintet was also recorded when he was ailing but never put on sale. Everything in his considerable output is for pf or has a pf part. Recorded *HMV* and *Columbia*.

Pupils included: Phyllis Palmer.

MEHLIG, Anna (1846–1928)
b. Stuttgart, Germany. Pupil of Cons. there, then of F. Liszt at Weimar. Successful concert artist throughout Europe, visiting USA from 1870. In six appearances for the London Phil. Soc. between 1866 and 1877 she played mostly lightweight works by Hummel, Mendelssohn and Weber. Exceptions were one performance of the Beethoven *Emperor* and one with W. Bache of the Mozart pf concerto for two pfs.

MEJIA, Omar (1950–)
b. El Salvador. Prodigy who made his début at age of 9. After studying there went to London as pupil of C. Smith at R. Coll. of Music. Received tuition also from L. Kentner and G. Agosti. Toured worldwide with a repertory ranging from classics to contemporary Latin American composers. Additionally administered affairs of the El Salvador SO.

MELCER, Henrik (1869–1928)
b. Kalisch, Poland. Pupil of Warsaw Cons. before studying with T. Leschetizky in Vienna 1891–3. Became well known as a touring pianist, taught at Helsinki before becoming a pf prof. at Vienna Cons. 1903–6. Director of Warsaw Cons. from 1922, and was also conductor of the Warsaw Phil. Soc. Compositions included two pf concertos, the first winning a Rubinstein prize, the second being awarded a Paderewski prize.

Pupils included: Mieczyslaw Horszowski.

MELGOUNOV, Julius (1846–93)
b. Vetlouga, Russia. Studied pf with A. Dreyschock and composition with Laroche; friend and champion of Tchaikovsky. Besides being a brilliant pianist and popular teacher wrote Russian songs based on folk-melodies, and made an edition of some of Bach's preludes and fugues.

MELIK-ASLANIAN, Emmanuel (1915–)
b. Tabriz, Iran. Studied there and in Berlin, where he made his début 1940. Career largely confined to Iran with appearances solo and with orch.; also broadcasting.

MENASCE, Jacques de (1905–60)
b. Bad Ischel, Austria. Pf pupil of E. von Sauer. Performed in Europe from 1932, settling in USA from 1941 as concert pianist and, after the war, in Europe. Composed two pf concertos and a *Divertimento* for pf and strings, chamber music and pf pieces.

MENDELSSOHN, Felix (1809–47)
(Jacob Ludwig Felix Mendelssohn-Bartholdy)
b. Hamburg, Germany, of wealthy cultured Jewish family. One of those personages who arrive on earth supremely gifted and seemingly all but fully equipped to perform the task in the sphere allotted to them.

At the age of 7 he received some pf lessons from M. Bigot while the family was on a visit to Paris, followed by tuition from L. Berger in Berlin. That was the extent of his training on the instrument. More importantly perhaps he was a composition pupil of Karl Zelter who was a friend of Goethe, to whom he introduced M in 1821. They became friends.

His début as pianist took place in 1818, by which time he had begun writing a quantity of precocious music. He was extraordinarily gifted in other respects: for instance, in the facility to read complicated scores, to memorize quickly, to transpose and to extemporize. His memory was retentive. By the time he was 15 he had written concertos, chamber-music, a pf sonata and symphonies. When he was on tour in 1822 he met F. Hiller. They became lifelong friends and occasionally played works on two pfs.

He toured as pianist and conductor and, in 1829, paid his first visit to the UK, appearing at a (R.) Phil. Soc. concert in his pf concerto for two pfs in E major, Op. post., the other pianist being I. Moscheles. Some of M's biographers suggested he received lessons from Moscheles, whereas records of the latter indicate he found young M so accomplished that only a little advice was given. It was during that visit to England that he journeyed north to Scotland, whence sprang the *Scottish Symphony* and *Hebrides Overture*.

To 1831 belongs his 1st pf concerto in G minor, Op. 25, which he premièred in Munich the same year. He returned to Paris and met the cream of its musical circle including Chopin and Liszt. He also appeared in concerts. He re-visited London the following spring, giving the first performance of his *Capriccio brillante*, Op. 22, for pf and orch. When his old composition teacher Zelter died that summer, he hoped he would be asked to take the vacant post of conductor of the Singakademie in Berlin, but it was not to be. However he was commissioned by the Phil. Soc. in London to write a symphony and an overture.

In 1833 he duly conducted the première of the *Italian Symphony* and also played the Mozart pf concerto K.466. That summer he was engaged to conduct at the Lower Rhine Festival, Düsseldorf, with such success that he was appointed its director. A few years later he took over the Gewandhaus Orch., Leipzig. He met the Schumanns in Düsseldorf in 1835, the year Chopin visited the festival.

M was the star of the Birmingham Festival in 1837 as composer, conductor and pianist. The première of his pf concerto in D minor, Op. 40, was given and much acclaimed. Earlier that year he had married, and his professional life became more and more busy as his services as both conductor and pianist continued to grow. Most of Beethoven's concertos were in his repertoire; he frequently played his own concertos as well as those of Mozart, and he had re-introduced the Bach D minor klavier concerto into the concert repertoire after it had lain neglected for decades. Here also is the appropriate place to record the fact that in 1839 he was responsible for giving a performance of Bach's *St Matthew Passion*, the first since the composer's death. He founded, in 1843, the Leipzig Cons., further adding to his workload. In his last years he was an extremely popular concert attraction, especially in Britain, whose audiences he found more congenial than those of Germany. He also frequently undertook the direction of his oratorios *St Paul* and *Elijah*.

News of the death of his favourite sister Fanny (Hensel) which reached him on tour in the summer of 1847 was a grievous blow. Within six months he was dead. It was speculated that the state of unconsciousness into which he fell when the news of Fanny's death came may in fact have been a stroke, for already his health had been undermined by overwork.

With his cultured and wealthy background M must have been a most civilized musician, belonging in time to the Romantic era yet incapable of adding much of significance to piano literature when all around him mighty things were either happening or about to happen. His refined and orderly mind made it difficult if not impossible for him to be otherwise, and he was not wholly in tune with leading lights like Berlioz, Chopin, Liszt and Schumann. Undoubtedly he was a brilliant player and in closer affinity to Weber than to his contemporaries. The hallmark of his compositional style may reflect the shallow-toned and comparatively fragile instruments of his day, but against that must be set the fact that Beethoven, Chopin, Liszt and Schumann had similar instruments to work on yet composed far more prophetically. Furthermore it is ironic that a composer who was so gifted and popular an executant should have earned immortality in the concerto field only by the brilliant violin concerto in E minor.

Besides works already mentioned, he composed a *Rondo brillante* for pf and orch., Op. 29, much chamber-music with a pf part, of which the most durable is the pf trio in D minor; many pf solos including 48 *Lieder ohne Worte* in eight books and which in a minor way can be regarded as a new art form; six preludes and fugues of which the first, in E minor, is occasionally heard, and several sonatas which are not; the fine *Variations sérieuses*; also over 80 songs with pf accompaniment in which professional singers are no longer interested.

Pupils included: Ludwig Ehlert, Johann Eschmann, Karl Evers, Eduard Franck, August Gockel, Hermann Krigar.

MENDELSSOHN-BARTHOLDY, Fanny: *see* **HENSEL, Fanny**

MENGES, Herbert (1902–72)
b. Hove, UK. Brother of the violinist Isolde Menges (1893–1976) and actually began learning the violin. Turned to pf and became a pupil of M. Verne, then of A. de Greef. Studied composition at R. Coll., London. Main career

was conducting, chiefly in London and Brighton.

MENTER (**Menter-Popper**), **Sophie** (1848–1918)

b. Munich, Germany. Studied there, début 1863. A successful concert in Frankfurt in 1867 was attended by K. Tausig who subsequently gave her tuition. Also received guidance from F. Liszt. In 1872 married the cellist David Popper. Was pf prof. at St Petersburg Cons. 1883–7. Thereafter toured. In 1894 in London gave first British performance of Tchaikovsky's *Fantaisie* for pf and orch. and at the same concert played her *Zigeuner-weisen* for pf and orch., orchestrally scored by Tchaikovsky. In the same visit gave a performance with her pupil V. Sapellnikov of Liszt's *Concerto Pathétique*. In 1890 Shaw wrote of her effect of magnificence, producing 'a perfectly rich, full and even body of sound'. She played 'with splendid swiftness, yet she never plays faster than the ear can follow; it is the distinctness of attack and intention that makes her execution so irresistibly impetuous'.

Pupils included: José Vianna da Motta, Alice Ripper, Vassily Sapellnikov, August Schmid-Lindner.

MENUHIN, Hepzibah (1920–81)

b. San Francisco, USA. Sister of Yehudi M. Studied there and with M. Ciampi in Paris. Début San Francisco 1928. Toured as soloist and with Yehudi throughout Europe and USA, having first appeared with him in joint recital in Paris in 1934. Settled in Australia 1938 for a time, living finally in London where she died. Recorded *HMV* and EMI.

MENUHIN, Jeremy (1951–)

b. San Francisco, USA. Pupil of M. Gazelle and M. Ciampi. Has appeared as soloist and with members of his family. Recorded EMI and Ades.

MENUHIN, Yaltah (1921–)

b. San Francisco, USA. Younger sister of Yehudi M and Hepzibah M. Studied with M. Ciampi, also K. Friedberg. Performed widely as soloist and with members of family, also duo work with husband J. Ryce. Recorded *HMV*, EMI, Everest and DG. Additionally a painter whose works have been exhibited.

MERKEL, Johannes Gottfried (1860–)

b. Leipzig, Germany. Student at Leipzig Cons. and Univ., then of F. Liszt at Weimar. Taught in Riga 1888–92, in Berlin 1892–8, after which he returned to Leipzig. Was an accomplished pianist and sound teacher. Composed much, including a concerto and a sonata, chamber music and other pieces. Wrote a course on counterpoint.

MÉRÖ-IRION, Yolanda (1887–1963)

b. Budapest, Hungary. Student of Cons. there from age of 6. Début 1902 Dresden, followed by European tour. American début 1909 in New York, in which year she married Herman Irion of Steinway piano firm. Lived thereafter in USA and performed extensively on that continent. Recorded *RCA*.

MERRICK, Frank (1886–1981)

b. Bristol, UK. Pupil of parents then of T. Leschetizky. Début 1895 Bristol; London 1903. Pf prof. at R. Manchester Coll. from 1911, the year he married the pianist-teacher Hope Squire with whom he gave many two-pf recitals. From 1929 pf prof. at R. Coll., London. Tried to rekindle public interest in J. Field. Composed prolifically, some of which attracted attention at the time, including two movements to complete Schubert's 8th symphony on the occasion of the centenary in 1928. CBE 1978. Recorded *Parlophone* and Rare Recorded Editions. Wrote *Practising the Piano* (1958).

Pupils included: Eileen Broster, Gordon Green, Paul Hamburger, Thomas Johnson, Alan Rawsthorne.

MERTKE, Eduard (1833–95)

b. Riga. Was child prodigy and after studying performed throughout eastern Europe. Became teacher at Cologne Cons. from 1870. Composed pf pieces and technical exercises; edited Chopin's works.

MERZHANOV, Victor (1919–)

b. USSR. Came 10th in 1949 Chopin Int. Comp., Warsaw. Recorded MK (Russian label).

Pupils included: Allan Schiller.

MESIEROW-MINCHIN, Nina (1901–)

b. Chicago, USA. Student of Lewis Inst. there, and with M. Rosenthal, F. Bloomfield-Zeisler, J. Lhevinne and L. Godowsky. Performed widely and was especially interested in chamber music, founding the Pro Musica Trio and the Chicago Chamber Music Soc.

MESS, Philibert (1929–)
b. Malines, Belgium. Student there and at Antwerp R. Cons., also with G. Anda. Recitalist and teacher. Currently prof. at Brussels.

MESSAGER, André (1853–1929)
b. Montluçon, France. Conductor and composer of charming operettas and comic opera, and dedicatee of Debussy's *Pelléas et Mélisande* which he conducted at its première. As a pianist (and his studies at Paris Cons. included the instrument) he performed duets with Debussy, took the pf part in the first performance of Chausson's *Trio in G minor* and with the composer gave the première of Chabrier's *Trios Valses* in 1883.

MESSIAEN, Olivier (1908–)
b. Avignon, France. Largely self-taught pianist though received advice from R. Lortat. Composition student at Paris Cons., where he wrote eight pf preludes in 1929. Wrote *Visions de l'Amen* in seven movements for two pfs (1942), performed in Paris by composer and Yvonne Loriod in 1943. *Vingt Regards sur l'enfant Jésus* (1944) was premièred by Yvonne L 1945, again in Paris. Other works with or for pf: *Réveil des Oiseaux* (1953) with orch., and *Oiseaux exotiques* (1956) with small orch.; *Première Catalogue des Oiseaux* (1958), also *Quatre Études de rhythme*. Wrote *Le Technique de mon langage musicale* (1944) and *La Traite du rhythme* (1954). R. Phil. Soc. Gold Medal 1975.

MEWTON-WOOD, Noel (1922–53)
b. Melbourne, Australia. Pupil of Melbourne Cons., then of R. Acad., London. Studied with A. Schnabel. Début 1940 London was highly successful. Wide-ranging musical sympathies and good chamber-music player. Prom début 1947. Dedicatee of the Bliss pf sonata (1952) out of recognition for the fine performances MW had given of the Bliss concerto. Dedicatee of 3rd pf sonata by Antony Hopkins. Recorded Weber and Schumann on *Decca*; Chopin, Bliss and Tchaikovsky on Nixa label. Committed suicide.

MEXIS, Konstantin Filotas (1913–)
b. Trieste, Italy. Studied at Vienna Acad. Début there 1959. Toured Europe as recitalist. Pf prof. Composed pf works. Recorded Preiser.

MEYER, Brigitte (1944–)
b. Bienne, Switzerland. Studied at Cons. there, and Lausanne; also at Vienna Acad. Début 1955 with orch. Performed in Europe and won prizes for her playing.

MEYER, Leopold von (1816–83)
b. Vienna, Austria. Studied pf with K. Czerny and J. Fischhof. Became famous travelling pianist including long tours in USA. Prolific composer of pieces in Victorian drawing-room style which were prominently featured in his recitals and which can still be occasionally found in second-hand shops. Appeared once in UK, in 1845, when he played his *Fantasia on Lucrezia Borgia*.

MEYER, Marcelle (1897–1958)
b. Lille, France. Pupil of Paris Cons. and of A. Cortot and R. Viñes. A fine pianist especially identified with interpreting the works of 'Les Six' as well as of Stravinsky and Ravel. One of the four pianists in the first performance of Stravinsky's *Les Noces* in 1923. Dedicatee of Poulenc's *Cinq Impromptus* (1920). Recorded *HMV* and *Columbia* – mostly contemporary French, and especially the *Scaramouche Suite* for two pfs with the composer.

MEYERBEER, Giacomo (1791–1864)
b. Berlin, Germany. Began as a pianist, studying with M. Clementi. Début at the age of 7 led to studying theory at Darmstadt alongside K. Weber. Composed an opera, *Abimelek*, which was produced in Vienna whence he moved. There he heard Hummel whose technique and style so impressed him that he postponed plans to give further concerts while he studied further. He pursued pianism until 1826 when he settled in Paris, finally concentrating on the career of operatic composer.

MEYERS, Emerson (1910–)
b. Washington, USA. Studied at Peabody Cons. Début Washington 1922. Toured widely as pianist and lecturer. In addition to being pf prof. specialized in electronic music.

MEZZENA, Bruno (–)
b. Trento, Italy. Began learning the violin before turning to the pf. Pupil of M. Long and A. B. Michelangeli. Awarded diploma for composition at Monteverdi Cons., Bolzano. Toured solo and with orch., also ensemble player with Quintetto Italiano. Recorded Dischi Ricordi.

MICHAŁOWSKI, Aleksander (1851–1938)
b. Kamieniec Podolski, Poland. Student of Leipzig Cons. with I. Moscheles and K. Reinecke. In 1869 went to Berlin to study with K. Tausig and the following year settled in Warsaw where he had a successful life as pianist and teacher. His technique was reputed to be prodigious, an assessment borne out by a legendary old gramophone record on which he played the Chopin D flat waltz. Composed in a brilliant manner; also made an edition of Chopin. Recorded *G & T* and *Muza*, also Syrena.

Pupils included: Victor Chrapowicki, Zbigniew Dymmek, Wanda Landowska, Mischa Levitzki, Piotr Maszynski, Heinrich Neuhaus, Piotr Rytel, Antoinette Szumowska, Julius Wolfsohn, Boleslav Woytowicz, Alexander Zakin, Georg Zurawlew.

MICHELANGELI, Arturo Benedetti (1920–)
b. Brescia, Italy. Pupil of his father and of Milan Cons., having already appeared in public as a prodigy. Won 1st Prize at the Geneva Int. Comp. for Musical Performers in 1939, the year in which he became a prof. at Bologna Cons. His career was interrupted by World War II, in which he served in the Italian Air Force. He resumed performing in 1946 with a tour of Europe, and the release of a number of remarkable recordings also helped to establish his reputation. He toured the USA in 1948 and by then held a secure place amongst the greatest virtuosi of his time. Also conducted his own school of young pianists of remarkable talent.

A wide-ranging repertoire reflected especial sympathy with the music of Scarlatti, Mozart, Debussy and Ravel in which the unfailing precision of technique showed to remarkable effect. A legendary figure whose concerts sold out in advance without any certainty that he would be there to carry out the engagement. Recorded *HMV* and DG.

Pupils included: Martha Argerich, Noretta Conci, Joerg Demus, Ludwig Hoffman, Walter Klein, Anthony Lindsay, Francisco Marigo, Bruno Mezzena, Maurizio Pollini.

MICKWITZ, Paul Harald (1859–1938)
b. Helsinki, Finland. Studied at St Petersburg Cons. under L. Brassin and in Vienna with T. Leschetizky. Was pf prof. at Karlsruhe then Wiesbaden. Settled in the USA from 1897,
holding teaching posts in Texas and Chicago. Retired to Finland.

MIEROWSKI, Henryk (1905–)
b. Jaroslav, Poland. Studied in Lvov and Vienna; taught at Lvov Cons. before World War II. Was in UK during hostilities, performing and teaching at Trinity Coll., London. Later settled in S. Africa. Was billed as a Chopin specialist.

MIETELSKI, Mark (1933–)
b. Cracow, Poland. Student of Acad. there, winning Diploma for pf. Début Cracow 1963. Thereafter gave recitals at home and abroad, solo and ensemble. Has worked in films, radio and television. Taught at Cracow Acad.

MIGDAL, Marian (1948–)
b. Poland. Studied at Warsaw Cons., then was a pupil of H. Leygraf 1964–6 in Sweden before spending four years at Cologne followed by three years at the Juilliard School, New York, with A. Dorfmann. Graduated with honours and has since played throughout Europe and the USA. Came joint 2nd with M. Tirimo in the Int. Musikwettbewerb, Munich, in 1971. Recorded EMI.

MIGNONE, Francesco (1897–)
b. São Paolo, Brazil. Pupil of Cons. there where he became prof. of pf and harmony. Concert tours included USA. Has written much pf music including sonatas, also ensemble and songs.

MIKOWSKY, Solomon (1935–)
b. Havana, Cuba. Studied there, also at Juilliard School, USA, and later Columbia Univ. Début Havana 1956. Concert pianist and teacher.

MIKULI, Karl (1819–97)
b. Czernowitz, Poland. Began life as medical student but turned to music and in 1844 went to Paris to study pf with F. Chopin and composition with Reicha. Left Paris on outbreak of 1848 revolution, touring eastern Europe with success before settling as Director of the Lemberg Cons., later establishing his own pf school. Made one of the first authentic editions of Chopin. Composed prolifically for the instrument.

Pupils included: Stanislas Niewiadomski, Moritz Rosenthal, Mieczyslaw Soltys, Yaroslav Zielinski.

MILDNER, Poldi (1915–)
b. Vienna, Austria. Pf pupil of Hedwig Kanner-Rosenthal. Début Vienna 1927, followed by extensive tours of Europe. US début 1931. Taught in Leipzig. Recorded *HMV*.
Pupils included: Amadeus Webersinke.

MILHAUD, Darius (1892–1974)
b. Aix-en-Provence, France. Pupil of Paris Cons. In 1917 went to Rio as a secretary in the French Legation. Later toured USA as concert pianist before returning to France. Took up career as composer (was a member of 'Les Six') and often appeared as conductor and pianist in performances of own compositions. Wrote two pf concertos and other works for same, suites, chamber music, dances in the Brazilian idiom and a sonata etc. Recorded *HMV* and other labels. Wrote autobiography, *Notes sans musique* (Paris, 1949).

MILKINA, Nina (1919–)
b. Moscow, USSR. Studied in London under T. Matthay and H. Craxton, then Paris Cons. Settled in UK and is naturalized. Well-known concert pianist and broadcaster with especial affinity for Scarlatti and Mozart. Recorded Decca and Pye.

MILLS, Sebastian Bach (1838–98)
b. Cirencester, UK. Allotted inflated baptismal names. Pupil of C. Potter and S. Bennett, then studied at Leipzig Cons. under I. Moscheles and later with F. Liszt. Début 1858 Leipzig. Appeared in New York the following year and was so well received that he settled there. Was a successful pianist and teacher and performed in USA and Germany regularly. Was soloist at the inaugural concert of Steinway Hall, New York, when it opened in 1866.

MINAMI, Chiseko (1957–)
b. Otsu, Japan. Studied at Soai Coll. of Music and at the Liszt Acad. in Budapest where she was a pupil of P. Kadosa.

MIROWITSCH, Alfred (1884–1959)
b. St Petersburg, Russia. Pf pupil of A. Essipova at Cons. there, graduating with 1st Prize in 1909. Began concert career and made many world tours. Taught at Juilliard School of Music, New York, 1944–53 before moving on to Boston Univ. Edited for Schirmer edition.

MITROPOULOS, Dimitri (1896–1960)
b. Athens, Greece. Studied pf and theory there, graduating at 22 with Gold Medal for pf-playing. Studied composition with Paul Gilson before joining Busoni's master-class in Berlin where he became *répétiteur* at the Opera. Took up conducting additionally to pf-playing and teaching and in the former role became famous. Probably the only pianist-conductor to play the Prokofiev No. 3 pf concerto conducting it from the pf stool when a soloist failed to appear at a concert by the Berlin Phil. which M was conducting.

MITTLER, Franz (1893–1971)
b. Vienna, Austria. Trained there and in Germany where his most distinguished teacher was K. Friedberg. Noted pianist and accompanist in Austria up to the outbreak of World War II, when he settled in New York. Wrote a variety of pf pieces over a wide range including popular.

MOHAUPT, Richard (1904–57)
b. Breslau, Germany. Studied in Berlin before creating a career as pianist, conductor and composer. Settled in USA on outbreak of World War II. Compositions included a pf concerto, pf works and songs.

MOISEIWITSCH, Benno (1890–1963)
b. Odessa, Russia. Student of Odessa School of Music where he won the Rubinstein Prize at the age of 9; then of T. Leschetizky in Vienna. Début in UK 1908, where he settled, becoming naturalized in 1937. Toured extensively throughout the world, and during World War II gave over 100 concerts for Mrs Churchill's *Aid to Russia Fund*, for which he received CBE in 1946. His first wife was Daisy Kennedy, the Australian violinist. Recorded *HMV*, EMI and Brunswick.
Pupils included: Alan Bush, Sir Malcolm Sargent.

MOKE,   Marie-Félicité-Denise: *see* **PLEYEL, Marie-Félicité-Denise**

MOKREIS, John (1875–1968)
b. Cedar Rapids, USA. Pf pupil of L. Godowsky. Taught in New York until 1945 when he moved to California before settling once more at Cedar Rapids. Composed chamber music, songs and educational pf pieces.

MOLL, Philip (1943–   )
b. Chicago, USA. Trained at Harvard and in Texas. Widely accomplished pianist especially accompanying. Toured throughout the world. Recorded EMI as accompanist.

MÖLLENDORFF, Willy von (1872–1934)
b. Berlin, Germany. Concert pianist who early on experimented in quarter-tone system as well as composing conventional works.

MOLLOVA, Milena (1940–   )
b. Ragard, Bulgaria. Début 1946 as prodigy. Pupil of Bulgarian Acad., then of Moscow Cons. Pupil of E. Gilels. Has performed extensively throughout Europe and the Americas, having won numerous prizes.

MOMPOU, Federico (1893–   )
b. Barcelona, Spain. Studied music at Cons. there, then, from 1911, in Paris where his pf teacher was I. Philipp. Returned home on outbreak of World War I, then in 1921 went back to Paris. Apart from a few songs has written mainly for pf in sketches whose scores lack bar lines and key signatures.

MONTIGNY-RÉMAURY, Fanny (1843–1913)
b. Pamirs, France. Student of Paris Cons. and of F. Le Couppey, winning 1st Prize for pf in 1858 followed by other prizes. Was also pupil of her elder sister who married the composer Ambroise Thomas. Had successful concert career. British début 1880 in Schumann concerto.

MOÓR, Emanuel (1863–1931)
b. Kecskemet, Hungary. Was a remarkable prodigy on the pf and organ. Studied in Budapest and Vienna and was a pupil of F. Liszt. Gave pf recitals. US début 1885. London début 1888. His concert career and composition occupied his time up to World War I when he settled in Switzerland, inventing and developing the Moór Duplex (double-keyboard) pf, seemingly inspired by his love of Bach's music. The invention was taken up in a limited way by several pf-makers including Bechstein and Bösendorfer, and the instrument was publicly demonstrated by artists of the calibre of Donald Tovey, Max Pirani and Winifred Christie, who married Moór in 1923 and enthusiastically devoted her life to the cause of the instrument until the outbreak of World War II. There have been sporadic

demonstrations since but, despite the interest shown, and optimistic predictions made, by a plethora of important pianists, the invention has been largely forgotten despite the setting-up of trust funds. *The History of the Emanuel Moór Double Keyboard Piano* (1978) by Herbert A. Shead deals exhaustively with the subject.

MOORE, Gerald (1899–   )
b. Watford, UK. Studied pf in Toronto and appeared in Canada as pianist before returning home to take up career as accompanist. Became distinguished collaborator with singers like Dawson, de los Angeles, Schwarzkopf and Dieskau. Lectured on art of accompanying. CBE 1954. Retired from public platform 1967. Wrote *The Unashamed Accompanist, Careers in Music, Singer and Accompanist, Am I too Loud?, The Schubert Song Cycles, Poet's Love, Farewell Recital* and *Furthermore*.
Pupils included: Phyllis Spurr.

MORALES, Angelica: *see* **SAUER, Emil von**

MORALES, Olallo Juan (1874–1957)
b. Almeria, Spain. Early life spent in Sweden where he studied music in Stockholm; then in Berlin 1899–1901 under H. Urban and T. Carreño. Returned to Sweden to teach in Gothenberg, later becoming prof. at Stockholm Cons. in addition to conducting and writing.

MORAVEC, Ivan (1930–   )
b. Prague, Czechoslovakia. He studied there at the Cons., graduating at age of 18. Performed in Europe with success. US début 1964. Taught at Prague Acad. from 1967 and conducted a master-class from 1969. Widely known as teacher and adjudicator. Recorded Connoisseur Soc.

MOREIRA-LIMA, Arthur: *see* **LIMA, Arthur Moreira**

MORERA, Enrique (1865–1942)
b. Barcelona, Spain. Studied at Brussels Cons., then in Barcelona under I. Albéniz for pf. Prolific opera composer who also wrote chamber music and pf pieces with a pronounced Catalan flavour.
Pupils included: Manuel Infante.

MORHANGE, Charles Henri Valentin: *see* **ALKAN, Charles Henri Valentin**

MORHANGE, Napoléon: *see* **ALKAN, Napoléon**

MORILLO, Roberto (1911–)
b. Buenos Aires, Argentina. Pf pupil of J. Aguirre. Lived and worked in Paris in late 1920s. Mainly composer but performed own works including a pf concerto which he premièred in 1940, an overture *Bersaerks* for pf and chamber orch., chamber music, a pf suite *Conjuros* and other pieces.

MOROUGES, Marie Bigot de: *see* **BIGOT, Marie**

MORRIS, Harold Cecil (1890–1964)
b. San Antonio, USA. Pupil of Texas Univ. and Cincinnati Cons. From 1921 taught in New York as well as performing throughout the USA and Canada. Composed a pf concerto which won a Juilliard award in 1932, also chamber music, four pf sonatas and other pf works.

MORRISON, Stuart Angus (1902–)
b. Maidenhead, UK. Studied at R. Coll. of Music, London, under H. Samuel for pf. Début Wigmore Hall, London, 1923. Pf prof. at R. Coll. from 1926. Appeared regularly as recitalist and at London Proms, made worldwide tours including Far East and broadcast regularly. CBE 1979. Dedicatee of the *Rio Grande* by Constant Lambert which he played frequently before World War II.

MORSZTYN, Helena (*c*.1880–1953)
b. Warsaw, Poland. Studied there and later in Vienna with E. von Sauer. Début 1912 Berlin. Toured Europe in substitution for her teacher von S who, luckily for her, fell sick. The tour led to a successful career. Visited USA later, settling there as concert pianist and teacher.

MORTIER DE FONTAINE, Henri Louis Stanislav (1816–83)
b. Volhynia, Poland. Of Franco-Polish descent. Lived in St Petersburg 1853–60; also lived in Munich and Paris before settling in London where he died. Was reputed to be a fine pianist with exceptional technique who pioneered the music of Bach and Beethoven in his recitals. In a write-up of 1881 on von Bülow, Hanslick mentions M de F, 'who made a name for himself with his (rather inept) performance of the great B flat Sonata (1847), and remained without a successor for a long time'.

MOSCHELES, Ignaz (1794–1870)
b. Prague, Czechoslovakia. His father was a cloth merchant and a music-lover who put his son to the pf from an early age. When the boy was 7, Dionys Weber, founder of Prague Cons., was asked to judge his talents and became his teacher, to such good effect that M made a successful début in Prague at the age of 14. On the death of his father, he went to Vienna, spending eight years studying, performing and laying the foundations of a highly disciplined and successful career. He became a friend and disciple of Beethoven as well as a keyboard rival of J. N. Hummel.

In the autumn of 1816 he began a long tour of Europe carrying a sheaf of influential letters of introduction. Everywhere he was received with friendship and acclaim, finally, at the end of 1817, reaching Paris then the most prestigious art centre of Europe. He met the élite and had several months of artistic success before journeying on to London, which delighted him as much as Paris had done. His concerts at this time featured the works of Mozart, whom he admired, and he was among the first concert pianists to promote the sonatas of Beethoven, whom he revered. He was also successful with his own compositions, especially *Variations über den Alexandermarsch*.

He settled in London in 1826, finding it an ideal centre from which to operate as virtuoso, teacher and composer. He remained there for twenty years, leading a very full artistic life. It was M who persuaded the Phil. Soc. to relieve Beethoven's straitened circumstances when the composer was dying; he who took over as conductor of the Soc. in 1845, making his only appearance as pianist in its concerts the following year in a performance of a *Concerto for pianoforte (MS) in D* (sic) by Bach.

In 1846 he joined Mendelssohn in founding Leipzig Cons., remaining on after M's death. It has been said Mendelssohn was a pf pupil of M, but contemporary records indicate that the man found the youth so perfected in talent and technique that only an occasional word of advice was necessary. Mendelssohn's *Fantasia* Op. 28 is dedicated to M.

Much respected and admired, M was a prolific composer of sonatas, concertos, studies and many other pf works running to some 140 opus numbers. Little has survived. Of his pf-playing a contemporary said: 'an incisive, brilliant touch, wonderfully clear, precise phrasing, and close attention to the careful accentuation of every phrase of the composer's meaning'. And Grieg wrote: 'He could and did play beautifully. Specially fine were his renderings of Beethoven whom he adored.' M translated Schindler's work on Beethoven into English under the title *Life of Beethoven* (1841).

Pupils included: Joseph Ascher, Woldemar Bargiel, Friedrich Baumfelder, Francesco Berger, Oscar Beringer, Leopoldine Blahetka, Bernardus Boekelmann, Jan Boom, Louis Brassin, Sir Frederick Cowen, Edward Dannreuther, Élie Delaborde, Felix Dessoff, Ferdinand Dulcken, Johann Eschmann, Louis Farrenc, Zdenko Fibisch, Henry Forbes, Eduard Ganz, Friedrich Gernsheim, Guillaume Gibsone, Edvard Grieg, Sir George Henschel, Richard Hoffman, Karl von Holten, Johann Horzalka, Alfred Jäell, Rafael Joseffy, Anton Krause, Emil Krause, Edouard Langer, Henry Litolff, Karl Lütschg, William Mason, Aleksander Michałowski, Sebastian Mills, Rudolf Niemann, Arthur O'Leary, Albert Parsons, Ernst Perabo, Carlyle Petersilea, Marie Pleyel, Ernst Rudorff, Erik Siboni, Otto Singer Snr, Edward Sloper, Sydney Smith, Constantin Sternberg, Franz Stockhausen, Sigismund Thalberg, Louis Thern, Willy Thern, Max Vogrich, Simon Waley, Karl Wehle, Richard Zechwer, Bruno Zwintscher.

MOSSOLOV, Alexander Vassilievich (1900–73)
b. Kiev, Russia. Pupil of Moscow Cons. and pursued career of pianist-composer. Wrote five pf sonatas, two concertos and several chamber works. Practically unknown outside Russia apart from the poem *Music of Machines* for orch. which was in vogue during World War II.

MOSZKOWSKI, Moritz (1854–1925)
b. Breslau, Germany. Studied music in Dresden, then in Berlin at Stern's and the Kullak Cons. Début there 1873. Became successful pianist, conductor and teacher, making friends in high places by virtue of his talent, culture and personality. Was always helpful to fellow-musicians. Prolific composer in most genres, his pf works being in the repertoire of leading pianists of the day. Retired in 1896 to Paris on the proceeds of considerable funds which, however, were lost during World War I because they were invested in Germany. He was reduced to penury. To relieve his straits a gala concert was organized in Carnegie Hall where the following appeared in one evening: Bauer, Bloomfield-Zeisler, Friedman, Gabrilowitsch, Ganz, Godowsky, Grainger, Hutcheson, Lambert, Lhevinne, Merö, Schelling, Schnitzer and Stojowski. The concert was repeated in Philadelphia.

Pupils included: Isabella Beaton, Gustav Becker, Theodor Bohlmann, Algot Haquinius, Harold Henry, Josef Hofmann, Carl Lachmund, Wanda Landowska, Joaquín Nin, José Rolón, Ernest Schelling, Wilson Smith, Josef Szulc, Teresita Tagliapietra, Joaquin Turina, Julius Wertheim, Wesley Weyman.

MOTTA, José Vianna da (1868–1948)
b. St Thomas island, off Africa. Pupil of Lisbon Cons. until the age of 14 when, on orders from the King, he was sent to Berlin to study with S. Menter, X. Scharwenka; then later with F. Liszt, and finally with H. von Bülow. Début 1902, followed by tours of Europe and S. America with immediate success. Was for a time court pianist in Berlin where, in 1905, he gave first performance of Otto Singer's pf concerto in A, Op. 8, under the composer's baton. Succeeded B. Stavenhagen at Geneva Acad., afterwards settling in Lisbon where he directed the Cons. and conducted symphony concerts. His compositions include a *Ballada*, a *Barcarolle*, a set of Portuguese scenes and a *Rhapsody*.

Pupils included: Sequeira Costa, Alf Hurum, Sverre Jordan, Nils Larsen, Vincente Pablo, Beryl Rubinstein.

MOTTU, Alexander (1883–1943)
b. Geneva, Switzerland. Pf pupil of T. Carreño in Berlin and from 1907 was pf prof. at Geneva Cons.

MOULART, Raymond (1875–1962)
b. Brussels, Belgium. Pupil of Cons. there under A. de Greef. Joined the Cons. and taught up to outbreak of World War II. Composed a pf concerto, chamber music and songs.

MOYINE, Suraya (–   )
b. Cairo, Egypt. Studied there with a pupil of T. Leschetizky and later with K. Taylor in London where she settled. Performed throughout Europe, and in 1983 gave in a London recital the world première of *Sonatina semplice No. 1* by the Maltese composer Charles Camilleri.

MOZART, Leopold (1719–87)
b. Augsburg, Austria. Of humble stock, was

musical and studied the hard way from chorister to violinist and keyboard player. Held appointments at the court of the Archbishop of Salzburg. Taught the two survivors of his seven children: Anna Maria M and Wolfgang Amadeus the elder, and took them on tours of Europe as prodigies. Was a prolific composer in most genres including 'pf' music, some dozen pieces being published.

Pupils included: Anna Maria Mozart, Wolfgang Amadeus Mozart, Josef Wölfl.

MOZART, Maria Anna (Marianne or 'Nannerl') (1751–1829)

b. Salzburg, Austria. Pupil of her father on the harpsichord; became renowned keyboard player, rated the equal of her brother Wolfgang Amadeus the elder, with whom she played duets. Adopted the pf as it evolved and in 1784 married Baron Berchtold zu Sonnenburg who died in 1801. Taught until about 1820 when her eyesight began to fail. She had already withdrawn from the musical scene. Died in Salzburg blind and in straitened circumstances.

MOZART, Wolfgang Amadeus (1756–91)

b. Salzburg, Austria. Highly proficient on the violin, viola, clavichord and organ; learned the rudiments of the harpsichord from his father, Leopold, when the latter was teaching his elder child, Maria Anna. As young children both performed in public and at court, where Wolfgang moved in aristocratic circles with the same nonchalance as Chopin did later. Leopold also took them abroad, where they appeared as duettists, notably in Paris and London, returning to Salzburg via Switzerland and Germany, in all a tour of almost three years.

M was already composing and had already shown he possessed absolute pitch, an infallible memory and a perfect architectural sense of musical form. In company with his father he toured Italy 1769–71, exhibiting his skills at the harpsichord in such feats as playing new works at first sight, transposing and spontaneously composing a sonata using a theme supplied to him on the spot by another musician. He performed before capacity audiences and received great acclaim for each demonstration of genius.

Early successes were matched by later disappointments, unfulfilled ambitions and other tribulations. After the death of the Archbishop of Salzburg (under whom M and his father had enjoyed much good), he lacked patronage, suffering merciless rejection at the hands of the succeeding prelate. A return visit to Paris 1777–8 in company with his mother (who died there) proved a fiasco. The brilliant child had become a man: the novelty had worn off.

Because M was naïve over money matters, he was obliged, again like Chopin, to earn a living largely by spending precious hours teaching when, in more financially secure circumstances, he might have been composing.

The consensus of M literature suggests he adopted the pf following a visit to the workshop of Johann Stein in Augsburg. This is based on information contained in a letter to his father in 1777 in which the writer enthuses upon the skill of the instrument-maker; but there is evidence that even before the visit M had had experience of playing on other pfs, e.g. those of Franz Späth and Anton Walter. Without such experience how could he have attested to Stein's superiority in the way in which he wrote?

At that period – the dawn of the pf as an important musical instrument – it is difficult to trace with any precision Mozart's commitment to it. Some scholars affirm he played the fortepiano; some generalize behind the term 'clavier'; while others boldly say he wrote pf concertos and pf sonatas. The works are described thus by publishers whose editions encompass more octaves than ever the composer had at his disposal on Stein's keyboard. The great Sir Donald Tovey in his writings about M's keyboard works never deviates from the term 'pianoforte'. And M himself was not exactly reliable in this respect: of two original MSS of the sonata in C minor, K.457, he autographed one as *'pour le Forte-piano'*, the other *'Sonata per il Piano forte Solo'*.

Once he turned to the Stein and Walter instruments, M discarded the harpsichord while retaining affection for the clavichord. For concerts he took travelling pfs around, described by one authority as 'in the shape of a couched harp with a single row of strings, transposable by means of a shifting keyboard'. He also used the pedal-board, a device placed on the floor under the fortepiano or pf and comprising up to 29 keys which were operated by the feet in the manner of the organ, and giving additional power of tone when applied as octaves. (See illustration pp. 96–7.)

Listening to Mozart's later concertos and sonatas, one may easily accept his eulogies on

Stein's instruments as expressed in that famous letter of 1777 to his father. True, Stein had improved the method of escapement and damping. But it also has to be remembered that in M's day the pf keyboard had a limited compass of less than six octaves; furthermore the keys were very narrow, the frame of the instrument was wooden, and the sound was thin if bright because the tensile strength of strings was poor by present-day standards, and hammers were covered with membrane and only the size of peas.

In style of playing the period was transitional too. Beethoven, for instance, told Czerny that M 'had a jerky touch, without legato, the touch of a harpsichordist'. In 1781, in Vienna, M had met Clementi who was touring Europe with a Broadwood pf (*sic*) and a harpsichord of the same make. He and M performed duets and fought duels in improvisation. Yet M described Clementi's sonatas as worthless.

During his last three years M virtually ceased performing, appearing only once in Vienna before his death.

Besides 27 pf concertos and a Rondo in D for pf and orch., a concerto for two pfs and one for three pfs, as well as 20 solo sonatas and one for two pfs in D, he wrote much chamber music with a pf part including over 40 violin sonatas; trios, quartets and a pf and wind quintet; sets of variations for violin and pf and 15 sets for pf, *fantaisies*, rondos etc; 5 sonatas for pf duet and one for two pfs. Some 35 of his own cadenzas for the pf concertos are also available.

Ludwig Köchel (1800–77) systematically investigated the MSS to create order out of chaos, leading to the publication of a first complete edition by Breitkopf & Härtel in 1877 and using the Köchel numbering. Even so, more works continued to be discovered, and Alfred Einstein (1880–1955) updated Köchel's list; a fresh edition of the catalogue was republished in 1937.

Pupils included: Ignaz Seyfried.

MOZART, Wolfgang Amadeus (1791–1844)
b. Vienna, Austria. Born a few months before the death of his incomparable father. A pupil of J. Hummel and a talented pianist. In later life settled around Lemberg where he taught when not on tour playing the pf. Founded the Cecilia Soc. there and composed several pf concertos, chamber music and pf pieces. Contributed variations to the Diabelli waltz for the set of 30 published by Diabelli in 1824.

Pupils included: Ernst Pauer.

MUCK, Dr Karl (1859–1940)
b. Darmstadt, Germany. His doctorate was for philology gained at Heidelberg and Leipzig Univs. Studied pf firstly with father, then with Kissner at Würzburg. Pf début 1880 Leipzig. Shortly after turned to conducting and became one of the great exponents of Wagner.

MUCZYNSKI, Robert (1929–)
b. Chicago, USA. Pf pupil of A. Tcherepnin at De Paul Univ. Composed works for pf and orch. as well as chamber music and pf pieces in French neo-Classic style.

MUDIE, Thomas Molleson (1809–76)
b. London, UK. Student of R. Acad. there under C. Potter 1823–32. Was pf prof. of the R. Acad. of Music 1832–44, and later in Edinburgh 1844–63, in which latter year he returned to London. Throughout his two academic posts he regularly performed. Composed pf pieces and chamber music.

MUKLE, Anne (1884–1941)
b. London, UK. Sister of May Mukle, cellist, with whom she appeared mainly in duo recitals.

MULLINAR, Michael (1895–1973)
b. Bangor, UK. Pupil of R. Coll. of Music, London. Worked in Birmingham and acquired a reputation as accompanist, later removing to London. Frequent broadcaster. Dedicatee of Vaughan Williams' 6th symphony.

MÜNZ, Mieczyslaw (1900–76)
b. Cracow, Poland. Studied there under J. Lalewicz and later at Vienna Acad.; also with F. Busoni at Berlin Hochschule. Début 1920 Berlin in three works with orch. US début 1922. Toured extensively thereafter. Joined Curtis Inst. 1941–63 and thereafter was prof. at Juilliard School until 1975 when he held master-classes in Tokyo. Had high reputation as virtuoso in the best sense, and as teacher. Married Aniela Mlynarska who later became Mrs Arthur Rubinstein.

Pupils included: Emanuel Ax, Ann Schein, Ilana Vered.

MURDOCH, Dennis (1914–)
b. Nuneaton, UK. Pupil of L. England at R. Acad., London, where he won the Macfarren Prize, also of E. von Sauer and E. Steuermann. Début 1946 London. Performed and broad-

cast, taught at R. Acad., where he became a Fellow; also examiner and adjudicator.

MURDOCH, William Daniel (1888–1942) b. Bendigo, Australia. Studied in Melbourne before becoming a pupil of R. Coll., London, winning in 1909 both Challen and Hopkinson Gold Medals. Début London in 1910. Had successful career as concert pianist and teacher, with extremely wide range of taste and sympathies. Frequently teamed up with Albert Sammons, W. H. Squire and Lionel Tertis in chamber-music recitals and recordings. Wrote excellent books on Brahms for the 1933 centenary, and Chopin – part 1, the second part never completed. Recorded *Columbia* and *Decca*.

MUSSORGSKY, Modest Petrovitch (1839–81) b. Karevo, Russia. Pf pupil of his mother and continued to receive regular tuition after embarking on a military career. Was a good pianist all his life, especially accompanying. Received lessons from M. Balakirev, who was the founder of the new national Russian School of composers. After leaving the army he tried to exist as a composer but was forced to take a government post to subsist. Composed *Boris Godunov*. Most famous composition for pf is *Pictures from an Exhibition*, a set of impressions in music of artwork by his friend Victor Hartmann, the pieces linked by a Promenade. Like most of his work, *Pictures* has been held to have blemishes yet is an uniquely imposing *œuvre* in the mainstream of Russian pf music and towers above the other short character pieces he wrote for pf. Also some 60 songs including the three important cycles: *Sunless, In the Nursery* and *Songs and Dances of Death* which are still performed, as is his *A Night on the Bare Mountain* for orch.

NACCIARONE, Guglielmo (1837–1916)
b. Naples, Italy. Son of Nicola N. Taught pf in
home town and composed chamber music, pf
solos and songs. Was a member of Florence
Acad. and visited Britain in 1861 when he
appeared at the (London) Phil. Soc. in the
Mendelssohn D minor concerto.

NACCIARONE, Nicola (1802–76)
b. Naples, Italy. Performed and taught pf; also
composed, especially vocal works.
    Pupils included: Guglielmo Nacciarone.

NADEZDA, Kolundzija (1952–   )
b. Belgrade, Yugoslavia. Studied at the Music
Acad. there and was later a pupil of Z. Kocsis
in Budapest. Won 3rd Prize in the Arnold
Schoenberg Int. Pf Comp. 1979.

NAGINSKI, Charles (1909–40)
b. Cairo, Egypt. Studied pf first with father,
then under a Juilliard Fellowship. Performed
and composed works for pf as well as songs.

NAPOLEON, Arthur (1843–1925)
b. Oporto, Portugal. His only pf teacher was
his father. Played in public as a prodigy at the
age of 6, touring Europe as a virtuoso. Made
extended visit to the Americas, joining forces
in 1860 with L. Gottschalk to give concerts in
the W. Indies. Returned to Europe but later
settled in Brazil where he helped to establish
the pf firm of Napoleão & Miguez. Composed
numerous works including *fantaisies* and
studies. In his autobiography Arthur Rubinstein recalled that N at the 'ripe age of ninety-
eight, played for me, with astonishing precision, a piece by Gottschalk'. Alternative
spelling of name: Napoleão.

NAPRAVNIK, Eduard Franz (1839–1916)
b. Beišt, Czechoslovakia. Learned the pf

locally, later studying at Maidel School where
he taught for a time before going to St Petersburg performing as pianist and as conductor.
Composed prolifically including chamber
works, pf pieces and songs.

NASEDKIN, Alexei (1942–   )
b. USSR. Student of Central School of Music
then of Moscow Cons. under H. Neuhaus.
Début while still a schoolboy. In 1959 won a
Gold Medal in Vienna VII Int. Festival of
Youth. Other prizes included joint 6th in the
Int. Tchaikovsky Comp., Moscow, of 1962
and 3rd in Leeds Comp., 1966; also in Vienna
for his playing of Schubert in which he specializes. Appeared solo, with orch. and in chamber
concerts. Recorded Melodiya.

NAT, Yves (1890–1956)
b. Béziers, France. A prodigy who attracted
the attention of Gabriel Fauré. Studied at Paris
Cons. under L. Diémer, winning 1st Prize for
pf playing. Performed, taught and composed.
Prof. of master-class at Cons. from 1937.
Recorded *HMV* and *Columbia* (for the latter
label Schumann major works and the concerto).
    Pupils included: Gerardus van Blerk, Yuri
Boukoff, Theo Bruins, Joerg Demus,
Genviève Joy, Jacques Loussier.

NAZIROVA, Elmira Mirza (1928–   )
b. Baku, USSR. Student of Cons. there,
graduating 1954, and afterwards taught pf at
same place. Assisted Fikret Amirov with some
of his pf compositions.

NEATE, Charles (1784–1877)
b. Brighton, UK. Studied pf with J. Field.
Début 1800 London. Became established as a
fine pianist. Was a founder member of (R.)
Phil. Soc. 1813, and in 1815 spent some

months in Vienna becoming acquainted with Beethoven. It is claimed that when in 1820 he played the C major concerto at a Phil. concert in London it was the first performance of any Beethoven pf concerto in Britain. Appeared as pianist in 13 of the early Soc. concerts as well as conducting.

Pupils included: Charles Salaman.

NEEFE, Christian Gottlieb (1748–98)
b. Chemnitz, Germany. Studied music in Leipzig alongside law. Was organist, concert pianist in the early days of the instrument, and composer. One of Beethoven's teachers. Compositions include a concerto for violin, pf and orch., pf sonatas, variations and a number of fantasias, also pf duets.

NEITZEL, Otto (1852–1920)
b. Falkenburg, Germany. Pupil of Kullak Acad. and of Berlin Univ. After graduation toured for a few years as accompanist to artists like P. Sarasate. Later took up conducting. Taught pf successively at Moscow and Cologne Cons. Toured USA 1906–7. Composed a concerto and a *Capriccio* for pf and orch. Wrote a life of Saint-Saëns (1898).

NEMENOFF, Genia (Mrs Pierre Luboschutz) (1905–)
b. Paris, France. Studied at Paris Cons. with I. Philipp and made her début there followed by appearances throughout Europe, solo and with other instrumentalists. Married the pianist P. Luboschutz and they established a duo-team, settling in USA. Recorded Everest.

NEMES, Katalin (1915–)
b. Debrecen, Hungary. Pupil of B. Bartók; gained diploma at Budapest Music Acad. Début there 1937. Recitalist throughout Europe displaying wide repertoire. Founder member of Ferenc Liszt Soc. Recorded various.

NEPOMUCENO, Alberto (1864–1920)
b. Fortaleza, Brazil. Studied in Rio and also in Europe. When he returned home he devoted his energies to promoting the cause of Brazilian music and, allying the formal training he had received in Europe with the folk-music of his native land, wrote a large quantity of pf pieces, songs and chamber-music which are characteristic of an emergent national culture.

NERIKI, Shigeo (1951–)
b. Tokyo, Japan. Studied at Toho Gakuen School of Music, Tokyo, and Indiana Univ., USA. Pupil of G. Sebok.

NETTO, Barrozo (1881–1941)
b. Rio de Janeiro, Brazil. Student at Nat. Inst. of Music there, took up career of concert pianist and in 1906 was appointed prof. at the Inst. Composed large quantity of pf pieces and songs.

NEUBRAND, Heinz (1921–)
b. Vienna, Austria. Pupil at Acad. there. Début Vienna 1933 followed by concert tours. Has evoked lighter side of music as well as serious, and is an examiner for pf and composition.

NEUHAUS, Gustav (1847–1938)
b. Germany. Pf student of F. Hiller. Married Olga Blumenfeld.

Pupils included: Karol Szymanowski.

NEUHAUS, Heinrich Gustavovich (1888–1964)
b. Elisavetgrad, USSR. Pupil of his father Gustav N, also of A. Michałowski. Performed at an early age and toured Europe. Studied composition in Berlin and was a pf pupil in Vienna of L. Godowsky. Subsequently taught at Kiev Cons. 1918–22, then became pf prof. at Moscow Cons. where he remained until his death. Nephew of F. Blumenfeld and cousin of K. Szymanowski. Did not pursue concert career because he suffered from stage fright. Wrote *The Art of Piano Playing* (1958) which is full of interesting sidelights. Recorded various Russian labels (78s).

Pupils included: Leonid Brumberg, Emil Gilels, Radoslav Kvapil, Radu Lupu, Alexei Nasedkin, Stanislav Neuhaus, Sviatoslav Richter, Julitta Slendzinka, Igor Zhukov.

NEUHAUS, Olga (–)
b. USSR. Sister of Felix Blumenfeld. Married Gustav N. Their son Heinrich N became celebrated pf teacher in Moscow.

NEUHAUS, Stanislav (1927–80)
b. Moscow, USSR. Son and pupil of Heinrich N. Début 1949. Toured Europe and was held by critics to play in the Russian grand tradition, specializing in Chopin. Pianist, teacher and adjudicator. Recorded Melodiya.

Pupils included: John Bingham, Radu Lupu, Eugeny Malinin, André Nikolsky.

NEUKOMM, Sigismund (Chevalier von) (1778–1858)
b. Salzburg, Austria. Received tuition from both Haydns and was highly regarded by Josef H. Toured Europe as pianist and conductor, settling, in 1809, in Paris where Prince Talleyrand appointed him his pianist in place of Dussek. Was ennobled in 1815 and a year later went to Brazil as music director to the court of the President. Returned to Paris in 1821 and rejoined Talleyrand. Was also known in London. Wrote a pf concerto, chamber music and pf pieces, also many songs.

NEUPERT, Edmund (1842–88)
b. Oslo, Norway. Of German parentage. Pupil first of father, then with T. Kullak, Berlin, at whose Cons. he taught on graduation, then, 1866–8 at Stern's Cons. German critics likened him to Liszt and Tausig. He went to Copenhagen Cons. for two years and in 1880 was appointed prof. at Moscow Cons. and gave highly successful concerts. Returned to Norway in 1881 but after giving some fine concerts in USA the following year decided to settle there and proceeded to build a fresh reputation as concert pianist and teacher. Was regarded as the greatest Norwegian pianist, and he evolved the 'Neupert Method' of teaching based on a logical development of technique which was taught by other Northern teachers after his death. Prolific composer of pf works, mostly studies and exercises. Probably his most important musical task was to give the première of Grieg's pf concerto in Copenhagen in 1869.
Pupils included: Agnes Adler, Anton Hartvigson.

NEVEU, Jean (–1949)
b. Paris, France. Fine young pianist who accompanied his sister the famous violinist Ginette N. Both were killed at an early age in a airplane crash in the Azores. Recorded *EMI* (as accompanist).

NEVIN, Arthur Finley (1871–1943)
b. Edgeworth, USA. Studied pf with father and in Boston, then, 1893–7 with K. Klindworth in Berlin. Thereafter music prof. at Kansas, Memphis and Pittsburgh. Visited Montana reservations in order to study Indian

music. Wrote chamber music and pf pieces. Younger brother of Ethelbert N.

NEVIN, Ethelbert Woodbridge (1862–1901)
b. Edgeworth, USA. Studied in Pittsburgh, then pf under B. J. Lang in Boston; took singing lessons in Dresden, later pf with von Bülow and K. Klindworth in Berlin. Lived thereafter in USA and Europe. Was a prolific composer of pf pieces and songs, of which *Narcissus* and *The Rosary* were best-sellers in their day. Addicted to tippling and died early of a stroke.

NEVINS, Marion: *see* **MACDOWELL, Marion**

NEWBY, Charles Henry (1891–1952)
b. Newcastle-upon-Tyne, UK. Studied pf locally and later under E. Bainton. Settled in London working in classical field as well as in light music and films. Also chamber-music player.

NEWCOMB, Ethel (1875–1959)
b. New York, USA. Studied in Vienna with T. Leschetizky 1895–1903. Début that year with Vienna PO. Was Leschetizky's assistant 1904–8. London début 1904 when she played the Schumann, the Chopin E minor and the Saint-Saëns' C minor concertos under the baton of Richard Strauss. US début 1905, to which country she eventually returned for good, dying in New York. Wrote *Leschetizky as I knew him* (1921).

NEWMAN, Alfred (1901–70)
b. New Haven, USA. Pf pupil of S. Stojowski. Was fully graduated student who turned to vaudeville before going to Hollywood as composer and arranger.

NEWMAN, William (1912–)
b. Cleveland, USA. Pupil of A. Loesser. Gave recitals and appeared with orch. Became important teacher including head of pf instruction at Univ. of N. Carolina. Wrote *The Pianist's Problems, A History of the Sonata Idea* (three volumes) and *Handbook for Piano Teachers*.

NEWMARK, John (1904–)
b. Bremen, Germany. Musically educated in Leipzig. Became leading accompanist to many celebrity singers and instrumentalists. Resident of Canada. Recorded various labels as accompanist.

NEWTON, Ivor (1892–1981)
b. London, UK. Studied pf in London with various teachers, including Y. Bowen, and in Amsterdam. Studied the art of accompanying with C. von Bos. Became internationally famous as accompanist to many of the greatest singers and instrumentalists. Wrote interesting autobiography *At the Piano* (1966). CBE 1966. Recorded most labels as accompanist.

NEY, Elly (1882–1968)
b. Düsseldorf, Germany. Student of Cologne Cons., then studied in Vienna with T. Leschetizky and E. von Sauer, winning Mendelssohn and Ibach Prizes. Début Vienna 1905. Taught at Cologne Cons. and toured Europe and the USA as soloist and with orch. A powerful technician who specialized in the German classics but who played the Tchaikovsky 1st pf concerto at 1930 London Proms and made the first recording of the R. Strauss *Burleske* for pf and orch. Recorded *German HMV*, *Polydor*, Pye and Hallmark.
    Pupils included: Helmut Brauss.

NICODÉ, Jean-Louis (1853–1919)
b. Jerozig, Germany. Pupil of T. Kullak at Kullak's Acad. from 1869, settling in Berlin as concert pianist and teacher. Taught at Dresden Cons. 1878–85 when he took over as conductor of the concerts there and became more interested in that role. Retired 1900 in order to compose. Wrote a pf sonata and studies, chamber-music and songs. Arranged Chopin's *Allegro de Concert* Op. 46 for pf and orch., also for two pfs and orch.

NICOLAEVA, Tatiana: *see* **NIKOLAYEVA, Tatiana Petrovna**

NICOLAIEV, Leonid (1878–1942)
b. Kiev, Russia. Student of Moscow Cons. under V. Safonov for pf. Pf prof. at Leningrad Cons. 1909–26; Dean of the Music Inst. thereafter. A fine concert pianist and teacher who composed chamber music, pf pieces and songs.
    Pupils included: Nadia Reisenberg, Dmitri Shostakovich, Vladimir Sofronitzky, Paul Stassevich, Vera Vinogradova, Alexander Zakin.

NICOLOSI, Francesco (1954–   )
b. Italy. Winner of La Spezia Concurs 1971. Incumbent principal at the Verdi Cons., Turin. Joint 3rd Prizewinner of 1980 Concurso 'Paloma O'Shea', Spain. Joint 2nd of Int. Comp., Geneva, 1980.

NIEDZIELSKI, Stanislas (1905–   )
b. Warsaw, Poland. Studied at Cons. there and his pf teachers were J. Slivinski, H. Opienski and I. Paderewski. Performed throughout Europe from 1925 and was awarded the Polish Gold Cross in 1938 for services to Polish music. Worked on Allied side during World War II and settled in Paris. In 1956 made extensive recital tour playing Schumann programme to commemorate the centenary of Schumann's death. Only artist known to us to be fined for assaulting a critic (B. Gavoty of Paris *Figaro*), who accused him of 'massacring' Chopin. Recorded *HMV* and Decca.

NIELSEN, Finn (1919–   )
b. Bergen, Norway. Studied at Bergen Cons. later in Stockholm, then Copenhagen and with I. Kabos in London. Début Oslo 1947. Thereafter toured Europe and USA. Has participated in films and television presentations of Grieg's music.

NIEMAN, Alfred (1913–   )
b. London, UK. Pf student of R. Acad. of Music there. Performed, taught and lectured in London, and for a time was on BBC staff. Compositions include two pf sonatas and variations, chamber music and songs.

NIEMANN, Rudolf Friedrich (1838–98)
b. Wesseburen, Germany. Pf pupil of I. Moscheles in Leipzig, then of A. Marmontel in Paris, and finally of H. von Bülow in Berlin. Performed mainly as celebrity accompanist besides teaching pf at Wiesbaden Cons. Prolific composer of chamber music, pf works and songs.

NIEWIADOMSKI, Stanislas (1859–1936)
b. Galicia, Poland. Pupil of K. Mikuli at Lwow, and of S. Jadassohn in Leipzig. Taught at Lwow Cons. and was also music critic and teacher later in Warsaw. Prolific composer of pf pieces and songs, as well as biographer of F. Chopin.

NIGGLI, Friedrich (1875–1959)
b. Aarburg, Switzerland. Studied in Germany, then in 1899 spent one year with G. Sgambati in Rome, followed by sojourns in Paris and Berlin. From 1901 taught pf and composition

at Zurich Cons. Composed chamber works, pf pieces and songs.

NIKISCH, Artur (1855–1922)
b. Szent Miklos, Hungary. Began studying the pf at the age of 6, and from an early start could correctly write out scores of pf music heard only once. Début when he was 8. Went to Vienna Cons. at 11, winning 2nd Prize for his playing. Became a great conductor of his generation but did on occasion accompany leading singers, especially Elena Gerhardt, whom he heard in Leipzig in 1902, accompanying her on her début and on many subsequent occasions.
Pupils included: Mitja Nikisch.

NIKISCH, Mitja (1899–1936)
b. Leipzig, Germany. Son of Artur N, from whom he received first pf lessons. Later studied at Leipzig Cons. under R. Teichmüller. Début Leipzig 1912. Gave two-pf recitals with father, under whose baton he also played concertos. Performed widely. US début New York 1923, having toured S. America 1921, and gave two recitals in London in 1933.

NIKOLAYEV, Leonid: *see* **NICOLAIEV, Leonid**

NIKOLAYEVA, Tatiana Petrovna (1924–)
b. Bezhitz, USSR. Studied in Russia pupil of A. Goldenweiser, touring E. Europe after World War II, winning 1st Prize at Leipzig **Bach Bicentennial Festival**. Gave première of the Shostakovich 24 preludes and fugues. Has composed pf concerto and pieces.

NIKOLSKY, André (1959–)
b. Moscow, USSR. Entered Moscow Cons. at the age of 17, S. Neuhaus being one of his teachers. Début Moscow 1977, playing an all-Scriabin programme. Came 2nd in the M. Long-J. Thibaud Pf Competition in Paris in 1979 where he also made his orchestral début. London début 1984, in which year he settled in New York.

NIN, Joaquín (1879–1949)
b. Havana, Cuba. Studied pf in Barcelona with C. Vidiella, then with M. Moszkowski in Paris. Taught at Schola Cantorum after receiving lessons from V. d'Indy there; was made hon. prof. Toured Europe as pianist, visited Cuba and founded a music society there in 1910;

returned to Paris and became member of Legion of Honour. G. Jean-Aubry described him as a 'remarkably gifted pianist, with an active mind, sincere and alive'. Began modern revival of Antonio Soler's sonatas written for harpsichord by including over a dozen of them in an edition he published of *Spanish Classics of the Piano* around 1925–8. Retired to Havana 1939. Wrote pf pieces with Spanish flavour. Arthur Rubinstein described him as a good-looking man, well-built and with regular features and a beautiful head of hair worn neck-length, and conscious of his good appearance.
Pupils included: Ernesto Lecuona.

NIN-CULMELL, Joaquín (1908–)
b. Berlin, Germany. Son of Joaquín N. Studied pf with Braud in Paris at Schola Cantorum, composition with Dukas. Spent time with de Falla in Spain, then gave concert tour throughout Europe, Cuba and USA. New York début 1936. He had a work performed at ISCM 1938, from which year he took up teaching in USA. His works for pf include a sonata (1934), rewritten 1955, a pf quintet and pf concerto as well as sets of variations and other pieces.

NISSEN, Erika (*née* **Lie**) (1845–1903)
b. Kongsvinger, Norway. Studied first with her sister, Ida L, then, from 1861, at Kullak's Acad., Berlin. Took lessons in Paris during 1868 and gave recitals in London. Became a popular artist throughout Europe, eventually settling in Oslo where she taught. With the Böhn string quartet gave première of Sinding's pf quintet in Oslo in 1888 and, in 1890, the première of his pf concerto in D which is dedicated to her. On numerous occasions played the Grieg concerto under the composer's baton. Dedicatee of Grieg's *Holberg Suite* (pf version).

NISSEN, Karl (1879–1920)
b. Oslo, Norway. Son of Erika Nissen. Pupil of his mother then of F. Busoni. Was a brilliant and popular pianist.
Pupils included: David Johansen.

NODA, Ken (1963–)
b. New York, USA, of Japanese-American parentage. Began studying pf at the age of 5, and two years later became a student of the Juilliard School. Début at the age of 8. Later

studied with D. Barenboim. European début 1979.

NOKE, Peter (1955–)
b. Cirencester, UK. Student of R. Manchester Coll. of Music and pupil of M. Clementi and G. Agosti.

NORDOFF, Paul (1909–)
b. Philadelphia, USA. Studied pf with O. Samaroff there; later was pupil at the Juilliard School, New York, receiving Guggenheim Fellowship. Held teaching post at Philadelphia Cons. and composed pf pieces and two pf concertos.

NORDRAAK, Rikard (1842–66)
b. Oslo, Norway. Studied pf there, then later with F. Kiel and T. Kullak in Berlin. Was imbued with strong national feelings. Met Grieg and together they formed Euterpe, a society for the advancement of Northern music. Composed pf pieces and songs but is remembered as creator of the Norwegian national hymn *Ja, vi elsker*. While still studying in Berlin, died of tuberculosis at a tragically early age. Dedicatee of Greig's *Humoresque*, Op. 6.

NORTON, Eunice (1908–)
b. Minneapolis, USA. Initial pf studies there. In 1930 went to London for tuition from T. Matthay, then, in Berlin, from A. Schnabel 1931–3. Début 1924 in London, followed by tour of France, Netherlands and Germany. American début 1932 New York. Thereafter her concert career was established. Recorded Honegger's *Concertino* with Minneapolis SO under Ormandy on *RCA*.

NOTTEBOHM, Martin Gustav (1817–82)
b. Lüdenscheid, Germany. Pupil of L. Berger, theory under Dehn. Later studied with Schumann and Mendelssohn in Leipzig. Settled in Vienna as a highly successful pf teacher; also made special study of Beethoven and produced several valuable volumes on him, and on Mozart and Schubert.

NOVAÈS, Guiomar (1895–1979)
b. São João da Boã Vista, Brazil. Began playing pf at age of 4 and was a prodigy. In 1909 she beat 400 contestants in Paris, playing Schumann's *Carnival* before a panel consisting of Debussy, Fauré and Moszkowski, to gain a place at the Cons. under I. Philipp. Graduated

1911 with 1st Prize. Paris début same year, followed by European tour before returning to S. America. US début 1915 and appeared throughout the continent. Was fine technician with deep sense of poetry, specially in sympathy with Romantic composers. Married Octavio Pinto. Recorded *Brunswick*, *Columbia*, Vox and RCA.

NOVÁK, Vitezslav (1870–1949)
b. Kamenice, Czechoslovakia. Studied at Prague Cons. with J. Jiránek. Was composition student of Dvořák. Some early pf works of N impressed Brahms who influenced Simrock to publish them. A pf concerto followed in 1895. Pursued an academic career and composed in most genres including many pf pieces and songs.
Pupils included: Alois Hába, Václav Kaprál.

NOVELLO, Marie (1898–1928)
b. UK. Studied in London and later with T. Leschetizky in Vienna. Performed without apparently receiving the success her talents merited and was obliged to play in theatres and music halls. Recorded *Edison* and *HMV*.

NOVOTNÝ, Jan (1935–)
b. Prague, Czechoslovakia. Pupil of Cons. there and later at the Acad. of Musical Arts. Début Prague 1954. Won 2nd Prize in the Spring Musical Festival in Prague in 1957. Taught at Prague Cons. and performed widely, notably in S. America and Far East. Specialized in Czech pf music. Recorded Supraphon.

NOWAK, Lionel (1911–)
b. Cleveland, USA. Pf teachers were B. Rubinstein and E. Fischer. Taught at Syracuse and Bennington. Pf compositions include a concertino, a trio and pieces.

NOWAKOWSKI, Josef (1800–65)
b. Warsaw, Poland. Pupil of Warsaw Cons. and of J. Elsner; fellow pupil of F. Chopin and lifelong acquaintance. Concert pianist and composer in the Polish idiom of the time. Visited Chopin in Paris in 1847 when Franchomme and Chopin played him the cello sonata Op. 65 still in MS. Was pf prof. at Alexander Inst., Warsaw. Wrote a pf method.

NOYES, Edward Hibbard (1867–1923)
b. London, Canada. From age of 20 spent eight years with K. Barth in Berlin; was then one year as court pianist in Russia before studying

further with A. Essipova in Vienna. Toured mostly in chamber music recitals before settling in USA as Head of Hartford Music School, continuing to perform in chamber-music concerts.

NYGAARD, Eline (1913–)
b. Sandefjord, Norway. Pf pupil of N. Larsen and S. Barere. Début Oslo 1939. Toured USA 1949. Taught pf at Oslo Univ.

NYIREGYHAZI, Ervin (or Edwin) (1903–)
b. Budapest, Hungary. Pf pupil of E. von Dohnányi at the Cons., then, later, of F. Lamond in Berlin. A child prodigy who was excessively cossetted and exploited, and who won fame wherever he appeared until finally, in 1925, he quarrelled with the manager of his US tour and gave up concert work, thereafter leading an impoverished and obscure life until he re-emerged in 1973, astonishing the musical public by his Liszt playing. Recorded Desmar and CBS.

OAKEY, Maggie: *see* **PACHMANN-LABORI, Marguerite de**

OBERHOFFER, Emil (1867–1933)
b. Munich, Germany. Pf pupil of I. Philipp in Paris, later emigrating to USA, where he developed career as concert pianist and conductor.

OBERSTADT, Carolus Detmar (1871–1940)
b. Tilburg, Netherlands. Pf pupil of K. Schumann. From 1894 taught at R. Cons., The Hague. Composed a pf concerto, chamber music and pf works.

OBORIN, Lev Nikolaevich (1907–74)
b. Moscow, Russia. Pupil of Gnessin School, then of Moscow Cons. under C. Igumnov, graduating 1926. Won 1st Prize in the Chopin Int. Comp. in Warsaw 1927, and taught at Moscow Cons. 1928–34, becoming prof. in 1935. Won various USSR prizes and toured widely as soloist; also played ensemble. Gave première of Khachaturian pf concerto (dedicated to O) in 1937 in Moscow. Composed a pf sonata and pieces.
  Pupils included: Vladimir Ashkenazy, Boris Berman.

O'CONOR, John (1947–   )
b. Dublin, Eire. Studied there at the Coll. of Music and also Univ. Coll.; later attended Vienna High School under a scholarship. Teachers included C. Zecchi, N. Magaloff, and W. Kempff. Won 1st Prize in 1973 in the International Beethoven Pf Competition, Vienna; also the Bösendorfer Prize in 1975. Appeared worldwide before settling in Dublin as pf prof. at R. Irish Academy of Music. Recorded Claddagh and others.

ODÉ, Jan (1906–   )
b. Delft, Netherlands. Student of Cons. at The Hague, then pupil of C. Arrau. Well-known recitalist and teacher. Was appointed Director of the Amsterdam Cons. 1956.

OFFERGOLD, Robert: *see* *under* **GOTTSCHALK, Louis**

OGDON, John Andrew Howard (1937–   )
b. Manchester, UK. Pupil of R. Manchester Coll. of Music and of I. Elinson and G. Green, later receiving tuition from E. Petri and D. Matthews. Won 2nd Prize in a Liverpool pf competition in 1959, in which year he made his formal début at Wigmore Hall, London. His career was launched at the Int. Tchaikovsky Comp. in Moscow in 1962, when he came joint 1st with V. Ashkenazy. Afterwards toured five continents. Had the facility for memorizing extraordinarily wide repertoire and playing many divergent works in the course of a season. Gave first performances of works by contemporary composers, including A. Rawsthorne's *Ballad* in Cardiff in 1967. Own compositions include three pf sonatas and a sonatina, preludes, a dance suite, *Theme and Variations* and a concerto, also a flute sonata. From 1975 taught a master-class at the Music School of Indiana Univ., USA, and for a time his concert work was curtailed on account of ill-health. Married the pianist Brenda Lucas (b. Manchester), also a pupil of the R. Manchester Coll. of Music, who had her own career as soloist and teacher as well as appearing in duo recitals with her husband. Wrote *Virtuoso*, the story of John O, in collaboration with Michael Kerr (1981). Malcolm Williamson dedicated his 3rd pf concerto to John O, who premièred it with the Sydney SO, and his two-pf sonata is dedicated to husband and wife jointly. John O recorded various labels.

OHE, Adele aus der (1864–1937)
b. Hanover, Germany. Studied pf with F. Kullak and T. Kullak and, from 1876 to 1886 with F. Liszt at Weimar. Performed extensively in Europe and America, pioneering the Tchaikovsky 1st pf concerto in the USA under the composer's baton. Composed much pf music and songs.

OHLSSON, Garrick (1948–)
b. New York, USA. Studied at the Juilliard School, being a pupil of S. Gorodnitzki then of R. Lhevinne. Won the Busoni Prize at Bolzano in 1966 and came first in the Int. Chopin Comp. in Warsaw in 1970, the first American to gain top in that competition. The same year he made his début with Ormandy and the Philadelphia Orch. Toured N. America and Europe and built a successful career. Became associated with festivals, e.g. Saratoga and Tanglewood. At 6 feet 4 inches reputed to be the tallest pianist in the business, and with a huge hand-stretch to match. Recorded EMI.

OLDBERG, Arne (1874–1962)
b. Youngstown, USA. Pf pupil of A. Hyllested and later of T. Leschetizky in Vienna. Was in charge of pf teaching at Evanston 1900–41. Wrote two pf concertos, chamber music and pf pieces.

OLDHAM, Arthur (1926–)
b. London, UK. Studied R. Coll. there, composition under H. Howells and pf under K. Long. Also had private lessons from Benjamin Britten. Subsequently turned to ballet direction and composition.

O'LEARY, Arthur (1834–1919)
b. Tralee, Ireland. Studied at Leipzig Cons. under I. Moscheles and entered the circle of the Schumanns. From 1852–6 was pupil W. S. Bennett at R. Acad. of Music, London, after which he became prof. there until 1903. Was associated with Nat. Training School. Composed pf pieces and made edition of Bennett's pf works.

OLIVEIRA, Jocy de (1936–)
b. Curtiba, Brazil. Studied in USA; then went as pupil of M. Long in Paris. Début São Paulo 1944. Performed S. America, USA and Europe solo and with orch. Recorded various.

OLIVERA, Mercedes (1919–)
b. Montevideo, Uruguay. Studied there, and made début 1932. UK début 1946. Has toured extensively, sponsoring Latin American music.

ONSLOW, George (1784–1852)
b. Clermont-Ferrand, France. Pf pupil of J. Dussek and of J. B. Cramer in London. Became especially interested in chamber music, performing and composing prolifically.

OPIENSKI, Heinrich (1870–1942)
b. Cracow, Poland. Musicologist, pianist, conductor and teacher. Studied successively with d'Indy, Urban, Riemann, Nikisch and I. Paderewski. During World War I lived in Switzerland, then was Director of Poznan Cons. 1919–26, after which he returned to Switzerland. Made an edition of Chopin's letters (French and Polish trans.), and a thematic catalogue of Chopin's works. Wrote *Chopin* (Lwow 1909, Warsaw 1910), a book on Paderewski and other books, including one on the Polish composer Moniuszko.

Pupils included: Stanislas Niedzielski.

OPPENS, Ursula (1944–)
b. New York, USA. Student of Radcliffe Coll. and later of the Juilliard School under R. Lhevinne. Début 1969 New York. Was founder member of Speculum Musicae and has featured much contemporary music, appearing with F. Rzewski. Won Busoni 1st Prize Bolzano in 1969, and in 1976 the Avery Fisher award. Toured extensively through the Americas and Europe. Premièred Elliott Carter's *Night Fantasies* in Bath, UK, 1980, and gave first performance of *The People United will never be Defeated* by F. Rzewski in 1976. Recorded RCA.

ORGER, Caroline: *see* **REINAGLE, Caroline**

ORLOV, Nicolas (1892–1964)
b. Jelec, Russia. Studied at Moscow Cons. under C. Igumnov, also receiving private tuition from S. Taneiev. Taught pf in Moscow 1913–15, during which period he gave the first performance of the Glazounov 1st concerto in F minor. Left Russia after the revolution and took up career as concert pianist in Europe. Toured USA. Settled in London. Claimed to have no speciality but was noted for beautiful interpretation of Chopin and Scriabin. A London critic wrote of a 1930 Chopin recital: 'Playing such as this disarms criticism; one

simply enjoyed every phrase for its revitalised beauty.' Tended to be overshadowed by his more famous Russian contemporaries. Recorded *Decca*.

ORNSTEIN, Leo (1895–   )
b. Krementchug, Russia. Precocious pupil of St Petersburg Cons. Went to New York at age of 11 and continued studies under F. Tapper. Début 1911 New York. Then toured USA and Europe solo and with leading orchs. Taught for many years in Philadelphia, having founded the Ornstein School of Music. Outside USA his name is now legendary. At one time his recital programmes, which contained many of his own compositions, caused a furore through being too advanced for their time. Critics took sides, but the furore subsided when he confined himself mainly to teaching and composing. Wrote mainly for pf but there are chamber works and songs.
Pupils included: Andrew Imbrie.

OROZCO, Rafael (1946–   )
b. Cordoba, Spain. Studied at Cons. there, then in 1959 went to Madrid Cons. under J. Cubiles and others, winning 1st Prize. Subsequently received lessons from A. Weissenberg. In 1966 won 1st Prize in Leeds Comp., and a successful concert career began. Recorded EMI and Philips.

ORTIZ, Cristina (1950–   )
b. Bahia, Brazil. Studied in Rio, winning prize to study in Paris with M. Tagliaferro. Won awards there and in Bucharest. Won 1st Prize in the Van Cliburn Int. Comp., 1969, and in 1971 made successful appearances in New York and Philadelphia. Studied a further two years with R. Serkin. Appeared in Europe in 1973 and settled in UK. Recorded EMI, Decca and Pantheon.

ORTMANN, Otto Rudolf (1889–   )
b. Baltimore, USA. Pupil of G. Boyle and E. Hutcheson at Peabody Cons., where he subsequently taught. Director there 1928–42 and founded its Research Dept. in 1925, being much involved, through laboratory experiment, in pf technique and methods. Was on teaching staff of Goucher Coll. 1942–57, and Chairman of its Music Dept. from 1948. After 1957 taught privately. Writings included *The Physical Basis of Piano Touch and Tone* (1925) and *The Psychological Mechanics of Piano Technique* (1929).

OSBORN, Franz (1905–55)
b. Berlin, Germany. Pupil of L. Kreutzer and later of A. Schnabel. Performed throughout Europe, becoming British citizen 1934. Concert soloist who also formed duo team with Max Rostal (violin). Recorded *Decca*.

OSBORNE, George Alexander (1806–93)
b. Limerick, Ireland. Studied in Brussels and for a time taught there. Went to Paris in 1826 to study with J. Pixis and F. Kalkbrenner, and moved in the musical circle of Chopin, Liszt and Berlioz. At Chopin's concert at Pleyel's house in 1832 the programme included a *Grand Polonaise with Introduction and March* by Kalkbrenner for six pfs, and O was one of the pianists. Settled in London in 1843 where he actively propagated the music of Chopin. Was an early influence in Trinity Coll., London, acting as chairman for a time. Wrote *Reminiscences of Chopin*, (1880).
Pupils included: Simon Waley.

OSTROWSKI, Felix (1802–60)
b. Lublin, Poland. Student of W. Würfel at Warsaw Cons. and a contemporary of Chopin. Concert pianist and composer of pf works with titles such as nocturne, polonaise and mazurka, and at least one sonata.

O'SULLIVAN, Patrick (1874–1947)
b. Louisville, USA. Studied in Paris under H. Bauer, later in Berlin with X. Scharwenka. Début in Europe before returning to USA. Became mainly teacher and composer, works including a *Fantaisie irlandaise* for pf and orch.

OSWALD, Henrique (1852–1931)
b. Rio de Janeiro, Brazil, of Swiss-Italian parentage. Studied music in Italy and spent nearly 30 years in Europe before returning to Rio. A capable pianist who became Head of the Nat. Inst. of Music in Rio. Compositions included a pf concerto and pieces said to show French and German influences from the period of his student days in Europe.

OUSSET, Cécile (–   )
b. Tarbes, France. A prodigy who first appeared in public aged 5, she studied at Paris Cons. and with M. Ciampi, winning 1st Pf Prize there. Won other international competitions and has toured worldwide including behind the Iron Curtain. Was described by one London critic in 1982 as 'clearly among the

world's most remarkable virtuosi'. Recorded Aurora and Cambridge.

OVERTON, Hall (1920–72)
b. Michigan, USA. Pupil of Chicago Music Coll., then of Juilliard School. Taught, performed and composed, including a pf sonata and much chamber music. Became specialist in jazz.

PABLO, Vicente (1880–)
b. Montevideo, Uruguay. Studied at Cons. there before going to Europe to continue with F. Busoni and V. da Motta. When he returned to Montevideo, he co-founded the Uruguay Cons. which became most successful.

PABST, Louis (1846–1903)
b. Königsberg. Elder brother of Paul P. Musical education details obscure. Début at age of 16. Established a school in Riga, then found his way to Australia, where he established the Melbourne Acad. of Music. Ten years later returned to Russia and taught thereafter.
Pupils included: Alexander Goldenweiser, Percy Grainger, Tina Lerner, Sergei Liapunov.

PABST, Paul (1854–97)
b. Königsberg. Younger brother of Louis P. Went to study with F. Liszt before joining staff of Moscow Cons.
Pupils included: Constantine Igumnov.

PACHER, Josef (1816–71)
b. Daubrowitz, Czechoslovakia. Well-known pianist of his day and composer of one-time popular salon music.

PACHLER-KOSCHAK, Maria Leopoldine:
see **KOSCHAK, Maria Leopoldine.**

PACHMANN, Adrian de (*c.*1893–1937)
b.   . Son of Vladimir and Marguerite de P. Became a concert pianist and pursued own career. Did not, however, appear to receive any tuition from father, and their careers were unconnected. Domiciled in Paris most of his life.

PACHMANN, Vladimir de (1848–1933)
b. Odessa, Russia. Son of an Austrian lawyer and amateur musician; his mother a Turk. Studied initially under the father. At the age of 18 he went to Vienna Cons. for two years, becoming a pupil of J. Dachs, and graduated with a Gold Medal. Début 1869 Odessa led to a tour of Russia and some appearances in Germany. However, hearing Karl Tausig, he at once became dissatisfied with his own attainments and retired for further study, re-emerging only to go back into retreat for another two years. At the age of 34 he finally resumed his concert career in 1882 (by which time Tausig had been dead some years) and proceeded to capture musical hearts throughout the capitals of Europe. His British début occurred that same year in St James's Hall. When he toured the USA, he met with similar success.

He revelled in beauty of tone and elegance of interpretation above all other qualities, spending endless time working out fingering that would secure those ideals without necessarily having regard for the musical intentions of the composers. As time went by, he played Chopin more and more to the exclusion of other composers. It is true he occasionally performed pf concertos like the Chopin E minor and Mendelssohn G minor, and records show he actually played the Beethoven C minor in London in 1892. Conductors, however, found his melodic line too subtle to follow even when he played in strict time.

Right up to the end of the first quarter of this century he toured, celebrated and esteemed worldwide as the supreme Chopin interpreter. It has been said that the only composition by Chopin which he hated playing was the Funeral March of the 2nd sonata because he held the superstition that, whenever he did so, someone, somewhere, would die. He received the R. Phil. Gold Medal in 1916. His last tour of the USA was in 1925, his last British appearance in the R. Albert Hall in 1928, the year he assumed Italian citizenship, dying in Rome.

He married the Australian pianist who had been his only pupil, Maggie Oakey (*see* PACHMANN-LABORI, Marguerite de). The marriage lasted about a decade, and there were two sons. One of them, Adrian de P, became a pianist and teacher but was always outmanœuvred by the garish reputation of his father.

When P died, his annotated scores passed into the possession of Mme Pachmann-Labori who caused a selection of Chopin bearing the master's fingerings to be published (Augener). Recorded *Columbia* and *HMV*. He and the Frenchman F. Planté were the only pianists born during Chopin's lifetime to live long enough to make gramophone recordings by the electrical process.

Only known pupil: Maggie Oakey.

PACHMANN-LABORI, Marguerite de (Maggie Oakey) (1864–1952)

b. Sydney, Australia. Studied pf and became a pupil of V. de Pachmann. They married in 1884 and she accompanied him on his first tour of USA in 1892. There was a pianist son, Adrian de P. She was considered a fine pianist in her own right and continued her career after she divorced him around 1895. She later married a French barrister, Maitre Labori, who had been counsel to Dreyfus. On P's death she came into possession of his music library especially scores of Chopin showing P's fingering. In 1934 Augeners commenced publishing an edition.

PACHULSKI, Henryk (1859–1921)

b. Lasa, Russia. Studied in Warsaw, then at Moscow Cons. where his pf teacher was N. Rubinstein. Taught there from 1886 and composed much, including chamber works and many pf pieces, some of which used to be included in collections of Russian music.

PADEREWSKI, Ignace Jan (1860–1941)

b. Podolia, Poland. Showed interest in the instrument as a child, entering Warsaw Cons. at the age of 12. Among his teachers was N. Janotha, a pupil of K. Schumann. At the age of 16 he and a violinist friend, Ignace Cielewicz, decided to try their luck in a year-long tour of Russia from which they gained more experience than money. He returned to Warsaw for further tuition, graduating in 1879 and becoming a teacher at the Cons. Married in 1880, his wife died in childbirth the following year leaving a sickly boy, Alfred, who did not survive beyond the age of 20. He spent a year studying composition in Berlin then went to Vienna as a pupil of T. Leschetizky and later obtained a teaching post in Strasbourg, which alleviated his chronic state of penury.

His adult début occurred in Vienna in 1887 when he played at a concert in which the star of the bill was Pauline Lucca, a famous Viennese soprano. He was a sensation overnight, his physical appearance – a slight figure with pale, artistic features surmounted by a mane of red hair (many contemporaneous accounts called it 'golden'), capturing ardent public admiration especially among women. The conductor Lamoureux was in the audience and booked him to appear in Paris, where his success was every bit as great as it had been in Vienna. Saint-Saëns made the famous remark: 'He is a genius who also plays the piano.' He settled in Paris for a time before acquiring an extensive property in Switzerland which he retained up to his death.

His London début came in 1890 where, after a faltering start, the cream of society showered him with favours. He was admired as much in public concerts as in the private *salons* of the wealthy where he used his own prestige to raise the status and earnings of hired musicians. The London Press called him 'the lion of Paris', but critical opinions were sharply divided. Two contrasted facets of his playing – a hard-hitting gruffness which vied with a gentle, romantic sweetness – recall the duality of Schumann's own nature.

It has been said that the suddenness of his sensational success caught him unprepared and with a woefully inadequate repertoire committed to memory. If that were so, he made good the deficiency within a short space of time. In 1891 he crossed the Atlantic and conquered N. America in a coast-to-coast tour, travelling with an entourage worthy of royalty. For the rest of his career he bestrode the Atlantic, a colossus of his art whose name, second to none, was capable of selling out the largest halls. Throughout a long life he was to exude a particular and unique charisma before which people instinctively genuflected.

He became involved in politics during the Great War when he espoused the cause of a free Poland and indeed was for a short time Prime Minister of that newly liberated country and an important figure among post-war European politicians. His status derived from recognition of his patriotism, innate dignity and wisdom. Nevertheless he had opponents, and his new career was not an entire success so, at the age of 63, he left the political scene and resumed concert work.

Those who heard him thereafter or who have relied on gramophone records have marvelled how a man who made such clumsy-sounding music could ever have captured the hearts of the public as P undoubtedly did. At the outset of his musical apprenticeship he acquired his own technique, and later tutors seem not to have eradicated what this age judges to be bad habits. Yet when we listen to the very first recordings he made between 1911 (when he was already 51 years old) and 1918, not happily transferred to LP, we discover many facets of masterful playing which could have captivated audiences of today, never mind those of pre-World War I. We can also hear mannerisms which later became more pronounced and distressing: bad rhythm and timekeeping, curious liberties with *rubato*, spread chords and left hand before right. In her historical recording of the Schumann concerto, F. Davies plays practically every chord as an arpeggio and advances one hand before the other. She was one of the best pupils of K. Schumann, so could these affectations demonstrated by P have been inherited indirectly from R. Schumann's wife through Mme Janotha?

He was associated primarily with the music of Chopin, yet recordings reveal a fine grasp of Liszt. William Mason, a pupil of that composer, once remarked that P, who never heard Liszt let alone studied with him, was nevertheless 'the finest living exponent of Liszt'. The gramophone repertory also demonstrates that his Schubert and Schumann were most exquisitely wrought.

He once expressed an opinion that success in music was a compound of one per cent talent, nine per cent luck and ninety per cent work, and he certainly practised assiduously before every concert, leaving nothing to chance. Yet for all that conscientious preparation, he was ever a victim of nerves.

He yearned to go down in history as a composer but, because of all the time spent playing the pf to earn money, his creative output is very modest. Besides the opera *Manru* and a symphony – both long, he wrote one pf concerto which Saint-Saëns thought highly of and which A. Essipova helped to make familiar; the *Polish Fantasy* also for pf

and orchestra, and a one-time popular piece in the concert repertoire; a pf sonata, sets of variations, and numerous solos including the famous minuet; also a sonata for violin and pf, and songs.

He received the Gold Medal of the R. Phil. Soc. of London in 1897 as well as more honours and awards for music and politics than any other musician. He was an active participant of the Chopin edition of the Fryderyk Chopin Inst., Warsaw, which supervised a complete edition of the Polish composer's works. The *Paderewski Memoirs* (1938) were ghosted by Mary Lawton. With Marie Tempest he starred in the film *Moonlight Sonata* (1936), playing the Beethoven work and the Chopin A flat polonaise.

He joined the *émigré* Polish Government in France in 1940, and when that country was overrun, the US Government exerted its influence so the old man could withdraw across the Atlantic. He died in New York the following year. Recorded *HMV* and *Decca*.

Pupils included: Harold Bauer, Zygmunt Dygat, Henry Eames, Maryla Jonas, Lennart Lundberg, Witold Malcuzynski, Stanislas Niedzielski, Heinrich Opienski, Ernest Schelling, Homer Simmons, Sigismund Stojowski, Stanislas Szpinalski, Henryk Sztompka, Antoinette Szumowska, Adela Verne.

PADWA, Vladimir (–)
b. Krivyakino, Russia. Student of St Petersburg Cons. and with F. Busoni in Berlin and M. von Zadora. Performed throughout Europe, America and Far East. Pf prof. at New York Univ. Compositions include a concerto for two pfs.

PAIK, Kun Woo (–)
Request to last-known concert agents for biographical details met with insufficient response.

PALENICZEK, Josef (1914–)
b. Travnik, Czechoslovakia. Student of Prague Cons., later training and working for a while in Paris. Was one-time pianist in Czech Trio. Taught at Prague Cons. from 1963. In his concert career specialized in the pf music of L. Janácek. Own compositions included a pf concerto.

PALLEMAERTS, Edmundo (1867–1945)
b. Malines, Belgium. Pupil of Brussels Cons.;

studied pf with A. de Greef. In 1889 went to Argentina and later founded the Argentina Cons. of Music in Buenos Aires, of which he was first Director. Wrote orch. works, pf music and songs.

PALMER, Phyllis (1920–   )
b. Petersfield, UK. Student of R. Acad. of Music and of Tobias Matthay School, London, also of N. Medtner. Recitalist, concerto- and ensemble-player. Taught.

PALMGREN, Selim (1878–1951)
b. Bjorneborg, Finland. Student at Helsinki Cons. 1895–9. Continued pf studies in Berlin under K. Ansorge and F. Busoni, returning home 1902. Toured USA 1921 and was prof. of pf and composition at Eastman School of Music, New York 1921–6, when he returned to Helsinki, continuing to teach and compose; also toured N. Europe regularly as pianist. Wrote much pf music of romantic type including five concertos, two sonatas and a set of preludes.
Pupils included: George Godzinsky.

PALUMBO, Constantino (1843–1928)
b. Naples, Italy. Studied at Cons. there. Gave concerts with success in UK and Italy, and appeared elsewhere on the Continent. Pf prof. at Naples Cons. from 1873. Wrote a concerto and much pf music.
Pupils included: Mario Vitali.

PANENKA, Jan (1922–   )
No details available.

PANHOFER, Walter (1910–   )
b. Vienna, Austria. Studied there and toured widely thereafter, solo and with leading orchs. Pf prof. at Vienna Univ. from 1971 and international adjudicator.

PANKIEWICZ, Eugene (1857–98)
b. Siedice, Poland. Studied pf at Warsaw Cons., then went on as a pupil of T. Leschetizky in St Petersburg. Returned to Warsaw to complete his musical education and in 1881 joined the teaching staff in succession to I. Paderewski, who had left for Berlin.

PAPADOPOULOS, Marios (1954–   )
b. Cyprus, where he studied from an early age. Worked in London from 1967 where his teachers included I. Kabos. Was 'Young Musician 1973' by Greater London Arts Assn,

the year of his début there, followed by concerts throughout Europe. USA début New York 1976, subsequently touring that country. Later appeared in S. Africa and Far East including Japan.

PARADIES, Pietro Domenico (1707–91)
b. Naples, Italy. Pupil of Porpora and composer for keyboard instruments who early became involved in the pf and taught the instrument in London from 1747 until returning to Naples shortly before his death. Composed 12 *sonate di gravicembalo* which have become early pf works.

PARADIS, Maria Theresia (1759–1824)
b. Vienna, Austria. Godchild to the Empress Marie Theresa and was blind. Studied pf and composition under leading musicians of the time and made her début by way of appearing at most of the royal courts of Europe during 1784. Was successful pianist, teacher and composer using a form of notation invented to overcome the handicap of blindness. Joseph Haydn composed his 2nd concerto for clavecin or pf for her which was first performed at a Concert Spirituel in Paris around 1783. Wrote sonatas, chamber music and songs.

PARDO, Rosa Lily de la: *see* **MIRANDA.**

PARKHOUSE, David (1930–   )
b. Teignmouth, UK. Student at R. Coll. of Music, London; won Chappell Gold Medal 1948. Début in London followed. Has performed widely as soloist and in ensemble. Married the cellist Eileen Croxford. Recorded various labels.

PARKIN, Eric (1924–   )
b. Stevenage, UK. Studied at Trinity Coll., London. Début Wigmore Hall 1948. Performed thereafter. Gave première of Kenneth Leighton's *Household Pets*, Op. 86, in London in 1982. Recorded various.

PARRATT, Sir Walter George (1841–1924)
b. Huddersfield, UK. Noted in his day as organist, teacher of the instrument and Master of Queen's and Kings' (Edward VII and George V) Musick; knighted 1892. Was pf pupil of E. Dannreuther and is included in this volume because by the age of 10 he had given evidence of possessing a prodigious memory, having learned all of Bach's '48', thereby being the original object of the phrase: 'to learn

Parratt fashion', it being subsequently amended to 'parrot'. Also credited with ability to play chess while playing from memory anything in the pf repertory from Bach to Brahms.

PARRY, Wilfrid (1908–79)
b. Birmingham, UK. Pupil at Trinity Coll., London, where he later taught. Became well-know accompanist in concerts and for BBC. As such recorded on various labels.

PARSONS, Albert Ross (1847–1933)
b. New York, USA. Studied in New York, then at Leipzig Cons. under I. Moscheles, K. Reinecke and E. Wenzel; and finally in Berlin with K. Tausig and T. Kullak. On his return to New York in 1871, became probably the most prestigious pf teacher there. Propagated the cause of Wagner. Wrote a treatise on pf practice; translated Wagner's *Beethoven* into English, also Lessmann's *Liszt*.

PARSONS, Geoffrey Penwill (1929–)
b. Sydney, Australia. Pupil at New South Wales State Cons. Became accompanist to Essie Ackland and Peter Dawson, accompanying latter to UK 1950, where he stayed to become internationally famous accompanist. Recorded various labels. OBE 1978.

PASDELOUP, Jules Étienne (1819–87)
b. Paris, France. Studied pf at Paris Cons., mainly under P. Zimmerman, winning 1st Prize in 1834. Taught the instrument 1847–50, relinquishing it in order to organize the celebrated concerts bearing his name.

PASSY, Edvard (1789–1870)
b. Stockholm, Sweden. Pf student of J. Field in Moscow, performing throughout central Europe before returning to Stockholm to teach and play. Composed several works for pf and orch., and a large number of solos and songs.

PASTORY, Ditta: *see* **BARTÓK, Ditta.**

PATTISON, John Nelson (1845–1905)
b. New York, USA. Studied pf with F. Liszt, S. Thalberg, A. Henselt and H. von Bülow. Was well-known concert soloist and accompanist in USA and composed much pf music. Worthy of remembrance for having published his memoirs at the age of 23.

PATTISON, Lee (1890–1966)
b. Grand Rapids, USA. Student of New

England Cons. and later under A. Schnabel in Berlin. Début 1913 Boston. Performed many years solo and as duo with Guy Maier. Toured throughout Europe and America. Taught in Chicago, later Columbia Univ. and Juilliard School. Composed works for pf.
Pupils included: John Browning.

PAU, Maria de la (1950–)
b. Prades, France, at the time of the first Festival there, founded by the cellist Pau Casals who became her godfather and from whom she adopted the surname. Daughter of the French cellist Paul Tortelier and member of a highly musical family. Orch. début in Belfast 1961. Student of Paris Cons. and of J.-M. Darré and L. Gousseau, later of the Volkwang Hochschule, Essen and of D. Kraus. Taught for one year in Bochum before embarking on a worldwide concert career. Recorded EMI.

PAUER, Ernst (1826–1905)
b. Vienna, Austria. Pf pupil of Wolfgang A. Mozart the younger. Settled in London 1851 as pianist and teacher, and was pf prof. at the R. Acad. 1859–64, and afterwards at the R. Coll. Developed a series of historical recitals and was an examiner and adjudicator for many years. Wrote volumes of studies, also chamber-music. Arranged Beethoven and Schumann symphonies, and Mendelssohn's orch. works, for two, four and eight hands on pf. Father of Max Pauer.
Pupils included: Max Pauer, Joseph Speaight, Agnes Zimmermann.

PAUER, Fritz (1943–)
b. Vienna, Austria. Studied at Vienna Cons. and had career in jazz and classical. Début in jazz club in Vienna. Taught pf at Vienna Cons. and played and broadcast jazz. Has composed much pf music in all fields, winning 1st Prize at Int. Comp. for Modern Jazz, Vienna, 1966.

PAUER, Max (1866–1945)
b. London, UK. Son of Ernst P who taught him until he was 15. Studied theory with V. Lachner. Pf prof. at Cologne Cons. from 1887; at Stuttgart from 1897, and thereafter at Leipzig and Mannheim. Retired 1934. Made an edition of Schumann's pf works and, in the manner of his father, arranged Haydn and Mozart symphonies for two and four hands. Recorded *Polyor* (chamber music).
Pupils included: Eugen d'Albert, John

Dunn, Walter Georgii, Margarete Hawkins, Felix Rath.

PAUL, Lady Dean: *see* **POLDOWSKI.**

PAUL, Oscar (1836–98)
b. Leipzig, Germany. Music student at Cons. there as well as private pupil of L. Plaidy. Taught at the Cons. from 1869 and later became prof. at Leipzig Univ. Was an authority on harmony, also on pf construction.
    Pupils included: Fanny Davies.

PAUL, Reginald William (1894–   )
b. London, UK. Studied at R. Acad. of Music there where he later taught as prof. and an Examiner for Association Board. Lectured, adjudicated. Recorded *Broadcast* and *Decca*.

PAUR, Marie (1862–99)
b. Gengenbach, Germany. Pf pupil at Stuttgart Cons., then studied in Vienna with T. Leschetizky and A. Essipova. Became successful concert pianist, especially in USA, where she had accompanied her husband Emil P, a conductor who succeeded A. Nikisch in Boston in 1893.

PAYNE, Albert (1842–1921)
b. Leipzig, Germany. Student of Cons. there and of A. Dreyschock. Took over his father's music publishing business, later introducing a range of pocket scores which proved so popular that the titles totalled over 200 by the time he sold out to Eulenburg in 1892.

PEEBLES, Antony (1946–   )
b. UK. Studied music at Trinity Coll., Cambridge; later was pf pupil of P. Katin, then of Yvonne Lefébure. Won BBC Pf Comp. 1971 and performed extensively. Recorded Unicorn label. Début London 1969.

PEKINEL, Güher and Süher (1954–   )
b. Ankara, Turkey. Identical twins who commenced to learn the pf at the age of 6, making their début three years later with orch. in Ankara. Studied in Frankfurt Hochschule, graduating with highest awards in 1972, after which they studied with R. Serkin at Curtis Inst. and later at Juilliard School. Prizewinners who as a duo have appeared widely in Europe and the USA. London début 1982. Recorded DG.

PELLEG, Frank (1910–   )
b. Prague, Czechoslovakia, where he studied before settling in Israel, becoming first Director of Music Dept in the Ministry of Education and Culture. Helped to establish music in that country very considerably. Gave first performance of Ben-Haim's pf concerto with Israel PO 1950.

PELLETIER, Louis-Philippe (1945–   )
b. Montreal, Canada. Studied at Cons. there, also with L. Kolessa and C. Helffer. Performed widely in N. America and in Europe. Pioneered performances of contemporary music. Winner of 1st Prize of Arnold Schoenberg Pf Concours 1979.

PELLETIER, Romain (1843–1927)
b. Montreal, Canada. Was extensively and thoroughly trained in European musical centres and was one of Canada's outstanding early musicians. One of the first pianists to perform Chopin convincingly in that country thanks to his training in Paris. Was additionally a fine organist and teacher.

PELTRE, Bruno (1956–   )
b. Nancy, France. Studied at Paris Cons. where his teachers included Y. Loriod.

PEMBAUER, Joseph (1875–1937)
b. Innsbruck, Germany. Pf pupil of J. Rheinberger and L. Thuille, Munich Acad. Taught there 1897–1900 after graduation while continuing studies with A. Reisenauer. Taught at Leipzig Cons. 1902–21, and thereafter at Munich Acad. Performed widely and had a severe 'professorial' approach to his art. Recorded *Parlophone*.
    Pupils included: Julian von Karólyi.

PÈNE, Léontine Marie: *see* **BORDES-PÈNE, Léontine Marie.**

PENNARIO, Leonard (1924–   )
b. Buffalo, USA. Pf pupil of G. Maier and later in New York of I. Vengerova. Début at the age of 12 in the Grieg concerto with Dallas Orch. New York début 1943 with New York PO. Has performed throughout the world solo and with orch. Chamber music concerts with Heifetz, Piatigorsky and Primrose from 1961 and in 1967 gave première of Rozsa's pf concerto Op. 31 which is dedicated to him. Latterly involved himself in the music of Gottschalk whom he

has portrayed in television appearances. Recorded various labels.

PEPPERCORN, Gertrude (1878–1974)
b. West Horsley, UK. Student of R. Acad., London, where she was taught by T. Matthay and became a prizewinner. Début in Edinburgh in 1896 followed by a tour of UK. Became well-known in Europe and USA. New York début 1907. Was pf prof. at Matthay's School in London; also taught at the R. Acad., where she was elected Fellow in 1902.

PEPPIN, Geraldine and Mary (–   )
b. Marston Magna, UK. Début at 17, followed by many appearances as duo-team. Both pf prof. at Guildhall School, London. Gave first performance of C. Lambert's *Trois Pièces Nègres pour les Touches Blanches* in London in 1949.

PERABO, Ernst (1845–1920)
b. Wiesbaden, Germany. German pianist whose family settled in USA 1852. Studied in Leipzig Cons. with I. Moscheles and F. Wenzel for pf. Went back to USA 1865 and became successful concert pianist. Taught in Boston and wrote pf music.
   Pupils included: Mrs H. H. A. Beach.

PERAHIA, Murray (1947–)
b. New York, USA, of Sephardic ancestry. Played from an early age, seeming to be more interested in conducting and composition. Studied at Mannes School and received guidance from eminent pianists. Played chamber-music with some of the greatest artists of his time, probably a potent factor in the extraordinary precision of his playing. Orch. début in New York in 1972, and first London appearance the following year, in which capital he later settled. Highly sensitive virtuoso who is especially distinguished in the music of Mozart. Came 1st in Leeds Int. Pf Comp. 1972. Recorded CBS.

PEREZ de GUZMAN, Enrique (–   )
b. Madrid, Spain. Studied at the Cons. there and later in Paris with M. Long and M. Tagliaferro. Won prizes in a number of European pf competitions and was awarded a Knighthood of the Order of Queen Isabel la Catolica in 1968. A distinguished performer in solo recital and with major orchestras. US début Detroit, 1973, London début 1976. Transcribed in suite form for pf solo both

sections of de Falla's ballet *The Three-Cornered Hat*.

PERKIN, Helen (1909–)
b. UK. First taught by mother up to age of 11, when she received lessons from A. Alexander. At 16 won scholarship to R. Coll., London, remaining there until 22, when she went to Vienna to study pf with E. Steuermann and composition with A. Webern. Broadcast own *Theme & Variations* for pf when 19. On return from Vienna began performing and was especially identified with contemporary music, notably the John Ireland pf concerto which she premièred 1930 Queen's Hall Prom concert under Wood. Composed chamber music, many pf pieces, also songs.

PERLEMUTER, Vlado (1904–)
b. Lithuania. Lived in France from 1907. Became a pupil of Paris Cons. 1917, winning 1st Prize at 15. Studied with A. Cortot and taught at Paris Cons. until 1977. Concert pianist and adjudicator. Légion d'Honneur 1968. Recorded Vox and Nimbus.
   Pupils included: Michel Dalberto, Vanessa Latarche, Ken Sasaki, Charles Timbrell, Ilana Vered.

PERRY, Edward Baxter (1855–1924)
b. Haverhill, USA. Blind pianist who studied in Boston, and later in Berlin with T. Kullak, K. Schumann and finally F. Liszt at Weimar. His career in the USA encompassed numerous pf recitals, and he also instituted there the lecture-recital, in all probably around 6,000 appearances. Composed chamber music and pf pieces, including technical exercises.

PERSICHETTI, Vincent (1915–)
b. Philadelphia, USA. Studied from an early age, later working under A. Jonás at Combs Coll. and with O. Samaroff for two years from 1939. In 1941 married Dorothy Flanagan, and together they propagated contemporary music for two pfs. Head of composition at Philadelphia Cons. from 1942 and at Juilliard School from 1948. Prolific composer including eleven pf sonatas, the first of which dates from 1939, many pf works, chamber music and songs.
   Pupils include: Hugh Aitken.

PERTICAROLI, Sergio (1930–)
b. Rome, Italy. Pf student at S. Cecilia Acad. there and later taught at Rome Cons. Has performed throughout the world.

PETERSILEA, Carlyle (1844–1903)
b. Boston, USA. Pupil of Leipzig Cons. under
I. Moscheles and K. Reinecke, later spending a
summer with F. Liszt in Weimar. Established
own academy of pf in Boston, later teaching at
New England Cons. before settling in
California, where he died. Was known as
concert pianist in Germany.

PETRI, Egon (1881–1962)
b. Hanover, Germany, of Dutch parentage.
His father was concertmaster of Hanover R.
Opera Orch. and a string-quartet player, his
mother a notable singer. When the father
moved to the post of leader of the Leipzig
Gewandhaus Orch., the family came in contact
with F. Busoni and many equally famous
personages in the world of music of the time. P
studied with T. Carreño from the age of 3 and
was also tutored in organ-playing and the violin
(Busoni composed a set of *Bagatelles* for violin
and pf for, and dedicated to, his young friend),
performing in orchestras and in his father's
quartet. He finally decided to concentrate on
the pf and studied successively with R.
Buchmayer, F. A. Draeseke and Busoni, and
worked on composition with Hermann
Kretzschmar. Undoubtedly the greatest
musical influence was Busoni, towards whom
he became virtually a disciple.

He made his début in 1902 and from the
outset showed the Busoni penchant for recitals
that were long and made intellectual demands
upon his audience. Nevertheless he quickly
established a pre-eminent position and reputation among the more serious members of the
musical public. He was a virtuoso, a consummate technician and musician.

In 1905 he spent a year in Manchester as pf
teacher in succession to W. Backhaus at the R.
Coll. of Music there, but left because the post
interfered with his concert career. He took
another teaching position at Basle Cons. later
and accepted a professorship at Berlin Hochschule, which he held 1921–6. He also later
taught in Poland.

In 1923 he visited the USSR, and it is
claimed he was the first soloist from the West to
visit that country after the Revolution. He
toured the USSR a number of times thereafter.
His US début was in 1932, and his concert
career on both sides of the Atlantic continued
until 1940 when he decided to settle in the
USA. He taught at Malkan Cons., Cornell
Univ. and Mills Coll., California, while continuing to give recitals, making occasional

return visits to Europe. His last recital was
given in 1960 at the ripe age of 79. Recordings
of his art at an advanced age show no diminu-
tion of his powers. As a recitalist he always
seemed possessed of an energy unmatched
today, thinking nothing of resuming his seat at
the end of a long programme as advertised and
playing by way of an encore item a late
Beethoven sonata or all 24 preludes of Chopin!

In his time he championed much unfamiliar
music by great technicians of formidable
intellect like Alkan, Busoni and Medtner.
With his mentor Busoni he made a monumental edition of Bach's keyboard works
amounting to 25 volumes in the Breitkopf &
Härtel edition. He also prepared cadenzas for
Mozart concertos and transcribed Busoni's
five-movement pf concerto for two pfs. Among
his own compositions is a *Konzertstück* for pf
and orch. which he performed in London in
1906. Recorded *HMV*, *Columbia*, Westminster, dell'Arte and others.

Pupils included: Luc Balmer, Victor Buesst,
William Busch, Joseph Cooper, Gordon
Green, Franz Hirt, Jan Hoffman, Leonard
Isaacs, Eugene Istomin, Grant Johannesen,
Gunnar Johansen, Ernst Levy, Charles
Lynch, John Ogdon, Alan Rawsthorne, Anton
Rudnytsky, Roman Rudnytsky, Verdina
Shlonsky, Ruth Slenczynska, Karol Szreter,
Norman Tucker, Earl Wild, Alexander Zakin.

PETROV, Nikolai (1943–   )
b. USSR. Student first of Moscow Central
Music School then of Moscow Cons. His pf
teachers included A. Goldenweiser and J. Zak.
Came 2nd in Van Cliburn Comp. in USA in
1962, and 2nd in Concours Musical Int. Reine
Elisabeth, Brussels, in 1964. An important
figure in the younger school of Russian pianists
and who toured widely. Gave première of
Aram Khatchaturian's *Konzertrhapsodie* for pf
and orch. (1968). Recorded various.

PETYREK, Felix (1892–1951)
b. Brno, Czechoslovakia. Studied pf in Vienna
under L. Godowsky and E. von Sauer. Taught
in Salzburg then at Berlin Hochschule. Conducted a master-class in Athens 1926–30 before
returning to Germany to work in Stuttgart.
Composed chamber music, pf works and
songs.

PETZET, Walter (1866–1941)
b. Breslau, Germany. Studied in Augsburg
and Munich. Moved to the USA in 1887, per-

forming and teaching, first in Minneapolis then later at the Scharwenka School in New York. In 1896 was appointed prof. at Helsinki in succession to F. Busoni. Returned to Germany at the end of the century, filling several posts. His output included pf works and two concertos.

PFEIFFER, Theodor (1853–1936)
b. Heidelberg, Germany. Pupil of Stuttgart Cons. and later of H. von Bülow. For ten years from 1889 taught privately in Baden, then, from 1899, at Mannheim Cons. Composed studies and pf pieces that once had a vogue. Wrote his recollections of H. von Bülow (1894).

PFITZNER, Hans (1869–1949)
b. Moscow, Russia, of German parentage. Family returned to Frankfurt when he was young. Studied at Hoch's Cons. from 1886 under J. Kwast, whose daughter he married at the turn of the century. Taught pf at Coblenz Cons. 1892–3, and during the latter year gave a concert of own works in Berlin. Became composer, conductor and teacher of composition. Composed a pf concerto and many songs. Appeared as accompanist in song recitals featuring his works. Recorded *Polydor* as conductor and accompanist.

PFLUGHAUPT, Robert (1833–71)
b. Berlin, Germany. Studied there, and later was a pupil of A. Henselt and F. Liszt. A concert pianist of brilliance whose early death ended a promising career. Composed facile pf pieces. Married Sophie P (*née* Shchepin, 1837–67, b. Dvinsk, Russia) who also studied with Henselt and Liszt and was a noted concert artist of the day.

PHILÉAS, Roy (1857–1939)
b. Montreal, Canada. Studied pf with C. Lavallée. Settled in New York 1899, performed and taught at New York Coll. of Music.

PHILIPP, Isidore (1863–1958)
b. Pest, Hungary. Was taken to Paris at the age of 3; studied at the Cons. there under G. Mathias, winning 1st Pf Prize in 1883. Became celebrated pf teacher, made many tours solo, with orch. and in chamber music throughout Europe and USA. Became naturalized French citizen. Appointed pf prof. at Paris Cons. 1903. Wrote textbooks on the instrument, composed much pf music including a concerto

for three pfs without orch. Also made transcriptions and edited. Settled in USA 1940, teaching actively there and in Canada up to 1955, when he gave farewell concert in New York. Undoubtedly one of the great teachers of pf of this century. Edited works of Debussy, Fauré, Kabalevsky, MacDowell and Rachmaninov for Int. Music Co.
Pupils included: Jef Alpaerts, Kenneth Amada, Stell Andersen, Henry Bellman, M. de la Bruchollerie, Dinora de Carvalho, Sergei Conus, Volga Cossack, Jeanne-Marie Darré, Henri Deering, Ania Dorfmann, Maurice Dumesnil, Sixten Eckerberg, Ulvi Erkil, Felix Fox, Jean Français, Norman Fraser, Noël Gallon, Margaret Grummitt, Youra Güller, John Kirkpatrick, Fernando Laires, João de Souza Lima, Nikita Magaloff, Colin McPhee, Federico Mompou, Genia Nemenoff, Guiomar Novaës, Emil Oberhoffer, Octavio Pinto, Morris Ruger, Phyllis Sellick, Ruth Slenczynska, Reginald Stewart, Soulima Stravinsky, Louise Talma, Alexander Tcherepnin, Madeleine de Valmaléte, Beveridge Webster, Victor Young.

PHILLIPS, Donald (1919–)
b. London, UK. Studied music there and made a career as composer, pianist and accompanist in light music, many numbers of which were published.

PHILLIPS, Jean (1942–)
b. London, UK. Studied at R. Coll. of Music, London. Début 1965 London. Performed throughout UK, with emphasis on teaching children. Won several prizes. Lectured on pf and harpsichord.

PIAGGIO, Celestino (1886–1931)
b. Concordia, Argentina. Pupil of J. Aguirre and of A. Williams at Buenos Aires Cons. In 1908 won scholarship to study in Paris. During World War I he lived and worked in Romania as concert pianist and conductor, returning home in 1921, teaching and performing. Composed pf works in classical style, also a few songs.

PIAZZINI, Edmundo (1857–1927)
b. Miscaglia, Milan, Italy. Student of Milan Cons. and under C. Angeleri, V. Appiani and G. Andreoli. Obtained diploma following splendid performances of a series of pf concertos and toured until 1878 when he went to Buenos Aires. There he performed and

founded the Sociedad del Cuarteto; also, in 1904, the pf Cons. Thibaud-Piazzini, his partner being Alfonso Thibaud. Composed pf pieces and songs, and prepared a pf method. Retired 1921.

PICK-MANGIAGALLI, Riccardo (1882–1949)
b. Strakonice, Czechoslovakia, of Czech–Italian parentage. Studied at Milan Cons. and began his career as a concert pianist before he started composing. Succeeded Pizzetti in 1936 as head of Milan Cons. Brilliant pianist who composed in most genres: for pf and orch. a *Humoresque*, Op. 35, also *Sortilegi*, Op. 39, described as a symphonic poem. Solos include the two *Lunaires*, Op. 33, of which the second, a scherzo, *La Danza di Olaf*, is occasionally heard.

PIERNÉ, Gabriel (1863–1937)
b. Metz, France. Pupil of Paris Cons. and of A. Marmontel for pf, taking 1st Prize for playing in 1879. Subsequently concentrated on conducting, composing and teaching. Composed in most genres including a pf concerto and a *Fantaisie-Ballet* for same, chamber music and pf pieces including a large-scale set of *Variations in C minor*, Op. 42. Recorded *Columbia*.

PIGGOTT, Audrey (1906–)
b. London, UK. Studied at R. Coll. of Music, London, and in Paris. Had equal facility with pf and cello and was well known in UK, Europe and Canada, in which country she took up residence in 1947. A noted chamber-music player.

PIMSLEUR, Solomon (1900–1962)
b. Paris, France. Family settled in USA in 1903 where his musical education culminated at Columbia Univ. Pupil of R. Goldmark. All-round musician who made many pf recital tours. Composed much chamber music with pf parts, as well as solo works.

PINELLI, Oreste (1844–1924)
b. Rome, Italy. Pf prof. at R. Liceo S. Cecilia, Rome, for many years.

PINNER, Max (1851–87)
b. New York, USA. Studied at Leipzig Cons. 1865–7, then in Berlin with K. Tausig. After touring as concert pianist settled in New York ten years before his death.

PINSONNEAULT, Bernard (1930–)
b. Montreal, Canada. Studied there, and in UK with A. Alexander, J. Isserlis and N. Medtner. Toured as soloist, accompanist and lecturer. Specialist on Medtner's music.

PINSUTI, Ciro (1829–88)
b. Sinalunga, Italy. Pupil of his father; a child prodigy. Studied pf in UK with C. Potter, returning home in 1845 and studying with Rossini while assistant pf teacher. Settled in Newcastle, UK, 1848 and began career as singing teacher as well as organizing concerts. Became prof. of singing at R. Acad., London, in 1856. Rest of career spent between UK and Italy.

PINTO, Octavio (1890–1950)
b. São Paolo, Brazil. Studied pf with I. Philipp and married Guiomar Novaës who also was a pupil of Philipp. Wrote pf miniatures mainly for children.

PIRANI, Eugenio (1852–1939)
b. Bologna, Italy. Studied at Liceo there and at Kullak's Acad. in Berlin, where he later taught in addition to performing throughout Europe. Settled for a time in Germany in the roles of teacher and musical correspondent. In 1905 founded a school in New York with the singer Alma Powell, later returning to Berlin where he died.

PIRANI, Max (1898–1975)
b. Melbourne, Australia. Won scholarship to study at the Cons. there. Went to UK in 1911 for a couple of years, then to New York. Served back home with Australian forces during World War I, was demobilized there and performed until 1920 when he returned to UK. Formed the Pirani Pf Trio which was successful for many years. In 1925 was appointed to R. Acad., London. Was Head of Music, Banff School, Alberta, 1941–7, and founded Music Teachers' Coll., Ontario, 1945. Returned to UK 1948 and resumed teaching career. Recorded *Columbia*.
  Pupils included: Peter Cowderoy, Richard Markham.

PIRNER, Gitti (1943–)
b. Immenstadt, Germany. Pupil of Munich Cons. and of E. Then-Bergh, later of W. Kempff. Début 1950 Augsburg. Performed throughout Europe and made cadenzas to Mozart concertos.

PISHNA, Johann (1826–96)
b. Erdischowitz, Czechoslovakia. Pf student of Prague Cons. Became famous teacher there and in Moscow. Wrote important technical exercises.

PIXIS, Johann Peter (1788–1874)
b. Mannheim, Germany. Studied pf with his father and gave joint recitals with brother, who was a violinist. Settled in Paris in 1825 as pianist and teacher, moved in the Chopin–Liszt circle, wrote fantasias and variations in idiom of the times and contributed a piece to the *Hexameron* variations of Liszt. In 1845 settled in Baden-Baden, continuing his career. Dedicatee of Chopin's *Grande Fantaisie on Polish Airs*, Op. 13. Appeared in UK in 1828, playing a concerto of own composition.
Pupils included: Ignace Leybach, George Osborne, Sigismund Thalberg.

PIZZETTI, Ildebrando (1880–1968)
b. Parma, Italy. Pf pupil of father before becoming student at Parma Cons. Composer, conductor, pianist, teacher and critic. Composed *Canti della stagione alta* (1933) for pf and orch., a trio, sonatas, pf pieces and songs.
Pupils included: Nicolas Flagello.

PLACHY, Wenzel (1795–1858)
b. Klopotowitz, Czechoslovakia. Studied pf in Vienna where he taught the instrument and from where he toured. A prolific composer whose works have long since been forgotten.

PLAIDY, Louis (1810–74)
b. Wermsdorf, Germany. Studied pf and violin in Dresden. After playing the violin in an orch. in Leipzig, he concentrated on the pf, developing his technique in the course of teaching. Joined the staff of Leipzig Cons. in 1843 at the invitation of Mendelssohn, remaining there until 1865. A successful teacher who returned to private tuition for his remaining years. Wrote a number of technical works.
Pupils included: John Alden, Francesco Berger, Heinrich Döring, August Gockel, Edvard Grieg, Karl von Holten, Emil Krause, Oscar Paul, William Rockstro, Ernst Rudorff, Herman Scholtz, Nicolas Wilm.

PLANTÉ, Francis (1839–1934)
b. Orthez, France. At the age of 10 entered Paris Cons. under A. Marmontel, winning 1st Prize in his first year. Became pianist in a trio with Alard and Franchomme. From 1853 to

1863 studied privately before resuming his concert career. Retired in 1900, making occasional appearances. Created for himself an image of eccentricity not unlike that enjoyed by V. de Pachmann. In 1928 made a series of electrical recordings for *French Columbia* in his home. Is known to have visited London in 1878, playing works by Mendelssohn and Liszt, and his own arrangement of Boccherini's *Minuet*. With Pachmann the only two pianists born during the lifetime of Chopin to live to make gramophone records by the electrical process.
Pupils included: Alfonso Thibaud, José Usandizaga.

PLEETH, Margaret: *see* **GOOD, Margaret.**

PLETNEV, Mikhail (1957–)
b. Archangel, USSR. Pupil of Moscow Cons. and of Y. Flier. 1st Prizewinner of the Int. Tchaikovsky Comp., Moscow, 1978. UK début following year. Concerts and recordings have elicited high praise. Made pf transcription of Tchaikovsky's *Nutcracker Suite*. Recorded Melodiya.

PLEYEL, Camille (1788–1855)
b. Strasbourg, France. Studied with his father, Ignaz P, and with J. Dussek. Married the concert pianist Marie Moke and in 1824 took over his father's pf business. Became associated with leading pianists of the time in Paris including Chopin and Kalkbrenner and Liszt. Wrote pf works.

PLEYEL, Ignaz Joseph (1757–1831)
b. Rupperstal, Austria. Was trained as pianist, violinist and composer, studying at one time with Haydn. Resided in Paris from 1795 and formed his pf business in 1807, handing over to his son Camille in 1824. A prolific composer in diverse forms including two pf concertos and several pf sonatas, as well as one for duet.
Pupils included: Camille Pleyel.

PLEYEL, Marie-Félicité-Denise (*née* **Moke**) (1811–75)
b. Paris, France. Studied pf with H. Herz, I. Moscheles and F. Kalkbrenner. Début at 15, causing a sensation everywhere she went in the course of touring Russia, Belgium, Austria and Germany. Berlioz fell in love with her but she married Camille Pleyel, son of the founder of the French pf firm which was so intimately connected with Chopin in Paris. Dedicatee of

the latter's *Nocturnes* Op. 9. Visited the UK in 1846 and played Weber's *Concertstück* at a Phil. Soc. concert. Taught at Brussels Cons. from 1848 until her death.

PLOWRIGHT, Jonathan (1959–)
b. Doncaster, UK. Studied pf from the age of 5, gaining his first scholarship at the age of 13. Pupil of F. Wibaut in Birmingham before attending the R. Acad. in London under A. Kelly, where he won a number of awards and scholarships, one of which provided studies in the USA from 1983 at the Peabody Inst. under Julio Esteban. Awarded 1st Prize the same year in the R. Overseas League Music Festival.

POGORELICH, Ivo (1958–)
b. Belgrade, Yugoslavia. Studied there before spending eleven years in Moscow. Prizewinner in pf competitions in Yugoslavia and Italy before winning the Montreal Int. Comp. in 1980, having already toured in Europe, the USSR and the USA. Entered the Int. Chopin Comp. in Warsaw in 1980 and was received by the audience like some pop star. His elimination in the third round caused a furore and the resignation of one member of the jury. In the event obtained more publicity perhaps than if he had won, for it led to escalating record sales and additional concerts in 1981 including his London début. Of his competitive performance in Warsaw the *New York Times* critic said: 'He ignored the score and did everything wrong. Except for one thing: he is clearly a genius.'

POHLIG, Karl (1864–1928)
b. Teplitz, Czechoslovakia. Pupil of F. Liszt and made concert tour of Europe before becoming *Kapellmeister* at Graz, when he turned to the baton.

POISOT, Charles Émile (1822–1904)
b. Dijon, France. Pupil of L. Adam and S. Thalberg in Paris, where he remained active 1850–68 as pianist and teacher. In 1868 founded Dijon Music School. Wrote works on technique, also a *History of Music in France*.

POLDINI, Eduard (1869–1957)
b. Budapest, Hungary. Pupil of Cons. there and studied pf later with J. Epstein in Vienna. Wrote many salon pieces, some of which, like *Poupée valsante*, achieved remarkable popularity.

POLDOWSKI (1879–1932)
b. Brussels, Belgium. Real name Irene Regine Wieniawska, daughter of Henryk Wieniawski, the Polish violinist-composer. Studied composition with Gevaert in Brussels and with Percy Pitt in London, and pf with M. Hambourg. Married Sir Aubrey Dean Paul and later studied with d'Indy in Paris. Composed a work for pf and orch., chamber music, a pf suite and songs.

POLLACK, Daniel (1935–)
b. Los Angeles, USA. Child prodigy, later studying with E. Leginska. Début 1942 Los Angeles. Went on to study with R. Lhevinne at Juilliard School, winning prizes. New York début 1957. Later studied in Europe with W. Kempff. Won 8th place in the Tchaikovsky Pf Comp., Moscow, 1958. Toured USSR before returning to USA to resume concert career. Recorded Columbia.

POLLINI, Francesco Giuseppe (1763–1846)
b. Laibach, Austria. Studied music with W. A. Mozart in Vienna (not positively known if it included pf), then later in Milan with N. Zingarelli. Settled in Milan as pf teacher and composer, and was made pf prof. when Milan Cons. began in 1809. Composed for the instrument, and it is claimed he was the first to use three staves. Dedicatee of Bellini's *La Sonnambula*.

POLLINI, Maurizio (1942–)
b. Milan, Italy. Pupil of the Cons. there, receiving a diploma for pf playing in 1959, having the previous year entered the Int. Comp. for Musical Performers at Geneva in which he shared 2nd place for male contestants with Ronald Turini. Was a pupil of A. B. Michelangeli and won 1st Prize in the Chopin Pf Comp. in Warsaw in 1960, being the youngest contestant that year. Among the jurors was A. Rubinstein, who declared that technically Pollini already played better than any of the jury. He rapidly attained the top rank of his profession, possessing formidable technique and intellect – so much so that, as time went on, his playing became magisterial. As one London critic wrote in 1979: 'Two hours in the company of Pollini can prove almost as demanding on the listener's attention as they are on the pianist's technique.' His repertoire ranged through the Classics and Romantics to the contemporary scene. Luigi

Nono wrote works for him. Additionally took up conducting. Recorded DG and Philips.

POMMIER, Jean-Bernard (1944–)
b. Beziers, France. Pupil of Nat. Cons. of Paris. Has appeared worldwide and is a chamber-music artist as well as soloist. Recorded EMI.

Pupils included: Katia Labèque, Marielle Labèque.

PONCE, Manuel (1882–1948)
b. Fresnillo, Mexico. His early training was in Mexico, later studying pf with M. Krause at Stern's Cons., Berlin. In 1909 appointed pf prof. at Mexico Cons., where he founded the Mexican Composers' Soc. Later resided in Paris. Composed chamber music, a pf concerto, a pf sonata and solos using Mexican rhythms, especially the *Canciones Mexicanas* and *Cuatro Danzas Mexicanas*.

PONG, Grace (1955–)
b. Hong Kong. Studied pf there and later in New York where she made her début 1978. Has won numerous awards and has toured widely. Taught in Toronto.

PONG, Lily (1913–)
b. Hong Kong. Studied there, performed and lectured widely in Far East in universities and colleges.

PONSE, Luctor (1911–)
b. Geneva, Switzerland. Studied Valenciennes Cons., France, winning prizes for theory and pf playing. Prizewinner Geneva 1935 and Brussels 1936. Performed in Europe. US début 1948; also toured Far East same year. Taught in Netherlands from 1964. Own compositions include a pf concerto for two pfs, pf pieces and much chamber music.

PONTI, Michael (1937–)
b. Freiburg, Germany, of American parentage (father in diplomatic service). Brought up in the USA and launched a concert career on a number of European prizes including a 2nd at the Int. Musikwettbewerb in 1958, another 2nd in the Int. Pf Comp. in Geneva in 1959; 1st in the Busoni Comp., Bolzano, in 1964, and a place in the Concours Int. Reine Elisabeth in Brussels, also in 1964. Performed all over the world including the Far East. Recorded Vox, specializing in disinterring obscure romantic

concertos. Fine technique and musicianship and, presumably, a prodigious repertoire.

PORTNOV, Mischa (1901–)
b. Berlin, Germany. Pupil of Stern's Cons. there; later at Stockholm Acad. Toured with violinist brother Vassili P before settling in New York as composer-teacher. Wrote pf music including a pf concerto which was premièred by the New York PO 1941.

POSTNIKOVA, Victoria (–)
Last known agents had no information to offer when approached.

POSTON, Elizabeth (1905–)
b. Highfield, UK. Student of R. Coll., London, and of H. Samuel for pf. Composed chamber music, songs and other works, and worked for the BBC.

POTTER. (Philip) Cipriani (Hambly) (1792–1871)
b. London, UK. Trained in pf and composition there before studying with J. Wolf in Vienna, where he also received help and friendship from Beethoven. Taught pf at the R. Acad., London, from 1822, becoming Principal ten years later. Gave British premières at (R.) Phil. Soc. concerts of Beethoven's 3rd and 4th concertos in 1824 and 1825 respectively. Robert Schumann described him as 'a master'. Composed a set of pf *études* and other pieces.

Pupils included: Sir William Cusins, Jane Dorrell, William Dorrell, Walter Macfarren, Sebastian Mills, Thomas Mudie, Ciro Pinsuti Charles Stephens, Robert Thomas, Agnes Zimmermann.

POUGNET, Rene (1911–)
b. London, UK. Pf pupil of M. Verne and T. Matthay. Had successful career in light music and in films. Compositions included a *Rhapsody* for pf and orch.

POUISHNOV, Lev (1891–1958)
b. Tiflis, Russia. Studied pf under A. Essipova at St Petersburg Cons. (also with Liadov, Rimsky-Korsakov and Glazounov for composition), where he gained the Gold Medal and the Rubinstein prize on graduation in 1910. Assumed career as concert pianist while becoming pf prof. at Tiflis for three years. Settled in UK after the Russian revolution; début Wigmore Hall 1921. Established reputa-

tion in five recitals there followed by 'mystery' radio broadcast as a stand-in at short notice. Toured Europe regularly, also USA from 1923. Gave entire Chopin repertoire in London in 1926 in seven recitals which were fated to coincide with the General Strike. Did much to propagate pf music of Rachmaninov, giving the première of 4th pf concerto in Liverpool and in London and elsewhere. Made first recording of Schubert *Fantaisie* sonata (D.894) for *Columbia* centenary issue (1928). Was first classical pianist to televise from London 1938 (Liszt E flat concerto). Naturalized British subject 1935. Married twice, his second wife being the pianist Dorothy Hildreth, a former pupil. Recorded *Columbia*, *HMV* and Saga.

Pupils included: Erik Chisholm, Dorothy Hildreth, Anne Taylor.

POULENC, Francis (1899–1963)
b. Paris, France. Of artistic ancestry, his mother being an excellent pianist. Studied pf from the age of 5, and at 16 became a pupil of R. Viñes, who was a profound influence as teacher and mentor besides giving first performances of Francis's early works. *Rapsodie Nègre*, reflecting influences of the time as its title indicates, was heard in 1917 at the Théâtre du Vieux Columbier in Paris, where new works were performed under the auspices of Jane Barthori, a notable mezzo and active propagator of the works of Debussy, Ravel and Satie. Therefore while still a teenager P came in contact with important figures of French musical and literary circles, and when he was composing mainly pf music, of which the three short *Mouvements perpétuels* have always been popular with pianists and their public.

After service in the French Army, 1918–21, he studied composition with Charles Koechlin, from which time came the sonata for two pfs and the six songs of *Le Bestiaire*. The work of the Vieux Columbier was only one aspect of gatherings of composers and performers to study and perform, both privately and in public, post-Debussy music. Many works were to receive their première, and the movement embraced European contemporaries and was also associated with painters and writers. Out of all this activity emerged the group known as *Les Six*: Auric, Durey, Honegger, Milhaud, P and Tailleferre. In the early days the leading lights were Honegger and Milhaud. Today they are eclipsed by P.

With Milhaud he toured Austria and Italy to survey the music scene. One work stimulated by travel is the three-movement pf suite *Napoli* (1925), with its highly evocative endpiece, *Caprice italien*. Several chamber works belong to this period, also the songs *Cinq Poèmes de Ronsard*, performed in Paris in 1926 by Pierre Bernac with the composer at the pf. That was their début, and from 1935 they appeared together frequently, P accompanying many French *chansons* in Bernac's repertoire.

Deux Novelletes, the *Trois Pièces* (*Pastorale*, *Toccata* and *Hymne*) and the *Concerto Champêtre* for harpsichord (or pf) and orch., written for W. Landowska, as well as *Aubade* for dancer, pf and chamber orch., all belong to the late 1920s, the concerto being played often by the composer in concert using a pf. Important works of the 1930s are *Les Soirées de Nazelles* (a fine set of pieces for pf comprising *Préamble* and *Cadence* followed by eight portraits or variations of which Nos. 4–6 were suppressed later by the composer); *Suite Française* – a pf arrangement of a work by the same title for nine wind instruments, side-drum and harpsichord; and the concerto for two pfs and orch. which was premièred in 1932 at the Venice Festival with P and J. Février, who became much identified with the composer's music.

The important song-cycle *Tel jour telle nuit* belongs to 1937 and was performed often in public by Bernac and P along with other groups of songs from the same period. Two sets of piano pieces, *Huit Nocturnes* and *Douze Improvisations*, took a decade to complete, by which time World War II was in progress. The violin sonata received its première in 1943 in Paris with Ginette Neveu and the composer; and in the spring of 1945 a concert devoted entirely to his songs was given in Paris to his accompaniment.

With the end of the war he resumed touring abroad as composer-pianist, and in 1948 he and Bernac spent three months in the USA. He wrote a pf concerto for a return visit the following year, giving the première in Boston. It has proved less than successful. Later pf works include *Thème Varié* (each of the eleven variations uniquely entitled by a mood, e.g. *joyeuse*, *noble*, *sarcastique*, *ironique* etc), sonata for two pfs (1952–3), one for flute and pf (1947), also one for cello and pf (1940–8). He wrote pieces for film music, from one of which came an adaptation for two pfs of *L'Embarquement pour Cythère*, popular with duettists.

The music reflects his style as an instrumentalist who, although not in the virtuoso class, was nevertheless the most accomplished French composer-pianist of his age in the triple role of soloist, ensemble player and accompanist. His art has wit, vitality, freshness, elegance and an audacity in keeping with the French idiom of the time. The melodic line often seems trite, yet there is an underlying streak of romanticism capable of producing harmonies of unforgettable rich beauty. Such music, with a warmth of feeling like the Nocturne in C, has an eternal quality so that it stands apart from trends at the time of its conception.

His unmistakable style harks back to early French harpsichord composers yet reflects contemporaneous tendencies. Thus admiration for Prokofiev's pianism is mirrored in the first of the three *Intermezzi*, while the third could well have been written by Fauré. His latterday romanticism is but one perspective of a highly civilized art which never passes beyond the comprehension of the ordinary musical person. Recorded *Columbia*, *HMV*, Columbia, Vega, Aurora and CBS.

POUMAY, Juliette (1934–   )
b. Verviers, Belgium. Studied at Liège Cons., also with L. Lévy in Paris. Winner of numerous awards, toured Europe widely, also taught.

POWELL, Ioan Lloyd (1888–19   )
b. Ironbridge, UK. Studied pf from early age; later pupil of R. Coll. of Music, London, winning scholarships as well as the Hopkinson Gold Medal 1908. Went on to study with F. Busoni. Toured widely as concert pianist and also as Association Board examiner. In his concert work propagated contemporary British pf composers.

POWELL, John (1882–1963)
b. Richmond, USA. Graduate of Univ. of Virginia before becoming a pupil of T. Leschetizky in Vienna 1902–7. Début in Berlin in 1908 followed by appearances in other European capitals. US début 1912, then regular concert tours. In 1919 composed *Rhapsodie Nègre* for pf and orch. which had phenomenal success and in 1920 was included in a European tour by the New York PO under Damrosch with Powell as soloist. Wrote several pf concertos and violin sonatas; three pf sonatas of which the one called *Teutonica* was first performed in London in 1914 by B. Moiseiwitsch: also pf pieces and songs. Recorded Royal and John Powell Foundation.

POZNIAK, Bronislaw (1887–1952)
b. Lwow, Poland. Student at Cracow Cons. before becoming a pupil of K. H. Barth in Berlin. Début there 1908. Performed solo and with a pf trio he founded. Taught in Breslau and Leipzig. Wrote on musical subjects.

PRADÈRE, Louis (1781–1843)
b. Paris, France. Student of Cons. where he became pf prof. 1802. Was court pianist to Louis XVIII and Charles X, pensioned off in 1827. Wrote much music including sonatas, rondos, a pf concerto, chamber music and songs.

Pupils included: Henri Herz, Jacques Herz.

PRADHER, Louis: *see* **PRADÈRE, Louis.**

PRÄGER, Ferdinand (1815–91)
b. Leipzig, Germany. Studied pf and taught in Germany and Netherlands. In 1834 went to London, where he performed and taught, as well as contributing to *Neue Zeitschrift für Musik* at Schumann's request. Toured Europe 1851–2 and became interested in the Wagner cause. Wrote *Wagner as I knew him* (1885) which caused a furore and was withdrawn. Composed chamber music, pf pieces and songs.

PRATT, Ross (1916–   )
b. Winnipeg, Canada. Student at Quebec Cons., then R. Acad. of Music, London, where he made his début; later became pf prof. at R. Acad. and at Quebec Cons. Recorded *Decca* and York.

PRATT, Silas Gamaliel (1846–1916)
b. Addison, USA. Studied first in Chicago, then under T. Kullak in Berlin. Taught, conducted and composed thereafter. Was pf prof. at New York Metropolitan Cons. 1890–1902. Composed pf pieces and songs.

PRESSLER, Menahem (1928–   )
Request to last known concert agents for biographical details met with no response.

PRESSMAN, Matvei (1870–1941)
b. Rostov, Russia. Pupil of V. Safonov at Moscow Cons., also of N. Zverev. Graduated in 1891 when he was appointed to a teaching post in Tiflis. From 1895 directed Rostov Music School. Was fellow-pupil, under Zverev, of S. Rachmaninov who dedicated his 2nd pf sonata to P.

PREVIN, André (1929–)
b. Berlin, Germany of American parentage.
Began studying there but moved with his
family to California on outbreak of World War
II. In 1945 joined MGM and proceeded to win
awards for film scores. Took up serious study
of composition and conducting, as well as
playing brilliantly as a jazz pianist. Was
appointed conductor of Houston Orch. in
1967, then, the following year, of London SO.
Continued to play pf in concertos and in works
for two pfs, and has composed pieces that span
the whole range from light to serious.
Recorded RCA, EMI, CBS and Decca.

PREYER, Karl Adolf (1863–1947)
b. Baden, Germany. Pf pupil of H. Urban and
of H. Barth in Berlin. Went to USA in 1893,
joining the teaching staff of Kansas Univ.,
where he remained.

PRICE, Florence (1888–1953)
b. Little Rock, Arkansas, USA. A coloured
pianist-composer who attended New England
Cons. and Chicago Univ., won the Wanamaker
Prize and taught in addition to a concert career
which embraced the general pf repertoire as
well as her own compositions which included a
pf concerto, pf quintet, a *Rhapsody* for pf and
orch. etc.
    Pupils included: Margaret Bond.

PROENÇA, Miguel (–   )
b. Rio Grande, Brazil. Studied successively at
the Kollischer Cons., Montevideo, and
through scholarships in Rio and in Germany.
Performed in S. America and Europe both solo
and in chamber music with leading associates.
Pf prof. at the Cons. in Rio as well as other
official posts. Recorded the set of 16 *Cirandas*
by Villa-Lobos and the complete pf works of
Lorenzo Fernandez on Brazilian labels.

PROHASKA, Karl (1869–1927)
b. Mödling, Austria. Studied in Vienna, then
with E. d'Albert in Berlin. Taught subsequently at Strasbourg Cons., then, after a spell
as conductor in Warsaw, went in 1908 to
Vienna as pf prof. Compositions include
chamber music and songs.

PROKOFIEV, Sergei Sergeievich
(1891–1953)
b. Sontzovka, Ukraine. His mother played the
pf, and he showed musical promise from a very
early age. When he was 10 he was examined at

Moscow Cons. by Taneyev who mapped out
his musical instruction, beginning with study
under Glière. Already the boy was composing
juvenile works, of which nothing prior to 1907
seems to have survived. In 1904 it was decided
he should go to St Petersburg Cons. under
Rimsky-Korsakov. The discipline of learning
proved irksome to his spirited and impulsive
nature. When Miaskovsky examined students'
work, including some of P's, he said he had not
realized what a viper the Cons. was nursing in
its bosom. The teachers were more than a little
afraid of his precocity.
    He played the pf in public for the first time in
1908, including the original version of *Suggestion diabolique*. About that time he became a
pupil of A. Essipova, who set herself the task of
trying to rectify early defects of his technique.
In 1912 his first pf sonata was published and he
also gave the première of his first pf concerto.
Next year the 2nd concerto was completed and
performed. The score later became lost or destroyed, and the composer re-wrote it in 1923,
in which form it is probably far more mature
than the original. *Sarcasmes* for pf solo belong
to this period, which was neatly rounded off in
1914 when he won the Rubinstein Prize.
    In 1914 also he met Diaghilev for whom he
was to begin writing music for the stage.
During the war years he played, composed and
conducted, while his mercurial temperament
made some enemies. He fled St Petersburg as
the Russian armies disintegrated and the
Revolution began. He sold compositions to
Sergei Koussevitzky to raise money to travel to
the USA via the eastern route.
    New York audiences and critics did not
enjoy his pf playing, which must have sounded
too fierce and vigorous to their ears. His repertoire was confined almost entirely to his own
works and so, unlike Rachmaninov, he presented only one facet of his pianism. It is
probable that, able player though he appeared,
he never quite rid himself of boyhood technical
defects which unconsciously became an
integral part of his compositional style. One
virtue of that style was unflagging rhythm.
Poulenc said that P 'had a nervous power like
steel, so that on a level with the keys he was
capable of producing sonority of fantastic
strength and intensity, and in addition the
tempo never, never varied'; an opinion fully
borne out by his recording of the 3rd concerto.
    In 1920 he visited Paris to meet Diaghilev
again, and his life was thereafter, until 1933,
spent between the USA and Paris. His 3rd

Nicolas Medtner

Gerald Moore

Hephzibah Menuhin – a family portrait

Adela Verne

Rosalyn Tureck

Leff Pouishnov

Maurice Ravel

Sergei Rachmaninov in consultation with Eugene Ormandy, 1939

Anton Rubinstein

Arthur Rubinstein

Camille Saint-Saëns

Alexander Scriabin; drawing by Myrrha Bantock

Artur Schnabel with his wife

Klara Schumann

Sigismund Thalberg

Solomon

Yitkin Seow

Earl Wild

Maurizio Pollini

Krystian Zimerman

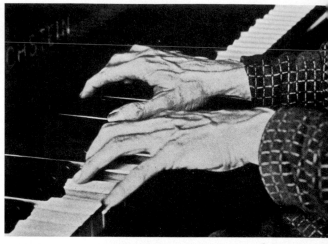
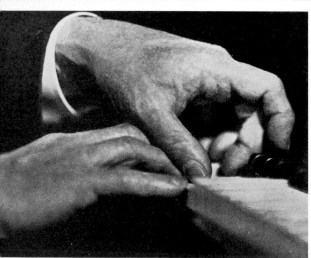
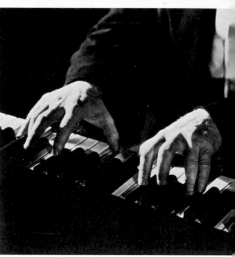

Hands: (*top left*) Wilhelm Backhaus; (*top right*) Ferruccio Busoni; (*above left*) Frederick Lamond; (*above right*) Ignace Paderewski; (*below left*) Sergei Rachmaninov; (*below right*) Artur Schnabel

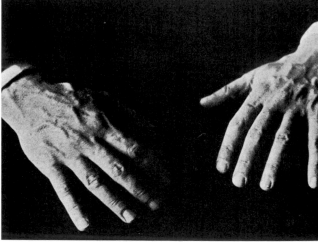

concerto, the most popular, had its première in Chicago in 1921. He toured Europe and America playing with orchestras and giving solo recitals. Fame and genuine appreciation overcame the image of an *enfant terrible*, and by 1925 he was able to undertake a coast-to-coast tour of the USA when, in addition to recitals and concerto performances, he accompanied his first wife, the singer Lina P.

Two years later the exile returned to visit the USSR. Everywhere he was received with friendship and enthusiasm, but he was not ready to settle: he went back to France and the Diaghilev environment. His 4th symphony was performed in Boston in 1930, and he was also commissioned to write a concerto for the left hand for Paul Wittgenstein – who on its completion refused to have anything to do with it. This ill-starred work, fourth of its *genre*, remained unperformed until after the composer's death, when it was premièred in Berlin in 1956. In 1932 he gave recitals in London and played his 3rd concerto, which he recorded under the baton of Piero Coppola. At the time a London critic wrote of his music: 'No doubt ignorance of it explains much of the puzzled, and puzzling writing we see in his music, crediting him in general with a desire to play the *enfant terrible*.' It was a viewpoint that endured virtually all his days, aided by the steely glitter surrounding his music and pf-playing. (Fifty years on, it has lost the initial novelty.) The same year (1932) saw the production of the 5th concerto in which, typical of his time, he introduced a jazz element with no discernible greater success than his contemporaries.

In 1933 he returned for good to the USSR, continuing to follow his creative muse despite official criticism and a final public recantation. He employed his time on all manner of new creations as well as actively participating in concerts, and had come to enjoy the status of a senior composer. In 1944 he was awarded the Gold Medal of London's R. Phil. Soc. At the beginning of the following year he conducted the première of his 5th symphony and shortly afterwards was stricken by complications following a heart attack that eventually proved fatal.

His compositions include five concertos and nine sonatas for pf, many pieces including the famous *Toccata* of 1912, *Sarcasmes*, *Visions fugitives*; also arrangements from the stage works *Romeo and Juliet*, *Love for* (or *of the*) *Three Oranges* and *Cinderella*. Among chamber works are two sonatas for violin and pf, one for cello and pf, and one for flute and pf. There are twelve groups of songs with pf accompaniment. Wrote own memoirs *Prokofiev by Prokofiev* (published Moscow; English trans. New York 1979). Recorded *HMV*.

PROKSCH, Josef (1794–1864)
b. Reichenberg, Czechoslovakia. Concert pianist and teacher who became blind at 13 but nevertheless developed technique through the system of Logier (q.v.) then being introduced into Germany. Founded own pf academy in 1830. As a composer he produced a concerto for three pfs, and a sonata; also transcribed orch. works for up to eight pfs for performance by pupils. The Acad. was continued by his descendants until the 1930s.
Pupils included: Katharina Kolař, Bedřich Smetana.

PROSNIZ, Adolf (1829–1917)
b. Prague, Czechoslovakia. Studied music there and was a pf pupil of J. Tomáschek. For over thirty years was pf prof. at Vienna Cons., living on in that capital in retirement for 17 years.

PROUT, Ebenezer (1835–1909)
b. Oundle, UK. Pf studies included a period with C. Salaman. Became pf prof. at Crystal Palace School of Art, later of Guildhall School. Conductor, lecturer and theoretical writer on all manner of musical subjects whose books were for long indispensable. Composed for pf, mainly in chamber works. A son, Louis Beethoven P (1864–19), was born London, taught by father and became pianist and teacher, following in father's footsteps to Crystal Palace School and in writing theoretical works.
Pupils included: Louis Prout, Herbert Sharpe.

PRUCKNER, Dionys (1834–96)
b. Munich, Germany. Début Leipzig 1851; later had lessons from F. Liszt. Performed and taught first in Vienna, later in Stuttgart. Appointed prof. 1868. Edited the pf works of Field and Hummel for the Stuttgart publisher Cotta.
Pupils included: Henry Lang.

PRUDENT, Émile Racine Gautier (1817–63)
b. Angoulême, France. Pupil at Paris Cons. under P. Zimmerman for pf and won 1st Prize

in 1833. Is said to have emulated Thalberg in style and enjoyed high regard for the technical polish of his performances. Made several successful tours of Europe as well as UK, taught in Paris and composed efficient but not over-inspired works.

PRÜWER, Julius (1874–1943)
b. Vienna, Austria. Studied pf there under A. Friedheim and later M. Rosenthal. Took up conducting under H. Richter.

PRYOR, Gwynneth Ruth (1941–   )
b. Sydney, Australia. Student at New South Wales State Cons. and later at R. Coll. of Music, London, winning the Hopkinson Gold Medal and Norris Prize in 1963. Début London 1965. Settled in UK and toured Europe, the Americas and Australasia solo and with orch. Taught at Morley Coll. and R. Coll. of Music. Chamber-music player; recorded various labels.

PUCHALSKI, Vladimir (1848–1933)
b. Minsk, Russia. Student of St Petersburg Cons. under T. Leschetizky for pf. Was appointed to teaching staff there on graduation. Became Director of Music School, Kiev, from 1876. The name is still to be found in albums of Russian salon pf music.
Pupils included: Julius Isserlis. N. Tutkovski.

PUCHAT, Max (1859–1919)
b. Breslau, Germany. Student of F. Kiel in Berlin where he won the Mendelssohn Prize in 1884. Took up role of teaching with conducting additionally. From 1910 ran own school in Breslau.

PUDDICOMBE, Henry (1870–1953)
b. London, Canada. Studied in Leipzig from 1892 under M. Krause and returned to Canada where he began teaching in Ottawa in about 1896, since he was not strong enough to undertake concert tours. In 1902 he founded there the Canadian Cons. and directed it until 1937, continuing to teach privately. Date of birth uncertain to within a year.

PUEYO, Eduardo del (1905–   )
b. Saragossa, Spain. Pf student of R. Cons., Madrid. Pf prof. at Brussels Cons. and toured as concert pianist.
Pupils included: Steven de Groote, Liliane Questel.

PUGNO, Raoul (1852–1914)
b. Montrouge, France. Showed precocious aptitude for the pf from early childhood, obtaining a scholarship at École Niedermeyer. From 1866 to 1869 studied at Paris Cons. under G. Mathias, winning 1st Prize. In 1893 he played at a Cons. concert and caused a sensation by the delicacy, fire and power of his playing. Immediately became a prof. at the Cons. and rapidly established a fine reputation as a pianist throughout Europe and America. Appeared six times at London Phil. Soc. concerts early this century before World War I, playing only one French work, the rest being by Mozart, Beethoven, Mendelssohn, Grieg and Rachmaninov. Also gave duo recitals with artists like Ysaÿe and Kreisler. Responsible for the Universal edition of Chopin, and dedicatee of Saint-Saëns' *Étude*, Op. 111/6 (the famous *Toccata*).
Pupils included: André Benoist, Camille Decreus, Ernst Levy, Germaine Schnitzer, Evelyn Suart, Andrée Vaurabourg, Julius Wolfsohn.

PURGOLD, Nadezhda Nikolaievna (1848–1919)
b. St Petersburg, Russia. Pf pupil of A. Rubinstein. Married Rimsky-Korsakov. Successful concert artist in own right who also made numerous pf arrangements of Russian orch. works, including those of her husband.

PYCHOWSKI, Jan (1818–1900)
b. Grazen, Czechoslovakia. Pf pupil of J. Tomásek at Prague Cons. After performing in Central Europe, toured USA in 1850 and decided to settle there. Composed chamber music and songs.

QUAILE, Elizabeth (1874–1951)
b. Omagh, Ireland. Educated in New York where she subsequently taught before undertaking further study in Paris with H. Bauer. Stayed on as his assistant. In 1921 co-founded the Diller-Quaile School in New York.

QUAILE, Leo (1918–   )
b. Pretoria, S. Africa. Pupil of father, later of Isadore Epstein. Won scholarship to R. Coll., London, studying pf under H. Fryer (also C. Lambert for conducting and G. Jacob for composition). Winner Hopkinson Gold Medal 1946. Later turned to conducting and in 1960 went back to S. Africa as prof. Compositions include a pf trio and songs.

QUEFFÉLEC, Anne Tita (1948–   )
b. Paris, France. Pf student at Paris Cons. under L. Gousseau, where she obtained 1st Prize for pf-playing in 1965 with another similar prize a year later for ensemble-playing. Winner of prizes in Munich (1968) and Leeds (1969). Has toured Europe, USA and Far East. Recorded Erato.

QUESTEL, Liliane (1951–   )
b. Haiti. Studied at Brussels R. Cons. and Peabody Cons., Baltimore. Teachers included E. del Pueyo and L. Fleischer.

QUIDANT, Alfred (1815–93)
b. Lyons, France. Studied there and at Paris Cons. Became renowned concert pianist of his day and composed pf pieces and songs.

QUINEY, Enid (1928–   )
b. London, UK. Pupil of R. Acad. there. Concert pianist, accompanist and lecturer; also harpist.

RAAD, Virginia (1925–   )
b. Salem, USA. Pupil at N. England Cons. and later of École Normale, Paris. Concert pianist, teacher, lecturer and writer.

RABCEWICZ, Sofia (1870–1947)
b. Poland. Believed to have studied with Anton Rubinstein, graduating from St Petersburg Cons. 1890. Début same year. Performed only in eastern Europe and made few public appearances after her marriage.

RABES, Lennart (1938–   )
b. Eskilstuna, Sweden. Studied in Stockholm, then with B. Siki in Zurich, M. Tagliaferro in Paris, and L. Kentner in London. Concert pianist and conductor who has toured Europe.

RABINOVICH, David (1900–   )
b. Kharkov, Russia. Student of St Petersburg Cons. and pupil of A. Essipova. Début there 1913 and continued studies with C. Igumnov. Graduated at age of 30 and later turned from career of pianist to musicology.

RABINOVICH, Max (1891–   )
b. Libau, Russia. Student of St Petersburg Cons., principal pf teacher A. Essipova. Graduated 1913 and commenced concert touring. After Revolution emigrated to USA, where he became distinguished accompanist to celebrity artists.

RACHLEW, Anders (1882–1970)
b. Drammen, Norway. Studied pf in Scandinavia, then with X. Scharwenka and T. Carreño in Berlin. Toured extensively, especially Scandinavia, and taught pf in Copenhagen. Composed pf works, chamber music and songs.

RACHMANINOV, Sergei Vasilyevich (1873–1943)
b. Oneg, Novgorod, Russia. Of a musical family, his grandfather having studied pf with J. Field. Attended St Petersburg Cons. from the age of 10, and developed his skill as a pianist while non-musical subjects were neglected. On the advice of A. Siloti he became a pupil of Zverev at Moscow Cons., rapidly turning into a brilliant pupil. He became well acquainted with Tchaikovsky's music, which he loved, as well as with the music of the Russian Orthodox Church, which exerted an abiding influence upon his life and creative output. At the age of 13 he played before Anton Rubinstein in company with leading pupils. In return the celebrated composer-pianist gave a short recital, and his playing left an indelible impression on the young musicians present.

At Moscow Cons. R studied harmony with Arensky, counterpoint with Taneyev and advanced pf-playing with Siloti, a distinguished prof. then teaching at the Cons.; in 1891 he received a Gold Medal. A year later he won the composition award with the opera *Aleko* which was performed at the Bolshoi Theatre the same year. He had already made his pf début in Moscow in a movement of the Rubinstein 4th concerto and solos of his own composition. Later that year the deaths of Zverev and Tchaikovsky occurred, both of them friends and mentors. His trio Op. 9 is dedicated to the memory of Tchaikovsky, whose passing he especially mourned deeply.

Until World War I he was as well-known as a conductor of opera and concerts as he was for playing the pf. and although, after exiling himself from Russia in 1917, he rarely took up the baton, recordings of his own works, notably the 3rd symphony, prove that, had he not become the greatest pianist-composer of his generation, he could have been a celebrated conductor.

His London début in the three roles occurred at a R. Phil. Soc. concert in 1899, by which time his *Prelude* was already famous worldwide. Most of his mature compositions came between then and 1914, including the C minor concerto first performed in 1901. He married in 1902 and lived in Dresden 1906–9, occupying much of his time with composition, the rest in performing throughout Europe, having appeared in Paris in 1906 in the triple role in Diaghilev's impressive season of Russian music.

He first toured the USA in 1909 and, with the New York SO under Walter Damrosch, premièred his D minor concerto, dedicated to J. Hofmann. At the end of the tour which kept him busy and tired, and having suffered adverse criticism over the new concerto, while turning down all offers for the following season including the baton of the Boston SO, he returned to Russia.

In 1917 he gave his last concerts in his mother country, revised a student work, the 1st pf concerto, then accepted an offer of ten engagements in Scandinavia. That assignment completed, he and his family turned their backs on Russia for ever and sailed from Oslo to the USA, where he settled in New York to earn his living in a new career as touring virtuoso in the western world. Only seven opus numbers were to be added to the list between that time and his death twenty-six years later. The strain of maintaining first position among pianists fully taxed the mental and physical powers of this melancholy perfectionist. In the period up to 1939 his year was organized on the basis of three seasons of touring: autumn and winter in the USA, with the spring in Europe, leaving the summer for recuperation and a little composition. From 1931 until 1939 the family spent the summers at Lake Lucerne at a villa which he had had built. There, in 1934, he composed his immediately successful work for pf and orch., the brilliant *Rhapsody on a theme of Paganini*, Op. 43. After 1939 his activities were of necessity confined to the USA, and in 1942, in addition to having a home in New York, he rented a property in Hollywood, where he died the following year just as, ironically, it seemed likely that the Soviet Government was ready to offer complete rehabilitation to its musical son in exile.

In his lifetime his works – the *Prelude* aside – as a whole enjoyed rather less popularity than they do today. The 2nd concerto, always appreciated by players and audiences, was a regular feature of the concert repertoire, while the 3rd appealed more to the serious musician but is now heard as frequently as the resplendent 2nd. The 1st, an Op. 1 revised in 1917, began to attract attention in the late 1930s. Perhaps the success story of the *Rhapsody* caused pianists to look for yet another work for pf and orch. from the same stable. At one time the morose and restless 4th seemed completely moribund. New York critics disliked it when the composer performed it there for the first time in 1927, and it met with similar displeasure when Pouishnov introduced it in Britain the same year.

Today his stock has never been higher, because the ordinary music-lover derives pleasure from the bitter-sweet elements of his rich melodies wrapped around with opulent sound – sound which reflects no other influence than that of Tchaikovsky (and who better to follow?), as well as the indelible hallmark of a strong, if sad, personality. There is strength and nobility, two qualities that always abounded in R's pf-playing.

At the keyboard everything he essayed went through the alchemy of a keenly analytical mind, so that a powerful and highly individual style was brought to bear upon a Beethoven sonata or Chopin scherzo. For the time being, the noble logic of his interpretation compelled the listener to accept the performance as gospel truth. Yet rarely did he give the impression that he was enjoying his task; perhaps it was because he had to undergo the added ordeal of playing to an audience containing the cream of his profession, there to receive a lesson from the hands of the undisputed master of the art.

The *Prelude* already referred to, the first of five pieces of Op. 3, achieved a popularity such as he could not have foreseen when, as a youth of 19, he sold the MS outright for a handful of roubles. Throughout his recital career there was a ritual, fully understood by him and the audience, that, whatever encores he gave, the *Prelude* had to come last, the signal that his recital was at an end. The renown it enjoyed during his lifetime tended to overshadow its superb qualities as the work of a teenager.

He was awarded the R. Phil. Soc. Gold Medal in London in 1932 at a Society concert in which he played his 3rd concerto under Sir Henry Wood.

His compositions for pf include four pf concertos and the *Rhapsody on a theme of Paganini*,

Op. 43, 24 *Preludes* spanning three opus numbers, two sonatas, sets of variations (one on a theme of Chopin, the other on a theme of Corelli); sets of *Moments Musicaux* and *Études-tableaux*: a sonata for cello and pf, and a pf trio; for two pfs there are two suites, and three *Symphonic Dances*, Op. 45: a number of transcriptions of a wonderful quality, and over 70 songs with sterling pf accompaniments. Recorded *Edison Bell* and *RCA Victor*.

He gave advice to many but did not teach the instrument in the accepted meaning of the phrase, and so there is no R school of playing. Those to whom he gave advice included: Gina Bachauer, Hans Ebell, Ruth Slenczynska.

RAFF, Joseph Joachim (1822–82)
b. Lachen, Switzerland. Mostly self-taught because of lack of means. Received help when Mendelssohn recommended his early compositions to Breitkopf & Härtel, who published them. H. von Bülow performed his *Koncertstück*. Visited Liszt in Weimar in 1850 who gave friendship and moral support. His works began to be performed. In 1856 settled in Wiesbaden playing, teaching and composing, in which he was prolific and popular. After his death his reputation plunged.
Pupils included: Anton Urspruch, Marie Wurm.

RAIF, Oskar (1847–99)
b. Zwolle, Netherlands. Studied locally then became pf pupil of K. Tausig. Taught at Berlin Hochschule and performed. Composed a pf concerto, chamber music and pieces.

RAJNA, Thomas (1928–)
b. Budapest, Hungary. Pupil of F. Liszt Acad. there and under S. Veress; then, from 1947, studied at R. Coll., London. Became noted exponent of Hungarian pf music, performing throughout Europe. Broadcast and has composed a pf concerto and chamber music. Recorded crd.

RALF, Eileen (1913–)
b. Perth, W. Australia. Went to UK to study at R. Acad., London. Début there 1936. Toured Europe and Commonwealth. Married the violinist Thomas Matthews.

RAN, Schulamit (1949–)
b. Tel Aviv, Israel. Studied at Mannes Coll. Début New York 1967. Taught at Chicago

Univ. from 1973. Composed works for pf and orch. as well as chamber music.

RANDEGGER, Giuseppe Aldo (1874–1946)
b. Naples, Italy. Pf student of R. Cons. there. Settled in USA where he toured as concert pianist as well as worked as Director of Atlanta Music Club 1893–7. After other teaching posts founded own school in New York. Composed chamber music and songs.
Pupils included: Paul Creston.

RANDELL, Sheila (1930–)
b. High Wycombe, UK. Studied locally and at Lucerne Cons. Début London 1947. Performed and broadcast frequently; also taught. Recorded Lyrita.

RANDOLPH, Harold (1861–1927)
b. Richmond, USA. Student of Peabody Cons. and one of the few of his generation who did not complete studies in Europe. Début Baltimore 1885 and soon became well-known concerto-player and recitalist, also gave two-pf recitals with Ernest Hutcheson. From 1898 directed Peabody Cons. with conspicuous success.

RANKI, Dezso (1951–)
b. Budapest, Hungary. Pf student at Bartók Cons. and later from 1967 at the Liszt Acad. under P. Kadosa. Winner of a number of European pf competitions and appeared in concert tours throughout Europe, America and the Far East both solo and with orch. Taught at Liszt Acad. since 1973. Recorded Hungaroton.
Pupils included: Gabor Csalog.

RAPEE, Erno (1891–1945)
b. Budapest, Hungary. Student of Acad. there and of E. von Sauer. Worked as pianist (both solo and accompanying). Went to USA 1912 and took up conducting opera, later becoming musical director of Radio City.

RAPPOLDI, Laura (*née* **Kahrer**) (1853–1925)
b. Mistelbach, Austria. Pupil of J. Dachs at Vienna Cons., then of F. Liszt, A. Henselt and H. von Bülow. In addition to her concert career she taught at Dresden Cons. until 1911 and thereafter privately.

RATH, Felix (1866–1905)
b. Cologne, Germany. Pupil of Cologne Cons. under M. Pauer and K. Reinecke. Performed

and taught pf. Composed a pf concerto, chamber music, pieces and songs.

RAUBENHEIMER, Marc (1952–84)

b. Durban, S. Africa. Studied there, making his début with the Durban SO at the age of 13. Studied later in Munich, Vienna and London and at the Juilliard School, New York. Teachers included F. Gulda and R. Lhevinne. Winner of numerous competitions including 1st Prize in the O'Shea Int. Comp. 1982. Début in London 1980, the same year in which he appeared at Carnegie Hall. Appeared in Europe, the USA, S. Africa and S. America. Killed in airplane crash at Madrid.

RAUCEA, Dario (1914–   )

b. Syracuse, Sicily. Pupil of A. Casella in Rome where he also studied pf before receiving tuition in Vienna from E. Fischer and E. von Sauer. Début 1930 followed by concert tours of Italy. After World War II toured Europe extensively and visited S. Africa. British début 1954. Besides classical repertoire was an active propagator of Italian music.

RAUCHEISEN, Michael (1889–   )

b. Rain-on-the-Lech, Germany. Began musical career as violinist and received tuition in conducting. Turned to pf and by World War I had become a most accomplished German pf accompanist, touring with artists of the calibre of Fritz Kreisler and Erna Sack. During the 1930s Telefunken issued a series of recorded accompaniments by R of selected *lieder* and songs and in groups according to soprano, tenor etc so that amateur vocalists could sing to his accompaniment, a novel extension of the 'one missing' idea. Recorded various labels as celebrity accompanist. In 1933 married the famous Hungarian coloratura soprano Maria Ivogun.

RAVEL, Maurice (1875–1937)

b. Ciboure, Pyrenees. While he was still an infant, his parents moved from the Basque country to Paris, and at the age of 7 he took pf lessons from H. Ghys. He also received lessons in composition and soon began composing, mostly for the pf. In 1889 he entered Paris Cons., and two years later, on winning a medal for his playing of a Schumann pf sonata, moved into the class of C. de Bériot. In the Cons. he met fellow-artists like Debussy, Satie, Chabrier and R. Viñes, the famous French pianist who performed signal service in

premièring so much French pf music including R's. He also took part in a students' exhibition at Salle Érard, playing a movement of a Moscheles pf concerto. Records indicate that, although he did not practise assiduously, he was able to perform well works by Chopin and Mendelssohn. He failed the examination in composition and then the pf examination in 1895, thereupon leaving the Cons. By then he had written his first compositions including *Menuet antique* and *Habañera*, the latter for two pfs and destined to appear later as the third section of *Rapsodie espagnole* for orch. of 1907.

In 1898 he returned to the Cons. to study composition with G. Fauré and was also a private pupil of André Gédalge for counterpoint and orchestration. Both teachers seem to have been of immense value to the young composer at that impressionable stage of his career, and a dictionary of earlier this century records that he owed to Gédalge his unfailing firmness in technique, and to Fauré an ability to combine respect for classical formulae with the most extraordinary liberty of invention in harmony and rhythm.

He failed to win the Prix de Rome in 1900 and again in 1901, in which latter year came the marvellous *Jeux d'eau*, premièred by Viñes along with *Pavane pour une infante défunte* which became popular with amateur pianists, although in later life its composer espied more faults than virtues in the work. Among his next compositions were a string quartet and *Sheherazade* for voice and orch. (1903); some songs, the *Sonatine* and *Miroirs* for pf, and *Introduction et Allegro* for harp with accompaniment of string quartet, flute and clarinet (1905–6). In 1908 came *Ma Mère l'Oye* – a charming set of children's pieces for four hands premièred in 1910 in Paris by Jeanne Leleu and Geneviève Durony. *Gaspard de la Nuit* was also composed in 1908. At this time, although Viñes seems to have given first performances of most of the pf solo works, R was pursuing an active career as pianist in his and other composers' works, if mainly in salon performances.

In 1911 he completed *Valses nobles et sentimentales*, dedicated to L. Aubert who gave the first performance at a Société Nationale de Musique concert of new works at which composers' identities were hidden during performance, the audience being invited to guess each at the end.

The important choreographic symphony *Daphnis et Chloé* occupied him 1909–12, together with songs and the orchestration of

Ma Mère for ballet. A pair of pf solos, *À la Manière de . . .*, in the styles of Borodin and Chabrier, came in 1913 followed next year by the pf trio.

World War I was a difficult time for R. He joined the French army and was eventually invalided out. Then, in 1917, his beloved mother died. That year he finished *Le Tombeau de Couperin*, each of the six pieces bearing a dedication to a soldier-friend who died on active service – *Toccata* (No. 6), for instance, being inscribed to the memory of the husband of M. Long who premièred the work in 1919 in Paris. By then he had embarked upon *La Valse*, the choreographic poem Diaghilev would have nothing to do with.

The war and death of his mother coincided with a change in R's outlook and habits. Composition came more sparingly, at the rate of less than one work per year. He undertook more engagements as composer-pianist and began visiting Britain, where he came to love the countryside. He appeared in Belgium and Italy, and by then concerts devoted to his own works were becoming fairly common.

In 1924 he visited Spain, playing and conducting his compositions. This was the year of *Tzigane* for violin and pf dedicated to Jelly d'Aranyi who premièred it in London, then, later that year, gave the first performance of the version with orch. The three *Chansons madécasses* for voice, flute, cello and pf, and the violin sonata belong to the same period, the sonata being first performed by Georges Enesco and Ravel in 1927. He took it to N. America the following year with Joseph Szigeti in a long tour of four months which was most successful. After the famous *Bolero* for orch. of 1928, a year in which he toured Britain and Spain playing, accompanying and conducting, his last important works, both pf concertos, belong to 1931. The one in G major was begun first, and he had every intention of introducing it with himself at the keyboard throughout Europe and possibly the USA. While working on it, however, he was commissioned by the one-armed Austrian pianist P. Wittgenstein to write one for the left hand. And so this one, in D major, was completed first and received its first performance by Wittgenstein in Vienna in November 1931, followed by repeats in other European capitals. The work was dedicated to Wittgenstein, who had exclusive rights over concert performances for five years. Without reference to the composer, he made alterations which displeased R, who later preferred J. Février in the work above all others.

Meantime, despite hard practice to try to restore his technique to concerto standard and with his health no longer capable of sustaining such a tour as he had envisaged, the G major work was offered to M. Long, who became its dedicatee and who gave the première in Paris with the composer conducting. They proceeded to perform it throughout the major centres of Europe, and to record it. He wrote little else, and from 1933 his health deteriorated. In 1937 brain surgery was decided upon. R did not recover consciousness and died on 28 December.

H. Gil-Marchex maintained that R never practised and that he sat incredibly low at the instrument. The fingers were long and agile, and he could twist his thumb into the palm of the hand with unbelievable facility, which enabled him to press down three keys at a time. M. Delage remarked on the great suppleness of R's wrist and how he sat very low at the keyboard with fingers stretched out flat.

Among his transcriptions are Debussy's *Nocturnes* and *L'Après midi d'un Faune*, both for two pfs. Only traceable recordings were accompanying the soprano Madeleine Grey in *Chansons hebraiques* marketed through *Polydor*.

RAVINA, Jean Henri (1818–1906)
b. Bordeaux, France. Studied at Paris Cons. Performed and taught. Composed for the instrument including four-handed arrangements of Beethoven symphonies.

RAVNKILDE, Niels (1823–90)
b. Copenhagen, Denmark. Studied there and later at Leipzig Cons. Settled in Rome, teaching and performing.

RAWICZ, Maryan (1898–1970)
b. Poland. Studied there, and in Vienna with R. Roberts. Distinguished career solo and later with the Rawicz and Landauer team. See also under Walter LANDAUER.

RAWSTHORNE, Alan (1905–71)
b. Haslingden, UK. Abandoned dentistry at the age of 21 to study at R. Manchester Coll., pf teacher F. Merrick. In 1930 he went to Berlin to work with E. Petri and on return home took a teaching appointment at Dartington Hall for some years before concentrating on composition. A distinguished output

includes two pf concertos, some pf solos and a handful of songs. CBE 1961.

RAYBOULD, Clarence (1887–1972)
b. Birmingham, UK. Studied at Birmingham Univ., being the first to attain Mus. Bac. there. His career began as pianist and accompanist. After service in World War I joined Beecham Opera Company. Later toured Australia and New Zealand as pianist and accompanist before becoming coach and assistant conductor at Covent Garden. Thereafter conductor and teacher. Musical adviser to Columbia Graphophone Co Ltd from 1927 until its merger with HMV 1931. Recorded *Columbia*.

REBIKOV, Vladimir (1866–1920)
b. Krasnoyarsk, Russia. Pupil of Moscow Cons. Afterwards taught in Berlin and Vienna until turn of century when he returned home and devoted his time to composition, mostly pf works. Some of the earlier pieces have been published in collections of Russian music; his later work became highly experimental, introducing mimicry not only in pf works but also in songs.

REBNER, Wolfgang Eduard (1910–   )
b. Frankfurt, Germany. Studied at Cons. there, then at Berlin Hochschule. Début Frankfurt 1930. Toured Europe, the Americas and Far East. Taught in USA and in Munich. Composed chamber-music and pf works.

RÉCHID, Djémac: *see* **REY, Cemal Resid**

REE, Anton (1820–86)
b. Aarhus, Denmark. Danish pianist, teacher and composer.

RÉE, Louis (1861–1939)
b. Edinburgh, UK. Went to Vienna to study pf with T. Leschetizky. Stayed there as concert pianist and teacher. Married Susanne Pilz and they developed duo appearances for which he wrote a concerto and made arrangements.

REEVES, Betty (1913–   )
b. London, UK. Studied at London Acad. and taught at the pf school founded by J. Ching, whom she married. Edited and composed albums of teaching emphasis.

REEVES, George (*c.*1900–60)
b. UK. Earliest biographical information unavailable. Worked in London as accompanist from age of 16; also appeared in solo capacity and did a spell of teaching at R. Coll. of Music from 1918. Afterwards became internationally established as an accompanist for leading soloists and singers especially Lehmann, Schumann, Gerhardt and Teyte. Was mainly resident in USA from 1940 and worked for a time as prof. at Urbana Univ., Illinois, visiting London annually where he eventually died suddenly.

REGER, Max (1873–1916)
b. Brand, Germany. Received some pf instruction from his father who was an organist. Appears to have been highly proficient at the instrument even though the teachers who helped him acquire technical mastery in composition were not noted for pianistic prowess. From 1901 undertook concert tours in addition to teaching and composing. Gave two recitals in London in 1909. His works run to 150 opus numbers. After his death Max Reger societies were formed in Germany and the USA to promote his cause. Compositions included four pf sonatinas, sets of variations on themes of Bach and Telemann, and an Op. 17,523 which parodies a popular piece of the day, *Eternally Yours!* and which is directed to be played faster than is possible. Also arrangements for two pfs (as well as duet), including the Bach Brandenburg concertos and four orch. suites.

REHBERG, Walter (1900–1957)
b. Geneva, Switzerland. Son of Willy R, who was his pf teacher; then pupil of E. d'Albert. Well-known concert pianist with a fine technique and a broadly classical repertoire. Recorded *Polydor*.
Pupils included: Johann Jacomet.

REHBERG, Willy (1863–1937)
b. Morges, Switzerland. Pf pupil of his father, then of K. Reinecke and S. Jadassohn at Leipzig Cons., where he became a teacher. Later was Principal at Geneva; prof. at Frankfurt then Mannheim, taking over the master-class at Basle in 1921. In addition to teaching had distinguished career as soloist. Also edited keyboard works of Handel, Schubert and Brahms, being a notable interpreter of the latter. Composed chamber music, pf pieces and songs. Father of Walter R.
Pupils included: Walter Frey, Lottie Krebs, Nikolai Lopatnikov, Walter Rehberg, Ernst Toch.

REICHA, Anton (1770–1836)
b. Prague, Czechoslovakia. Played a number of instruments and was in the Bonn Orch. in which Beethoven played viola. Taught pf in Hamburg 1794–9, then resided in Paris and Vienna, leaving the latter city when the French army arrived. Back in Paris resumed teaching. In 1818 became prof. of counterpoint and fugue at Paris Cons. Became naturalized Frenchman, and in 1835 took over as prof. of composition at the Cons. when Boildieu resigned because of ill-health. His chamber-music and pf works were highly esteemed.

Pupils included: Charles Dancla, Jeanne Louise Farrenc, Charles Gounod, Henri Herz, Franz Hünten, Charles Lefebvre, Franz Liszt, Ludwig Schunke.

REIMANN, Aribert (1936–   )
b. Berlin, Germany. Studied there and in Rome. Became concert pianist and specialized in accompaniment. Wrote a number of concertos including two for pf.

REINAGLE, Alexander (1756–1809)
b. Portsmouth, UK, of Austrian parentage. Studied music in Edinburgh and London. Settled in Philadelphia, USA, 1786, where American records show he played a *Sonata for Pianoforte* of own composition, first mention of the instrument in that country. Following year introduced four-hand music. Performed and taught pf. Conducted the orch. of the first theatre in Philadelphia from the pf keyboard around 1790s.

REINAGLE, Caroline (*née* **Orger**) (1818–92)
b. London, UK. Début there 1840. Gave first performance of own pf concerto there in 1843 and was one of first women composer-pianists. Wrote chamber music and pf pieces, also a pamphlet on technique.

REINECKE, Karl (1824–1910)
b. Altona, Germany. Pupil of his father, touring Scandinavia 1843, after which he stayed in Leipzig where Mendelssohn and Schumann befriended him. A period as court pianist in Denmark was followed by a visit to Paris. Thereafter he made Leipzig his home. He taught there and conducted Gewandhaus Orch. As one of the leading pianists of the day, he toured Europe each year and was especially successful in Mozart. Became famous as teacher and composer, wrote several textbooks as well as articles on music for the Press. Was editor for many of Breitkopf & Härtel pf publications including concerto cadenzas. Played Mozart's *Coronation* pf concerto in London in 1869. Dedicatee of Busoni's *Variations and Fugue on Chopin's C minor Prelude, Op. 22*.

Pupils included: Isaac Albéniz, Marie Bailey-Apfelbeck, Algernon Ashton, Hans Barth, Ernest Consolo, Fanny Davies, Karl Fiqué, Felix Fox, Gottfried Gal, Amina Goodwin, Glenn Gunn, Philip Halstead, Aloys Hennes, Hans Huber, Ernest Hutcheson, Siegfried Karl-Elert, Oliver King, Ivan Knorr, Gennari Korganov, Martin Krause, Emil Kronke, James Kwast, Adele Lewing, Louis Maas, Aleksander Michałowski, Albert Parsons, Carlyle Petersilea, Felix Rath, Willy Rehberg, Alfonso Rendano, Julie Rivé-King, Julius Röntgen, Ernst Rudorff, Cornelius Rybner, Leander Schlegel, Eduard Schütt, Frank Shepard, Oscar da Silva, Christian Sinding, Constantin Sternberg, Robert Teichmüller, Marcian Thalberg, Louis Thern, Willy Thern, Max Vogrich, Theodor Wiehmayer, August Winding, Marie Wurm.

REINHOLD, Hugo (1854–1935)
b. Vienna, Austria. Pf pupil of J. Epstein at Vienna Cons., graduating in 1874 with Silver Medal. Taught there and composed songs, pf pieces, chamber music and works for orch.

REISENAUER, Alfred (1863–1907)
b. Königsberg, Norway. Studied pf with L. Köhler, also F. Liszt. Début Rome 1881. Turned to law in Leipzig but resumed concert career in 1886 and toured practically the entire world before taking post at Leipzig Cons. as pf prof. Shaw heard him in London in 1892 and considered he had acquired a huge superfluity of technical power which he was resolved to take out in speed rather than in thought. Returned to London in 1896 and played Beethoven's 3rd concerto at Phil. concert.

Pupils included: Clarence Adler, Sergei Bortkievicz, Josef Pembaur jnr, Anna Schytte.

REISENBERG, Nadia (1904–   )
b. Vilna, Russia, of Russian American parentage. Studied at St Petersburg Cons. under L. Nicolaiev. Left Russia 1920 and toured Europe. Settled in USA 1922 and took further tuition from A. Lambert. US début 1924. Performed thereafter and taught at Curtis Inst.

REIZENSTEIN, Franz (1911–68)
b. Nuremberg, Germany. Took to music from an early age, studying at Berlin Hochschule 1930-4, where Hindemith was one of his teachers. When the Nazis came to power, he settled in UK and became naturalized. Continued study at R. Coll., London, and took pf lessons from Solomon. A fine concert artist with wide range from Beethoven to the *Ludus Tonalis* as well as chamber music. Compositions include sonatas, chamber music and pf pieces both brilliant and difficult. Recorded *Decca* and Lyrita.

Pupils included: Peter Cowderoy, Lyndon Davies, Eric Hope, Benjamin Kaplan, Jeffrey Siegel, David Wilde.

REMMERT, Martha (1854–1928)
b. Gross-Schwein, Poland. Studied at Warsaw Cons. then with F. Liszt at Weimar. Toured regularly as concert pianist until 1900 when she founded the Franz Liszt Acad., Berlin, where she subsequently settled.

RENARD, Rosita (1894–1949)
b. Santiago, Chile. Pupil of M. Krause in Berlin. Made a brilliant début, especially in the Americas. When she reappeared in Berlin around the age of 27, she received such hostile criticism that she gave up concert work. She returned to Chile and taught until her re-emergence in 1945. Her one and only Carnegie Hall recital occurred within four months of her death and was a resounding success.

RENDANO, Alfonso (1853–1931)
b. Carolei, Italy. Studied pf at Naples Cons. and toured as a prodigy. In Paris met S. Thalberg, who taught him, befriended him and introduced him to Rossini who helped his career. London début 1868 at a Phil. Soc. concert. Spent a few years in further study with K. Reinecke at Leipzig Cons. Thereafter his concert career was a triumph until eventually he settled in Naples as a teacher. He invented the Rendano Independent Pedal, placed between the usual foot pedals and manipulated by the left heel applied after pressing down a key, the effect being to prevent the damper returning to the strings until the independent pedal is released. Not to be confused with the middle pedal on Steinway and Bösendorfer concert grands. Composed a small number of select works mostly for pf.

RENESSE, Georg van (1909–   )
b. Amsterdam, Netherlands. Studied at Cons. there, Prizewinner 1928. Pupil of R. Viñes in Paris and L. Kreutzer in Berlin. Performed in Europe thereafter. US début 1949. Also partnered famous string players in duo recitals.

Pupils included: Hans Henkemans.

RESEL, Peter (1945–   )
b. Dresden, E. Germany. Pf pupil of Hochschule there, then of Moscow Cons. Joint 6th in Int. Tchaikovsky Comp., Moscow, 1966.

RESPIGHI, Ottorino (1879–1936)
b. Bologna, Italy. A string-player with practical experience in orch. and chamber music who also played the pf, and among whose works are an early *Fantasia*, a concerto (1923), and a *Toccata* (1928), all for pf and orch.; a concerto for oboe, horn, violin, double-bass, pf and string orch. (1934); works for violin and pf, an *Adagio con variazioni* for cello and pf, a pf quintet, pf pieces and songs.

REUBKE, Julius (1834–58)
b. Hausneindorf, Germany. Son of Adolf R, organ-builder. Pupil of T. Kullak in Berlin and later of F. Liszt in Weimar. A finished artist and fine pianist who seemed set for a brilliant career when he died suddenly at an early age. Wrote a pf sonata, pf pieces and songs.

REUSS, Eduard (1851–1911)
b. New York, USA. Pupil of F. Liszt; taught at Karlsruhe 1880–96, then at Wiesbaden Cons., 1896–1902, Director from 1899. Married the soprano Luise Reuss-Belce whom he accompanied in recitals. In final years was pf prof. at Dresden Cons. Wrote a biography of Liszt (1898).

REUTER, Rudolph Ernest (1888–1953)
b. New York, USA. Studied at Berlin Hochschule, pf teachers being K. Barth and E. Rudorff, winning Mendelssohn Prize on graduation 1910. Début year earlier with Hamburg Phil. From 1910 to 1913 was in Tokyo where he restructured the Acad. of Music. Returned to USA, where he taught in Chicago 1913–21. Held other posts besides performing widely and serving a term as President of the Soc. of US Musicians.

REUTTER, Hermann (1900–   )
b. Stuttgart, Germany. Studied in Munich; début 1923. Performed solo and as accom-

panist, early in career touring Europe and USA with the soprano Sigrid Onegin. Taught successively at Stuttgart and Frankfurt. From 1956 prof. at Munich Hochschule. Compositions include a number of pf concertos, chamber music, pf pieces and songs.

REV, Livia (–   )
b. Budapest, Hungary. A child prodigy who studied in Budapest and Leipzig. Performed in Europe during World War II, settling in Paris. London début 1948. Taught pf in addition to concert career. Recorded Saga.

REY, Cemal Resid (1904–   )
b. Istanbul, Turkey. Studied pf there and in Paris with M. Long. Début Paris 1922, returning home following year when he was appointed pf prof. at the Cons. Later became Director of Music Ankara Radio and after World War II founded Istanbul Phil. Wrote pf concerto and chamber-music, and used the style Djémac Réchid for concert and publishing purposes.

REY, Colaço (1854–1928)
b. Tangiers, N. Africa, of Portuguese ancestry. Studied in Madrid and Berlin. Performed and taught pf in Lisbon.

RHEINBERGER, Josef (1839–1901)
b. Vaduz, Liechtenstein. A prodigy of pf and organ. Pupil at Munich Cons., where he studied both instruments as well as composition, graduating with distinction. Taught pf for a while there; also accompanied, conducted and played the organ. Late-Romantic composer best known for his organ works although he wrote much chamber music, also works for pf including a concerto and some difficult sonatas.
    Pupils included; Josef Pembauer jnr, Hermann Scholtz, Max Schwarz.

RICHARDS, Henry Brinley (1817–85)
b. Carmarthen, UK. Early pf pupil of R. Acad., London, winning scholarships in 1835 and 1837. Lived in London and enjoyed a highly successful career as concert pianist and composer of popular Victorian light music.

RICHARDS, Kathleen: *see* **DALE, Kathleen.**

RICHARDS, Lewis Loomis (1881–1940)
b. Michigan, USA. Studied there and at

Brussels Cons. under A. de Greef. Toured Europe before returning to USA to take up concert career with teaching at Michigan State Coll. and later the Inst. of Music there.

RICHARDSON, Alan (1904–78)
b. Edinburgh, UK. Pupil of R. Acad., London and of H. Craxton for pf. As a young man worked for BBC in Edinburgh as pianist. Compositions included pf pieces. Transcribed Rachmaninov's song *Vocalise* for pf.

RICHEPIN, Elaine (–   )
b. Paris, France. Pf pupil of M. Long and A. Cortot. Performed extensively, lectured and adjudicated.

RICHNER, Thomas Benjamin (1911–   )
b. Point Marion, USA. Studied at Columbia Univ. and at Frankfurt-am-Main. Performed extensively as pianist and organist, also lecturer. Has written works on various musical subjects especially one on interpretation of Mozart pf sonatas.

RICHTER, Francis William (1888–1938)
b. Minneapolis, USA. Studied pf there and later in Vienna under T. Leschetizky and J. Labor. Début 1909 Paris and toured Europe and America thereafter until returning home, where he lived in Portland. Nephew of Hans R, the conductor.

RICHTER, Sviatoslav Teofilovich (1914–   )
b. Zhitomir, Russia. Studied in Odessa and made his début 1934. In 1937 went to Moscow Cons. and became a pupil of H. Neuhaus, graduating ten years later. Awarded Stalin Prize 1949. Through the medium of gramophone records his reputation as an outstanding Soviet musician preceded his concert tours in the West. His US début did not in fact occur until 1960 and British a year later. Since then has appeared regularly in the West, especially at festivals. Prokofiev's 9th pf sonata is dedicated to him. Recorded most labels.

RICHTER-HASSER, Hans (1912–80)
b. Dresden, Germany. Début there 1928 and began performing. Career interrupted by World War II. When it ended, he took classes at Detmold Music Acad. and conducted local concerts. His international career began in the Netherlands, leading to tours of America, the Near and Far East, Africa and Australia. A noted Beethoven exponent who composed two

pf concertos, chamber music, pf pieces and songs. Recorded Columbia and Philips.

RIDOLFI, Vico (1863–1920)
b. Ancona, Italy. Studied at Milan Cons., went to Rome, knew Sgambati and was famous for his fine touch and perfection of execution.

RIEFLING, Robert (1911–   )
b. Oslo, Norway. Studied there and in Hanover, and later in Berlin with W. Kempff and E. Fischer. Début Oslo 1925. Toured widely through Europe and USA. Founded and ran own pf school for a time, later becoming prof. at R. Danish Cons., Copenhagen. Recorded various. Wrote *Pianoforte Pedalling* (English edition 1962).

RIES, Adolf (1837–99)
b. Berlin, Germany. Pf pupil of T. Kullak. Settled in London, performed and taught there.

RIES, Ferdinand (1784–1838)
b. Frankfurt-am-Main, Germany. Was pf pupil of L. van Beethoven in Vienna 1801–5. Visited Paris and toured Germany, Scandinavia and Russia. Settled in London 1813–24 where he was befriended by Salomon who secured his début with the Phil. Soc. He began a successful career as soloist, teacher, composer and conductor, and worked hard to popularize the music of Beethoven in Britain. His compositions include 52 pf sonatas, pf concertos, of which the No. 3 was once highly popular, perhaps because it reflects Beethoven's style, and pieces.
Pupils included: Ludwig Schunke.

RIFKIN, Joshua (1944–   )
b. New York, USA. Student of Juilliard School of Music and of Princeton Univ. Spent some time in Europe as Fulbright Scholar. As pianist in a wide and versatile career he successfully linked a classical outlook with ragtime and jazz and is equally well known in all fields. Was on the faculty of Brandeis Univ. and musical consultant to Nonesuch Records. Specialized in the music of Scott Joplin. Recorded various labels.

RILEY, Howard (1943–   )
b. Huddersfield, UK. Educated at Bangor Univ and in USA, receiving Arts Council grant to pursue jazz composition. Became prof. at Guildhall School, London, and in 1970

founded jazz dept there. Made many appearances and tours in various groups, including own trio which was formed in 1967. Recorded CBS and other labels.

RINGEISSEN, Bernard (1934–   )
b. Paris, France. Student of Paris Cons., where he was a pupil of M. Long and J. Février, winning 1st Prize 1951. Competition prizes included a 1st at Geneva in 1954, and 4th at the Int. Chopin Comp. in Warsaw in 1955. Toured throughout Europe, USSR and America. Adjudicator at international competitions.

RINGNES, Inge Rolf (1894–1971)
b. Oslo, Norway. Studied there, then in Germany under A. Schnabel. Well-known pianist throughout Scandinavia who gave concerts in Germany and Austria. Took a keen interest in propagating contemporary music. Taught in Oslo.

RIPPER, Alice (1889–   )
b. Budapest, Hungary. Pupil of Cons. there and of Sophie Menter. Settled in Munich as concert pianist and teacher.

RISLER, Édouard (1873–1929)
b. Baden-Baden, Germany. Family settled in Paris in 1874 where he became a pf pupil at the Cons. under L. Diémer, winning 1st Prize 1889. Later studied in Germany with K. Klindworth, B. Stavenhagen and E. d'Albert. Début Paris 1894. Toured Europe and became a leading pianist specializing in recital series, e.g. Beethoven '32', Bach '48' and the entire output of Chopin. Propagated contemporary French music as well. Dedicatee of Chabrier's *Bourrée Fantasque* and of Granados' *Goyescas* No. 2. Premièred the Dukas sonata in Paris in 1901 and the *Variations Interlude et Finale sur un thème de Rameau* in 1903. Arthur Rubinstein in his autobiography said he never heard anyone play Beethoven better than on the occasion when Risler played the entire series in Buenos Aires.
Pupils included: Jacques Février, Noël Gallon, Dagmar Rybner.

RITTER, Theodore (1841–86)
b. Paris, France. Pupil of F. Liszt. Successful touring artist who wrote pieces which were once popular, also operas and dramatic works that had no success whatsoever.
Pupils included: James Huneker.

RIVÉ-KING, Julie (1857–1937)
b. Cincinnati, USA. A prodigy who studied in New York before going to Europe to become a pupil of K. Reinecke. Début in Leipzig in 1874 before having a short period of tuition with F. Liszt, returning home in 1875, when her New York début took place. It is recorded that she gave upwards of 4,000 concerts during her career. Wrote a few popular pf pieces.

RIVERA, Héctor Alejandro Daniel (1952–   )
b. Rosario, Argentina. Studied with L. Hoffman in Munich. In 1975 won 1st Prize in the Ettore Pozzoli Pf Comp. in Italy and prizes in other competitions. Performed in Europe and the USA. Came 3rd in the Int. Beethoven Pf Comp. in Vienna 1981.

ROBERT, Richard (1861–1924)
b. Vienna, Austria. Studied at the Cons. there, where he later taught. Pupils included famous persons who became mainly conductors.
Pupils included: Julius Chajes, Walter Landauer, Rudolf Serkin, Georg Szell.

ROBERTS, Bernard (1933–   )
b. Manchester, UK. Studied at R. Coll., London. Pf prof. and Association Board examiner. Recorded Nimbus.

ROBERTSON, Rae (1893–1956)
b. Ardersier, UK. Studied pf with P. Halstead, then at the R. Acad., London, with T. Matthay, winning the Chappell Gold Medal. After World War I service, resumed his career, specializing in two-pf recitals with E. Bartlett whom he married. They became internationally known and settled in the USA. Was MA and FRAM. Recorded *HMV*, *Columbia* and others.

ROBINSON, Thelma (1914–   )
b. London, UK. Studied pf there, especially with E. Howard-Jones. Mainly known as accompanist, and taught widely including Edinburgh.

ROCKEFELLER, Mrs John D. Jr: *see* **BAIRD, Martha.**

ROCKSTRO, William Smyth (1823–95)
b. London, UK. Studied pf there and later, 1845–7, at Leipzig Cons. under L. Plaidy. Returned to London, performed and taught. Lived in Devon 1866–91, then returned to the capital. A prolific writer on theoretical matters as well as criticisms, he wrote a book on Handel and one on Mendelssohn, both important in their day.

ROECKEL, Edouard (1816–99)
b. Treves. Studied pf with J. Hummel, who was R's uncle. Début 1836 in London. Toured Europe, settling in UK 1848.

ROECKEL, Josef Leopold (1838–1923)
b. London, UK. Younger brother of Edouard R and nephew of J. Hummel. Spent most of career in Bristol area.

ROGÉ, Pascal (1951–   )
b. Paris, France. Began learning to play at the age of 4. Début Paris 1962, when he entered the Cons., studying with L. Descaves and graduating four years later with 1st prizes for pf and chamber music. Studied thereafter with J. Katchen for three years. Paris and London débuts 1969, and was awarded joint 1st Prize in the Concours Int. Long-Thibaud 1971. Regularly toured Europe and the USA and visited the Far East. Recorded Decca.

ROGER-DUCASSE, Jean Jules (1873–1954)
b. Bordeaux, France. Student of Paris Cons. and of C. Bériot for pf, winning 2nd Prix de Rome 1902. Taught, composed and wrote pedagogic works. Pf compositions include preludes, a barcarolle and studies, also chamber music and songs; for pf duet more studies and an early *Petite Suite*.

ROGOFF, Ilan (1943–   )
b. Tel Aviv, Israel, of musical family. Studied at Acad. there, début 1955, then with S. Askenase in Brussels and with L. Shure in New York. Also received advice and help from V. Horowitz and C. Arrau. US début 1970 in Pittsburgh followed by appearances in other American cities. Resided in UK from 1974, from which he toured worldwide. Dedicatee of John McCabe's 3rd pf concerto which he premièred in 1977 in Liverpool. Recorded Nimbus, Unicorn and Desmar.

ROHARD, Jutta (1927–   )
b. Copenhagen, Denmark. Studied there, début 1950. Toured Scandinavia, Europe and parts of Africa; also visited London and Birmingham. Prof. at R. Acad., Copenhagen.

ROLL, Michael (1946–)
b. Leeds, UK, of Austrian parentage. 1st
Prizewinner of inaugural Int. Pf Comp.,
Leeds, 1963, having already made his London
début in 1958. US début 1974 in Boston.
Toured widely throughout Europe, USSR,
America and Far East. Also chamber-music
player.

ROLÓN, José (1883–1945)
b. Guzman, Mexico. Studied locally then later
went to Paris where he became a pf pupil of M.
Moszkowski and Gédalge for composition. He
combined the Impressionist style with native
folk-music and rhythms. Works included a pf
concerto and pf pieces.

ROMANIELLO, Luigi (1858–1917)
b. Naples, Italy. Pupil of B. Cesi and had a
successful playing career. Went to Buenos
Aires in 1898 as concert pianist and teacher,
founding a pf school which he directed with
distinction. A noted chamber-music player.
Wrote *Técnica Pianistica* for students.

RONALD, Sir Landon (1873–1938)
b. London, England. (Real name Landon
Ronald Russell.) Pupil of R. Coll. of Music,
London, 1885–90, being taught pf by F.
Taylor. Début 1890 London. Soon after began
to conduct and rapidly acquired a reputation
for pf accompanying. In 1894 accompanied
Melba on a US tour and by the turn of the
century he and H. Harty led in this work in
London. Gradually turned to the baton and
was noted for conducting concertos with
instinctive accuracy. As musical adviser to
HMV helped build the pre-1939 catalogue to
eminence. Principal of Guildhall School,
London, 1910–37. Knighted 1922. Among
many compositions are pf pieces and over 300
songs. Wrote *Variations on a Personal Theme*
(1922 – two volumes), followed later by *Myself
and Others*.
Pupils included: Harry Farjeon.

RONCAL, Simeon (1870–1953)
b. Sucre, Bolivia. Pianist whose most important work for the instrument, *20 Cuecas* (based
on the Bolivian dance of that name), is in the
repertoire of S. American pianists.

RÖNTGEN, Julius (1855–1932)
b. Leipzig, Germany. Pf pupil of K. Reinecke
and studied composition with Franz Lachner.
Début 1875 Stuttgart. Went to Amsterdam in

1878 where he settled and taught at the Music
School. Co-founded Amsterdam Cons. in
1885, taught there and was Director 1918–24.
Wrote in most genres including a pf concerto
and pieces. Was a friend of Brahms and edited
his letters.
Pupils included: Coenrad von Bos, Martin
Sieveking.

ROSA, Dario de (1919–)
b. Trieste, Italy. Studied pf at Cons. there,
where he became pf prof. Pianist of the famous
Trio di Trieste and as such recorded for various
labels.

ROSCOE, Martin (1952–)
b. Halton, Cheshire, UK. Studied under a
scholarship at R. Manchester Coll. of Music
with M. Clementi and G. Green. Came 2nd to
T. Judd in the Liszt Society of England Comp.
of 1976, and 9th in the Sydney Int. Pf Comp. of
1981. Début Wigmore Hall, London, 1973.
Performed extensively thereafter and taught in
Manchester.

ROSE, Fred (1897–1954)
b. St Louis, USA. Self-taught in light music,
playing in groups and solo from age of 10.
Added song-writing and pursued the craft of
pf-playing until he was pianist in Paul White-
man's band. Worked in Hollywood on successful film scores and founded a music publishing
company. Recorded Brunswick and others.

ROSE, Jerome (1938–)
b. Los Angeles, USA. Pf pupil of Mannes Coll.
and of Juilliard School. Won 1st Busoni Prize
1961. Performed since and has taught.

ROSELLEN, Henri (1811–1876)
b. Paris, France. Pupil of Paris Cons. under P.
Zimmerman. Went on to become a pupil of H.
Herz. Became a favourite pianist, popular
teacher and composer of numerous and varied
trifles in keeping with the age, as well as author
of a technical work on pf-playing.

ROSEN, Charles (1927–)
b. New York, USA. Pupil of Juilliard School
and of Princeton Univ., and especially with M.
Rosenthal and Hedwig Kanner-Rosenthal.
Début 1951 New York. Thereafter performed
solo and with leading orchs. throughout USA
and Europe. Pf prof. 1972. Recorded various,

and has written technical works, including *The Classical Style* (1971).

Pupils included: Yonty Solomon.

ROSENBLOOM, Sydney (1889–1967)
b. Edinburgh, UK. Studied at the R. Acad., London, where he graduated and became a teacher. Début London 1911. Taught for some years at Blackheath Cons., then privately. Emigrated to S. Africa where he performed and taught, finally settling in Bloemfontein. Composed interesting pf music that requires skill and polish to perform.

ROSENFELD, Moritz (1865–1939)
b. Vienna, Austria. Taken by family to USA when a child, studying at Chicago Music Coll., winning the Pf Medal. Taught there until 1911. Later opened own school which he ran until 1930 in addition to performing, lecturing and writing for the Press.

ROSENHAIN, Jakob (1813–94)
b. Mannheim, Germany. Studied pf there and later at Frankfurt. Performed throughout Europe. Wrote a *Capriccio* for pf and orch., which he played in London at a Phil. Soc. concert in 1837; also chamber music and technical pieces. A younger brother Eduard R (1818–61) was also a concert pianist, teacher and composer.

ROSENSTEIN, Mayer (–   )
b. London, UK. Teachers included I. Epstein. Début London 1933. Toured extensively thereafter as soloist and with orch.

ROSENSTOCK, Josef (1895–   )
b. Cracow, Poland. Studied at the Cons. there with J. Lalewicz, and later at the Vienna State Acad. Pursued dual career of concert pianist and opera conductor, and for a time was pf prof. in Berlin. Composed a pf concerto and sonata, also a set of variations on Chopin's C minor prelude; and works for two pfs.

ROSENTHAL, Hedwig KANNER-: *see* **KANNER-ROSENTHAL, Hedwig.**

ROSENTHAL, Moritz (1862–1946)
b. Lemberg, Poland. A leading pianist of his generation who studied under three illustrious masters: (1) Karl Mikuli, one-time pupil of F. Chopin; (2) Rafael Joseffy, himself a pupil of K. Tausig and of F. Liszt; and (3) F. Liszt himself. Mikuli taught at the Cons. in

Lemberg, where the young R was brought up; Joseffy was in Vienna where R made his début in 1876 before studying with Liszt 1876–8.

After that he went to Vienna Univ. to study philosophy, graduating in 1884. He returned to his concert career at once. Of his performance in Vienna of the Paganini-Brahms *Variations*, Eduard Hanslick wrote: 'To report that Rosenthal mastered them faultlessly, and with utter security and freedom, is to rank him automatically amongst the first pianists of the time.' He proceeded to tour Europe and pick up equally fine Press notices. It was the same when he made his US début in 1888 in Steinway Hall, New York. Most critics wrote of his perfect execution and style. In 1912 the Austrian Emperor Franz Josef appointed him court pianist, and throughout his career R rubbed shoulders with most eminent musicians, being respected and admired alike for his general culture, wit and brilliant pf playing.

The fabulous technique was subservient to a delicate musical sensibility. His repertoire was completely catholic, and he propagated a series of seven 'Historial Recitals' featuring masterworks from Scarlatti to Debussy. But he is especially remembered for his exquisitely turned Chopin, of which he left some notable recordings. In 1935 Neville Cardus wrote: 'The exquisite melancholy of his Chopin is nostalgic. We feel the presence of a man left over from a proud, glamorous civilisation, meditating on the "pathos of distance", glancing back, not sentimentally but as a connoisseur in rare emotions. His touch at such moments is aromatic. He distils fine fragrance. It was no accident that at this recital his playing became lovelier, deeper in poetry, as the afternoon turned to twilight and the lights were lit in the hall.'

In 1938 he celebrated the 50th anniversary of his American début. He decided to settle in that country and founded a school of pf-playing assisted by his wife, the concert pianist Hedwig Kanner-Rosenthal. By that time it was estimated he had given close on 4,000 concerts, embracing many hundreds of works. In an interview he once said: 'People ask me who my teachers were. I tell them Mikuli, Joseffy and Liszt, but please note this. I have learned all I know about piano playing from the music of Chopin.' Recorded *Odeon, HMV, RCA, Edison.*

Pupils included: Kenneth Amada, Josephine Innis, Nina Mesierow-Minchin, Julius Prüwer, Charles Rosen, Hilde Somer.

ROSSI, Karl (1839–1906)
b. Lemberg, Poland. Lived most of his life in Venice as pianist and composer.

ROSS-OLIVER, Charmion June (–   )
b. London, UK. Teachers included P. Garratt, L. England, J. Cooper and C. Arrau. Performed and taught at London Coll. of Music.

ROSSOMANDI, Florestano (1867–1933)
b. Bovino, Italy. Pf pupil of Naples Cons. under B. Cesi. Subsequently taught there. Was fine pianist and founded an association in Naples to prepare young artists for professional career.

ROSTAL, Peter (–   )
b. UK. Student of R. Coll., London, where he met P. Shaefer. Subsequently both went to the Juilliard School, New York, on scholarships, and on returning to UK teamed up in what was to prove one of the most successful pf duos ever in the light field, taking them all over the world, on land and afloat, since they appeared on luxury liners. In addition to their own two-pf arrangements, John Rutter wrote for them a concerto based on music of the Beatles which has proved popular. Recorded EMI.

ROSTROPOVICH, Mstislav (1927–)
b. Baku, USSR. Most famous as cellist and conductor but accompanied his wife the soprano Galina Vishnevskaya. Resided in France after being stripped of Russian citizenship in 1978, becoming member of Légion d'Honneur in 1981 in recognition of his services to music.

ROTERS, Ernst (1892–1961)
b. Oldenburg, Germany. Pf pupil of M. Mayer-Mahr; also studied at the Klindworth-Scharwenka Cons. in Berlin. Taught in Danzig, Hamburg and finally Berlin. Composed suite for pf and orch., chamber music and pf pieces.

ROTH, Bertrand (1855–1938)
b. St Gallen, Switzerland. Student at Leipzig Cons. and later with F. Liszt. Performed and taught at Frankfurt Cons., also at Dresden. Was one of the founders of the Raff Cons. Composed pf pieces and songs.
    Pupils included: Percy Sherwood.

ROUGNON, Paul (1846–1934)
b. Poitiers, France. Student at Paris Cons. 1862–70. Had long career as virtuoso and teacher. Composed chamber music and pf pieces, and wrote technical works.

ROWLANDS, Alan (1929–)
b. Swansea, UK. Student of R. Coll., London; Chappell Gold Medallist 1959, and award of Worshipful Company of Musicians. Taught at R. Coll. and performed. Recorded Lyrita.

ROWLEY, Alec (1892–1958)
b. London, UK. Student at R. Acad., London. Pianist, teacher and composer, being for many years associated with Trinity Coll. Wrote two pf concertos, one of them with military band, *Three Idylls* for pf and orch. which were first performed in London in 1942, chamber music and many intrumental pieces and songs. Chiefly remembered for educational works published in examination albums. Died while playing tennis.

ROZHDESTVENSKY, Gennadi (1931–)
b. Moscow, USSR. Trained at Cons. there and is mainly a conductor. Has appeared as pianist with his wife, V. Postnikova. UK début as duettists 1978 in London.

RUBACKITYE, Muza (1955–)
b. Kovno, Lithuania, USSR. Student of Vilna Cons. and of Moscow Cons. Won 2nd Prize in Liszt Bartók Comp., Budapest, 1981.

RUBBRA, Edmund (1901–)
b. Northampton, UK. Important British composer and fine pianist who often performed especially in chamber music and performances of own works. Studied for a time under C. Scott in London, putting on a concert of his master's works in Northampton when he was an adolescent. Also studied with Holst, John Ireland and Vaughan Williams, becoming a composer of great skill and elegance of expression. Compositions include pf concerto and *Sinfonia Concertante* for same combination, premièred 1943 in London, *Prelude and Fugue* on a theme of Cyril Scott written at the time of the latter's 70th birthday, a set of eight preludes, four *Études*, as well as other works, much distinctive chamber music and songs. Wrote a work on *Counterpoint* (1960). The preludes were first performed by the composer in 1967 during Cheltenham Festival.

RUBINSTEIN, Anton (1829–94)
b. Viykhvatinets (Wechwotinez), Moldavia, Russia, of Polish-Jewish origin. Mother an excellent pf-player under whom he began studying. Making rapid progress, he was placed under the tuition of A. Villoing in Moscow and after 18 months made an outstanding début there in 1839. One newspaper spoke of the ease with which he overcame difficulties and of the beautiful tone and power displayed by one so young. After further study he went on tour 1841–2 with his master, visiting Paris where he met the great personalities including Chopin and Liszt before whom he played. He made quite an impression in the French capital and went on to repeat it in London where I. Moscheles wrote of the 'Russian boy with fingers light as feathers yet strong as a man's'. Of that London début in 1842 a contemporary account said: 'His countenance, though somewhat impaired by a profusion of long hair, beams with frankness and intelligence, and affords an apt index to his remarkable talent.'

The tour continued triumphantly in Scandinavia, Germany and Austria. In 1843 his mother took him to Berlin to seek advice from G. Meyerbeer. As a result he stayed there to study composition. Then, for several years, he hovered between Berlin and Vienna and was reduced to teaching.

In 1848 he arrived in St Petersburg with a portfolio of his own compositions made during his travels and quickly established a reputation as pianist and composer. Then in 1854, at the zenith of his powers and fame in both capacities, he began a grand tour of Europe to consolidate that reputation more widely. On that occasion he avoided Britain because of the Crimean War, but he visited London regularly from 1857, in which year a Viennese critic likened him to none other than Beethoven. R's compositions by then included four symphonies, four pf concertos and four operas. In 1862 he founded the St Petersburg Cons., initially known as the Russian Musical Soc. It received a government grant and was the first great Russian school of music. As Director he poured his own wealth as well as time and effort into the project, in which he was joined by his brother Nikolai R.

In 1867 he relinquished the directorship to resume his international career. He toured America in 1872, giving well over 200 concerts and including performances of his own works.

By now conducting had been added to his list of accomplishments.

His farewell tour of European centres occupied 1885–6, when his series of seven 'Historical Recitals' (see below) were widely performed. He was the first important Russian professional pianist and was primarily responsible for founding the Russian school of pf-playing. As a performer he made a profound impression upon many who heard him including Tchaikovsky, Josef Hofmann, Rachmaninov and Lhevinne. In an obituary notice G. B. Shaw described him as 'a player of stupendous manual dexterity, with immense power, passion, and spontaneity'.

As a composer he wrote prolifically in most genres. A few pf solos as well as his 4th pf concerto enjoyed a vogue in his lifetime and for some time afterwards. Today his music is very rarely heard. He was regarded as an inspiring teacher who sought to reach the heart of musical interpretation. He had little time for fanciful editions and eschewed von Bülow's edition of Beethoven, and Klindworth's Chopin, saying: 'I want Beethoven, I want Chopin, as they give themselves to us. They are good enough for me and must be good enough for my pupils.' Recipient of the R. Phil. Soc. Gold Medal in 1876. Dedicatee of Busoni's only pf sonata. A performance of his 4th pf sonata in Wigmore Hall in 1981 was billed as '1st London performance'.

The seven 'Historical Recitals' for which he was famous comprised:

1. Works by Byrd, John Bull, Couperin, Rameau, D. Scarlatti, J. S. Bach (two *Preludes & Fugues*, *Chromatic Fantasia & Fugue* and miscellaneous pieces), Handel, C. P. E. Bach, Haydn (*F minor Variations*); and Mozart (*C minor Fantasia*, *Gigue in G*, *Rondo in A minor* and *Alla Turca* (*sic*)). 36 works in all without encores.
2. Beethoven sonatas – Opp. 27/2, 31/2, 53, 57, 90, 101, 109 and 111.
3. Schubert (*Wanderer Fantasia*, six *Moments musicaux*, a minuet in B minor and two *Impromptus* – in C minor and E flat), Weber (Sonata in A flat Op. 39, a *Momento capriccioso*, *Invitation to the Dance* and *Polacca brillant in E*) and Mendelssohn (*Variations sérieuses*, *Capriccio in E flat minor*, ten *Songs without Words* and *Scherzo Capriccio*).
4. Schumann – *Fantaisie in C major*, *Kinderscenen*, *Études symphoniques*, Sonata in F sharp minor, four pieces from Op. 12: *Des Abends, In*

der Nacht, Traumeswirren, and *Warum?*; *Vogel als Prophet, Romance in B flat minor Op 28/1* and *Carnaval Op 9*.
5. Clementi (Sonata in b flat), three nocturnes by J. Field, four works by Moscheles, five by Henselt, two by Thalberg including the *Fantasia on 'Don Juan'*; and Liszt (*Étude* in D flat, *Valse caprice*, two *Consolations, Au bord d'une Source, Rhapsodies Nos. 6* and *12, La Gita, La Danza* and *La Regatta*, three transcriptions of Schubert *lieder*, a *Soirée de Vienne* and *Fantasia on 'Robert le Diable'*.
6. Chopin – *Fantaisie in F minor*, six preludes, four *Ballades, Barcarolle*, three waltzes, two impromptus, *Scherzo in B minor*, three nocturnes, four Mazurkas, *Berceuse*, sonata in B flat minor and three polonaises.
7. Miscellaneous: eleven *études* by Chopin, the rest Russian works by Balakirev, Cui, Glinka, Liadov, Rimsky-Korsakov, both Rubinsteins and Tchaikovsky. 32 works in all.

Pupils included: Platon Brounov, Teresa Carreño, Frederick Dawson, Sandra Droucher, Artur Friedheim, Ossip Gabrilowitsch, Eduard Hesselberg, Richard Hoffman, Josef Hofmann, Katarzyna Jaczynowska, Alberto Jonás, Sophia Malozyomova, Nadezhda Purgold, Sofia Rabcewicz, Cornelius Rybner, Samuel Sanford, Josef Slivinski, Carlos Sobrino, Vera Timanova. (See also under J. Hofmann for comments on Rubinstein as teacher.)

RUBINSTEIN, Arthur (1887–1982)
b. Lodz, Poland. First played in public 1894 locally. After a spell under L. Rozycki in Warsaw, went to Berlin under K. H. Barth privately, where the musical life of the capital proved more stimulating and rewarding than the stodgy tuition. The early days as concert pianist were difficult; having hated the uninspired curriculum under Barth, he failed to acquire the necessary self-discipline early in his career. He roamed Europe for a time in futile pursuit of fame and fortune but meeting with and hearing the greatest artists of the day, clearly imbibed at too many founts. Was fortunately blessed with long life and career and so harnessed discipline to brilliant musicianship to become one of the greatest virtuosi of all time as well as a marvellous personality and raconteur. Very wide repertory, sponsoring the work of contemporary composers especially Szymanowski and Villa-Lobos. Was also excellent ensemble player with world's leading instrumentalists. Retired 1976 in his 90th year.

Recorded *HMV, RCA* and RCA. Began autobiography, first volume, *My Young Years* (1973), second *My Many Years* (1980). R. Phil. Soc. Gold Medal 1961. Returned to Wigmore Hall in June 1976 to give farewell London recital. The occasion also celebrated the 75th anniversary of the opening of this, the original Bechstein Hall, in 1901, which was the scene of his first London recitals in 1912. His farewell recital comprised:
Beethoven: Sonata in E flat op 31/3.
Schumann: Carnaval.
Ravel: Valses nobles.
Chopin: Étude Op. 10/4; Nocturne Op. 27/2; Scherzo Op. 31.
Pupils included: Dubravka Tomsic, Jan Wolmer.

RUBINSTEIN, Beryl (1898–1952)
b. Athens, USA. Pf pupil of his father then of A. Lambert. Touring the USA as a prodigy. Studied in Europe 1911–16 with F. Busoni, then J. da Motta, reappearing in New York 1916. Head of pf dept. at Cleveland Inst. of Music 1921–5, Dean of the Faculty 1929, Director 1932. A remarkable pianist who composed two pf concertos, a sonatina, studies, a suite for two pfs and other pf pieces. Wrote *Outline of Piano Pedagogy*.
Pupils included: Lionel Nowak.

RUBINSTEIN, Josef (1847–84)
b. Starokonstantinov, Russia. Studied pf in Vienna under J. Dachs, then later with F. Liszt. Came under the influence of Wagner's music and made pf reductions of *The Ring* and *Parsifal*. Died by own hand in Switzerland.

RUBINSTEIN, Nikolai (1835–81)
b. Moscow, Russia. Younger brother of Anton (and fourth son). Studied pf under T. Kullak 1844–6. As a pianist never attained the eminence of his brother but was a notable teacher as well as conductor. Founded the Imperial Musical Soc., Moscow, in 1859, and became head of Moscow Cons. when it was created in 1866. Gave annual recitals in St Petersburg.
Pupils included: Ernst Jedliczka, Henryk Pachulski, Emil von Sauer, Alexander Siloti, Heinrich Spanenberg, Sergei Taneiev.

RUDNYTSKY, Anton (1902–75)
b. Luka, of Ukrainian–American parentage. Pf pupil of A. Schnabel and E. Petri. Mainly

conductor but accompanied his wife, the soprano Maria Sokil. Composed pf works.

RUDNYTSKY, Roman (1942–)
b. New York, USA. Studied in Philadelphia, then at the Juilliard School, New York. Leventritt Prizewinner. Held succession of teaching posts, and toured widely in N. America and Europe, solo and with leading orchs.

RUDORFF, Ernst Friedrich Karl (1840–1916)
b. Berlin, Germany. Studied pf privately till the age of 17, then went to Leipzig Cons. under I. Moscheles and L. Plaidy; also took private lessons from Reinecke. Taught at Cologne Cons., then 1869–1910 head of Hochschule, Berlin, when he retired. Edited works of Mozart and did research on Weber.
Pupils included: F. Backer-Gröndahl, Leopold Godowsky, Elsie Hall, Rudolph Reuter, Eugenie Schumann, Bernhard Stavenhagen, Lazzaro Uzielli.

RÜFER, Philippe (1844–1919)
b. Liège, Belgium. Pupil of Cons. there. On graduation moved to Berlin, where he taught successively at Stern's, Kullak's and Scharwenka's.

RUFF, Herbert (1918–)
b. Vienna, Austria. Studied in Berlin, notably under W. Gieseking. Début 1930 Berlin. Made distinguished career in film industry as pianist, conductor and composer.

RUFFER, Magdi (1924–)
b. Berne, Switzerland. Studied there and at École Normale, Paris. Début 1943 Basle. Performed throughout Europe. Recorded Durium.

RUGER, Morris (1902–)
b. Superior, USA. Composer who studied with I. Philipp in Paris and wrote chamber music.

RUMMEL, August (1824–86)
b. Wiesbaden, Germany. Second of four generations of concert pianists. Younger son of Christian R and brother of Josef R. Settled in London and was much in vogue as concert pianist.

RUMMEL, Christian (1797–1849)
b. Brichsenstadt, Germany. First of four generations of concert pianists. Fine performer solo and in chamber-music. For many years *Kapellmeister* at Wiesbaden.
Pupils included: Josef Gregoir, August Rummel, Josef Rummel.

RUMMEL, Franz (1853–1901)
b. London, UK. Father of Walter Morse R. Student of L. Brassin at Brussels Cons., winning 1st Prize 1872, then taught there. Début Antwerp 1872. Appeared in London following year, later touring Europe several times. Lived in USA 1878–81, finally settling in Berlin where he taught between concert tours. Played the Dvořák pf concerto in London in 1885 while it was still a comparatively new work.
Pupils included: Clayton Johns.

RUMMEL, Josef (1818–80)
b. Wiesbaden, Germany. Second of four generations of concert pianists. Elder son of Christian R. Distinguished concert artist and prolific composer for the pf.

RUMMEL, Walter Morse (1887–1953)
b. Berlin, Germany. Son of Franz R, and grandson of the inventor of telegraph code. Went to the USA with his mother in 1901 on the death of his father, but returned to Europe to study with L. Godowsky 1904–9. Later toured Europe regularly, living for many years in Paris where he became close friend of Debussy. Composed pf works and chamber-music; made transcriptions of Bach and of French songs of earlier centuries. Recorded *Polydor* and *German HMV*.

RUSSELL, Landon Ronald: *see* **RONALD, Sir Landon.**

RUTHARDT, Adolf (1849–1934)
b. Stuttgart, Germany. Pupil of Stuttgart Cons. Taught at Geneva and later was pf prof. at Leipzig Cons. Wrote many pf pieces and especially studies of graded difficulty according to opus number. Also acted as publishers' editor.

RHYBNER, Cornelius (1855–1929)
b. Copenhagen, Denmark. Studied at Cons. there, then at Leipzig with K. Reinecke, H. von Bülow and Anton Rubinstein. Toured Europe and directed Karlsruhe Cons. Settling in USA, he took over from E. MacDowell as head of music at Columbia Univ. in 1904, remaining there until 1919. Performed solo

and with orch. and composed chamber music and pf works.

Pupils included: Dagmar Rybner.

RYBNER, Dagmar de Corval (1892–1965)
b. Baden, Switzerland. Daughter of Cornelius R. Studied at Karlsruhe and Columbia Univ., USA. Pf pupil of father and of É. Risler. Début 1906 Karlsruhe. Toured USA and Europe as soloist, with orch. and as accompanist to her singer husband. Taught at Curtis Inst., then Columbia Univ.

RYCE, Joel (1933–)
b. Sterling, USA. Studied at Am. Coll. Chicago, and Curtis Inst., Philadelphia; pupil of W. Kapell, R. Serkin and M. Hess. Début New York 1956. Performed widely solo and with wife Yaltah Menuhin. Recorded Everest, EMI, etc.

RYTERBAND, Roman (1914–)
b. Lodz, Poland. Studied there and in Switzerland where he taught and performed before moving successively to Canada and the USA. Has written a variety of works with a pf part, often featuring the harp as well.

RZEWSKI, Frederic (1938–)
b. Massachusetts, USA. Graduate of Princeton Univ. and studied with leading US composers. Commenced touring in 1958 and has been associated with serialism, working mainly in Europe between 1960 and 1970. Founded Musica Electronica Viva 1966. Own compositions include sonata for two pfs (1959), *No Place to go but Around* (1975) and *The People United will never be Defeated* (1976). Taught in USA and Cologne and has appeared at most festivals. Recorded numerous labels.

SADOFF, Simon (1919–   )
b. Hoboken, USA. Student at Mannes School, later with E. Steuermann. Toured from 1941 and became involved in ballet principally as pianist and conductor.

SAFONOV, Vassily Ilyitch (1852–1918)
b. Itsyrusk, Russia. Studied locally, then 1878–80 at St Petersburg Cons. under T. Leschetizky and L. Brassin for pf, and under Zaremba for theory. Also took pf lessons from A. Villoing. Début St Petersburg 1880. Taught at Cons. there 1881–5 and then until 1905 at Moscow Cons., Director for 17 years. A brilliant teacher and pianist who became successful conductor not only in the USSR but also in Europe and America.

Pupils included: Grigorii Beklemischev, Alexander Goedicke, Alexander Gretchaninov, Julius Isserlis, Wiktor Labunski, Josef Lhevinne, Nicolai Medtner, Leonid Nicolaiev, Matvei Pressman, Alexander Scriabin.

SAGALOV, Leonid (1910–40)
b. Russia. 6th Prizewinner in Chopin Comp. Warsaw, 1932. No further details found.

SAINT-SAËNS, Camille (1835–1921)
b. Paris, France. His father died from tuberculosis two months after Camille's birth, and it was feared the child might not live long. Brought up in the care of the mother and an aunt, he showed an early and strong attraction towards the pf, demonstrating a sense of perfect pitch. Before he had attained the age of 5, he was playing sonatas by Mozart and Beethoven and had begun composing. At seven he began lessons from C. Stamaty, former disciple of Kalkbrenner, and in 1846 made his début at the Salle Pleyel, playing Beethoven's concerto No. 3 in C minor and the Mozart in B flat, K.450, as well as solos, the whole performed from memory. The Press next day hailed him as a second Mozart.

He entered Paris Cons., adding organ study to pf and composition. At 17 he became organist at the Church of St Mary. A youthful symphony created friendships with Berlioz and Gounod. He met Liszt on one of the latter's rare visits to Paris, and the meeting proved fruitful in both furthering his career and cementing their friendship. His third symphony in C minor is dedicated to the memory of Liszt. He was also introduced to Rossini and spent much time with the elderly composer, where S-S's early chamber music was performed. A number of works composed around this period remain unpublished. Twice he failed to gain the Prix de Rome, but he was appointed prof. at École Niedermeyer 1860–3, where Fauré and André Messager were among his pupils.

In 1868 he gave the première of his 2nd and most popular pf concerto in G minor, Op. 22, in Paris under the baton of Anton Rubinstein. It was sketched out in just three weeks, was an immediate success and led to the two musicians becoming firm friends. Around this time S-S became a member of the Légion d'Honneur. During the Franco-Prussian war when the Commune seized Paris, he, along with Gounod and other artists, sought refuge in Britain until the Commune was defeated. He appeared as pianist in London ahead of his official début with the R. Phil. Soc. which occurred in 1874 in Beethoven's concerto No. 4 in G. The concert took place in the course of an extensive tour of Europe, with S-S in the triple role of pianist, composer and conductor. Compositional work in this period seems to have been largely opera.

Returning to London in 1886, he conducted the première of his 3rd symphony in C minor, commissioned by the R. Phil. Soc., and the following year appeared for them in his pf concerto No. 4 in C minor under the baton of Wilhelm Ganz. It is dedicated to Anton Door. In 1893 he received an honorary degree in music at Cambridge along with Boito, Bruch, Grieg and Tchaikovsky (Grieg was not present). At Cambridge he played his new fantasy, *Afrique*, for pf and orch., written during one of his visits to N. Africa, as was the pf concerto No. 5 in F minor, completed in 1896 and dedicated to Louis Diémer. *Afrique* enjoyed a vogue for a time but has now sunk into oblivion.

His US début occurred in 1906, and he was well received. In 1910 a concert of chamber music in London marked the 25th anniversary of his first chamber concert in the capital, and Ysaÿe, Joseph Hollman, the Belgian cellist for whom S-S wrote his 2nd cello concerto, and the pianist Pugno all took part. The following year, at the age of 76, he played at the Liszt centenary celebrations in Heidelberg. He returned to London in 1913 and in a concert otherwise devoted to his works played the pf in a Mozart concerto. It is recorded that he performed with undiminished vitality and prowess. From then until his death, which occurred in Algiers, whither he had gone as usual to weather the winter, he continued to practise at least two hours a day.

According to contemporary reports he had no peer in the line of French pianists, being a good all-rounder with the facility to read a score at sight, as well as highly developed powers of improvisation. Something of his fluency and style can distantly be gauged from his early acoustical records. His style of composition combined the classical with brilliance, both now regarded as somewhat facile. Thus he stood aside from the mainstream of the developing French School. Busoni said that S-S 'seemed to indulge in composition as a pleasant mental exercise; he was a cheerful priest of the art. One cannot gather from his music whether he was good, kind or capable of suffering'. Certainly his art is civilized, versatile and highly fertile, and his instrumental writing is very effective. He was sensitive to tone colour, and it has been said that this feeling 'not always expressed by original methods but unfailingly correct, drapes his lesser creations with a shimmering garment of illusion which blinds us, perhaps to the commonplaceness of an accompaniment figure'.

Besides the six works for pf and orch., he wrote much chamber music with pf part embracing the posthumous *Carneval des animaux*, duets and works for two pfs including a set of variations on the theme from the trio of the slow movement of the Beethoven pf sonata in E flat, Op. 31 No. 3; also numerous solos with romantic titles, apart from the two sets of *Six Études*, Opp. 52 and 111. Two of these which have survived in the repertoire are the study in the form of a waltz, and the *Toccata* which is an adaptation of the last movement of the 5th pf concerto. Recorded *G & T* and *HMV*.

Pupils included: Gabriel Fauré, Eugène Gigout, André Messager.

SAKO, Akiyoshi (1957–)
b. Japan. Student of Tokyo Univ. and 1st Prizewinner there. Bronze medallist of Int. Comp., Geneva, 1980.

SALAMAN, Charles Kensington (1814–1901)
b. London, UK. Studied at R. Acad., London, and with C. Neate. Début there 1828. Went to Paris for further tuition from H. Herz, returning to London in 1831 where he performed, taught and conducted. Co-founder of the Music Soc. of London in 1858. Took part in chamber-music concerts, wrote for journals and lectured.

Pupils included: Ebenezer Prout.

SALMON, Alvar Glover (1868–1917)
b. New York, USA. Studied at New England Cons. and in Berlin before going to St Petersburg to concentrate on Russian pf music. Toured the USA extensively, playing, writing and lecturing on his speciality.

SALZMAN, Pnina (–)
b. Tel-Aviv, Israel. Studied pf there and at Paris Cons. Toured globally solo and with orch.

SAMAROFF, Olga (1882–1948)
b. San Antonio, USA. Studied with C. Sternberg in Philadelphia, then at Paris Cons. before returning home for further tuition from E. Hutcheson. Début 1905 New York. Toured USA and Europe, becoming a celebrity through orch. appearances and joint recitals with famous fellow-artists. Married the conductor L. Stokowski in 1911, then temporarily gave up her career on account of a breakdown. When she resumed, she taught in a succession

of important pf schools, later adding newspaper criticism to her activities. Wrote a number of books on music. Recorded *RCA*.

Pupils included: Richard Farrell, William Kapell, Eugene List, Paul Nordoff, Vincent Persichetti, Thomas Schippers, Rosalyn Tureck, Alexis Weissenberg.

SAMAZEUILIH, Gustav (1877–1967)
b. Bordeaux, France. Studied with E. Chausson, V. d'Indy and P. Dukas, and made close study of Ravel's pf technique. Included here because he transcribed for pf numerous orch. works by French composers such as Franck, Debussy, Duparc, Dukas, d'Indy, Fauré etc; all told in excess of 100, as well as songs. Pf works included a large suite in three movements, *Le Chant de la Mer*, which, in the words of Norman Demuth, 'combines the impressionism of Debussy with the pianism of Ravel'; chamber works included a violin sonata dedicated to E. Ysaÿe and first performed by the latter and R. Pugno in 1904; also a *Fantaisie* for same combination premièred by J. Thibaud and A. Cortot. Despite such auspicious beginnings, his works, for all their elegance and distinctiveness, have remained in obscurity. He also contributed much to the musical Press, published a book on Dukas (1913) and made a pf arrangement for four hands of de Falla's *Nights in the Gardens of Spain*.

SAMPER, Baltasar (1888–   )
b. Palma de Mallorca, Spain. Went to Barcelona in 1907 and became pf pupil of E. Granados. An accomplished pianist who gave a series of recitals featuring first performances there of Cyril Scott's music. Composer in Balearic style including a set of *Danzas Mallorquinas* for pf. In addition to performing, taught at the Granados Acad.

SAMUEL, Clotilde: *see* KLEEBERG, Clotilde

SAMUEL, Harold (1879–1937)
b. London, UK. Pupil of M. Verne before studying at the R. Coll., London, under E. Dannreuther for pf, and Sir C. Villiers Stanford for composition. Début London 1894. As time went on, he developed into a specialist in Bach's keyboard works *on the pf*, something of a novelty in those days. He had a splendid technique, very necessary for Bach, and it is probably true to say that had that same technique been applied to Chopin and Liszt, he would have been hailed as a virtuoso in the top flight.

He also had an extraordinarily retentive memory and it is claimed that at any given moment he could sit down, without music, and play any keyboard work of Bach, a feat in which he rivalled M. Rosenthal in Chopin. His view of Bach was essentially robust rather than religious. He enjoyed playing and conveyed that impression to audiences.

But over the years he encompassed Beethoven concertos and sonatas and was a noted exponent of Brahms. His US début was in 1924, and he became exceedingly popular there, returning every year to perform and teach. He was pf prof. at the R. Coll. and gave first performance of Herbert Howell's pf concerto at a R. Phil. Soc. concert in London in 1925. Recorded *HMV* and *Columbia*.

Pupils included: David Branson, Benjamin Britten, Howard Ferguson, Angus Morrison, Elizabeth Poston, Norman Tucker.

SANCAN, Pierre (1916–   )
b. Mazamet, France. Studied at Paris Cons., winning Prix de Rome 1943. Concert pianist and pf prof. at Paris Cons.

SANDOR, Arpád (1896–1972)
b. Budapest, Hungary. Studied pf with B. Bartók, graduating in 1914. Lived in Berlin before going to the USA as accompanist in 1922, returning to Berlin for some years before finally settling in USA as accompanist to artists like Heifetz. Naturalized in 1943.

SANDOR, György (1912–   )
b. Budapest, Hungary. Studied pf with B. Bartók at the Cons. there. Toured Europe before World War II, then settled in USA in 1939. Premièred Bartók's 3rd pf concerto (posthumously) in Philadelphia, 1946. Made pf transcription of Dukas' *L'Apprenti Sorcier*. Wrote *On Piano Playing* (1981). Recorded Vox, including Prokofiev sonatas and the complete pf works of Bartók.

Pupils included: Guy Johnson, Peter Simon.

SANDT, Maximilian (1863–1934)
b. Rotterdam, Netherlands. Studied there and was pupil of F. Liszt. Made reputation as touring pianist and taught successively in Berlin, Cologne and Bonn. Composed pf pieces of above-average difficulty.

SANFORD, Samuel (1849–1910)
b. Bridgeport, USA. Pupil of W. Mason. Went to Russia to receive tuition from Anton Rubinstein and later studied in Paris. Reputedly a highly finished executant but made rare public appearances. Was prof. at Yale Univ.

SANGIORGIO, Victor (1959–)
b. Italy. Lived in Australia from 1962, studying pf in Perth and then in Melbourne at the Victoria Coll. of the Arts. In 1979 toured China with the Australian Youth O., and the following year went to Italy to study with G. Agosti in Rome. Joint winner of the Aust. Musical Overseas Scholarship at the R. Over-Seas League Music Festival, London, 1984. Performed widely solo and in ensemble.

SANROMA, Jesús María (1902–)
b. Carolina, Puerto Rico. Granted facilities by his government to go to New York where he studied with A. Szumowska, and later with A. Cortot and A. Schnabel. Won pf prize in 1920, and in 1924 made successful début in Boston, followed by career as concert pianist and teacher. Among premières he gave was the Vernon Duke pf concerto (*Dedicaces*) in 1938 under Koussevitzky. Dedicatee of pf concerto by Ferde Grofe. Recorded *Victor* (including first versions of Paderewski A minor and MacDowell D minor concertos); also Everest.

SAN SILVESTRO, Barone Napolino di: *see* **FLORIDIA, Pietro.**

SAPELLNIKOV, Vassily (1867–1941)
b. Odessa, Russia. Pupil of St Petersburg Cons. and of L. Brassin and S. Menter. Début 1888 in Hamburg in the Tchaikovsky pf concerto No. 1, composer conducting. Became friend of Tchaikovsky and propagated his pf music. British début 1889 with same concerto at R. Phil. Soc., London, concert and between concert tours spent three years 1897–9 as pf prof. at Moscow Cons. Gave British première of Tchaikovsky's 2nd pf concerto in 1890 at a Crystal Palace concert, and was a very popular pianist in UK. Shaw spoke of his 'amazing' performance of the Chopin A flat polonaise, 'the middle episode in which comes from his puissant hands like an avalanche'. In 1902 gave first British performance of Rachmaninov's 2nd concerto. Lived on in UK after retiring from the platform. Recorded *Vocalion*.

SAPERTON, David (1889–1970)
b. Pittsburgh, USA. Studied pf with his grandfather, theory with father. Début there with orch. in 1899 at the age of 10. New York début 1905. Toured Europe 1910–12. Married Vanita, daughter of L. Godowsky, in 1921, and three years later joined Curtis Inst. as pf teacher. Wrote *The Science of Transposition* and *Score Reading and Writing*.
Pupils included: Jacques Abram, Orlanda Amati, Jorge Bolet, Sydney Foster.

SARGENT, Sir Malcolm (1895–1967)
b. Ashford, UK, of parents normally living in Stamford, Lincs. Studied pf locally, then in Peterborough, learning also to conduct and play the organ. His official concert work began in Leicester where with a local orch. he performed a number of pf concertos. Was a pupil of B. Moiseiwitsch in 1922 and later confined the pf role in concert work to chamber music. Knighted 1947, R. Phil. Soc. Gold Medal 1959.

SARNECKA, Jadwiga (1878–1913)
b. Slawuta, Poland. Pupil of F. Szopski in Cracow, and of T. Leschetizky in Vienna. Concert pianist in Poland and prolific composer of pf pieces.

SASAKI, Ken (1943–)
b. Sendai, Japan. Began playing pf from an early age. Won 2nd Prize in a Japanese Radio pf comp. and went on to study at Tokyo Cons., where he graduated in 1966, the year of his début there. Was awarded a two-year course at Warsaw Cons., where his teachers included Z. Drzewiecki. From 1969 he studied in Paris with V. Perlemuter; also won a silver medal in the Viotti Comp. in Italy. US début 1979. London début 1972. Toured widely thereafter, solo and with major orchs. Recorded Nimbus.

SATIE, Erik (1866–1925)
b. Honfleur, France. Of mixed parentage, his mother being Scottish. Largely self-taught although he spent a short time as a pf pupil of G. Mathias at Paris Cons. Was dubbed eccentric because he chose a way of humility and near poverty while playing in Montmartre cafés. Attracted the friendship of Debussy and Ravel, becoming the spiritual leader of 'Les Six', and was for a short time involved in the antics of a bogus mystic by the name of Joseph Péladan which has caused S to be described incorrectly as a member of the Rosicrucian

Order. Composed a string of pf works under novel titles which were regarded highly by his contemporaries, being performed by leading pianists like R. Viñes and which continue to enjoy consistent if quiet popularity. F. Poulenc said of him: 'Satie played the piano very badly, especially towards the end of his life. He was very fond of the piano for sure, but most of his pieces were written on café tables.'

SATTER, Gustav (1832–79)
b. Vienna, Austria. Studied pf there. Went to Paris to study medicine but, stimulated by the musical life of the capital, resumed lessons. Gave concerts and composed, and spent some time in the Americas before returning to Paris. Later toured Europe before going back to the USA, finally settling in Georgia as pianist, teacher and lecturer. Is credited with giving first New York performance of the Beethoven *Emperor* in 1855. Composed much chamber music and pf works including three sonatas.

SAUER, Emil von (1863–1942)
b. Hamburg, Germany. Pf pupil of N. Rubinstein at Moscow Cons. 1879–81. Toured Europe for several years, then went for tuition with F. Liszt at Weimar 1884–5. Became internationally famous virtuoso and teacher and received the R. Phil. Soc. Gold Medal 1910. Recorded *Parlophone* and *Columbia* and is dedicatee of *Goyescas* No. 1 by Granados. Composed two pf concertos and many pieces including studies. Edited the works of Brahms and Liszt for Peters, also some of Pishna, Kullak and others. Wrote *Meine Welt* (1901). One wife, Angelica Morales, was a concert pianist who was recorded on *Columbia* in the Beethoven 'Triple Concerto' (Weingartner). She later lived and taught in the USA.
   Pupils included: Webster Aitken, Stefan Askenase, Edoardo Celli, Sixten Eckerberg, Gunnar de Frumerie, Anita Harrison, Ignace Hilsberg, Maryla Jonas, Lubka Kolessa, Walter Landauer, Jacques de Menasce, Helena Morsztyn, Dennis Murdoch, Elly Ney, Felix Petyrek, Erno Rapee, Dario Raucea, Germaine Schnitzer, Marie Varro, Desider Vecsey, Paul Weingarten, Olof Wibergh.

SAVERY, Karl Maria (1897–)
b. Hamburg, Germany. Pf teachers included J. Stockmarr and I. Friedman. Settled in Copenhagen as concert pianist and teacher and founded a music society there in 1946.

SAVYTSKY, Roman (1907–60)
b. Sokal, Russia. Studied at Lysenko Ins., Lviv, and later at Prague Cons. Début there 1932. Toured central and eastern Europe as concert pianist in addition to teaching in Lviv. In 1949 settled in USA, where he taught in Philadelphia, performed and founded Ukrainian Musical Inst. of America.

SAWALLISCH, Wolfgang (1923–)
b. Munich, Germany. Studied there privately. Became noted as conductor of opera and orch. concerts but has accompanied recitals by international artists, e.g. E. Schwarzkopf and Fischer-Dieskau.

SAXBY, Joseph (1910–)
b. London, UK. Student of R. Coll. of Music, London, who had dual career with pf and harpsichord. Toured Europe and USA several times as accompanist to leading celebrities; was chamber-music player and interested in early keyboard music. Recorded various.

SCARLATTI, Domenico (1685–1757)
b. Naples, Italy. Son of Alessandro S and noted composer who wrote well in excess of 600 works for harpsichord on which his enduring reputation rests. His free style of composition opened out digital technique, and it has been well said that he founded modern pf technique. His sonatas have enjoyed great popularity by pianists, and numerous editions and collections have been published. This work was completely accomplished by Alessandro Longo in what has become known as the Longo edition with its own numbering. A later edition, the Kirkpatrick, now supersedes the Longo in scholastic circles.

SCARPINI, Pietro (1911–)
b. Rome, Italy. Studied at S. Cecilia Acad., Rome; début there 1936. Toured up to World War II, during which he taught at Florence Cons. and until 1967 when he moved to Milan. Has wide repertoire including works like the Busoni pf concerto. Compositions include concertos, chamber music etc. as well as an arrangement for two pfs of Mahler's 10th symphony.

SCHACHNER, Rudolf Josef (1821–96)
b. Munich, Germany. Pf pupil of J. B. Cramer and established reputation as touring virtuoso in Europe before settling in London. Was a

good teacher and composed numerous works for the instrument.

SCHAD, Josef (1812–79)
b. Steinbach, Germany. Pupil of A. Schmitt and subsequently settled in France as pf teacher. Wrote mainly for pf, and his published works enjoyed a vogue at the time.

SCHAEFER, Paul (–   )
b. UK. Pf studies at R. Coll., London. With Peter Rostal was awarded scholarship for further study at Juilliard School in New York. Subsequently teamed up in successful pf duo in the field of light music. Toured N. America several times in addition to Europe and the Far East. Well-known broadcasters and recorded EMI.

SCHÄFER, Dirk (1873–1931)
b. Rotterdam, Netherlands. Studied music there and in Cologne. Won Mendelssohn Prize, Berlin 1894. Settled in The Hague performing and teaching throughout the Low Countries. Removed to Amsterdam in 1904, the year in which his pf quintet had its première in Frankfurt. From 1913 gave series of historical recitals numbering 11 in which he featured major works from Byrd to Schoenberg. Composed a pf concerto and chamber music. Recorded *Columbia*.

SCHALK, Josef (1857–1911)
b. Vienna, Austria. Pf pupil of J. Epstein and taught pf at Vienna Cons. Met Anton Bruckner as a young man, and his arrangements for four hands of the Bruckner symphonies made history. Also wrote a book on the Austrian composer published in 1885. Elder brother of Franz S, conductor and later director of Vienna Opera.

SCHARFENBERG, William (Wilhelm) (1819–95)
b. Cassel, Germany. Pf pupil of J. Hummel at Weimar. Début Cassel 1837. The following year appeared in New York with such success that he settled there, speedily taking a prominent part in the musical life of the city. Also taught, and was editor and adviser to the publishers G. Schirmer.

SCHARRER, Irene (1885–1971)
b. London, UK. Pupil of R. Acad., London, under T. Matthay. Début 1900 at Proms under Wood. Became very successful artist touring UK, Europe and USA as soloist, with orch. and in chamber music. Appeared with M. Hess in two-pf recitals. Had wide repertoire with perhaps special emphasis on Chopin and Schumann, being a finely sensitive interpreter with good technique and warm tone. Made a memorably beautiful record of Chopin E flat *étude*, Op. 10, No. 11; also rescued from oblivion the *Scherzo* of Litolff's 4th pf concerto in a brilliantly executed and best-selling disc. Recorded *HMV* and *Columbia*.
Pupils included: Dorothy Wilson.

SCHARWENKA, Xaver (1850–1924)
b. Samter, Poland. Studied pf from age of 3. When he was 15 the family removed to Berlin, and he and his brother Philipp (1847–1917), who became a teacher of composition, began studying at Kullak's Acad. there. S took pf with T. Kullak and composition with Richard Wüerst. He graduated in 1868 and was appointed a pf teacher there, making his début the following year in Berlin.

From 1874 he toured Europe and USA as a virtuoso, and his brilliant technique and handsome presence soon made him a favourite. In 1881 he opened his own school in Berlin and was joined in the project by his brother. However, they gave it up to start a Cons. in New York. Philipp stayed there only one year, returning to Berlin; Xaver went back in 1898 to take over the Klindworth-Scharwenka Cons. which had amalgamated in 1893. In 1914 he founded a master school. His concert career continued throughout the spells of teaching; he composed prolifically and because of his popularity as a concert pianist was a favourite performer in court circles in Germany and Austria.

His compositions include four pf concertos (the first of which was dedicated to F. Liszt and which the composer made popular); two pf sonatas, 2 *Ballades*, two sets of *études*, sixteen *Polish National Dances* over five opp nos. (the first dance of which, in E minor, was phenomenally popular, the sheet music selling in millions), other miscellaneous pieces, a quantity of chamber music, and songs. In association with K. Klindworth he edited one Augener edition of Chopin. Produced a *System of Piano Playing* (1908) and wrote his autobiography, *Klänge aus meinem Leben* (1922). Recorded *Columbia*.
Pupils included: Gustav Becker, Halfdan Cleve, Minnie Coons, Albert von Doenhoff, Judith Heber, Jessie S. Kelley, Fritz Linde-

mann, Isidore Luckstone, José V. da Motta, Patrick O'Sullivan, Anders Rachlew, Edward Schneider, Kurt Schubert, Wilson Smith.

SCHEIN, Ann (1939–)
b. New York, USA. Pf pupil of various teachers. Début 1946 in Washington at age of 7. Further tuition from M. Munz. Adult début Mexico City 1957. Toured thereafter, visiting Europe from 1958.

SCHELLING, Ernest (1876–1939)
b. Belvedere, USA. An infant prodigy who, 1882–5, studied with G. Mathias at Paris Cons., before having lessons from M. Moszkowski, T. Leschetizky, H. Barth and I. Paderewski. Toured Europe and S. America 1903–4, then the USA from 1905. In later years turned additionally to conducting and was prof. at Halle Univ. Composed suite for pf and orch. as well as pf pieces and chamber music. Was soloist in the suite which he introduced to London audiences in 1910 at a concert which included the British première of Rachmaninov's 2nd symphony, and some songs by Richard Strauss sung by Elena Gerhardt accompanied by Artur Nikisch.

SCHENCK, Peter (1870–1915)
b. St Petersburg, Russia. Pupil of Cons. there where he later taught in addition to concert career as pianist. Composed chamber music and pf pieces.

SCHICHT, Johann (1753–1823)
b. Zittau, Germany. Early German pianist who played at concerts in Leipzig even before the founding of the Gewandhaus and who succeeded Hiller as conductor of the society. Accompanied his wife who was a soprano. Composed two pf concertos, sonatas and other pieces; also translated into German the pf methods of Pleyel and Clementi.

SCHIFF, András (1953–)
b. Budapest, Hungary. Student of F. Liszt Acad. there with P. Kadosa; also received tuition from G. Malcolm. Début 1972 in Budapest and subsequently toured Europe, the USA and Japan. Joint 4th Prizewinner of Int. Tchaikovsky Comp., Moscow, 1974; joint 3rd, Leeds Int. Pf Comp., 1975. Recorded Hungaroton and Decca.

SCHIFRIN, Lalo (1932–)
b. Buenos Aires, Argentina. Came of musical family and studied at Buenos Aires Univ., later in Paris, becoming involved in the jazz scene there. On returning to Buenos Aires formed own group on Count Basie lines and achieved success in Latin-American tours. Became additionally successful composer including much film music. Settled in California and claimed to seek a reconciliation between straight music and its jazz counterpart.

SCHILLER, Allan (1943–)
b. Leeds, UK. Début at the age of 10 with the Hallé Orch. and Sir John Barbirolli. Student of D. Matthews and, later, of V. Merzhanov in Moscow and of G. Agosti in Rome. Toured Europe and N. America, also behind the Iron Curtain. Awarded Harriet Cohen medal 1966. Concert pianist and chamber music player; pf prof. at Guildhall School, London. Recorded various labels.

SCHIØLER, Victor (1899–1967)
b. Copenhagen, Denmark. Pf pupil first of his mother, then of I. Friedman and A. Schnabel. Début 1914 thereafter performed throughout Europe. US début 1948. Recorded *HMV* and *Tono*.
    Pupils included: Victor Borge, Gunnar Johansen.

SCHIPPERS, Thomas (1930–77)
b. Kalamazoo, USA. Studied at Curtis Inst., Yale Univ. and Juilliard School. Pf pupil of O. Samaroff. Early pf career gave way to conducting.

SCHLEGEL, Leander (1844–1913)
b. Overveen, Netherlands. Studied at The Hague before going to Leipzig Cons. under K. Reinecke. Toured for a while before taking over a music school in Haarlem which he ran with success for nearly 30 years, finally founding own school in his home town. Composed chamber music and pf pieces.

SCHLÖSSER, Adolf (1830–1913)
b. Darmstadt, Germany. Son of Louis S, the composer, who had studied with Salieri. Toured Europe with success 1847–54 when he went to London, joined R. Acad. of Music and taught there until he retired. Composed chamber music and pf pieces.

SCHLOTTMANN, Louis (1826–1905)
b. Berlin, Germany. Pupil of K. Taubert and successful concert pianist. Taught in Berlin

additionally. Composed chamber music, pf pieces and songs.

SCHMID-LINDNER, August (1870–1959)
b. Augsburg, Germany. Student of Munich Acad., winning the Mendelssohn Prize in 1889 in Berlin. Received additional tuition from S. Menter before rejoining Munich Acad. as a teacher in 1893, becoming pf prof. 1903. Well-known local performer, propagating the music of Reger. Edited works of Liszt for Schott.

SCHMIDT, Franz (1874–1939)
b. Pressburg, Austria. Studied at Vienna Cons. and was pf pupil of T. Leschetizky. Taught cello and pf at Vienna Cons.; also Director of Vienna Acad., then Rector of the Hochschule, retiring 1937. Among numerous compositions were pf works written for the Austrian pianist P. Wittgenstein including *Konzertante Variations* for left hand (first performed by P. W. in Vienna in 1924), pf concerto for left hand (first performed in Vienna 1935) and a *Toccata*. There is also chamber music including a pf quintet.
Pupils included: Friedrich Wührer.

SCHMITT, Aloys (1788–1866)
b. Erlenbach, Germany. Pupil of his father, and an accomplished pianist by the age of 14. Settled in Frankfurt in 1816 as pianist, teacher and composer. Wrote four pf concertos, much chamber music and pf pieces; also studies and a method.
Pupils included: Heinrich Enckhausen, Charles Flabell, Heinrich Henkel, David Koning, Josef Schad, Georg Schmitt, Karl Wolfson.

SCHMITT, Florent (1870–1958)
b. Blamont, France. Pupil of Paris Cons. 1889–96. Played mainly own compositions, including a large-scale pf quintet, the *Symphonie concertante* for pf and orch. which he took to USA in 1932. Wrote numerous works for two and four hands, as well as songs.
Pupils included: Pierre Ferroud.

SCHMITT, Georg Aloys (1827–1902)
b. Hanover, Germany. Son of Aloys S, who was his teacher. Toured Europe as concert pianist from 1848; also accompanied his wife, Cornelia S, who was a soprano. Took up conducting additionally later in life. Composed chamber music, pf pieces and songs.

SCHMITT, Hans (1835–1907)
b. Koben, Czechoslovakia. Student of Vienna Cons., where on graduation he was appointed teacher and eventually prof., being head of the senior pf class. Composed numerous exercises, studies and pieces of a pedagogic nature; also prepared an edition of Clementi's *Gradus*.
Pupils included: Artur Schnabel.

SCHMITT, Jakob (1803–53)
b. Obernburg, Germany. Younger brother of Aloys S. Performed, taught and composed prolifically, including sonatinas, pieces, a Method and numerous studies.
Pupils included: Henry Timm.

SCHMITZ, Elie Robert (1889–1949)
b. Paris, France. Pf pupil of Paris Cons. under L. Diémer, winning 1st Prize. Accompanied operatic stars before embarking on solo career. US début 1919 where he became popular. In 1920 founded a French-American music soc. Regularly toured Europe and America thereafter. Taught in Canada and USA and arranged an American edition of Chopin studies. Gave première of Henri Barraud pf concerto in 1946 in New York under Manuel Rosenthal. Wrote *The Piano Works of Claude Debussy* (1950) and *The Capture of Inspiration*.

SCHNABEL, Artur (1881–1951)
b. Lipnik, Austrian Silesia. As a child received tuition from H. Schmitt of Vienna Cons. At the age of 9 entered the Leschetizky domain, at first under A. Essipova until Leschetizky divorced her, when she returned to Russia. He then worked under a Mme Bree, who was on the staff and who had studied with Liszt but had never performed in public. In due course came under the personal tuition of Leschetizky and formed lifelong friendships with contemporaries like R. Bühlig, Mark Hambourg, I. Friedman and O. Gabrilowitsch. He was 12 when he met Brahms, from which sprang his interest in that master's compositions. His début took place in 1897 in Vienna. Important persons were in attendance, and he received highly complimentary reviews.

He then stayed in Berlin with friends, making contacts and securing concert dates. His début there was in 1898, but thereafter the going was slow. About this time he met a *lieder* singer Therese Behr and accompanied her in a number of recitals. They fell in love. Orch. dates came slowly and were interspersed with recitals. Then, in 1902, he formed his first pf trio in Berlin, which was successful. He began to be taken up by conductors like Nikisch and Richter, but a performance of his youthful pf concerto with the Berlin PO was not a success. He also played in London without conspicuous success and around this time appeared as often in ensemble work as solo.

In 1905 he married T. Behr. They settled in a large flat in Berlin with ample room to practise and teach either end without disturbing the other. His reputation as a teacher grew, and so the flat became a Mecca for aspiring students of pf and song until the Nazi threat drove them from Germany.

He had passed 50 when HMV made the famous scoop of adding his name to their list of recording artists, having up till then resisted all offers to record. In 1931 he recorded the complete Beethoven concertos and sonatas and variations for a limited edition. The series made his name in the international sense for it was the first time the Beethoven pf repertoire had been recorded complete by one artist. By this time the pianist, who had started his career with a wide repertoire from Bach to Rachmaninov and taking in Chopin, Weber and many another, had gradually narrowed his interests to the Austro-German group of Mozart, Schubert, Brahms and Beethoven with some occasional Schumann.

In 1939 he withdrew to the USA. He survived the war years and lived to resume performing in Europe once more, dying in Switzerland after a number of severe illnesses. Besides the concerto already mentioned, he composed pf pieces, chamber music and songs. Lectures given in the USA were transcribed and published in book form under the title *My Life of Music* (1961), based on twelve talks given in 1945 at the Univ. of Chicago and followed by question-and-answer sessions.

Sir Clifford Curzon said of him as a teacher that: 'He really taught one how to teach oneself – to stand on one's own feet; for he never imposed his own interpretation of the music.' Other pupils have said of his method of teaching that it constituted a system. Recorded *HMV* and *RCA*.

Pupils included: Adrian Aeschbacker, Webster Aitken, Victor Babin, Martha Baird, Ethel Bartlett, Alan Bush, Sir Clifford Curzon, Henri Deering, Maria Donska, John Duke, Rudolf Firkusny, Leon Fleischer, Claude Frank, Sir Wm. Glock, Francizek Goldenberg, Boris Goldowsky, Lajos Hernadi, Betty Humby-Beecham, John Hunt, Eileen Joyce, Natalia Karp, Reuben Kosakov, Lili Kraus, Guy Maier, Noel Mewton-Wood, Eunice Norton, Franz Osborn, Lee Pattison, Inge Rignes, Anton Rudnytsky, Jesús María Sanroma, Victor Schiøler, Shulamith Shafir, Verdina Shlonsky, Leon Shure, Ruth Slenczynska, Vitya Vronsky, Nelly Wagenaar, Nancy Weir, Konrad Wolff, Carlo Zecchi.

SCHNABEL, Helen (*née* **Fogel**): *see* **SCHNABEL, Karl Ulrich.**

SCHNABEL, Karl (1809–81)
b. Breslau, Germany. Family made pianos. In due course was put to work in the factory, additionally learning pf and composition. Is very probably the only pianist ever to make the instrument upon which he publicly performed his own pf concerto, thereafter leaving the business to pursue a musical career. History does not record at which vocation he excelled.

SCHNABEL, Karl Ulrich (1909–   )
b. Berlin, Germany. Pupil of Hochschule there under L. Kreutzer for pf. Début 1925 Berlin. Thereafter toured worldwide before World War II. New York début 1937. Settled in USA 1938 and took citizenship 1944. Married Helen S (*née* Fogel, 1911–74, who wrote pf pieces including a sonata) and formed duo-team. Later became interested in electronic music. Wrote *Modern Technique of the Pedal*. Recorded *HMV* (duets with father) and various LP labels. Edited pf works of Schubert and Weber.

Pupils included: Harold Heiberg.

SCHNABEL-TOLLEFSEN, Augusta (1885–1955)
b. Boise, Idaho, USA. Began studying pf at an early age and toured Europe as a prodigy. Studied in Frankfurt before becoming a pupil of L. Godowsky in Berlin, and of P. Gallico in New York. Adult début with New York PO in 1906. In 1907 married the violinist Carl Tollefsen, and with the French cellist Paul Kefer they formed the Tollefsen Trio which toured successfully for many years.

SCHNEEVOIGT, Sigrid Ingeborg (1878–1953)
b. Helsinki, Finland. Student of the Cons. there and later pupil of F. Busoni. Performed throughout Scandinavia and European countries and taught pf at Helsinki Cons. from

1911. Married the distinguished Finnish conductor Georg Schneevoigt.

SCHNEIDER, Edward Faber (1872–1950)
b. Omaha, USA. Studied pf with X. Scharwenka in New York, then H. Barth in Berlin. Returned to USA and pursued career as teacher as well as writing pf pieces and songs.

SCHNEIDER, Friedrich (1786–1853)
b. Alt-Waltersdorf, Germany. Successful pf teacher who founded own school in 1829. An exceedingly prolific composer in most fields. On his death the pupils joined the Leipzig Cons. and his school was closed.
   Pupils included: Michael Bergson, Fritz Spindler, Heinrich Willmers.

SCHNITZER, Germaine (1888–   )
b. Paris, France. Pupil of Paris Cons. under R. Pugno, winning 1st Prize 1902. A year spent with E. von Sauer in Vienna resulted in another 1st. Début Berlin 1904 and from there visited European capitals. US début 1906 led to further tours until finally she settled in New York. Date of birth also given as 1889 in US references.

SCHOBERLECHNER, Franz (1797–1843)
b. Vienna, Austria. Pupil of J. Hummel and became successful pianist and composer, travelling throughout Europe. Prolific composer of chamber music, sonatas and pf pieces.

SCHOENBERG, Arnold (1874–1951)
b. Vienna, Austria. Largely self-taught and not strictly speaking a concert pianist. Nevertheless as leader of what has been called the Second Viennese School, his sets of *Klavierstücke*, written in 1908, 1911, 1923, 1929 and 1932, are regarded as important landmarks on the pf scene as well as marking stages in his individual development. Other works include the pf concerto (1942).

SCHOLTZ, Hermann (1845–1918)
b. Breslau, Germany. Studied there, then at Leipzig Cons. under L. Plaidy, and later at Munich with H. von Bülow and J. Rheinberger. Knew Liszt. Taught at R. School, Munich, becoming prof. in 1910. Principally remembered as an editor of Chopin for Peter's as well as for some of Augener's editions.
   Pupils included: Otto Thümer.

SCHOLZ, Erwin Christian (1910–   )
b. Vienna, Austria. Studied at Acad. there. Début 1934 followed by extensive touring and taught in Vienna as pf prof. Compositions include pf studies, sonatas etc and chamber music. Also wrote extensively on technique.

SCHÖNBERGER, Benno (1863–1930)
b. Vienna, Austria. Pupil of Vienna Cons. and of A. Door; then worked with Liszt at Weimar before returning to Door to complete his training. Début 1878, and for the next two years toured Europe from Belgium to Russia. After a spell of teaching in Sweden, he taught in London, made an American tour during 1894, and returned to London as prof. at R. Acad. Was judged to play with remarkable brilliance and elegance, and besides solo work appeared with artists like Ysaÿe. A critic said of him in 1893: 'His passion for the mechanical part of his art seems to have filled him with an ambition to play like clockwork; and all I can say is that if he is not very careful he will succeed.' In his latter days took up operatic conducting in UK, where he died.
   Pupils included: Henry Geehl.

SCHRÖTER, Johann Samuel (1750–88)
b. Warsaw, Poland. Early pianist who visited London in the course of touring and decided to settle there. On death of J. C. Bach he took over as teacher to royal family. Composed a quantity of pf concertos, chamber music and sonatas which were published in London at the time. Had a sister, Corona Elisabeth (1751–1802), who was renowned soprano of her day.

SCHUB, André-Michel (1953–   )
b. France, but has lived in USA since he was an infant. Studied pf from early age. His teachers included J. Zayde, and R. Serkin at the Curtis Inst., Philadelphia. Début 1974 New York followed by wide touring, solo and with orch. Awarded 1st Prize in Van Cliburn Comp. 1981. European début 1982. Recorded Vox. Harold Schonberg described him as a 'formidable pianist with a fierce integrity who will respect the traditions of the Cliburn Competition at its best'.

SCHUBERT, Franz (1797–1828)
b. Lichtenthal, Vienna, Austria. Taught himself pf, receiving aid from an older brother. Had no public career as soloist although he played his works in company with associates. From the style of his pf works and *lieder* accom-

paniments, it could be deduced he was a highly sensitive player. This century the pf sonatas (some are still coming to light) have slowly found favour with soloists and audiences; and he foreshadowed the Romantic era in his *Impromptus* and *Moments Musicaux*. Also composed much for two pfs, chamber music and over 600 *lieder*, many of which were arranged for pf by Liszt, who also made a version of the *Wanderer Fantaisie* for pf and orch.

SCHUBERT, Kurt (1891–)
b. Berlin, Germany. Pupil of parent, then of X. Scharwenka at Klindworth-Scharwenka Cons., where he taught.

SCHULHOFF, Erwin (1894–1942)
b. Prague, Czechoslovakia. Pf pupil of Cons. there 1902–4, then spent four years in Vienna under W. Thern, continuing at Leipzig Cons. 1908–10 under R. Teichmüller, and finishing at Cologne with K. Friedberg. Won the Mendelssohn Prize twice, 1913 and 1918, and made a number of successful tours of Europe. Was arrested by the Nazis and died in a concentration camp. Wrote a pf concerto, chamber music and pf solos, some in eccentric dance rhythms. His creative work included quarter-tone research. Was descendant of Julius S. Recorded *HMV*.

SCHULHOFF, Julius (1825–98)
b. Prague, Czechoslovakia. Pupil of the Cons. there, studying pf with J. Tomáschek. Début 1842 Dresden. Appeared in Leipzig, then went to Paris, where, according to one source, he managed to introduce himself to Chopin and to play one of his works to the master. Thus he was able to enter the Parisian musical circle, becoming a popular pianist and fashionable teacher. Made a long and involved tour through Europe, absorbing several years, finally settling in Berlin. Composed a pf sonata, studies, and pieces with titles *à la* Chopin.

SCHULTZ, Arnold (1903–72)
b. Minnesota, USA. Studied at Carleton Coll. and in Minneapolis. An exponent of pf technique, devoting most of his working years to that aspect of the art. Wrote *The Riddle of the Pianist's Finger* (1936) and *A Theory of Consciousness* (1973).

SCHULTZ-EVLER, Adolf (1854–1905)
b. Warsaw, Poland. Pupil of K. Tausig.

Brilliant pianist who wrote original compositions as well as transcriptions in the idiom of the times and of his teacher, notably the one on *The Blue Danube*.

SCHULZ-SCHWERIN, Karl (1845–1913)
b. Schwerin, Germany. Student of Stern's Cons. and of H. von Bülow. After touring and a spell as a court pianist, returned to Stern's in teaching capacity. Later moved to Mannheim.

SCHUMACHER, Thomas (1937–)
b. Montana, USA. Pf pupil of Manhattan and Juilliard Schools at which latter he taught from 1967. Toured throughout USA and Europe.

SCHUMANN, Eugenie (1851–1938)
b. Düsseldorf, Germany. Youngest child of R. and K. Schumann. Pupil at Berlin Hochschule für Musik under E. Rudorff, later of her mother; also had lessons from J. Brahms. Few public appearances but taught as assistant to her mother. Wrote *Erinnerungen* (1925), and *Robert Schumann: ein Lebensbild meines Vaters* (1931).

SCHUMANN, Klara (*née* **Wieck**) (1819–96)
b. Leipzig, Germany. Pupil of her father, Friedrich Wieck, appearing as a prodigy and touring from an early age. Married Robert Schumann 1840 and after his death resumed concert career and also taught. Worked hard to propagate the music of her husband, of Brahms and of Chopin with German audiences besides being the first woman to play the Beethoven *Hammerklavier* in public, in the process earning contumely for her unladylike behaviour. Became a legendary teacher and founded the Schumann school which taught Robert's pf music with authenticity. Was a lifelong friend of Johannes Brahms and dedicatee of his 2nd pf sonata. Among her compositions are cadenzas for Beethoven's 3rd and 4th pf concertos as well as Mozart's D minor K.466, and a dear little concerto in A minor which she wrote at the age of 9 and lacked the judgment to destroy at 10. Daughter Eugenie described her mother at practice directly after breakfast: 'Scales rolled and swelled like a tidal sea, legato and staccato; in octaves, thirds, sixths, tenths, and double thirds; sometimes in one hand only, while the other played accompanying chords. Then arpeggios of all kinds, octaves, shakes, everything prestissimo and without the slightest break, exquisite modulations leading from key to key. The most wonderful feature of this

practising was that although the principle on which it was based was always the same, it was new every day, and seemed drawn ever fresh from a mysterious wellspring. Irresistible inspiration, perfect rhythm, such as springs from the souls of only the greatest artists, combined with absolute mastery of technique, made these exercises a wonderfully spiritualised achievement.' Klara disapproved of fingered editions, and held that one should have acquired the right feeling for fingering through study of scales, arpeggios and other exercises.

Pupils included: Richard Andersson, Leonard Borwick, Fanny Davies, Henry Eames, Ilona Eibenschütz, Adolf Frey, Karl Friedberg, Amina Goodwin, Clement Harris, Natalia Janotha, Louise Japha, Walter Lampe, Carolus Oberstadt, Edward Perry, Oscar da Silva, Anton Strelezky, Franklin Taylor, Lazzaro Uzielli, Mathilde Verne, Marie Wurm.

SCHUMANN, Marie (1841–1929)
b. Leipzig, Germany. Eldest of the eight children of R. and K. S who accompanied her mother's career and taught as an assistant. Little in the way of public performances.

SCHUMANN, Robert (1810–56)
b. Zwickau, Germany. One of four great Romantic composers for the instrument born within a year of each other, with F. Chopin, F. Mendelssohn and F. Liszt. Showed early interest in the instrument and in composition. An important step in his life was in 1830 when he went to Leipzig to study with F. Wieck in whose house he lived and later married the daughter, Klara W. Using a contraption of his own device to aid digital agility, he permanently damaged a finger of the right hand and was forced to turn to composition. His early works are all for pf and he was fortunate to have the backing of influential artists like his wife and Liszt to perform his music in public. Founded and edited the *Neue Zeitschrift für Musik* in 1834, famous in its day for lively criticism and sharp outlook. From 1840, when he married Klara, he branched out into songwriting, symphonies and chamber music. Later toured as a conductor and taught. His last years were overshadowed by mental ill-health leading to a final breakdown of sanity. Compositions for pf include the other Schumann concerto in A minor; *Introduction and Allegro appassionato*, and an *Introduction and Allegro*, both with orch.; three sonatas, the

great *Fantaisie* in C Op 17 dedicated to Liszt and written in memory of Beethoven; a set of *Études symphoniques* in the form of a theme and variations with finale, and a resplendent Op 1 set of variations on the name *Abegg*; groups of pieces – *Papillons* Op 2, *Davidsbündlertanze* Op 6, *Carnaval* Op 9, *Kinderscenen* Op 15, Kreisleriana Op 16, *Faschingsschwank aus Wien* Op 26, *Waldscenen* Op 82; also eight Novelletten Op 21, three *Romances* Op 28, and a splendid early *Toccata* in C. Chamber music includes violin sonatas, trios, quartets (all with pf part), and the distinguished pf quintet Op 44. There are works for two pfs and many lovely sets of songs whose lasting fragrance ranks amongst the best flowers in the German *lieder* garden. The childlike side of the composer's nature is shown in *Kinderscenen*, while other early sets reflect the fantastic contrast of character between Florestan and Eusebius – a contrast carried further in his writings on music.

Pupils included: Ludwig Ehlert, Harmann Krigar.

SCHUNKE, Karl (1801–39)
b. Magdeburg, Germany. Cousin of Ludwig S. Taught by his father, then studied pf with F. Ries, who took him to London. In 1828 he moved to Paris and was pianist to the court, but is not mentioned in contemporary records of the artistic circles of the capital. Apparently committed suicide.

SCHUNKE, Ludwig (1810–34)
b. Cassel, Germany. Pupil of F. Kalkbrenner and of A. Reicha in Paris. Made successful appearances in main European musical centres. His compositions included a pf concerto which he played in London at a Phil. concert in 1826, Weber conducting. Settled in Leipzig and assisted R. Schumann with *Neue Zeitschrift für Musik*. Died at early age; at the time Schumann described him as 'a master in pianoforte playing, the enchanter who held us spellbound within his circle'. Dedicatee of Robert Schumann's *Toccata* which the composer related Schunke played perfectly, not from the score but from listening several times to its creator's performance.

SCHURMANN, Gerard (1928–   )
b. Java, Indonesia, of Dutch parentage. Educated at Radley Coll., UK; studied pf with K. Long, composition with Alan Rawsthorne. Embarked upon career as concert pianist, composed and for a time was conductor of

Hilversum radio orch., eventually settling in London as a composer. Works include *Contrasts* for pf, also a pf concerto which was first performed in 1973 in Bournemouth by J. Ogdon.

SCHÜTT, Eduard (1856–1933)

b. St Petersburg, Russia. Spent two years (1876–8) at the Cons. there, followed by another two years at Leipzig Cons. with K. Reinecke. Studied privately with T. Leschetizky in Vienna. Toured Central Europe with the violinist Wilma Neruda (later Lady Hallé), and appeared in St Petersburg in 1881 as soloist in his 1st pf concerto. Next year he accompanied Leopold Auer in a tour of Hungary but shortly after retired from the concert platform in favour of composition, among which are two pf concertos, pieces and chamber music. Prepared Schumann's pf works for the Universal edition.

SCHWALB, Miklós (1909–)

b. Budapest, Hungary, Pf pupil of E. von Dohnányi at R. Acad. there. Début 1923 in Budapest, thereafter touring as concert pianist. US début 1942. Settled there after World War II. Taught at New England Cons. from 1947. Recorded *Duophone* and *HMV*.

SCHWARZ, Heinrich (Max) (1861–)

b. Dietenhofen, Germany. Studied pf in Munich with J. Rheinberger and K. Bärmann, later teaching in Frankfurt and Munich where he became pf prof. Was also known as concert pianist who toured Europe, visiting UK 1892. Appointed to the court of Bavaria 1900. Wrote a pedagogic work on pf teaching.

Pupils included: Frederic Lamond.

SCHYTTE, Ludvig Theodor (1848–1909)

b. Aarhus, Denmark. Studied in Copenhagen, then with W. Taubert in Berlin and finally with F. Liszt in Weimar. Taught at Horak's Inst., Vienna, 1887–9, remaining in the Austrian capital until 1907 when he took a teaching post in Berlin. Was successful concert pianist, teacher and prolific composer including a pf concerto (first British performance 1902 at London Proms), studies, pieces and works for two pfs. A daughter, Anna Johanne (b. Copenhagen 1887–), was taught by him and later by A. Reisenauer and became a concert pianist.

SCOTT, Cyril Meir (1879–1970)

b. Birkenhead, UK. Was a natural pianist from an early age. Studied composition in Germany under Knorr and Humperdinck, and had a few lessons on pf from L. Uzielli. As concert pianist he performed only own works which include two pf concertos, much chamber music, songs and numerous pf works which were once popular, if held to derive from Debussy, an opinion with which, according to S, the Frenchman emphatically disagreed when the composer played some of them to him. Gave première of his 1st concerto in 1915 in London and toured USA in 1920 as soloist in the same work. Recorded *HMV* and *Columbia*.

SCRIABIN, Alexander Nicolas (1872–1915)

b. Moscow, Russia. Born on Christmas Day 1871 (OS). His mother, Lubov Petrovna – *née* Stchetinin – had not long graduated with a Gold Medal from St Petersburg Cons. where she had studied pf with T. Leschetizky. Her musical talents had already attracted favourable attention from the Rubinstein brothers. She was actively planning a concert career when she married but by the time she was carrying Alexander she was suffering from tuberculosis and in fact died a few months after he was born.

It is recorded that he took to the pf naturally from the earliest age, 'producing soft and delicate sounds with his elegant little fingers'. At that age he memorized music on sight or at one hearing. He began serious studies in 1883, later entering Moscow Cons. to study with N. Zverev then V. Safonov. His composition teachers were A. Arensky and S. Taneiev, while fellow-students included J. Lhevinne and S. Rachmaninov. In 1891 he won a Gold Medal for pf playing, and at a pupils' concert that year he performed a mazurka of his own. It is said that A. Rubinstein who was present at the concert promptly sat down at the keyboard and improvised a series of variations on the mazurka.

Around this time his right hand suffered a passing form of paralysis due to overstrain from practice. Gradually it was nursed back to efficiency but throughout his life was apt to trouble him.

Early in his career Scriabin attracted the interest of the influential publisher Mitrofan Belaiev who quickly put into print a whole selection of the young man's early work. He went further by sponsoring the composer-pianist in a European tour extending over 1895–6, featuring his own works and taking in Germany, France, Belgium, the Netherlands and Switzerland. On his return to Moscow, S continued to perform and taught pf at the Cons. 1897–1903. In 1897 he had married Vera Ivanovna Isakovich, a pupil of the Cons. They appeared in joint recitals of his music, notably in Paris later in the year of the marriage.

In 1903 a wealthy patron provided funds which released him from teaching, enabling him to concentrate on composition. The Scriabins settled in Switzerland where his father was living. By 1903 he had become involved with Tatiana Schloezer, who also had been a pupil at Moscow Cons. Safonov thoughtfully found a place for Vera Ivanovna as a pf teacher. Vera herself appears in the light of a saint, for in addition to never reproaching the composer with infidelity, she devoted time and energy to propagating his music in her public recitals. Meantime his interest in mysticism in general and Theosophy in particular was growing apace.

He was invited to the USA in 1906 to fulfil engagements and was so well received that he sent for Tatiana. New York society was scandalized when the news of their relationship broke. Outstanding concerts were cancelled and the couple returned to Europe in straitened circumstances.

All this time his output was steadily growing, and he even managed a number of concerts. With the death of Belaiev in 1903, all contact with the publishing house had abruptly ceased, and it was not until 1908 that Koussevitzky founded the Russian Music Edition in Berlin and offered S a regular income in return for the right to publish his works. The Scriabins, who had been living in Brussels, returned to Moscow in 1909, where he gave a very successful concert and for a short while basked in adulation. The truth is that he had passed beyond the comprehension of his audience both musically and occultly. By 1910 *Prometheus* ('Poem of Fire') was taking shape, and this was destined to be his final major orch. work. In the middle of this work Koussevitzky arranged a tour of nineteen concerts along the Volga in which the composer was featured playing his pf concerto; a number of his orchestral works were also played.

The première of *Prometheus* took place in 1911 in Moscow. It is a poem for pf, orch. and colour organ, and he performed the pf part. He appeared in London in 1914 playing his pf concerto as well as the pf part of *Prometheus* under Sir H. Wood. On that same visit to the British capital he gave two recitals of his own works in Wigmore Hall (then called Bechstein, being owned by the German firm of pf-manufacturers). The first recital consisted of eight preludes from Op. 13, two mazurkas Op. 3 and three *études* from Op. 8; the F sharp minor sonata Op. 23; *Poème* Op. 32 No. 1, *Ailé* Op. 51 No. 3, *Désir* Op. 57, *Étrangeté* Op. 63, *Feuillet d'Album* Op. 59 and *Poème satanique* Op. 36. The second recital comprised ten preludes selected from Opp. 11, 16, 17 and 35, two mazurkas Op. 25 and three *études* from Op. 8; *Sonata Fantaisie* Op. 19; both *Poèmes* of Op. 32 and the one of Op. 69 No. 1, *Masque* Op. 63, and the 9th sonata Op. 68.

Already, in London, he was suffering a painful lip that within a year was to lead to toxaemia and death. He returned to Moscow in the spring of 1914 to commence what he intended to be the crowning work of his creative life, which became known as *The Act*. He produced little more than a sketch of the prelude.

He wrote ten pf sonatas (two early ones being discovered long after his death and published c. 1940–50) and many sets of pieces most complex and difficult, as well as symphonic works and the early single pf concerto, but no chamber music or songs. No published composition of his bears a dedication. As a Russian composer he was unique in that he set out from what might loosely be termed the Chopin Romantic style but rapidly developed his own idiom which came to be identified with the 'mystic' chord built on fourths, leading to his discarding key signatures. (It is of interest to detect that Debussy in his *études* had reached a similar point). In Scriabin fiercely passionate themes and restless sections alternate with softly dreamy interludes of ineffable beauty. *Prometheus* was one manifestation of his research into a connection between the psychic vibrational scale of psychic colours with that of sound. His scale, adhering to the customary musical cycle of fifths, is as follows:

C major	Red
G major	Rosy-orange
D major	Yellow
A major	Green
E major	Pearly-blue
B major	Pearly-blue
F sharp	Bright blue
D flat	Violet
A flat	Purple

E flat	Steely, metallic
B flat	Steely, metallic
F major	Dark red

SCRIABIN, Vera Ivanovna (1875–1920)
b. Moscow, Russia. Pf pupil of Cons. there, whose playing deeply impressed musical circles of the capital, including A. Scriabin who married her in 1897. She was already playing his music in recitals and continued, sharing a recital with him in Paris during the honeymoon. Her career was interrupted as children arrived. The marriage proved transient, and S deserted her for Tatiana Schloezer, a former pf pupil with whom he associated until towards the end of his life, because official annulment to Vera was withheld. She in the meantime resumed her career and appears to have been of a forgiving nature for she continued to feature S's music in her recital programmes, visiting Paris for the première of his 3rd symphony. She also taught at Moscow and St Petersburg Conss.

SEBOK, Gyorgy (1922–)
b. Seged, Hungary. Pupil of Budapest Acad. and later taught at the Béla Bartók Cons. there, before settling in USA as prof. at Indiana Univ. Recorded Philips, Erato and others.
Pupils included: Sumiko Hioki, Shigeo Neriki.

SEELING, Hans (1828–62)
b. Prague, Czechoslovakia. Studied music there, toured extensively as pianist, eventually returning to Prague as teacher. Composed light pf pieces which had a vogue.

SEEMAN, Friedrich Karl (1910–)
b. Breme, Germany. Concert pianist who toured worldwide solo and with leading instrumentalists, e.g. E. Mainardi. Taught pf additionally. Recorded *Siemans*.

SEISS, Isidor Wilhelm (1840–1905)
b. Dresden, Germany. Pf pupil of F. Wieck in Leipzig. Settled in Cologne as teacher at the Cons., becoming prof. seven years later. Composed difficult studies and other pf pieces.
Pupils included: Carl Lachmund, Gustav Lazarus, Frank Liebich.

SEITZ, Ernest (1892–1978)
b. Hamilton, Canada. Pf pupil of Toronto Cons., then, for four years, with J. Lhevinne in Berlin. Spent some time with E. Hutcheson in New York. In 1916 became teacher at Toronto and proceeded to build up career as concert pianist in N. America.

SELLICK, Phyllis (1911–)
b. Essex, UK. Pupil of R. Acad., London, then of I. Philipp. Taught and performed thereafter. In 1937 married Cyril Smith with whom she often appeared in works for two pfs (and latterly three hands), especially written by British composers, e.g. Vaughan Williams and Lennox Berkeley. Gave première of M. Tippett's 1st pf sonata in 1938 in London. Recorded *Rimington van Wyck*, *Columbia*, EMI and Nimbus.
Pupils included: Adrian Sims.

SELVA, Blanche (1884–1942)
b. Brive, France. Student of Paris Cons. at an early age, thereafter of Schola Cantorum where she was to teach 1901–22. Début 1897. Also taught successively in Strasbourg, Prague and Barcelona. In 1904 gave a series of 17 recitals devoted to the entire keyboard works of Bach. Was also a specialist in contemporary French music, and was the first to play the Albéniz *Iberia* Suite. Wrote a number of books including *La Sonate* (1913) and a biography of de Sévérac. Recorded for *Columbia* (Bach and, with Joan Massia, the Beethoven *Spring* Sonata and the César Franck). Dedicatee of A. Roussel's *Suite pour piano*, Op. 14.

SEMPRINI, Fernando Riccardo Alberto (1908–)
b. Bath, UK. Of Italian father and English mother, both musicians. Studied pf and cello and at the age of 10 won a scholarship to study at the R. Verdi Cons., Milan, where his father became librarian to La Scala Opera House. Graduated 1928 as concert pianist, composer and conductor and with a wide and practical knowledge gained in association with some of the greatest Italian musicians. In 1933 formed a pf duo with an Italian pianist, Bormioli, who died 1944. Returned to UK after the end of World War II, having spent three years in Spain working and studying Iberian music. Became widely known for his accomplished pf playing and excellent arrangements. Also gave recitals in London and other musical centres. Recorded *HMV* and EMI. *Semprini's Serenade* was a popular feature of BBC Radio for many years until he retired in 1982. OBE 1983.

SEMSEY, Maria (1943–)
b. Budapest, Hungary. Student of Béla Bartók Cons. there and of Vienna Hochschule. Début 1969 Vienna. Performed in Europe.

SEOW, Yitkin (also **Yit Kin**) (1955–)
b. Singapore. Played in public from age of 5 and won several competitions. Formal début in Singapore 1967, and was accepted as a pf and violin student at the Menuhin School in UK. Made provincial appearances and in Europe. US début 1972. Won BBC Pf Comp. in 1974 and made his London début with orch. the following year. In 1977 won a Bronze Medal at the Arthur Rubinstein Int. Pf Comp., Tel-Aviv, after which he toured Europe, America and the Far East, solo and with orch. Recorded various.

SEREZS, Rezso (1899–1968)
b. Budapest, Hungary. Pianist, singer and nightclub entertainer who composed many of the songs in his repertoire including *Gloomy Sunday*, a number that became notorious through its influence on listeners to commit suicide. He himself committed suicide.

SERKIN, Peter (1947–)
b. New York, USA. Pupil of his father, Rudolf S. Début at the age of 10. UK début 1965 and thereafter performed successfully. Much identified with the contemporary scene. Recorded RCA.

SERKIN, Rudolf (1903–)
b. Eger, Czechoslovakia, of Russian parentage. Studied in Vienna under R. Robert, most of whose pupils who became famous being conductors. Début 1915 in Vienna. Began touring 1920 after World War I. US début 1933, and settled there when he joined the Curtis Inst., becoming Director 1968. Dedicatee of Martinu pf sonata (1954) which he premièred in New York in 1957. Also gave US première of Prokofiev 4th concerto (left hand) in 1958, but was known principally as one of the greatest exponents of the classical repertory of his time. Was also chamber music player in association with his father-in-law Adolf Busch. Director of Marlboro School of Music, Williams Coll., Oberlin Coll. and Univ. of Rochester. Awarded Presidential Medal of Freedom, 1963. Recorded *HMV*, *Columbia*, CBS and others.
Pupils included: Paul Berkowitz, Ronald Brautigam, Yefim Bronfman, Evelyn Crochet,

Gary Graffman, Steven de Groote, Cecile Licad, Seymour Lipkin, Frederick Marvin, Cristina Ortiz, Güher Pekinel, Süher Pekinel, Joel Ryce, Peter Serkin, Hilde Somer, Piet Veenstra.

SERMET, Huseyin (–)
b. Turkey. Won 1st Prize in the Jaen Pf Comp. in Spain in 1981. Enquiries addressed to sources in Turkey met with no response.

SEROCKI, Kazimierz (1922–)
b. Toruǹ, Poland. Studied pf and comp. in Lodz before gaining further training and experience in Paris. Toured as a virtuoso and was also prominent in Warsaw festivals of *avant-garde* music. Co-founder of Group 49. Compositions include a concerto, a sonata, a sonatina and other works for pf, also music for small ensembles with pf part.

SERRANO Y RUIZ, Emilio (1850–1939)
b. Vittoria, Spain. Student of R. Cons., Madrid, where he taught 1870–1920. Founded the concerts of the Circulo de Bellas Artes, and for a time directed the R. Opera, Madrid. Composed a pf concerto and pieces.

SESSIONS, Roger (1896–)
b. Brooklyn, New York, USA. Pupil of E. Bloch, and became his assistant. Teacher and composer. Pf works include three pf sonatas (1930, 1946 and 1965).
Pupils included: Vivian Fine.

SÉVÉRAC, Déodat de (1873–1921)
b. St Félix de Caraman, France. Received pf lessons from his father; went to Toulouse Cons., then Schola Cantorum, Paris, where his tutor in composition was d'Indy. Spent rest of his life composing, and the numerous pf works are now regarded as the best of his output.

SEYFRIED, Ignaz Xavier (1776–1841)
b. Vienna, Austria. Received pf lessons from W. A. Mozart; also studied composition with J. Albrechtsberger, whose theoretical works he edited. Taught pf and conducted.
Pupils included: Eduard Marxsen, Adalbert Sowinski.

SGAMBATI, Giovanni (1841–1914)
b. Rome, Italy. A prodigy who played in public at the age of 6. Was taught in Rome and received pf lessons from F. Liszt. Through him S came to know Wagner and began con-

ducting concerts of German works in addition to playing pf and teaching. Toured throughout Europe and was acclaimed. Played much chamber music and was co-founder of the Liceo Musicale and head of its pf dept up until his death. Composed many works in most genres including a pf concerto which he introduced to London in 1882. Now remembered only for his arrangement of the Gluck melody from *Orfeo*.

Pupils included: Dante Alderighi, Francesco Bajardi, Mary L. Barratt, Maria Bianco-Lanzi, Maria Carreras, Edoardo Celli, Ernesto Consolo, Giuseppe Ferrata, Hector Forino, Aurelio Giorni, Friedrich Niggli, Lydia Tartaglia, Enrico Toselli, Orsini Tosi.

SGOUROS, Dimitris (1969–)
b. Athens, Greece. Began learning the pf when 7 years old; début the following year. Appointed pf prof. at the Cons. there in 1979. US début at Carnegie Hall in 1982 and first appearance in London in 1983, on both occasions playing the Rachmaninov D minor concerto under Msitislav Rostropovich. As a prodigy of this century, critics have likened him to Horowitz, Barenboim and Menuhin. In 1983 was credited with having 35 concertos in his repertoire.

SHAFIR, Shulamith (1923–)
b. Odessa, USSR. Studied privately in Palestine, then with A. Schnabel and Solomon. Début 1934. Wide repertoire including the Bliss pf concerto played a number of times under the composer's baton.

SHAPIRO, Joel (1934–)
b. Cleveland, USA. Pupil at Columbia Univ., then of Brussels R. Cons., where he won 1st Prize, and privately with S. Askenase. Début 1963 New York followed by extensive tours. Taught at Illinois Univ. from 1970.

SHARPE, Ethel (*née* Hobday): *see* **HOBDAY, Ethel.**

SHARPE, Herbert Francis (1861–1925)
b. Halifax, UK. Pupil of R. Coll. of Music, London, under E. Prout and others. Appointed prof. there 1884. Composed pf works and duets as well as songs.

SHATTUCK, Arthur (1881–1951)
b. Wisconsin, USA. Studied in Vienna 1895–1902 with T. Leschetizky. Début same year

Copenhagen. Settled in Paris and toured extensively as soloist and with orch. Returned to USA during World War I.

SHAVICH, Vladimir (1888–1947)
b. Moscow, Russia. Pf pupil of L. Godowsky, and of F. Busoni in Berlin. Toured before World War I and was in USA when that war started. Settled there and acquired additional reputation as conductor, touring as such globally. Married Tina Lerner.

SHEARING, George (1919–)
b. London, UK. Primarily a jazz musician who toured USA and Europe in concerts and clubs, solo and with groups. Also performed classical works with principal symphony orchs. Recorded various.

SHEDLOCK, John (1843–1919)
b. Reading, UK. Studied in Paris under E. Lubeck for pf and E. Lalo for composition. Finished education in London where he settled as concert pianist, teacher and writer. Made valuable translations of Beethoven's letters from the collection by Kalischer, and of the dictionary of musicians by Riemann; wrote a work on Beethoven's sonatas and edited *Monthly Musical Record* at the beginning of the century. Composed pf works and a pf quartet.

SHELLEY, Howard (1950–)
b. London, UK. Pupil at R. Coll. of Music there under H. Craxton, L. Crowson and I. Kabos. Début 1971 Wigmore Hall. Has performed since. Recorded various. With his wife Hilary S (*née* Macnamara) made two-pf recital tour of Mongolia in 1981, said to be 'the first Western musicians in living memory to visit the country'. Announced in the autumn of 1983 a series of five recitals at Wigmore Hall devoted to the complete cycle of solo pf music by S. Rachmaninov, described in the advertising as 'a world first'.

SHEPARD, Frank (1863–1914)
b. Bethel, USA. Studied in Boston, then in Leipzig, where he was a pupil of S. Jadassohn and K. Reinecke. Returned to USA and founded own pf school, which he ran until his death.

SHEPPARD, Craig (–)
b. Philadelphia, USA. Student of Curtis Inst. and of the Juilliard School. Won prizes in Los Angeles and Dallas, and came second in Leeds

Int. Pf Comp. 1972, thereafter appearing solo and with leading orchs. of USA and Europe. Recorded EMI.

SHER, Daniel Paul (1943–   )
b. New York, USA. Student of Oberlin Coll. and of the Juilliard School. Début New York in 1974 (in duo recital with his wife). Performed in Europe and the USA; also taught.

SHERIDAN, Frank (1898–1962)
b. New York, USA. Studied pf privately with R. Goldmark and H. Bauer. Début in New York in 1924. Toured the USA and Europe in addition to teaching.

SHERWOOD, Percy (1866–1939)
b. Dresden, Germany. Student of Cons. there; pupil of F. Draeseke and of B. Roth. Taught at the Cons. while performing. Compositions included a pf concerto, a pf quintet and a sonata for two pfs.

SHERWOOD, William Hall (1854–1911)
b. New York, USA. Was prepared by many teachers in the USA and Europe, culminating with F. Liszt in Weimar. Performed in Europe before returning to the USA in 1876 where he became a distinguished pianist and teacher, in 1897 founding his own school.
Pupils included: Arthur Whiting.

SHIMIZU, Kazune (1960–   )
b. Japan. Took pf lessons from the age of 4 and came under professional training at 5. In 1974 won 3rd Prize at 28th East Japan Middle High School student concours, and two years later was enrolled in the Music Dept of Toho High School. By the time he was 20 he was a student of Geneva Cons. and the following year won 1st Prize of the M. Long–J. Thibaud Concours, Paris. Concentrated on concerts and recitals.

SHLONSKY, Verdina (1905–   )
b. Kremenchug, Russia. Studied pf in Berlin under E. Petri and A. Schnabel. Later studied composition with Milhaud and became a composer.

SHOSTAKOVICH, Dmitri (1906–75)
b. St Petersburg, Russia. Taught pf by mother before training at Glassov Music School, then at the Cons. there, which he entered in 1919, his pf teacher being L. Nikolaiev. Graduated in pf in four years, and for composition diploma wrote his 1st symphony (which has a

pf part), which had its première under N. Malko in 1926. The following year he entered the Chopin Pf Comp. in Warsaw, and composed pf sonata and *Aphorisms* (set of 10 pieces) shortly afterwards. The 24 preludes belong to the same period as the 1st concerto for pf, trumpet and strings, Op. 35 (1933) and first performed the same year with the composer as soloist. A 2nd sonata for pf was written in 1942 and 24 *Preludes & Fugues* belong to 1951. The 2nd pf concerto was written 1956–7 and was premièred by the composer's son Maxim S. in the latter year. Also composed chamber music, songs and pf pieces. Works for 2 pfs included a *Tarantella* and Concertino. Most of his student works were destroyed but 3 *Fantastic Dances* of 1922 were allowed to survive. R. Phil. Soc. Gold Medal 1966. Recorded Columbia.

SHOSTAKOVICH, Maxim (1938–   )
b. Leningrad, USSR. Son of Dmitri S. Showed musical talent from early age especially for pf and later studied at Moscow Cons. Concert pianist and teacher who gave première of his father's pf concerto No. 2 on his 19th birthday. It is dedicated to him, as is the concertino for two pfs. Recorded Melodiya. Defected to West 1981. His son Dmitri S (1961–   ) is a concert pianist who also in 1981, on tour in Western Europe, sought asylum.

SHOSTAKOVSKI, Peter Adamovich (alias SHOSTAKSKY) (1853–   )
b. Riga. Student of St Petersburg Cons. before becoming pupil of T. Kullak in Berlin and of F. Liszt at Weimar. Was pf prof. at Moscow Cons. before setting up own school in 1878 which was incorporated in Moscow Phil. Soc. in 1883. Besides concert and teaching activities, also conducted opera for a time. Was a friend of Rimsky-Korsakov who in his autobiography rated S highly as a concert pianist.

SHRAGER, Pyta (–   )
b. London, UK. Musically educated in Paris, and privately with G. Chavchavadze. Début 1966. Broadcast and performed throughout Europe. Specializes in French and Spanish music. Recorded EMI.

SHTARKMAN, Naum (1927–   )
b. USSR. Pupil of C. Igumnov and won 1st Prize in da Motta Pf Comp., Lisbon, 1954. Came 5th in Chopin Comp., Warsaw, 1955.

Performing confined mainly behind the Iron Curtain.

SHTCHEPIN, Sophie: *see* **PFLUGHAUPT, Robert.**

SHUKOV, Igor: *see* **ZHUKOV, Igor.**

SHURE, Leonard (1910–)
b. Los Angeles, USA. Studied there and later with A. Schnabel in Berlin. From 1933 taught successively at New England Cons. and Texas Univ., while carrying on concert career.
Pupils included: Harold Heiberg, Ilan Rogoff.

SIBONI, Erik Anton (1828–92)
b. Copenhagen, Denmark. Pupil of I. Moscheles in Leipzig. Performed and taught in Denmark becoming pf prof. at Sorö Acad. Wrote chamber music with pf parts, also a concerto and two-pf pieces.

SIEGEL, Jeffrey (1942–)
b. Chicago, USA. Student of R. Ganz, F. Reizenstein, R. Lhevinne and I. Kabos, winning 3rd Prize in the Concours Reine Elisabeth, Brussels, 1968. Appeared widely in the USA, Europe and the Far East solo, with orch. and as chamber-music player. Recorded Vox and Orion.

SIEVEKING, Martin (1867–1950)
b. Amsterdam, Netherlands. Pupil of J. Röntgen. Spent early years as an accompanist, working for celebrities like Patti. Went to America, performing and teaching. Was interested in virtuosic aspects and wrote technical music requiring a high degree of ability to perform.

SIKI, Bela (1923–)
b. Budapest, Hungary. Student of Liszt Acad. there, where he made his début. Performed thereafter. Pf prof. Recorded various labels.
Pupils included: Lennart Rabes.

SIKORSKI, Tomas (1939–)
b. Warsaw, Poland. Son of the composer Kazimierz S, who was one of his teachers, with N. Boulanger in Paris. In the vanguard in respect of contemporary music in both performing and composing in which the piano is much featured.

SILAS, Édouard (1827–1909)
b. Amsterdam, Netherlands. Studied pf with L. Lacombe in Frankfurt, then with F. Kalkbrenner in Paris, later studying organ and opera at the Cons. there. In 1849 won 1st Prize for organ, beating Saint-Saëns. Settled in London 1850, establishing fine reputation as pianist and organist before later taking up teaching. Composed three pf concertos, chamber music and pf pieces. His B minor concerto was premièred 1892 in London with composer as soloist. Shaw said the work had brilliance and cleverness that was not matched by the technical quality of playing on account of age.

SILKOFF, David Michael (1949–)
b. London, UK. Studied at R. Coll. there, with K. Taylor and C. Smith; also at R. Acad. with G. Green. Début 1975 London. Prizewinner and recitalist.

SILOTI, Alexander (1863–1945)
b. Kharkov, Russia. Pupil of Moscow Cons. under N. Sverev and N. Rubinstein. During the period 1883–6 studied with F. Liszt and on the latter's death returned to Moscow Cons., becoming pf prof. Left in 1890 to pursue concert career. UK début 1895. Settled in the USA after World War I where he taught at the Juilliard School for many years. Elder cousin of S. Rachmaninov and friend of many of the musical giants of his time. Made more arrangements and transcriptions than original compositions. Dedicatee of Rachmaninov's 1st pf concerto and of his ten preludes Op. 23.
Pupils included: Marc Blitzstein, Alexander Goldenweiser, Ilmari Hannikainen, Constantine Igumnov, Alexander Kelberine, Sergei Rachmaninov.

SILVA, Oscar da (1872–1958)
b. Lisbon, Portugal. Pupil of K. Reinecke in Leipzig, then of K. Schumann. Settled in Lisbon as teacher and composer, occasionally touring Europe. Worked in Brazil 1932–52, then returned home to retire.

SILVER, Millicent (1905–)
b. London, UK. Student of R. Acad. of Music, London, and of T. Matthay. Pianist but better known as harpsichordist.

SILVESTRI, Constantin (1913–69)
b. Bucharest, Romania. Studied pf, conducting and composing at the Cons. there. Pf début

1924, conducting 1930. When appointed to Bucharest Opera in 1935, gradually gave up pf playing.

SILVESTRI, Renzo (1899–)
b. Modena, Italy. Studied at Parma Cons. In between a concert career was pf prof. at Cagliari Cons. and S. Cecilia Cons., Rome. Composed for the pf and made transcriptions for two pfs of the Paganini-Brahms *Variations* and the Franck *Prélude, Aria et Finale*. Wrote technical works. Lectured at summer school at Mozarteum, Salzburg.

SIMMONS, Homer (1900–)
b. Evansville, USA. Pupil of J. Grunn followed by study in Europe including some lessons from I. Paderewski. Composed a *Phantasmania* for pf and orch., two works for two pfs and string quartet as well as pieces and songs.

SIMON, Abbey (1922–)
b. New York, USA. Pupil of Curtis Inst., Philadelphia. Toured worldwide solo and with orch. Won Elizabeth Sprague Coolidge Medal. Taught at Indiana Univ. from 1962. Recorded various.
    Pupils included: Philip Thomson.

SIMON, Anton (1850–1916)
b. Paris, France. Student of Paris Cons., settling in Russia from 1872 mainly as teacher. Compositions include a pf concerto and pieces.

SIMON, James (1880–1941)
b. Berlin, Germany. Pupil of K. Ansorge for pf and of Max Bruch for composition at R. High School there. From 1907 taught at Klindworth-Scharwenka Cons. Composed pf concerto and chamber music. Died in a Nazi concentration camp.

SIMON, Peter (1949–)
b. place unknown. Studied at Univs. of Toronto, Western Ontario and Michigan, also at Juilliard School of Music. Teachers included G. Sandor and L. Kentner.

SIMONDS, Bruce (1895–)
b. Bridgeport, USA. Student of Yale Univ. then in Paris and at the Matthay School, London. Début there 1921. Returned home and performed as well as joining Yale, becoming pf prof. 1938 and later Dean. Married the concert pianist Rosalind Simonds.

SIMONS, John (1911–)
b. Birkenhead, UK. Studied with H. Craxton and T. Matthay in London, then in Paris with W. Landowska and R. Casadesus. Début 1934 Wigmore Hall, London. Performed extensively and taught. Examiner at Trinity Coll.

SIMS, Adrian (1960–)
b. London, UK. Pupil of R. Coll. there and with P. Sellick, winning the Chappell Gold Medal in 1981. Also won the main award for pianists in The Royal Over-Seas League Music Festival, London, 1984, as well as prizes in other competitions.

SINDING, Christian (1856–1941)
b. Königsberg, Norway. Studied in Oslo, then later in Leipzig Cons., where his pf teacher was K. Reinecke. Decided concert work was not for him and turned to composition, the first major work being the pf quintet in E minor. There followed the D flat pf concerto and many pf works and songs. Was assisted by Peters when they took over publication of his compositions. Lived for a time in Berlin; also had a spell as prof. of composition at Eastman Cons., USA. In outlook not so national as E. Grieg. Remains primarily the composer of *Rustle of Spring*.

SINGER, Otto snr (1833–94)
b. Saura, Germany. Pupil of I. Moscheles and F. Liszt. Emigrated to USA, where he spent most of remaining lifetime at Cincinnati Coll.
    Pupils included: Otto Singer jnr.

SINGER, Otto jnr (1863–1931)
b. Dresden, Germany. Son of Otto S. Pupil of father before studying in Paris, then with F. Kiel in Berlin, and later composition under Rheinberger. Conductor and pianist. Composed chamber music and pf works including potpourri of themes from R. Strauss' *Der Rosenkavalier* for two pfs; also arranged Strauss tone poems for two hands for Breitkopf edition.

SIROKAY, Zsuzsanna (1941–)
b. Ungvar, Hungary. Studied at the Franz Liszt Acad. in Budapest where she was a pupil of P. Solymos, graduating with honours. Later attended master-classes with A. Brendel, G. Anda, P. Badura-Skoda and J. Demus. Prizewinner in Vienna and Leeds and later toured Europe solo and in concertos. Domiciled in Switzerland from 1968, assuming Swiss

nationality in 1983. Recorded Hungaroton and Jecklin.

SIROTA, Leo (1885–1965)
b. Kiev, Russia. Studied at St Petersburg Cons. and later under F. Busoni. Toured as fine concert pianist and for a time taught in Poland before settling in Vienna.

SITSKY, Larry (1934–)
b. Tientsin, China, of Russo-Jewish parentage. Studied at New South Wales Cons. of Music, Australia, winning a diploma. Début 1945. Performed in China for a time after that, then returned to Australia, where he became a noted virtuoso specializing in music of the Romantic period and 20th century. Compositions include *Fantaisie in memory of Egon Petri* (1962), *Petra*, 12 *Mystical Preludes* and a concerto for two pfs.

SKOLOVSKY, Zadel (1926–)
b. Vancouver, Canada. Studied at Curtis Inst. and with L. Godowsky and I. Vengerova. Performed solo and with major orchs. Dedicatee of Milhaud's 4th pf concerto which he premièred. Pf prof. at Indiana Univ., USA. Recorded various.

SLADE, Heather (1947–)
b. Birkenhead, UK. Studied at Liverpool Univ. and was a pupil of G. Green and C. Helliwell. Toured widely as pianist, harpsichordist and accompanist.

SLAVKOVSKY, Karel ze (–1919)
b. Czechoslovakia. Little known about this Bohemian virtuoso of the 19th century other than he propagated Czech pf music, giving first performance of Dvořák's pf concerto in 1878 which is dedicated to him; also premièred other works by Dvořák.

SLENCZYNSKA, Ruth (1925–)
b. Sacramento, USA. Infant prodigy who toured Europe 1931–2 solo and with leading orchs. Retired to study further, receiving tuition from J. Hofmann, E. Petri, S. Rachmaninov, A. Schnabel, A. Cortot, L. Lévy, M. Long and I. Philipp. Having possibly broken the record for the number of teachers she had sought help from, she re-emerged on the concert platform for a time but gave up that career in favour of teaching. Wrote *Music at Your Fingertips*, and an autobiography, *Forbidden Childhood*.

SLENDZINKA, Julitta (1927–)
b. Vilna, Lithuania. Pupil of Warsaw Cons. and later of H. Neuhaus at Moscow Cons. Début 1945. Additionally studied harpsichord and pursued dual career, touring widely. Recorded Muza.

SLIVINSKI, Josef (1865–1930)
b. Warsaw, Poland. Pupil of Warsaw Cons. before spending four years with T. Leschetizky in Vienna and finishing with Anton Rubinstein in St Petersburg. Début 1890 was followed by tours. Début in London and New York in 1892. Taught in Riga until 1918 when he settled in Warsaw. Was noted for the beauty of his playing of the Romantic composers and was at one time a rival to Paderewski. Shaw described him as 'prodigiously swift and with that air of deliberate, undistraught purpose which a man can only maintain when he is at something well within his physical power'.
Pupils included: Stanislas Niedzielski, Julius Wertheim.

SLOBODYANIK, Alexander (1942–)
b. Kiev, USSR. Pupil of Moscow Cons. Has toured outside USSR including USA. Last known agents had no information to offer when approached. Recorded Melodiya.

SLONIMSKI, Nikolai (1894–)
b. St Petersburg, Russia. Student of the Cons. there, and pf pupil of his aunt, I. Vengerova. Settled in the USA 1923, giving up a concert career in Europe to teach at Eastman School. Additionally took up writing and conducting. Wrote *Music since 1900*. Composed pf pieces and songs. Recorded Orion.

SLOPER, Edward Hugh Lindsay (1826–87)
b. London, UK. Studied with I. Moscheles. Début 1846 London. Rapidly became fashionable accompanist and composer of Victorian drawing-room trifles. Also played concertos. Late in life taught at Guildhall School.

SLUSZNY, Naum (1914–)
b. Geneva, Switzerland, of Belgian parentage. Pf student at Antwerp and Brussels Conss. Successful pianist and taught at Brussels Cons. Recorded EMI and Decca.

SMEBYE, Einar Henning (1950–)
b. Norway. Studied there, and later at Vienna Acad. and the École Normale, Paris. Début

Oslo in 1968. A leader among Norway's younger pianists who is equally at home solo, with orch. and in ensemble. Repertoire ranges from Bach to Bartók and Shostakovich.

SMENDZIANKA, Regina (1924–)
b. Toruń, Poland. Studied in Cracow under Z. Drzewiecki. Début there 1947 followed by widespread tours. Teacher and lecturer in Warsaw. Recorded Muza.
    Pupils included: Kyoko Koyama.

SMETANA, Bedřich (1824–84)
b. Leitomischl, Czechoslovakia. Initially self-taught on the pf because of parental opposition to music as a career. Later received lessons from J. Proksch through introduction of a friend, Katharina Kolař, who was a pupil and who married S. He taught for a time, then gave it up to tour as a concert pianist. History says he was a good pianist with special sympathy for Chopin. The tour was a disaster, and in despair he turned to F. Liszt, who helped S open his own pf school in 1848. Eight years later he took up conducting in Göteberg, but his wife's health was affected by the climate and she died in 1859. S returned to Prague in 1862 and became involved in the formation of national opera there. He became totally deaf at the age of 50, and ten years later was insane. As a national composer his greatest works are the opera *The Bartered Bride* and the six symphonic poems under the title *Ma Vlast*. He did, however, write sets of polkas and Bohemian dances for pf at three stages in his career which indicate what a fine pianist he must have been. He wrote them at a time when the polka had swept Europe as a craze, but these pieces seem to have been later overshadowed by the Dvořák *Symphonic Dances*.
    Pupils included: Josef Jiránek.

SMETERLIN, Jan (1892–1967)
b. Bielsko, Poland. Studied in Vienna, winning a prize in 1913; also pupil of L. Godowsky there. Toured Europe and USA with wide-ranging repertoire. An advocate of Szymanowski's works, giving the first London performance of the *Symphonie Concertante*, Op. 60, in 1933 under N. Malko. Chiefly remembered as a Chopin exponent whose playing was described as intellectual yet warmly human in appeal. Took out British nationality and settled in London prior to World War II. His Jubilee Concert of 1951 in the Wigmore Hall

was devoted to Chopin. Reputed to be an excellent chef. Recorded *HMV*.

SMIT, Leo (1921–)
b. Philadelphia, USA. Studied at Curtis Inst. and with I. Vengerova. Following the award of the Guggenheim Fellowship in 1950 spent time on further study in Rome. Has performed widely and written works for pf and songs. Identified with the contemporary musical scene, especially A. Copland whose four *Piano Blues* were premièred by him in New York in 1950, the first one dedicated to him.

SMITH, Cyril James (1909–74)
b. Middlesbrough, UK. Studied locally and was successful in local festivals before winning scholarship to R. Coll., London, studying pf with H. Fryer. Played Brahms B flat concerto at college concert under Boult, who invited him to repeat it with Birmingham Orch. Won further medals, also 1st Prize in *Daily Express* Pf Contest of 1928, following which he made recordings, broadcasts and a successful recital début in London. Became pf prof. at R. Coll. 1934 and in 1936 toured Europe, having already made provincial British tour with Elisabeth Schumann. In 1937 married P. Sellick and later they became known as duettists. In 1956 during Russian tour suffered a thrombosis which incapacitated left arm. Thereafter gave three-handed performances with his wife, and many notable composers supplied them with original works and arrangements. Also continued to teach. OBE 1971. Recorded *Columbia*, *Decca*, EMI and Nimbus.
    Pupils included: Clifford Benson, Eileen Broster, Julia Cload, Robert Ferguson, Eric Harrison, Antony Hopkins, Niel Immelman, Kay Lam, Gillian Lin, Iris Loveridge, Omar Mejia, David Silkoff, David Ward.

SMITH, (Edward) Sydney (1839–89)
b. Dorchester, UK. Student of Leipzig Cons. under distinguished teachers including I. Moscheles. Settled in London, becoming renowned as pianist, also composer of frothy salon trifles as well as transcriptions which were popular in Victorian drawing-rooms and for a long time after.

SMITH, Ronald (1922–)
b. London, UK. Studied at R. Acad. there, also in Paris, Début 1942 in London. Recitalist and broadcaster, specializing in the music of

Alkan about whom he has written several authoritative works. Recorded EMI.

SMITH, Wilson George (1855–1929)
b. Elyria, USA. Musically educated in Germany, mainly by X. Scharwenka and M. Moszkowski. Spent rest of his life as music teacher in Cleveland.

SMULDERS, Carl (1863–1934)
b. Maastricht, Netherlands. Pupil of Liège Cons. in 1873 from age of 10, and taught there from 1887. Became Belgian citizen. Used time as a concert pianist to demonstrate the keyboard of his friend Pierre Hans, an electrical engineer at Liège Univ. The Klavier–Hans comprised two keyboards, the front one being tuned as normal while the one behind, otherwise identical, was tuned a semitone higher throughout. The invention was designed to simplify pf technique by passing the hands from one keyboard to the other and so avoid the use of black keys whether ascending or descending the scale. A pf concerto for the Klavier-Hans keyboard was composed by René Barbier, a minor Belgian composer.

SOBRINO, Carlos (1861–1927)
b. Pontevedra, Spain. Showed pianistic ability from an early age and with the help of I. Albéniz appeared at a concert at 11. Student of R. Cons., Madrid, before travelling in search of experience. Met Anton Rubinstein who gave him lessons, after which he began touring widely solo and with artists of the calibre of Ysaÿe and Sarasate. Settled in London in 1898 performing and teaching. Was a pf prof. at Guildhall School there from 1905.
Pupils included: Maurice Cole.

SOFRONITZKY, Vladimir Vladimirovich (1902–61)
b. St Petersburg, Russia. Pupil of Cons. there under L. Nicolaiev, passing in 1921. Performed throughout Europe and taught; prof. at Leningrad Cons. 1936–42 and thereafter at Moscow Cons. Notable exponent of Scriabin, whose son-in-law he was.

SOKORSKI, Jerzy (1916–)
b. Yalta, Russia. Début 1936. Settled in Warsaw 1945 and performed solo and in chamber music, also accompanying his wife, the soprano Bogna Sokorska. Compositions include a pf concerto.

SOLARES, Enrique (1910–)
b. Guatemala City. Pupil of E. Bacon and of A. Casella. Carried on musical career in addition to diplomatic work.

SOLC, Karel (1893–)
b. Milevsko, Czechoslovakia. Student in Prague and especially of V. Štěpán. Début there 1917. Distinguished career as concert pianist and accompanist, retiring 1966 on account of left hand disability. Arranged and edited.

SOLOMON (1902–)
b. London, UK. Pupil mainly of M. Verne in early years; début Queen's Hall, London, in 1910 in Tchaikovsky 1st pf concerto. Performed as prodigy until 1916 when a committee was formed to provide funds for further studies in London and Paris, including with A. Cortot. Resumed career in 1921 in a recital at Wigmore Hall, London, and thereafter became established as a leading British pianist. Gave first London performance of G. Gershwin's 2nd *Rhapsody* in 1933, and world première of the Bliss pf concerto in 1939 in New York under Sir Adrian Boult. CBE 1946 for services during World War II. In his fifties, and at the height of his powers, suffered a stroke and was forced to retire from the concert platform. Recorded *Columbia*, *HMV* and EMI. Sir Neville Cardus said: 'He wasn't a Schnabel and he wasn't a Horowitz, but he had some of the elements of greatness and he wove them into the marvellous Solomon synthesis. Nobody of his period played the "Moonlight" Sonata so beautifully.'
Pupils included: Eric Hope, Franz Reizenstein, Shulamith Shafir, David Wilde.

SOLOMON, Yonty (1937–)
b. Cape Town, S. Africa. Student of Cape Town Univ. Went to London 1963 and became a pupil of M. Hess. After her death in 1965 he studied in Rome and later in California with C. Rosen. Performed in N. America, Europe, Israel and S. Africa. Wide repertoire included Bach and the entire published pf works of C. Ives. Gave première of 2nd sonata by Usko Meriläinen at Camden Arts Festival 1967. Played the solo version of the Gershwin *Rhapsody*, also works by Sorabji.
Pupils included: Piers Lane, Doreen Yeoh.

SOLTI, Sir Georg (1912–)
b. Budapest, Hungary. Studied at Cons. there

with Kodály, Bartók and, for pf, E. von Dohnányi. Began musical career as pianist, then gradually took up conducting initially through the opera house. As pianist recorded in role of accompanist and duo, especially Brahms sonatas with G. Kulenkampff on *Decca*.

SOLTYS, Mieczyslaw (1863–1929)
b. Lwow, Poland. Student of Lwow Univ., where he studied pf under K. Mikuli. Completed musical education in Vienna and Paris. From 1899 was Director of Lwow Cons. and conductor of local orch. Composed much music including pf concerto, pieces and chamber works.
Pupils included: Mieczyslaw Horszowski.

SOLYMOS, Peter (1910–)
b. Torokbecse, Hungary. Studied Budapest and Vienna. Début Budapest 1934. Concert pianist, teacher and editor of classical works. Recorded various.
Pupils included: Zsuzsanna Sirokay, Gergely Szokolay, Kenji Watanabe.

SOLYOM, Janos (1938–)
b. Budapest, Hungary. Student of Béla Bartók Cons. and Liszt Acad. under I. Kabos and others, also with M. Tagliaferro in Paris. Début Stockholm 1959, having settled in Sweden in 1956. Toured Europe and USA. Performed regularly. Recorded crd.

SOMER, Hilde (1930–)
b. Vienna, Austria. Child prodigy who, when family moved to the USA before World War II, became a pupil of R. Serkin at Curtis Inst., and later with M. Rosenthal and C. Arrau. Her career was dominated by interest in new music of which she gave a number of first performances.

SOMERS, Harry (1925–)
b. Toronto, Canada. Student of R. Cons. there. Wrote a pf concerto, several sonatas and songs.

SORABJI, Kaikhosru Shapurji (c.1892–)
b. Chingford, UK. A mysterious person whose musical education was private but included the pf. Also his name cropped up from time to time in the musical Press, usually in connection with some controversial matter. Began composing around 1910, giving public performances of his works up to c.1936 when he withdrew from

public life and put a ban on performances of his music, which was admired by persons as diverse in outlook as E. Petri, J. Ireland, E. Chisholm and Y. Solomon, who was permitted by S to include some pf solos in Wigmore Hall recitals 1976–7. Pf compositions included five sonatas, a set of variations and fugue on the *Dies Irae* theme; *Opus Clavicembalisticum* which the composer premièred in 1930; various transcriptions, *fantaisies*, toccatas, nocturnes and 100 *Transcendental Études*.

SORIANO, Gonzalo (1916–72)
b. Alicante, Spain. Student of R. Cons., Madrid. Début there in 1935. After the Civil War ended, his career went ahead, and rapidly he became a foremost Spanish pianist, touring extensively throughout Europe, USA and the Far East. Recorded *HMV* and Decca, also EMI as accompanist to the soprano V. de los Angeles.

SORMANN, Alfred (1861–1913)
b. Danzig. Studied Hochschule, Berlin, and later with F. Liszt at Weimar. Performed and was on staff of Stern's Cons. Wrote a pf concerto and chamber music as well as songs.

SOWERBY, Leo (1895–1968)
b. Michigan, USA. Pf pupil of P. Grainger. Début 1917 in Connecticut was followed by engagements solo and with orch. before war service. On release resumed his career and in 1920 gave première of his 1st pf concerto in Chicago. In 1921 was awarded the Prix de Rome and on his return home resumed a dual role as concert pianist and composer. Works included two pf concertos, a *Ballad* for two pfs and orch., and a variety of works for two and four hands.

SOWINSKI, Adalbert (1803–80)
b. Lukasowka, Poland. Studied pf in Vienna under Czerny and I. Seyfried. After a concert tour of Europe stayed in Paris establishing a reputation as teacher. Was one of the six pianists who played the Kalkbrenner polonaise etc at Chopin's first concert in Paris, but is especially remembered for compiling the first encyclopedia of Polish musicians in French, published in 1857. Composed a pf concerto, chamber music and light pf pieces.

SPADA, Pietro Salvatore (1935–)
b. Rome, Italy. Student at S. Cecilia Cons. there. Performed widely and taught in USA

from 1966, holding various univ. appointments. Recorded RCA.

SPANGENBERG, Heinrich (1861–1925)
b. Darmstadt, Germany. Studied in Frankfurt, then with N. Rubinstein in Moscow and with T. Leschetizky in Vienna. Taught successively in Mainz and Wiesbaden before founding own school. Performed and composed songs and chamber music.

SPANUTH, Auguste (1857–1920)
b. Brinkum, Germany. Pf student at Hoch's Cons., Frankfurt. Début 1874. Performed and taught in Germany until 1886 when he visited the USA, remaining there for twenty years as player, teacher and correspondent for a German journal. Returned to Berlin in 1906 to teach at Stern's Cons. Made an edition of Liszt's pf works, composed pf music and songs, wrote exercises and other pedagogic works.

SPEAIGHT, Joseph (1868–1947)
b. London, UK. Pupil of Guildhall School there, studying pf with E. Pauer. Appointed pf prof. at the School in 1894, moving in same capacity to Trinity Coll., London, in 1919. Composed chamber music and pf works.

SPEIDEL, Wilhelm (1826–99)
b. Ulm, Germany. Pf pupil of W. Kuhe. Performed and taught at Munich and Ulm. Co-founder of Stuttgart Cons. where he taught pf until founding own school in 1874. On the death of S. Lebert both schools were amalgamated. Prepared the Chopin edition for the publisher Cotta.

SPENCER, Allen Hervey (1870–1950)
b. Fair Haven, USA. Studied and taught all his life in Chicago, latterly as Dean of American Cons. Wrote a treatise on pf technique.

SPENCER, Eleanor (1890–1973)
b. Chicago, USA. Pupil of W. Mason and H. Bauer before spending five years in Vienna with T. Leschetizky. Début London 1910. New York début 1913. Thereafter toured Europe and the USA from her home in Paris.

SPENCER, Vernon (1875–1949)
b. Durham, UK. Pupil at Leipzig Cons., settling in USA 1903. Taught in Nebraska, then Los Angeles, where he died. Composed pf pieces and songs.

SPENCER-PALMER, Florence (1900–)
b. Thornbury, UK. Pf student of Matthay School, teachers V. Langrish and B. Dale. Performed, taught, gave lecture recitals, composed pf works for solo and two pfs, chamber music and prepared works on technique.

SPINDLER, Fritz (1817–1905)
b. Wurzbach, Germany. Pupil of F. Schneider at Dessau. Resided in Dresden from 1841 as concert pianist, teacher and composer. Composed a pf concerto, chamber music and hundreds of salon pieces, also sonatinas, several of which once had a vogue as teaching material.

SPITZENBERGER, Herbert (1927–)
b. Munich, Germany. Studied at Augsburg and Munich. Début 1950 Augsburg. Thereafter performed solo and with leading orchs. in Europe and Far East. Teacher and prof.

SPIVAKOVSKY, Jascha (1896–)
b. Kiev, Russia. Pupil of the Klindworth-Scharwenka Cons. in Berlin, also of M. Mayer-Mahr. Performed and taught pf, settling in Australia from 1934, where he worked at the Cons. of Melbourne Univ.

SPRY, Walter (1868–1953)
b. Chicago, USA. Pf pupil of T. Leschetizky. Performed and taught in USA, founding own school in Chicago in 1905. Later taught at Columbia School of Music.

SPURR, Phyllis (1910–)
b. Sittingbourne, UK. Student of R. Acad. of Music, London, and of G. Moore. A noted accompanist (especially of the contralto K. Ferrier) and singing coach. Recorded various.

SQUIRE, Hope: *see* **MERRICK, Frank.**

STADLEN, Peter (1910–)
b. Vienna, Austria. Studied at Vienna Acad., then at Berlin Hochschule under L. Kreutzer, winning 3rd Prize at an Int. Comp. for pianists in Vienna, 1933. Début 1934 there. London début the following year after settling there. Toured Europe, specializing in both Viennese schools of composition. Premièred Webern's *Variations*, Op. 27, in 1937 and, after World War II introduced works of Schoenberg and Webern to Germany. In 1948 gave première of Krenek's 3rd pf concerto in Frankfurt. Wrote

musical criticism, becoming chief critic of London's *Daily Telegraph*.

STAMATY, Camille-Marie (1811–70)
b. Rome, Italy, of Franco-German parentage. His mother took him to Paris on the death of his father and supervised his musical tuition. Taught by F. Kalkbrenner. Début 1835 with signal success. One of the pianists who played Kalkbrenner's *Grande Introduction, Polonaise et Marche* played on six pfs at Chopin's first concert in Paris in 1832. Later studied with Mendelssohn in Leipzig, becoming a celebrated teacher in Paris. His compositions included many sets of difficult studies.
Pupils included: Louis Gottschalk, Camille Saint-Saëns.

STANCZYK, Anna Maria (–   )
Request to last-known concert agents for biographical details met with no response.

STANLEY, Helen (1930–)
b. Tampa, USA. Student of Cincinnati Cons. and of E. von Dohnányi. Concert pianist and lecturer. In composition moved into electronic field.

STARCK, Ingeborg: *see* **BRONSART, Ingeborg von**

STARR, Suzan (1942–)
b. Philadelphia, USA. Student at Curtis Inst. Début 1948 with Philadelphia Orch. Made many appearances as prodigy solo and with leading American orchs. Toured throughout the world and won numerous prizes.
Pupils included: Michael Ford.

STASNY, Karl Richard (1855–1920)
b. Mainz, Germany. Prodigy who studied with I. Brüll, W. Krüger and F. Liszt. Toured Europe as concert pianist and taught, especially 1885–91 at Hoch's Cons., Frankfurt. Settled in the USA in 1891 and was pf prof. at New England Cons.

STASSEVICH, Paul (1894–)
b. Simferopol, Russia. Studied violin and pf simultaneously, the latter under L. Nicolaiev. Career thereafter alternated between the two instruments but after moving to USA he caused a considerable stir by being billed to appear in New York on 16 Dec. 1924, playing in the same programme the Tchaikovsky 1st pf

concerto and the Brahms violin concerto. Took up teaching and became noted pedagogue.

STAVENHAGEN, Bernhard (1862–1914)
b. Greiz, Germany. Studied privately in Berlin, then at the Hochschule under E. Rudorff, winning the Mendelssohn Prize 1880. Then, 1885–6, was one of the last pupils of F. Liszt. Began brilliant career as a touring virtuoso rapidly gaining a reputation as a Liszt specialist. Held court positions as pianist and conductor. Accompanied his wife Agnes. In 1890 G. B. Shaw rated him as 'the finest, most serious artist of them all', in the context of comparison with Paderewski and Sapellnikov. Composed two pf concertos and much pf music.
Pupils included: Max Anton, Edvard Fazer, Philip Halstead, Ernest Hutcheson, Nora Drewett de Kresz, Loris Margaritis, Edouard Risler, Otto Urbach.

STECHER, Melvin (1931–)
b. New York, USA. Studied there and later linked up with N. Horowitz to form the Stecher and Horowitz duo; also co-founder of pf school of same name from 1960. Toured and devoted much time to tuition of the young via compositions and writings. Recorded Everest.

STEFANSKA, Halina: *see* **CZERNY-STEFANSKA, Halina.**

STEHLE, Margarete: *see* **LEYGRAF, Hans.**

STEIBELT, Daniel (1765–1823)
b. Berlin, Germany. Colourful character who learned keyboard technique from an instrument-maker. Paris début 1790. Became a leading pianist in the city after challenging other contenders and beating them. In 1797 left Paris because of hostility to his obnoxious behaviour, settling in London. In 1799 he began a tour of Germany, leading on to Vienna, where he challenged Beethoven to a pf contest and was badly beaten. Returned to Paris, went on to London and then, in 1808, began a wandering tour through Europe which ended at St Petersburg, where he settled. Composed five pf concertos, numerous sonatas, rondos etc. One concerto has a *Bacchanalian Rondo* requiring chorus and was performed in London in 1822 with C. Neate as pianist.

STEIN, Hedwig: *see* **ELINSON, Hedwig.**

STEIN, Nanette: *see* **STREICHER, Nanette.**

STEIN, Richard Heinrich (1882–1942)
b. Halle, Germany. Studied at Berlin Hochschule and led mainly academic career in Spain and Berlin and finally Las Palmas. Was one of the first researchers into quarter-tones, and his *Zwei Konzertstücke* for cello and pf (1906) was the first publication in the system. Wrote upon the subject and composed many pf works.

STEIN, Theodor (1819–92)
b. Altona, Germany. Taught during latter part of his life at St Petersburg Cons., Russia, where he died.

STENHAMMAR, Wilhelm Eugen
(1871–1927)
b. Stockholm, Sweden. Son of a successful song-writer. Pf pupil of R. Andersson, then of K. Barth in Berlin. Début 1893 Stockholm in own pf concerto which enjoyed local success for some time. Became distinguished soloist and chamber music player as well as conductor of R. Opera, Stockholm.

ŠTĚPÁN, Pavel (1925–)
b. Brno, Czechoslovakia. Début 1941. Distinguished recitalist and chamber-music player throughout Europe. Recorded extensive repertoire on Supraphon.

ŠTĚPÁN, Vaclav (1889–19)
b. Pecky, Czechoslovakia. Student of Prague Univ., studies in pf and composition being private and continued in Berlin and Paris. Specialized in Czech pf music and was a leading exponent, giving many first performances. Toured Europe in early days as concert pianist. Composed much chamber music and pf works.
Pupils included: Karel Solc.

STEPHENS, Charles Edward (1821–92)
b. London, UK. Pf pupil of C. Potter. Concert pianist, teacher and organist, very much involved with the Phil. Soc. and hon. member of R. Acad. Composed pf pieces, chamber music and songs.

STERNBERG, Constantin Ivanovich
(1852–1924)
b. St Petersburg, Russia. Pupil of I. Moscheles and K. Reinecke at Leipzig Cons. Later studied with T. Kullak and received some lessons from F. Liszt. Conducted opera, toured as pianist and taught. The tours took him through Europe, Asia and America. Following the USA tours 1880–5 he was Director of the Coll. of Music at Atlanta for four years. Then in 1890 opened his own school in Philadelphia. Wrote *The Ethics and Aesthetics of Piano Playing* (1917).
Pupils included: George Antheil, Olga Samaroff.

STEUERMAN, Jean-Louis (1949–)
b. Rio de Janeiro, Brazil. Began studying pf from age of 4 and made his orchestral début when he was 14. Won prizes in S. America and in Europe. London début 1976. Toured widely in the Americas, Europe and Far East.

STEUERMANN, Eduard (1892–1964)
b. Lwow, Poland. Studied pf there, finishing with F. Busoni. Was also a composition pupil of Schoenberg. Returned to Poland, teaching and performing throughout Europe. Emigrated to USA in 1936 where he taught at the Juilliard School and continued concert work, undertaking the performance of new music especially of the contemporary Viennese scene. Gave the première of Schoenberg's pf concerto in 1944 and made pf arrangements of Schoenberg's orch. works as well as recording all the pf music. Own compositions included a pf sonata, a suite, chamber music and songs.
Pupils included: Kenneth Amada, David Bean, Alfred Brendel, Jakob Gimpel, Lili Kraus, Julius Lepiankiewicz, Dennis Murdoch, Helen Perkin, Simon Sadoff, James Tenney.

STEURER, Hugo (1914–)
b. Munich, Germany. Studied at the Music High School there. Established a reputation as an interpreter of Beethoven. Was pf prof. at Leipzig Acad. and from 1958 held a masterclass in Munich High School.

STEVENSON, Ronald (1928–)
b. Blackburn, UK. Studied pf and composition at R. Manchester Coll. and at S. Cecilia, Rome. Composer-pianist who taught for a time at Cape Town Univ. A prolific output of original work includes pf concertos, sonatinas, solos like *Variation Study on a Chopin Waltz* and *Canonic Caprice on 'The Bat'*, also a long *Passacaglia on DSCH*, chamber music and song cycles. Recorded EMI.

STEWART, Reginald (1900–84)
b. Edinburgh, UK. Pf pupil of M. Hambourg, and of I. Philipp in Paris. Worked in Canada in 1930s as concert pianist and teacher; also founded Toronto Orch. Then became Director of Peabody Cons., USA, 1941–58. Later head of pf dept at Santa Barbara, California, and Director of Peabody Cons.

STOCKHAUSEN, Elisabeth von: *see* **HERZOGENBERG, Heinrich von.**

STOCKHAUSEN, Franz (1839–1926)
b. Alsace, France. Studied with C. Alkan in Paris, then with I. Moscheles at Leipzig Cons. Director of Strasbourg Cons. Brother of Julius S, famous baritone who was a friend of Brahms and gave many early public performances of that composer's works.

STOCKMARR, Johanne (1869–1944)
b. Copenhagen, Denmark. Studied there and later at Paris Cons. under A. Fissot. Début 1889 Copenhagen, rapidly becoming a leading woman pianist on account of technical brilliance and musical sensibility. Toured Europe regularly as soloist, chamber music player and with orch. Recorded *HMV*.
Pupils included: Karl Maria Savery.

STOJOWSKI, Sigismund (1870–1946)
b. Strzelce, Poland. Pupil of L. Zelenski in Cracow, then of L. Diémer at Paris Cons., winning 1st Prize for pf playing. Later studied with I. Paderewski, who used to play pf pieces by S in his recitals. In 1891 in Paris he premièred a pf concerto of his own. Performed in Europe until 1911 when he settled in USA, holding teaching posts in New York from which he periodically toured. Became US citizen 1938. Composed two pf concertos and a *Rhapsody* for pf and orch., as well as solos.
Pupils included: Emanuel Balaban, Manna Friedberg, Oscar Levant, Arthur Loesser, Harriet Ware.

STORM, Nanne (1873–1953)
b. Horten, Norway. Studied in Copenhagen under Agathe Backer-Gröndahl, and then with F. Busoni in Berlin, finishing in Paris. Début 1900 Oslo. Performed and taught. In addition espoused the cause to raise the status of teaching in Norway.

STOTT, Kathryn Linda (1955–)
b. Nelson, UK. Pupil of the Menuhin School.

Début London 1978 after winning several scholarships. Gave première of George Lloyd's 4th pf concerto, RFH London, 1984.

STRADAL, August (1860–1930)
b. Teplice, Czechoslovakia. Studied pf at Vienna Cons. under A. Door before becoming a pupil of F. Liszt. Toured extensively until joining staff of Horak's Cons., Vienna. Had the reputation of very fine Liszt player. Composed pf pieces and songs; arranged Liszt's orch. works for pf, edited klavier works of Bach, Handel, etc and wrote books on Bruckner and Liszt.

STRASFOGEL, Ignace (1909–)
b. Warsaw, Poland. Studied at Berlin Hochschule. Accompanist to leading artists, e.g. Szigeti, Huberman, Piatigorsky, Lehmann. For a time pianist with New York PO.

STRAUSS, Noel (1880–1959)
b. Chicago, USA. Studied there then later with L. Uzielli in Frankfurt and with L. Godowsky in Berlin. Returned to USA, taught in Chicago and later in New York. Was also eminent music critic.

STRAUSS, Richard (1864–1949)
b. Munich, Germany. Studied pf as part of his musical education, reaching the stage in 1885 of playing a Mozart concerto in public under H. von Bülow whom S had in mind when composing the *Burleske* for pf and orch. Bülow never played it and, since it was beyond the composer's powers, the first performance went to E. d'Albert in 1890. Was accompanist at occasional *lieder* recitals, e.g. with his wife Pauline on tours in Europe and the USA before World War I, and with Elisabeth Schumann in the USA after World War II. Composed chamber music and pf works including an early sonata; also for P. Wittgenstein *Panatenäenzug* and *Parergon zur Sinfonia domestica*; and many beautiful songs with fine pf accompaniments. Fritz Busch in his memoirs describes Richard S as 'an excellent pianist'.

STRAVINSKY, Igor (1882–1971)
b. Oranienbaum, Russia. Studied pf from an early age as one of the musical disciplines, and doubtless used it in the course of composition. Later returned to study the instrument afresh, probably as a means of attaining security of income by developing a triple career as com-

poser-conductor-pianist. He premiered his concerto for pf and wind in 1924 in Paris and *Capriccio* for pf and orch. in 1929 in the same city, subsequently appearing in both works many times throughout the world during the 1920s and 30s. Also appeared with J. Iturbi in works for two pfs and partnered the violinist Dushkin especially in the *Duo Concertante* (1932). Other works for pf include a concerto for two pfs without orch., two sonatas and chamber music with pf part, *Serenade in A*, *études*, *Piano Rag Music*, a sonata and pieces for two pfs, and songs. Published autobiography, *Chroniques de ma vie* (Paris, 1935; English version 1936; republished 1975). Took French nationality in 1934 and became an American citizen in 1945. Recorded *Columbia* and CBS.

STRAVINSKY, Soulima (1910–)
b. Lausanne, Switzerland. Younger son of Igor S. Pf pupil of I. Philipp. Début in 1933 in Barcelona. First appeared in New York 1948. Taught pf at Illinois Univ. Concert career mainly associated with performances of father's works. Composed a pf sonata, sonatinas for beginners, 24 preludes etc. Recorded *Columbia*.

STREICHER, Johann Andreas (1761–1833)
b. Stuttgart, Germany. An early pianist who married Nanette, daughter of Georg Andreas Stein, piano-maker to Mozart. Moved the pf business from Augsburg to Vienna and gradually took over interest in pf construction, showing inventiveness. See also Nanette S.

STREICHER, Nanette (*née* **Stein**) (1769–1838)
b. Augsburg, Austria. Pianist who married Johann Andreas S, son of the founder of the Viennese pf business of that name.

STRELEZKY, Anton (1859–1907)
b. Croydon, UK. Studied pf at Leipzig Cons., then with K. Schumann. Toured Europe and USA as concert pianist. Composed pieces best suited to Victorian drawing-rooms and wrote his memoirs on meetings with Liszt.

STRIGELLI, José (1844–1916)
b. Milan, Italy. Student of the Cons. there. Performed and taught, especially members of the royal family. At 26 became conductor at Montevideo Opera House. In 1875 settled in Buenos Aires as concert pianist, conductor and prof at the Escuela de Música.

SUART, Evelyn (1881–1950)
b. India. Pf pupil of R. Pugno in Paris and of T. Leschetizky in Vienna. Thereafter toured Europe, settling in UK. In her concerts featured works of contemporary British composers. Was President of Soc. of Women Musicians, daughter of Brig. W. H. Suart CMG, and wife of Admiral Sir Cecil Halliday Harcourt KCB. Her daughter Griselda Gould became second wife of L. Kentner in 1946.

SUNDGREN, Sigrid Ingeborg: *see* **SCHNEEVOIGT, Sigrid Ingeborg.**

SUROWIAK-POLISZEWSKA, Bozena Maria (1949–)
b. Katowice, Poland. Pupil at Warsaw Acad., graduating 1973. Début Cracow 1968. Has performed extensively in own country as well as Europe.

SUSSKIND, Walter (1913–80)
b. Prague, Czechoslovakia. Student of Cons. there, also of J. Hofmann. Pianist of London Czech Trio (1932–42), soloist and chamber-music player, later turning to conducting with distinction. Adopted British nationality 1945 and in later years conducted successively in Toronto and St Louis. Compositions included pf works.

SUTCLIFFE, Doris (1911–)
b. Cape Town, S. Africa. Studied at Univ. there and commenced career as soloist, accompanist and teacher. Taught at Cons. of Music, Nairobi, from 1956.

SUTHERLAND, Bruce (–)
b. Florida, USA. Educated at Univ. of S. California. Pupil of E. Leginska and A. Iturbi. Concert pianist, teacher and adjudicator. Has written chamber music, pf pieces and songs.

SUTHERLAND, Margaret (1897–)
b. Adelaide, Australia. Studied at Melbourne Cons. under various pf teachers. Performed and taught pf until gradually turning to composition. Spent 1923–5 in Europe gaining experience. Works include a *concertino* for pf and orch., chamber music, pf pieces including a sonata and a sonatina, several suites, works for two pfs and songs.

SUTRO, Ottilie and Rose (1872–1970, 1870–1957)
b. Baltimore, USA. Careers ran parallel in that

they worked at the pf under their mother before studying at Berlin Hochschule under H. Barth. Début as duettists 1894 in London followed by USA the same year. Toured both continents thereafter.

SVEREV, Nikolai Sergei: *see* **ZVEREV, Nikolai Sergei.**

SWAIN, Freda Mary (1902–)
b. Portsmouth, UK. Pupil of Tobias Matthay School, and of R. Coll., London, under A. Alexander whom she married in 1921. Joined R. Coll. of Music teaching staff and besides solo appearances gave two-pf recitals with her husband. Founded British Music Movement in 1936 for propagating new music. Prolific composer including *Airmail* concerto for pf, chamber music, works for one, two and three pfs, and songs.

SWINNERTON-HEAP, Charles: *see* **HEAP, Charles Swinnerton.**

SWINSTEAD, Felix Gerald (1880–1959)
b. London, UK. Studied at R. Acad. there under T. Matthay. Became pf prof. in 1910. Made occasional concert appearances and was a successful composer of pf pieces with educational interest.

SZALKIEWICZ, Kyril (1914–)
b. Helsinki, Finland, of Polish descent. Pf pupil of L. Lévy and of A. Cortot in Paris. Performed in Europe before returning to Finland.

SZÁNTÓ, Theodor (1877–1934)
b. Vienna, Austria. Pupil first of J. Dachs at Vienna Cons., then of R. High School, Budapest. Worked with F. Busoni 1897–1901 in Berlin. Resided in Paris 1905–14, becoming friend of F. Delius whom he assisted in the revision of the Delius pf concerto which is dedicated to S, who gave the first performance at a London Prom concert in 1907. During World War I lived in Switzerland and thereafter in Budapest, performing throughout his career. Composed pf works of brilliance and technical difficulty which include *Essays and Studies* based on Japanese themes.
    Pupils included: Géza Frid.

SZASZ, Tibor (–)
b. Romania. Won 1st Prize in Univ. of Mary-

land Int. Pf Festival 1974. Enquiries addressed to sources in Romania met with no response.

SZEKELY, Imre (1823–87)
b. Matyasfalva, Hungary. Studied pf in Budapest, toured Europe as virtuoso and composed works for pf and orch., also *études* etc.

SZÉKELY, István (1960–)
b. Dunaújváros, Hungary. Studied at the Bartók Cons. and Liszt School there, teachers including P. Kadosa and Z. Kocsis. Prizewinner of Liszt-Bartók Comp. 1981.

SZELÉNYI, István (1904–72)
b. Zolyom, Hungary. Pupil of Budapest Acad. Début there 1926. Performed and taught pf. Featured contemporary composers in programmes and composed pf pieces and songs.

SZELL, Georg (1897–1970)
b. Budapest, Hungary. A prodigy who received all-round musical education, his teachers including R. Robert for pf, and Reger. Played and composed from *c.*1908 with astonishing facility. Then Richard Strauss took a hand and steered him into opera houses and to conducting. Recorded CBS (Mozart violin sonatas with R. Druian).

SZENDY, Arpad (1863–1922)
b. Szarvas, Hungary. Studied at Music Acad., Budapest, also with F. Liszt. Became pf prof. at the Acad. from 1890. Composed a *Concert Fantasia* for pf and orch., and pieces which are said to reflect the Hungarian idiom.
    Pupils included: Alexander László, Dezider Lauko.

SZIDON, Roberto (1941–)
b. Porto Alegre, Brazil, of Hungarian parentage. A prodigy who began a career in medicine before returning to music and finishing his studies in the USA. Afterwards toured globally especially the Americas. Recorded DG.

SZOKOLAY, Gergely (1953–)
b. Budapest, Hungary. Studied there at the Béla Bartók Cons., also at the Liszt Acad. and later at Moscow Cons., teachers including P. Solymos.

SZOPSKI, Felician (1865–1939)
b. Krzeszowice, Poland. Studied with L. Zelenski for seven years then with H. Urban in Berlin. From 1894 taught pf and harmony at

Cracow Cons.; also wrote musical criticisms. Later was music adviser to government. Wrote pf pieces, songs and an opera.
Pupils included: Jadwiga Sarnecka.

SZPINALSKI, Antoni (1901–)
b. Podlaski, Poland. Pupil at Chopin School, Warsaw. Performed; also composer of popular music including *Evening Tales* for pf and orch.

SZPINALSKI, Stanislas (1901–57)
b. Krasnodar, Russia, of Polish parentage. Studied at Mosow and Warsaw Conss., graduating in 1924. Won 2nd Prize at 1st Chopin Comp., Warsaw, 1927. Studied with I. Paderewski for four years then toured Europe. Prof. at Vilna Cons. 1934–40 and later taught at Poznan. Director of Warsaw State Music School from 1951. Recorded *HMV*.

SZRETER, Karol (1898–1933)
b. Poland. Studied there and later with E. Petri. A brilliant pianist who performed throughout Europe but whose career sadly ended through leukaemia at the early age of 35. Recorded *Odeon* and *Parlophone*.

SZTOMPKA, Henryk (1901–64)
b. Boguslawiec, Poland. Student of Warsaw Cons. under J. Turczynski for pf, graduating 1926. Obtained distinction in 1st Int. Chopin Comp., Warsaw, 1927 with a state scholarship enabling him to study with I. Paderewski in Switzerland. Début Paris 1932, followed by extensive tour of Europe. After World War II was pf prof. at Cracow Cons. while continuing to perform widely. Fine exponent of Chopin. Recorded Muza.

SZULC, Josef (1875–1956)
b. Warsaw, Poland. Studied at Warsaw Cons. before receiving tuition from M. Moszkowski in Paris where he remained as pianist, composer and teacher. Acquired success writing operettas.

SZUMOWSKA, Antoinette (1868–1938)
b. Lublin, Poland. Studied at Warsaw Cons. with A. Michałowski and from 1890–5 with I. Paderewski in Paris where she made her début 1891. Toured Europe appearing in London 1892 where according to G. B. Shaw she played 'beautifully and intelligently'. Settled in USA 1895, marrying the cellist Adamowski follow-

ing year. Was pianist in the Adamowski Trio.
Pupils included: Jesús María Sanroma.

SZYMANOWSKA, Maria (1790–1832)
b. Warsaw, Poland. Pf pupil of J. Field in Moscow. Lived for most of her life in Warsaw when not touring as concert pianist, becoming well-known and popular in western Europe. Composed pf pieces but according to one reference is better remembered for her ardent love affair with Goethe. Her name is mentioned twice in passing in the Hedley collection of Chopin letters, and Phil. Soc. records show she was in London in 1824 and played a Hummel concerto.

SZYMANOWSKI, Karol (1882–1937)
b. Timoshovka, Ukraine (Russia). Of Polish parentage and of a wealthy family with cultural background. Musical studies included pf with G. Neuhaus, and by 18 was composing music in the Chopin idiom. Went to study further in Warsaw, met a number of young Poles who formed an association to propagate their compositions. His early *études*, preludes and *Theme and Variations* were heard at public concerts and achieved popularity. Resided in Berlin 1906–9, finding especial interest in the work of R. Strauss. After returning home he continued to tour and compose. Met Arthur Rubinstein who liked his pf works and put some of them into his repertoire. Spent 1912–14 in Vienna and then proceeded to Paris. The Russian Revolution ruined the family, and S toured as composer-pianist, visiting Paris and London and, then, in 1921, made his US début in New York. In 1926 he became Director of Warsaw Cons. but was obliged to resign three years later on account of ill-health. He composed works for violin and pf, three pf sonatas, poems, dances and mazurkas. Among the last Opp. is *Symphonie Concertante* for pf and orch. premièred with S as soloist in Poznan in 1932. A Polish edition of his works was published in Cracow from 1973.

SZYMONOWICZ, Zbiguiew (1922–)
b. Lwow, Poland. Studied at Music Acad. there, where he later taught. Performed throughout Europe. Compositions include *Variations and Fugue on a theme of B-A-C-H* for two pfs, a pf concerto, a *Dialogue* for pf, strings and percussion, also pf pieces.

TACCHINO, Gabriel (1934–)
b. Cannes, France. Studied there and in Paris, winning 1st Prize at the Cons. Début 1953, and won a prize at the Busoni Comp. in Bolzano the following year. Awarded 4th place in the Concours Int. M. Long–J. Thibaud, Paris, 1957. Toured widely. Recorded Vox.

TAGLIAFERRO, Magda (1890–)
b. Petropolis, Brazil. Pupil of São Paulo Cons., later student of Paris Cons., winning 1st Prize for pf in 1907. Distinguished career as concert pianist and teacher before being appointed to a master-class at the Cons. in 1937. Two years later, at the invitation of the French Government, undertook an extended tour of the Americas where she remained during World War II, resuming her career in Paris in 1949. This legendary lady returned to London after half a century in January 1983 to give a recital of Debussy, Fauré, Franck and Chopin, a recording of which performance is preserved in the BBC archives. Recordings include Mozart's *Coronation* (*Decca*) and works by R. Hahn (*Pathé*) and H. Villa-Lobos (Columbia), conducted by the composers. Recorded also on Erato. Dedicatee of the Villa-Lobos *Momoprecoce* (1929) for pf and orch., which she premièred. Her autobiography was published in Portuguese.

Pupils included: Wladyslaw Kedra, Jean Laforge, Cristina Ortiz, Enrique Perez de Guzman, Lennart Rabes, Janos Solyom.

TAGLIAPIETRA, Gino (1887–1954)
b. Ljubliana, Italy. Pf pupil of J. Epstein in Vienna, then of F. Busoni in Berlin. From 1906 was pf prof. at the Liceo, Venice. Composed a concerto and pieces for pf and edited for Ricordi a monumental anthology of pf music through the ages.

TAGLIAPIETRA, Teresita (1883–)
b. New York, USA. Daughter of the famous T. Carreño and her second husband. Studied pf with her mother, then with J. Hofmann and, later, in Paris with M. Moszkowski. Début 1901 Stockholm followed by concerts throughout Europe and USA.

TAILLEFÈRE, Germaine (1892–1983)
b. Paris, France. Pupil at Paris Cons., winning distinction in harmony, counterpoint and accompanying. As a composer became a member of 'Les Six'. Wrote chamber music including two violin and pf sonatas, the first of which was premièred by Thibaud and Cortot in Paris in 1922, two works for pf and orch., and a composition for two pfs (with alternative orch. version). Settled in USA in 1942.

TAKACS, Jeno (1902–)
b. Siegendorf, Austria. Pf pupil of Vienna High School. Début 1926 in Sopron followed by career as touring pianist. Taught in Cairo 1927–32, then in Manila for three years. Returned to Europe 1942, then, in 1951, settled in USA, working at Cincinnati Cons. Toured Far East as well as USA and Europe. Recorded various labels and wrote extensively on eastern music.

TAKACS, Peter (–)
b. Romania. Won 1st Prize in Univ. of Maryland Int. Pf Festival 1973. Enquiries addressed to sources in Romania met with no response.

TAKAGI, Toroku (1904–)
b. Okayama, Japan. Studied at Tokyo Acad. and Paris Cons. Compositions included pf concertos, *Japanese Dance Music* for two pfs, other pieces and songs.

TAKAHASHI, Yoriko (or Yugi) (1937–)
b. Kanazawa, Japan. Pupil of Tokyo Univ. and of Cons. there; also of the Juilliard School, New York, and in Vienna. Prizewinner in several international pf competitions and appeared solo and with orch. both sides of the Atlantic as well as in own country. Also known as accompanist. Recorded RCA.

TAL, Josef (1910–)
b. Poznan, Poland. Studied in Berlin under M. Trapp and settled in 1934 in Israel, teaching, performing, conducting and composing. Works include five pf concertos, pieces, chamber music and songs.

TALMA, Louise (1906–)
b. Arcachon, France. Student of New York and Columbia Univs., pf pupil of I. Philipp; also student of N. Boulanger. Was on staff of Hunter Coll., New York; also performed. Works include two pf sonatas and pieces, also song cycles.

TAMAS, Janos (1936–)
b. Budapest, Hungary. Studied there and later in Switzerland. Début 1958 in Zurich. Won Bach Prize, Budapest, 1949, and 2nd Prize Bartók Comp. 1954. Appeared solo, with orch. and as accompanist. Has conducted. Compositions include chamber music and works for pf.

TAMIR, Alexander (1931–)
b. Israel. Student of Jerusalem Cons. with Alfred Schroeder, a pupil of A. Schnabel. Formed duo partnership with Bracha Eden, making their US début in 1955, developing into an international career with tours throughout the world. Became Head of chamber music section of the Israel Broadcasting Authority. Recorded Decca.

TANEIEV, Sergei Ivanovich (1856–1915)
b. Vladimir, Russia. Student of Moscow Cons. under N. Rubinstein for pf and P. Tchaikovsky for composition. Début 1875 in Moscow in Brahms D minor pf concerto, then toured Russia with the violinist Leopold Auer. In 1878 succeeded Tchaikovsky as prof. of harmony at Moscow Cons., then, when N. Rubinstein died in 1881, took over the masterclass. A brilliant pianist much admired by Tchaikovsky who entrusted first performances of many of his pf works to T, including the 2nd pf concerto in Moscow in 1882. He completed Tchaikovsky's 3rd concerto – many hold not

very successfully; was a famous teacher and wrote much music and valuable educational works on counterpoint, canon and fugue.
Pupils included: Arseni Koreshtchenko, Nicolas Orlov.

TANSMAN, Aleksander (1897–)
b. Lodz, Poland. Studied in Lodz then at Warsaw Cons., winning Polish State Prize for composition. Pf pupil of K. Lütschg. Début 1912 Warsaw. Settled in Paris after World War I. Toured Europe and composed. Visited USA 1927, giving première of his 2nd pf concerto in Boston followed by extensive tour. Toured Far East 1933. Settled in USA during World War II, returning to Paris in 1946. A distinguished pianist and composer, works included two pf concertos and two *Partitas* for pf and orch., a suite for two pfs and orch., five sonatas and many other works including *Sonatine transatlantique* dating from his first visit to USA and showing influence of jazz; chamber music and an opera. Recorded own *Mazurkas* on *HMV*.

TAPPER, Bertha (*née* Feiring) (1859–1915)
b. Oslo, Norway. Pf pupil of A. Backer-Gröndahl before continuing studies at Leipzig Cons. until 1878 when she became a pupil of T. Leschetizky. Settled in USA in 1881 where she taught as well as performed. In 1895 married the writer and lecturer Thomas Tapper. Composed pf pieces and songs; also edited Grieg's pf works.
Pupils included: Leo Ornstein.

TARENGHI, Mario (1870–1938)
b. Bergamo, Italy. Studied pf at Milan Cons. Became Director of Milan school of music and composed prolifically, especially a set of variations for two pfs on themes by Chopin and Schumann, also for duet a set of variations on *Santa Lucia*.

TARNOWSKY, Sergei (1888–1976)
b. Russia. Known to have been a pupil of A. Essipova. Pianistic career interspersed with teaching and settled in the USA later in life. Recorded Genesis.
Pupils included: Vladimir Horowitz.

TARTAGLIA, Lydia (1898–)
b. Rome, Italy. Studied at St. Cecilia, Rome, and with G. Sgambati and A. Casella. A popular concert artist in Italy who toured Germany and visited London.

TAUBERT, Wilhelm (1811–91)
b. Berlin, Germany. Pf pupil of L. Berger. Performed solo and as accompanist. Composed two pf concertos, chamber music, pf sonatas and many songs. Taught and later conducted at the Berlin Court.

Pupils included: Michael Bergson, Felix Dreyshock, Alexander Fesca, Hermann Genss, Louis Schlottmann, Ludvig Schytte.

TAURIELLO, Antonio (1931–)
b. Buenos Aires, Argentina. Studied there, and also with W. Gieseking. Wrote two pf concertos and other works.

TAUSIG, Aloys (1820–85)
b. Prague, Czechoslovakia. Pupil of S. Thalberg and father and first teacher of Karl T. A well-known and proficient pianist of his day though for a time outshone by his son, whom he survived. Composed showy pf pieces which exploited technique.

Pupils included: Karl Tausig.

TAUSIG, Karl (1841–71)
b. Warsaw, Poland. A pupil of father Aloys T and a prodigy. In 1855 he went to F. Liszt and on completion of studies appeared in a concert in Berlin in 1858 under H. von Bülow. Liszt furnished him with a letter of introduction to Richard Wagner who took the teenager under his wing only to find that T interrupted his composing by playing the pf violently and for long periods. Wagner wrote: 'His furious piano playing makes me tremble,' and he despatched T to practise elsewhere. By this time some contemporaries vowed he surpassed Liszt and S. Thalberg in sheer digital perfection, and the former described him as 'the infallible, with fingers of steel'. Others, however, were dubious about his temperament and methods. In 1862 he made a number of appearances in Vienna and was received with great acclaim.

Eduard Hanslick, a famous Viennese musicologist of the time, had reservations, saying of one recital that T was uncommonly gifted and extraordinarily enterprising, with astonishing bravura, power and endurance in 'so frail a youth. Similarly astonishing is his memory, which permits him to present a long succession of the most varied compositions with consummate security. . . . Not one single piece left a pure, satisfactory or even profound impression. He has a habit of striking single notes with a force which simply makes the piano groan'.

During that visit to Vienna, T formed a friendship with J. Brahms. From 1862 to 1865 he retired to study further and to compose. In 1864 he married Seraphine von Brabely and from 1865 resumed his concert career to renewed approbation, although critics continued to have reservations. That same year the Tausigs settled in Berlin, and he founded an Acad. for master pupils. He toured widely throughout Germany, Austria and Russia, dying of typhoid fever in Leipzig.

His original works are forgotten, but transcriptions of works by Bach, Schubert, Strauss and Weber continue to attract the attention of concert pianists. He made an arrangement of Chopin's E minor pf concerto, setting the fashion of truncating the opening orch. *tutti*.

Pupils included: Karl H. Barth, Oscar Beringer, Beniamino Cesi, Amy Fay, Anton Hartvigson, Rafael Joseffy, Aleksander Michałowski, Albert Parsons, Max Pinner, Oskar Raif, Adolf Schultz-Evler, Vera Timanova.

TAUSIG, Seraphine (*née* **von Brabely** (1843–1931)
b. place unknown. Pf pupil of A. Dreyschock and fine pianist in own right who married Karl T in 1864 and survived him.

TAWASTSTJERNA, Erik Verner (1916–)
b. Mikkeli, Finland. Pupil of Sibelius Acad., Helsinki. Début there 1943. Has performed throughout Europe and is prof. at Helsinki Univ. Has written much on the national hero Sibelius and is considered an authority.

TAYLOR, Anne (–)
b. Johannesburg, S. Africa. Studied in London and with L. Pouishnov. Teacher, concert pianist and accompanist, especially in S. Africa. Leading musical figure there.

TAYLOR, Franklin (1843–1919)
b. Birmingham, UK. Studied pf at Leipzig Cons. three years before becoming a pupil of K. Schumann. Settled in London performing and teaching for a time at R. Coll., and was generally a pillar of the London academic world as well as a director of the R. Phil. Soc. Published works on technique and prepared many editions for Augeners including Bach and the sonatas of Clementi, Haydn, Mozart and Schubert.

Pupils included: Frederick Cliffe, Thomas Dunhill, Rupert Erlebach, Herbert Fryer,

Ethel Hobday, Sir Landon Ronald, Mathilde Verne.

TAYLOR, Kendall (1902–   )
b. Sheffield, UK. Student of R. Coll., London, under H. Fryer for pf. Chappell Gold Medal 1925. Concert pianist and teacher. Recorded various labels.

Pupils included: Vanessa Latarche, Suraya Moyine, David Silkoff.

TAYLOR, Marie del Pico (1935–   )
b. Havana, Cuba. Studied at Univ. and Cons. there. Début Carnegie Hall 1975 as member of trio. Performed in N. America and became pf prof. at Havana Temple Univ.

TCHAIKOVSKY, Andre (1935–82)
b. Warsaw, Poland. Studied at the Cons. there, and later in Paris with L. Lévy, then with S. Askenase. Début Paris 1948, and began his concert career which was to take him throughout Europe, America and the Far East. 3rd Prize in the Concours Int. Reine Elisabeth, Brussels, 1956. Domiciled in UK from 1977. Died in Oxford and bequeathed his skull to R. Shakespeare Theatre, Stratford-upon-Avon, for use in *Hamlet*. The theatre accepted it. Composed pf concerto, chamber works and pf pieces. Recorded various.

TCHAIKOVSKY, Peter Ilyich (1840–93)
b. Kamsko-Votkinsk, Russia. Learned pf from age of four. Family removed to St Petersburg in 1848, and in 1862 he entered the Cons. which had just been opened, studying with the two Rubinsteins. In 1865 N. Rubinstein opened Moscow Cons. and invited him to join as prof. of harmony. T was always a good pianist although his public appearances were mainly as a young man and as accompanist. Wrote two pf concertos (a third was abandoned but posthumously completed by S. Taneiev), a *Concert Fantasia*, a pf trio in memory of N. Rubinstein, two sonatas, solo pieces numbering around 100, a collection of Russian *Folksongs* numbering 50 arranged for pf duet, chamber works and many exquisite songs that have been unjustly neglected.

TCHEREPNIN, Alexander (1899–1977)
b. St Petersburg, Russia. Son of the composer Nicholas T (1873–1945). Received some instruction from the Cons. there until the father was appointed to a teaching post in Tiflis. There young T studied further until the

revolution forced the family to take ship to France where they settled in Paris. Received pf lessons from I. Philipp. Début 1922 in London in own compositions. He premièred his 1st pf concerto in Monte Carlo in 1923, the year in which his 2nd concerto was written. US début 1927. In 1933 he made a world tour, and the following year carried out a long and exhaustive tour of USA. Returned to Paris where he lived throughout World War II thereafter resuming his concert career. Married the pianist Lee Hsien-Ming. Between the wars studied Oriental music in China and Japan and as a result wrote a *Method for piano on the Pentatonic Scale*; also developed the nine-tone scale (C-Dfl-Efl-E-F-G-Afl-A-B-C), as well as interpoint – note between notes as opposed to counterpoint, note against note. Prolific composer in most genres. Recorded EMI and RCA.

Pupils included: Robert Muczynski.

TEDESCO, Ignace (1817–82)
b. Prague, Czechoslovakia. Pupil of J. Tomáschek. Highly successful concert pianist who finally made his base in Odessa. Composed pf pieces in a light idiom.

TEICHMÜLLER, Robert (1863–1939)
b. Brunswick, Germany. Pupil of K. Reinecke at Leipzig Cons. where he taught from 1897 and was Director of the master-class from 1907. A nervous disease forced him to abandon concert work. Supervised editions of classical pf works and wrote a book on pf musical interpretation.

Pupils included: Dante Alderighi, Edgar Barratt, Marjorie Blackburn, Rudolf Breithaupt, Victor Buesst, Glenn Gunn, Eileen Joyce, Viggo Kihl, Paul Kovalev, Jean Kürsteiner, Jaroslav Kvapil, Mitja Nikisch, Erwin Schulhoff, Felix Wolfes.

TELLEFSEN, Thomas (1823–74)
b. Trondheim, Norway. One of Chopin's last pupils in Paris and, according to Arthur Hedley, accompanied the composer on his visit to Britain in 1848, being sent back from Scotland with a letter from Chopin to Pleyel begging the recipient to take good care of his pupil. Subsequently performed and, with Mikuli, embarked upon a Chopin edition for the Paris publisher Richault. A number of MSS of Chopin works in T's handwriting are known to exist, and after the Polish composer's death his sister gave the Norwegian a genuine

copy of the *Scherzo in B flat minor* Op. 31 which is now in the possession of the Paris Cons.

TEMPLETON, Alec Andrew (1909–63)
b. Cardiff, UK. Blind pianist who studied at R. Coll. and R. Acad., London, won a national contest in 1927 and performed solo and with most British orchs. US début 1936, by which time he had developed an act at the pf including songs. Was highly successful. Became a US citizen 1941. In his compositions a jazz influence is reflected in works like *Bach goes to Town*. Recorded RCA.

TENNEY, James (1934–)
b. Silver City, New Mexico, USA. Studied pf under E. Steuermann, performed and taught in California.

THALBERG, Marcian (1877–)
b. Odessa, Russia. Studied 1894–9 at Leipzig Cons. under K. Reinecke for pf. Toured Europe then settled in London for two years before moving to Paris (début 1903), living there until 1913 when he went to USA, teaching at Cincinnati Cons. until 1932. Before World War II was teaching privately in Paris.

THALBERG, Sigismund (1812–71)
b. Geneva, Switzerland. Son of Austrian prince who had resided temporarily while on diplomatic work. Showed aptitude for music from an early age and by the time he was 10 had progressed to studying with J. N. Hummel in Vienna. Even at such an early age his fingerwork was remarkable for great precision, and he seemed to have no difficulty in commanding absolute mastery of the keyboard. In 1826 he went to London, where his father had become ambassador, and studied under I. Moscheles, who regarded the teenager as one of his most gifted pupils. Soon he was demonstrating his skills before society as well as professionals, such as Clementi, who were most impressed.

About this time he started composing, mainly pf *fantaisies* and adaptations of opera. On his return to Vienna he continued to play in salons and was received with acclaim. His public début took place in the Austrian capital and in 1830 he commenced a tour of Europe taking him through Germany, France and the UK. The artistic life in Paris was at its height but it has been said that 'the splendid, calm beauty' of his style instantly captivated all who heard him, and from that moment began the

rivalry with F. Liszt. He composed a pf concerto designed precisely to show off his capabilities, but the work was not a success. At the same time he tried his hand at opera, writing two in quick succession. They also failed, and thereafter he confined his creative talents to solo pf works. In 1834 he became court pianist in Vienna, receiving the plaudits of most of the crowned heads of Europe in the form of magnificent presents of land, houses, jewels and decorations. His official duties did not interfere with brilliant concert tours. He appeared five times for the Phil. Soc. of London between 1836 and 1850, in four of them playing operatic *fantaisies*. In only one did he perform a concerto, the Mozart D minor (K.466). His popularity was then at its zenith.

In London, where he gave several recitals in 1842, *The Dramatic and Musical Review* recorded rooms densely crowded and with many unable to gain admission. At one of them: 'His first piece was a fantasia on subjects from Lucrezia Borgia; this was followed by the andante in D flat Op. 32, and a new study for the piano-forte, in the latter of which he was encored; and his third and last piece was his favourite capriccio on subjects from *Norma*. The extraordinary power and command over his instrument, the ease with which he masters passages written to shew that there is nothing the performer cannot achieve on his instrument, the perfect repose and finish by which M. Thalberg's playing is distinguished, were never more apparent; each note is played with precision, and no passage is slurred over; the formation of his hand, no less than his intellectual gifts, give him a superiority, in mastering difficult effects, over all his competitors.'

He visited America in 1853 and again in 1857, very extended tours reaching into Cuba, Mexico and the South, during which he earned fabulous praise and rewards. During his last years he restricted his appearances mainly to the European capitals and lived on a splendid estate in Naples where he assiduously tended a vineyard. A contemporary wrote, 'Imagination in its higher functions he seemed to lack. A certain opulence and picturesqueness of fancy united in his artistic being with an intelligence both lucid and penetrating, and a sense of form and symmetry almost Greek in its fastidiousness.' Schumann wrote at length on a recital in Leipzig in 1841, ending: 'The public did not seem to be there to judge, but only to enjoy; they were as certain of enjoyment as the master was of his art.' He was an exact antithesis of most of his contemporaries, being 'smoothly shaven, quiet, eminently respectable-looking, his handsome, somewhat Jewish-looking face composed in an expression of unostentatious good breeding, he was wont to seat himself at the piano with all the simplicity of one doing any commonplace thing'. He composed three pf sonatas, rondos, nocturnes, *études* etc, but the most important were some thirty fantaisies on operas which were very popular in his lifetime.

It had been claimed he was the first to divide the melody between the hands so that the right could carry out scintillating figuration while the left supported with a full and rich bass part. In fact Francesco Pollini (1763–1846) was the first to use three staves, and one of his Toccatas Op. 42 has the melody between the hands in the centre of the keyboard while intricate passages weave on either side. Whether or not Thalberg was acquainted with that work, the style which brought him fame was copied by others. He published an instructional method called: *The Art of Singing as Applied to the Piano*, and Liszt, referring to his singing tone, described T as 'the only artist who can play the violin on the piano'.

Pupils included: Paul Bernard, Beniamino Cesi, Heinrich Ehrlich, Eduard Ganz, Arabella Goddard, Wilhelm Kuhe, Tito Mattei, John Pattison, Charles Poisot, Alfonso Rendano, Aloys Tausig.

THEMELI, George (1915–)
b. Cairo, Egypt. Studied there and later at Paris Cons., winning 1st Prize. Début 1926. Performed throughout the world.

THEN-BERGH, Erik (1916–)
b. Hanover, Germany. Concert pianist and pf prof. Recorded *German HMV*.
Pupils included: Gitti Pirner.

THERN, Louis (1848–1920)
b. Budapest, Hungary. Younger brother of Willy T. Studied with father, then with I. Moscheles and K. Reinecke in Leipzig. Had duo career with Willy, later additionally teaching in Vienna.

THERN, Willy (1847–1911)
b. Ofen, Austria. Pupil of father then of I. Moscheles and K. Reinecke in Leipzig. Formed duo with brother, Louis T, and toured

Europe as such as well as teaching at Vienna Acad.
Pupils included: Erwin Schulhoff.

THIBAUD, Alfonso (1861–1937)
b. Paris, France. Pf pupil at Paris Cons. and of F. Planté and A. Marmontel, obtaining 1st Prize in 1876 for his performance of Beethoven's Op. 111. Subsequent public appearances aroused public acclaim. Toured UK and Low Countries 1879 solo and with the famous violinist P. Sarasate. Appeared in 1881 in Paris with C. Saint-Saëns, playing the latter's *Variations on a theme of Beethoven*. Settled in Buenos Aires from 1885. Co-founder in 1904 of the Thibaud-Piazzini Cons. Was regarded as a fine pianist with something of the temperament of L. Gottschalk.

THIBAUD, Joseph (1875–)
b. Bordeaux, France. Elder brother of the violinist Jacques T. Pupil of L. Diémer at Paris Cons., winning 1st Prize after first year there. Was noted concert pianist in Parisian circles. Also gave duo recitals, e.g. with Marsick the violinist; Carl Flesch in his *Memoirs* mentions giving a recital with T in the Salle Pleyel in 1896.

THIBERGE, Raymond (1880–1968)
b. Le Mans, France. Blind pianist who turned teacher and through a long life developed own method, working in Paris from 1913. Taught at École Normale from 1921 for a decade, opening own school in 1931. His principles later became linked to general education. Wrote tracts and made films on his theses.

THOMÁN, Stefan (1862–1940)
b. Homonna, Hungary. Pupil of F. Liszt 1881–5. Thereafter pf prof. at R. High School, Budapest. Composed sets of pf studies.
Pupils included: Béla Bartók, Ernst von Dohnányi.

THOMAS, Ambroise (1811–96)
b. Metz, France. Pupil first of his father, then entered Paris Cons. in 1828 to study pf with P. Zimmerman and F. Kalkbrenner, winning 1st Prize for his playing in 1829. Wrote a *Fantaisie* for pf and orch. and other pf works, also chamber music, but is remembered for his work in the theatre.

THOMAS, Margaret Betty: *see* **HUMBY-BEECHAM, Lady Betty**

THOMAS, Robert Harold (1834–85)
b. Cheltenham, UK. Pupil of C. Potter at R. Acad., London, where he became pf prof., then later at Guildhall School. Performed extensively and composed pf pieces and songs.

THOMÉ, François (1850–1909)
b. Mauritius. Studied at Paris Cons. 1866–70, his pf teacher being A. Marmontel. Settled there as pianist, teacher, composer and critic. Wrote music in diverse fields. One of his pf pieces, *Simple Aveu*, became extremely popular.

THOMPSON, John Sylvanus (1889–1963)
b. Williamstown, USA. Student at Philadelphia, then Pennsylvania Univ. Became concert pianist who toured USA and visited Europe. Successful teacher who wrote prepared courses and treatises on practice and technique.

THOMSON, Philip (1952–)
b. St John, New Brunswick, Canada. Student of Univ. of Toronto, (Mus.Bac): and later of the Juilliard School under A. Simon. Winner of a number of awards including the Juilliard Liszt Comp. Performed throughout N. America following début with Toronto SO in 1973. New York début 1980, and first toured Europe 1984, visiting London, Brussels, Amsterdam and Paris. A London critic wrote: 'his fingers found the notes with seemingly minimal effort, so that the maturity of his musicianship was allowed to emerge as the dominating feature'.

THUILLE, Ludwig (1861–1907)
b. Bozen, German Tyrol. Student of his father, then, at the age of 15, of J. Pembauer senior at Innsbruck. Went to Munich to teach pf and in 1883 became pf prof. at the Music School. Composed numerous pf pieces, chamber music and songs and, under the influence of Richard Strauss, tried his hand at opera. Also prepared a pf transcription of *Der Cid*, an opera by Peter Cornelius. His *Threnodie* is occasionally heard. In association with R. Louis published a textbook on harmony (1907).
Pupils included: Josef Pembauer Jnr, Hermann Waltershausen.

THÜMER, Otto Gustav (1848–1917)
b. Chemnitz, Germany. Pf pupil of H. Scholtz. Taught in Dresden and performed. Was famous editor of music editions of his day; also composed pf pieces including studies.

TICCIATI, Francesco (1893–1949)
b. Rome, Italy. Pf pupil of St. Cecilia Acad. there, and of F. Busoni. Performed and composed in various genres. Was Musical Director of London Univ. His *Poema gregoriano* for pf and orch. was premièred by him in London in 1921. Dedicatee of the second of Busoni's *Drei Albumblätter* for pf.

TICHMAN, Nina (1949–)
b. New York, USA. Student of Juilliard School from the age of 12, graduating in 1971 with the E. Steuermann Prize and making appearances in the USA and Europe. The following year was 1st in the Casagrande Int. Pf Comp., Terni, and began steadily to extend concert work. New York début 1977. Appeared in US festivals such as Tanglewood and Marlboro, and from 1977 was on the Faculty of Amherst Coll. Music Festival. In 1979 a *Washington Star* critic described her as 'an intensely dramatic and sensitive performer, with warmth, musicality, and understanding'.

TIDDEN, Paul (1861–1938)
b. New York, USA. Studied there and in Germany. Début 1886 New York. Thereafter toured USA and Europe solo and as accompanist.

TIMANOFF, Vera: *see* **TIMANOVA, Vera**

TIMANOVA, Vera Viktorovna (1855–1942)
b. Ufa, Russia. Child prodigy at the age of 9. At 11 began studying with Anton Rubinstein, and later with K. Tausig in Berlin. Lived for a time in Prague, then in Vienna, spending two summers at Weimar in the school of F. Liszt. Continued touring before settling in St. Petersburg as teacher. Appeared in London in the seasons 1880–1 when her name was given as Timanoff.

TIMBRELL, Charles (–   )
b. New Jersey, USA. Student at Oberlin Cons., and graduated from Univ. of Michigan. Prizewinner several times over, enabling him to study in Rome with G. Agosti and in Paris with J.-M. Darré, M. Haas and V. Perlemuter. Since 1979 performed widely in Europe and USA solo and with orchs., and on radio. London début 1981.

TIMM, Henry Christian (1811–92)
b. Hamburg, Germany. Pupil of Jakob Schmitt there. Début 1828. Emigrated to USA

1835 and was one of the first touring concert pianists there. Founder member of New York Phil. Soc. and President for a time. Composed pf works.

TINEL, Edgar (1854–1912)
b. Sinay, Belgium. Taught by his father, an organist, before attending Brussels Cons. from 1863 as pupil of L. Brassin. 1st Prize for pf playing 1873. Taught at the Cons., eventually becoming Director. His compositions were mainly of a religious nature but there are pf pieces including a sonata for four hands.

TIOMKIN, Dmitri (1894–1979)
b. St Petersburg, Russia. Student of Glazounov at St Petersburg Cons.; later pf pupil of F. Busoni. Début Moscow. Toured Europe, appearing in New York in early 1920s. Gave first European performance of the Gershwin pf concerto in 1928 in Paris. Moved into the Hollywood film scene from 1933, writing many scores which were acclaimed and which earned him Oscar awards.

TIRIMO, Martino (1942–   )
b. Larnica, Cyprus. Pupil of R. Acad., London, and of Vienna State Acad. Début London 1965. Has since toured widely, solo and with orch. Specialized in Schubert's pf works. Recorded Saga and EMI.

TOCH, Ernest (1887–1964)
b. Vienna, Austria. Taught himself initially before studying pf with W. Rehberg in Frankfurt, winning the Mendelssohn Prize in 1910. Later taught theory in Mannheim and composed in addition to studying for doctorate in philosophy. In 1926 gave première of his pf concerto in Düsseldorf. Lived in Berlin until 1933 when the rise of Hitler obliged him to move to Paris and then to the USA, where he taught and composed, and became naturalized in 1940. He and the Roth Quartet had given the première of his pf quintet in Pittsfield in 1938. Revisited Europe for a while after the war, still active on the concert platform, but returned to USA in 1958. Works include also a symphony for pf and orch., other chamber music, and sonatas and studies for pf.

TOLLEFSEN, Augusta: *see*
SCHNABEL-TOLLEFSEN, Augusta

TOLLEFSON, Arthur (1942–   )
b. San Francisco, USA. Educated at Stanford Univ., also privately. Début 1954 San Francisco. Performed and taught at North Western Univ.

TOMÁSCHEK, Johann Wenzel (1774–1850)
b. Skuch, Czechoslovakia. Studied law before deciding on musical career, and was mainly self-taught. A fine all-round musician of tremendous industry, splendid pianist and teacher; friend of Beethoven. According to his pupil E. Hanslick, the student was required to prepare a Bach prelude and fugue from memory for each lesson. Composed well over 100 opus nos. of great diversity covering sonatas, pf pieces and chamber music. A pf concerto in C patently belongs to the Beethoven era but is well structured and has charm.

Pupils included: Alexander Dreyschock, Sigmund Goldschmidt, Hans Hampel, Eduard Hanslick, Wilhelm Kuhe, Siegmund Lebert, Adolf Prosniz, Jan Pychowski, Julius Schulhoff, Ignace Tedesco, Jan Voříšek, Karl Wels.

TOMSIC, Dubravka (1940–   )
b. Dubrovnik, Yugoslavia. Pf student of Ljubliana, then of Juilliard School of Music, New York. Pupil of Arthur Rubinstein. Won prizes including Mozart Comp., Brussels, 1967. Toured throughout the world and taught at Ljubliana Cons. from 1967. Recorded various.

TORNER, Eduardo Martinez (1888–1955)
b. Oviedo, Spain. Studied in Paris, performed and taught. Made many arrangements of 16th-century stringed music for pf.

TORTELIER, Maria: *see* **PAU, Maria de la**

TOSAR, Hector (1923–   )
b. Montevideo, Uruguay. Known in Latin America as composer-pianist in neo-Classical style, works including pf concertino and pieces, chamber music and songs.

TOSELLI, Enrico (1883–1926)
b. Florence, Italy. Pf pupil of G. Sgambati. Toured as concert pianist before 'hitting the jackpot' with his song *Serenata*. Married a Crown Princess.

TOSI, Orsini (1878–1938)
b. Rome, Italy. Pupil of St. Cecilia Acad. there

and of G. Sgambati for pf. Toured as concert pianist, becoming additionally a conductor.

TOVEY, Sir Donald Francis (1875–1940)
b. Eton, UK. Privately educated, including music, firstly under a pf teacher, Miss Sophie Weisse. Memorized Bach and Beethoven as blotting-paper absorbs ink. Went to Oxford in 1894 and began a brilliant career. From 1900 appeared in London and other capitals. Prom début 1903 playing his own concerto. Gave solo recitals and chamber music concerts regularly thereafter. In 1914 was appointed Reid Prof. of Music at Edinburgh Univ., where he remained until his death. Was an especially great interpreter of three Bs and a pillar in the BBC *Foundations of Music* series up to 1939, and wrote valuable analytical notes on a variety of works. Some brilliant series of lectures have been published in book form, remaining everlasting tributes to a deeply penetrating musical mind which profoundly influenced the thinking of those students who came in contact. Knighted 1935. In association with Harold Samuel edited *Das Wohltemperierte* and with Harold Craxton the Beethoven sonatas, both for Association Board. Compositions include a pf concerto in A minor (dedicated to Miss Weisse), chamber music, pf pieces including a set of variations on an original theme, and dances for pf duet. About Tovey, Casals once remarked to Ivor Newton: 'There is the greatest musician since Bach. I remember Joachim saying, "I can discuss music with Brahms and Schumann, but not with that young Tovey. He knows too much." '

TOWNSEND, William (1847–1925)
b. Edinburgh, UK. Student of R. Acad., London, and of Leipzig Cons. Performed and taught for many years from Edinburgh where he settled. Wrote pedagogic works on pf technique.

TOZER, Geoffrey (1950–)
b. Australia. Appeared with Melbourne SO as prodigy at age of 8. In 1970 was joint winner of Alex de Vries Belgian Prize and 1st Prize in the R. Over-Seas League Music Festival, London Following year made UK début at Prom concert, London; also appeared at Aldeburgh Festival. In 1977 won bronze medal in Arthur Rubinstein Int. Pf Comp., Tel Aviv. Has toured Australia several times and in 1974 made tour of the Far East. Settled in UK.

TRAGÓ, José (1856–1934)
b. Madrid, Spain. Pupil of R. Cons. there, winning 1st Prize for pf playing at the age of 14. Later studied at Paris Cons., where he won further prizes. Début Paris 1880. Public appearances were rare because he preferred to teach at Madrid Cons. Did, however, tour with F. Arbos (violin) and A. Rubio (cello) through Iberia and offshore islands, performing for the first time there trios by Schubert, Schumann and Beethoven.
Pupils included: Carmen Alvarez, Manuel de Falla, Francisco Furter, Joaquin Turina.

TRAPP, Max (1887–1971)
b. Berlin, Germany. Pupil of Berlin Hochschule where his pf teacher was E. von Dohnányi. Taught first at Benda Cons., Berlin, then was pf prof. at the Hochschule. From 1929 was member of Berlin Acad. of Arts where he taught a master-class.
Pupils included: Josef Tal.

TRAUTMANN, Marie (1846–1925)
b. Steinseltz, Alsace-Lorraine, France. Pf pupil of H. Herz and wife of A. Jäell. Composer of chamber music, pf pieces and songs, and a writer on musical subjects including pf technique. Dedicatee of Saint-Saëns' 1st pf concerto and of his *Étude en forme de Valse*, Op. 52/6.

TRENEČEK, Hanuš (1858–1914)
b. Prague, Czechoslovakia. Studied there and taught for a time in Schwerin, Germany, before returning to Prague where he was pf prof. at the Cons. for many years. Pf compositions included chamber music, sonatas and batches of studies. With Karel Hoffmeister compiled a *Piano School* and was a one-time editor of pf scores for Universal Edition.

TRIGGS, Harold (1900–)
b. Denver, USA. Studied at Bush Cons., Chicago, then under J. and R. Lhevinne at Juilliard School, New York. Début 1924 Chicago. Toured throughout USA, appearing many times with leading orchs. Taught at Juilliard and at Curtis Inst. and gave two-pf recitals with Vera Brodsky.

TRIMBLE Joan (1915–)
b. Enniskillen, N. Ireland, UK. Student of R. Irish Acad., Dublin, then of R. Coll. of Music, London, under A. Benjamin. Début London Proms. 1943 with sister Valerie T in Mozart E

flat (K.365). Famous duo-team at recitals, concerts and broadcasting. Gave first British performance of S. Dances (Rachmaninov), pf concerto (G. Frid), concerto for two pfs (Bartók) and Stravinsky sonata. *Jamaican Rumba* by A. Benjamin was written for them, and first performance was given at R. Coll. in 1938. Composed and arranged much for two pfs.

TRIMBLE, Valerie (1917–81)
b. Enniskillen, N. Ireland, UK. Student of R. Irish Acad., Dublin, then of R. Coll. of Music, London, under A. Benjamin. See Joan T for details of duo career.

TROIANI, Cayetano (or Gaetano) (1873–1942)
b. Castiglione, Italy. Family removed to Argentina when he was a child but he came back to study pf at Naples Cons., returning to S. America in 1898. Settled in Buenos Aires as teacher and composer, as well as giving many concerts of own works. Was pf prof. at S. Cecilia Inst. there.

TROUP, Malcolm (1930–   )
b. Toronto, Canada. Studied at Toronto R. Cons. and Guildhall School, London, then in Germany with W. Gieseking. Worked in London and was pf prof. at Guildhall School of Music. Examiner and broadcaster. Performed in Europe and Americas.

TRYON, Valerie Ann (1934–   )
b. Portsmouth, UK. Studied pf at R. Acad., London, and with J. Février in Paris. Début London 1953. Toured Europe and USA as well as broadcast. Recorded BBC. Taught at McMaster Univ., Hamilton, Canada.

TUCKER, Norman (1910–78)
b. Wembley, UK. Played pf from early age. Student of R. Coll., later pupil of H. Samuel, then of E. Petri. Début 1936 Wigmore Hall. Appeared in recitals and concertos up to World War II, which was spent in administration in Whitehall. Resumed pf career from 1945 before transferring to opera as an administrator. Appeared from time to time thereafter in chamber recitals and as accompanist. CBE 1956.

TURCZYNSKI, Josef (1884–1953)
b. Zytomierz, Poland. Studied with his father, then spent two years with F. Busoni in Vienna.

Début 1908. Won 1st Prize in pf competition in St Petersburg in 1911. Toured Europe. Taught at Kiev Cons. 1915–19, thereafter master-class Warsaw Cons. One of the assistant editors of the Chopin edition of the Fryderyk Chopin Inst.
Pupils included: Helina Czerny-Stefanska, Maryla Jonas, Witold Malcuzynski, Henryk Sztompka, Moise Vainberg.

TURECK, Rosalyn (1914–   )
b. Chicago, USA. Took naturally to the instrument and in 1924, at the end of a year's tuition with her first teacher, won a prize to give a public recital. Two years later she appeared with the Chicago SO. She became a pupil of Jan Chiapusso who was to have a profound influence on her musical development. In 1930 she began giving all-Bach recitals and in 1937 performed a series of six in New York. Meantime she studied at the Juilliard School under O. Samaroff, who continued Chiapusso's good work of laying the strong foundations of a solid technique allied to a vigorous musical sense.

She carried out tours of the USA and in 1947 made her European début in Copenhagen, becoming famous throughout Europe as well as further afield in the Far East, India and Australasia.

Her distinctive approach to the music of Bach ensured that she became the leading exponent of her generation, as H. Samuel had been in his. Each, albeit with a different approach, put an indelible and individual stamp upon the music. In her case this specialization has tended to overshadow the fact that, at her orch. début with the Philadelphia Orch., she played the Brahms B flat concerto and that her repertoire is wide-ranging. She played the pf, fortepiano, organ, harpsichord, clavichord and such modern electronic instruments as the theremin. Ever indefatigable, she was additionally a member of the Faculty of Philadephia Cons. 1935–42, Mannes School, New York, 1940–4, Columbia Univ. 1953–5 and Juilliard School 1963–4, while during the same period fulfilling a professorship at Washington Univ.; she lectured at the Univ of California, 1966. She settled in Britain for a time from 1956, and held fellowships at Oxford 1975–   .
Wrote *An Introduction to the Performance of Bach*, published in three volumes in several languages and in 1966 founded the Int. Bach Soc. Edited Bach for the Schirmer edition.

Dedicatee of the pf sonata (1947) by D. Diamond. Recorded various.
Pupils included: Philip Fowke.

TURINA, Joaquin (1882–1949)
b. Seville, Spain. Studied at Madrid Cons. under J. Tragó. Worked and studied in Paris 1905–14 and received pf lessons from M. Moszkowski. On outbreak of World War I settled in Madrid, becoming a leading musical figure in the life of the city. Was pianist of the Madrid Quintet, composed, taught at the Cons. and wrote criticism. As composer used pf in chamber music, solos and songs. Published *Enciclopedia Abreviada de Música* (1916).

TURINI, Ronald (1933–)
b. Montreal, Canada. Studied at Quebec Cons., graduating 1950, and later received tuition from V. Horowitz. Shared (with M. Pollini) 2nd Prize at Geneva Int. Comp., 1958; also came 2nd in Concours Reine Elisabeth, Brussels, 1960. Toured N. America 1961, and USSR the following year. Visited Europe for first time 1965. Recorded RCA.

TÜRK, Daniel Gottlob (1756–1813)
b. Claussnitz, Germany. Thoroughly trained in Dresden and Leipzig. An organist and early pianist-teacher who also composed a large number of pf sonatas and sonatinas, teaching works, pieces for four hands and a method; also songs.
Pupils included: Carl Loewe.

TURNER, Alfred (1854–88)
b. St Albans, USA. Studied there, performed and taught in New York and Boston. Composed chamber-music and pf pieces.

TUTKOVSKI, Nikolai (1857–)
b. Kiev, Russia. Pf pupil of V. Puchalski. Thereafter taught pf and performed. For a time was pf prof. at St Petersburg Cons. before founding own school in Kiev in 1893. Composed pf pieces and songs.

TVEITT, Nils (1908–)
b. Kvam, Norway. Pf pupil of Conss. at Leipzig, Paris and Vienna. Wrote six pf concertos, *Variations* for two pfs and orch., and 100 *Folk Tunes* for pf as well as a large number of pf sonatas and other works evoking the Norwegian folk idiom.

TYRER, Anderson (1893–1963)
b. Manchester, UK. Studied at R. Manchester Coll. Début with Hallé 1914 and, after military service in World War I, London début 1919. Fellow of Manchester and Trinity Colls., concert pianist, teacher and adjudicator who travelled worldwide in latter capacity. Advised and conducted in the 1940 Centennial Music Celebrations by the New Zealand Government who, in 1946, invited him to organize their first national orch. Composed pf works. Recorded *Edison Bell*.

UCHIDA, Mitsuko (1948–)
b. Tokyo, Japan. Studied in Tokyo and Vienna, where she made her début. Teachers included S. Askenase and W. Kempff. Won 1st Prize in the Beethoven Pf Comp., Vienna, 1969; 2nd in the Int. Chopin Pf Comp., Warsaw, 1970, and 2nd in the Leeds Int. Pf Comp. 1975. Toured throughout the world including appearances in China in 1979. Recorded Toshiba-EMI.

ULM, Franz (1810–81)
b. Tschaslau, Czechoslovakia. Studied music locally and had a solo career as well as that of accompanist, especially with the soprano Henriette Sontag. Taught pf and also wrote musical criticisms.

ULRICH, Boris (1935–)
b. Zagreb, Yugoslavia. Studied there, where he gave his début in 1965. Performed and composed numerous and varied works, specializing in music for stage, screen, radio and TV.

ULRICH, Hugo (1827–72)
b. Silesia. Student of Stern's Cons., Berlin. Composed chamber music and many pf pieces but is remembered for his arrangements of Beethoven symphonies for four hands.

UNGAR, Imre (1909–72)
b. Hungary. Pupil of E. von Dohnányi. Won 2nd Prize, Warsaw Chopin Comp., 1932. Triumphed in a concert career despite blindness and was rated a brilliant and sensitive musician. Recorded *Radiola*.

UNIA, Giuseppe (1818–71)
b. Dogliani, Italy. Pf pupil of J. Hummel. Became a virtuoso, living and teaching in Turin. Composed prolifically for pf, mainly studies and operatic transcriptions.

UNINSKY, Alexander (1910–72)
b. Kiev, Russia. Pupil of Cons. there and later of Paris Cons. where he graduated with 1st Prize. Début 1927. First prizewinner of Chopin Comp., Warsaw, 1932, touring Europe until outbreak of war when he went to S. America, then USA. In addition to performing was appointed pf prof. at Toronto Cons. 1955. Later taught in Dallas, where he died. Recorded Philips and others.

UPTON, William Treat (1870–1961)
b. Tallmadge, USA. Studied there and, 1896–8, with T. Leschetizky in Vienna. Began concert career and teaching but spent a further year's study with J. Lhevinne in Berlin prior to World War I. Taught at Oberlin Cons., USA.

URBACH, Otto (1871–1927)
b. Eisenbach, Germany. Pupil of B. Stavenhagen at Weimar; studied composition at Frankfurt and pf with K. Klindworth in Berlin. From 1898 taught pf in Dresden, being appointed prof. in 1911. Founded own pf school there in 1921. Composed pf works and songs.

URBAN, Heinrich (1837–1901)
b. Berlin, Germany. Studied under violin masters but taught pf, especially at Kullak's Acad., Berlin, from 1881. Wrote critical essays.

Pupils included: Arthur Bird, Olallo Morales, Ignace J. Paderewski, Karl Preyer, Felician Szopski.

URIBE-HOLGUIN, Guillermo (1880–1971)
b. Bogota, Columbia. Important S. American composer who studied with d'Indy in Paris and, although his instrument was violin, composed for pf a series called *Trozos en el sentimiento populaire* numbering over 300 as well as a

pf concerto, chamber works, pf pieces and songs.

URSPRUCH, Anton (1850–1907)
b. Frankfurt, Germany. Studied pf and composition there and later became pupil of F. Liszt and J. Raff. Had mainly academic career, firstly at Frankfurt Acad. and later at the Raff School. Wrote a pf concerto and works for four hands.

USANDIZAGA, José María (1887–1915)
b. San Sebastian, Spain. Studied at Schola Cantorum, Paris, under d'Indy for composition and F. Planté pf. When he returned to Spain in 1910, was fired by Basque cause and produced an opera which was successfully staged in Bilbao. Encouraged to work on another, *The Swallows*, he gave up concert career for time being. By the time second opera was produced in Madrid U was already mortally sick from tuberculosis. He left pf works among his compositions, including a *Basque Rhapsody*.

UZIELLI, Lazzaro (1861–1943)
b. Florence, Italy. Studied there with G. Buonamici, then with E. Rudorff in Berlin and K. Schumann in Frankfurt. Taught there and in Cologne. Noted chamber-music player.

Pupils included: Adolf Busch, Balfour Gardiner, Alfred Hoehn, Cyril Scott, Noel Strauss.

VAINBERG, Moise (1919–)
b. Warsaw, Poland. Pupil of Warsaw Cons.
under J. Turczynski. Lived in Moscow from
1943 mainly as composer. Output includes
chamber music, pf sonatas and pieces, as well
as songs.

VAKARELIS, Janis (1950–)
b. Salonica, Greece. Musically educated there
and at Vienna Music Acad., his teachers
included B. Gelber and N. Magaloff. Won a
number of prizes in European pf comps. including a distinction in the Jaen Comp. of
1975. Toured throughout Europe solo and
with orch., and in London in 1983 gave world
première of *Entrata, 1983* by Theodore
Antoniou. Recorded RCA.

VALCÁRCEL, Theodoro (1900–42)
b. Puno, Peru. European study of music took
place in Milan and Madrid. Returned home in
1920, performing and composing. Visited
Europe again in 1930 and gave a recital in Paris
of own works which was acclaimed. Compositions included many pf works, e.g. *Fiestas
andinas*, 12 *Estampas peruanas*, a suite for violin
and pf, and many songs.

VALENCIA, Antonio Maria (1902–52)
b. Cali, Colombia. Studied music at Bogota
Cons. and in Paris. When he returned home in
1933 he established a Cons. of Fine Arts and
performed, introducing to Colombians much
contemporary European pf music which is said
to have been carried as an influence in his own
mature works for pf. Also wrote chamber
music.

VALLE de PAZ, Edgardo Dell: *see* **DEL
VALLE DE PAZ, Edgardo**

VALLIER, John (1900–)
b. London, UK. Son of Adela Verne. Studied
with M. Verne, A. Cortot and E. Fischer.
Début *c*.1950. Taught and gave recitals. US
début New York 1983. Compositions include
works for pf solo and two pfs. Recorded
Argem.

VALMALÉTE, Madeleine de (1899–)
b. Montreuil, France. Student of I. Philipp at
Paris Cons., winning 1st Prize for pf playing.
Became well-known recitalist and concerto
player, touring Europe numerous times.
Taught at École Normale and was pf prof. at
Grenoble Cons. Recorded *Polydor*.

VAN BARTHOLD, Kenneth: *see*
BARTHOLD, Kenneth van

VAN BLERK, Gerardus (1924–)
b. Tilburg, Netherlands. Pupil of Amsterdam
Cons. and prizewinner for pf playing. Later
studied with Y. Nat in Paris. Performed and
was pf prof. at The Hague R. Cons.

VAN CLEVE, John (1851–1918)
b. Maysville, USA. Studied pf in Boston and
settled in Cincinnati, towards the end of his life
living in New York. Concert pianist and
teacher.

VAN HESSEN, Ro (1913–)
b. Groningen, Netherlands. Pupil of W.
Andriessen and S. Askenase. Performed
mainly as accompanist; and lectured.

VANNUCCINI, Luigi (1828–1911)
b. Fojano, Italy. Singing teacher and conductor who later took up pf and was successful
as soloist and accompanist. Composed for the
instrument, also songs.

VAN RENESSE, Georg: *see* **RENESSE, Georg van**

VAN WYK, Arnold: *see* **WYK, Arnold van**

VARELLA-CID, Sergio (1935–)
b. Lisbon, Portugal. Studied there and in Paris and Moscow, teachers including H. Craxton and I. Kabos. Widely toured.

VARRO, Marie Aimée (1915–70)
b. Brunoy, France. Pupil of Paris Cons., winning 1st Prize; then of R. Casadesus and A. Cortot. Studied Liszt with E. von Sauer before starting concert career in Europe and America, specializing in works of the Romantic composers. Recorded Orion.

VÁSÁRY, Tamas (1933–)
b. Debreczen, Hungary. Pupil of Budapest Acad. and of E. von Dohnányi; later of E. Fischer and C. Haskil. Taught at the Acad. until 1956 when he left Hungary at the time of the uprising, afterwards living in Switzerland. London début 1961. Built worldwide reputation as virtuoso, performing solo and with leading orchs. Recorded DG.

VAURABOURG, Andrée (Mrs Arthur Honegger) (1894–)
b. Toulouse, France. Student at the Cons. there, winning 1st Prize in 1902. Went to Paris in 1908 where she was a pupil of R. Pugno and also studied composition at Paris Cons., winning a prize. As pianist, teacher and composer was modern in outlook. Gave première of her husband's works, notably *Toccata et Variations* in 1916, and the *Concertino* for pf and orch. in 1925. Her own compositions include pf works, chamber music and songs.

VAZSONYI, Balint (1936–)
b. Budapest, Hungary. Studied at F. Liszt Acad. there, also with E. von Dohnányi. Début 1948 Budapest. Performed thereafter in Europe and USA. In 1977, to mark 150th anniversary of death of Beethoven, performed the entire cycle of 32 sonatas in London from memory, non-stop, within 36 hours. Recorded Vox, Genesis.

VECSEY, Desider (1882–1966)
b. Budapest, Hungary. Studied at Budapest Cons. and later under E. von Sauer. Was a child prodigy and continued to tour after graduation. Went to USA during World War I

and decided to settle there. Taught in the Hollywood area. Composed various pf pieces and songs.

VEENSTRA, Piet (1929–)
b. Rotterdam, Netherlands. Pf pupil of L. Fleisher and R. Serkin. Début The Hague 1955. Thereafter performed and toured. Recorded various.

VENGEROVA, Isabella (1879–1956)
b. Vilna, Lithuania. Pupil first of A. Goldenweiser, then of J. Dachs at Vienna Cons., becoming pupil of T. Leschetizky 1896–1900. Appointed to St Petersburg Cons. 1905 and made prof. 1907. Settled in New York 1921. Appointed pf prof. at Curtis Inst. 1924 when it was established.
Pupils included: Samuel Barber, Leonard Bernstein, Lukas Foss, Sydney Foster, Gary Graffman, Ignace Hilsberg, Norman Horowitz, Lilian Kallir, Leonard Pennario, Zadel Skolovsky, Nikolai Slonimski, Leo Smit.

VERED, Ilana (–)
b. Tel Aviv, Israel. Studied at Paris Cons. where she won 1st Prize at 15. Teachers included V. Perlemuter, M. Münz, R. Lhevinne and J.-M. Darré. Performed with great success throughout Europe and America. Recorded Decca.

VERESS, Sándor (1907–)
b. Kolozsvar, Hungary. Pf pupil of Budapest Cons., and studied with Z. Kodály and B. Bartók. Taught pf in Budapest. Left Hungary after World War II and settled in Berne, Switzerland, as prof. at the Univ. Composed a pf concerto which he premièred in 1954, also chamber music and songs.
Pupils included: Thomas Rajna, Jürg Wyttenbach.

VERNE, Adela (1877–1952)
b. Southampton, UK. Youngest of four sisters, all pianists and teachers. (Family name was Wurm and the eldest, Marie, retained it.) Studied with her sister Mathilde before becoming a pupil of Marie Schumann. Also received tuition from I. Paderewski. Début 1891 London. Achieved eminence as performer and teacher. Gave first London performance of Brahms 2nd pf concerto. Toured Europe and the USA solo and with artists of the calibre of Butt, Elman and Ysaÿe. Gave duo recitals with

Mathilde V, and they played the Mozart E flat concerto at Queen's Hall, London, on 28 Jan. 1906 to commemorate the 150th anniversary of the composer's birth. Taught and performed up to her death. Recorded *Columbia*.

VERNE, Alice (1868–1958)
b. Southampton, UK. Second eldest of the Verne sisters. Taught by her parents and was a pf teacher at Mathilde V's school. Composed pf pieces.

VERNE, Mathilde (1865–1936)
b. Southampton, UK. Pupil of parents then of F. Taylor before attending the R. Coll., London. Was heard by K. Schumann who taught her for six years in Frankfurt. Début London Proms 1903. Had extensive concert career and taught at R. Coll. before opening own school. Taught HM Queen Elizabeth the Queen Mother. Wrote autobiography *Chords of Remembrance*.
Pupils included: Joan Last, Moura Lympany, Herbert Menges, Rene Pougnet, Harold Samuel, Solomon, John Vallier, Adela Verne, Dushko Yovanovich.

VESELY, Roman (1879–)
b. Chrudim, Czechoslovakia. Pupil of S. Jadassohn in Leipzig, later in Prague. Late taking up career but from 1919 was pf prof. at Prague Cons. Made speciality of transcribing Czech orch. works for pf.

VETTER, Hermann (1859–1928)
b. Grossrebnitz, Germany. Pupil of Dresden Cons., where he taught pf from 1883, eventually as pf prof. Composed studies, edited works of Liszt and wrote pedagogic treatises.

VEUVE, Adolphe (1872–)
b. Neuchâtel, Switzerland. Studied at Berlin High School, then with T. Leschetizky in Vienna. One of the finest Swiss pianists with splendid technique and temperament. Regularly appeared in Germany, France and Low Countries. Composed sonatas, pieces and songs.

VIDAL, Paul (1863–1931)
b. Paris, France. Pianist, composer and teacher at Paris Cons., principally the art of accompaniment.
Pupils included: Nadia Boulanger.

VIDIELLA, Carlos (1856–1915)
b. Barcelona, Spain. Studied with F. Pujol there, and later with A. Marmontel at Paris Cons. Was successful concert pianist and teacher.
Pupils included: Joaquín Nin.

VIEIRA, José Antonio (1852–94)
b. Lisbon, Portugal. Concert pianist who taught at Lisbon Cons. from 1882.

VIGNOLES, Roger Hutton (1945–)
b. Cheltenham, UK. Studied at Cambridge. Concert career included recitals; also accompanied celebrities; chamber music work and broadcasting.

VILLA-LOBOS, Heitor (1887–1959)
b. Rio de Janeiro, Brazil. Largely self-taught composer and pianist, although he went to Paris in 1922 on Government grant and spent some years there. His compositional style incorporates exotic Brazilian folk-music based on study of itinerant bands of musicians. He originated two types: the *Chôros*, and the *Bachianas Brasileiras*, some quite modest in scope and for a single instrument, others highly complex and for big forces. Very prolific composer with many works for pf or with a pf part, all mostly of great difficulty. Sponsored by A. Rubinstein from 1918 who gave first performances of his compositions. Year of birth uncertain. Villa-Lobos himself maintained: 'The whole fabric of my style, the melody, the rhythm, even the harmony of my music is permeated by the basic elements of the music that is most truly and characteristically of my own country, Brazil.' And in his autobiography Arthur Rubinstein describes V-L as 'a short man of dark complexion, clean-shaven, with dark, disorderly hair and large sad eyes, but his hands were his most attractive feature with their lovely shape, sensitive and alive'.

VILLOING, Alexander Ivanovich (1804–78)
b. Moscow, Russia. Pupil of A. Dubuc. Celebrated pf teacher, especially of the brothers Rubinstein, accompanying Anton on tour 1840–43, taking in Paris where the wonderchild played to Chopin and Liszt. His *Practical School of Piano Playing* was for years the standard textbook in St Petersburg Cons.
Pupils included: Anton Rubinstein, Nikolai Rubinstein, Vassily Safonov.

VIÑES, Ricardo (1875–1943)
b. Lerida, Spain. Pupil of Barcelona Cons., obtaining 1st Prize for pf at age of 12. Went to Paris Cons., studying under G. de Bériot for pf and winning 1st Prize 1894. Had early and immediate success in Paris as pianist and, in the words of Pedro Morales, 'was the first virtuoso who placed his art at the service of the new school of Debussy, Ravel, de Séverac and others through his wonderful exposition of its piano works which for a long time he monopolised'. Had an enormous repertoire not only of Classical and Romantic periods but also of the new and difficult French School which owed much to his dedication. Recorded *Columbia*. Dedicatee of *Le Fandango* (Goyescas No. 3) by Granados, of *Nights in the Gardens of Spain* by de Falla, and of Poulenc's *Trois Pièces*.
Pupils included: Viking Dahl, Francis Poulenc, Georg van Renesse.

VINOGRADOVA, Vera (–)
b. St. Petersburg, Russia. Student at Cons. there under L. Nicolaiev. Toured internationally. Composed pf concerto, *Ballade* for pf and chamber orch., suite for violin and pf, and pf pieces.

VINTSCGER, Jürg von (1934)
b. St Gallen, Switzerland. Student of Vienna Acad., winning the Joseph Pembauer Prize in 1954. Début same year. His recitals featured the pf works of Honegger and Schoenberg. US début in Carnegie Hall in 1963 was highly successful. Toured widely; also taught from 1971 in Zurich.

VIOLE, Rudolf (1825–67)
b. Schochwitz, Germany. Studied in Germany and had lessons from F. Liszt. In addition to career as concert pianist, composed many works for pf, including ten sonatas and over 100 studies.

VIRSALADZE, Eliso (1942–)
b. Georgia, USSR. Student of Tbilisi Cons., winning prizes for her playing before graduating. Later joined Moscow Cons. as a pf teacher and toured Europe and America solo and with orch.; also performed in Scandinavia and the Far East. British début 1981, London, where a critic wrote: 'In Chopin a radiant tone explored the composer's poetic genius, the excitement being only just below the surface.'

VISCARRA, Monje Umberto (1898–1971)
b. Bolivia. Studied there and in Europe. Pianist-teacher and Head of the Music Acad. of La Paz. Composed mainly for pf, including *Impresiones d'Altiplano*.

VITALI, Mario (1866–1932)
b. Pausula, Italy. Studied at Naples Cons. with C. Palumbo. Appointed to Liceo Rossini, Pesaro, as pf prof. Formed a pf trio that gave many recitals. Composed in various forms including pf.
Pupils included: Adriano Ariani.

VLADIGEROV, Pancho (1899–)
b. Sofia, Bulgaria. Studied there and in Berlin, where he conducted before returning to teach at Sofia Cons. Composed five pf concertos, chamber music, pf pieces including a set of preludes, and songs.

VOEGELIN, Urs (1927–)
b. Aarau, Switzerland. Student there and also at Zurich Cons., being a pupil of W. Burkhard. Noted accompanist – vocal and instrumental.

VOGEL, Edith (–)
b. Austria. Studied at Acad. there. Début Vienna. Toured Europe. Became resident in UK. Recorded EMI and Decca. Prof at Guildhall School, London.

VOGEL, Wilhelm Moriz (1846–1922)
b. Sorgau, Silesia. Studied in Leipzig where he settled, performing and teaching. Became deeply involved in pedagogic career, preparing a method which eventually spanned the gamut from beginner to advanced student. Published in 12 parts, it contained his own compositions as teaching material. Also wrote critical essays for the Press.

VOGRICH, Max Wilhelm Karl (1852–1916)
b. Transylvania. A prodigy who later attended Leipzig Cons. (1866–9) studying pf under E. Wenzel, K. Reinecke and I. Moscheles. Toured Europe and USA 1870–8, later working in Australia, 1882–6, as concert pianist and teacher. The next six years were spent in New York. Afterwards he lived in Germany, then UK until 1914, when he returned to New York. Composed pf concerto and many pieces, besides arranging an edition of Schumann's pf music.

VOGT, Johann (1823–88)
b. Gross-Tinz, Germany. Studied pf in Germany but taught in St Petersburg on graduation, settling subsequently in Berlin. Toured as concert pianist, including USA. Composed chamber music and pf pieces.

VOIGT, Henriette (*née* **Kunze**): *see* **KUNZE, Henriette**

VOLAVY, Marguerite (1886–)
b. Brünn, Czechoslovakia. Pf pupil of A. Door at Vienna Cons., graduating 1901 with 1st Prize. Received instruction from T. Leschetizky. Début 1902 Prague, followed by tours of Europe. US début 1915 New York. Eventually settled in USA.

VOLCKLAND, Alfred (1841–1905)
b. Brunswick, Germany. Pupil of Leipzig Cons. Became court pianist and later added conducting to his career.

VOLKONSKY, Andrei (1933–)
b. Geneva, Switzerland of Russian descent. Pf pupil of D. Lipatti. Lived in Moscow from age of 15 and as a composer was severely criticized by the regime. From 1973 lived in Israel.

VON MEYER, Leopold: *see* **MEYER, Leopold von**

VON SAUER, Emil: *see* **SAUER, Emil von**

VON ZADORA, Michael: *see* **ZADORA, Michael von**

VOŘIŠEK, Jan Hugo (1791–1825)
b. Vamberk, Czechoslovakia. An early pianist who studied first with his father, then with J. Tomáschek. Went to Vienna in 1813 and was befriended by Hummel. When the latter moved on to Stuttgart, he recommended his pupils in Vienna to continue with V. Was appointed pianist to the Phil. Soc.

VOSS, Charles (1815–82)
b. Schmarsow, Germany. Learned the instrument in Berlin. Settled in Paris, where he was esteemed as concert pianist, teacher and composer of mainly salon pieces but also several pf concertos and books of studies.

VOTAPEK, Ralph (1939–)
b. Milwaukee, USA. Studied at Wisconsin Cons., later at Manhattan and Juilliard schools, at the latter under R. Lhevinne. Winner 1962 of 1st Van Cliburn Int. Pf Comp. Thereafter performed in USA and Europe as well as touring USSR in 1975. Taught at Michigan State Univ.

VRIES, Alexander de (1919–)
b. Amsterdam, Netherlands. Studied at Antwerp Cons., where he became pf prof. 1958 after teaching at Ghent Cons. Concert pianist and adjudicator.

VRONSKY, Vitya (1908–)
b. Evpatoria, Russia. Studied pf in Berlin with A. Schnabel where she met her future husband, Victor Babin. Embarked upon her concert career in Europe in 1930. London début at R. Albert Hall. After their marriage the Babins joined forces in a two-pf team, emigrating to the USA in 1937 where they rapidly established themselves in the forefront of the duettist profession. Toured both continents regularly. Recorded *HMV*, American Columbia, RCA and Brunswick.

VYSHNEGRADSKI, Ivan (1893–)
b. St Petersburg, Russia. Student of the Cons. there who became involved in quarter-tone music. Resided in Paris from 1922, becoming one of the leaders of the system. Constructed a pf on the quarter-tone principle with two keyboards, wrote a book on its harmony and composed numerous works for the system.

WAGENAAR, Nelly (1898–)
b. Utrecht, Netherlands. Pupil of Cons. there, also of A. Schnabel. Début 1920 Utrecht. Performed and taught at Amsterdam Cons., becoming pf prof. 1927–67. Performed both as soloist and with orch.

WAGNER, Manfred (1952–)
b. Vienna, Austria. Studied at Acad. there, where he became pf prof. Performed throughout Europe and Near East.

WAGNER, Oscar (1893–)
b. Corydon, USA. Studied pf in Chicago, then with E. Hutcheson in New York. Held teaching posts and toured. From 1925 on staff of Juilliard School.

WALDTEUFEL, Emil (1837–1915)
b. Strasbourg. Taught first by father, a prof. of Strasbourg Cons., before going to Paris Cons. where his pf teacher was A. Marmontel. Left before graduation, having been offered a post with Scholtus, pf-makers. Became court pianist to the Empress Eugénie. Began composing waltzes which met with such immediate success that he went on writing them, to the tune of 268, which he played and conducted throughout Europe.

WALEY, Simon (1826–75)
b. London, UK. Pf pupil of I. Moscheles, W. S. Bennett and G. Osborne. Career as concert pianist, teacher and composer, writing a pf concerto, chamber music and pf works for two and four hands.

WALKER, George (1922–)
b. Washington DC, USA. A pupil of Oberlin Coll. and of Curtis Inst. who numbered among his pf teachers C. Curzon, R. Casadesus and R. Serkin, and who studied composition with N.

Boulanger in Paris. Début New York, 1945. Toured N. America, the W. Indies and Europe, winning the Bok Award in 1963. Taught widely, especially at the Curtis Inst. His compositions included two pf sonatas and a sonata for two pfs, as well as solo pieces and chamber music.

WALLE-HANSEN, Dagmar (1871–1954)
b. Oslo, Norway. Studied with A. Backer-Gröndahl and later spent four years with T. Leschetizky, after which she remained as his assistant 1893–1914. Returned to Oslo from where she performed in Europe.

WALLENSTEIN, Martin (1843–96)
b. Frankfurt, Germany. Pupil of A. Dreyschock in Prague, continuing his studies in Leipzig. Became highly successful concert pianist and composed for the instrument including a concerto, studies and other pieces.

WALLERSTEIN, Lothar (1882–1949)
b. Prague, Czechoslovakia. Studied there and later taught pf at Geneva Cons. Concert virtuoso who settled in USA in 1941.

WALLFISCH, Peter (1924–)
b. Breslau, Germany, where he studied before emigrating to Israel in 1938. Under a scholarship he attended Jerusalem Acad. of Music, then in 1946 became a pupil in Paris of M. Long and J. Février, winning the Liszt Prize in 1947. In 1948 was awarded 1st Prize in the Concours Liszt-Bartók, Budapest. Other prizes followed. Début in Paris 1948, after which he began touring worldwide. Settled in London in 1951 and was pf prof. at R. Coll. there from 1974. Repertoire ranges from Arne to the contemporary scene solo, with orch. and in chamber music. Formed a trio with his son

Raphael W (cello) and Anton Weinberg (clarinet). Recorded various.

WALTER, Bruno (1876–1962)
b. Berlin, Germany. Showed musical ability from early age and studied at Stern's Cons. under H. Erlich for pf, and F. Dreyschock. Performed a Moscheles pf concerto with Berlin PO 1889. Was famous operatic and orch. conductor who preserved a fine pf technique throughout a long and distinguished career, giving joint recitals with artists of the calibre of Kathleen Ferrier, Lotte Lehmann, Arnold Rosé, Alexander Petschnikov, Jacques Thibaud, etc. A specialist in Mozart, he played the pf concertos, conducting from the keyboard in an age when critics frowned upon the practice. Recorded the K.461 with Vienna PO in this manner on *HMV*; also accompanied Lotte Lehmann on Columbia and Kathleen Ferrier on Decca. Took French nationality in 1938 after being driven out of Austria by Nazis, then in 1946 became US citizen. Composed chamber music and songs, wrote a work on Mahler, also memoirs *Theme & Variations* (1944). R. Phil. Soc. Gold Medal 1957. Composed chamber music and songs.

WALTERS, Teresa (1950–)
b. Lincoln, USA. Studied at Peabody Cons., Baltimore, and at Paris Cons. Was pupil of J. Esteban.

WALTERSHAUSEN, Hermann
(1882–1954)
b. Göttingen, Germany. Studied at Strasbourg before, in 1900, becoming pf pupil of L. Thuille in Munich. Mysteriously lost his right arm and right foot 'in a game', and adapted his pf playing (as well as conducting) accordingly. Founded own music school in Munich in 1917, and in 1920 was made prof. at Munich State Acad. of Music, and Director two years later. Composed a variety of works as well as wrote textbooks on interpretation of operas.

WALTHEW, Richard Henry (1872–1951)
b. London, UK. Student of the Guildhall School and of R. Coll. there. A pianist with highly cultured style and especially interested in chamber music being long connected with the Sunday series of South Place Concerts, London. His pf concerto was first performed as long ago as 1894 in London. Conductor, teacher and prolific composer, especially of chamber works, sonatas and pf pieces. Wrote *The Development of Chamber Music* (1909).

WAMBACH, Bernard (1948–)
b. Neuwied, W. Germany. Student of Bremen Cons. and of Hamburg High School. A pupil of F. Gulda and won 2nd Prize at Arnold Schoenberg Pf Concours of 1979.

WARD, David (–   )
b. Sheffield, UK. Student of R. Coll. of Music, London, and of C. Smith. Later was with N. Boulanger under a French Government scholarship. Performed widely, having special affinity with music of Mozart; also taught at R. Coll. Recorded Meridian.

WARE, Harriet (1877–1962)
b. Waupun, Wisconsin, USA. Pupil of Pillsbury Acad., then studied for two years in New York. Was a pupil of S. Stojowski in Paris from 1896, later studying in Berlin. Returned to USA 1906 where she lived in New York, working on own compositions. She made coast-to-coast tours giving programmes of her own music and in 1926 set up her own publishing house.

WARREN, Elinor (1908–)
b. Los Angeles, USA. Pf pupil of F. La Forge, then of P. Gallico. Performed in USA and Europe both solo and as accompanist to celebrity singers. Composed in various genres.

WATANABE, Kenji (1954–)
b. Gifu-shi, Japan. Studied pf at Tokyo High School and in Budapest, teachers including P. Solymos. A prizewinner in the Liszt-Bartók Concours 1981.

WATTS, Andre (1946–)
b. Nürnberg, Germany. Of American parentage, his father being a regular soldier. Began in music with the violin at the age of 4, then, after his parents returned home, he changed to the pf, studying at the Musical Acad., Philadelphia. Later he progressed to Peabody Inst., Baltimore, working with L. Fleisher. In a Young People's Concert on television, and with Leonard Bernstein conducting the New York PO, he made a highly successful appearance in the Liszt 1st pf concerto. Three weeks later, quite unexpectedly, he was called to take the place of an indisposed G. Gould with the same orch. and conductor.
Began touring the USA. London début

1966, then toured Europe in 1967 with the Los Angeles PO, and six years later the USSR with the San Francisco Orch. Possessed a powerful technique, his repertoire showing preference for big-boned music. Has been described as a risk-taker on the platform because of a highly charged Romantic temperament. 'No one,' he once remarked cryptically to an interviewer, 'will ever get to know me better than by listening to me play.' Recorded CBS.

WAYENBERG, Daniel (1929–)
b. Paris, France, of Dutch stock. Studied pf at The Hague and later with M. Long in Paris, where he won 2nd Prize in the 1949 Long–Thibaud Comp. Performed widely thereafter. US début 1953 in New York, since when has made extensive tours throughout America. Recorded various.

WEAVER, Powell (1890–1951)
b. Clearfield, USA. Studied in New York and Rome. Well-known accompanist. Compositions included *Dance of the Sand-Dune Cranes* and *Ode*, both for pf and orch., chamber music and pf pieces.

WEBER, Carl (1860–1938)
b. London, UK. One source of reference states he was born in St James's Palace, without offering an explanation. Pupil of T. Leschetizky. Début 1884 London. Performed and taught thereafter, becoming Director of Incorporated London Acad. of Music. Composed pf pieces and wrote *A Practical Pianoforte School*.

WEBER, Karl Maria von (1786–1826)
b. Eutin, Germany. There is no traceable justification for the assumption of 'von'. Because of the itinerant habits of the parents, his acquisition of musical knowledge was fragmentary, although he was highly talented and picked up crumbs of knowledge with alacrity. Received some tuition from Michael Haydn and George Vogler, a self-styled *abbé*. He nevertheless became a concert pianist who gave first performances of most of his pf works. With an enormous stretch he could encompass beyond a twelfth – hence the novel and striking effects in his works which are unjustly neglected. He is acknowledged founder of the German Romantic school, and his pf works are among the first genuine compositions for the instrument. It should be remembered that the pf was still relatively undeveloped when works like his beautiful A flat sonata were written. Early

compositions were mainly dances. Later came two pf concertos and *Konzertstück*, four sonatas, some half-dozen sets of variations, *Invitation to the Dance* and the *Rondo* in E flat which used to be in every pianist's repertoire. He also made pf scores of his operas. Was described by a contemporary as 'a distinguished and characteristic pianist capable of stretching wide intervals, introducing them in his keyboard music'.

WEBER, Margaret (1924–)
b. Switzerland. Studied in Zurich and toured Europe extensively. US début 1956 and gave première of Stravinsky's *Movements* for pf and orch. 1960 in New York under composer's baton.

WEBERN, Anton von (1883–1945)
b. Vienna, Austria. Protégé of A. Schoenberg and strictly speaking not a concert pianist. Composed pf *Variations*, Op. 27, and chamber music in the idiom of what is known as the Second Viennese School.

WEBERSINKE, Amadeus (1920–)
b. Broumov, Czechoslovakia. Studied in Leipzig where his teachers included P. Mildner. From 1946 lectured at Leipzig High School, and in 1966 became prof. at the Weber High School, Dresden. Later taught at Weimar and Tokyo Acad.

WEBSTER, Beveridge (1908–)
b. Pittsburgh, USA. Studied first with his father before becoming a pf pupil of I. Philipp at Paris Cons., where he graduated 1926 with 1st Prize for playing. Toured Europe for some years, returning home in 1934 where he developed a successful concert career. Taught at New England Cons. and at Juilliard School. Gave première of Quincy Porter's pf sonata in 1930. Edited various pf works for International Music Co., New York.
Pupils included: Michel Bloch, Raymond Jackson.

WEHLE, Karl (1825–83)
b. Prague, Czechoslovakia. Pupil of I. Moscheles in Leipzig, then of T. Kullak in Berlin. Performed throughout the world before settling in Paris as teacher, pianist and composer of salon works of considerable technical difficulty.

WEILL, Janine (1903–)
b. Paris, France. Studied at the Cons., Paris, and with A. Cortot and M. Long. Concert pianist and teacher at École Normale. Director and founder of French School of Music. Recorded *Decca*.

WEINBERG, Jakob (1879–1956)
b. Odessa, Russia. Distant relative of Anton Rubinstein through marriage. Pupil of Moscow Cons. under C. Igumnov, graduating in 1906 as pianist and composer. Later went to Vienna and studied with T. Leschetizky. Lived in Palestine 1925–8, then settled in New York. Was fine pianist and poured his creative energies mostly into Jewish liturgical works. For pf composed a concerto, chamber music and songs.

WEINER, Jean (1896–)
b. Paris, France. Studied privately and at the Cons. there. Fine pianist and arranger who worked in the contemporary field, both serious and light. Noted for his work in the creation of entertainment at the night club *Le Bœuf sur le toit* where his versatility solo and with Clement Doucet was much admired. Was associated with Doucet in two pfs over many years and was a friend of leading musicians including Ravel. Gave French première of Schoenberg's *Pierrot Lunaire*, also wrote *Concerto franco-américain*. Recorded *Columbia* with C. Doucet.

WEINGARTEN, Josef (1911–)
b. Budapest, Hungary. Pf pupil of F. Liszt Acad. under E. von Dohnányi, graduating 1934 with Diploma. Won successive distinction in competitions in Budapest, Vienna, Warsaw and Geneva. Settled in London, teaching, in addition to concert work and broadcasting. Became British subject.

WEINGARTEN, Paul (1886–)
b. Brünn, Austria. Studied at Vienna Acad., pf teacher E. von Sauer. Won Rubinstein Prize and from 1921 was pf prof. at the Acad. as well as making extensive tours in Europe.
Pupils included: Walter Landauer.

WEIR, Nancy (1916–)
b. Australia. Studied in Melbourne. Début there 1929 in Beethoven's 3rd concerto. Went to Europe to receive tuition from A. Schnabel, later winning scholarship to R. Acad., London, with H. Craxton.
Pupils included: Piers Lane.

WEISSENBERG, Alexis (1929–)
b. Sofia, Bulgaria. Settled in USA 1946. Won Leventritt Award there 1947, the year of his début with New York PO and Szell, having studied with O. Samaroff at Juilliard School. Toured with Philadelphia Orch., also worldwide tours commencing 1950 with Europe. Recorded RCA and EMI. A distinguished accompanist.
Pupils included: Robert de Gaetano, Rafael Orozco.

WELCH, Roy Dickinson (1885–1951)
b. Dansville, USA. Educated at Michigan Univ., then in Berlin under J. Lhevinne. Thereafter took up pedagogic career, firstly at Northampton, Mass., then from 1935 as head of the music dept of Princeton Univ.

WELLS, Paul (1888–1927)
b. Carthage, USA. Student at Peabody Cons. under Ernest Hutcheson, then in Berlin with J. Lhevinne. Début there with Berlin PO. Studied further in Vienna with L. Godowsky, returned to USA and made an extended tour. Went to Toronto Cons. in 1913 as teacher and was known as 'a brilliant concert pianist'.

WELS, Karl (1825–1906)
b. Prague, Czechoslovakia. Pupil of J. Tomáschek. Emigrated to USA, where he played pf and organ. Composed a pf concerto, pieces and songs.

WENDLING, Karl (1857–1918)
b. Frankenthal, Germany. Pupil of Leipzig Cons. Studied the Jankó pf keyboard and propagated the instrument in Germany. Taught at Leipzig Cons.

WENZEL, Ernst Ferdinand (1808–80)
b. Waldorf, Germany. Pf pupil of F. Wieck, in whose house he met R. Schumann and became his friend. Taught pf at Leipzig Cons. from its inception in 1843; knew Mendelssohn and wrote for Schumann's *Neue Zeitschrift für Musik*. Was a popular pf teacher.
Pupils included: Friedrich Baumfelder, Edvard Grieg, Sir George Henschel, Hans Huber, Rafael Joseffy, Martin Krause, Albert Parsons, Ernst Perabo, Max Vogrich.

WERKENTHIN, Albert (1842–1914)
b. Berlin, Germany. Studied pf with H. von Bülow at Stern's Cons., Berlin, where he later taught in addition to pursuing a concert career.

Composed for pf; also wrote songs and critical essays, as well as a pf method which ran to several editions.

WERNICK, Casimir (1828–59)
b. Warsaw, Poland. Pf pupil of J. Nowakowski there. Lived in Paris 1843–8 and studied with F. Chopin. Performed throughout Europe as he returned to Warsaw during the revolution of 1848. Finally settled in St Petersburg as concert pianist, teacher and composer, where he died. Composed pf pieces with the titles, and in the idiom, of Chopin.

WERTHEIM, Julius (1880–1928)
b. Warsaw, Poland. Piano pupil of M. Moszkowski and J. Slivinsky, winning Gold Medal at Warsaw Cons. in 1901. Thereafter taught there some years before settling in Berlin as composer. Besides four symphonies wrote a considerable quantity of pf music: sonatas, variations, etc.

WESTLAKE, Frederick (1840–98)
b. Romsey, UK. Student of R. Acad., London, under W. Macfarren for pf. Taught there from 1862 and composed pf pieces.
Pupils included: Joseph Holbrooke.

WEYMAN, Wesley (1877–1931)
b. Boston, USA. Pf pupil of W. Mason. Performed and taught for three years, then went to Europe to study with L. Godowsky and M. Moszkowski in Berlin and with T. Matthay and Y. Bowen in London. London début 1912 followed by touring in Europe until 1914 when he returned to USA and resumed concert work and teaching.

WHITE, Felix Harold (1884–1945)
b. London, UK. Self-taught pianist-composer who wrote much chamber and pf music which remains in MS. Was responsible for the Scriabin edition of Belaiev and compiled a *Dictionary of Musical Terms*.

WHITEHEAD, Percy Algernon (1874–)
b. Sevenoaks, UK. Student of R. Coll., London, under T. Matthay. Became pf teacher at the Coll. and later with the Matthay School. Composed pf pieces and songs.

WHITHORNE, Emerson (1884–1958)
b. Cleveland, USA. Was taught locally and played in vaudeville before studying with T. Leschetizky in Vienna 1904–6. Lived in

London until 1914 when he returned home and later concentrated on composing. His works included *Poem* for pf and orch. as well as chamber music, pf pieces and songs. Married the pianist E. Leginska in 1907, probably having met when they were pupils of Leschetizky (divorced 1909).

WHITING, Arthur (1861–1936)
b. Cambridge, USA. Pupil of W. H. Sherwood at New England Cons. and later of Munich Cons. Lived in Boston 1885–95, performing and composing, after which he settled in New York. Developed series of chamber concerts at principal universities, especially early works when he forsook the pf for harpsichord. Edited certain works of Brahms for Schirmer including the three pf sonatas. Composed a *Fantasy* for pf and orch., chamber music, pf pieces and songs, and wrote for the Press.

WHITTINGTON, Dorsey (1899–)
b. Effingham, USA. Pf teachers included K. Friedberg, E. Hughes and E. Hutcheson. Performed as pianist, also conductor, and taught in New York, Birmingham and Michigan. Composed pf studies and chamber music.

WIBAUT, Frank Stephen (1945–)
b. London, UK. Student at R. Coll of Music, London, winning prizes including Chappell Gold Medal 1964. Taught at R. Coll. of Music, London; also at Birmingham School of Music.
Pupils included: Jonathan Plowright.

WIBERGH, Olof (1890–1962)
b. Stockholm, Sweden. Student of Stockholm Cons. under L. Lundberg, then went to Berlin before finishing under E. von Sauer in Vienna. Début Stockholm 1914. Became successful recitalist at home and abroad as well as an influential teacher.

WIDOR, Charles-Marie (1844–1937)
b. Lyons, France. Famous organist, organ composer, writer and critic, who wrote pf pieces and a *Fantaisie* for pf and orch. which was first performed in UK in 1890 with I. Philipp as soloist and the composer as conductor.

WIECK, Alwin (1821–85)
b. Leipzig, Germany. Son of Friedrich W and brother of Klara and Marie. Pf pupil of his

father and taught in Dresden. Published methods.

Pupils included: Karl Ehrenberg.

WIECK, Friedrich (1785–1873)
b. Pretzsch, Germany. A gentleman of many parts beginning with theology, giving it up to be a private tutor with time to study music. Started a pf factory next in Leipzig but left it in order to teach pf playing, and became very successful at it, removing to Dresden. Then he studied a singing method and gave singing lessons too. By 1843 was sufficiently well known for Mendelssohn to offer him a post in the newly founded Leipzig Cons., which was declined. In the meantime R. Schumann had been one of his pupils and in 1840 married Klara W, a daughter by W's first wife. After the Wiecks were divorced, he married a second time and there was another daughter, Marie W. Busy teacher who found time to compose studies and write textbooks. Was described as 'a tall, spare man with prominent features, and eyes of a deep blue: fiery eyes and at the same time melancholy, such as are only found in Germans'.

Pupils included: Hans von Bülow, Robert Schumann, Alwin Wieck, Marie Wieck, Klara Wieck (later Klara Schumann), Ernst Wenzel.

WIECK, Klara: *see* **SCHUMANN, Klara**

WIECK, Marie (1832–1916)
b. Leipzig, Germany. Daughter and pupil of F. Wieck. Début at age of 11 with her elder sister Klara Schumann (*née* Wieck). Appointed court pianist to the Hohenzollerns at the age of 26 and began a series of successful tours of Europe. Settled as pf teacher in Dresden, where her final public appearance occurred in 1915 at the age of 83, playing the Robert Schumann pf concerto.

WIEHMAYER, Theodor (1870–1947)
b. Marienfeld, Germany. Pupil of Leipzig Cons. under K. Reinecke for pf. Début there 1890, then toured Europe before returning to Leipzig as teacher, firstly on own then at the Cons. Later taught at Stuttgart Cons. Wrote a number of pedagogic works on technique.

WIENIAWSKA, Irene Regine: *see* **POLDOWSKI**

WIENIAWSKI, Josef (1837–1912)
b. Lublin, Poland. Younger brother of Henri

W, famous violinist. Studied pf at Paris Cons. from 1847 under P. Zimmerman, A. Marmontel and C. Alkan. Toured with his brother in 1850 when aged 13 and 15 respectively. Studied for a time with F. Liszt, returning to Paris in 1857. Later was pf prof. at Moscow Cons. before founding own school. Settled in Brussels 1876 where he taught at the Cons. Throughout his career toured as pianist and was as famous as his brother. Composed pf concerto and many pieces. Invented a pf with double keyboard which was known as the Mangeot pf because it was constructed in Paris by Mangeot. There was public and professional interest in it for a time.

Pupils included: Léon Delcroix, Boleslaw Domaniewski.

WIERSZYLOWSKI, Jan (1927–)
b. Warsaw, Poland. Studied there and made his début 1960. Performed mainly in Poland, appearing solo and with orch., also in chamber music and on radio.

WIHAN, Dora (1860–1938)
b. Germany. Pianist and teacher who married the cellist Hanus W, and friend of R. Strauss who dedicated pf pieces to her and composed a cello sonata for him. The marriage ended in divorce, and after her concert career ended she taught the instrument, living for a time in the USA.

WIKLUND, Adolf (1879–1950)
b. Langserud, Sweden. Studied pf with R. Andersson at the R. Cons., Stockholm, winning a Jenny Lind scholarship enabling him to receive tuition from J. Kwast in Berlin. Performed but later turned to conducting opera. Composed two concertos and a *Konzertstück* for pf and orch., chamber music and pf pieces. Younger brother of Victor W.

WIKLUND, Victor (1874–1933)
b. Animskog, Dalsland, Sweden. Brother of Adolf W. Studied at Stockholm Cons., also with R. Andersson, and taught at his school 1896–8, also at Stockholm Cons. 1904–33. Additionally well known as accompanist and singing teacher.

WIKMAN, Bertil (1944–)
b. Stockholm, Sweden. Pupil of Andersson's School there. Début Stockholm 1967. Performed solo and in duet work with wife, Solveig W.

WIKMAN, Solveig (1942–)
b. Viskafors, Sweden. Studied pf in Stockholm, then in Salzburg. Was pupil of W. Kempff. Début 1965 Stockholm. Married Bertil W and performed solo and with husband.

WILCKENS, Friedrich (1899–)
b. Liezen, Austria. Pupil of J. Lalewicz in Vienna. Toured extensively thereafter as solo artist and also as accompanist in ballet.

WILD, Brigitte (1908–)
b. Rome, Italy. Studied there and at Stern's, Berlin, under C. Arrau. Performed and taught including at Guildhall School, London, from 1964.

WILD, Earl (1915–)
b. Pittsburgh, USA. Pupil of Carnegie Technical Coll. there, later of E. Petri, R. Bühlig and others. Virtuoso of legendary quality, in style and technique recalling pianists of the calibre of J. Lhevinne. Recorded RCA, EMI, dell'Arte and others. Compositions included a set of Rachmaninov songs exquisitely transposed for pf solo.

WILDE, David Clark (1935–)
b. Stretford, UK. Pf teachers included F. Reizenstein, Solomon and I. Elinson. Taught at R. Acad., London, and R. Manchester Coll. Soloist, accompanist and broadcaster. Recorded Saga.

WILKSTRÖM, Inger (1939–)
b. Gothenberg, Sweden. Studied in Stockholm and with I. Kabos. Performed extensively throughout Europe, USSR and Americas. Recorded RCA and Decca.

WILLIAMS, Alberto (1862–1952)
b. Buenos Aires, Argentina. Began musical studies there before going to Paris Cons., where he was a pf pupil of G. Mathias and composition pupil of C. Franck. Returned home in 1899 and gave recitals. Founded the Cons. of Music of Buenos Aires, which was so successful that he opened branches throughout the country. Popularized Chopin in Argentina in his recitals, and was also a conductor. Composed chamber music and pf pieces, also a *Sonata Argentina*; but his principal contribution to national music in this sphere was in the *Aires de la Pampa*, totalling about 50 works.
Pupils included: Celestino Piaggio.

WILLIAMS, Janice (1936–)
b. London, UK. Studied there with H. Craxton and in Brussels with S. Askenase. Won MacFarren Gold Medal.

WILLIAMSON, Malcolm (1931–)
b. Sydney, Australia. Student of Cons. there. Has appeared with leading orchs. Composed three pf concertos and three pf sonatas. Master of the Queen's Musick. Recorded Argo.

WILLMERS, Heinrich Rudolf (1821–78)
b. Berlin, Germany. Studied there and with J. Hummel in Weimar and F. Schneider in Dessau. Début Berlin 1844, followed by appearances in Paris and London in 1846. Became touring pianist as well as a teacher at Stern's Cons., Berlin, 1864–6. Thereafter lived in Vienna. Was reputed to have a remarkable technique which helped create a successful career. Wrote chamber music and much pf music of a showy if shallow quality. Is also reputed to have lost his sanity before he died.

WILLNER, Arthur (1881–1959)
b. Teplice, Czechoslovakia. Pf pupil of Leipzig Cons. Taught in Berlin 1904–24, then in Vienna 1924–38, when he moved to London where he died. Prolific composer in many fields including a pf concerto and four sonatas, chamber music, pf pieces and songs.

WILM, Nicolas (1834–1911)
b. Riga, Russia. Student of Leipzig Cons. and of L. Plaidy for pf. Conducted for a time in Russia but returned to Germany in 1875 where he settled in Wiesbaden as teacher and composer. Was prolific, including chamber music and pf works for one and two instruments as well as songs.

WILSON, Dorothy (1900–)
b. Wordsley, UK. Studied in London and with I. Scharrer, F. Dawson and T. Matthay, winning Gold Medal at latter's school. Performed and taught at home and abroad.

WINDING, August Hendrik (1835–99)
b. Lolland, Denmark. Pupil of K. Reinecke and A. Dreyschock. Début 1857 Copenhagen. In addition to performing was pf prof. at Copenhagen R. Cons. as well as on board of governors. Was regarded as one of finest Danish pianists of the time. Close friend and associate of E. Grieg. His compositions, which

are in the Romantic idiom, curiously include a pf concerto in A minor, Op. 16.

WINGHAM, Thomas (1846–93)
b. London, UK. Pupil of R. Acad., London, and of Sir W. S. Bennett for pf. Taught there from 1871, becoming a prof. Composed for pf and wrote songs.

WINKHLER, Charles (1802–46)
b. Hungary. Pianist, composer of pf pieces and chamber music. Performed throughout Austria and Hungary.

WINKLER, Alexander Adolfovich
(1865–1935)
b. Kharkov, Russia. Studied there and in Paris with V. Duvernoy; also in Vienna with T. Leschetizky. Returned to Kharkov in teaching capacity, then, from 1907, at St Petersburg Cons. Following the Russian Revolution he had a short spell in France before going back to settle in Leningrad as prof. of composition at the Cons. Composed variety of chamber music with pf part as well as works for two and four hands.

WINTERBERGER, Alexander (1834–1914)
b. Weimar, Germany. Pf pupil of Leipzig Cons. and of F. Liszt. Lived for a time in Vienna and was pf prof. at St Petersburg Cons. for three years from 1869. Returned to Leipzig and settled as teacher, composer and writer.

WITTASEK, Johann Nepomuk (1770–1839)
b. Horin, Czechoslovakia. Early Bohemian pianist who performed Mozart pf concertos in public and earned the composer's approbation. Additionally taught and composed.

WITTGENSTEIN, Paul (1887–1961)
b. Vienna, Austria. Pupil of J. Labor and T. Leschetizky. Début 1913 there. Promising career as concert pianist suffered through the loss of his right arm in action in World War I. In consequence a number of composers wrote works especially for him, e.g. Prokofiev No. 4, Strauss *Parergon* to *Symphonia domestica* Op. 73, Ravel concerto in D and Britten *Diversions*. Settled in USA 1940, teaching at Ralphe Wolfe Cons., New York. Brother of the philosopher Ludwig W and member of the famous family who had been patrons of the arts in Vienna for generations and especially of Brahms and Joachim. Erich Korngold wrote a concerto for

left hand for him. See also under Schmidt, Franz.

WOLF, Joseph (1772–1812)
b. Salzburg, Austria. Studied music with L. Mozart and M. Haydn. Became a highly skilled pianist, having large hands with enormous stretch which in his compositions caused problems to other players. Had a pf contest with Beethoven in the art of extemporization in which the outcome was said to have been a dead heat. Composed much pf music, most of which is lost.
Pupils included: Cipriani Potter.

WOLF, Wilhelm (1838–1913)
b. Breslau, Germany. Pf pupil of T. Kullak in Berlin where he settled as teacher, pianist and essayist.

WOLFES, Felix (1892–1971)
b. Hanover, Germany. Pupil of Leipzig Cons. and of R. Teichmüller for pf. Took to conducting in various centres in Germany, emigrating to USA in 1938 where he conducted and taught. Amongst his pf works are reductions of scores by Richard Strauss.

WOLFF, Auguste Désiré Bernard (1821–87)
b. Paris, France. Pf pupil of P. Zimmerman. Performed and taught pf, then, in 1852, joined the firm of Pleyel, later becoming its head when the style was changed to Pleyel-Wolff. Was noted executant and instituted the Pleyel-Wolff pf prize, an annual award for the best pf composition with or without orch.

WOLFF, Bernhard (1835–1906)
b. Schwetz, Germany. Pf pupil of H. von Bülow; performed and taught in Berlin and composed technical works, including simplified versions of Pischna's exercises.

WOLFF, Édouard (1816–80)
b. Warsaw, Poland. Student of Warsaw Cons. and pf pupil of J. Elsner as well as being a fellow-pupil of F. Chopin. Later completed studies in Vienna and settled in Paris from 1835 as a concert pianist, teacher and member of the Chopin-Liszt circle. Composed prolifically for pf, including many studies based on the Chopin style. In a letter written to Nowakowski he provides the only known evidence regarding Chopin's opinion of the playing of J.

Field. His sister was the mother of Henri and Josef Wieniawski.
Pupils included: Emmanuel Chabrier.

WOLFF, Erich (1874–1913)
b. Vienna, Austria. Pupil of A. Door at the Cons. there. Removed in 1906 to Berlin. Was pf accompanist for celebrities and died suddenly during a concert tour with Julia Culp just as they reached New York.

WOLFF, Ernst Victor (1889–1960)
b. Berlin, Germany. Pupil of Scharwenka School, Berlin, and also graduated at Berlin Univ. Performed as pianist and also harpsichordist in Germany until 1933 when he settled in London, removing three years later to USA, where he taught in New York.

WOLFF, Konrad (1907–)
b. Berlin, Germany. Studied privately with various teachers including B. Eisner; also received some tuition from A. Schnabel. Performed in Europe and USA, settling there as recitalist, lecturer and writer. Taught at Columbia Univ., USA, from 1957. Wrote *On Music and Musicians*.

WOLFF, Marguerite (–)
b. London, UK. Studied at R. Acad. and Trinity Coll. there, also with L. Kentner. Performed in Europe and taught.

WOLFRAM, Victor (1920–)
b. New York, USA, Pupil of Juilliard School. Début 1944 Chicago. Also noted harpsichordist.

WOLFSOHN, Julius (1880–1944)
b. Warsaw, Poland. Pf pupil of A. Michałowski, in Paris with R. Pugno, then with T. Leschetizky in Vienna. Performed in Europe until 1933 when he emigrated to USA. As a composer identified himself with Jewish folk-music, and pf works include a *Jewish Rhapsody*, 12 *Paraphrases on Folk Melodies* and other character pieces said to show the Romantic influence of Chopin and Liszt.

WOLFSON, Karl (1834–1907)
b. Germany. Pupil of A. Schmitt in Frankfurt. Début there 1848. Took further tuition while touring as concert pianist, moving to London before settling in USA in 1854. Was one of the first pianists to give public performances of the entire cycle of Beethoven sonatas, and later

complete cycles of Schumann and Chopin pf works. Was also chamber music player as well as teacher.

WOLLENHAUPT, Hermann Adolf (1827–63)
b. Leipzig, Germany. Studied there under J. Knorr. Went to USA in 1845 where he established a first-class reputation as concert pianist and composed salon pieces of considerable difficulty as well as arranging music in the trend of the times.

WOLMER, Jan (1909–)
b. Oslo, Norway. Studied pf in Riga and Berlin, also receiving tuition from Arthur Rubinstein. Performed in Europe and USA until 1960, when illness caused his retirement. Composed for the instrument.

WOLOWSKA, Maria: *see*
SZYMANOWSKA, Maria

WOOD, Sir Henry Joseph (1869–1944)
b. London, UK. Taught pf by his mother and later studied at the R. Acad. of Music. Early records of the 'Proms' show he played in concerto work and was a useful accompanist all his life, in addition to which he premièred, as conductor, many new works for pf and orch. during his long career.

WOOD, Noel Mewton-: *see* **MEWTON-WOOD, Noel**

WOODHOUSE, George (1877–1954)
b. Cradley Heath, UK. Studied pf in Birmingham, followed by a spell at Dresden Cons., culminating in tuition from T. Leschetizky. Established the Woodhouse Pf School in London and wrote pedagogic works on pf technique: *The Artist at the Piano* (1925), *Creative Technique* (1930), *Commonsense in Pianoforte Technique* (1948) and *A Realistic Approach to Piano Playing* (1953).

WOODWARD, Roger (1943–)
b. Sydney, Australia. Student of State Cons. there and later of Z. Drzewiecki at State Acad., Warsaw. Played in most Western countries and with leading orchs. Wide-ranging repertoire, especially contemporary. Recorded EMI, Decca, DGG and RCA.

WORDEN, Wilfred (1915–79)
b. Blackburn, UK. A prodigy who made début

in London in 1928 in a Mozart concerto. Subsequently performed there and in Europe. Taught at Fort Augustus Abbey School 1940–58, when he returned to London and interested himself in electronics and hi-fi, developing and patenting components. Recorded *Imperial* and *Decca.*

WORMSER, André Alphonse (1851–1926)
b. Paris, France. Pupil of Paris Cons., studying pf under A. Marmontel, winning 1st Prize for playing in 1872. Performed, taught and composed variety of works including pf pieces.

WOYTOWICZ, Boleslav (1899–1980)
b. Dunajowice, Poland. Student of the Chopin High School, Warsaw, and of A. Michałowski. Later studied composition in Paris. Appointed pf prof. at Chopin School, receiving the Polish State Music Award in 1937. Composed a pf concerto, chamber music and pf pieces. Recorded Muza.

WRIGHT, Desmond Elliston (1940–)
b. Durban, S. Africa. Studied at R. Coll. of Music, London, also with M. Hess. Concert soloist and chamber-music player in Europe and S. Africa. Taught at Hochschule Mozarteum Salzburg from 1972.

WRIGHT, Leslie (1938–)
b. Ecuador. Studied pf there and at S. Cecilia Acad., Rome, winning M. Long diploma. Performed extensively worldwide.

WRIGHT, Rosemary (1932–)
b. Chorley, UK. Student at R. Acad. of Music, London, and Vienna Acad. Pupil of E. Fischer and W. Kempff. Début 1960 Vienna. Toured Europe and USA and taught in UK.

WU, Enloc (1946–)
b. Shanghai, China. Studied pf in Hong Kong and at R. Coll. of Music, London, winning Chappell Gold Medal, also Commonwealth Prize of Overseas League 1966. Toured UK and Far East, also broadcast. Settled in UK.

WU, Mary (1964–)
b. Hong Kong. Pupil of the Menuhin School in UK from 1976, where she studied with L. Kentner. Appeared as soloist, accompanist and ensemble player (including Yehudi Menuhin) in several countries especially China. Won a number of awards as well as the

1st Overseas Prize in the R. Over-Seas League Music Festival of 1983.

WÜHRER, Friedrich Anton Franz (1900–)
b. Vienna, Austria. Studied pf with M. Szudolski from age of 6, thence to Vienna Cons. with F. Schmidt. Appointed pf prof. there 1925 but continued a career as concert virtuoso with interest mainly in the Austro–German classics to which he brought a finished technique and distinguished intellect. In London in 1960 a critic wrote of his 'magnificent playing in Beethoven, using a tremendous range of dynamics and completely without resort to special effects, he rendered the C minor Op 111 a most moving and human utterance'. Co-founder of Austrian section of ISCM 1922 and subsequently taught in Mannheim and at Salzburg Mozarteum. From 1955 pf prof. at State Acad., Munich. Recorded *HMV, Columbia* and *Vox.*
Pupils included: Hans Kann, Roman Rudnytsky, Siegbert Ziak.

WUORINEN, Charles (1938–)
b. New York, USA. Pupil at Columbia Univ. there, where he became a member of the Faculty in 1964. Taught at Manhattan School from 1971. Prolific composer in modern idioms including electronic and non-standard instruments, in public performances of which he has appeared widely as pianist. Helped form the Group for Contemporary Music in 1962. Pulitzer prizewinner. Pf concerto (1966) and a pf duet *Making Ends Meet.* Recorded CRI.

WÜRFEL, Wilhelm (1791–1852)
b. Planian, Czechoslovakia. Early Bohemian pianist and teacher who was a prof. at Warsaw Cons. before settling in Vienna where he added conducting to his activities. Composed a pf concerto and pieces.
Pupils included: Felix Ostrowski.

WURM, Marie (1860–1938)
b. Southampton, UK. Eldest of four sisters, all pianists and teachers. (The other three changed the surname to Verne.) Pf pupil of Stuttgart Cons.; also studied with J. Raff and K. Schumann, winning the Mendelssohn Scholarship enabling her to study in London, then with K. Reinecke. Début 1882 began a career at which she enjoyed great popularity. Percy Scholes records that in 1895 she gave a recital made up solely of extemporizations on themes handed in by persons in the audience.

Besides performing in UK and Germany, taught successively in Hanover, Berlin and, from 1925, Munich, until her death.

WYK, Arnold van (1916–83)
b. Calvinia, Cape Prov., S. Africa. From 1938 pupil of R. Acad., London, and of H. Craxton until joining BBC for the period of World War II. Returned to S. Africa and was lecturer at Univ. of Cape Town 1949–60, and then at Stellenbosch until 1978. Performed regularly as pianist. Compositions include *Night Music* for pf in memory of Noel Mewton-Wood.

WYTTENBACH, Jürg (1935–)
b. Berne, Switzerland. Student of S. Veress there and after further study in Paris was appointed to Berne Cons. as pf prof. Composed a pf concerto.

YABLONSKAYA, Oxana (1941–)
b. Moscow, USSR. Began studying from age of 6, then worked at Moscow Cons. 1957–62 and was a pupil of A. Goldenweiser. Took part in various competitions abroad, coming 2nd in the Long-Thibaud Comp. in Paris 1963. Performed in USSR and was pf prof. at Moscow Cons. 1965–75. Applied to emigrate to USA. The visa took two years to obtain, during which she was deprived of all professional activities. Finally reached New York and rapidly re-established her reputation as pianist. Recorded Melodiya.

YANKOV, Ventsislav (1926–)
b. Sofia, Bulgaria. Studied at Sofia Cons., then in Berlin with W. Kempff, later with E. Fischer and in Paris with M. Long; prize-winner. Toured Europe, Americas and Far East.

YANNICOSTA, Melita (1928–)
b. Athens, Greece. Student at Cons. there and in Switzerland. Gold medallist. Performed throughout Europe.

YARDUMIAN, Richard (1917–)
b. Philadelphia, USA, of Armenian parentage. Studied pf with an elder brother, then, from age of 22, with J. Iturbi. Pf compositions included a concerto *Passacaglia, Recitative and Fugue*; a *Burlesque* for pf and orch., a *Chromatic Sonata* and *Armenian Suite*.

YAZBECK, Peter (1930–)
b. Wallaceburg, Canada. Studied in Toronto, also at Mannes College, New York. Début Toronto. Concert pianist, lecturer and adjudicator.

YEOH, Doreen (1960–)
b. Penang, Malaysia. Played from age of 4, winning a scholarship from the Association Board in 1978 enabling her to undertake a graduate course at the R. Coll., London. Pupil of Y. Solomon and winner of several pf prizes.

YOUNG, Dalhousie (1866–1921)
b. Punjab, India, of British parentage. Pf pupil of T. Leschetizky. Was regarded as a pianist of remarkable delicacy and refinement, and his compositions bore similar characteristics.

YOUNG, Douglas (1947–)
b. London, UK. Pupil at R. Coll., London, and of A. Hopkins. Composer of chamber music and pf pieces.

YOUNG, Victor (1889–1968)
b. Bristol, USA. Pupil of I. Philipp in Paris. Mainly accompanist and teacher and was associated with production of pf recordings in the Edison organization. Composed pf pieces and later became involved in writing film music.

YOVANOVICH, Dushko (1907–)
b. Nosi Sad, Yugoslavia. Brother and pf accompanist of Bratza the violinist. Studied in Vienna and later in London at R. Coll. of Muic under I. Epstein and privately with M. Verne. Toured widely with Bratza in duo-recitals and also with international celebrities. Settled in UK and became British subject in 1929. Later worked for BBC while still accompanying artists. Recorded *Columbia* with Bratza.

YSAŸE, Theophile (1865–1918)
b. Verviers, Belgium, younger brother of Eugène, famous violinist. Studied at Liège Cons., then in Berlin with T. Kullak for pf and in Paris with César Franck for composition. From 1889 held post of pf prof. at Geneva Cons. but resigned when the duties interfered

with concert work. Lived in Brussels teaching, directing the Académie de Musique, touring solo and in duo recitals with Eugène. Composed two pf concertos, the first of which was performed by de Greef, especially in London 1921, a pf quintet and quantity of pf music.

YU, Chun Yee (1936–)

b. Shanghai, China. Studied at R. Coll., London. Début there 1962. Performed throughout Europe and the Far East. Pf prof. at R. Coll., London.

YUDINA, Maria (1899–1970)

b. Leningrad, Russia. Student of Cons. there and fellow-student of D. Shostakovich and V. Sofronitzky. A splendid if eccentric artist who confined her activities to USSR and mainly Moscow and Leningrad. Wide-ranging repertoire from Bach to moderns including Bartók and Hindemith. Gave Russian première of Krenek's pf concerto in F minor.

ZABALZA y OLASO, Don (1833–94)
b. Irurita, Spain. Concert pianist who also taught at Madrid Cons. Chiefly remembered for studies which enjoyed local vogue in pedagogic circles.

ZABRACK, Harold (1929–)
b. St Louis, USA. Pupil of R. Ganz in Chicago. Visited Europe under Fulbright grant, giving concerts, afterwards settling in home town. Performed, taught and became prof. in Missouri. Composed a pf concerto (premièred by him 1964), also a sonata and set of variations, and 2nd pf concerto.

ZADORA, Michael von (1882–1946)
b. New York, USA. Began playing from an early age, entering Paris Cons. in 1899. Later studied with T. Leschetizky and F. Busoni, featuring the latter's works in recitals. Successful concert artist who also taught Lvov Cons., Poland, 1910–11, and later at the Inst. of Musical Art, New York. Composed and made arrangements for pf. Recorded *Polydor*.
  Pupils included: Vladimir Padwa.

ZAIKO, Thomas Joseph (1943–)
b. Philadelphia, USA. Studied at Curtis Inst., also with B. Janis. Performed and took masterclasses. Special interest in works of Cherubini.

ZAK, Yakov Izrailevich (1913–76)
b. Odessa, Russia. Studied at the Cons. there and later at Moscow Cons. where he taught 1935–47. 1st Prizewinner of Chopin Int. Pf Comp., Warsaw, 1937. Performed widely and recorded Melodiya.
  Pupils included: Youri Egorov, Nikolai Petrov, Eliso Virsaladze.

ZAKIN, Alexander (1903–)
b. Tobolsk, Russia. Pf pupil of A. Michał-owski, Warsaw, 1911–14, then of L. Nicolaiev; later of E. Petri and L. Kreutzer. Has performed solo and with leading artists. Recorded CBS.

ZAKOTNIK, Breda (1945–)
b. Maribor, Yugoslavia. Prodigy. Début 1957. Studied in Ljubljana and Vienna; diploma there 1969. Performed throughout Europe, mainly chamber music. Has special affinity with Mozart.

ZANELLA, Amilcare (1873–1949)
b. Monicelli d'Ongina, Italy. Student of Parma Cons., graduating 1891. The following year toured S. America giving pf recitals and conducting opera. Returned to Parma Cons. in 1903 as director, then, in 1905, succeeded Mascagni at the Liceo Rossini, Pesaro. Composed chamber music, pf works and songs.

ZAREMBSKI, Julius (1854–85)
b. Zhitomir, Poland. A prodigy who performed own works in public at the age of 11. Pupil of J. Dachs in Vienna 1870–4 and winner of a Gold Medal. Studied at St Petersburg before going to Rome for lessons from F. Liszt. Toured from 1876 and acquired considerable reputation. Interested in the Mangeot pf invented by J. Wieniawski and built by Mangeot incorporating two keyboards. Demonstrated it at Paris Exhibition 1878. In 1879 became pf prof. at Brussels R. Cons. Died early from tuberculosis. Composed in style and titles of Chopin.

ZARZYCKI, Alexander (1834–95)
b. Lwow, Poland. Studied there and in Paris. Became famous in Europe as brilliant pianist and was Director of Warsaw Cons. from 1879. Composed works for pf and orch. and pf pieces using titles associated with Chopin's output.

ZATHEY, Janus (1927–)
b. Warsaw, Poland. Pupil at Cracow Cons., winning pf diploma 1953. Début 1948 there. Taught at Cracow Coll. from 1954. Well-known concert pianist in Poland.

ZAYAS, Juana (1940–)
b. Havana, Cuba. Studied at Havana Cons. and later in Paris, having made début as a prodigy. Won numerous prizes for pf playing in Americas and Europe and appeared widely in N. and S. America.

ZAYDE, Jascha (–)
b. New York, USA. Studied first with C. Adler and won a fellowship to the Juilliard School at the age of 14, his teachers being K. Friedberg, R. Goldmark and (for composition) Bernard Wagenaar. Had diverse and successful career as soloist, duettist with L. Hambro and pianist to the New York City Ballet Company. Conducted musical shows on Broadway. A gifted arranger, especially for two pfs. Recorded Command.

ZBINDEN, Julien (1917–)
b. Rolle, Switzerland. Pupil of Lausanne Cons. Was associated with radio there and composed pf concerto with orch. and another with strings, chamber music and a jazz sonata.

ZECCHI, Carlo (1903–)
b. Rome, Italy. Studied there with F. Bajardi and later in Berlin with A. Schnabel and F. Busoni. Performed from 1930. US début 1931. Later turned to conducting as well as teaching. Recorded *Cetra* and *Telefunken*.
Pupils included: Ivan Davis, Robin Harrison, Jerzy Marchwinski, John O'Conor, Siegbert Ziak.

ZECH, Frederick (1858–1926)
b. Philadelphia, USA. Studied pf in USA and later in Berlin at T. Kullak's Acad. where he taught before returning to USA in 1882. Settled in San Francisco as pianist and teacher. Composed a number of pf concertos as well as chamber music.
Pupils included: Julius Alsleben.

ZECHWER, Camille (1875–1924)
b. Philadelphia, USA. Pupil of his father, Richard Z, and later in Berlin at the Scharwenka School. Back home took up pedagogic career and composed a pf concerto, chamber music and pf pieces.

ZECHWER, Richard (1850–1922)
b. Stendal, Germany. Pupil of Leipzig Cons. under I. Moscheles. Settled in USA, where he taught in Philadelphia. Composed songs and pf pieces, and wrote a work on touch.
Pupils included: Camille Zechwer.

ZEISLER, Fannie Bloomfield: *see* **BLOOMFIELD-ZEISLER, Fannie**

ZELENSKI, Ladislaw (1837–1921)
b. Grodkowice, Poland. Studied music in Cracow, Prague and Paris. Taught pf and composition at Warsaw Cons., later became Director of Cracow Cons. Besides playing and teaching was prolific composer, including for pf a concerto, two sonatas, many pieces and chamber music.
Pupils included: Stanislas Lipski, Sigismund Stojowski, Felician Szopski.

ZELLAN-SMITH, Georgina (1931–)
b. Milburn, New Zealand. Studied in Dunedin and then at the R. Acad., London. Début there 1961. Performed in Europe and Far East, also S. America. Taught at Otago Univ. before settling in UK as pf prof. at R. Acad. of Music. Recorded Peerless.

ZELLER, Julius (1832–1900)
b. Vienna, Austria. Pianist, teacher and composer who wrote a pf concerto, chamber music, and numerous pf compositions for two and four hands.

ZELTER, Mark (–)
b. USSR. Pf pupil of J. Flier in Moscow. Winner of awards including 2nd Prize in Busoni Comp. in Italy in 1968. Appeared at Spoleto Festival in 1976. New York début 1978. Now settled in the USA.

ZEUNER, Karl Traugott (1775–1841)
b. Dresden, Germany. Studied in Halle, and was also a pupil of M. Clementi. Performed in France and Austria, and lived in Vienna for a time before going on to St Petersburg. Lived finally in Dresden but died in Paris while touring. Composed pf concertos, solo variations, polonaises, etc as well as chamber music.

ZHELOBINSKY, Valery Viktorovich (1912–46)
b. Tambov, USSR. A prodigy who studied locally, then at Leningrad Cons. Composed pf pieces including 24 preludes, songs, etc.

ZHUKOV, Igor (1936–)
b. Gorki, USSR. Student of Moscow Cons. as a pupil of N. Neuhaus, graduating with honours in 1960, the year of his début and commencement of career. 2nd Prizewinner in M. Long-J. Thibaud Comp. 1957. Special interpreter of Scriabin. Recorded Melodiya.

ZIAK, Siegbert (1909–)
b. Vienna, Austria. Student of Univ. there; studied pf with C. Zecchi and F. Wührer. Academic career and performed solo, with orch. and in ensemble, mainly in Austria.

ZICHY, Count Geza (1849–1924)
b. Sztara, Hungary. An extraordinary son of a nobleman who studied music and the legal profession. At the age of 14 lost his right arm in a hunting accident but continued literally to become a virtuoso with the left hand only, pursuing a concert career, the proceeds of which largely went to charities. Studied with F. Liszt and several times they performed in public a three-handed arrangement of the *Rakoczy March*. For a time was president of the Hungarian National Acad. Composed many works especially for left hand, and wrote an autobiography.

ZIELINSKI, Yaroslav (1844–1922)
b. Lubycza, Poland. Pupil of K. Mikuli. Left Poland after the revolution and settled in USA from 1864 where he was involved in the Civil War. Thereafter taught and performed eventually moving west to California. Composed pf pieces.

ZILCHER, Hermann (1881–1948)
b. Frankfurt, Germany. Pupil first of his father, then of Hoch's Cons. under J. Kwast for pf. Lived in Berlin 1901–8, performing and teaching (for a time at Hoch's). Pf prof. in Munich 1908–20 and continued to tour Europe and America. Composer of a wide variety of works including a pf concerto and solos.

ZIMERMAN, Krystian (1956–)
b. Katowice, Poland. Pf pupil first of his father then of Andrzej Jasinki. Winner of several prizes as a student, culminating in 1st Prize in the Chopin Int. Comp., Warsaw, 1975. London début 1977, followed by appearances in the USA. An internationally esteemed artist, especially in the music of F. Chopin. Recorded DG.

ZIMMERMAN, Pierre Joseph Guillaume (1785–1853)
b. Paris, France, Student of Paris Cons., winning 1st Prize for playing in 1800. Appointed pf prof. there in 1816 where he remained until retirement in 1848 when he was made Chevalier of the Legion of Honour. Composed two pf concertos, a sonata and studies. His most enduring work is the pedagogic *Encyclopédie du Pianiste*.
   Pupils included: Charles Alkan, Charles Angelet, César Franck, Alexandre Goria, Louis Lacombe, Martin Lazare, Antoine-François Marmontel, Jules Pasdeloup, Émile Prudent, Henri Rosellen, Ambroise Thomas, Josef Wieniawski, Auguste Wolff.

ZIMMERMANN, Agnes Marie (1847–1925)
b. Cologne, Germany. Student of R. Acad., London, under C. Potter and E. Pauer, winning two scholarships and a silver medal. London début 1863. German début Leipzig 1864. Performed thereafter regularly and had one of the longest unbroken spans before the public from the age of 16 to well over 75. Made edition of the complete pf works of Schumann, one of the Beethoven sonatas, and another of the Mozart sonatas.

ZSCHOCHER, Johann (1821–97)
b. Leipzig, Germany. Pf pupil of T. Kullak, A. Henselt and F. Liszt. Concert pianist and teacher.

ZUBRSYKI, Boguslav (1929–)
b. Cracow, Poland. Student of State Coll. there, winning Diploma 1956. Début same year in Cracow. Performed throughout Poland and composed much for pf.

ZUCKERMANN, Augusta: *see* MANA-ZUCCA

ZURAWLEW, Georg (1887–1980)
b. Rostov on Don, Russia. Studied at Warsaw Cons. with A. Michałowski. Début there with orch. in 1911. Performed thereafter successfully at home and abroad, solo and with orch. Became pf prof. His international reputation as virtuoso and teacher also rests on the fact that he was the inspiration behind the founding of the Chopin Int. Comp. for pianists in Warsaw, begun in 1927. Recorded Muza. Dedicatee of the Paraphrase on the D flat waltz of Chopin by A. Michałowski. Also known as Jerzy Z and George Jouravleff.

ZVEREV, Nikolai Sergei (1832–93)
b. Moscow, Russia. Student of A. Dubuc and von Henselt. Pf prof. at Moscow Univ. from 1870 until his death. Had reputation for being a hard taskmaster but his pupils afterwards spoke highly of his inspiration. Was friend of P. Tchaikovsky who had taught him theory.

Pupils included: Constantine Igumnov, Arseni Koreschenko, Matvei Pressman, Sergei Rachmaninov, Alexander Scriabin, Alexander Siloti.

ZWINTSCHER, Bruno (1838–1905)
b. Ziegenhain, Germany. Pf pupil of I. Moscheles. Taught at Leipzig Cons. 1875–96, thereafter on his own in Dresden. Published technical studies based on Plaidy's; also a work on ornamentation.

ZYKAN, Otto (1935–   )
b. Vienna, Austria. Pupil of Acad. there, winning the Darmstadt Comp. 1958. As concert pianist mainly interested in contemporary music.

ZYNOVYEV, Paul (1844–87)
b. St Petersburg, Russia. Pf pupil of T. Leschetizky and taught pf at the Cons. until 1887 when he became editor of the *Gazette* there. Contributed many freelance essays on music, and translated Liszt's *Chopin* into Russian.

ZYWNY, Adalbert (1756–1842)
b. Czechoslovakia. A violinist and keyboard player who had been court pianist and teacher in the old Poland before partition. Thereafter taught in Warsaw. The really important historical fact about his career is that he taught F. Chopin as a boy somewhere between 1816 and 1822. Some references record the year of his death as 1840.

Appendix

WINNERS OF INTERNATIONAL PIANO COMPETITIONS
and
MEDALLISTS OF CONSERVATOIRES AND SCHOOLS

(Note. This section is compiled from information supplied by officials of the various organizations to whom the author makes grateful acknowledgement. It will become apparent, however, that here and there names are spelt with slight differences from entries in the main sections of this Dictionary, and indeed on concert programmes and records. After due reflection the author decided not to attempt to alter the competition records in their original form.)

AUSTRALIA

Sydney International Piano Competition (presented under the auspices of the Sydney Conservatorium of Music). Macquarie Street, Sydney NSW 2000, Australia.

1977

1 Irina Plotnikova, USSR
2 Svetlana Navasardian, USSR
3 André Laplante, Canada
4 Marioara Trifan, USA
5 Philip Fowke, UK
6 Manana Doidzashvili, USSR
7 Daniel Blumenthal, USA
8 Dennis Lee, Malaysia
9 Diana Kacso, Brazil
10 Gary Steigerwalt, USA
11 Jenö Jandó, Hungary
12 Pawel Checinki, Poland
13 Piers Lane, Australia

1981

1 Chia Chou, Canada
2 Endre Hegedus, Hungary
3 Catherine Vickers, Canada
4 Daniel Blumenthal, USA
5 David Owen Norris, UK
6 Liora Ziv-Li, Israel
7 Marc Raubenheimer, S. Africa
8 Patrick O'Byrne, New Zealand
9 Martin Roscoe, UK
10 Alec Chien, USA

11 Yves Rault, France; Edward Newman, USA

(Best Australian pianist – Phillip Shovk; best chamber music pianist – Daniel Blumenthal, USA; Musica Viva special prize – David Owen Norris, UK; best accompanist – Endre Hegedus, Hungary.)

AUSTRIA

Bösendorfer-Klavierwettbewerbes (given as a prize after a competition for the piano students of Vienna Academy by the piano-makers Bösendorfer Klavierfabrik A.G., Vienna).

1890 Alexander Zemlinsky
1892 Roderich Bass
1893 Hugo Holik
1894 Elsa Prinz
1895 Marie Turzansky
1896 Emil Friedberger
1897 Julius Fischer
1898 Alexander Mandeltort
1899 Wilhelm Klasen
1900 Adolf Borschke
1901 Bruno Eisner
1902 Stefanie Rath
1903 Leopold Wagner
1904 Ingeborg Franzen
1905 Henriette Zettermayer
1906 Richard Glas
1907 Anna Nikel
1908 Bertha Engel
1909 Antonie Geiger
1910 Helene Matschek
1911 Friedrich Hilbrandt

1912 Marianne Lederer
1913 Agnes Dudik
1914 Margarethe Löwit
1915 Dorothea Josefovicz
1918 Georg Jokl
1919 Lilly Gutowski (Feb.)
1919 Lubka Kolessa (Nov.)
1920 Hilda Deutsch
1921 Eugenie Volek
1924 Hertha Gröger
1927 Hans Weber
1929 Roland Raupenstrauch
1930 Robert Spitz
1932 Hans Höpfel
1935 Taras Mykyscha
1949 Alexander Jenner
1951 Eduard Mrazek
1953 Walter Klien
1955 (Not awarded)
1957 Hans Petermandl
1960 Rosemarie Wright
1961 Ivan Eröd
1964 Friederike Grünfeld
1967 Rudolf Buchbinder
1971 Brigette Meyer
1973 Jesus Gonzales
1975 John O'Conor
1977 Emilio Angulo-Sanchez
1979 Naoko Nagaoka-Knopp
1981 Wessel van Wyk
1983 Dagmar Poeltl-Cesnik

International Beethoven Piano Competition. Held every fourth year. The upper age limit of entrants is 32 years, and emphasis is placed upon knowledge of style, creative power and instrumental skill in the performance of Beethoven's works. Generalsekretariat: A-1037 Wien, Lothringerstrasse 18, Austria.

1961

1 Not awarded
2 Dieter Weber, Austria
3 Blanca Uribe, Colombia

1965

1 Lois Carole Pachucki, USA
2 Edward Auer, USA
3 Joao Carlos Miranda de Assis Brasil, Brazil

1969

1 Mitsuko Uchida, Japan
2 Oksana Jablonska, USSR
3 Verena Pfenninger, Switzerland

1973

1 John O'Conor, Ireland (sic)
2 Seta Tanyel, Austria—Turkey
3 Oscar Tarrago, Mexico

1977

1 Natalia Pankova, USSR
2 Edson Elias, Brazil
3 Natalia Vlassenko, USSR

1981

1 Avo Kouyoumdjian, Lebanon
2 Ian Hobson, UK
3 Héctor Alejandro Daniel Rivera, Argentina

BELGIUM

Concours Musical International Reine Elisabeth. (Three different sessions in every three successive years and representing piano, violin and composition. Held under the patronage of HM the Queen of the Belgians and with the support of the Government.) Rue Baron Horta 11, B-1000 Brussels.

1952

1 Leon Fleischer, USA
2 Karl Engel, Switzerland
3 Maria Tipo, Italy
4 Frans Brouw, Belgium
5 Lawrence Davis, Australia
6 Lamar Crowson, USA
7 Theodore Lettvin, USA
8 Yuri Boukoff, Bulgaria
9 Jacques Coulaud, France
10 Philippe Entremont, France
11 Hans Graf, Austria
12 Janine Kinet, Belgium

1956

1 Vladimir Ashkenazy, USSR
2 John Browning, USA
3 Andrej Czajkowski, Poland
4 Cécile Ousset, France
5 Lazar Berman, USSR
6 Tamas Vasary, Hungary
7 Stanislav Knor, Czechoslovakia
8 Claude Coppens, Belgium
9 Gyorgy Banhalmi, Hungary
10 Hiroko Kashu, Japan
11 Hans Graf, Austria
12 Peter Frankl, Hungary

1960

1 Malcolm Frager, USA
2 Ronald Turini, Canada
3 Lee Luvisi, USA
4 Alice Mitchenko, USSR
5 Gabor Gabos, Hungary
6 Shirley Seguin, USA
7 Walter Kamper, Austria

8 Yuri Airapetian, USSR
9 Jerome Lowenthal, USA
10 Agustin Anievas, USA
11 Alberto Gimenez Attenelle, Spain
12 Kenneth Amada, USA

1964

1 Evgueni Moguilevsky, USSR
2 Nicolai Petrov, USSR
3 Jean-Claud Vanden Eynden, Belgium
4 Anton Kuerti, USA
5 Richard Syracuse, USA
6 Michael Ponti, USA
7 Eugen Rjanov, USSR
8 Evelyne Flauw, France
9 Dora Milanova, Bulgaria
10 Kou Chen Ying, Taiwan
11 John Covelli, USA
12 Krassimir Gatev, Bulgaria

1968

1 Ekaterina Novitzkaja, USSR
2 Valere Kamychov, USSR
3 Jeffrey Siegel, USA
4 Semion Kroutchine, USSR
5 André de Groote, Belgium
6 François-Joël Thiollier, USA
7 Edward Auer, USA
8 Eva-Maria Zuk, Venezuela
9 Elisaveta Leonskaja, USSR
10 Mikzuko Uchida, Japan
11 François Duchable, France
12 Waled Howrani, Poland

1972

1 Valery Afanassiev, USSR
2 Jeffrey Swann, USA
3 Joseph Alfidi, USA
4 David Lively, USA
5 Svetlana Navassardian, USSR
6 Ikuyo Kamiya, Japan
7 Emanuel Ax, USA
8 James Tocco, USA
9 Cyprien Katsaris, France
10 Jonathan Pervin, USA
11 Djeni Petrova, Bulgaria
12 Pi-Hsien Chen, China

1975

1 Mikhail Faerman, USSR
2 Stanislav Igolinski, USSR
3 Yuri Egorov, USSR
4 Larry Michael Graham, USA
5 Sergiu Iuchkevich, USSR
6 Olivier Gardon, France
7 Mikhail Petoukhov, USSR
8 Evelyne Brancart, Belgium
9 Harumi Hanafusa, Japan

10 Daniel Rivera, Argentina
11 Dominique Cornil, Belgium
12 Seta Tanyel, Australia

1978

1 Abdel-Rahman El-Bacha, Libya
2 Gregory Allen, USA
3 Brigitte Engerer, France
4 Alan Weiss, USA
5 Douglas Finch, Canada
6 Robert Groslot, Belgium
7 Natasha Tadson, Israel
8 Attila Nemethy, Hungary
9 Sylvia Traey, Belgium
10 Paulo Gori, Brazil
11 Urzula Mitrega, Poland
12 Bernd Goetzke, W. Germany

1983

1 Pierre Volondat, France
2 Wolfgang Manz, W. Germany
3 Boyan Vodenitcharov, Bulgaria
4 Daniel Blumenthal, USA
5 Eliane Rodrigues, Brazil
6 Sergei Edelmann, apatride
7 Rian de Waal, Netherlands
8 Huseyin Sermet, Turkey
9 David Buechner, USA
10 Uriel Tsachor, Israel
11 Megumi Umene, Japan
12 Alexander Kuzmin, apatride

CANADA

Concours International de Montreal. Institut
International de Musique du Canada, 106 Avenue
Dulwich, Saint-Lambert, PQ, Canada J4P 2Y7.

1965

1 Albert Lotto, USA; Jean-Claude Pennetier,
  France
3 Verda Erman, Turkey; Jeffrey Siegel, USA
5 Arthur Fennimore, USA
6 Catherine Silie, France; Michael Studer,
  Switzerland
8 Michael Rogers, USA; Csilla Szabo, Hungary
10 Eugene Pridonoff, USA; François Joël Thiollier,
   USA
12 Christiane Billaud, France

1968

1 Garrick Ohlsson, USA
2 Peter Rösel, E. Germany
3 Liubovj Timofeeva, USSR
4 Aleksey Liubimov, USSR
5 James Tocco, USA
6 Dan-Nicolae Grigore, Romania

7 Krassimir Gatev, Bulgaria
8 Jonathan Purvin, USA
9 Arthur Moreira-Lima, Brazil
10 Raul Sosa, Argentina
11 Christian Bernard, France; Vladimir Denisenko, USSR

1971

1 Not awarded
2 Peter Basquin, USA
3 William Tritt, Canada
4 Jeffrey Swann, USA
5 Zola Shaulis, USA
6 Janina Fialkowska, Canada
7 Jesus G. Alonso, Spain
8 Daria Hovora, France
9 Marta Deyanova, Bulgaria

1976

1 Eteri Andjaparidze, USSR
2 Nicolai Demidenko, USSR; Naum Grubert, USSR; Gerhard Oppitz, W. Germany
5 John Hendrickson, Canada
6 Michael Blum, USA
7 Marioara Trifan, USA
8 Evelyne Brancart, Belgium
9 Bogdan Czapiewski, Poland

1980

1 Ivo Pogorelich, Yugoslavia
2 Christopher O'Riley, USA; Vladimir Ovtchinnikov, USSR
4 Emma Tachmizian, Bulgaria
5 Andrei Diev, USSR
6 Boris Petrov, USSR
7 Ick-Choo Moon, Canada
8 Rémy Loumbrozo, France
9 Ruriko Kikuchi, Japan

CZECHOSLOVAKIA

Virtuosi per Musica di Pianoforte (an annual competition founded in 1968). LSU, CS 40001, Usti nad Labem, Kalininova 1, CSSR.

1968 I Category

1 J. Brhlíková, Czechoslovakia
2 H. Vokurková, Czechoslovakia
3 M. Hršel, Czechoslovakia
4 I. Dubnová, Czechoslovakia

II Category

1 M. Vítová, Czechoslovakia (Absolute winner of the Competition.)
2 J. Snítil, Czechoslovakia
3 I. Tomášová, Czechoslovakia; A. Skálová, Czechoslovakia; J. Vorlíček, Czechoslovakia

III Category

1 A. Binková, Czechoslovakia
2 J. Bajgar, Czechoslovakia; H. Snítilová, Czechoslovakia
3 M. Eben, Czechoslovakia
4 P. Klinecký, Czechoslovakia

IV Category

1 Not awarded
2 Not awarded
3 D. Šplíchalová, Czechoslovakia

1969 I Category

1 Zdeňka Kolářová, Czechoslovakia; Martin Hršel, Czechoslovakia
2 Not awarded
3 Ivana Polcarová, Czechoslovakia; Alena Tesařová, Czechoslovakia

II Category

1 Tomáš Víšek, Czechoslovakia; Ivana Tomášová, Czechoslovakia
2 Petr Hübner, Czechoslovakia; Magdaléna Ivanová, Czechoslovakia
3 Petr Zejfart, Czechoslovakia

III Category

1 Eva Virsíková, Czechoslovakia; Martina Vítová, Czechoslovakia
3 Jindřich Bajgar, Czechoslovakia
4 Eliška Beránková, Czechoslovakia

IV Category

1 Cyril Dianovský, Czechoslovakia
2 Not awarded
3 Olga Tittlová, Czechoslovakia; Svata Valešová, Czechoslovakia; Elena Mešková, Czechoslovakia

1970 I Category
1 Leoš Svárovský, Czechoslovakia
2 Monika Maňasová, Czechoslovakia
3 Alena Kociánová, Czechoslovakia; Ivanka Polcarová, Czechoslovakia

II Category

1 Hana Pěgřímková, Czechoslovakia; Yvetta Koláčková, Czechoslovakia; Jitka Hlobílková, Czechoslovakia
2 Hana Vokurková, Czechoslovakia; Alena Tesařová, Czechoslovakia
3 Věra Hájková, Czechoslovakia; Ivan Gajan, Czechoslovakia; Alena Kopčanová, Czechoslovakia; Iva Hincáková, Czechoslovakia

III Category

1 Tomáš Víšek, Czechoslovakia
2 Martina Kaplanová, Czechoslovakia

3 Jana Homolková, Czechoslovakia

IV Category

1 Not awarded
2 Aleš Zoulek, Czechoslovakia
3 Petr Kofroň, Czechoslovakia

1971 I Category

1 Margus Bubert, Estonia
2 Péter Nagy, Hungary; Signe Kübar, Estonia
3 Jana Vlková, Czechoslovakia; Pavlínaa
   Moskalyková, Czechoslovakia; Leoš Svárovský,
   Czechoslovakia

II Category

1 Kristina Kiss, Hungary
2 Martin Hršel, Czechoslovakia; István Kassai,
   Hungary
3 Hana Vokurková, Czechoslovakia; Hana
   Pěgřímková, Czechoslovakia

III Category

1 Kalle Randallu, Estonia; Tibor Kátai, Hungary
2 Zsuzca Bauer, Hungary
3 Jaromír Kubíček, Czechoslovakia; Pavel Matyáš,
   Czechoslovakia

1972 I Category

1 Martin Hršel, Czechoslovakia
2 Sarosi Orsolya, Hungary
3 Ondřej Černil, Czechoslovakia; Jitka
   Rakušanová, Czechoslovakia

II Category

1 Leoš Svárovský, Czechoslovakia; István Kassai,
   Hungary
2 Zdeňka Kolářová, Hungary; Marián Pivka,
   Czechoslovakia
3 Robert Szacsky, Hungary; Gerald Fauth, E.
   Germany; Laszló Erdélyi, Hungary

III Category

1 Rein Mets, Estonia
2 Tibor Pozsgai, Hungary
3 Christine Wildner, E. Germany

1973 I Category

1 Jana Vlková, Czechoslovakia; Simona Klučková,
   Czechoslovakia
2 Marie Mátlová, Czechoslovakia
3 Zuzka Pauleschová, Czechoslovakia; Jana
   Potočková, Czechoslovakia

II Category

1 Balasz Szokolay, Hungary
2 Kristina Schell, E. Germany

3 Iwona Karasinska, Poland; A. Tocheva Tocheva,
   Bulgaria

III Category

1 S. Michail Slavom, Bulgaria; Tibor Poszgai,
   Hungary; Piret Hurtova, Estonia
2 T. Baynov Nedelkovič, Bulgaria; Věra Hájková,
   Czechoslovakia
3 Not awarded

1974 I Category

1 Tomáš Tvaroh, Czechoslovakia
2 Zuzka Paulechová, Czechoslovakia' Jana
   Potočhová, Czechoslovakia
3 Miloš Hýsek, Czechoslovakia

II Category

1 Amad Weiland, E. Germany; Lani Pille, Estonia;
   Maria Krasteva, Bulgaria
2 Albena Hadjikrasteva, Bulgaria
3 Arunas Staškus, Lithuania; Ireneusz Jagla,
   Poland

III Category

1 Zsuzsa Kollár, Hungary; Zdeňka Kolářová,
   Czechoslovakia; Egle Perkumaite, Lithuania
2 Katrin Kaasik, Estonia; Gerald Fauth, E.
   Germany
3 Lolita Skirbutajite, Lithuania; Ilina Todorova,
   Bulgaria

1975 I Category

1 Ingrid Kalusová, Czechoslovakia
2 Luděk Šabaka, Czechoslovakia; Jana Kociánová,
   Czechoslovakia; Jana Potočková, Czechoslovakia
3 Martin Kotek, Czechoslovakia; Helena
   Suchárová, Czechoslovakia; Petra Šmejkalová,
   Czechoslovakia

II Category

1 Neringa Puisyte, Lithuania
2 Aleksandras Kovalskis, Lithuania
3 Arunas Giurkowa, Lithuania; Mariana
   Dimitrowa, Bulgaria; Robert Jens Melke, E.
   Germany

III Category

1 Boian Wodenitscharov, Bulgaria
2 Gábor Czalog, Hungary
3 Ludmila Franková, Czechoslovakia; Jana
   Macharáčková, Czechoslovakia; Larysa
   Molnárová, Czechoslovakia

1976 I Category

1 Luděk Šabaka, Czechoslovakia
2 Jitka Drobílková, Czechoslovakia; Monika
   Pecikievičová, Czechoslovakia

3 Almuth Krauser, E. Germany; Csoba Tunde, Hungary; Martin Kotek, Czechoslovakia; Rita Papp, Hungary

II Category

1 Zuzana Paulechová, Czechoslovakia; Jana Potočhová, Czechoslovakia; Jana Juliová, Czechoslovakia
2 Lala Filippova, USSR; Ivan Kováč, Czechoslovakia; Radoslawowa Dimitrowa, Bulgaria
3 Not awarded

III Category

1 Christina Schell, E. Germany
2 Lauri Vainmaa, Estonia; Heili Seppo, Estonia; Jaromír Klepáč, Czechoslovakia
3 Riina Piirsalu, Estonia

1977 I Category

1 Karin Ritschel, E. Germany; Martin Kotek, Czechoslovakia
2 Alexander Vassilenko, Bulgaria
3 Luděk Šabaka, Czechoslovakia; Monika Picikiewiczová, Czechoslovakia

II Category

1 Leonid Kuzmin, USSR; Zbignevas Tatolis, Lithuania
2 Cvetelina Nenkova, Bulgaria; Simona Klučková, Czechoslovakia
3 Iavor Konov, Bulgaria; Szymon Kowalczyk, Poland; Jana Potočková, Czechoslovakia

III Category

1 Lijana Baronaite, Lithuania; Ireneusz Jagla, Poland
2 Albina Šikšniute, Lithuania; Vladimír Dulov, USSR
3 Lora Angelova, Bulgaria

1978 I Category

1 Igor Ardašev, Czechoslovakia
2 Amadeus Gros, E. Germany; Wojciech Switala, Poland
3 Justas Dvrionas, Lithuania; Andreas Boyde, E. Germany; Rumjana Kirčeva, Czechoslovakia

II Category

1 Not awarded
2 Rita Papp, Hungary; Adrien Soŏs, Hungary
3 Ulrich Meining, E. Germany

III Category

1 Thomas Effner, E. Germany; Jana Potočková, Czechoslovakia
2 Zuzana Paulechová, Czechoslovakia; Tomáš

Hála, Czechoslovakia; Audroné Petručionyté, Lithuania
3 Not awarded

1979 I Category

1 Jan Pipek, Czechoslovakia; Anna Petrova, USSR
2 Not awarded
3 Adam Gren, Poland; Aniko Novák, Hungary

II Category

1 Igor Ardašev, Czechoslovakia
2 Tunde Csoba, Hungary
3 Ani Avramova, Bulgaria; Monika Pecikiewoczová, Czechoslovakia; Karin Ritschel, E. Germany; Gábor Legindi, Hungary

III Category

1 Roman Raithel, E. Germany
2 Cornelia Freese, E. Germany
3 Darius Burnekci, Poland; Michal Rezek, Czechoslovakia; Jana Melčová, Czechoslovakia

1980 I Category

1 Vladimír Hristov, Bulgaria
2 Iliana Rawanova, Bulgaria
3 Oksana Michajlova, USSR; Petr Jiříkovský, Czechoslovakia

II Category

1 Andreas Boyde, E. Germany
2 Wojciech Swvitala, Poland
3 Piotr Krajniak, Poland; Jana Pavlínová, Czechoslovakia

III Category

1 Martti Raide, Estonia
2 Ljudmila Tarasova, USSR; Martin Kotek, Czechoslovakia
3 Michal Rezek, Czechoslovakia; Elena Sidoreva, USSR

1981 I Category

1 Milada Přibylová, Bulgaria
2 Ilona Marchevič, USSR; Leila Petrova Naidenova, Bulgaria
3 Ivona Solonková, Czechoslovakia; Andrus Rang, Estonia

II Category

1 Miloš Bok, Czechoslovakia; Indrek Laul, Estonia; Cordula Schumann, E. Germany
2 Dénes Várjon, Hungary
3 Jan Pipek, Czechoslovakia

III Category

1 Vaida Kirvelyte, Lithuania

2 Dariusz Pawlas, Poland
3 Andrius Talimaa, Lithuania; Karin Ritschel, E. Germany

1982 I Category

1 Kollert Jiří, Czechoslovakia
2 Petr Jan, Czechoslovakia
3 Lysov Denis, USSR

II Category

1 Gerretz Marrit, Tallin
2 Alena Králová, Czechoslovakia; Pavlova Nikolaeva, Bulgaria
3 Halina Jančiková, Czechoslovakia

III Category

1 Darius Simkunas, Lithuania
2 Dimitrov Stefanov, Bulgaria
3 Randal Piret, Tallin

1983 I Category

1 Jitka Fraňková, Czechoslovakia
2 Petra Pospíšilová, Czechoslovakia
3 Not awarded

II Category

1 Izabela Alescandrova, Bulgaria; Michaela Oravcová, Czechoslovakia; Wesselina Boteva, Bulgaria
2 Daniela Erhartová, Czechoslovakia
3 Ivona Solonková, Czechoslovakia

III Category

1 Dan Vladescu, Romania
2 Halina Jančiková, Czechoslovakia
3 Miriam Fialová, Czechoslovakia; Daniela Hlinková, Czechoslovakia

DENMARK

Leonie Sonnings Musikfond. (An annual prize in cash awarded to composers, instrumentalists, conductors or singers of international reputation. Cannot be applied for.) Only recipients whose names appear in the main part of this volume are included hereunder.

1959 Igor Stravinsky
1965 Leonard Bernstein
1967 Witold Lutoslawski
1968 Benjamin Britten
1971 Arthur Rubinstein
1973 Dmitri Shostakovich
1977 Olivier Messiaen
1981 Mstislav Rostropovich

FRANCE

Concours International Marguerite Long–Jacques Thibaud (alternate years since the third concours, with prizes for violin and piano. Only piano finalists listed). Secrétariat Général, Immeuble Gaveau, 45 Rue la Boétie 75008, Paris.

1943

Grand Prix, Samson François, France
2 Marie-Thérèse Fourneau, France

1946

Grand Prix, Hedi Schneider, Hungary
2 Janine Dacosta, France
3 Myrielle Blancard, France
4 Olga Craen, W. Indies
5 Hélène Toinet, France

1949

Grand Prix, Aldo Ciccolini, Italy; Ventsislav Yankoff, Bulgaria
2 Daniel Wayenberg, Netherlands
3 Paul Badura-Skoda, Austria
4 Yuri Boukoff, Bulgaria
5 Pierre Barbizet, France
6 Marie Chairo-Georges, Greece
7 Selma Herscovici, France
8 Monique Mercier, France
9 Inge Mayerhofer, Austria

1951

Grand Prix, Janine Dacosta, France
2 Sequeira Costa, Portugal
3 Andrzej Vasowski, Poland
4 Lawrence Davis, Australia
5 Philippe Entremont, France
6 Alexander Jenner, Austria
7 Georg Solchany, Hungary
8 Joaquin Achucarro, Spain
9 Ronald Smith, UK
10 Lya de Barberiis, Italy

1953

Grand Prix, Not awarded
2 Eugeny Malinin, USSR; Philippe Entremont, France
3 Alberto Colombo, Italy
4 Kioko Tanaka, Japan
5 Barbara Hesse-Bukowska, Poland
6 Cécile Ousset, France
7 Walter Klien, Austria
8 Emmy Behar, Bulgaria

1955

Grand Prix, Not awarded
2 Dimitri Bachkirov, USSR; Bernard Ringeissen, France
3 Gabor Gabos, Hungary

4 Gleb Axelrod, USSR
5 Klaus Schilde, Germany
6 Peter Frankl, Hungary
7 Tamas Vasary, Hungary
8 Claude de Coppens, Belgium
Mentions, Joulian Goutmane, USSR; Milosz
 Magin, Poland

1957

Grand Prix, Peter Frankl, Hungary
2 Igor Zhukov, USSR
3 Klaus Schilde, Germany
4 Gabriel Tacchino, France
5 Ayse-Gul Saridja, Turkey
6 Milosz Magin, Poland
7 George Katz, USA
8 Alain Motard, France
Mentions, Nina Leltchouk, USSR; Midori Miura,
 Japan; John Blot, Netherlands

1959

Grand Prix, Toyoaki Matsura, Japan
2 John Blot, Netherlands
3 Milena Vesselinove, Bulgaria
4 Ayse-Gul Saridja, Turkey
5 Nicolai Constantinov-Evrov, Bulgaria
6 Tatiana Achot-Haroutounian, Iran
7 Marie-Claire Laroche, France
8 Olegna Fuschi, USA

1961

Grand Prix, Marina Mdivani, USSR
2 Jean-Claude Pennetier, France
3 Bruno-Leonardo Gelber, Argentina
4 Catherine Silie, France
5 Alice Michenko, USSR
6 Ralph Votapek, USA
7 Adrien Egorov, USSR
8 Csilla Szabo, Hungary

1963

Grand Prix, Victro Eresko, USSR
2 Oksana Jablonska, USSR
3 Anton Dikov, Bulgaria
4 Verda Erman, Turkey
5 Valery Kastelsky, USSR
6 Bruno Rigutto, Italy
7 Krassimir Gatev, Bulgaria
8 Maryse Charpentier, France
9 Yuko Fujimura, Japan
10 Mayne Miller, USA

1965

Grand Prix, Not awarded
2 Alexei Tcherkassov, USSR
3 Youliana Markova, Bulgaria; Elisabeth
 Leonskaya, USSR

4 Raymond Jackson, USA
5 Renata Arnetova, Czechoslovakia; Reynaldo
 Reyes, Philippines
6 Leslie Wright, Ecuador
7 Klaus Hellwig, Germany
Mentions, Suzanne Husson, France

1967

Grand Prix, Edward Auer, USA
2 Irène Smolina, USSR
3 Marc Zelter, USSR
4 Myriam Birger, France
5 Vitali Berson, USSR
6 Elisabetha Glabowna, Poland
7 François-Joël Thiollier, USA
8 Tigrán Alikhanov, USSR
Prix Rainier, Vitali Berson, USSR
Prix Lefébure, Irène Smolina, USSR
Prix Julliard, Myriam Birger, France
Mention, André Gorog, France

1969

1 Grand Prix, Loubov Timofeeva, USSR
2 Grand Prix, Dmitri Alexeev, USSR
3 Grand Prix, Nathalie Gabrilova, USSR
4 Takashi Hironaka, Japan
5 Jean-Philippe Collard, France
6 Brigitte Engerer, France
7 Frantisek Maly, Czechoslovakia
8 Cecilio Tieles Ferrer, Cuba
Prix Pasquier, Jean-Philippe Collard, France
Prix de la Sacem, Jean-Philippe Collard, France
Prix de Vries, Marina Khvitia, USSR

1971

1 Grand Prix, Vladimir Feltzmann, USSR; Pascal
 Rogé, France
2 Claude Cymerman, France
3 Vladimir Viardo, USSR; Jacques Rouvier,
 France
4 Yuri Egorov, USSR
5 David Lee Lively, USA
6 Ramzi Yassa, Egypt
Prix de Vries, Olivier Gardon, France
Prix Pasquier, Pamela Pia Paul, USA
Mention, Guadalupe Parrando, Peru

1973

Grand Prix, Not awarded
2 Olivier Gardon, France; Jacques Taddei, France
3 André Laplante, Canada
4 Hiroshi Tajika, Japan
5 Frantisek Maly, Czechoslovakia
6 Valentina Diaz Frenot, Argentina
7 Anne Mie Ghirandelli, France
8 Nancy Loo, UK
Mentions, Till Engel, Switzerland; José do Amaral,
 Brazil; Vincenzo Balzani, Italy

Prix Fauré, Valentina Diaz Frenot, Argentina
Prix Saussine, Olivier Gardon and Jacques Taddei,
   France; Pierre Pradier and Daniel Epstein,
   France

1975

Grand Prix, Michael Rudy, USSR
2 Akiko Ebi, Japan
3 Yuri Lissitchenko-Lissitza, USSR
4 Nina Kogan, USSR; Caroline Roussel, France
6 Abdel Rahman El Bacha, Lebanon
7 Marie-Paule Siruguet, France
8 Valida Rassulova, USSR

1977

Grand Prix, Jorge Luis Prats, Cuba
2 Katsumi Ueda, Japan
3 Hélène Varvarova, apatride; Chantal Riou,
   France
5 Dan Atanasiu, Romania
6 Elzbieta Tarnawska, Poland
7 Aïko Okamoto, Japan
8 Akira Sagawa, Japan
Prix Bonnaud, Jorge Luis Prats, Cuba
Prix M. Ravel, Jorge Luis Prats, Cuba
Prix de Vries, Ivo Pogorelich, Yugoslavia; Hélène
   Varvarova, apatride
Prix Darnel, Jorge Luis Prats, Cuba

1979

Grand Prix, Frédéric Aguessy, France
2 André Nicolsky, USSR
3 Irina Ossipova, USSR; François Kerdoncuff,
   France
4 Erik Berchot, France
5 Géry Moutier, France
6 Nino Katamadze, USSR
7 Yukiko Takahashi, Japan
Prix Rainier, Erik Berchot, France
Prix Bonnaud, Frédéric Aguessy, France
Prix M. Ravel, Gulsin Onay, Turkey
Prix Descaves, Erik Berchot, France
Prix Rachmaninoff, François Kerdoncuff, France
Prix Alain, Frédéric Aguessy, France
Prix de Vries, Bernard d'Ascoli, France
Mentions, Kristine Merscher, Germany; Jacques-
   Henri Gauthier, France; Jean-Yves Thibaudet,
   France

1981

Grand Prix, Kazune Shimizu, Japan
2 Jian Li, China
3 Kei Itoh, Japan
4 Alan James Ball, USA; Alain Jacquon, France
6 Ying Ming Qin, China
7 Johanna Domanska, Poland
Prix Descaves, Masako Nakai, Japan
Prix de Vries, Johannes Kropfitsch, Austria

1983

Grand Prix, Stanislav Bounine, USSR
2 Jania Aoubakirova, USSR
3 Hervé Billaut, France
4 Alexandre Fomenko, USSR
5 Vladimir Vinnitsky, USSR
6 Dan-Wen Wei, China
Prix Rainier, Hervé Billaut, France
Prix Descaves, Stanislav Bounine, USSR
Prix Jolivet, Jania Aoubakirova, USSR
Prix Vries, Marie-Noëlle Damien, Belgium
Prix Darnel, Hervé Billaut, France; Stanislav
   Bounine, USSR
Prix des Jeunesses Musicales de France, Hervé
   Billaut, France
Prix Hanlet–Steinway, Stanislav Bounine, USSR

GERMAN DEMOCRATIC REPUBLIC
(E. GERMANY)

Preisträger der Internationalen Robert-Schumann-
Wettbewerbe. (Held every three years with awards
in two musical subjects: piano and singing. Began in
Berlin in 1956 and 1960, and thereafter in Zwickau.)
Münzstrasse, 95 Zwickau, GDR.

1956

1 Annerose Schmidt, E. Germany
2 Irina Sijalowa, USSR
3 Michael Woskresenski, USSR; Lydia
   Grychtolowna, Poland

1960

Piano was not featured.

1963

1 Nelly Akopjan, USSR
2 Ruschka Tscharaktschijewa, Bulgaria; Peter
   Rösel, E. Germany
3 Aniko Szegedi, Hungary

1966

1 Elisso Wirsaladse, USSR
2 Swetlana Nawasardjan, USSR
3 Ewgenia Sachariewa, Bulgaria; Raina Padarewa,
   Bulgaria

1969

1 Dezso Ranki, Hungary
2 Tatjana Riumina, USSR
3 Okitaka Uehara, Japan

1974

1 Pawel Jegorow, USSR
2 Dina Joffe, USSR

3 Petru Tiberiu Grossmann, Romania

1977

1 Emma Tachmisjan, Bulgaria
2 Dana Borsan, Romania
3 Christoph Taubert, E. Germany

1980

1 Yves Henri, France
2 Susanne Grützmann, E. Germany
3 Kalle Randalu, USSR; Balazs Szokolay, Hungary

1983

No information available.

FEDERAL REPUBLIC OF GERMANY (W. GERMANY)

Internationales Musikinstitut Darmstadt (Kranichsteiner Musikpreis: established 1952 and awarded every two years for composition and interpretation of new music during an 'International Holiday Course for new music'. Prizewinning pianists only shown below). 6100 Darmstadt, Nieder-Ramstädter Strasse 190, FDR.

1952

2 André François Terrasse, France; Alexander Jenner, Austria

1953

2 Robert Alexander Bohnke, W. Germany; Winifred Patricia Carroll, UK

1954

1 Joan Rowland, Canada

1955

1 Marion Zarzeczna, Italy
2 Elly Jeremias, W. Germany

1956

1 Jorge Zulueta, Argentina

1957

Jerome Lowenthal, Switzerland
Karl Otto Plum, W. Germany
Helga Thieme, W. Germany

1958

1 Otto Zykan, Austria

2 Gabor Gabos, Hungary; Wolfgang Gayler, W. Germany; Rolf Kuhnert, W. Germany

1959

1 Erika Haase, W. Germany

1960

1 Thomas McIntosh, USA
2 Bruno Canino, Italy; Andor Losonczy, Hungary
3 Howard Lebow, USA

1961

2 Howard Lebow, USA

1969

Richard Trythall, USA

1972

Herbert Henck, W. Germany
Yukike Sugawara, Japan

1974

Peter Hill, UK
Cristian Petrescu, Romania

1976

David Arden, USA

1982

Bernhard Wambach, W. Germany

International Musikwettbewerb der Rundfunkanstalten der Bundesrepublik Deutschland (an annual competition begun in 1952 for instrumentalists and singers). Bayerischer Rundfunk, 8 Munich 2, FDR.

1952

Kurt Bauer, W. Germany
Alberto Colombo, Italy
Laurence Davis, Australia
Peter Wallfisch, Israel

1953

Alexander Sellier, W. Germany
Edoardo Vercelli, Argentina
Lamar Crowson (for duo with violin), USA

1954

Ingrid Haebler, Austria
Fernande Kaeser, Switzerland

1955

(for piano duo playing) Kurt Bauer, W. Germany;
Heidi Bung, W. Germany
Alfons and Aloys Kontarsky (duettists), W.
Germany
Arlette Eggmann (for duo with violin), Italy

1956

Robert Bohnke, W. Germany
James Mathis, USA
Eduard Mrazek, Austria
Joel Ryce (for duo with violin), USA

1957

1 Thérèse Dussaut, France
2 Sumiko Inouchi, Japan
1 Peter Frankl (for duo with violin), Hungary
2 Robert Henry (for duo with violin), USA

1958

1 Hans Eckart Besch, W. Germany
2 Michael Ponti, USA; Dieter Weber, Austria
1 Eleonore Wikarsky (for duo with cello), W.
Germany
2 Ursula Trede (for duo with cello), W. Germany

1959

1 Friedrich Schnurr, W. Germany
2 Gernot Kahl, W. Germany; Norman Shetler,
USA

1960

2 Thérèse Castaing, France
3 Evelyn Ursat, France
4 Yoko Kono, Japan
2 Susanne Szabo (for duo with violin), Hungary
3 Arlene Pach (for duo with violin), Canada

1961

2 Pavica Gvozdic, Yugoslavia
3 Alexandra Ablewicz, Poland; Maureen Beeken,
UK

1962

2 Christoph Eschenbach, W. Germany
3 Lis Smed Christensen, Denmark; Milena
Mollova, Bulgaria

1963

2 Edith Fischer, Chile–Switzerland; Evelyn Flauw,
France
3 Dolores Holtz, USA
1 Sylvaine Billie (for duo with violin), France

2 Ramón Walter (for duo with violin), Switzerland
3 Marylou Kolbinson (for duo with violin), Canada

1964

2 Marie-José Billard and Julien Azaïs, France;
Joanne and Joyce Weintraub (for piano duo
playing), USA

1965

1 Judith Burgänger, USA
2 Dag Achatz, Sweden; Hanae Nakajima, Japan

1966

1 Claude Savard, Canada
3 Mitsuko Uchida, Japan

1967

2 Elena Tatuljan, USSR
3 Anthony Goldstone, UK; Valerij Kastelskij,
USSR
1 Aleksej Nasedkin (for duo with cello), USSR
2 Justus Frantz (for duo with cello), W. Germany
3 Shuku Iwasaki (for duo with cello), Japan

1968

1 Anne Queffélec, France
3 Mériem Bléger, France; Yuko Fujimura, Japan
2 Tacko Ouchi (for duo with violin), Japan; Susan
Halligan (for duo with violin), USA
3 Naoyuki Inoue, Japan

1969

2 Wilfried Kassebaum, W. Germany; Erika Lux,
Hungary
3 Poitr Paleczny, Poland

1970

2 André de Groote, Belgium; Akiko Kitagawa,
Japan

1971

2 Marian Migdal, Poland; Martino Tirimo, UK
3 Carolyn Moran, USA
1 Clifford Benson (for duo with violin), UK
2 Boris Petruschanskij (for duo with violin), USSR
3 Katalin Váradi (for duo with violin), Hungary

1972

1 Pi-Hsien Chen, Taiwan
3 Roland Keller, E. Germany

1973

1 James Tocco, USA
2 Myung Whun Chung, S. Korea
3 Gottfried Hefele, E. Germany

1974

1 Anthony and Joseph Paratore, USA
2 Elif and Bedii Aran, Turkey
3 Marina Horak, Yugoslavia and Hakon Austbo, Norway, (for piano duo playing)
3 Krystyna Makowska (for duo with violin), Poland; Dorothee Snow (for duo with violin), UK

1975

1 Diane Walsh, USA
2 Natascha Tadson, Israel
3 Nina Tichman, USA

1976

No piano awards.

1977

3 Chieko Oku, Japan; Mario Patuzzi, Italy

1978

No solo piano awards.
2 Barbara Weintraub (for duo with violin), USA
3 Mathias Weber (for duo with violin), E. Germany

1979

1 Hans-Christian Wille, E. Germany
2 Marioara Trifan, USA
3 Kenji Watanabe, Japan
2 Konstantin Bogino (for duo with violin), USSR
3 Gabriel Rosenberg (for duo with violin), E. Germany

1980

2 Natalia Bagdassarov, USSR; James Winn, USA
3 Carlos Duarte, Venezuela and Varda Shamban, Israel (for piano duo playing)

1981

2 François Killian, France
3 Chisato Ogino, Japan; Rolf Plagge, E. Germany

1983

1 Kei Itoh, Japan
2 Not awarded
3 Andrei Nikolsky, USSR; Hai-Kyung Suh, S. Korea

HUNGARY

Concours International de Piano Liszt–Bartók. Originally the Liszt Ferenc Competition and reorganized from 1956 to include a work of Bartók. Competition held every five years and open to pianists of all nationalities of an age not above 32. Address: 1366 Budapest V, Pf 80., Vörösmarty ter 1.

1933

1 Annie Fischer, Hungary
2 Mykisha Taras, USSR
3 Louis Kentner, Hungary

1948

1 Peter Wallfisch, Israel
2 Paul Badura-Skoda, Austria

1956

1 Lev Vlaszenko, USSR
2 Mihály Bächer, Hungary
3 Lazar Berman, USSR

1961

1 David Wilde, UK; Gábor Gabos, Hungary
2 Dino Ciani, Italy
3 Thérèse Castaing, France

1966

2 Imre Antal, Hungary
3 Gabriella Torma, Hungary
4 Gyula Kiss, Hungary; Erika Lux, Hungary

1971

1 Reiko Matsuzaki, Japan; Nyikolaj Szuk, USSR
2 Jelena Szkuratovszkaja, USSR
3 Etsuko Tazaki, Japan; László Baranyay, Hungary

1976

1 Robert Benz, E. Germany
2 Gary Steigerwalt, USA; Frédéric Aguessy, France
3 Imre Rohmann, Hungary; Vagyim Monasztyirszkij, USSR

1981

2 Muza Rubackitye, USSR
3 Hortense Cartier-Bresson, France
4 István Székely, Hungary; Kenji Watanabe, Japan
5 Endre Hegedüs, Hungary; Krisztina Kiss, Hungary

ISRAEL

The Arthur Rubinstein International Piano Master Competition was founded in 1974 in honour of the great Polish pianist and with the object of fostering talent and aspiring young interpreters and to promote their true artistic careers. Held every three years and open to pianists of all nationalities between 18 and 32 years of age. There are six prizes divided into two groups and each carrying a cash prize. In addition, the first group consists of three laureates each with a gold medal, and the second group of three is awarded a silver medal. The Secretariat, Shalom Tower, 5th floor, POB 29404, Tel Aviv 61293, Israel.

1974

1 Emanuel Ax, USA
2 Eugene Indjic, USA
3 Janina Fialkowska, Canada; Seta Tanyel, Austria

5 Oscar Tarrago, Mexico
6 Arnaldo Cohen, Brazil

1977

1 Gerhard Oppitz, W. Germany
2 Diana Kacso, Brazil
3 Etsuko Terada, Japan

4 Larry Graham, USA
5 Natasha Tadson, Israel
6 Boris Bloch, USA
Additional Bronze Medal: Geoffrey Tozer, Australia; Craig Sheppard, USA; Yitkin Seow, Singapore; Alexandru Preda, Romania; Mioko Kato, Japan; Jahja Mursalim Indonesia

1980

1 Gregory Allen, USA
2 Ian Hobson, UK
3 Geoffrey Tozer, Australia

4 Lyras Panayis, USA
5 Trifan Mariora, USA
6 Yuguchi-Yonogi, Japan
Additional Bronze Medal: Daniel Adni, Israel; Christian Blackshaw, UK; Evelyne Brancart, Belgium; Sergei Edelman, apatride; Sandro de Palma, Italy; Alan Weiss, USA

1983

1 Jeffrey Kahane, USA
2 Hung-Kuan Chen, USA
3 Fei-Ping Hsu, USA

4 Alexander Kuzmin, USA
5 Barry Douglas, UK
6 Gregorio Nardi, Italy

ITALY

'F. Busoni' International Piano Competition was founded in 1949 with a committee of seventeen of the foremost living virtuosi. The Busoni Prize is awarded annually, being now held under the aegis of the Bolzano community and the Italian Ministries of Tourism and Entertainment. Conservatoire statale di musica 'Claudio Monteverdi', Piazza Domenicani 19, 39100, Bolzano, Italy.

1949

1 Not awarded
2 Lodovico Lessona, Italy
3 Rossana Orlandini, Italy
4 Alfred Brendel, Austria
5 Bela Siki, Hungary

1950

1 Not awarded
2 Karl Heinz Schlüter, W. Germany
3 Jacques Coulaud, France
4 Jean Franssen, Netherlands
5 Bruno Mezzena, Italy; Andrzej Wasowski, Poland

1951

1 Not awarded
2 Not awarded
3 Karl Engel, Switzerland; Walter Klein, Austria
4 Alfred Kremela, Austria
5 Maria Luisa Candeloro, Italy

1952

1 Sergio Perticaroli, Italy
2 Andrzej Wasowski, Poland
3 Marisa Candeloro, Italy; Agostino Orizio, Italy
4 Ingrid Häbler, Austria; Walter Klein, Austria
5 Eleanor Fine, USA

1953

1 Ella Goldstein, USA
2 Monte Hill Davis, USA
3 Esteban Sanchez Herrero, Spain
4 Vladimir Havsky, USA
5 Adriana Brugnolini Vecchiato, Italy

1954

1 Aldo Mancinelli, USA
2 Gabriel Tacchino, France
3 Günter Ludwig, W. Germany
4 Kurt Bauer, W. Germany
5 Alberto Colombo, Italy

1955

1 Not awarded

2 Germaine Devéze, France
3 Günter Ludwig, W. Germany; Maria da Penha, Brazil
4 Sylvie Mercier, France; Myrtha Perez, Uruguay
5 Monte Hill Davis, USA

1956

1 Jörg Demus, Austria
2 Ivan Davis, USA
3 James Mathis, USA
4 Bruno Canino, Italy; Michael Ponti, USA

1957

1 Martha Argerich, Argentina
2 Ivan Davis, USA; Jerome Lowenthal, USA
3 Jeaneane Dowis, USA
4 Ludwig Hoffmann, W. Germany
5 Alberto Colombo, Italy

1958

1 Not awarded
2 José Kahan, Mexico; Ronald Turini, Canada
3 Fabio Peressoni, Italy; Michael Ponti, USA
4 Bruno Canino, Italy
5 Marisa Candeloro, Italy

1959

1 Not awarded
2 Cécile Ousset, France; John Perry, USA
3 Imre Antal, Hungary; Leonhard Hokanson, USA
4 Joaquin Achucarro, Spain
5 Ruriko Tsukamoto, Japan
6 Virginia Hutchings, USA

1960

1 Not awarded
2 Agustin Anievas, USA; James Mathis, USA
3 Imre Antal, Hungary
4 Giorgio Sacchetti, Italy
5 John Ogdon, UK
6 Marie Claire Laroche, France; Françoise Parrot, France

1961

1 Jerome Rose, USA
2 Howard Aibel, USA; Norma Fisher, UK
3 Dubravka Tomsic, Yugoslavia
4 Thomas McIntosh, USA
5 José Maria Contreras, Philippines
6 Friederike Grünfeld, Austria

1962

1 Not awarded
2 Brenton Dale Bartlett, Canada

3 Ivan Eröd, Hungary; Reynaldo Reyes, Philippines
4 Virginia Hutchings, USA
5 Thomas Schumacher, USA
6 Mayne Miller, USA; Giorgio Sacchetti, Italy

1963

1 Not awarded
2 Gernot Kahl, W. Germany
3 José Maria Contreras, Philippines
4 Maxine Franklin, Jamaica
5 Robert Hamilton, USA
6 Gloria Lanni, Italy
Premio speciale – Sonderpreis; Jeffrey Siegel, USA

1964

1 Michael Ponti, USA
2 François-Joël Thiollier, USA
3 Ivan Drenikov, Bulgaria
4 Friederike Grünfeld, Austria
5 Sergio Varella-Cid, Portugal
6 John Covelli, USA; Maria Luisa Lopez-Vito, Philippines

1965

1 Not awarded
2 Bojidar Noev, Bulgaria
3 James Dick, USA
4 Israela Margalit, Israel; Franco Medori, Italy
5 Benedikt Köhlen, W. Germany

1966

1 Garrick Ohlsson, USA
2 Richard Goode, USA
3 Not awarded
4 Not awarded

1967

1 Not awarded
2 Ivan Klansy, Czechoslovakia
3 Pietro Maranca, Italy
4 Frantisek Maly, Czechoslovakia
5 Roman Rudnytsky, USA

1968

1 Vladimir Selivochin, USSR
2 Mark Zelter, USSR
3 Benedikt Köhlen, W. Germany; Craig Sheppard, USA
4 Adrian Ruiz, USA
5 Vadim Sacharov, USSR

1969

1 Ursula Oppens, USA
2 Annamaria Cigoli, Italy

3 Akiko Kitagawa, Japan
4 Not awarded
5 Not awarded

1970

1 Not awarded
Premio di selezione – Selektionspreis: Maria Luisa
Lopez-Vito, Philippines
Borsa-premio-Förderungspreis: Etsuko Tazaki,
Japan

1971

1 Not awarded
2 Nina Tichman, USA
3 Ilan Rogoff, Israel; Marioara Trifan, USA
4 Catherine Collard, France
5 Wilfried Kassebaum, W. Germany; Seta Tanyel,
Austria

1972

1 Arnaldo Cohen, Brazil
2 Not awarded
3 Peter Bithell, UK; David Oei, China
4 Dai Uk Lee, Korea
5 Marian Hahn, USA

1973

1 Not awarded
2 Roland Keller, W. Germany; Andrzej Ratusinski,
Poland
3 Not awarded
4 Kveta Novotna, Czechoslovakia
5 Pierluigi Camicia, Italy; Seth Carlin, USA

1974

1 Robert Benz, W. Germany
2 Pascal Devoyon, France
3 Diane Walsh, USA
4 Steven Mayer, USA
5 Daniel Rivera, Argentina
Premio speciale – Sonderpreis: Pascal Devoyon,
France

1975

1 Not awarded
2 Staffan Scheja, Sweden
3 Terence Judd, UK; Laszlo Simon, Sweden
4 Caroline Haffner, France
5 Marina Kapatzinskaja, USSR

1976

1 Roberto Cappello, Italy
2 Daniel Rivera, Argentina
3 Not awarded

4 Susan Ann Howes, UK; Adrienne Shannon,
Canada
5 Alexeii Golovine, USSR; Antony Peebles, UK

1977

1 Not awarded
2 Ayami Ikeba, Japan; Véronique Roux, France
3 Joop Celis, Netherlands; Kyoto Ito, Japan
4 Hans Christian Wile, W. Germany
5 Radu Toescu, W. Germany

1978

1 Boris Bloch, USA
2 Dennis Lee, Malaya
3 Arnulf von Arnim, W. Germany
4 Josep Colom, Spain
5 Edson Elias, Brazil; Daniel Blumenthal, USA
Premio 'Cesare Nordio Preis': Dennis Lee, Malaya

1979

1 Catherine Vickers Steiert, Canada
2 Not awarded
3 Alyce le Blanc, USA
4 Not awarded
5 Maria Teresa Carunchio, Italy; Hiroko Miki,
Japan

1980

1 Not awarded
2 Ruriko Kikuchi, Japan; Rolf Plagge, W.
Germany; Hai Kyung Suh, S. Korea
3 Margarita Höhenrieder, W. Germany
4 Giovanni Umberto Battel, Italy; Hüseyin Sermet,
Turkey
5 Eun Soo Son, S. Korea

1981

1 Margarita Höhenrieder, W. Germany
2 Lev Natochenny, USA
3 Boyan Vodenitcharov, Bulgaria
4 Maria Theresa Carunchio, Italy
5 Fred Höricke, W. Germany
6 Christopher O'Riley, USA

1982

1 Not awarded
2 Hung-Kuan Chen, Taiwan
3 Daniel Blumenthal, USA; Yukino Fujiwara,
Japan
4 Rainer Becker, W. Germany
5 Not awarded
6 Fred Höricke, W. Germany; Gülsin Onay,
Turkey

1983

1 Not awarded
2 Robert McDonald, USA
3 Frederick Blum, USA; Arthur Greene, USA
4 Gülsin Onay, Turkey
5 Rumi Shima, Japan; Bernard Glemser, W. Germany
6 Neil Rutman, USA

'Alessandro Casagrande' International Piano Competition was founded in 1966 in memory of A. Casagrande (1922–64), born in Terni and who was Director of the G. Briccialdi Musical Institute there. It is held annually and the 1st prizewinner gets additionally engagements at Italian Festivals. Commune di Terni, 05100 Terni, Italy.

1966

1 Giuliano Silveri, Italy
2 Grazia Barbanera, Italy; Vladimir Krpan, Yugoslavia

1967

1 Fausto di Cesare, Italy
2 Roberto Bianco, Italy; Melita Kolin, Bulgaria

1968

1 Not awarded
2 Bozidar Noev, Bulgaria
3 Melita Kolin, Bulgaria; Sun Kiung Lee, Korea

1969

1 Bozidar Noev, Bulgaria
2 Guila Kiss, Hungary
3 Cecilia de Dominicis, Italy
4 Manfred Fock, Germany

1970

1 Martha Deyanova, Bulgaria
2 Yoannis Wakarelis, Greece
3 Peter Sizmarovic, Czechoslovakia
4 Mario Argentieri, Italy; Victor Ciuckov, Bulgaria

1971

1 Luiz Medalha, Brazil; Laslo Simon, Hungary
2 Not awarded
3 Atanas Kareev, Bulgaria; Roman Rudnystky, USA
Mention, Paolo Conti

1972

1 Nina Tichman, USA
2 Elsa Kolodziej, Poland; Svetla Slavtcheva, Bulgaria

3 Andreja van Schaick, Netherlands
Mention, Cecilia de Dominicis, Italy

1973

1 Kathleen Solose, Canada
2 Alan di Cenzo, USA
3 Andrea Bonatta, Italy; Catherine Girod, France; Patricia Thomas, France

1974

1 Robert Groslot, Belgium
2 Golovine Alexei, USSR
3 Hector Rivera, Argentina; Pierre Reach, France

1975

1 Boris Petrushansky, USSR
2 Caroline Haffner, France
3 Dennis Lee, UK; Alexandre Toradze, USSR

1976

1 Takeda Makiko, Japan
2 Terence Judd, UK
3 Luigi Ceci, Italy

1977

1 Alexander Lonquich, Germany
2 Dennis Lee, UK
3 Not awarded

1978

1 Ivo Pogorelich, Yugoslavia
2 Not awarded
3 Marioara Trifan, USA

1979

Not awarded

1980

Devoted to four-hand duos and 2 pianofortes
1 Guher and Suher Pekinel, Turkey
2 Silvie Irla, France, and Yoko Katayama, Japan
3 Anacleto Ferrari and Giovanna Valente, Italy; Ivelina Ivancheva and Atanass Atanassov, Bulgaria

1982

1 Joanna Domanska, Poland
2 Francis Rayner, UK
3 Balazs Szokolay, Hungary; Sergei Markarov, USSR

Concorso Internazionale 'Alfredo Casella'. A biennial competition founded in 1952 in memory of one of Italy's leading 20th-century composers (1883–1947). Temporarily in abeyance owing to lack of official support. c/o Academia Musicale Napoletana, Villa Communale 80121, Napoli, Italy.

1952

1 George Solchany, Hungary

1954

1 Esteban Sanchez Herrero, Spain; Walter Blankenheim, Germany (*sic*)

1956

1 Gabriel Tacchino, Italian-French

1958

1 Ivan Davis, USA

1960

1 Pierre Ives le Roux, France

1962

1 Richard Syracuse, USA

1964

1 Sergio Varella Cid, Portugal

1966

1 Michele Campanella, Italy

1968

2 Franco Medori, Italy; Ewa Anna Osinska, Poland

1970

1 Alain Pierre Neveux, France

1972

1 Michel Krist, Germany (*sic*)

1974

1 Christian Blackshaw, UK

1976

1 Sandro de Palma, Italy; Gerhard Oppitz, Germany (*sic*)

Dino Ciani Prize – Teatro alla Scala. A competition held at intervals and founded in 1975. Co-sponsored by the Ente Autonomo Teatro alla Scala and the

Dino Ciani Association. Via Filodrammatici, 20121 Milano, Italy.

1975

1 Jeffrey Swann, USA
2 Jeno Jando, Hungary
3 Craig Sheppard, USA; Marioara Trifan, USA

1977

1 David Lively, USA
2 Daniel Rivera, Argentina
3 Verena Pfenninger, Switzerland

1980

1 Not awarded
2 Angela Hewitt, Canada; Endre Hegedus, Hungary
3 Pietro Rigacci, Italy; Sandro de Palma, Italy

1983

1 Andrea Lucchesini, Italy
2 Jean Marc Luisada, France
3 Dan Atanasiu, Romania

International Piano Competition 'Ettore Pozzoli'. A biennial competition founded in 1959 in memory of Prof. Ettore Pozzoli (1873–1957) who was a native of Seregno. c/o Palazzo Municipale, 20038 Seregno, Italy.

1959

1 Maurizio Pollini, Italy
2 Gino Brandi, Italy; Wally Rizzardo, Italy
3 Marie Françoise Boucquet, France
4 Francesca Meneghel, Italy; Augusto Parodi, Italy

1961

1 Pier Narciso Masi, Italy; Fabio Perossoni, Italy
2 France Redon, France
3 Lydia Rocchetti, Italy
4 Laura de Fusco, Italy

1963

1 Laura de Fusco, Italy
2 Alberto Colombo, Italy
3 Alessandro Specchi, Italy
4 Vittorio Rosetta, Italy

1965

1 François-Joël Thiollier, USA
2 Yoshiya Iwamoto, Japan; Riccardo Risaliti, Italy
3 Joaquin Soriano, Spain; Pier Vise Vulpetti, Italy
4 Sergio Marengoni, Italy; Ivan Darel, France
Special award – 'Rotary Club': Delia Pizzardi, Italy; Ivan Darel, France

1967

1 Not awarded
2 Speidel Sontraud, W. Germany; Wolak Eva,
  Poland
3 Angeleri Franco, Italy
4 Medori Franco, Italy; Steurman Jean Louis,
  Brazil

1969

1 Angeleri Franco, Italy; Cigoli Anna Maria, Italy
2 Bacchelli Antonio, Italy
3 Noev Bozidar, Bulgaria; Cesare Brunin, Chile
4 Midori Kasahara, Japan

1971

1 Pierre Reach, France
2 Vincenzo Balzani, Italy; Tajka Hiroshi, Japan
3 David Oei, Hong Kong; Bojidar Noev, Bulgaria
4 Vera Drenkova, Italy

1973

1 Raimondo Campisi, Italy
2 Michael Krist, Germany; Noemi Gobbi, Italy
3 Anne Pellerin, France; Roxana Bogdanova,
  Bulgaria
4 Bianca Bodalia, Yugoslavia; Nancy Loo, UK
5 Daniela Arpajou, France; Nadia Stoyanova,
  Bulgaria

1975

1 Daniel Rivera, Argentina
2 Boris Bloch, USSR; Roberto Cappello, Italy
3 Andrea Bonatta, Italy
4 Frantisek Maly, Czechoslovakia
5 Maria Luisa Lopez Vito, Philippines; Radu
  Toescu, Germany

1977

1 Pietro Rigacci, Italy
2 Elisabeth Rigollet, France
3 Keiko Katshura, Japan
4 Luigi Ceci, Italy; Pietro Soraci, Italy
5 Nicola Frisardi, Italy; Anna Khirlova Varbanova,
  Bulgaria
Confalonieri Award: Bruno Bizzarri, Italy

1979

1 Rolf Plagge, W. Germany
2 Giovanni Umberto Battel, Italy
3 Alain Jacquon, France
4 Colette Lanssens, Belgium; Sonoko Maejima,
  Japan; Reiko Tanaka, Japan
5 Mario Boselli, Italy; Vincenzo Taramelli, Italy
Confalonieri Award: Barbara Tolomelli, Italy

1981 and 1983

No response to request for information made.

NETHERLANDS

International Arnold Schoenberg Piano Concours
founded in 1977. Probably last one will be held in
1984. Foundation Gaudeamus, Contemporary
Music Centre, PO Box 30, 3720 AA Bilthoven,
Netherlands.

1977 (only one prize awarded)

1 Pi-Hsien Chen, W. Germany

1979

1 Louis-Philippe Pelletier, Canada
2 Bernard Wambach, W. Germany
3 Kolundzija Nadezda, Yugoslavia

1981

1 Jean-Jacques Dünki, Switzerland
2 Suzanne Fournier, Canada
3 Carmen Betancourt, Mexico

1983

No competition

NORWAY

Norsk kulturråds musikpris (Norwegian Cultural
Council Music Prize) was established in 1970 and is
awarded annually to a Norwegian citizen only. It is
not confined to pianoforte. Rosenkrantzgt 11, IV
Oslo 1, Norway.

1971

Robert Riefling, Norway

1973

Kjell Baekkelund, Norway

1977

Eva Knardahl, Norway

POLAND

International Frédéric Chopin Piano Competition
was founded in 1927 and is one of the greatest and
most prestigious piano competitions. Held every five
years, World War II period excepted. Frédéric
Chopin Association, ul. Okolnik 1, 00-368 Warsaw,
Poland.

1927 (26 entrants)

1 Lev Oborin, USSR
2 Stanislaw Szpinalski, Poland
3 Roza Etkin-Moszkowska, Poland
4 Grigori Ginzburg, USSR

1932 (89 entrants)

1 Alexandre Uninski, USSR
2 Imre Ungar, Hungary
3 Boleslaw Kon, Poland
4 Abram Lufer, USSR
5 Louis Kentner, Hungary
6 Leonid Sagalov, USSR
7 Leon Borunski, Poland
8 Theodore Gutman, USSR
9 Gyula Karolyi, Hungary
10 Kurt Engel, Austria
11 Emanuel Grossman, USSR
12 Josef Wagner, Germany
13 Maryla Jonas, Poland
14 Lily Herz, Hungary
15 Suzanne de Mayere, Belgium

1937 (79 entrants)

1 Yakov Zak, USSR
2 Roza Tamarkina, USSR
3 Witold Malcuzynski, Poland
4 Lance Dossor, UK
5 Agi Jambor, Hungary
6 Edith Azenfeld, Germany
7 Monique de la Bruchollerie, France
8 Jan Ekier, Poland
9 Tatiana Goldfarb, USSR
10 Olga Ilwicka, Poland
11 Lelia Gousseau, France
12 Halina Kalmanowicz, Poland

1949 (54 entrants)

1 Halina Czerny-Stefanska, Poland; Bella
  Davidovich, USSR
2 Barbara Hesse-Bukowska, Poland
3 Waldemar Maciszewski, Poland
4 Georgi Muravlov, USSR
5 Wladyslaw Kedra, Poland
6 Ryszard Bakst, Poland
7 Eugeny Malinin, USSR
8 Zbigniew Szymonowicz, Poland
9 Tamara Guseva, USSR
10 Viktor Mirzhanov, USSR
11 Regina Smendzianka, Poland
12 Tadusz Zmudzinski, Poland

1955 (77 entrants)

1 Adam Harasiewicz, Poland
2 Vladimir Ashkenazy, USSR
3 Fou Ts'ong, China
4 Bernard Ringeissen, France

5 Naum Shtarkman, USSR
6 Dmitri Papierno, USSR
7 Lidia Grychtołowna, Poland
8 Andrzej Czajkowski, Poland
9 Dmitri Sakharov, USSR
10 Kiyoko Tanaka, Japan

1960 (77 entrants)

1 Maurizio Pollini, Italy
2 Irina Zaritskaya, USSR
3 Tania Achot-Haroutounian, Iran
4 Li Min-Czan, China
5 Zinaida Ignateva, USSR
6 Valery Kastelsky, USSR

1965 (76 entrants)

1 Martha Argerich, Argentina
2 Arthur Moreira-Lima, Brazil
3 Marta Sosinska, Poland
4 Hiroko Nakamura, Japan
5 Edward Auer, USA
6 Elizbieta Głab, Poland

1970 (80 entrants)

1 Garrick Ohlsson, USA
2 Mitsuko Uchida, Japan
3 Piotr Paleczny, Poland
4 Eugene Indjic, USA
5 Natalia Gavrilova, USSR
6 Janusz Olejniczak, Poland

1975 (84 entrants)

1 Krystian Zimerman, Poland
2 Dina Yoffe, USSR
3 Tatyana Fedkina, USSR
4 Pavel Gililov, USSR
5 Dean Kramer, USA
6 Diana Kacso, Brazil

1980 (149 entrants)

1 Dang Thai Son, Vietnam
2 Tatyana Shebanova, USSR
3 Arutiun Papazjan, USSR
4 Not awarded
5 Akiko Ebi, Japan; Ewa Pobłocka, Poland
6 Eric Berchet, France; Irina Petrova, USSR

PORTUGAL

Vianna da Motta International Piano Competition is
held in Lisbon at irregular intervals. Enquiries to
various addresses there, as supplied by the Cultural
Counsellor of the Portuguese Embassy in London,
have failed to elicit a response. A further enquiry to
the Cultural Attaché of the British Embassy in
Lisbon produced a list of prizewinners, reproduced

below, from the British Council Office there, together with a disclaimer as to its complete accuracy.

1951

Naum Starkman

1955

Nelson Freire
Vladimir Karainev (? Krainev)

1959

No 1st Prize awarded

1963

Prize awarded to a violinist

1967

Victoria Postnikova

1971

? Keller

1975

Wilfrid Devan

1979

Arthur Papavian

1983 (information from newspaper reports)

No 1st Prize awarded
2 Florent Boffard, France; Pedro Burmester, Portugal
3 Suzanne Grützmann, E. Germany
4 Lilia Boyadjieva, Bulgaria; Faca Rossdo, Portugal
5 Kemal Gekic, Yugoslavia

SPAIN

International Piano Competition Prize 'Jaén' was founded in 1956, is usually annually, and is open to pianists of all nationalities, the first winner receiving a cash prize, a gold medal and concert engagements. Instituto de Estudios Giennenses, Palacio Provincial, Jaén, Spain.

1956

Jacinto Matute Narro, Spain

1957

Begoña Uriarte Pérez, Spain

1958

Clotilde Ortiz R. de Cellis, Spain

1959

Agustin Serrano Mata, Spain

1960

Carlos Santos Ventura, Spain

1961

Rafael de Solis y Peiró, Spain

1962

Joaquin Parra González, Spain

1963

Mario Monreal Monreal, Spain

1964

Rafael Orozco, Spain

1966

Joaquin Soriano Villanueva, Spain

1968

Boaz Sharon, Israel

1970

José Martinez Pinzolas, Spain

1971

Valentina Diaz de Frenot, Argentina

1972

Ewa Osinska, Poland

1973

Marioara Trifan, USA; Elza Kolodin, Poland

1974

Jean François Heisser, France

1975

Boris Bloch, USSR

1976

Michiko Tsuda, Japan

1977

Josep Colom, Spain

1979

John Salmon, USA

1980

Emilio Angulo Sánchez, Mexico

1981

Huseyin Sermet, Turkey

1982

Benedetto Lupo, Italy

1983

Akiyoshi Sako, Japan

Concurso Internacional de piano 'Paloma O'Shea' was established in 1974, has usually been held annually and carries various awards. The first winner receives a cash prize, a gold medal and concert engagements in Spain. Hernán Cortés 3, Santander, Spain.

1974

1 Rusiko Kikuchi, Japan
2 Jesus Gonzalez Alonso, Spain; José Martinez Pinzolas, Spain

1975

1 Marioara Trifan, USA
2 Peter Bithell, UK
3 Rebecca Penneys, USA
4 Silvie Carbonell, France

1976

1 Huseyin Sermet, Turkey
2 Ivan Klanski, Czechoslovakia
3 Paulo Gori, Brazil; Janina Drath, Poland

1977

1 Ramzi Yassa, Egypt
2 Jeremy Atkin, UK; David Wehr, USA

1978

1 Josep Colom, Spain
2 Frédéric Aguessy, France
3 Ana Manarasova, USSR
4 Andrei Diev, USSR

1980

1 Not awarded
2 Barry Douglas, UK
3 Franceso Nicolosi, Italy; Dan Atanasiu, Romania

1982

1 Marc Raubenheimer, S. Africa
2 Oleg Volkov, USSR
3 Yves Rault, France

1984

1 Hugh Tinney, Eire
2 José Carlos Cocarelli, Brazil
3 Rauf Kasimov, USSR
4 Fei-Ping Hsu, China

SWITZERLAND

Concours Géza Anda was founded in 1976 by the pianist's widow with the object of encouraging the younger generation of players to follow his example of inspiration. Age not above 32. The competition is triennial, and the winner is assured of a public engagement in Detroit, London, Lucerne, Paris, Salzburg, Vienna and Zurich. Géza Anda-Stiftung, CH-8002 Zurich, Bleicherweg 18, Switzerland.

1979

1 Georges Pludermacher

1982

1 Heidrun Holtmann

International Competition for Musical Performers began in 1939 as an annual event, and requirements vary from year to year. Piano prizewinners only are given below. 12 rue de l'Hotel de Ville, CH-1204 Geneva, Switzerland.
m=men; w=women

1939

1 m Arturo Benedetti-Michelangeli

1940

1 w Cécile Beguin
2 w L. Marcet-Filosa
1 m Rudolf am Bach
2 m Leo Nadelmann; Theodor Sack

1941

1 w Not awarded
2 w Nelly Roser; Madeleine Depraz
1 m André Perret
2 m Georg Solti

1942

1 w Not awarded
2 w Lilia Marcet-Filosa; Kitty Tschirren
1 m Georg Solti
2 m Harry Datyner

1943

1 w Not awarded
2 w Yvonne Schmit; Pina Pozzi
1 m Not awarded
2 m Not awarded

1944

1 w Not awarded
2 w Marguerite Viala-Brandt
1 m Harry Datyner

1945

1 w Not awarded
2 w Marthe Schneider; Marguerite Viala-Brandt;
    Kitty Tschirren
1 m Nico Kaufmann
2 m Wilfred de Boe; Albert Schneeberger

1946

1 w Not awarded
2 w Rossana Bottai; Dyna August; Annie D'Arco
1 m Friedrich Gulda
2 m Louis Backx; Paolo Spagnolo

1947

1 w Not awarded
2 w Marie-Madeleine Petit
1 m Paolo Spagnolo
2 m Gilbert Schuchter; Sergio Fiorentino; Ervin
    Laszlo

1948

1 w Not awarded
2 w Maria Tipo
1 m Not awarded
2 m Bela Siki; A. Franssen; Georges Szoltsanyi

1949

1 w Maria Tipo
2 w Selma Herscovici
1 m Robert Weisz
2 m Ronald Smith

1950

1 w Not awarded
2 w Not awarded
1 m Not awarded
2 m Hubert Harry; Sergio Berticaroli; Georges
    Alexandrovitch

1951

1 w Not awarded
2 w Fernande Kaeser
1 m Not awarded
2 m Ronald Smith, Georges Solchany, Alexander
    Jenner; Laurence Davis

1952

1 w Not awarded
2 w Kiyoko Tanaka; Ingrid Haebler
1 m Not awarded
2 m Walter Kamper; Alexander Jenner

1953

1 w Not awarded
2 w Ingrid Haebler
1 m Jacques Klein
2 m Kurt Bauer; Peter Stone

1954

1 w Not awarded
2 w Cécile Ousset; Ruslana Antonowicz
1 m Bernard Ringeissen
2 m Hans Graf

1955

1 w Not awarded
2 w Ruslana Antonowicz
1 m Not awarded
2 m Gabriel Tacchino; Malcolm Frager

1956

1 w Not awarded
2 w Ruslana Antonowicz; Danièle Dechenne
1 m Robert-Alexander Bohnke
2 m John Blot

1957

1 w Marta Argerich
2 w Thérèse Castaing
1 m Dominique Merlet
2 m Maurizio Pollini

1958

1 w Not awarded
2 w Sun-Ying Kou
1 m Not awarded
2 m Maurizio Pollini; Ronald Turini

1959

1 w Not awarded
2 w Catherine Silie
1 m Jean-Paul Sevilla
2 m Michael Ponti

1960

1 w Not awarded
2 w Lis Smed Christensen
1 m Not awarded
2 m Lucien Kemblinsky; Heinz Medjimorec

1961

1 w Not awarded
2 w Marise Charpentier; Ryoko Ohno
1 m Désiré N'Kaoua
2 m Jean Derbes; Fernando Lopes

1962

1 w Not awarded
2 w Not awarded
1 m Not awarded
2 m Radashi Kitagawa

1963

1 w Not awarded
2 w Meiko Miyazawa
1 m Not awarded
2 m Alberto Colombo
(After 1963 there is only one piano section for both sexes.)

1964

1 Robert Majek
2 Gernot Kahl

1965

1 Not awarded
2 Ruslana Antonowicz

1966

1 Not awarded
2 André Gorog; Virginio Pavarana

1967

1 Jerzy Sulkiowski
2 Ray Luck

1968

1 Not awarded
2 Jean-Claude Pennetier; Louis-B. Nagel

1969

1 Peter Efler
2 Christian Zacharias

1970

1 Margrit Pirner
2 Pascal Sigrist; Pamela Mia Paul

1971

1 Not awarded
2 David Lively

1972

1 Not awarded
2 Martino Tirimo; Guadalupe Parrondo

1973

1 Not awarded
2 Caroline Haffner; Alain Raes

1974

1 Not awarded
2 Alyce le Blanc

1975

1 Not awarded
2 William Westney

1976

1 Tatiana Chebanova
2 Cécile Hugonnard-Roche; Pierre-Laurent Aimard

1977

1 Not awarded
2 Yukie Irizuki; Yukiko Takahashi

1978

1 Not awarded
2 Anna Jaszyk; Hans-Christian Wille

1979

No piano prizewinners

1980

1 Not awarded
2 Francesco Nicolosi; Akiyoshi Sako

1981

No piano prizewinners

1982

1 Evgueni Krouchevsky
2 Daniel Blumenthal

1983

No piano prizewinners

Prix 'Clara Haskil' was created by the Clara Haskil Association in conjunction with the Festival de Musique, Montreux-Vevey and has run more or less biennially since 1965, The winner receives a cash prize and engagements. Avenue des Alpes 14, CH-1820 Montreux, Switzerland.

1965

Christophe Eschenbach, Germany

1967

Dinorah Varsi, Uruguay

1973

Richard Goode, USA

1975

Michel Dalberto, France

1977

Eugeny Koroliov, USSR

1979

Cynthia Raim, USA

1981

Konstanze Eickhorst, Germany

1983

No prizewinners

Prix de l'Association des musiciens Suisses pour les jeunes solistes was founded during World War II and is a competition for young musicians of Swiss origin of up to 30 years of age. It is not confined to piano, but only piano prizewinners are shown below. 1000 Lausanne 13, Avenue du Grammont 11 bis, Switzerland.

1942

Max Egger

1955

Georges-Henri Pantillon

1966

Urs Peter Schneider

1969

Nicole Wickihalder

1971

Pascal Sigrist

1977

Martin Christ

1979

Jürg Lüthy; Dagmar Clottu; Christoph Delz

1980

Werner Bärtschi

1981

Stefan Fahrni; Stéphane Reymond

1983

Olivier Sörensen

UNION OF SOVIET SOCIALIST REPUBLICS

(The help of Mrs Irina Stafford in transliteration of names from the Cyrillic alphabet is gratefully acknowledged.)

International Tchaikovsky Competition, established in 1958 and extended to cover string-players and singers. Prizes are also awarded for meritorious performances of music by the composer after whom the competition is named. Rules and prizes vary between competitions, and prizewinners undergo concert tours in the USSR. 15 Neglinnaya Street, Moscow, USSR.

1958

1 Van Cliburn, USA (Gold Medal)
2 Lev Vlasenko, USSR (Silver Medal); Lu Shi-Koon, China (Silver Medal)
3 Naum Shtarkman, USSR (Bronze Medal)
4 Edward Miansarov, USSR (Honours)
5 Milena Mollova, Bulgaria (Honours)
6 Nadia Gedda-Nova, France (Honours)
7 Toyoaki Matsoora, Japan (Honours)
8 Daniel Pollak, USA (Honours)

1962

1 John Ogdon, UK (Gold Medal); Vladimir Ashkenazy, USSR (Gold Medal)
2 In' Chen-Tszoon, China (Silver Medal); Suzan Starr, USA (Silver Medal)

3 Eliso Virsalatsze, USSR (Bronze Medal)
4 Marina Mdivani, USSR (Honours)
5 Valery Kamshov, USSR (Honours)
6 Alexei Nasedkin, USSR (Honours); Christian
   Biyo, France (Honours)

1966

1 Gregory Sokolov, USSR (Gold Medal)
2 Misha Dichter, USA (Silver Medal)
3 Victor Eresko, USSR (Bronze Medal)
4 Aleksander Slobodyanik, USSR; Georg Sirota,
   USSR
5 Edward Auer, USA; James Dick, USA
6 François-Joël Tiole, France; Peter Rezel, E.
   Germany
7 André de Groote, Belgium
8 Alen Karnesekka, France; Bruno Rigutto, France

1970

1 Vladimir Krainev, USSR (Gold Medal); John
   Lill, UK (Gold Medal)
2 Horacio Gutiérrez, USA (Silver Medal)
3 Arthur Moreira Lima, Brazil (Bronze Medal);
   Victoria Postnikova, USSR (Bronze Medal)
4 Arkady Sevidov, USSR (Honours)
5 James Tokko, USA (Honours)
6 Not awarded

1974

1 Andrei Gavrilov, USSR (Gold Medal)
2 Stanislav Igolinsky, USSR (Silver Medal);
   Myung-Whun Chung, USA (Silver Medal)
3 Yuri Egorov, USSR (Bronze Medal)
4 Eteri Anjaparidze, USSR (Honours); Andras
   Schiff, Hungary (Honours)
5 Dmitri Alexeev, USSR (Honours)
6 Bridjit Anjerer, France (Honours); David Laivly,
   USA (Honours)
7 Not awarded
8 Not awarded

1978

1 Michael Pletnev, USSR (Gold Medal)
2 Pascal Devoyon, France (Silver Medal); André
   Laplante, Canada (Silver Medal)
3 Evgeny Rivkin, USSR (Bronze Medal); Nicolai
   Demidenko, USSR (Bronze Medal)
4 Terence Judd, UK (Honours); Boris Petrov,
   USSR (Honours)
5 Christian Blackshaw, UK (Honours)
6 Naum Grubert, USSR (Honours)
7 Not awarded
8 Not awarded

1982 (No Gold Medal awarded)

1 Vladimir Ovchinnikov, USSR (Silver Medal);
   Peter Donohoe, UK (Silver Medal)

2 Michie Kayama, Japan (Bronze Medal)

UNITED KINGDOM

Incorporated Society of Musicians – Young Artists'
Recital Scheme provided opportunities to young
professionals who were members of the Society.
Auditions were held annually for artists of either sex
up to the age of 27 in the case of instrumentalists, for
the Society's series of recitals held in Wigmore Hall.
The scheme was terminated from 1982 and the
Society hope to replace it sometime in the future.
General Secretary, Incorporated Society of
Musicians, 10 Stratford Place, London W1N 9AE,
England.

1959

Elizabeth Ellwood; David Parkhouse; Geoffrey
   Buckley

1960

Eric Stevens; Keith Swallow

1961

Bryan Vickers

1962

John Barstow

1963

Ronald Lumsden

1964

Antony Hill; Michael Freyhen

1965

Joan Havill

1967

John McCabe

1968

Margaret Gulley; Margaret Newman

1970

Dennis Lee

1971

Stephanie Bamford

1972

Hilary Macnamara

1975

Paul Roberts; Richard Markham; Michael Redshaw

1977

Heather Dupre; Andrew Ball

1978

Martin Roscoe; Julie Adam

1979

David Mason

1981

Peter Bradley

1982

Benjamin Frith; Caroline Palmer

Leeds International Pianoforte Competition is a triennial event founded in 1963, open to professional pianists of any nationality up to the age of 30. In addition to cash the first prize carries a gold medal in memory of Princess Mary plus concert engagements. The competition is run in association with Harvey's of Bristol. Department of Education, Leeds City Council, Great George Street, Leeds LS1 3AE, UK.

1963

1 Michael Roll, UK
2 Vladimir Krainov, USSR
3 Sebastien Risler, France
4 Armenta Adams, USA

1966

1 Rafael Orozco, Spain
2 Victoria Postnikova, USSR; Semyon Kruchin, USSR
3 Alexei Nasedkin, USSR
4 Jean-Rodolphe Kars, Austria

1969

1 Radu Lupu, Romania
2 Georges Pludermacher, France
3 Arthur Moreira-Lima, Brazil
4 Boris Petrushansky, USSR
5 Anne Queffelec, France

1972

1 Murray Perahia, USA
2 Craig Sheppard, USA
3 Eugene Indjic, USA

1975

1 Dmitri Alexeev, USSR
2 Mitsuko Uchida, Japan
3 Andras Schiff, Hungary; Pascal Devoyon, France
4 Myung-Whun Chung, USA; Michael Houston, New Zealand

1978

1 Michel Dalberto, France
2 Diana Kacso, Brazil
3 Lydia Artimiw, USA
4 Ian Hobson, UK

1981

1 Ian Hobson, UK
2 Wolfgang Manz, W. Germany
3 Bernard d'Ascoli, France
4 Daniel Blumenthal, USA
5 Christopher O'Riley, USA
6 Peter Donohoe, UK

1984

1 John Kimura Parker, Canada
2 Ju Hee Suh, S. Korea
3 Junko Otake, Japan
4 Louis Lortie, Canada
5 David Buechner, USA
6 Emma Takhmizyan, Bulgaria

The Liszt Society of England was formed to spread knowledge and appreciation of the Hungarian composer-pianist. It sponsors periodically the British Liszt Piano Competition to afford pianists up to the age of 30 the chance to display their prowess in the composer's music. The Secretary, 32 'Chivelston', 78 Wimbledon Park Side, London SW19 5LH, UK.

1961

1 John Ogdon
2 David Wilde
3 Benjamin Kaplan

1968

1 John Owings
2 Stephanie Bamford
3 Richard McMahon

1976

1 Terence Judd
2 Martin Roscoe
3 Peter Donohoe
4 Anthony Green
5 Francis Reneau
6 Christopher Lee

Royal College of Music, medals awarded by British pianoforte manufacturers, now under the auspices of the College.

The Challen & Sons Gold Medal (1895–1943)

1895 Maud Branwell
1896 Gertrude King
1897 William Morgans
1898 Ethel Wilson
1899 Maud Gay
1900 Florence Smith
1901 Harold Samuel
1902 Daisy Jones
1903 Helen Boyd
1904 James Friskin
1905 Edmund Phillips
1906 Phyllis Emanuel
1907 Ellen Edwards
1908 Grace Humphrey
1909 William Murdoch
1910 Joseph Taffs; Emmie Gregory
1911 Douglas Fox; Norah Cordwell
1912 George T. Ball; Winifred McBride
1913 Kathleen Cooper
1914 Kathleen Long
1915 Cecil Dixon
1916 Maria Ramirez-Aguirre
1918 Dorothy Davies
1919 Doris Fell
1922 Evelyn Willis
1923 Belinda Heather
1924 Norman Greenwood
1925 Doreen Clark
1926 Hilda Noble
1927 Wilhelmina Arnott
1928 Isadore Goodman
1929 Dorothea Aspinall
1930 Jean Cotton
1931 Mabel Lovering
1932 Irene Kohler
1933 Pamela Norris
1934 Theodolinda Calburn
1935 Florence Channon
1936 Derek Kidner
1937 Lance Dossor
1938 Stephen Dorman
1939 Margaret Evans
1940 Natasha Litvin
1941 Barbara Hill
1942 Muriel Dixon
1943 Fanny Waterman

The Chappell Gold Medal (1921–)

1921 Kathleen McQuitty
1922 Edward Greenwood
1923 Eileen Parker
1924 Cornelius Fisher (Gold); Harold Rutland (Silver)
1925 Kendall Taylor
1926 Edwin Benbow
1927 Theresa Walters
1928 Isadore Goodman
1929 Nancy Reed
1930 Fredericka Hartnell
1931 Ruth Pasco
1932 Mabel Lovering
1933 Robert South
1934 Irene Crowther
1935 Jean Norris
1936 Barbara Kerslake
1937 Edith Astall; Maria Donska
1938 Margaret Fleming
1939 George Malcolm
1940 Cyril Preedy
1941 Raymond O'Connell
1944 Valerie Dossor
1945 Hilary Reeve
1946 Margaret Evans
1947 Leila Ashcroft
1948 David Parkhouse
1949 A. Broomhead
1950 Lamar Crowson
1951 Patricia Carroll
1952 Pamela Stickley
1953 Sally Mays
1954 John Roberts
1955 Ivan Melman
1956 Malcolm Binns
1957 Ian Lake
1958 Douglas Paling
1959 Alan Rowlands
1960 John Barstow
1961 Herbert Nuala
1962 Jonquil Glenton
1963 John Lill
1964 Frank Wibaut
1965 Hilary Macnamara
1966 Peter Hampshire
1967 William Enloc
1968 Howard Shelley
1969 Niel Immelman
1970 Etelvina Rodriques
1971 Peter Hill
1972 Yuriko Marakami
1973 M. Wu
1974 Carol Cooper
1975 Jan Koenig
1976 Elizabeth Hammond
1977 Kathryn Stott
1978 David Green
1979 Ian Gaukroger
1980 Lidla Ziv-Li
1981 Adrian Sims

1982 Helen Choi
1983 James Lisney
1984 Nicholas Unwin

Hopkinson Gold Medal (1886–1900)

1886 Marmaduke Barton
1887 Marian Osborn
1888 Polyxena Fletcher
1889 Annie Grimson
1890 Augusta Spiller
1891 Amy Grimson
1892 Edith Green
1893 Gwendolyn Toms
1894 Maud Branwell
1895 Evlyn Howard-Jones
1896 Beatrice Cerasoli
1897 Maud Gay
1898 Florence Smith
1899 Hester Hardman
1900 Edgar L. Bainton

Hopkinson Gold and Silver Medals (1904–   )

(First named=Gold Medal winner(s); second named=Silver Medal winner(s))

1904 Helen Boyd; Ethel Brigstock
1905 James Friskin; Edmund Phillips
1906 Edmund Phillips; Phyllis Emanuel
1907 Ellen Edwards; Winifred Gardiner
1908 Ioan Powell; William Murdoch
1909 William Murdoch; Grace Humphrey
1910 Grace Humphrey; Grace de Rozario
1911 Mary Graham; Joseph Taffs
1912 Jennie Wilson; Bertha Nottingham
1913 Rosalie Stokes; Norah Cordwell
1914 George T. Ball; Kathleen Long
1915 Kathleen Long; Winifred McBride
1916 Irina Meyrick; Kathleen Cooper
1917 Doris Fell; Cecil Dixon
1918 Cecil Dixon; Dorothy Davies
1919 Margery Newborn; Betty Powell
1920 Not awarded; Laura Loughman
1921 Angus Morrison; Maria Ramirez-Aguirre
1922 Kathleen McQuitty and Evelyn Willis; Phyllis Price
1923 Not awarded; Not awarded
1924 Irene Sweetland; Kendall Taylor
1925 Edwin Benbow; Christobel Fullard
1926 Mary Noble; Gwendo Paul, Jean Cotton and Audrey Piggott
1927 Leonard Isaacs; Fredericka Hartnell
1928 Fredericka Hartnell; Millicent Silver
1929 Irene Kohler; Dorothea Aspinall and Nancy Reed
1930 Kathleen Collins; Mabel Lovering
1931 Josephine Southey-John; Robert South
1932 Robert South; Nan Pulvermacher
1933 Nan Pulvermacher; Celia Morris
1934 Cynthia Hemmerde; Barbara Kerslake and Jean Norris
1935 Celia Morris; Freda Firth

1936 Maria Donska; Margaret Fleming
1937 Margaret Evans; G. M. Jewel Evans
1938 Not awarded; Not awarded
1939 Cyril Preedy; Brian Douglas
1940 Raymond O'Connell; Douglas Hoops
1941 Joan Rimmer; René Selig
1942 Gladys Jones; Fanny Waterman
1943 Pamela Larkin; Freda Caplan
1944 Hilary Reeve; Barbara Hill
1945 Patricia Sutton-Mattocks; Sheila Mossman
1946 Leo Quayle; Pamela Kitchen
1947 Pamela Kitchen; Peggy Gray
1948 Peggy Gray; Elsie Jacobs
1949 Doreen Stanfield; Shirley Welch
1950 Stanislav Heller; Harold Rich
1951 Harold Rich; Peris Jayasinghe
1952 Patricia Bishop; Bridget Saxon
1953 Michael Matthews; Hilary Leech
1954 Ivan Melman; Gwen Davies
1955 Carelina Carr; Nellie Bailey
1956 Sonya Franke; Ian Lake
1957 Douglas Paling; David Rowlands
1958 Constance Currie; Margaret Gully
1959 John Barstow; Gideon Shamir
1960 Ray Odette; Herbert Nuala
1961 Ruth Stubbs; Ronald Lumsden
1962 Judith Lambden; Barry Morgan
1963 Gwenneth Pryor; John Havill
1964 Roger Smalley; Stephen Savage
1965 Raymond Alston; Francis Steele
1966 Julia Cload; Dennis Lee
1967 Dennis Lee; A. Zuk
1968 Dennis Lee; Bryan Sayer
1969 Robert Ferguson; David Helfgott
1970 Maria Czyrek; Margaret Scott
1971 Andrew Ball; Carol Cooper
1972 Andrew Ball; Peter Wild
1973 Michael Redshaw; Andrew Haigh
1974 Ronan Magill; Not awarded
1975 Simon Nichells; Kenneth Lewis
1976 Melvyn Tan; Michael Cook
1977 Margaret Finghut; Adrian Williams
1978 Noriko Kawai; Michael Cook
1979 Eva Luc; Philip Honlihan
1980 Vivian Choi; Noriko Kawai
1981 Graham Fitch; John Lenehan
1982 James Lisney; Mark Bebbington
1983 Kaven Briscoe; Nigel Clayton
1984 Iwan Llewellyn Jones; Amanda Hurton

The Royal Over-Seas League Music Festival began in 1952 and is an annual event for professional musicians of UK and Commonwealth origin under the age of 25 in the case of instrumentalists. Piano winners only are listed below. Over-seas House, Park Place, St James's Street, London SW1A 1LR, UK.

1952

Robert Cooper, Australia

1953

Geoffrey Parsons, Australia

1954

Oswald Russell, Jamaica

1958

Audrey Cooper, Jamaica

1959

Patsy Toh, Hong Kong

1960

Yonty Solomon (runner-up), S. Africa

1963

John Lill, UK

1966

Enloc Wu, Hong Kong

1967

David Bollard, New Zealand

1968

Dennis Lee, Malaysia; Frank Wibaut, UK

1969

Penny Scott, UK

1970

Geoffrey Tozer, Australia; Andrew Haigh, UK

1971

Andrea Kalanj, Canada; Jan Latham Koenig, UK

1972

Tessa Uys, S. Africa

1974

Francis Reneau, Belize

1975

Jonathan Dunsby, UK

1977

Aydin Onac, India

1979

Surendran Reddy, S. Africa; Barry Douglas, UK

1981

Simon Shewring, UK

1982

Piers Lane, Australia

1983

Jonathan Plowright, UK; Mary Wu (1st Overseas Prize), Hong Kong

1984

Adrian Sims, UK

UNITED STATES OF AMERICA

Gina Bachauer International Piano Competition, established in 1976 and usually held annually; open to pianists of any nationality between the ages of 18 and 32. Symphony Hall, 123 West South Temple, Salt Lake City, Utah 84101, USA.

1976

1 Douglas Humphreys, USA
2 Christopher Giles, USA
3 Andrew Willis, USA
4 Del Parkinson, USA

1977

1 Christopher Giles, USA
2 Jeffrey Shumway, USA
3 Marilyn Collard, USA
4 Della Ming Lin, USA

1978

1 Arthur Greene, USA
2 Edward Newman, USA
3 Steven Mayer, USA

1979

1 Panayis Lyras, USA
2 Marc Silverman, USA
3 Gregory Allen, USA

1980

1 Duane Hulbert, USA
2 James Barbagallo, USA
3 Marco Antonio Almeida, W. Germany.

1981

No competition

1982

1 Michael Gurt, USA
2 Diana Kacso, USA
3 Alexander Kuzmin, USA

1983

No competition

Van Cliburn Quadrennial Piano Competition, established in 1962. 3505 West Lancaster, Fort Worth, Texas 76107, USA.

1962

1 Ralph Votapek, USA
2 Nikolai Petrov, USSR
3 Mikhail Voskresenski, USSR
4 Cécile Ousset, France
5 Marilyn Neeley, USA
6 Sergio Varella-Cid, Portugal
7 Arthur Fennimore, USA
8 Takashi Hironaka, Japan

1966

1 Radu Lupu, Romania
2 Barry Snyder, USA
3 Blanca Uribe, Colombia
4 Maria Luisa Lopez-Vito, Philippines
5 Rudolf Buchbinder, Austria
6 Benedikt Köhlen, W. Germany

1969

1 Cristina Ortiz, Brazil
2 Minoru Nojima, Japan
3 Mark Westcott, USA
4 Gerald Robbins, USA
5 Diane Walsh, USA
6 Michiko Fujinuma, Japan

1973

1 Vladimir Viardo, USSR
2 Christian Zacharias, W. Germany
3 Michael Houston, New Zealand
4 Alberto Reyes, Uruguay
5 Eugeny Korolev, USSR
6 Krassimir Gatev, Bulgaria

1977

1 Steven de Groote, S. Africa
2 Alexander Toradze, USSR
3 Jeffrey Swann, USA

4 Christian Blackshaw, UK; Michel Dalberto, France
5 Ian Hobson, UK; Alexander Mndoyants, USSR

1981

1 André-Michel Schub, USA
2 Santiago Rodriguez, USA; Panayis Lyras, USA
4 Jeffrey Kahane, USA
5 Christopher O'Riley, USA
6 Zhu Da Ming, China

University of Maryland International Piano Festival and Competition was established in 1971 and is a member of the International Music Competitions in Geneva, Switzerland. It is an annual event. The University of Maryland, College Park 20742, Maryland, USA. ·

1971

1 Mark Westcott, USA
2 Diane Walsh, USA
3 Not awarded
Also: Emanuel Ax (Baldwin Prize), Poland; David Wasser (Macke Prize), USA; Edward Newman (Macke Prize), USA

1972

1 Ellen Wasserman, USA
2 Marian Hahn, USA
3 Kimberley Kabala, USA
Also: Jane Coop (Baldwin Prize), Canada

1973

1 Peter Takacs, Romania
2 Alan Marks, USA
3 Margie Huffman, USA
Also; Gary Steigerwalt (Baldwin Prize), USA; Stefan Scaggiari (Baldwin Prize), USA

1974

1 Tibor Szasz, Romania
2 Dickran Atamian, USA
3 Mari-Elizabeth Morgen, Canada
Also: William Martin (Baldwin Prize), USA

1975

1 Santiago Rodriguez, Cuba
2 David James, New Zealand
3 Julian Martin, USA
Also: Peter Amstutz, USA; Pamela Paul, USA

1976

1 Pan Lyras, Greece
2 Peter Orth, USA

3 Stephen Mayer (Baldwin Prize), USA
Also: Neil Rutman, USA; Stephen Mayer (Gisriel Prize), USA

1977

1 Myung-Hee Chung, Korea
2 Edward Newman, USA
3 Liliane Questrel (Baldwin Prize), Haiti
Also: Robert Chumbley (Irwin Freundlich Prize), USA; Charles Abramovic (Irwin Freundlich Prize), USA; Edward Newman (Gisriel Prize), USA

1978

1 Enrique Graf, Uruguay
2 James Barbagallo, USA
3 William Koehler (Baldwin Prize), USA
Also: Jeffrey Campbell (Irwin Freundlich Prize), USA; William Koehler (Gisriel Prize), USA; Edith Nahas (Bladensburg Rotary Club), Austria

1979

1 Marioara Trifan, USA
2 Ian Hobson, UK
3 Michael Blum, USA
4 Jeffrey Chappell USA
5 Eric Himy (Irwin Freundlich Prize), USA
6 Marc-André Hamelin (Baldwin Prize), Canada
7 John Salmon (L. Eiseley Memorial Prize), USA
Also special prizes: Marioara Trifan (Organization of American States Prize); Ian Hobson (Gisriel Prize); Eric Himy (Chas. E. Morganston Memorial Award)

1980

1 Not awarded
2 Meral Guneyman, Turkey; Robert McDonald, USA
3 Michael Korstick, USA
Also: Robert McDonald (Organization of American States Prize)

1981

1 Boris Slutsky, USSR
2 Nina Tichman, USA
3 Vladimir Levtov, Israel

Also: Clipper Erickson (Bela Bartók Prize), USA; Brian Zeger (Gisriel Prize), USA; Dmitri Rachmanov (Freundlich Prize), USSR; Kuei Pin Yeo (L. Eiseley Memorial Prize), Indonesia

1982

1 Not awarded
2 Dmitri Feofanov (US citizenship applied for); Michael Lewin, USA
3 Daniel Lessner, USA
Also: Clive Swansbourne (Baldwin/Gisriel Prize), UK; Diana Kacso (Freundlich Prize), Brazil; Ira Levin (Alumni Prize), USA; Paul Maillet (Monday Night Musicales, inc. Prize), USA; Fei-Ping Hsu (G. M. Hinson Prize), China; Eun Soo Son (C. E. Morganston Memorial Prize), Korea; Fei-Ping Hsu (L. Eiseley Prize), China

1983

1 Alexander Kuzmin, apatride
2 Liora Ziv-Li, Israel
3 Remy Loumbrozo, France
Also: Thomas Duis (Alumni Prize), W. Germany; Mihae Lee (Boucher Memorial Prize), Korea; Noriko Ogawa (Boucher Memorial Prize), Japan; Christoph Ullrich (Boucher Memorial Prize), W. Germany; Akira Imai (Monday Night Musicales inc. Prize), Japan; Arthur Greene (L. Eiseley Memorial Prize), USA

C. Pulitzer Prizes in Music are for composition, and entries below refer to works for a piano part. The award is usually annual. 702 Journalism, Columbia University, New York, NY 10027, USA.

1954 to Quinch Porter for Concerto for two pfs and orchestra, first performed the same year by the Louisville Symphony Orchestra.
1959 to John Lamontaine for a Concerto for pf and orchestra, first performed in 1958 by the National Symphony Orchestra in Washington DC.
1963 to Samuel Barber for Piano Concerto No. 1, first performed by the Boston Symphony Orchestra in 1962.
1976 to Scott Joplin. A special award bestowed posthumously for his contribution to American music.

ADDENDA

ITALY

'F. Busoni' International Piano Competition

1984
1. Louis Lortie, Canada
2. Matthias Fletzberger, Austria
3. Bernard Glemser, West Germany
4. Neil Rutman, USA
   John Salmon, USA
5. Jean-Baphtiste Müller, Switzerland
   Boris Slutsky, USA
6. Luigi Ceci, Italy
   Riccardo Zadra, Italy

'Alessandro Casagrande' Piano Competition

1984
1. Not awarded
2. Balasz Szokolay, Hungary
3. Fabio Bidini, Italy
   Cristian Beldi, Romania
Mention: Anjela Tocheva, Bulgaria
         Narada Hideyo, Japan
         Balasz Szokolay, Hungary

UNITED STATES OF AMERICA

University of Maryland Int: Piano Festival and Competition

1984
1. Angela Cheng, Canada
2. Christian Beldi, Romania
3. Eduardus Halim, Indonesia
Also: Alan Chow (Adele Marcus Prize), USA; Paul Maillet (Monday Musicales), USA; Frederick Blum (Alumni Prize), USA; Philip Hosford (Loren Eisley Memorial), USA; Alvin Chow (Boucher Prize), USA; Clive Swansbourne (Boucher Prize), UK; Jennifer Tao (Boucher Prize), USA; Michael Schmidt (Lynell Gordon Mem. Prize), Israel-USA; Liani Larose (Frank Kopp Mem. Prize), USA; Yukiko Hori (Lynell Gordon Mem. Prize), Japan; Jean Saulnier (Lynell Gordon Mem. Prize), Canada; Anthony Padilla (Frank Kopp Mem. Prize), USA.